SOUNDINGS

Gary K Wolfe
is also the author of

The Known and the Unknown:
The Iconography of Science Fiction (1979)

Critical Terms for Science Fiction and Fantasy (1986)

Harlan Ellison: The Edge of Forever (with Ellen Weil; 2002)

SOUNDINGS

REVIEWS 1992-1996

GARY K WOLFE

For Charles —
(see the intro) —
for causing all
ol this to happen!

Gary

BECCON PUBLICATIONS
2005

Beccon Publications
75 Rosslyn Avenue
Harold Wood
Essex RM3 0RG, U.K.
beccon@dial.pipex.com

Printed by Antony Rowe Ltd., Chippenham, England

CONTENTS

REVIEWS: 1994

REVIEWS: 1995

INTRODUCTION
REVIEWS 1992
REVIEWS 1993
REVIEWS 1994
REVIEWS 1995
REVIEWS 1996
INDEX OF TITLES

Trainspotting

For anyone who grows up passionately involved with reading, it can be oddly liberating to discover that you have no particular talent for writing fiction. If one devotes part of one's professional career to being a critic, of course, such an admission invites all sorts of canards and snowballs, ranging from the familiar accusations of simple parasitism to darker scenarios of Iago-like malignity. Criticism, in this view, may be cavalierly divided into two categories: sniping, malicious reviews on the one hand, and cluelessly arcane academic theorizing on the other. Both are more plentiful than they ought to be, but neither has much to do with the real politics of engagement that has long made responsible criticism an interesting and provocative part of the literary game. To be sure, such attitudes are heard less often these days (outside of the occasional fan convention, where they're still good for cheap applause lines), and a measure of the maturation of genre fiction may well be the extent to which it's become possible to talk about it without the risk of betraying the home team, or of driving away tourists by noting that it's raining, or of violating the corporate mission statement by acknowledging that some products lack nutritional value. Mentioning in a public venue that a particular SF novel is problematical is no longer *necessarily* taken to imply that SF itself is a bad idea, nor does celebrating a particular novel imply that SF is somehow therefore a superior breed of fiction. For SF – or more properly, the *reading* of SF – to mature, it isn't necessary to adopt Theodore Sturgeon's overquoted dictum that ninety percent of everything is "crud," but it might be necessary to accept that mediocrity will always far outweigh either the crud or the diamonds.

The problem, for both the reviewer and the academic critic, is that mediocrity is not very interesting to write about. Books that are truly, spectacularly dire – what we might call the literature of emesis (as opposed to mimesis) – are perhaps too easy to write about, and are among the critic's most unsavory temptations; the sharper the barb, the wittier the riposte, the better. But with endless piles of books staring balefully from the desk, and with only a handful that can be carefully read before deadline, the question arises as to why the critic would even *finish* such a book, much less take the time to write about it. A certain sign of a facile critic is one who habitually takes on such books merely as a preening display of weaponry; such reviews are seldom more useful than those of the hungry puppy reviewer who praises everything out of a desire for acceptance or for blurbs on the paperback edition. Usually, though, if favorable or mixed reviews outnumber bad reviews, it's because many of the bad reviews never get written, since the book never gets completely read. Far more interesting to me are the books that set out honorably to express or shape a particular vision, and which at times succeed astonishingly well, but more often generate mixed results, or raise more questions than they answer. For such books, context may often be as important as content, and even a book which isn't quite firing on all cylinders may nevertheless move the vehicle forward into interesting new territory.

This, I think, is where that lack of a particular fiction-writing gene might almost become an asset. It helps to retain a certain measure of awe at the entire enterprise of fiction, to remain free of the temptation to think one might have done it better oneself, and to recognize that even the most undistinguished book will have its appreciative readers. This last point is a significant one, since another temptation the reviewer sometimes faces is the temptation to review a book's readership rather than the book itself, especially when that readership seems singularly undemanding. I've been a teacher for far longer than I've been a reviewer, and it's led me to believe that the most serious hazard facing fiction is not a degradation of taste — can one seriously argue that the readers of *Varney the Vampire* are significantly more sophisticated than readers of Anne Rice? — but rather the wholesale abandonment of reading altogether. University teachers who regularly assign novels to their classes, if they are honest with themselves, will recognize that the last novel assigned in the last class will, for a fair number of students, be the last novel they will ever read. This is a reality not always evident within the relatively sheltered provinces of literature and academia, but it's an important perspective to maintain. As a critic, I can afford to show little patience for the formulaic sentimentality of a Danielle Steele; as a teacher, I have to try to understand what power such novels wield, since the student reading a Steele novel may be the only member of the class who is voluntarily reading *anything*. The mysterious alchemy that may exist between a particular reader and a particular novel is something we critics have little access to, and in some important sense it's none of our business.

What *are* we good for, then? For many years before I began writing book reviews in a monthly column, I published a good deal academic criticism in a variety of venues. During these decades — essentially the 1970s and 1980s — the scholarly enterprise about SF and popular fiction in general grew from a relative handful of books, articles, and conventions to a vigorous, polyphonic dialogue informed by resources ranging from textual and bibliographical scholarship to various postmodern theories, feminism, Marxism, and multicultural and postcolonial sensibilities. While this dialogue often remains stimulating, it's also remarkably insular, with major journals in the field numbering their circulation in the hundreds and the attendance at academic conventions often even lower than that. In a disturbingly large measure, the production of academic literary scholarship is driven less by its readership than by the demands of tenure committees, and in a real sense there is almost no market demand at all. Nor, at least in the United States (though the situation seems somewhat more salutary in the U.K.), is there much overlap between this academic dialogue and the parallel dialogues about SF among the readers, writers, editors, and publishers in the field. When I began to find myself involved in these other dialogues, first through the occasional fan convention and later through such mixed-use developments as the International Association for the Fantastic in the Arts, I discovered there a kind of passionate immediacy, a sense that the literature was constantly reforming itself in the light of its own critical discourse, and that this discourse was often only tangential to what we academics were doing. I thus drifted into reviewing, first in the academic journals and in the now-defunct *Fantasy Review*, and eventually in *Locus*. It was over a lunch at ICFA in 1991 that Charles Brown invited me to submit a couple of test reviews, and at the end of that year I became a monthly contributor.

Still, many academic colleagues have never ceased to wonder why I do this, and more than a few times I've been given earnest career advice suggesting I'd be better off spending my time on "real" work. But for someone who remains intrigued with what science fiction and fantasy can be and who has no intention of becoming a fiction writer, the question of finding the most rewarding level of engagement can be a very personal one. I never agreed with the "real work" argument, and I do still write academic pieces now and then, but even less can I countenance the cliché that critics are all failed artists (which, among other things, demeans those quite successful novelists who also write reviews). The notion that a review written under a deadline *necessarily* involves less engagement and rigor than a critical essay is demonstrably naïve, and a repeated flaw in much academic criticism of SF has been the failure of many scholars to cite reviews as critical sources in cases where they would be appropriate. While serving on the editorial boards of a number of academic journals, I've seen entire essays constructed around some revelatory insight about a novel or writer, carefully marshalling the usual endnotes and works cited, but with the author blissfully unaware that his or her central insight is essentially a recapitulation of what the reviews said in the first place; those reviews themselves are almost never among the citations. The failure to regard the central reviewers of the last few decades — Damon Knight, James Blish, Algis Budrys, John Clute, and many others — as legitimate scholarly resources is in many cases a simple failure of scholarship, particularly when these reviewers have assembled selections of their reviews in more widely available book form.

Furthermore, I'd long admired the stylistic freedom of reviewers both in and out of the field, ranging from Pauline Kael and Edmund Wilson to Budrys and Clute. Not only were such writers simply enjoyable to read, but they demonstrated a fierce engagement with their subjects in a manner that frankly is hard to bring off in the constrained formalities of academic writing, and that usually sounds strained when attempted, like an eager professor's effort at boogalu. And a constantly churning field such as SF seemed to *invite* such engagement. Charles Brown, the editor of *Locus*, seemed to feel the same way, and wanted his magazine, in the most literal way, to become a locus of discourse on what he persistently terms the "philosophy" of the field. He often challenged and cajoled his reviewers to connect with the field as it is lived, month by month, by those who write it. Many of the reviews which follow are the direct result of arguments or discussions on the nature of the field with the editor of *Locus* and others.

That engagement with the living substance of the field is what keeps alive the surprises of monthly reviewing, even after more than a decade, even after repeated encounters with The Thousand Page Novel That Arrives A Week Before Deadline,

The Kindly Author Who You Love To Drink With But Would Rather Not Engage In Print, The Author Who Of Course Never Reads Reviews But Somehow Writes Two-Thousand-Word Rebuttals To Every One, The Writer Whose Novels You Admire But Whom You Would Cross The Street To Avoid Talking With, The Experimental Novel That You Find Thoroughly Opaque But Have To Say Something About Anyway, The Angry Fans Convinced You Are Biased Against Their Favorite Subgenre, The Angry Publisher Convinced You Are Hopelessly Out Of Touch With Popular Taste, The Condescending Fellow Professor Convinced You Are Hopelessly In *Thrall* Of Popular Taste, and so on. One doesn't take up reviewing with the expectation to be lionized, and one ought not to take up reviewing out of an illusory sense of power or influence; surveys repeatedly indicate that "recommendation of authority" falls far behind author name recognition, word of mouth, and even cover design in influencing book sales. One writes reviews because reviews are what one writes: they are essays about literature, and literature is worth writing essays about. They are generally essays written for a somewhat wider audience than academic and theoretical pieces, and under far more oppressive deadlines, but they may collectively provide a kind of chronicle of an evolving literature in a way that the academic pieces are never intended to. Put in more crudely metaphorical terms, the academic critic considers a passing train, often long after it's passed; the reviewer must try to leap on. Sometimes we miss the train entirely, but that risk is part of the exhilaration. Sometimes, if we're lucky, we make sense.

What follows consists of most, but not all, of the reviews written for *Locus* magazine during the five years between 1992, my first full year as a reviewer, and 1996. (The reviews since 1996 would fill two additional volumes of this size.) For the most part, I have omitted reviews of specialized interest – academic, nonfiction, or art books – although a few of these are included when they seemed to contribute significantly to ongoing dialogues developing in the field or in the culture at large (hence, for example, a discussion of a few spectacularly ephemeral *Star Trek* memoirs). Observant readers will no doubt note that some important books are not covered, while works by authors already almost forgotten are included. Part of this has to do with the vagaries of monthly reviewing, and which books crossed or did not cross my desk, but the intent here is not to provide "best" or "recommended reading" lists (though a bit of that goes on in the overviews that preface each year's chapter) so much as to offer a chronicle of fairly consistent reading in SF and related fields over a half-decade during which the field began to shape itself into something like what it is today. Context seems to me to be a crucial feature of any act of criticism, and the extent to which these pieces are worth revisiting today largely derives from their possible value in suggesting a history of emerging contexts, of exploring issues not yet fully resolved, questions not yet answered, books not yet written.

REVIEWS 1962

1992 – Overview: The Year in Review
~ originally published in Locus #385 (Feb 1993) ~

Victorian critics used to worry about whether fiction was capable of the same kind of measurable progress as science or industry – whether, for example, Walter Scott represented a faltering step on the road to George Eliot, with Dickens somewhere in between – and every time I see a year-end summary of any kind of literature, I wonder if something of the same sort may be going on. If the characters in a novel like Greg Bear's *Anvil of Stars* annihilate solar systems with considerably more *angst* than characters in Doc Smith, does that mean the genre has morally advanced by so many spaces? Do Joe Haldeman's more fully realized characters and sophisticated psychosocial themes in *Worlds Enough and Time* demonstrate that he's outgrown his Heinleinian forebears? Does the self-conscious "literariness" of Dan Simmons's *The Hollow Man*, with its allusions to Dante and T.S. Eliot, mean that SF has matured beyond the kind of dogged self-referentiality that has helped to isolate it from the mainstream? In short, is SF really going anywhere, and has the past year brought us any closer to wherever that may be?

The answer, I think, is that it's a stupid question. SF is characterized by so many obtusely stubborn individualists, and shaped by so many market forces and multiple audiences, that to try to identify purely literary trends gets hopelessly confusing very quickly. Last year, for example, I speculated in this space that SF's increasing fascination with history might be a trend worth watching, and subsequently felt happily vindicated when one of this year's top novels turned out to be Connie Willis's *Doomsday Book*, which embeds a fully-realized and utterly convincing Black Plague historical novel in a suspenseful time-travel adventure with a near-future setting – sort of a fictional version of Barbara Tuchman's *A Distant Mirror*. Mike Resnick, too, seemed to keep this tradition alive with his *Alternate Presidents* and *Alternate Kennedys* anthologies. But then Kim Stanley Robinson, whose collection *Remaking History* was one of my pre-eminent examples of this trend, had to go off and write a dyed-in-the-wool hard SF Mars colonization epic, *Red Mars*, which certainly ought to be on anyone's list of the top three or four novels of the year. Robinson's interest in historical forces and utopian thought is everywhere in evidence in this novel, but it doesn't take control of the narrative, which is one of the most accomplished mixes of science, social thought, and character development we've seen in a long time. The other big Mars novel of the year, Ben Bova's *Mars*, demands much less of readers, and will probably prove to be far more popular among those who just want to know "what it will be like."

A novel that shares many of Robinson's virtues is Joe Haldeman's *World Enough and Time*, which finally concluded his "Worlds" trilogy after a nine-year hiatus. By completing his fictional biography of Marianne O'Hara and elevating her to near-mythic status, Haldeman has produced one of his best novels — better, in fact, than the trilogy of which it's a part. Haldeman's greater maturity and self-assurance shows markedly when one goes back and compares this novel with the original 1981 *Worlds*. It is both the ambition and the hazard of any writer of series or sequels that the last volume should be the best — after all, there are always going to be some readers who would enjoy the last volume but may not find the first as enthralling — and Greg Bear faced a similar problem with *Anvil of Stars*, his sequel to *Forge of God*. Bear's strategy was to write a different kind of novel altogether, linked by character and motivation to the first but far less conventional in form. *Anvil of Stars* deals effectively with the theme of young people coming to grips with issues of justice and vengeance, but those who relished the cataclysmic special effects of *Forge of God* will find them very nearly shunted offstage in this new novel.

While those two important series were closed out during 1992, other important series got underway. In addition to Kim Stanley Robinson's projected Mars trilogy, which began with *Red Mars*, Orson Scott Card began his five-novel "Homecoming" saga with *The Memory of Earth* and *The Call of Earth*. Set on a distant human colony some 40 million years in the future, these first two novels suggest a setting and theme vaguely reminiscent of Arthur C. Clarke's *The City and the Stars* — the rediscovery of human will in a society whose technological control begins to falter — but overlays this with an odd mix of Biblical overtones and Machiavellian militarism. There seems little doubt that the whole series will prove as readable — and as morally committed — as we've come to expect from Card, but we'll have wait and see if he can fill the whole expansive canvas that he's outlined. Elisabeth Vonarburg's *The Silent City* was new only in the States (it had been published in Canada in 1988 and Paris in 1981), but deserves mention for its haunting evocation of a future urban redoubt and the social consequences of assigned vs. chosen gender roles. I found the novel's followup, *In the Mothers' Land*, considerably tougher going, however.

Another 1992 trend I was anticipating (if not actively dreading) was an increase in virtual reality fiction. But the major novel of the year to use this theme, Neal Stephenson's *Snow Crash*, proved to be so inventive and spirited in its hilarious portrayal of a near-future California that the cybernet sequences very nearly paled by comparison. Stephenson delivered on Big Concepts, too, although his elaborate exposition of a religion-as-mind-virus theme slowed the frenetic pace almost to a standstill at times.

Embedding complex ideas in fast-action narratives, in fact, turned out to be one of the few clear trends in technique during the year, and perhaps the only one that we could legitimately call progress (we've come a long way from the days in which Van Vogt's goofy "science" needed only sound just credible enough to get us to the next action scene). Both Dan Simmons's *The Hollow Man* and Greg Egan's *Quarantine* suggested that *all* reality may be a kind of virtual reality, at least in a quantum mechanical sense. Both novels also work out their notions of standing wavefronts in ingenious and provocative terms, and both contain enough flat-out action for a Mel

Gibson movie – at least in their initial chapters. But the Robocop crowd would be heading out for popcorn as soon as Egan begins patiently explaining all of quantum theory, or when it grows apparent that Simmons has packed everything from *The Inferno* to an inverted version of Silverberg's *Dying Inside* into a novel which is astonishingly complex for its length. In the fantasy arena, the master of fast-paced myth fiction remains Tim Powers, whose *Last Call* superimposes his myth-drenched paranoid narrative universe onto the near-ideal setting of Las Vegas, and delivers a rousing cosmic battle involving poker-playing Fisher Kings.

A trend which I did not foresee, but which is more than welcome (if two novels are enough to make a trend), shows up in part in Robinson's *Red Mars* but more clearly in Ian McDonald's *The Broken Land* (aka *Hearts, Hands, and Voices*) and Ernest Hogan's *High Aztech* (which is near the top of my list of the most-likely-to-be-overlooked novels of the year). This trend involves a growing awareness of the experience of Third World countries, of the imaginative potential of such experience, and of the almost certainly increased role of the Third World in the future (although I wonder if the term Third World may not already be outdated, seeing as how there's not much of a Second World left). McDonald's novel vividly draws on everything from Northern Ireland to South Africa to Asian boat people to Nazi Germany, and yet his future world seems as consistent, and makes at least as much sense, as more familiar SF futures drawn from urbanized western societies; it's a powerful and depressing book. Hogan's *High Aztech* is less gloomy and more ironic, with a high-tech Mexico in the grip of an Aztec revival, Africa as a mecca of biology and genetics, and all the world's gods hauled on stage in a rousing finale. Oddly, it shares with Stephenson's *Snow Crash* the religion-as-virus idea, but its most vivid aspect is its portrait of a post-U.S.-dominated world order.

At least one non-SF novel deserves mention, not only because it represents the year's most haunting meditation on why we need fantasies at all, but because it's in many ways clearly the work of a fantasy writer. Geoff Ryman's *Was* re-imagines the story of *The Wizard of Oz* as a grimly naturalistic tale of abandonment and abuse, then intercuts this with narrative fragments detailing the growth of the Oz legend in Hollywood and on television, and with a modern tale of an AIDS patient which just might end on a note of real fantasy. It's not genre work, but it is speculative fiction of a high order. The year's other big experiment with realism as a bridge to fantasy was Orson Scott Card's *Lost Boys*, which isn't speculative at all, but rather revelatory in structure: the fantastic becomes a way of imaging the very real agonies of trying to hold a family together, particularly following the loss of a child.

To return to the dumb question with which I began: is all this "progress"? Well, look at it this way. Underlying this list of books that I found worthwhile – and, I would wager, underlying the lists of my fellow reviewers – there is a substantial reservoir of SF novels whose plot, characters, and setting have not advanced measurably beyond last night's episode of *Star Trek*, whose authors are busily at work even now to assure your local retailer that shelf space need not go vacant, and whose publishers are any day going to start stamping these books with consumer expiration dates just like those on milk cartons. A reviewer can easily get caught up in questions of whether serious writers are doing the absolute best they can, and whether they've really given us anything new. But when I actually look on the shelves, I'm quickly reminded of the real context of SF, and am that much more impressed at what a Willis, a Robinson, a Haldeman, a Simmons, a McDonald, is able to accomplish.

– January 1992, Locus #372 –

Storming the Reality Studio: A Casebook of Cyberpunk and Postmodern Science Fiction ~~ ed. Larry McCaffery

He, She and It ~~ Marge Piercy

Every time I almost convince myself "the mainstream" is little more than a phantom fortress conjured up by envious genre writers, I find myself face to face with something that makes me want to cop an attitude. There is this recurring notion, for example, that SF is some-how too good for itself – that it's a wonderful house except for the people who live there. This notion isn't confined to mainstream reviewers who want to praise a Doris Lessing or a Paul Theroux despite their science fictional borrowings; it also shows up among some of the genre's most enthusiastic defenders – the historians who want to lay claim to everything from Plato to Swift, or the anthologists who slip in stories by Steve Allen or Shirley Jackson to up the ante on the remaining stories in the volume (these last examples are from Judith Merril's first best-of-the-year anthology back in 1956, but she continued the practice for years). Actually, the relationship between science fiction and the mainstream has become far more complex and interesting over the last several years, and shows up in a lot of different ways.

Larry McCaffery's **Storming the Reality Studio** (the title is from William Burroughs' *Nova Express*) consists of 29 literary selections and 20 essays, all designed to illustrate the proposition that cyberpunk is nothing less than the fruition of an aesthetic and ideological movement that encompasses everything from Mary Shelley and Olaf Stapledon to Thomas Pynchon, *Robocop* and MTV. Eleven of the pieces originally appeared in a cyberpunk issue of *Mississippi Review* which McCaffery edited in 1988; 14 more are excerpts from novels, often little more than two or three pages long. The only substantially complete pieces of fiction are Pat Cadigan's "Rock On," Samuel R. Delany's "Among the Blobs," Harold Jaffe's "Max Headroom," Lewis Shiner's "Stoked," John Shirley's "Wolves of the Plateau," and Bruce Sterling's "Twenty evocations." The critical essay section also leans a bit much on excerpts, mostly from texts in postmodern theory by the weighty likes of Jacques Derrida, Frederick Jameson, and Jean-Francois Lyotard. There are clear and cogent arguments being made in the essays by Veronica Hollinger, Joan Gordon, and and Tom Maddox, but much of the rest of this section depends on what Bruce Sterling has called "heavy dudism" – the idea that you can't write about fiction unless you sound at least as hip as the fiction you're writing about. Timothy Leary even shows up here, pointing out that early cyberpunks included Christopher Columbus, Mark Twain, and Charles Lindbergh. In a long interview with McCaffery, William Gibson cheerfully admits that he often doesn't know what he's talking about when it comes to the logical and scientific background of his novels, but this doesn't stop his enthusiasts from filling it in for him.

Near the end of the book, when we've been nearly inundated with the idea that cyberpunk's true fathers are Hammett, William Burroughs, and Pynchon, and that its closest living relatives are Don DeLillo and Ted Mooney, it comes as a surprise to encounter Bruce Sterling's view (in the introduction to his *Mirrorshades* anthology) that cyberpunk is almost purely an SF phenomenon. He acknowledges Pynchon, to be sure, but he also acknowledges Ellison, Moorcock, Spinrad, Aldiss, Ballard, Niven, Heinlein, Farmer, Varley, Dick, and Bester. A few of these writers get discussed in terms of the punk canon McCaffery is trying to establish, but the main thrust of the whole book is to suggest that the movement's true origins lie outside the genre. I'm reminded of similar anthologies from 20 or 30 years ago that tried to show how the beat movement started with Dostoyevsky, or the '60s counterculture with Antonin Artaud. Incidentally, the "post-modern" of the title doesn't refer to a postmodern period of SF itself; it refers to those works of postmodernist culture that resemble or use the tropes of SF or to SF which in turn resembles (or can be made to resemble) these works. All this cross-pollination is supposed to be good for everyone concerned. Barriers come down, everybody gets weird, and culture is liberated all over again. The only thing is, it already seems like history.

I don't think Marge Piercy is generally counted as a postmodern writer, but she certainly is an accomplished mainstream novelist with some ties to science fiction. Her *Woman on the Edge of Time* created something of a stir in 1976 when it appropriated SF devices for its feminist/ecotopian purposes. Now Piercy is back with **He, She and It**, a novel which is neither as daring as some mainstream readers are likely to think nor as irredeemably awful as SF readers will expect. To be sure, Piercy's first several chapters are rough going; she hasn't a clue as to how to set up SF exposition except for Gernsbackian subordinate clauses, and her mid-21st-century America is a paste-up collage made partly of recycled William Gibson (who even gets an acknowledgement), partly of 1940s *Astounding* (with moving strip-roads, no less), partly of *Logan's Run*, partly of *Frankenstein*, and partly of *Brave New World*. There's a cyborg who sometimes talks just like Frost from Zelazny's "For a Breath I Tarry," and he has a lover whose attitude toward him seems borrowed from the movie *Making Mr. Right*. Most of these aren't *hommages*, though; Piercy seems to think she's making the whole thing up, and it's easy to lose patience.

This is unfortunate because Piercy is a very talented writer, and there is a pretty good novel imbedded inside *He, She and It*. As in *Woman on the Edge of Time*, Piercy splits her narrative between two time frames, and again the nonfuturistic time is the more compelling. The framing narrative (the futuristic one) concerns Shira Shipman, who after losing a painful custody battle retreats from the male-dominated, corporate urban "dome" where her career has been stalled and returns home to the "free town" where she was raised, an egalitarian Jewish enclave called Tikva. Tikva is partly a refuge against anti-Semitism following a nuclear war in the Middle East which destroyed Israel (but for which Israel nonetheless gets blamed). There Shira becomes involved in the social training of an illegal cyborg named Yod, built to help protect the community from both physical predators and corporate data pirates.

Obviously, we are in for a version of the Golem legend, and indeed much of the novel consists of Shira's grandmother Malkah retelling this legend to Yod. Malkah's narrative, set in Prague in 1600, is really the core of the novel — which seems meant to be more an exploration of Jewish identity and survival than a portrayal of a dystopian future. The Prague chapters are as effective and suspenseful a retelling of the story of Rabbi Loew and his Golem as any modern treatment I've seen, and their portrayal of an embattled Jewish community seems much more contemporary than the parallel story of Yod, with all its cybernetic bells and whistles. For one thing, anti-Semitism isn't the real threat to the town of Tikva; instead, it's the secret of how Yod was built that seems to attract the data pirates from the domed city. In other words, Yod is built to protect the city from danger, but most of the danger is caused by his presence. The noble sacrifice that ends the novel thus seems rather pointless. But Piercy's main problem isn't a conundrum of plotting — it's simply that her future world isn't consistently derived from any clear set of imaginative premises. It's simply a place to put a Golem, and not nearly as interesting a place as Prague.

— February 1992, Locus #373 —

Sheltered Lives ~~ Charles Oberndorf

There Won't Be War ~
~ eds. Harry Harrison & Bruce McAllister

Lafferty in Orbit ~~ R A Lafferty

A professional gigolo is hired by a woman whose lover has recently committed suicide under suspicion of terrorist activities, gradually falls in love with his client, and finds himself caught up in a cat-and-mouse game between government agencies and the suspected terrorist group. This is the plot of Charles Oberndorf's first novel, **Sheltered Lives**, and the obvious question is, what makes it science fiction? Well, for one thing, all this is set in an unspecified near-future Ohio in which cities have been turned into vast "Constructs" and *Nineteen Eighty-Four*-style television "monitoring" has become an accepted part of everyday life. The gigolo works for a unit of government called "Personal Services," set up to provide controlled outlets for sexual behavior in the wake of a virulent epidemic of sexually-transmitted diseases collectively called "Hives." Hives victims are routinely rounded up and sent away to relocation camps, and these relocation camps are what the terrorists seek to abolish. Most of this information is revealed through conversations of the main characters, and none of it is foregrounded. The relocation camps, for example, are never seen except through a brief virtual reality experience which is meant to be more tragic than horrifying. The question of whether this novel is SF, at least in its basic conception, still stands.

Oberndorf has extrapolated the AIDS epidemic (or something very much like it), fears of crime and terrorism, and the trend toward socially sanctioned voyeurism into a future society that is generally consistent and quietly persuasive. Although he has borrowed openly from *Nineteen Eighty-Four* and even has his characters discuss Orwell, he avoids presenting this future as a nightmarish dystopia; the various curtailments of liberty seem like unfortunate compromises designed to protect a rapidly dissolving social contract. He even provides an almost-satisfactory answer to a question that always plagues me about these spy-camera societies – namely, how can such intensive surveillance of almost everyone be supported economically? In Oberndorf's version, a sophisticated artificial intelligence system nick-named Tricky Dick does most of the actual watching and culling of tape; human operators only look at the good parts. Oberndorf has worked out other details of his inflationary economy pretty well, too; we learn that a "quarter" means 25 dollars, and we believe it because it's consistent with other prices we are given. All this is handled confidently and with some grace, but none of it is what the novel is about. And this is why I'm still not sure it's science fiction.

What the novel is about is Rod Lawrence, the male prostitute who narrates the story, and Anna Baxter, the woman who hires him as her companion after her lover kills himself. Lawrence is an alienated, undereducated, Camus-type narrator who passionlessly lets himself be guided by events and by other people. Anna tries to get him to connect with the realities of human suffering by making him read Dostoevsky and Hardy, and eventually by undergoing "Relocation Experience," a taped recreation of life in the relocation camps. But is she trying to humanize him because she's fallen in love, or is she preparing him for involvement with the terrorists who oppose the camps? Lawrence isn't sure, and even as he's beginning to suspect he loves her back, he secretly reports on her activity to an anti-terrorist official, rationalizing the betrayal by not accepting the money offered for it. The characterization of Lawrence is the novel's greatest strength; we can understand how such an existential protagonist can emerge from the society we see described.

On the other hand, we can understand how such a character might emerge from any number of societies, past or present; Oberndorf himself reminds us of this with his references to *Jude the Obscure* and *Crime and Punishment*. This is where the SF dimension of the novel frequently fails. Interested in exploring themes of love and betrayal, Oberndorf borrows only his setting from SF. His plot comes from the espionage novel, and when the plot seems to demand it, a futuristic subway system turns right back into something out of the 1940s film noir. The relocation camps, with all their resonances of Nazi genocide and contemporary gay-bashing, never horrify us; they're issues, not nightmares. Even the ever-present cameras don't seem very spooky, and the artificial intelligence that monitors them often seems positively benign.

In short, Oberndorf pulls too many punches. In order to keep us focused on Rod and Anna, he glosses over the most powerful implications of his imagined world – how it came about, and how it might change. The result is disappointing as SF, but rewarding in other ways. Oberndorf has a strong sense of character and a good ear for dialogue. He knows how to plot, even though the pacing of his first half is far too slow and too much depends on a contrived showdown at the end. He is in every way the proverbial "talent to watch." But on the basis of *Sheltered Lives* I could not begin to guess whether his next novel will be SF or mainstream – or whether he will really achieve the synthesis he seems to striving for.

For the past several years, faculty members at Notre Dame and several other universities have been trying to develop curricula in what they call "Peace Studies." The problem they keep coming up against is that what students almost invariably end up studying in such courses is war. Harry Harrison and Bruce McAllister have much the same problem in **There Won't Be War**, a collection of 14 original and five reprint stories that are supposed to provide, or suggest, or at least get us thinking about, models for a "postwar world." At least 11 of the stories draw most of their effect from depictions of war or the effects of war, and the fact that the authors adopt an anti-war attitude doesn't necessarily show us the way to peace. By these standards, novels from *All Quiet on the Western Front* to *Catch-22* ought to be reclassified as peace novels.

McAllister's introduction and Harrison's afterword make it clear that they were aware of the problems inherent in this anthology concept, and they wisely chose to avoid somber utopian prescriptions in favor of entertainment. It was a wise choice in terms of making a readable book, but the price is that most of the stories are pretty lightweight. Asimov's brief "Frustration" simply restates the theme of his "The Evitable Conflict" by suggesting that everything be left to well-programmed computers. Joe Haldeman's "Beachhead" sets up an interesting situation in which aggressive children are isolated until they're ready to re-enter the world, but ends in an abrupt flurry of exposition before the ambiguities of the premise can be explored. His brother Jack implies that enough check-off boxes on income tax forms I might save the world, and Timothy Zahn makes essentially the same point about insurance contracts. Charles Stross, in "SEAQ and Destroy," doesn't exactly propose an end to war, but shows how future wars might take the form of computerized stock market raids. None of these stories are much more than clever premises, I although Stross works his out in such maddening detail that it begins to lose its satiric charm.

Not surprisingly, satirists have an easier time of it with this kind of material. William Tenn's classic "The Liberation of Earth" is here, and should be, but his "Generation of Noah" shouldn't; it's a badly dated early cold war bomb shelter parable. Robert Sheckley has a lot of fun with "There Will Be No War After This One," but the plot is the old chestnut of a bellicose earth being taught a lesson by the Galactic Empire — probably not a very useful model for current governments. The only Eastern European story, Ratislav Durman's "The Long-Awaited Appearance of the Real Black Box," suggests that a perfect defensive weapon might defeat its purpose by permitting soldiers to desert with impunity, and Frederik Pohl's "The Rocky Python Christmas Video Show" presents what is essentially Buffy Sainte-Marie's old song "The Universal Soldier" done up as a bizarre version of TV's *The Dating Game.* Pohl's story is more cynical than funny, but it gets at an idea that is reflected in the book's most serious and ambitious stories. Put simply, this is that individuals have choices which make not only their own fates, but the fates of others as well. This is most effectively dramatized in two reprints — Kim Stanley Robinson's alternate-Hiroshima "The Lucky Strike" and J.G. Ballard's classic "The Terminal Beach" — but it also shows up in Marc Laidlaw's "Wartorn, Lovelorn," Nicholas Emmet's "Brains on the Dump" (an especially unpleasant vignette), James Morrow's "Known But to God and Wilbur Hines," and Nancy A. Collins' "Iphigenia." Morrow's story is a mainstream World War I tale narrated by the ghost of an "unknown" soldier, and shares with Jack McDevitt's "Valkyrie" and Gregory Frost's "Attack of the Jazz Giants" a supernatural dimension that seems way out of whack with the general tenor of the anthology — although the stories work well enough on their own terms. But Nancy Collins' "Iphigenia" is a real zapper, easily the most unforgettable story in the book, despite the fact that its premise doesn't seem credible for a minute.

Only one story, George Zebrowski's "Sacred Fire," engages in any thoughtful way the notion that conflict may be inherent in human freedom, and that transcending conflict might be as much an evolutionary problem as a political one. I suspect that the editors wanted more of this kind of debate, but simply didn't get it in the stories submitted (they could have found plenty of it in *Astounding* in the late '40s and early '50s, but that would have meant a different kind of anthology). Judging from their title, McAllister and Harrison want to offer an upbeat counter-balance to Jerry Pournelle's *There Will Be War* anthologies, but the stories in those anthologies never were as bellicose as the title suggests, and some of these stories might have been right at home there. Pournelle's books didn't offer much serious thinking about war, and this one doesn't offer much serious thinking about peace, but it does have some entertaining stories, and one or two haunting ones.

One of the best examples of SF's general lack of neatitude is the work of R.A. Lafferty. Those who came to Lafferty late and wonder what all the fuss was about should take a look at **Lafferty in Orbit**, a collection of 18 stories originally published in the series of *Orbit* anthologies edited by Damon Knight between 1966 and 1980. (Knight also provides a brief introduction here.) Many of these stories will be familiar to Lafferty readers, and a few, such as "Interurban Queen," are among the most familiar of all his stories. But bringing them together in this way shows clearly why Lafferty made such a unique impact during the period usually associated with the New Wave. Lafferty wasn't really New Wave; he was a wave all his own—a kind of cracker-barrel Calvino whose disarmingly folksy style masks sophisticated intellectual games in which evolutionary theology and cultural anthropology get transformed into tall tales about cupless cups of coffee and bush-league baseball pitchers. It's as though Borges and Chesterton had decided to collaborate on a new round of Pecos Bill yarns.

You can't blame Knight for wanting a crafty Lafferty story in almost every *Orbit*; there's absolutely no danger that any of them will look like anything else in the anthology. But you know what? Putting them all together like this and reading them in one big gulp is another whole ball of wax! And why is that? Well, for one thing, it sure is exhausting! For another, it builds up in your system until your prose turns weird and you risk alienating your friends by trying to describe the plots. For a third, it can't help but take the edge off some of the stories, until what at first seemed fresh and liberating begins at times to seem merely uncontrolled. Taken in abundance, the little rhymes sprinkled throughout the stories get on your nerves, and the underlying Irish Catholic moralism begins to weigh them down. Ironically, this doesn't interfere much with such straightforward fables as "Bright Coins in Never-Ending Stream" or "Royal Licorice," which play variations on the old get-your-wish-and-see-what-happens theme; but a story such as "Great Day in the Morning," a kind of antic critique of Teilhard de Chardin's mystical theology, needs a lot of helium to keep it airborne.

Looking back on these stories, we can also see that Lafferty wasn't as isolated from the SF community at large as his myth suggests. Clarke gets mentioned by name; other stories suggest links with Le Guin and Delany; and a few (notably "All Pieces of a River Shore") resolve themselves into the kind of wild surmises that we used to call the sense of wonder. At the same time, it's clear that Lafferty was interested early on in the kinds of issues that ought to endear him to the postmodernists. The map literally becomes the territory in "Entire and Perfect Chrysolite," image subsumes reality in "The Hand With One Hundred Fingers," and the power of naming is made absolute in "And Name My Name." In all the stories, Lafferty's fascination with languages, signs, and names provides ample evidence that he was ahead of his time; none of them seem in the least dated. It's a collection worth having and worth reading – even if only in controlled doses.

Doomsday Book ~~ Connie Willis

Worlds Enough and Time ~~ Joe Haldeman

The Memory of Earth ~~ Orson Scott Card

Last Call ~~ Tim Powers

Readers who drift away from science fiction sometimes complain that the genre has lost sight of the old-fashioned virtues of simple storytelling, by which they usually mean the kinds of narrative hooks and wires that keep the pages turning and the adrenaline pumping. Exposition in such stories is handled by means of a series of widening revelations, often presented as chapter-ending cliffhangers, and characters are tested by what seem to be insoluble dilemmas and out-and-out villains. To some extent, these are pulp virtues, but they are virtues shared by many mainstream bestsellers, and they're not necessarily incompatible with SF's long uphill struggle toward mainstreamdom. The fact is that during the last 20 years or so, SF has produced as talented a crop of storytellers as one could hope for, as some of this month's titles attest.

Readers of Connie Willis' "Firewatch," about time-traveling historians in the London blitz, probably noticed that the narrator's roommate Kivrin was assigned to do her practicum in England in 1349, during the Plague. It seemed an obvious set-up for another story, and now it's apparent why we've had to wait ten years for it. **Doomsday Book** is an ambitious, finely detailed, and compulsively readable novel that ought to land Willis on the bestseller list. The novel has enormous potential for mainstream appeal, but Willis has made no attempt to disguise its science fiction content. There's no elaborate set-up explaining the possibilities of time travel, no detailed backstory about the 21st-century society which has suffered its own viral epidemics and which provides the setting from which the time travelers operate, no apology for the novel's central fantastic premise. Willis simply sets us down in the cozy academic community of a future Oxford (which looks a lot like the real present-day Oxford), where Kivrin is making her preparations for her practicum. The novel starts at a gallop and doesn't slow down until somewhere in the middle, when the narrative line gets stretched a little thin to permit Willis to develop her detailed and convincing portrait of a 14th-century English village.

The novel works wonderfully, even when we can see how we're being manipulated. It's structured as a dual story, taking place over the same two-week period in the future and in the past, much as in Benford's *Timescape*. The future story depicts a viral epidemic in Oxford which disables those supervising the time travel and threatens to leave Kivrin stranded in the past. By itself, this is a convincing tale of academic politics and epidemiology, and it provides a suspenseful counterpoint to the medieval narrative. The medieval sections, which hinge on the question of whether Kivrin has been accidentally sent to the plague year instead of to the relatively safe year of 1320 as intended, work by means of old-fashioned dramatic irony, with the reader guessing the truth long before Kivrin does, and long before Willis reveals it to us. Sometimes the set-ups are overplayed a bit — the "rules" of time travel are conveniently exactly what they need to be for the narrative to work, and in order to withhold a crucial piece of information, Willis keeps one poor character in a feverish delirium for nearly 400 pages — but they're never shaky enough to make us question the novel's fundamental integrity. Nor does the fact that some of the medieval characters think and act a little too modern at times — identifying the brain as the controller of behavior, for example.

There are plenty of things in the novel that ought not to work, but they all do work, and that's the power of good storytelling. Despite Willis' obviously meticulous research, there are probably anachronisms that a reader more conversant with medieval history than I am would pick up, but I'm not sure it makes much difference. The essential form of *Doomsday Book* is not that of an historical novel or even of a time-travel story, but rather that of the end-of-the-world tale. That at least is the belief Willis' medieval characters come to adopt, and by the time we've lived with Kivrin through the harrowing series of tragedies that lead to the book's climax, we're convinced.

Joe Haldeman is another first-rate storyteller, but one who works much more closely within the traditions of SF. **Worlds Enough and Time** completes the fictional biography of Marianne O'Hara that began with *Worlds* in 1981 and continued with *Worlds Apart* in 1983. I could have said "epic," because by the end of the trilogy O'Hara emerges as a true epic heroine, but "fictional biography" better describes the extraordinary depth of character with which Haldeman invests these novels. I deliberately didn't reread *Worlds* and *Worlds Apart* before taking on this new novel, but I was amazed at how much I share O'Hara's memories of her earlier life, and how well I know her. She's one of SF's few great characters, and maybe the most fully-realized female character I've seen anywhere in the hard-SF field. *Worlds Enough and Time* is easily readable on its own terms, but infinitely richer for those who have read the first two novels.

Apart from its convincing cast of characters, the trilogy taken as a whole is almost a catalog of SF themes: the earth in the 21st-century, nuclear holocaust, life in a space station, artificial intelligence, virtual reality, cryogenics, space travel, generation starships, the colonization of other planets, alien contact, even, at the end, a touch of good old-fashioned inexplicable superscience. Several of these themes are introduced for the first time in *Worlds Enough and Time*, which takes up O'Hara's story after she has witnessed the near-destruction of Earth, along with many of its orbiting space colonies, and helped plan the long voyage to a new planetary home. The story of this voyage is told principally through extracts from O'Hara's diaries and through the narration, some 2000 years later, of her computer "clone," O'Hara Prime. There are also a number of documents, transcripts, charts, and maps that help flesh out an exceptionally convincing picture of what life in a starship must be like. Haldeman has so meticulously worked out the details of the starship and its course that even the most obsessive hard SF readers should be satisfied.

The plot may not be what hard SF readers expect, however. While there are plenty of voyage-threatening crises along the way – a massive computer failure, a mutagen which destroys the crops needed for food, a religious movement which turns people into cosmic couch potatoes – the real story concerns O'Hara's coming to terms with her age, her relationships, and her values. This last point is especially important, since the fate of the whole human race comes to depend on O'Hara's values, and since Haldeman takes his greatest risks with the novel in dramatizing the means by which they are finally tested. The final chapters of any star-voyage novel face these same risks – how to keep planetfall from seeming anticlimactic, how to introduce new wonders without violating the carefully built-up credibility of the spaceship society, how to expand the thematic scope of the narrative without betraying its original terms. Haldeman doesn't play it safe in handling these problems, but he does handle them, and he brings it all off brilliantly.

Orson Scott Card has a very different approach to SF. In a relatively short span of years, he's made himself into SF's pre-eminent author of boys' books – no mean achievement if one accepts Leslie Fiedler's proposition that the boys' book is the characteristic form of classic American literature. Card's latest novel, **The Memory of Earth**, is the first in a projected five-book series collectively titled "Homecoming," which promises to be a full-scale epic of how the inhabitants of Harmony, a planet settled by humans some 40 million years earlier, rediscover and return to their home planet. Nafai, the 14-year-old hero of *The Memory of Earth*, bears similarities to Card's Ender Wiggins and Alvin Maker, but he also has much in common with Arthur C. Clarke's Alvin in *The City and the Stars* or Heinlein's Hugh Hoyland in "Universe." In other words, this is Card's version of one of the great SF character archetypes, The Kid Who Suspects There's More To Everything.

Nafai lives in a city called Basilica on the planet Harmony, and early on we learn that the name "Harmony" has ominous overtones. Like Clarke's Diaspar or Aldiss's Malacia, Nafai's society represents another grand old SF archetype – The City That Never Changes. The harmony on Harmony, it turns out, is maintained by an orbiting computer called the Oversoul, which sends signals to the genetically altered brains of the inhabitants, preventing them from thinking in directions that might lead toward the kind of technological development that destroyed Earth millions of years earlier.

While this results in a highly stable, non-evolving society (although it's not clear exactly how biological evolution is prevented), it also leads to an odd combination of high and low tech. For example, Harmony has magnetic antigravity devices to assist the disabled, but no motorized transportation. It has sophisticated computers and solar energy systems, but no long-distance communication systems. Card's implicit argument that war is made possible by transportation and communications is a compelling one, but is it worth the trade-off? This is where Card seems more ambivalent than earlier SF writers like Clarke. He's gone to a great deal of trouble to work out the details of his imaginary society — kinship systems, education, economics — and the society isn't all that unattractive. When it begins to break down, it's not because of a heroic Galileo-figure who fights his way toward the truth, but because the master computer itself is beginning to fail, and *arranges* for Nafai to begin discovering the truth. Only with human help can the computer find its way back toward Earth, possibly to be repaired.

The question then is whether Nafai can lead his people out of darkness before society is again too far gone in the direction of self-destruction. Card sets this up well, and there's more than enough intrigue and suspense in this first volume to suggest that the series will turn out to be as readable and gripping as the Alvin Maker or Ender Wiggins novels. But, as with those novels, the adventure is presented in a context that tries to redefine the whole moral universe of SF. The persistent transcendental themes — names like Oversoul and Harmony, Nafai's computerized predestination and his willingness to become a servant of the Oversoul — suggest that there may be more here than meets the eye. The story itself is grand enough to make us want to read the forthcoming "Homecoming" novels, but part of the suspense is going to be in seeing how Card works through his morality play, and in seeing if he can convince us that Moses makes as effective an SF hero as Galileo.

[Obviously this review missed the central significance of the Book of Mormon to this series of Card novels, but I caught on eventually: future volumes in the series are reviewed in January 1993 and February 1995.]

Speaking of mythical heroes, when did Bugsy Siegel become a cultural icon? First we have two movies in the last two years (*The Marrying Man* and *Bugsy*), and now here's Tim Powers in **Last Call** telling us that Bugsy was really the Fisher King and that Las Vegas is the Siege Perilous. Or something like that. Powers is the kind of storyteller who entertains by sheer bravado, throwing everything into the pot, introducing a welter of bizarre characters, and keeping violent incidents coming at breakneck speed. There's a touch of hardboiled detective fiction in the latter technique, and there's a good dose of Lovecraft, too, with vast cosmic forces struggling unseen for possession of us and our world. Now imagine that Thomas Pynchon had been raised on a diet of Lovecraft and Spillane, and you've got a good sense of what *Last Call* feels like. The novel does for poker what *The Drawing of the Dark* did for beer.

There hasn't been a good epic poker fantasy since Edward Whittemore's *Jerusalem Poker* back in 1978, although there have been plenty of tarot novels. Powers has it both ways. Recognizing that modern playing cards are simplified versions of the tarot deck, he constructs a scenario in which gambling becomes a kind of cosmic metaphor of the forces of chaos and randomness in the universe, and whoever controls the gambling capital – Las Vegas – becomes the mythic king able to restore fertility to the land. Powers' protagonist, Scott Crane, discovers that his natural father had usurped this role from Bugsy Siegel in the forties and has grown increasingly corrupt in the years since. Aided by his adoptive father, his moon-goddess sister, a next-door neighbor who hopes to cure his cancer through exposure to randomness, and at one point the ghost of Bugsy himself, Crane finds himself embroiled in an epic struggle to unseat the old king while fending off various other pretenders who have converged on Las Vegas with the same purpose. This use of Las Vegas as the stage for such an epic confrontation cannot help but call to mind Stephen King's *The Stand*, but Powers's vision is very much his own, more cyclical and less apocalyptic than King's.

Powers' appeal is in his wealth of invention and his elaborately convoluted plotting. But there is also a genuine mythic sensibility at work in his fiction. For all the characters' talk about randomness and chaos, the universe of *Last Call* is almost the complete opposite of randomness. Even the most trivial incidents are invested with meaning: pick up a ringing pay phone and the call is for you (and it's from a ghost); follow the direction of your spit and you'll find salvation; look at anyone's hand of cards and discover what cosmic forces are at work in the neighborhood. It's an almost totally paranoid universe, where nothing is quite as it seems – in other words, a universe of myth. That Powers has us buying into it completely by the end of his first few chapters is evidence of the power of his kind of storytelling.

– April 1992, Locus #375 –

Anvil of Stars ~~ Greg Bear

Ishmael ~~ Daniel Quinn

Child of the Light ~~ Janet Gluckman & George Guthridge

Was ~~ Geoff Ryman

Once you've destroyed the world, what do you do for a sequel? The challenge is at least as old as Wylie and Balmer's *After Worlds Collide* (1934), and now Greg Bear has taken it up in **Anvil of Stars**, which details the efforts of surviving earth children to find and destroy the civilization that produced the killer robots which gobbled up the earth in *The Forge of God*. But even though the ending of *The Forge of God* carefully sets up the premise for a sequel and even offers a little preview, Anvil of Stars is conceptually quite a different novel. Some sequels – most recently, Joe Haldeman's *Worlds Enough and Time* – complete an extended narrative arc, the shape of which was already apparent in the original novel. Others are spinoffs, taking a situation or unresolved plot element in the original and using it as the basis for a fundamentally new story.

Anvil of Stars belongs in the latter group. Whereas *The Forge of God* was a first-rate disaster novel, using multiple viewpoints and settings to build to a (literally) shattering conclusion, Bear's new novel is more focused and introspective, confining itself mostly to the moral development of a single character — Martin Gordon, the son of the main viewpoint character in *The Forge of God* — and setting most of its action in the interior of a single starship, the Ship of the Law. Whereas *The Forge of God* repeatedly called attention to its context as a work of SF, with allusions to SF writers and films and an SF writer as a minor character, *Anvil of Stars* is full of references to children's literature — Oz, Peter Pan, Pooh, Robin Hood, Narnia (the starship is even named the *Dawn Treader* by the children). There's even a touch of *Hamlet* in this tale of sometimes reluctant youngsters, aided by mysterious forces, coming to grips with the ambiguities of justice and vengeance. Clearly, Bear is after something of a quite different order from a disaster epic.

This doesn't mean that *Anvil of Stars* lacks the kind of large-scale spectacle that Bear does so well; he's one of the few modern writers willing to annihilate whole solar systems with the abandon of a Doc Smith — and make it seem plausible and almost reasonable. He also has a wonderful sense of tragic incident, such as an episode in which Martin's lover Theresa, trapped in her "bombship," is transformed into antimatter and irrevocably separated from him. But the central issue of the book remains a moral one — will these young adults, whose whole culture is defined by images of their childhood, be able to identify and destroy whole civilizations in order to satisfy a vague and mysterious Law enforced by superior aliens who refuse to even identify themselves? And would it be the right thing to do, anyway? Bear handles the dilemma masterfully, and gives us a moving and insightful portrait of an emerging society aboard the starship, but the questions he's set up are almost unanswerable. Some readers may feel that the ending of the novel involves a cop-out, but what leads up to that ending is a substantial, inventive, and satisfying coming-of-age novel.

After all the publicity and controversy surrounding the awarding of Ted Turner's huge "Tomorrow Fellowship" — for a work of fiction that "proposes positive solutions to global problems" — to Daniel Quinn's **Ishmael**, it's probably inevitable that the book itself should seem something of an anticlimax. *Ishmael* certainly expresses some heartfelt ideas about global problems — although they are neither particularly original nor particularly immediate — and it does so in an accessible and readable way. But it's the "work of fiction" rubric that seems most likely to upset the losers. Cast in the form of an extended philosophical dialogue between a sincere but sometimes hopelessly obtuse narrator and a giant telepathic lowland gorilla named Ishmael, the book is almost all talk. The only narrative elements are the queer way the narrator meets the gorilla (Ishmael advertises in the paper for pupils, and meets with them in an abandoned office), a brief account of Ishmael's background, and a short bit at the end that we can see coming a mile away. The rest consists of Ishmael leading the straw-man narrator toward Quinn's views of what's wrong with the world. It's Candide going at it with Pangloss, or the Little Prince interviewing the fox, or (in terms closer to SF), C.S. Lewis's Ransom debating Weston or the Un-man. Quinn loads the dice in his favor by making his spokesman a noble example of a mistreated and endangered species, but this doesn't disguise the fact that he's lecturing us mercilessly. It's My Dinner With King Kong.

The philosophical dialogue has a long and noble literary history, of course, and it remains popular today as one of the few purely didactic literary forms left, popular with logicians and philosophical conundrum-makers like Douglas Hofstadter. But Quinn is no Hofstadter. Ishmael draws his knowledge of human history from such semi-popular writers as Peter Farb and Marshall Sahlins, and the narrator seems to get his knowledge of science from Nova. At his best, Ishmael sounds like Joseph Campbell explaining things to Bill Moyers, and the main things he explains turn out to be the Book of Genesis and the invention of agriculture. As humanity's first and most powerful technology for dominating the environment, agriculture and its consequences – civilizations, cities, division of labor, technology, overpopulation – is viewed by our culture as one of the key achievements of human history. But the myth of Genesis, in Ishmael's view, portrays this invention as a curse – as western agricultural society being cast out of the garden of hunter-gatherer societies and made to fend for itself. Only a return to hunter-gatherer values, he implies, can free humanity of its self-constructed prison and the impending end of the world. And the main hunter-gatherer value seems to be "take no more than you need."

"Take no more than you need" sounds a lot like one of the principles elucidated in Robert Fulghum's enormously bestselling *All That I Really Need to Know I Learned in Kindergarten* ("share everything"; "clean up your own mess," "don't take things that aren't yours"). It's entirely possible – probable, even – that many readers will also regard this book as a similar fount of simple wisdom, buying copies for their friends and keeping it in print forever. Science fiction readers are more likely to view it as naive, if not quaint – a trendier version of those late nineteenth century utopias in which intractably dense protagonists listen for hundreds of pages to explanations of what's wrong with their world. At the same time, some readers may react sharply to Quinn's comment about how *all* SF endorses and perpetuates the myth of human possession of the universe ("hasn't he heard of Le Guin?"). But here's the rub: for most of SF, Quinn is *exactly right*, and in broad strokes his arguments are compelling enough not to be ignored. For all the klutziness of its presentation, *Ishmael* is not a stupid book, and if its message that environmental salvation depends upon a complete rethinking of our notions of how we relate to the world gets across to the Jonathan Livingston Seagull crowd, it could do worse.

I suspect one reason why SF novelists like to play with the logic of history is that there isn't any. There are no immutable laws of physics as in hard SF, and no one is going to write in correcting your calculations; almost anything you make up stands a good chance of sounding at least as rational as actual historical events. But there's a big risk with this kind of imaginative freedom, especially when the historical event in question is something as wildly irrational and barely imaginable as the Holocaust. Simply put, the risk is that the historical source material carries so much emotional weight that it overwhelms almost any fictional variations. This is the main problem with Janet Gluckman and George Guthridge's **Child of the Light**, which appears to be the first in a series of novels collectively titled *The Madagascar Manifesto*. The main premise of this "alternate Holocaust fantasy" is that the Nazi High Command implements a plan – actually proposed – to resettle all European Jews in Madagascar. Whether or not this is supposed to mean that the Holocaust never happens is unclear from this first volume, which ends with the first shipload of Jewish exiles arriving on the African island. For most of its length, *Child of the Light* is a straight historical novel leavened by a couple of fantasy elements involving telepathic dog training and Jewish mysticism.

The formulaic plot concerns two boyhood friends, Solomon Freund and Erich Weisser, who love the same girl. Solomon is Jewish, and is plagued by visions. Erich has a strange psychic power over dogs, which enables him to rise quickly through the Nazi ranks as a trainer. Needless to say, circumstances test their friendship and their mutual love of Miriam Rathenau, niece of the assassinated (and historical) Jewish Weimar leader Walther Rathenau. Throughout the novel, which covers the years 1918 to 1939, such connections with real figures are made much of. Miriam's tennis teacher is Vladimir Nabokov. While singing in a cabaret she meets Bertolt Brecht. Erich works on films with Leni Riefenstahl, and is accompanied on his mission to Madagascar by Juan Peron. Even though an afterword explains that most of these people could have been where the novel says they were, the overall effect is like *Ragtime* gone berserk. There's no doubt that Gluckman and Guthridge have done their research, but the research begins to weigh down the narrative; none of the historical characters have much depth, nor is their thematic significance immediately apparent. Of the main characters, Erich's growing corruption is far too predictable, and Miriam is far too gullible, staying with Erich even after he rapes her and lies to her about Solomon's being in a concentration camp. Only Solomon, with his provocative visions of horror, seems a compelling character who holds out some promise of development.

But the larger question is, what's the point? There's an enormous body of fiction and memoirs about the Holocaust, and recent years have seen an increasing number of writers using fantasy to explore this difficult topic – Jane Yolen and Martin Amis being two recent examples. In the best of these works, the fantasy forces us into a new perspective and gives us an imaginative framework with which to handle tough material; even Elie Wiesel in *Night and Twilight* uses fantasy elements. *Child of the Light* contains some striking scenes of horror, but the psychic fantasy doesn't add much to it, and the larger alternate-history scenario just doesn't make sense to me

– at least not yet. The novel is dedicated "to the survivors," but it's not clear how their pain is going to be served by imagining something far less horrible than what actually happened. Maybe the next volume in the series – which promises to be about struggles for the control of the Madagascar colony – will make this clear.

A completely different way of using history is represented by Geoff Ryman's **Was**, which gives us a pretty good idea of what might have resulted had Dorothy Gale been invented by Thomas Hardy rather than L. Frank Baum. An unusually powerful novel which is neither fantasy nor SF, *Was* nevertheless seems right in keeping with SF's recent fascination with reinventing history – in this case, the history of a real Dorothy Gael (not Gale) in Kansas, intertwined with episodes from the life of Judy Garland and her mother and with a contemporary story of an AIDS-afflicted actor and his therapist, who come to discover that Dorothy had in fact been a real person. Ryman's only fudging with history consists of placing L. Frank Baum where he wasn't, as a substitute teacher in Dorothy's school, and his only concession to the fantastic is an unresolved disappearance and a few hallucinatory sequences. What all these threads have in common is the question, formulated late in the book, of "what the world does to children." An aging Dorothy, encountered in a mental hospital in the 1950s by the teenager who will later become the AIDS therapist, rambles on about a place called Was, and how you can't get there from Is.

For Dorothy, Was consists of a half-remembered life in St. Louis, before her father disappeared and her mother died of diptheria. Sent with her dog Toto to live with her Auntie Em and Uncle Henry near Manhattan, Kansas, Dorothy's life turns into a nightmare of abuse and loneliness in a landscape that seems eerily congruent with Baum's own descriptions of Kansas grayness and desolation. Baum himself appears only briefly in the novel, but his enthusiasm and imagination transform him into a symbol of unrealized possibilities that haunts Dorothy for the rest of her life – he's like the Technicolor door-opening in the movie. As a substitute teacher, he assigns Dorothy to write a theme which we recognize is the germ of *The Wizard of Oz*, but then he, too, disappears into Was.

Ryman's other storylines explore with irony and great compassion the ways in which the great myth that Dorothy has unwittingly entered affect the lives of other characters, historical and fictional. A key event linking all these stories is the November 1956 TV premiere of the Judy Garland movie, which is crucial to the development of the two main contemporary characters and which indirectly sets up the historical mystery that concludes the novel. It's a brilliant stroke. Even though Baum enthusiasts may want to take exception to Ryman's emphasis on the movie rather than the books in his account of the Oz myth, the fact is that those annual TV showings universalized Oz as part of all our childhoods – as part of a Was that we all share. Through such inspired touches, Ryman's epic fable of lost innocence finally draws us all into the story. It isn't fantasy, but it uses realism as *though* it were fantasy – to show us what we've lost.

The Hollow Man ~~ Dan Simmons

Snow Crash ~~ Neal Stephenson

High Aztech ~~ Ernest Hogan

While many science fiction readers and critics worry over science fiction's unrewarding struggle to get accepted into the mainstream, an increasing number of writers seem to be setting out to do almost exactly the opposite — incorporating the mainstream into SF. One of the most ambitious such writers is Dan Simmons, whose *Hyperion* novels sent readers scurrying back to their Keats, and whose *Phases of Gravity* was one of those novels which sought to erase SF/mainstream boundaries altogether. Now, with **The Hollow Man**, he sets out to do what many literate SF readers must have thought about over the years — namely, taking the apocalyptic imagery of a T.S. Eliot poem and turning it into an apocalyptic narrative. Simmons's novel is remarkably consistent with the feel and imagery of the Eliot poem from which it draws its title and chapter headings, but right away it runs into a rather obvious problem — namely, that "The Hollow Men" doesn't have a plot.

For this, Simmons turns to Dante, whose *Inferno* is another canonical classic that seems to have natural ties to SF (I once saw a copy of John Ciardi's translation — the one Simmons apparently uses — displayed in the SF section of a used bookstore). The story is the spiritual odyssey of Jeremy Bremen, a math professor at Haverford, following the death of his wife — the only other telepath he had ever met. Their marriage not only provided a uniquely intimate relationship for both of them, but protected each from what Bremen calls the "neurobabble" of the troubled minds that surround them (and that serve as stand-ins for the damned souls of hell during Bremen's journey). Adding to the tragedy — and giving the novel its primary SF focus — is the fact that Bremen was on the verge of discovering a mathematical model that would not only explain their telepathy, but that suggested that personality, and hence projected reality, was nothing more than a complex standing wave-front. This research becomes crucial to the denouement of the novel, and is revealed in flashback chapters which alternate with Bremen's infernal odyssey.

Lest there be any doubt that Dante is at work here, Bremen's first stop is Florida, where a fishing guide named Verge ferries him to a remote island. There he inadvertently witnesses a body being dumped in the water by a mafioso named Vanni Fucci (another name from Dante). In the first of a series of improbably stupid moves on the part of the novel's gangsters, Fucci kidnaps Bremen to Disney World, where Bremen escapes disguised as Goofy. I don't think any of this is meant to be funny; *The Hollow Man* is peppered with such idiot-plot conveniences and unlikely coincidences, and Simmons's tone is erratic as well — most notably in a long central sequence set in a desert ranch meant to correspond to Dante's ninth circle. As Ciardi realized in translating *The Inferno* for the modern reader, Dante was out to horrify, but the only modern rhetoric we have for doing this is – well, the horror story. Simmons constructs his horror sequence in such a way that he ends up with stunning images of Cerberus and the frozen lake, but by then we feel like we're in a different novel altogether. How Simmons gets out of all this to provide an essentially upbeat ending consistent with neither Dante nor Eliot is a testimony to his considerable storytelling talent. (His ending, in fact, invokes another, uncredited modernist poet – Wallace Stevens – in its vision of imagination ordering chaos.) Whether it works or not will depend upon the degree to which readers are willing to accept such an unlikely brew of SF, horror, gangster chase adventure, modernist poetry, and medieval mysticism.

Is it steam-engine time for the notion that religion is a virus? 1992 isn't half over, and already here are two very different novels – Neal Stephenson's Snow Crash and Ernest Hogan's *High Aztech* – built around that central conceit. Stephenson's novel is the more nominally ambitious of the two, coming from a mainstream writer and dressed up in the finery of Bantam's Spectra imprint, but both are remarkable for the ways in which they portray highly original 21st century societies, and both are further examples of SF importing influences from outside itself. *Snow Crash* begins in a wildly Pynchonesque future America in which centralized government has given way to semi-autonomous "burbclaves" and private enterprise has taken over everything from jails (competing franchises called The Hoosegow and The Clink) to international relations ("Admiral Bob's Global Security," "General Jim's Defense System"). The Mafia is in the pizza delivery business, and hires armed Deliverators to get the pies there on time. Streets and highways are full of high-tech skateboarding messengers called Kouriers, who harpoon passing traffic to gain speed. The sheer bravado of Stephenson's invention in these opening chapters is exhilarating. Hiro Protagonist, a freelance hacker and intelligence stringer who is working as a Deliverator, meets a fifteen year old girl Kourier named Y.T. when she "poons" his truck, and they're off on what seems to be an series of endlessly funny adventures.

But then the novel changes focus, as Hiro enters a virtual reality program called the Metaverse, a kind of VR bulletin board which is this society's main source of entertainment and fantasy fulfillment. Stephenson's VR world is no less inventive than his 21st century California – but it's no more interesting, either. (One of the potential problems with VR fiction is that fiction, by its very nature, is *already* a kind of virtual reality, and VR thus becomes a fiction within a fiction, competing with the novel's primary world for the reader's interest.) In the Metaverse, Hiro first encounters the Snow Crash of the title – a computer virus that can disable the "software" of the brain itself, but that also exists as a biological virus (the term "snow crash" itself is apparently a hacker's term for a system crash so severe that only snow appears on the video monitor). As Hiro investigates the source of Snow Crash, the novel shifts focus again, and becomes a kind of extended, *Foucault's Pendulum*-style infodump as a near-omniscient program called The Librarian provides Hiro with evidence that something like this virus may have been at the root of early religions – and that someone may be trying to use it to take over the world.

Much of the rest of the novel becomes a chase-and-capture adventure as Hiro and Y.T. try to foil the bad guys in a series of adventures reminiscent of everything from *Videodrome* to *Ghostbusters*. It's remarkable that Stephenson can bring this all off, veering from Pynchon to Eco to pulp adventure complete with a too-plucky punk Nancy Drew – but he does, and the result is great fun.

The religion virus in Ernest Hogan's **High Aztech** is more or less purely biological, but as both Hogan and Stephenson observe, the distinction between biology and information at the molecular level is pretty arbitrary. Hogan's hero (!) is Xolotl Zapata, a cartoonist living in 21st century Mexico City, which has been renamed Tenochtitlan in the wake of an Aztec revival following the collapse of the United States as a superpower and the growth of former third-world countries. Mexico has become the center of high-tech, and Africa the center of biological and genetic research. African scientists have isolated a virus which can be programmed with the beliefs of any religious system and – needless to say – someone wants to use it to take over the world.

Although both Hogan and Stephenson share the commonly-held SF view that religion is mainly an instrument of social control, Hogan is a bit more interested in the kinds of intolerance competing religious systems can generate. Zapata, for example, is already under a death threat for having published a comic satirizing aspects of Aztec belief (in case the parallel misses anyone, Salman Rushdie himself shows up in a hallucinatory sequence near the end of the book), and Ishmael Reed's 1972 novel *Mumbo Jumbo* – about the resurgence of Voodoo as an empowering religion for African-Americans – provides one of the novel's epigraphs and also gets mentioned in that hallucinatory sequence. To make matters worse for Zapata, he is infected by a former lover with the Aztec virus and becomes the prime carrier, sought by both Aztec nationalists and North American fundamentalists who want to infect him with *their* virus to prove their religion is superior.

What all this leads up to is an astonishing tour-de-force of an ending, in which Zapata envisions a wild party of all the world's gods in the skies over Tenochtitlan. This ending alone is worth the price of the book, but getting to it may be a bit of a challenge for many readers. It's a rewarding change to see the third world brought to the forefront of a 21st century scenario, but Hogan has chosen to give this world texture by means of the most complicated array of multilingual neologisms since Burgess's *A Clockwork Orange*. Every page is peppered with Spanish-Nahuatl words, often impossible to decipher from context and frequently unnecessary; sentences sometimes seem awkwardly constructed just to accommodate them. Hogan provides a glossary, but urges us not to consult it until we've read the whole novel. Fat chance.

The Year's Best Fantasy and Horror: Fifth Annual Collection ~
~ edited by Ellen Datlow and Terri Windling

Children of the Night ~~ Dan Simmons

An interesting characteristic of the vampires in Dan Simmons's *Children of the Night* (more about which in a moment) is that they can survive for long periods of time without infusions of fresh blood — but sooner or later the body will begin to cannibalize itself for nutrients. Maybe this self-cannibalization is the problem with horror fiction itself, and to some extent with fantasy as well. It's not that there aren't plenty of talented new writers in the field — Ellen Datlow and Terri Windling's fifth outing of **The Year's Best Fantasy and Horror** provides ample evidence of that — but any genre that carries so much market clout is bound to find the market pushing back, and markets always want more of the same. So it's not surprising to see a few Dracula and Frankenstein variations showing up in this latest annual volume, and even Hollywood seems to be getting into the act: the collection includes stories about Robin Hood and Peter Pan, as well as two variations on the "Little Mermaid" theme. What is most striking about *The Year's Best Fantasy and Horror*, though, is not just that many talented writers are devoting energy to these recyclable materials, but that the editors have also tracked down a huge number of truly inventive stories. They've cast an impressively wide net over original anthologics (seventeen are represented here), story collections, chapbooks, genre magazines (both fantasy and mystery), mainstream magazines, even "little" magazines. Not even the most omnivorous reader is likely to complain that much of this looks too familiar, and some of it raises interesting questions of genre definitions.

Ellen Datlow's selection of horror fiction seems to take the most risks. In her very comprehensive survey of the year in horror, she makes (but does not explain) a distinction between horror fiction and what she calls "horrific" fiction (which sounds a lot like what Robert Bloch calls "terror"). This permits her to include several mystery and crime novels in her recommended list, and to include a handful of mainstream stories whose effect is decidedly unsettling despite their lack of teeth and claws. David Morrell's "The Beautiful Uncut Hair of Graves" is the most haunting of these, although Stephen Gallagher's "The Visitors' Book," Gloria Ericson's "The Witch of Wilton Falls," and Dennis Etchison's "Call Home" are also models of what can be done by indirection. In additional to Morrell, the collection also includes several other stories — both fantasy and horror — by authors with substantial mainstream reputations, such as Joanne Greenberg's "Persistence of Memory," which explores a fascinating Borgesian idea in a not-too-convincing prison setting, and Lisa Mason's moving "Hummers," which deals with the very real horror of ovarian cancer. Perhaps not surprisingly, several of the stories at least mention such real-life horrors as AIDS, cancer, or child abuse. Ordinary vampires, if you'll pardon the expression, begin to seem pale by comparison.

Eroticism is another theme which seems to being gaining favor — at least among horror writers — and which is central to stories by Kathe Koja, Karl Edward Wagner, S.P. Somtow, Grant Morrison, Poppy Z. Brite, and Pierrette Fleutiaux. Of these, the most substantial is Fleutiaux's "The Ogre's Wife," translated from the French, which calls to mind the best of Angela Carter's explorations of the hidden sexuality of folklore. The most disturbing is Grant Morrison's sadomasochistic nightmare "The Braille Encyclopedia," with its extreme development of the blind-girl-as-victim theme, and the most disappointing is Karl Edward Wagner's fantasia on girlie model Betty Page, "The Kind Men Like," which is a weaker version of Fritz Leiber's classic "The Girl with Hungry Eyes" (which also inspired a Harlan Ellison story — god help us, another incipient theme anthology!). Eroticism is also a subtext in several of the anthology's clutch of vampire stories, four of which are from Datlow's own *A Whisper of Blood* and the most impressive of which is Pat Cadigan's "Home by the Sea" — which actually draws most of its power from its eschatological imagery, not its bloodsuckers.

Given the intensity of some of the horror pieces, it's disarming to come across, in the same volume, fairly wispy treatments of the Little Mermaid (by Charles de Lint) or Robin Hood (by Midori Snyder); mythological romances by Nancy Springer, Robert Holdstock and Garry Kilworth, Alison Fell, and C.J. Cherryh; or the complete text of Nancy Willard's children's book *Pish, Posh, Said Hieronymus Bosch*. (What kind of Jekyll-and-Hyde audience is out there, anyway?) The fantasy selections, and Terry Windling's overview of the year in fantasy (I mention these introductions because they add enormous value to the book as a reference source), are eclectic in a different way from the horror: whereas the horror selections sometimes reach into related genres, the fantasy selections draw on several non-genre (or non-market) based traditions of the fantastic. Magic realism is well represented by Rosario Ferre's Cortazar-like "The Poisoned Story" and Sandra Cisneros's "Little Miracles, Kept Promises"; Japanese legends by S.P. Somtow's "The Pavilion of Frozen Women"; Russian social satire by Nina Katerli's "The Monster"; surrealism by Kobo Abe's "The Life of a Poet"; the tall tale in Terry Bisson's delightful (and totally unpredictable) "The Coon Suit"; even Georgia O'Keeffe's imagism in A.R. Morlan's highly original "The Second Most Beautiful Woman in the World." Several pieces tread what Windling calls the "shadowland" between fantasy and horror, and there are several poems as well, including a moving Holocaust meditation by Jessica Greenbaum. The best poem in the book, however, is disguised as a story: Steve Rasnic Tem's apocalyptic elegy "At the End of the Day," about a deliveryman with a last, undeliverable package, is a minor classic.

There are, to be sure, enough traditional dragons and princesses and monsters to keep genre freaks happy, but the real strength of *The Year's Best Fantasy and Horror* is in showing the enormous range that is possible in fantasy and horror – but that is too seldom visible on bookstore shelves laden with fantasy trilogies and horror novels the size of pot roasts. Datlow and Windling go a long way toward showing us that what is wrong with these genres is not inherent in the genres themselves, but in what writers and publishers do to them.

One writer who's been doing a lot with and to the horror genre lately is Dan Simmons, whose *Summer of Night* last year was a thoroughly competent, suspenseful, and ultimately not very interesting excursion into Stephen King's horror/nostalgia territory. This doesn't mean that Simmons isn't an interesting writer. Far from it: certainly no one can accuse him of being unwilling to try new recipes. In **Children of the Night**, his band of ghostbusting kids from that earlier novel have grown up into an old boy network, and one of them – now a world-weary, disillusioned Vietnam vet and priest – is ready to take on Dracula himself. But Simmons isn't about to leave it at that. Before it's over, *Children of the Night* segues from an historical catalog of Vlad Tepes' atrocities to an indictment of Romanian orphanages to a medical thriller to a romance to a James Bond capture-and-pursuit adventure. The vampires hardly get a moment's breath to do any old-fashioned vampiring at all.

In *Song of Kali*, Simmons did a brilliant job of integrating the horrors of real-life Calcutta with the supernatural forces – a conspiracy to bring the goddess Kali back to earth – which threaten the narrator and his wife and kidnap their baby. *Children of the Night* also begins in an impoverished, corrupt society (Romania), involves a conspiracy to bring back into power an unholy terror (Dracula), and revolves around a man and woman and her adopted baby – who also gets kidnapped. Simmons's opening indictment of medical practices in Romania – which sounds convincing – is so powerful and graphic that it already threatens to overwhelm whatever imaginary horrors he can come up with later on, but he ups the ante on himself even more by introducing a possible cure for AIDS and cancer in his medical subplot. This subplot, which concerns a recessive gene for vampirism that might also help the body rebuild its immune system, almost gets out of hand in whole chapters of medical dialogue obtuse enough to send Robin Cook reeling for his PDR. Dr. Kate Neuman, a physician from the Centers for Disease Control on assignment in Romania, enlists the aid of Father Mike O'Rourke to help her adopt a Romanian infant with a strange blood disorder. Back in the States, she begins enlisting other medical researchers and sets up a high-security lab – but then the baby is stolen, the lab destroyed, and a fellow researcher killed (along with Kate's ex-husband) by intruders with apparently supernatural powers.

Enter Father O'Rourke again – Mike – getting more macho by the minute. He returns with Kate to Romania, where they uncover a conspiracy of strigoi plotting to make the child (who is of course a vampire) the heir to Dracula's throne. The plot thins, as repeated cliffhangers are resolved by unlikely coincidences: a protest rally conveniently provides cover for an escape from a car chase; Mike seems to know everything about Romanian history except whatever pertains to the current problem; the one model of helicopter that Mike knows how to fly is the one on the vampires' front lawn. Simmons handles all this with gusto, and his interpolated chapters in which Dracula recalls his various historical atrocities are equally juicy, if just a bit gratuitous. The problem isn't that Simmons can't handle thriller material well; it's just that along the way he's giving us glimpses of how he could do so much more.

− July 1992, Locus #378 −

Hearts, Hands and Voices ~~ Ian McDonald
(as *The Broken Land* in the U.S.)

Tales of Chicago ~~ R.A. Lafferty

For those of us raised on Shaw, Yeats, and Joyce, it's a bit unsettling to be reminded that Ireland today is virtually a third-world country, with its own history of oppressive colonialism, violence, famine, and poverty. Despite a rich heritage of visionary literature and mythology, not to mention an unparalleled tradition of satirical fantasy from Swift to Flann O'Brien, it's hard to think of a clearly Irish tradition in science fiction − one that takes account of both the fabled Irish love of language and more bitter economic and historical realities. Ian McDonald seems to have set out to remedy this situation single-handedly. Last year, he took on most of modern Irish history in *King of Morning, Queen of Day*, a novel whose unfortunate title may have steered away readers who thought it sounded like another generic fantasy trilogy. The American title of his new novel, **The Broken Land**, isn't much better − it sounds like a Donaldson rip − but the novel itself is a complete original, and a startling extension of McDonald's concerns about oppression, violence, and redemption.

In one sense, the novel is a depressing catalogue of twentieth-century atrocities, displaced to a distant setting that sometimes resembles Northern Ireland, sometimes Nazi Europe, sometimes South Africa, and sometimes southeast Asia. The chief antagonists are the Proclaimers, who rule their empire using more or less traditional technology, and the Confessors, who seek home rule and are masters of the most thoroughly imagined biotechnology since Harry Harrison's *West of Eden* trilogy. If this political background suggests the Catholic-Protestant conflict in Northern Ireland, McDonald's cultural and mythic background suggests a whole panoply of oppressed peoples. His character and place names seem to draw on African, aboriginal, and oriental languages; his themes of ancestor-worship and apocalyptic revolutionary movements call to mind everything from Yoruba mythology to the Native American ghost dance movement. Villages are destroyed in ways that remind us of Vietnam; certain populations are restricted to South African-style "townships";

prisoners are hauled in darkened trucks for days and then "selected," in the manner of Nazi Germany.

McDonald holds all this together through the story of Mathembe, a girl whose response to the world she has inherited is the same as that of Oskar in Gunter Grass's *The Tin Drum*: she refuses to speak. When her village is destroyed by imperial forces for harboring members of a resistance movement called the Warriors of Destiny, she sets out with her family to seek refuge with an uncle in the city – a vivid amalgam of Dickensian London and *Bladerunner* L.A. – only to be displaced again when the revolution comes and her adopted neighborhood is burned. Separated from her remaining family, she becomes, literally, a boat person, attaching herself to an enormous riverboat which is a society unto itself. After winning acceptance into this society through her skills with biotechnology, she sets out to find her family, journeying first to sprawling D.P. camps and finally to a mysterious Borderland, where her mother has joined a movement to end violence through a new advance in genetic engineering.

McDonald's ending is problematical, and raises moral questions that trouble Mathende herself. Even though it's well set up thematically, and serves to make sense out of the organic vs. mechanical opposition that permeates the narrative, it's still a science fiction solution to all-too-real social and economic problems. It's a tribute to McDonald's skill that he has made these problems so convincing and so vivid that his own ending can't quite handle them, but there's enough wisdom and thoughtfulness in the rest of the novel to more than make up for a facile resolution. There's another reason to recommend the book: for all its violence and depredations, its style is intensely poetic, even hypnotic. As familiar as its aspects are, McDonald's world is entirely original, entirely consistent, and entirely his own. The Irish language is very much alive, and it can do wonders for SF.

R.A. Lafferty is another Irishman, of sorts, and he certainly has his own facility with language, but he properly belongs more in the Irish-American tradition of loudmouthed storytelling – the tradition that gave us "Finnegan's Wake" (the song, not the novel) and Finley Peter Dunne. Lafferty's **Tales of Chicago** comes to us from United Mythologies Press, which promises that it is only the first in a trilogy of illustrated novels (to be followed by *Tales of Midnight* and *Argo*) collectively titled *More than Melchisedech*. That title comes from a poem by G.K. Chesterton, whose passion for wordplay, goofy satire, and arcanely disguised Catholic mysticism would seem to make him an unlikely influence on much modern sf, but who is much in evidence not only in Lafferty but in the work of Gene Wolfe. In the Bible, Melchisedech is a legendary king of Jerusalem whose life is seen as prefiguring that of Christ; in Lafferty's story, he is Melchisedech Duffey, an Iowa-born magus who can create gold by banging his hands together, absorb the memories and skills of others, create human beings, and summon invisible giants to his aid. *Tales of Chicago* details the first forty-odd years of Duffey's life (uncertain, since Duffey claimed to have been five years old when he was born), from the turn of the century through World War II.

Duffey is one of Lafferty's familiar tall-tale characters, establishing a hugely successful men's club in St. Louis by the time he is fifteen, becoming a boxer, musician, and balloonist, enjoying a succession of women, finally getting married and creating a "golden age" in Chicago in the late twenties. All the while, he is capable of periodically summoning supernatural forces to his aid, and all the while he is plagued by three mysterious slant-faced men who have been trying to kill him since childhood. In the end, he even undergoes psychoanalysis. All of this is presented in Lafferty's usual let's-have-another-round style, with his usual preoccupations (the world has already ended, but we don't know it yet, golden ages come and go without our noticing, the world is run by conspiracies of anonymous men, etc.).

In short, *Tales of Chicago* (which isn't a collection of tales and has little to do with Chicago) is as wildly enjoyable and maddeningly elliptical as most of Lafferty, and at times almost too whimsical to bear. R. Ward Shipman's pen-and-ink illustrations, reminiscent of Mervyn Peake, are well-chosen and appropriate, but the volume does suffer some of the production problems characteristic of small presses (several typos, chapter headings that appear in the contents but not on the chapters themselves). United Mythologies press deserves credit for a good job, but at the same time it's unfortunate that Lafferty has begun to disappear into small presses which reach only a limited portion of the SF audience, and probably none of Lafferty's true audience – which may lie outside the SF field altogether, probably in some magic realist barroom somewhere.

– August 1992, Locus #379 –

Mars ~~ Ben Bova

Lost Boys ~~ Orson Scott Card

Fatherland ~~ Robert Harris

About once a decade, it seems, science fiction decides it hasn't had enough of Mars, and we get an outbreak of new Martian novels and stories. In the late forties and early fifties, of course, it was Bradbury, Clarke, and Heinlein, with a supporting cast including Leigh Brackett and "Cyril Judd"; the early sixties saw Heinlein again, along with Dick and Zelazny; and the mid-seventies had important works by Pohl, Varley, and Ian Watson. The latest flurry of Mars novels may have begun with Terry Bisson's *Voyage to the Red Planet*, and its most ambitious entry, at least in terms of market potential, may be Ben Bova's **Mars**. Bova has set out to do for Mars what James Michener has done for most of the pages in your world atlas, but he lacks Michener's long-windedness and passion for history. The result, from the point of view both of the novel's mainstream ambitions and of its SF content, is both good and bad.

From a science fiction perspective, Mars belongs in the tradition of counter-mythic texts that seek to show us how inhospitable the planet really is and how heroic its first explorers must be — much like Clarke's *The Sands of Mars* provided a realistic balance to Bradbury's *The Martian Chronicles* forty years ago. As is usual in such novels, the technological extrapolation is much more convincing than the political and economic scenarios. Bova has an impassioned Brazilian statesman virtually shaming the nations of the earth into mounting a joint Mars expedition, which subsequently is threatened by political jockeying and the presidential ambitions of a female American vice-president. Meanwhile, a genuine crisis emerges among the Martian explorers, as their attempts to alter the exploration schedule to visit a likely life-supporting region are plagued by a mysterious malady. (It would be unfair to reveal just what this malady turns out to be, but some readers may be disturbed, as I was, by how it is inadequately set up and how the explanation, when it comes, fails to account for a key factor that should have prevented it all along.)

The multinational expedition gives Bova a chance to assemble the most politically correct cast of characters imaginable — men, women, a Black, Asians, Russians, etc. — but this political correctness also nearly backfires on him. Jamie Waterman, the half-Navaho hero of the story, is admirably steeped in Native American lore (Tony Hillerman is credited in the acknowledgments), but insists repeatedly he was brought up as a white man in an academic family. Still, he sometimes verges on a stereotype: when he learns of his acceptance on the Mars team, his impulse is to let out a war whoop, and later he thinks the Martian wind sounds like the spirit of his ancestors. Bova also has an understandably difficult time imagining what the Russians would behave like in the twenty-first century, and several of the tensions among crew members have a cold-war edge to them that already seems dated.

Nevertheless, for the most part, Bova accomplishes what he sets out to do, which is to write an SF novel as close to the mainstream side of the envelope as possible. The technology of space travel and Martian exploration is detailed and thoroughly researched, and his Mars is believable, if not quite awe-inspiring. The sheer wonder of planetary exploration, which comes through in even the most hardwired narratives of a romantic like Clarke, seems always just a bit beyond the reach of Bova's rather pedestrian prose, and the various romances and jealousies of his characters are standard bestseller fare. All this may bode well for the novel's chances in the mainstream arena, but it doesn't challenge us as SF. Bova has mastered the real-life details of Mars better than any current SF writer; he just isn't in love with it.

Orson Scott Card's approach to the mainstream is quite different from Bova's, and **Lost Boys** is even being touted as Card's first work of mainstream fiction. But it isn't quite his first (unless you discount 1984's *Woman of Destiny*), and it isn't quite mainstream. The novel is an expansion and reworking of Card's controversial 1989 *Fantasy and Science Fiction* story of the same title, and although he has eliminated the direct autobiographical references, invented a family in place of his own, and shifted from a first-person to a third-person narrative voice, the novel in some ways seems more autobiographical than ever; the story at least had the distancing tone of folklore about it. As a novel, the weight of realistic detail — Card's vivid feel for places and characters, mixed with a believable account of the computer marketing wars of the early eighties in a subplot — somehow brings the pain of losing a child (or losing touch with a child) even closer to the surface.

Card writes about kids as well as almost anyone, and Stevie Fletcher, the increasingly morose eight-year-old who has trouble adjusting to his family's move to North Carolina, is the focus of *Lost Boys*. The viewpoint character, however, is Stevie's father Step, forced to take a job as a manual writer for a small computer software firm after royalties from a successful game program begin to dry up. Step is miserable in his new job, not only because of the office politics but because it draws him away from his family — especially Stevie, whose attempts to make a new life are derailed by an unhinged teacher, and who increasingly withdraws into a favorite computer game and begins to talk of imaginary friends. Step eventually learns that there's something preternatural about Stevie's computer game, and that his imaginary friends may not be all that imaginary. The novel's conclusion is essentially the same as that of the story, but now it must carry the weight of several hundred pages of family drama, with little foreshadowing beyond a few haunted-house style bug invasions. Card makes it work — he's a brilliant storyteller — but it doesn't quite warrant calling this a "mainstream" book, even though there's a good argument here for the silliness of that distinction in the first place.

One aspect of the novel that will make some readers uncomfortable is the importance of Christian belief in the life of Step and his family. The small Mormon community provides their only support system, and Step's wife DeAnne at times seems almost immobilized by her devoutness. The moral didacticism implicit in all of Card's work is here directly linked to religious faith, and as usual there's not a trace of irony in his approach. An important subtext of the novel is the struggle to adhere to a received moral code in an impure world, and there's no good reason why Card shouldn't be allowed to make his characters practicing Mormons in order to explore this; after all, it's his moral code. Christians have long complained that they're almost invisible in modern literature, and they may have a point. The irony is that in *Lost Boys*, which deliberately explores the limits of what faith can do, that faith turns out to be less intrusive and Card's use of it less manipulative than in many of his other novels.

While Bova and Card mount their approaches to the mainstream from such differing perspectives, the mainstream itself continues to cheerfully recycle SF scenarios. The most recent *cause celebre* is London Sunday Times columnist Robert Harris's first novel, **Fatherland**, already at the top of British bestseller lists, already optioned for film by Mike Nichols, already translated into a dozen languages, already rejected by a score of German publishers because of its portrayal of a Nazi-dominated Europe in 1964. Victorious-Nazi tales date back to the thirties, and may be the largest single subcategory of the alternate-history motif, but Harris does manage to add some new twists to the formula, even though he's apparently unaware that it's a formula at all.

In the first place, Harris sets his story in Berlin itself, rather than in a defeated Britain or America, which is more often the case. This is the Berlin that Albert Speer wanted to build, and in its overblown monumentality it very nearly becomes the star of the story. In the second place, Harris casts his narrative as a police procedural; his protagonist is a disillusioned SS police officer whose investigation of a murder, aided by an American woman journalist, leads him to uncover first a conspiracy involving stolen art treasures and eventually to a much broader cover-up which has kept the extermination of the Jews from public knowledge. Harris's thesis is that even if Hitler had won, a government built on such massive crimes could not sustain itself for long if the crimes were known; presumably, this is why he chooses 1964, only eighteen years after the war, for his setting. (Victims of Stalinist Russia might want to debate this thesis as being a bit naive.) Harris's emphasis on the good cop working within a corrupt system gives the novel a tone more like Stuart Kaminsky's or Martin Cruz Smith's Soviet mysteries than the alternate histories of Philip K. Dick and others.

In fact, except for his descriptions of Berlin, Harris keeps the details of his alternate history firmly in the background. Hitler and Heydrich (Harris's history diverges in 1942, before Heydrich's assassination) are kept offstage, and we only learn bits and pieces about the rest of the world. Churchill has fled to Canada; the war on the Eastern front continues with Russia aided by America; a cold war has developed between Germany and America, but there is talk of detente. President Kennedy is about to visit Berlin for the first time, but it isn't John Kennedy — it's his dad Joseph, whose pro-German sentiments have led him to appoint Charles Lindbergh as ambassador to Berlin. Other aspects of popular culture seem relatively unaltered: the Beatles are gaining popularity, and Barbara Cartland is grinding out her romances, only now with German settings.

For all the publicity surrounding it, *Fatherland* is actually a rather modest suspense novel with modest ambitions. By compressing what in reality were several years' worth of revelations about the Holocaust into a single police investigation, Harris effectively conveys the enormity of the crime, and he makes the telling point that questions about the fate of the Jews were not pressed simply because most Americans didn't care much. While some might object that Harris is guilty of using the Holocaust as a trendy macguffin in a suspense tale, it's at least a pretty good suspense tale, with an ending ambiguous enough to make us think.

The Oxford Book of Science Fiction Stories ~
~ edited by Tom Shippey

Foundations of Fear: An Exploration of Horror ~
~ edited by David G. Hartwell

Quarantine ~~ Greg Egan

The Silent City ~~ Elisabeth Vonarburg
(translated by Jane Brierly)

Beauty ~~ Brian D'Amato

Long before there was anything resembling a coherent critical dialogue concerning SF, fantasy, or horror (if there is one yet), anthologies served as a means of shaping our views of these fields and presenting implicit arguments about their nature. Groff Conklin's thematic anthologies and thematic divisions of his general anthologies promoted the idea that SF might best be understood by means of folklore-like taxonomies — invasions of earth, time travel, marvelous inventions, etc. Judith Merril, through her best-of-the-year selections, argued that SF and fantasy were not wholly defined by genre markets and could sustain a wide variety of stylistic experiments. Back in the thirties, Dorothy Sayers did much to legitimize horror and supernatural fiction by including it on an equal footing with the detective and mystery story in her *Omnibus of Crime* anthologies. Now, with such recent books as Gardner Dozois's *Modern Classics of Science Fiction* and such forthcoming books as projected Norton anthology of Ursula Le Guin and others, the Big Anthology seems to be re-emerging as a theoretical platform.

Tom Shippey's **Oxford Book of Science Fiction Stories** (carefully titled to avoid the implication that this is the "Oxford Book of Science Fiction") will undoubtedly be a major player in this sweepstakes, especially on college campuses where names like Oxford or Norton carry the same patina of safe respectability as IBM. Far from retreating into the obvious "classics," however, Shippey has produced an unusual and in some ways even quirky anthology, organized not around the common understanding of American SF's evolution — Heinlein, Asimov, and Bradbury are nowhere in sight, and only two of the selections overlap with *The Science Fiction Hall of Fame* — but around stylistic and structural matters, and in particular around his notion that SF is part of a literary mode which he names by the neologism "fabril." "Fabril" (from the Latin faber, or artificer) is supposed to be the opposite of "pastoral," and represents literature that is urban, future-oriented, concerned with the making of artifacts.

It's an intriguing notion, even though Shippey has to do some footwork to account for his inclusion of several stories that look awfully pastoral to me, such as Simak's "Desertion," Weinbaum's "A Martian Odyssey," James H. Schmitz's "The Second Night of Summer," Le Guin's "The Dowry of the Angyar" (more familiar to most readers as "Semley's Necklace"), or Paul J. McAuley's "Karl and the Ogre." Other stories, such as Wells's "The Land Ironclads," Spinrad's "A Thing of Beauty," or David Brin's "Piecework," admirably illustrate the thesis. But as in all such anthologies, the broader principal of finding good, varied stories inevitably gets away from the proposed argument, and Shippey has done an excellent job of providing some unusual and provocative selections.

Some of the stories seem to reveal Shippey's own unacknowledged interests. Overpopulation, for example, is addressed by Harry Harrison's "A Criminal Act," Ballard's "Billennium," and Disch's "Problems of Creativeness." Religion is a major theme in Walter M. Miller's "Crucifixus Etiam," Gene Wolfe's "How the Whip Came Back," and George R. R. Martin's "The Way of Cross and Dragon." Other stories are a mix of the surprising and the obvious. Frank L. Pollack's "Finis" is a stilted but vivid world-cataclysm tale from 1906; Jack Williamson's 1928 "The Metal Man" seems intended only to represent the flavor of the early *Amazing Stories*; James Blish's "How Beautiful with Banners" is an odd exploration of symbolic sexuality; and Hilbert Schenk's "Silicon Muse" shows up as what is otherwise part of the cyberpunk section of the book. Mainstream forties *Astounding* is represented by the Simak, one of Kuttner and Moore's Baldy stories, and Van Vogt's "The Monster." And the selections by Weinbaum, Campbell, Pohl, Aldiss, Cordwainer Smith, Alice Sheldon, and William Gibson are pretty much what you'd expect. In all, this is an excellent mix of stories that — while it may not reflect what many think of as the standard SF canon — retains a distinctively individual flavor without presenting a seriously distorted view of the genre's possibilities.

Horror fiction is in an even stranger position than SF in regard to its literary pedigree; it's at once both more and less respectable. On the one hand, paperback racks are full of quarter pounders with cheese and embossed covers, while on the other an apologist such as David Hartwell, in putting together **Foundations of Fear**, can find superb mainstream works by the likes of Thomas Hardy, Carlos Fuentes, and E.T.A. Hoffmann to claim as part of horror's lineage. Like Shippey with SF, Hartwell regards horror as more a "mode" than a genre, and like Shippey, he provides a thoughtful, intelligent, and informative introduction. (Unlike Shippey, he also provides useful introductions to each selection). Hartwell began his historical exploration of horror in 1987 with *The Dark Descent*, which included most of the predictable Big Names and still stands as the one horror anthology anyone needs to read unless they're going to get serious about it. In *Foundations of Fear*, Hartwell casts his net a bit wider and comes up with some truly eye-opening examples of what he calls "horrific" writing. (Awkward as it sounds, "horrific" is fast becoming the adjective of choice among horror critics, presumably to parallel "fantastic" and to avoid the obvious *double entendre* of simply calling a story "horrible.")

Although more than half of Hartwell's thirty selections were originally published after 1950, the tone of the anthology is dominated by the seven stories that date from before 1900, giving it a feel not unlike those old Sayers anthologies. The oldest story is Hoffmann's "The Sand-Man," which provides a nice bridge between the Gothic and the SF horror tale, which is represented by Campbell's "Who Goes There?," George R. R. Martin's "Sandkings," Dick's "Faith of Our Fathers," and stories by Silverberg, Pohl, and Octavia Butler (whose "Bloodchild" is still one of the most harrowing uses of horror in SF that I know). Thomas Hardy's "Barbara, of the House of Grebe," a monumentally depressing tale of an inhumanly cruel husband, sets the stage for a number of non-supernatural tales of psychological horror and connects thematically to stories by Violet Hunt, Theodore Sturgeon, and Elizabeth Engstrom. Gertrude Atherton, the only author with two stories in the collection, explores themes of obsessiveness and loss of identity that later become common in modern horror. This is the general pattern of the anthology — establishing thematic and stylistic links between diverse works, and thus constructing a sense of the traditions of "horrific" writing.

There are a few familiar classics in the book — Daphne Du Maurier's "Don't Look Now," Lovecraft's "At the Mountains of Madness," Heinlein's "They," Campbell's "Who Goes There?," Arthur Machen's "The Great God Pan," Richard Matheson's "Duel" — but the real strength of the book is its presentation of lesser-known texts by authors such as Jean Ray, Madeline Yale Wynne, Harriet Prescott Spofford, and Edgar Pangborn. Carlos Fuentes' "Aura," the only representation of Latin America's tradition of the uncanny, is a true masterpiece, and possibly the best-crafted story in the book. Another notable strength is the attention paid to women writers, who make up nearly a third of the selections and whose contribution to the evolution of modern horror literature is convincingly demonstrated. What is not apparent — and it's fine by me — is the post-George Romero school of horror-as-special-effects-in-prose. Even the Clive Barker selection ("In the Hills, the Cities"), if not quite restrained, is thoughtful and provocative.

Foundations of Fear clearly represents a lot of care and thought, and it pays off admirably. More than just a worthwhile sequel to *The Dark Descent*, the book extends and deepens our understanding of a literary tradition that has perhaps become too easy to dismiss. Hartwell has not only found a good bunch of stuff for us to read, but he has also made a significant contribution to the theory and criticism of the field. Genre. Mode. Whatever.

The many-worlds interpretation of quantum mechanics has proved invaluable for a generation of SF writers seeking a vague rationalization for parallel-universe tales, even though the parallel universe theme was there long before Hugh Everett's influential 1957 paper; one thinks of Murray Leinster's 1934 story "Sidewise in Time," for example. Greg Egan views the theory as something more than a world-generating machine, however, and his first novel **Quarantine** makes the collapse of the wave function itself the pivotal event, giving it almost the status of a character. As such, *Quarantine* has more in common with a much lesser-known Leinster story, "The Laws of Chance" (1947), which concerned a kind of radiation which could alter probabilities. It also contains echoes of Philip K. Dick. The main difference is that Leinster and Dick had very little scientific notion of what they were talking about, while Egan knows — and is willing to share — almost more than his narrative can handle.

The plot is initially set up as a kind of existential mystery reminiscent of Lem's *The Investigation*. In 2068, the solar system has been inexplicably isolated from the rest of the universe by an immense bubble beyond the orbit of Pluto, giving rise to various millenarian movements and endless scientific speculation. The narrator, Nick Stavrianos, has been hired by an anonymous client to investigate the disappearance of a woman, severely retarded by congenital brain damage, from the institution where she has lived since childhood. Aided by various neural modifications (all of which have brand names and are listed complete with price, giving the early chapters of the novel the odd tone of a chatty mail-order software catalogue), Nick is able to trace the woman to a mysterious research institute in New Hong Kong. But before he can rescue her, he himself is captured and "reprogrammed" by something called the Ensemble. In good superscience tradition, the macro and micro narratives are brought together as Nick comes to realize the connection between the woman's disappearance and the presence of the bubble around the solar system.

The first half of the novel is a model of the investigation-leading-to-ever-widening-revelations suspense plot. But the infodump, when it comes, very nearly derails the rest of the narrative. It begins with an elementary lecture on Schrodinger's Cat, which leads to speculation that the collapse of the wave-function is centered in the human brain (an idea also touched upon in Dan Simmons's recent *The Hollow Man*), which in turn suggests that infinities of universes are destroyed each time a wave function collapses, which means that if humans learn to sustain an uncollapsed wave-front, all possibilities become real. By the time Egan gets his plot going again with some business about a mad scientist who wants to infect the whole world with the ability to maintain uncollapsed states — a kind of quantum version of Greg Bear's *Blood Music* — we're almost dizzy with theory. Still, Quarantine qualifies as grand speculation in the purest sense, and despite a few structural problems, it's a stunning first novel.

Another first novel, Elisabeth Vonarburg's **The Silent City**, has taken an inordinately long time to see print in the U.S. Published originally in France in 1981 as *Le Silence de la Cité*, the novel won the Grand Prix de la SF Française and appeared in Jane Brierly's English translation in 1988 in Canada, where Vonarburg has lived since 1973. It's an elegant and moving work, which begins with the standard SF trope of a young person raised in a high-tech underground city isolated from the outside world for several generations following a massive ecological cataclysm. At first one wonders whether Vonarburg can do anything original with this hoary scenario, but the novel soon opens up into a thoughtful and complex exploration of the relations of mind, body, identity, and society that calls to mind Kate Wilhelm and Ursula Le Guin more than E.M. Forster and Arthur C. Clarke.

In the novel's early chapters, the city's few surviving adults live largely through robot surrogates, even though genetic advances permit them to regenerate their bodies on a limited basis. One such surrogate acts as a grandfather to Elisa, whose father Paul sees her as the greatest genetic hope of permitting the human race to survive and eventually repopulate the outside. Paul occasionally sends robots, or "ommachs," into the surrounding tribal communities to gather samples of genetic material for this project. As Elisa grows older, she gradually learns about her true nature, her relationship with Paul, and her growing ability to manipulate her body at will – even to the point of changing herself into a man. Aided by a robot programmed with the personality of her "grandfather" and fearing Paul's growing madness, Elisa flees the city in the form of a man – in order to increase her chances of survival, since on the outside four girls are born for every boy and women are devalued – and eventually finds herself sexually involved with a young woman, Judith, whom she (he?) impregnates. Paul reappears, wanting to kidnap the mother and unborn child for his genetic project, and Elisa kills him.

Later, Elisa returns to the city and undertakes her own version of the Project, creating generations of children who are all born as girls but who can later change sexual identity at will. While this is going on, Judith has led a revolt among the women and established an independent women's village which is preparing to go to war against the male-dominated enclaves. The contrast between the society in which sex roles are chosen freely and the society which traps its members into predetermined roles according to sex could easily lead to a schematic feminist tract, but Vonarburg handles all this without losing sight of the ambiguities involved and in particular the character of Elisa. The novel is one of the most sensitive explorations of gender and identity since *The Left Hand of Darkness*, and Jane Brierly's fine translation lends it a haunting, evocative tone. Bantam deserves credit for finally giving us a look at one of the major works of recent French-language SF.

Still another accomplished first novel is Brian D'Amato's **Beauty**. D'Amato is a young New York artist whose work was featured in the virtual reality exhibition in Manhattan's Jack Tilton Gallery last July – one of the first such exhibits in a commercial gallery – and whose mother is the successful mystery novelist Barbara D'Amato. But *Beauty* is neither a mystery nor a virtual reality tale – unless you regard radical, computer-assisted plastic surgery as a form of virtual reality. D'Amato's narrator, Jamie Angelo, is a successful New York artist and former medical student who makes a fortune doing unlicensed facial reconstructions, using unorthodox techniques which he and his colleagues have developed. His masterpiece is Penny

Penn, a film actress loosely based on Jodie Foster, but he becomes obsessed with the idea of creating the perfect beauty for the age, and eventually persuades his lover, Jaishree, to undergo such a transformation. She becomes a phenomenal success, but eventually something goes wrong with the reconstructed tissue, and Jamie becomes a fugitive from his former clients, from the law, and from the medical profession.

On the horror-story level, then, D'Amato's plot is something straight out of an old EC comic — which in fact once ran a similar story about plastic surgery gone awry. It also calls to mind both Kobe Abe's *The Face of Another* and Patrick Suskind's *Perfume* in its exploration of the cosmetic nature of identity. But the novel is much more complex and rewarding than such comparisons suggest. It is one of the few recent works of fiction to recognize the implicit links between the Frankenstein and Pygmalion myths, and its portrayal of the New York art scene is at once cynical and convincingly trendy. The obsessiveness and eventual disintegration of the narrator, who grows increasingly revolted by the imperfections of real human flesh as he is consumed by the pursuit of beauty, is handled brilliantly, and is far more disturbing than the more conventional horror elements. Jamie's preoccupation with Mesoamerican blood sacrifices, his compulsive viewing of old movies on themes of transformation — *Island of Lost Souls* in particular — his looking for rationalizations in the theoretical works of Adorno, Bataille, Barthes, and others, all add up to a three-dimensional portrait of a genuinely scary character. Beauty may be only marginally SF in terms of its technology, but its theme traces a straight line back to Shelley, Wells, and even *Metropolis*. It's a worthwhile and innovative addition to a noble tradition.

— October 1992, Locus #381 —

The Collected Stories of Robert Silverberg,
Volume One: Secret Sharers

Speaking in Tongues ~~ Ian McDonald

Mirror to the Sky ~~ Mark S. Geston

A Deeper Sea ~~ Alexander Jablokov

Back in the days when aliens were still called Space Monsters!, Robert Silverberg made his initial reputation by turning out millions of words for post-pulp digest-sized magazines which often featured lurid covers depicting girl-snatching tentacled aliens. They were the sort of magazine that many modern SF enthusiasts tend to discreetly ignore. Now, of course, Silverberg is SF's consummate craftsman, well on his way to stateliness if he isn't there already. The very title of his **Collected Stories: Volume One** seems almost ostentatiously understated for a writer whose actual collected works would sink a small boat. Silverberg's output of stories has slowed in the wake of his successful novels, and each one is a model of structure, control, and sophistication. Of the twenty-four stories in this volume, more than half were originally sold to *Playboy* or *Omni*, almost that many made one or more "best of the year" collections, and a sizable handful won Hugo or Nebula nominations or awards – and all this from a collection which only covers the years between 1981 and 1988! Nearly all of them are self-assured, literate, elegant, precise. And what are they about? Well, girl-snatching tentacled aliens, among other things.

Those particular girls get snatched in "Against Babylon," which to be fair is a complex and sensitive story which presents the alien landing as part of a larger scenario involving a failing romance and brooding L.A.-*angst*, but there's no question that Silverberg likes to write about meetings with aliens of one sort or another: aliens who digest humans and take on their form ("Amanda and the Alien"), aliens who are art collectors ("Tourist Trade"), horrible aliens who slide up your nostrils and live in your brain ("Symbiont"), primitive little aliens found on Pluto ("Sunrise on Pluto"), giant aliens who land in Central Park ("Hannibal's Elephants"), aliens who are superpowerful computers ("Hardware"), aliens who enslave the whole world ("The Pardoner's Tale"), aliens with whom first contact is made in deep space ("The Iron Star"). If some of this sounds like it might have come from the pages of *Super-Science Fiction*, it shouldn't be surprising. More than any other writer, Silverberg has been able to take the basic materials of SF pulpdom and transform them into something resembling mainstream literature. He's immensely popular because he validates the guilty pleasures of anyone who has ever loved SF, and he knows how to deliver the clear exposition and satisfying payoff that non-hardcore readers of *Playboy* or *Omni* expect. (Only a couple of stories, such as "Sunrise on Pluto," tend to fizzle after presenting their initial premise.)

This isn't meant to suggest that Silverberg comes off as a cynic who merely recycles slicked-up versions of familiar scenarios. There is genuine affection and care evident in his treatments of these old themes, and he specifically acknowledges that "Symbiont" is meant as a kind of tribute to *Planet Stories*. Nor is it meant to suggest that his recent short fiction is confined to this mode: the collection contains at least an equal number of stories that represent characteristic Silverbergian preoccupations. Variant or simulated history, for example, shows up in "Sailing to Byzantium," "House of Bones," "To the Promised Land," "A Sleep and a Forgetting," and the Hugo-winning "Enter A Soldier. Later: Enter Another." "Dancers in the Time-Flux" returns to the bizarre, David Lindsay-like world of *Son of Man*. "The Asenion Solution" is his ingenious, in-joke tribute to Asimov. And Silverberg's almost obsessive fascination with shared or disembodied consciousness crops up in so many stories that the book's subtitle, *Secret Sharers*, is far more than an allusion to his masterful take on Conrad which provides the collection's centerpiece. Silverberg's inventiveness in exploring this theme is endless: minds can be shared or liberated through time travel ("Homefaring"), symbiosis ("Symbiont"), multiple personalities ("Multiples"), telepathy ("Snake and Ocean, Ocean and Snake," an especially appealing romance), absorption ("Amanda and the Alien"), data storage ("The Secret Sharer"), microchips ("Chip Runner"). Silverberg is as good as anybody at imagining what it would feel like to have someone else inside your head, but I leave it up to future scholars to ponder on why it's so important to him.

Even though many of the stories here have been previously anthologized, Silverberg's engaging and informative introductions help knit the *Collected Stories* into something of a single piece, placing each tale in the context of Silverberg's other work and constituting a kind of literary autobiography for the eighties. The end result is not only a good lesson in craft and style, but a clear picture of a highly professional writer who knows exactly what he's doing – even when he plays it safe.

Ian McDonald is a newer Irish writer who's interested in anything but playing it safe, and many of the readers who enjoy Silverberg's stories might find themselves puzzled or confused by some of the pieces in McDonald's second collection, **Speaking in Tongues**. McDonald is an energetic, try-anything writer who at times seems intoxicated by the sound of his own incantatory prose, but he's capable of achieving great effects with that prose, and his stories are almost always original and challenging. When he does call to mind earlier texts, they're likely to be quirky masterpieces. "Gardenias" explores the suicide-and-resurrection implications of "mattercasting" in a way that suggests Budrys's *Rogue Moon*; "Rainmaker Cometh," written in a kind of transmogrified middle American idiom, suggests early Bradbury (in theme only); "Fragments of an Analysis of a Case of Hysteria" almost reads like an explication of the SF subtext of D.M. Thomas's *The White Hotel*; and "Toward Kilimanjaro" echoes the setting and imagery of Ballard's *The Crystal World*.

But McDonald is by no means a derivative writer, and even in those cases when his theme seems familiar, his rhetoric doesn't. He's fascinated with trying out different modes of expression, and sometimes his imagined world is so poetically compelling that the SF infodump, when it comes, seems especially jarring; this, at least, is what happens in "Listening," an apocalyptic tale of a world transformed by spore-like microscopic nanocomputers. The title story, "Speaking in Tongues," is almost entirely an experiment in juxtaposing distorted rhetorical modes – a computer, a propagandist, a religious witness, a schizophrenic. In "Floating Dogs," the speech is that of genetically altered animals conditioned to fight wars (not surprisingly, they sound a lot like Dr. Moreau's beast-men). And in "Approaching Perpendicular," perhaps the most bizarrely original story in the book, the protagonist is a poet trying to grapple with a topological paradox.

If there's a recurrent preoccupation in McDonald's work, evident in his novels as well as many stories, it's an acute awareness of the plight of the dispossessed. This is most evident in "Atomic Avenue," a bitter rock-lyric of a story about a working-class youth who learns his place while visiting a futuristic Vegas-like city, but it's also evident in the most genuinely moving story in the collection, "Winning," which describes the plight of a Muslim athlete who finds his talent and his beliefs compromised by the surgical and psychological manipulations that have become integral to the future Olympics. Failing to compete, he knows, will strip him of what status he has been given and return him to third-world anonymity. McDonald is fully in control of his style and subject matter here, and shows us that there's a lot to look forward to as his fiction continues to mature.

Twenty years ago, after complaining about the scrounging necessary to put together an anthology of art-related SF, James Blish predicted a forthcoming "invasion" of SF by the arts, and vice versa. He may have been a bit premature, and he certainly couldn't have foreseen the way in which virtual reality would come to co-opt almost any discussion of traditional art forms in the genre. But now here comes Mark S. Geston, who's been laying relatively low of late, with a novel constructed entirely around the power of representational painting. To be sure, the paintings in **Mirror to the Sky** are the work of an advanced alien civilization, and involve something called "chronic perspective" which gives them almost catastrophic psychological power, but Geston is to be credited for confronting the narrative implications of his thesis head-on: where many writers resort to abstract metaphors and stylistic tricks to describe the appearance and effects of such art, Geston gives us detailed descriptions of what the paintings look like and exactly what their effect is on different viewers. At its best, the novel is an elegant exploration of the act of seeing.

The novel begins with a familiar enough scenario: alien spaceships have moved into orbit around the Earth, and the aristocratic aliens (so handsome they are called "gods" by earthlings) have shared scientific and medical miracles and thoroughly ingratiated themselves. Five years after their arrival, a Washington bureaucrat named Andrew Cavan arranges for an exhibit of alien paintings and sculpture at the National Gallery, and discovers that the works displayed – especially a reproduction of a triptych by a legendary alien artist named Blake – have powerful psychological effects on certain viewers, including his son Timothy. An effort to expand the exhibit leads to disaster, however, as a terrorist explodes a bomb while the aliens are unloading works for display. Timothy is killed in the explosion, and the aliens decide to evacuate – accompanied by Cavan and hundreds of other "gifted" earthlings.

Geston shifts the action to a violence-torn post-alien Earth, where Rane, one of the few gods to remain behind, begins work on another epic painting that will prove as powerful as Blake's masterpiece. Gradually, we learn the true meaning of both paintings, as a resurrected Timothy and other characters await the aliens' return (it seems the Blake reproduction was actually the original, and they want it back). The ending perhaps smacks a bit too much of the kind of species chauvinism we get in stories like Clarke's "Rescue Party" or Van Vogt's "The Monster," but along the way Geston makes enough cogent observations about the connections between art, imperialism, and civilization to make *Mirror to the Sky* a worthwhile – and very unusual – contribution to the arts-in-SF tradition.

Alexander Jablokov is another author whose attention to the role of art gave an unusual dimension to his first novel, *Carve the Sky*. His new novel, **A Deeper Sea**, is expanded from his 1989 novella of the same title, and it may be expanded a bit too much. Like the novella, it works toward the wonderfully romantic image of a whale in orbit around Jupiter, but in tracing back the events that lead to this image, Jablokov introduces so much material that you begin to suspect he worked out several alternative ideas for dolphin novels, then decided to use them all. He begins by introducing us to Ilya Stasov, a colonel in a shakily reborn twenty-first century Soviet Union, who has been assigned to a remote dolphin research station. Though criticized for his brutal methods, he succeeds in re-establishing communication with the dolphins, who it turns out had talked quite freely with humans up until the time of the ancient Minoan civilization, when a kind of geologic apocalypse occurred. Meanwhile, Stasov begins to develop a relationship with an American scientist who has done some work on puzzling evidences of life in the atmosphere of Jupiter. It's clear that all this is going to come together somehow, but before it does Jablokov veers off into a lengthy future war scenario, complete with harrowing scenes of P.O.W. camps.

Stasov is able to train (or more accurately, persuade) the dolphins to participate in a territorial war against Japan and the United States, and many of the dolphins are modified with sophisticated weapons systems. Some of these remain at large, having gotten a taste for war, after the war ends and Stasov is imprisoned by the Japanese for his war crimes and his putative crimes against dolphins and whales. He finds himself being defended by his erstwhile American lover, and with her aid he re-establishes his contact with the dolphins by enlisting their aid in understanding the ambiguous Jovian communications. The dolphins, who by now have become major players in world finance by virtue of their ability to locate sunken treasure, inform him that they want to send an orca whale to Jupiter, accompanied by a representative of their own. The reasons the dolphins and whales want to explore space is fuzzy, but it's clear that they've had it with tuna nets.

A Deeper Sea has much to recommend it, especially for those interested in the growing subgenre of dolphin stories. Jablokov carefully avoids sentimentalizing his dolphins — when they talk, they sound like surly, rebellious teenagers — and has intelligently thought through the sorts of things they would likely know and care about. His characterization of Stasov is also complex and not entirely sympathetic, and it's refreshing to see a twenty-first century world presented from something other than an American point of view. (The portrayal of the Japanese, especially in the prisoner-of-war chapters, makes very little concession to politically correct sensibilities.) But trying to handle ancient civilizations, volcanic catastrophes, cetacean language, future war, future politics, P.O.W. tortures, space travel, and alien contact all in one narrative is a bit much. Despite its compelling images and original ideas, *A Deeper Sea* finally accretes so much thematic baggage that it's exhausting — a tuna-net of a novel.

Inside the Funhouse: 17 SF Stories about SF ~
~ edited by Mike Resnick

After all the scholarly attempts to make some kind of order out of the chaos of SF and fantasy, it's interesting to explore how SF comments on itself. Anthony Lewis's *Annotated Bibliography of Recursive Science Fiction* (1990) lists more than 200 stories about SF and the SF world. Mike Resnick provides a good sampling of these in **Inside the Funhouse: 17 SF Stories about SF**, which is actually a collection of 16 stories and a short poem by Jane Yolen. The stories range from 1952 to 1990 and from playful jokes about the agony of getting published (three of the stories are in the form of exchanges of letters between writers and editors) to the depressive but sharply insightful meditations of Barry Malzberg, whom Resnick rightly dubs the "master of the recursive science fiction story." (Technically, I suppose, "recursive" describes only stories which refer to themselves, and by that standard only Malzberg's "A Galaxy Called Rome" and Resnick's own "His Award-Winning Science Fiction Story" meet that criterion, but all the other stories are certainly "about" SF in some form.)

I've long believed that some of the most revealing commentary about SF lies in what some critics would call its intertextuality, and Resnick's collection couldn't have come at a better time, following a spate of anthologies and novels re-imagining and rethinking everyone from Asimov to Bradbury to Farmer. While Resnick leans heavily toward good-time fiction, there are serious points made in several of the stories. Frederik Pohl and C.M. Kornbluth's "Mute Inglorious Tam," for example, implicitly argues that the speculative imagination requires the proper social conditions to flourish, while Edmond Hamilton's classic "The Pro" offers a bitter dose of reality for an aging SF writer. A few of stories are set all or in part at Worldcons; Ian Watson's "The World Science Fiction Convention of 2080" hilariously shows how universal cataclysm can be liberating for SF writers wanting to return to their pulp roots, and Philip K. Dick's "Waterspider" presents deft caricatures – and a few biting critical comments – on some major writers and editors of the early fifties. "Corridors," one of two Barry Malzberg stories, portrays the bitterness and despair of a Worldcon guest of honor in what amounts to an essay disguised as a story. While some of the other stories recycle tired fannish cliches about, for example, how Shakespeare would have been an SF fan, these and a few other selections help make the collection as a whole both delightful and provocative, a contribution to SF criticism as well as to SF.

The Lifted Veil: The Book of Fantastic Literature
by Women ~~ ed. A. Susan Williams

Modern Ghost Stories by Eminent Women Writers ~
~ ed. Richard Dalby

Belladonna ~~ Michael Stewart

Tales of the Lovecraft Mythos ~~ ed. Robert M. Price

The Ugly Little Boy ~~ Isaac Asimov & Robert Silverberg

Despite the sometimes heroic efforts of Peter Straub and others to bring it into the mainstream of horror fiction, the gothic ghost story somehow retains its identity, and apparently its audience. Among the fantastic genres, it's like a kindly but slightly goofy maiden aunt, clinging to an aura of genteel respectability long after the younger relatives have moved uptown and started sporting punk hairdos. Like the English detective story, it seems to favor form over invention, atmosphere over plot, tone over style. And like the English detective story, for whatever reasons, it seems to be largely the province of women writers. By my rough count, more than a third of the 60 stories in A. Susan Williams's massive **The Lifted Veil: The Book of Fantastic Literature by Women** are ghost stories, although this includes a few variations such as doggie-ghosts (Edith Wharton's "Kerfol") and haunted cars (Mary O'Malley's "The Buick Saloon"). (This affinity between women writers and ghost stories has not escaped the attention of academic critics).

The Lifted Veil did not set out to be an historical survey of women's ghost fiction, although that's practically what its first half amounts to. It set out to be a "grand anthology" of fantastic literature by women, and perhaps an answer to such earlier grand anthologies of the fantastic by Jorge Luis Borges, Alberto Manguel, and others, which severely underrepresented women writers. To a great extent it succeeds in this mission, and in doing so almost unwittingly addresses another imbalance in those earlier collections — the underrepresentation of science fiction as a modern mode of the fantastic. Williams's selection of science fiction stories is surprisingly broad-ranging and knowledgeable, including pulp classics such as C.L. Moore's "Shambleau" and Leigh Brackett's "The Lake of the Gone Forever" along with more predictable "literary" selections from Le Guin, Russ, Tiptree, Carol Emshwiller, and Kit Reed. There is also a good sampling from the middle range of writers not quite liberated from their generic reputations yet: Anne McCaffrey, Joan Vinge, Lisa Tuttle, Tanith Lee, and Suzy McKee Charnas (whose "Boobs" is one of the treasures of the collection's dozen post-1980 selections). This final third of the collection, including some 21 stories published after 1960, constitutes by itself a first-rate overview of contemporary fantastic literature by women, and doesn't seem to duplicate many selections from other anthologies.

The main problem with the collection — at least for anyone who tries to read it straight through, as I did — is all those haunted priories and ghostly lovers that weigh down the front end. This sea of gothic prose does serve to highlight the extraordinary imagination of Mary Shelley ("The Mortal Immortal") or the solid style of George Eliot (whose "The Lifted Veil" gives the collection its title), and makes a utopian tale such as Rokeya Sakhawat Hossain's 1905 "Sultana's Dream" seem a positive revelation. But Williams virtually ignores one of the richest mines of 19th-century fantasy by women — the fairy tale. Edith Nesbit is represented by the uncharacteristic "Man-Size in Marble," and Angela Carter's revisionist "Peter and the Wolf" is included, but writers like Anne Thackeray Ritchie, Frances Hodgson Burnett, or Christina Rossetti are nowhere in evidence. Nor has Williams provided significant representation to minority women writers; Opal Palmer Adisa's "Widow's Walk" seems added almost as an afterthought, and Octavia Butler is a notable omission from the SF selections. Williams's other criterion — that all works had to be written in English — also tends to put blinders on what in many other ways is a monumental anthology, and one that will be an important point of reference for anyone seeking to trace the history of women's fantastic literature.

If Williams's anthology seems haunted by the specter of the ghost story, Richard Dalby's **Modern Ghost Stories by Eminent Women Writers** makes no bones about its celebration of the form. Dalby's collection is a follow-up to his 1988 *Victorian Ghost Stories by Eminent Women Writers*, and while "eminent" in that earlier collection generally meant "dead," here it merely seems coy. Along with such heavy hitters as A.S. Byatt, Rebecca West, Antonia Fraser, Edith Wharton, Daphne Du Maurier, Ruth Rendell, Jean Rhys, and Joan Aiken, Dalby also includes newer writers such as Elizabeth Fancett and Pamela Sewell — representatives, as he puts it, of a new generation of ghost-story writers. He establishes without doubt that the ghost story is form is alive and well in England, but for the life of me I can't see that it's making much progress. Fancett's overripe revenge-western, for example, could have been written by Max Brand fifty years ago.

If one can get through all the Skeptical Narrators Who Didn't Believe In The Supernatural Until That Night In The Rectory and Stationmasters Who Tell You The Folks You Just Had Dinner With Have Been Dead For A Year, there are some treasures in this book. A.S. Byatt is simply a wonderful writer, and her "The July Ghost" is a gem, although it offers few surprises. Celia Fremlin's "Don't Tell Cissie" offers a much-needed comic respite, and Margaret Irwin's "The Book" — better known for being praised by Joanna Russ than for being widely read — is genuinely chilling. D.K. Broster's "The Pestering," which contains enough material for a 700-page epic by several horror writers I can think of, is a model of pacing and economy, as is Jean Rhys's very brief "I Used to Live Here Once." Dorothy Haynes's "Redundant" offers a nice, Bartleby-like edge to a plot that could have been lifted from EC comics. And old masters like Du Maurier, Ruth Rendell, and Joan Aiken are always at least competent. But what is perhaps most striking in the collection as whole is the sense of change-ringing, of working a genre so proscribed by its formalism that ingenuity has long since replaced invention.

Michael Stewart appears to be one of those attracted to the formal elements of the classic ghost story, but dissatisfied with its anemic disposition. His latest novel, **Belladonna**, begins with a classic situation – a modern scholar researching the life of a 17th-century alchemist finds himself involved with the ghost of the alchemist's mistress – but from the very beginning promises a lot more than a standard haunting. For one thing, the ghostly Isabel is incredibly sexy, and it's clear that her initial hold on the scholar Matthew Cavewood is purely carnal. For another, Cavewood's predecessor in researching the alchemist Nathaniel Shawcrosse was a particle physicist, and there are plenty of hints that Shawcrosse's alchemical discoveries had something in common with modern quantum theory. This near-SF element doesn't really go anywhere – what physics there is in the book is decidedly fuzzy – but it's clear that Stewart wants to develop his novel in several directions at once. It's partly an academic novel, partly history of science, partly sexual soap opera, partly a horror story about reincarnation (Isabel eventually manages to land in someone else's body). But it's still mainly a ghost story.

What Stewart does handle well is the character of Cavewood's wife Hazel, who's cast in the usually thankless role of the devoted wife facing a supernatural rival. A successful photographer, Hazel is a far cry from the confused, innocent victim of formula, and her determination to fight Isabel makes for the novel's most interesting conflict. By the time Cavewood has gone through his fourth or fifth period of serious goofiness, however, the question is not so much who'll win the cosmic struggle for his soul as why Hazel is wasting her time with him in the first place. Belladonna is an enjoyable diversion which sets up its plot elements well, but once the machinery is in place, it turns into an elevator-novel: you know where you're going and when you'll get off, but you're trapped for the ride.

The peril of researching arcane historical texts, which is what initially causes the trouble in *Belladonna*, is also one of the central precepts of Lovecraftian horror fiction, and it seems to be such an attractive theme that virtually everyone from Robert Bloch to Colin Wilson has had a whack at the so-called "mythos"; it's become a kind of borscht belt for horror writers. In 1969, August Derleth put together a collection of Lovecraft stories by various hands under the title *Tales of the Cthulhu Mythos*, and since then various other collections have shown how younger writers have joined the band long after the leader's death. Now Robert Price shows us what pulp-era gems Derleth and the others left out with **Tales of the Lovecraft Mythos**. In the past few years, Derleth's pre-eminence as Lovecraft's interpreter has been challenged by a number of scholars and writers, and the term "Lovecraft mythos" is supposed to be more accurate by dethroning the undeserving Cthulhu from center stage. (If he objects, presumably we'll hear about it.) The term also gives editor Price a chance to open up the field to include not only stories that tried to expand upon Lovecraft's own cosmology, but those which show a heavy Lovecraft influence (such as C. Hall Thompson's "Spawn of the Green Abyss") or those which Lovecraft simply *liked*, whether or not they relate directly to his system (such as Mearle Prout's "The House of the Worm.")

Even those who don't have a taste for Lovecraft have to admit that he was good at what he did, which was to write forty-thousand word stories that ended with italicized punchlines. The authors rounded up by Price all seem to have mastered the basics, even down to the one-from-column-A, one-from-column-B title formulas: "The Thing on the Roof" (Robert E. Howard), "Fane of the Black Pharaoh" (Robert Bloch), "The Lair of the Star-Spawn" (August Derleth and Mark Schorer), "The Guardian of the Book" (Henry Hasse). Like the master himself, they're all very big on forbidden books and surly old professors, and the main variations that most of them offer consist of expanding Lovecraft's rather provincial geography into new areas: Mexico (Howard's "The Thing on the Roof"), Egypt (Bloch's "Fane of the Black Pharaoh"), California (Henry Kuttner's "The Invaders" and "Bells of Horror"), Canada (Derleth's "The Thing that Walked on the Wind"), Washington state (Duane Rimel's "Music of the Stars"). The stories date from as early as 1929, and Price has gone to the trouble of uncovering such things as restored versions of Howard's "The Fire of Asshurbanipal," Prout's "The House of the Worm," Robert Lowndes's "The Abyss," and Carl Jacobi's "The Aquarium," E. Hoffmann Price's original story draft for what became his Lovecraft collaboration "Through the Gates of the Silver Key," and Richard Seabright's unpublished "The Warder of Knowledge." All of which makes this an indisputably valuable book for pulp-era collectors and Lovecraftians.

One has to be grateful, however, that Donald Wollheim's parody and Fritz Leiber's good-natured tribute are saved for the end of the book. Although Wollheim's punchline misfires, his line on Lovecraft's stylistic excesses would make the whole book seem like a parody if you were to read it first. And Leiber is simply so far superior a writer to anyone else here that his waggish version of a faculty get-together at Miskatonic University makes it that much harder to take seriously much of the hysterical prose that precedes it. For those of us who enjoyed this sort of stuff when younger, *Tales of the Lovecraft Mythos* can provide some fun, but at the same time I'd as soon not be reminded that an old hero like Clark Ashton Smith could write a line (in "The Seven Geases") like "'How now varlet!' said Ralibar Vooz." Maybe Dr. Seuss was a closet Lovecraftian, too.

The Ugly Little Boy is the latest in what threatens to be a series of Silverberg novelizations of Asimov stories, and in an odd way it makes more sense for Silverberg than it ever did for Asimov. Asimov's original story, published as

"Lastborn" in *Galaxy* in 1958, was unusual in that it posed a problem that Asimov could not reasonably solve within the scope of his own narrative rules, giving him no option but to crank up the pathos; it's one of his most unabashedly sentimental tales. It's also an unwitting testament to Asimov's difficulty in creating any female character who isn't Susan Calvin. Edith Fellowes, a brilliant, unmarried children's nurse, devoted only to her patients, is hired to care for a Neanderthal child snatched into the present by a corporation which has devised a method of hijacking bits of the distant past. She grows attached to the boy and, having no life of her own, chooses to go with him when she discovers he must be returned to the past. The story never really worked, but it gained an enduring reputation as evidence that the good doctor had his soft side.

Silverberg, who's been fascinated with similar themes in stories like "A Sleep and a Forgetting" and "Enter a Solder. Later: Enter Another," leaves whole chunks of the Asimov story intact but adds a few characters, fleshes out everyone's background, and develops two new subplots. One concerns a publicity-seeking child-rights advocate and seems to portray the whole child-rights movement as a kind of lunatic fringe. The other, set among the Neanderthals from whom the boy was snatched, is a version of what many readers will recognize as the standard Neanderthal vs. Cro-Magnon plot, dressed up with a kind of proto-feminist (*really* proto) tribal seer and gerrymandered to provide an unlikely happy ending in place of Asimov's ambiguously tragic one.

One can see how Silverberg's interest in anthropology, in staging historical confrontations, and in re-examining old modes of SF might attract him to this story, and perhaps this explains why he's devoted so little effort to updating the 1950s flavor of the original, with its secretive private research foundations and references to "sub-etheric" mass communications. One can also admire the seamlessness with which he's merged his own style with that of 1950s Asimov. But the novel does little to allay the nagging suspicion that its real genesis, like that of the earlier *Nightfall*, lies in the fact that novels are marketable sales units whereas short stories aren't.

1993 – Overview: The Year in Review

~ originally published in Locus #397 (Feb 1994) ~

I've been asked to provide a summary overview of the year's trends in SF and fantasy, and already I'm feeling the kind of anxiety that must regularly afflict people with such an assignment: namely, what if there *are* no trends? What if, one year, the field suddenly randomized itself totally, with no two authors or publishers moving remotely in the same direction? Or what if everyone simply kept doing pretty much what they'd been doing before? What are the possibilities of a trendless literature? What would it look like? *Analog*?

But no. There are *always* trends and patterns, even though these patterns may have their roots some years back and only gradually percolate to the surface of publishing. (Publishing, after all, is only the storm-tossed surface of the vast and still Sea of Literature, and – well, forget it.) The pattern that I have in mind here is one that we might term – should we choose to be alarmist about it – Creeping Mainstreamism. Creeping Mainstreamism is the increasing tendency of SF and fantasy writers to write, and their editors and readers to accept, mainstream literary fiction as though it were SF or fantasy. One of the best examples dates from 1992, when Geoff Ryman, in an afterword to his novel Was, described himself as a fantasy writer who'd fallen in love with realism. Last year, *Was* showed up as a finalist for the World Fantasy Award, as did Jane Yolen's *Briar Rose*, which isn't a fantasy either (even though both novels were based on famous works of fantasy). Connie Willis's Hugo-winning *Doomsday Book* incorporated a full-length historical novel in a science fiction frame largely provided for point of view and texture, and her new collection, *Impossible Things*, contains a handful of stories that are powered not by fantasy or SF, but by close observation of ordinary people in domestic settings. Similar kinds of stories appeared in collections from two other major writers during the year, Brian Aldiss (*A Tupolev Too Far*) and John Crowley (*Antiquities*). Datlow and Windling's *Year's Best Fantasy* and Dozois' *Year's Best Science Fiction* each contained a generous sampling of stories which are "literary" in this sense, and – in what was certainly the most widely publicized anthology of the year – Ursula Le Guin and Brian Attebery's *Norton Book of Science Fiction* virtually set out to redefine the last 30 years of North American science fiction in something close to such terms.

Does this mean that "literariness" (whatever that might be) is threatening to infiltrate the good innocent fun of old-time SF? Has somebody at, say, *The New Yorker* finally "gotten to" our favorite writers with evil promises of Guggenheims? More likely the opposite is true. After decades during which SF tried to legitimize itself by pointing to everyone from E.M. Forster to Margaret Atwood, it seems to have awakened to the fact that its own home-grown writers can compete admirably outside the ghetto – even if most of their recognition for such accomplishments still comes from inside. But there are signs that even this is changing. Harlan Ellison's "The Man Who Rowed Christopher Columbus Ashore" shows up not only in the Datlow/Windling annual, but in Louise Erdrich's *Best American Short Stories* collection. William Gibson gets lionized in Time magazine and even plays himself in an incoherent TV-movie, something even Amy Fisher wasn't able to pull off. In terms of both serious literature and pop culture, the ghetto is growing less easily defined. Instead of clear boundaries, we have what mathematicians call a fuzzy set.

At the same time, there have been more than enough books published this past year to assure us that SF in all its guises is still around. Some of it is so conventional – so trendless – that it hasn't been reviewed by Locus at all. Some of it, such Kim Stanley Robinson's ongoing Mars trilogy or Greg Bear's contrasting *Moving Mars*, has shown that idea-driven SF can not only prosper, but successfully incorporate many of the virtues of literary fiction. Rather than the mainstream infiltrating SF, SF is showing signs of wanting to stake out territory in the mainstream. In both of my previous annual-review columns I made a similar point regarding historical fiction; almost the only short fiction concerning history which gets published anymore is published as SF, and historical novels seem to prosper in the U.S. only when embedded in some SF/fantasy framework (Delia Sherman's *The Porcelain Dove* may be 1993's most persuasive and accomplished example of this). Now I'm beginning to suspect that historical fiction may only be the tip of the iceberg. SF – some SF writers, at least – want to be able to do everything the mainstream does, in the mainstream's own terms, but without sacrificing either the freedom or the discipline imposed by traditional SF values. Of course, this is what SF's most ardent champions have claimed it's done all along, but in fact it's done it all too rarely, and too often at the margins of the field. This is one of the implicit arguments in the pattern of stories selected for *The Norton Book of Science Fiction*.

It's interesting, then, that while SF seems to be redefining its literary identity in new ways, another notable trend of the year should prove to be the return of several names from the past. For me the most accomplished fantasy novel of the year was Peter Beagle's *The Innkeeper's Song*, a masterpiece of minimalist world-building. Beagle may not exactly be a name from the past – his previous novel dates from only 1987 – but *The Innkeeper's Song*, through its multiple viewpoints and complex character relationships, develops a resonance and depth that we have not seen from this author since 1968's *The Last Unicorn*, and in some ways actually surpasses that acknowledged masterpiece. My candidate for the most likely-to-be-underrated SF novel of the year is Algis Budrys's *Hard Landing*, an unexpectedly moving and tightly written novel of aliens trying to survive on earth in the decades that led up to Watergate. It had been more than 15 years since we'd seen a new Budrys novel. Less successful, but still quite promising, was Alfred Coppel's return to the field – after more than a decade as a successful thriller writer and more than three decades since his last adult SF novel – with *Glory*, an energetic but not altogether convincing tale of a troubleshooting spaceship crew and a South African planetary colony.

If such works demonstrate that there is still much to be done with the traditional materials of SF and fantasy, another healthy trend was the attempt to rescue major names from out-of-print limbo. Small presses brought out Cordwainer Smith's collected short fiction (*The Rediscovery of Man*) and David R. Bunch's *Bunch!*; both authors, in retrospect, seem to presage the stylistic sophistication I mentioned earlier (and both show up in *The Norton Anthology*). R.A. Lafferty's unpublished work continued to trickle out with *Tales of Midnight*, and the so-called "Sturgeon Project" got underway with a modest memoir titled *Argyll*.

Several large-scale series or sequels kept some of the field's current big names visible during the year; I've already mentioned the second volume of Kim Stanley Robinson's Mars trilogy, *Green Mars*; and Greg Bear's *Moving Mars* is essentially part of a series with *Queen of Angels* and *Heads*. Arthur C. Clarke and Gentry Lee (but mostly Gentry Lee, who's finally putting his own unmistakeable stamp on the series) provided a fourth Rama novel, *Rama Revealed*, which actually concludes a trilogy that began with the *second* Rama, not the first. (Clarke's own *The Hammer of God*, while an enjoyable catalog of his imagination, was hardly a major work.) Gene Wolfe and Orson Scott Card continued work on multivolume epics which probably can't be fairly judged until all the books are in. But for me, the most impressive and original sequel I reviewed during the year was David Zindell's *The Broken God*, a followup to Neverness which matches the original in complexity of texture and high drama; it's old-fashioned big-scale SF done with panache and style.

Zindell doesn't quite qualify as a new author (although I count him as among my personal discoveries of the year, since I hadn't read *Neverness* before), but two brand-new authors who published impressive first *and* second novels during the year are Mary Rosenblum and Patricia Anthony. Rosenblum's *The Drylands* was a fine ecological catastrophe tale set in the same drought-stricken northwest as her popular series of stories; her *Chimera* showed she could make good use of more high-tech themes as well. Anthony's *Cold Allies* was a stunningly original conception combining very strange aliens with very convincing future war; her *Brother Termite* was no less original in its straight-faced treatment of tabloid-style aliens in the White House. (I don't know if two novels make a trend, but aliens in the White House showed up in Budrys's *Hard Landing* as well. Maybe it really is the influence of the tabloids, or maybe it was just twelve years of Reagan and Bush.)

In nonfiction, there's no room for discussion. John Clute and Peter Nicholls's *The Encyclopedia of Science Fiction* was the event not only of the year, but probably of the decade. Almost twice the length of the 1979 first edition and with many of that editions entries revised or rewritten, it's an essentially new work, filled not only with an astonishing amount of information, but with solid critical insights (one can easily get so overwhelmed by its scope as a reference as to overlook its value as a work of criticism). Clute did most of the author entries and Brian Stableford most of the theme entries, and neither makes much effort at the bland "consensus" tone you so often get in reference works; it's actually a book you can argue with. Though I was initially disappointed by the exclusion of many minor authors to make room for too-generous media coverage, I note my own copy is already getting dog-eared from overuse; the book defined the field in a far more comprehensive and inclusive way than any anthology could hope to.

I've written this without having yet read books by several authors that – on the basis of my fellow reviewers' comments – I intend to get to soon: Octavia Butler's *Parable of the Sower*, Pat Cadigan's *Dirty Work*, William Gibson's *Virtual Light*, Poul Anderson's *Harvest of Stars*, Nancy Kress's *Beggars in Spain*, to name a few. Whether my thesis of "Creeping Mainstreamism" holds up with a wider sample remains to be seen, but it's becoming clear that many SF writers seek to be judged by broader aesthetic standards than the ones they grew up with, while at the same time holding on to what they've got. In a convoluted way, one recent reminder of how far SF has come is the epic film *Gettysburg*, which brought back into paperback its source, Michael Shaara's Pulitzer Prize winning 1974 novel *The Killer Angels*. Shaara, one of the promising SF writers of the early fifties, had long since abandoned the field when he gained that pinnacle of mainstream recognition; he'd escaped the ghetto back in the days when you were either an SF writer or you weren't. Today, Shaara wouldn't have to choose. It's no longer a matter of escape, it's a matter of tearing down the walls altogether, like in Berlin. Maybe it's not Creeping Mainstreamism at all. Maybe it's reunification.

– January 1993, Locus #384 –

Deus X ~~ Norman Spinrad

The Call of Earth: Homecoming, Volume 2 ~~ Orson Scott Card

Kingdoms of the Wall ~~ Robert Silverberg

Live from Golgotha ~~ Gore Vidal

Et Tu, Babe ~~ Mark Leyner

Tales of Midnight ~~ R.A. Lafferty

Argo ~~ R.A. Lafferty

It's no wonder that religion has long been for SF what the Amazon rainforest has been for the pharmaceuticals industry. If writers can't borrow what they need from the holy books themselves (extraterrestrial intelligences, mysterious strangers with secret powers, cosmic struggles, resurrections, epic apocalypses), they can probably find it in the history of religious institutions (labyrinthine bureaucracies, secret cabals, internecine power struggles, exiled leaders, and the psychological manipulation of whole populations). Given this affinity, it's surprising that there isn't much genuinely religious SF; more often than not, SF writers either fall into an embarrassing kind of apologetics (such as Clarke's "The Nine Billion Names of God"), or else seem content to find new ways of giving religion a hotfoot by asking impertinent questions. Do aliens (or robots) have souls? Is God learning disabled? Was Jesus a time traveler — or an alien? Can computers (or neoterics, or big sandworms) become as gods?

Norman Spinrad's short novel **Deus X** starts off as a hotfoot for Catholicism, but never really develops a strong satiric edge. In a 21st century dying from ecological catastrophes, people can achieve a kind of immortality by downloading their personalities into computers prior to death. A private detective named Marley Philippe is hired by the first female Pope to track down the missing "software zombie" of Father De Leone, which has disappeared from the Vatican computer. Father De Leone had agreed to be downloaded in order to challenge the proposition that such entities have souls — a proposition the Church has denied in an unpopular doctrine that has caused its membership to dwindle drastically. With rather unconvincing ease, Philippe's cyberpunk-detective skills lead him to a system-wide intelligence called the Vortex, which has kidnapped the Father Leone program in hopes of proving its own existence through a kind of Cartesian Turing test.

Philippe's narrative alternates with the narrative of Father De Leone himself, both before and after his death and transfiguration into a superprogram called Deus X (from "deus ex machina"), and by the time the two narratives come together, things begin to get a bit mystical and — suprisingly for Spinrad — even sentimental. The Church seems to find a way to save itself and maybe even redeem the world. Spinrad's initial conundrum — and the one that makes the novel worth reading as a philosophical *tour de force* — is the question of whether the "soul" or identity is located in the brain's software or in the body, and whether a replicated consciousness is still a consciousness. The debates over these issues are well thought out and clearly presented, but they're made to carry the weight of a cyberpunk detective ecology parable that seems to want to go off in all directions at once. Spinrad has set up a genuinely provocative situation, but I'm not sure he's done himself a favor by trying to resolve it in such a conveniently SF-nal manner.

Orson Scott Card's use of religion in his "Homecoming" series promises to be both more and less subtle than Spinrad's. It's more subtle in that he makes no overt reference to any religious text or system — after all, we're 40 million years in the future and on another planet — and it's a lot less subtle in that Card seems to have no problem with taking whole chunks of his central narrative conflicts right out of the Old Testament and the Book of Mormon. (In fact, this series is beginning to look like it might do for those books what Asimov's "Foundation" series did for Gibbon.) The Oversoul, that diseased orbiting computer that began meddling in the affairs of the planet Harmony in *The Memory of Earth*, is still at work in the series' second volume, **The Call of Earth**. Although the boy Nafai remains a central character, by far the most interesting and complex figure in this novel is General Moozh, a brilliant tactician who defies the Oversoul even as he comes to suspect he's inadvertently acting out its plan.

After learning that the legendary women's city Basilica has been destabilized by Nafai's actions in the first volume, Moozh seizes this opportunity to march on the city, with the hopes of taking it over as a bastion from which he can dominate all the cities of the plain, and possibly challenge the Imperator himself.

Card loves writing about strategy and tactics, both military and political, and the most rewarding aspects of *The Call of Earth* are the accounts of how Moozh's mind works and his cat-and-mouse game with Nafai's mother Rasa, the moral leader of Basilica. These two characters dominate the novel, and by contrast the simplistic motivations of the other characters, most notably Nafai's brothers, seem almost cartoonish. (One assumes Card is setting these characters up for greater complexity in later volumes.) While all this is going on, Nafai, his father, and his brothers, are exiled in the desert, waiting for the Oversoul to tell them how to get back to earth (where it needs to go to repair itself) and thinking about getting some wives.

Card's novel seems closer than Spinrad's to a kind of religious SF, because religion is here a part of form more than of content. He has to keep reminding us that the Oversoul is an imperfect machine, because its behavior − sending detailed dreams to people, arranging for the conception and birth of its own virgin priestesses, causing people to abandon their families or commit murder or choose particular mates − seems at times indistinguishable from that of a Sunday-school Jehovah. Card also must take pains to maintain a level of indeterminacy in the narrative; some actions may be free will, while others may stem from false inspiration, others are clearly the work of the Oversoul, and still others may be inspired by a mysterious and even more remote intelligence. All this seems to point in a direction in which the human characters will have to eventually assume the responsibilities of godhood; we'll have to wait and see if later volumes bear this out. Meanwhile, Card has done a masterful job of addressing the classic mid-book-in-a-series problem: giving us a good, driving narrative while quietly setting up the stage machinery for the next act.

To a certain extent, Card seems to be working a variation on what may be the oldest SF/religion formula of all: myth tested by empiricism. This is the theme of innumerable generation-starship or lost-colony tales, and the structure is fairly simple: you invent a society drenched in myth and ritual, then think of a reason to have some smart-aleck kid set out on a quest which eventually leads to the discovery of the historical or technological realities underlying the myths. The religious belief that knits the whole society together comes unraveled, but in its place is the rediscovery of lost knowledge, and the realization that Man Must Make His Own Destiny. I don't think it's giving too much away to note that this is also the basic structure of Robert Silverberg's **Kingdoms of the Wall**, a rather strange, dreamlike epic that for much of its length might as well be straight fantasy (multiple suns and moons are the only clear SF codes we get at first, though the characters all have six-fingered hands and limited shape-changing abilities).

The book has a great central image – an almost unimaginably vast mountain range called the Wall, which so dominates the lives of the villagers who live near it that they regard it as the abode of the gods and ritually select 40 young people from each generation to set about climbing it. Almost none of these pilgrims return, and those that do are often insane or at best surly. Nevertheless, it is a great honor to be chosen, and the narrator, Poilar Crookleg, makes a childhood vow with his best friend Traiben that they will not only be selected, but will succeed in meeting the gods face to face. Encouraged by portents – such as a dream shared by the whole village that he will succeed (maybe they're picking up signals from Card's orbiting computer over in that other novel) – Poilar does become the leader of a "Forty," and most of the narrative details his group's adventures as they climb through one bizarre "kingdom of the wall" after another, seeking the abode of the gods. With its succession of stark landscapes and the distorted humans who inhabit them, the novel owes much of its imagery and tone to David Lindsay's *A Voyage to Arcturus* or Silverberg's own *Son of Man* – but it lacks the unifying philosophical vision of those works, and as the plot gradually comes to look more and more familiar, we begin to just want them to get on with it. By the time the pilgrims climbed to a kingdom resembling Shangri-la, I found myself irrationally hoping for a helicopter to show up.

Silverberg's considerable power of invention is in fine form here, and *Kingdoms of the Wall* could make for a good quest fantasy, but at times it seems that Silverberg is treating invention as its own reward; one looks in vain for ideas to match the power of the images. For example, Silverberg dedicates the book to Ursula Le Guin, and his pilgrims resemble the Gethenians in *The Left Hand of Darkness* in that they lack secondary sexual characteristics until it's time to mate, when they undergo "the Changes." But they are always clearly male or female: the males boast of physical prowess, the females are more spiritual and sensitive, and nothing in their biology is enough to save one female character from being repeatedly raped by neighboring villagers. It's not clear how this half-baked monosexuality serves any science fictional evolutionary purpose or carries any metaphoric weight; it's just there. Nor is it clear whether the various transformed beings the pilgrims encounter along the way are supposed to represent Bunyanesque (John, not Paul) moral hazards, or if they are merely freaks of mutation (although the novel strongly suggests the latter). Silverberg's ending is anything but transcendent, and seems to suggest in good old-time SF fashion something that Card deliberately stops short of – namely, that religion is simply myth in need of explication.

Gore Vidal is a storyteller of a radically different sort from either Card or Silverberg (though somewhat closer in spirit to Spinrad), and his **Live from Golgotha** is a good example of how even a mainstream satirist turns to science fiction tropes when he wants to take potshots at religious belief and practice. This isn't a new game for Vidal; he used SF scenarios to indict the death-worshipping nature of much religious belief in both *Messiah* in 1954 and *Kalki* in 1978. Both of those novels were closer to being SF than this one; here he simply uses time travel as a convenience to get modern TV networks back to the time of the Crucifixion. Stylistically, *Live from Golgotha* is more of a piece with *Myra Breckenridge* and *Duluth* than with Vidal's SF or historical fiction. He does come up with the interesting notion of combining time travel with cyberpunkish data manipulation: it seems a mysterious hacker has been "erasing" Christian texts from the timestream, and St. Timothy is commissioned by visitors from the future to write his own gospel and hide it away where it won't be discovered until the 21st century. He's also invited to anchor a planned telecast of the crucifixion itself, and in preparing for the media event of the millenium, he encounters everyone from Nero to Shirley Maclaine.

Even though Vidal has to play out a fairly sophisticated time-travel scenario to tie up the threads of his plot, it isn't the science fiction content that drives any of the book's ideas. Vidal's main target doesn't even seem to be religion – I don't think anyone these days is really likely to be shocked by the notion that Timothy and Paul were bedmates – but rather the cult of celebrity and the power of the media to distort history. He offers cynical and funny portraits of Jesus, the disciples, Nero, and others, and his supply-side account of the crucifixion itself is wonderful – it seems Jesus really sealed his fate when he drove the moneylenders from the temple, thus lowering the prime rate. The best parts of the novel have this stand-up comedy-shtick tone to them, and owe a lot more to Lenny Bruce's old "Religions, Inc." routine than to any science fictional treatments of religious themes – although readers who remember Michael Moorcock's *Behold the Man* will see one of the major plot twists coming a mile away.

As long as we're on the topic of stand-up comedy fiction, Mark Leyner's **Et Tu, Babe** is another mainstream novel about celebrity which makes occasional use of SF conceits (although it has nothing in particular to do with religion). Leyner's first novel, *My Cousin, My Gastroenterologist*, contained enough science-fictionoid elements to get Leyner kidnapped for cyberpunk purposes in Larry McCaffrey's anthology *Storming the Reality Studio*. But whereas Vidal knows enough about SF devices to use them in a focused way, Leyner simply grabs them off the shelf along with whatever other icons of pop culture seem within reach – TV game shows, Carl Sagan, Connie Chung, Christiaan Barnard, near-death experiments, Paula Abdul, trendy hallucinogens, the FBI, celebrity endorsements. The novel is all shtick, and while some of the individual bits are quite funny, the conceit that loosely strings it all together – that Leyner has become a multibillion-dollar celebrity as a result of the success of his first novel – wears thin pretty quickly, as does the clunky self-referentiality of the text. (Self-disintegrating metafiction isn't exactly news anymore, much as some of us academics would like to believe it is.)

Despite this novel's near-future setting and relentless surrealism, I don't see how Leyner is connected to SF at all; he seems instead to be working in the superhip gonzo tall-tale tradition of Richard Brautigan and Tom Robbins, with more than a little of Buckaroo Banzai thrown in. The sheer inventiveness of some of his episodes — a weight loss camp for terrorists, a sudden outbreak of poets murdering movie stars — almost calls to mind Pynchon as well, but it's Pynchon redone for MTV, and the whole book can be enjoyed by someone with the attention span of a gnat. Last year's *Snow Crash*, by Neal Stephenson, shares some of this same kind of free-for-all comic invention, but Stephenson goes to the trouble of working things out, and ends up with a pretty good SF novel. Leyner just changes channels.

There's nothing wrong with writing tall tales, of course; it's just that they don't always work well in the context of the sort of discipline imposed by SF. (The classic examples which everyone cites, by Clarke or de Camp and Pratt, are really only SF stories *disguised* as tall tales.) I suspect that this accounts for part of the trouble with R.A. Lafferty, the first volume of whose *More than Melchisedech* was reviewed here last year under the title *Tales of Chicago*. Lafferty seems to be fast receding into an undeserved obscurity, in part because he gained his reputation in science fiction circles when most of his stories never made the slightest amount of sense as SF. (It could turn out that the worst thing that ever happened to him was being "discovered" by Damon Knight in those *Orbit* anthologies back in the 60s.) Lafferty's now in danger of becoming a genuine cult writer, commanding intense loyalty among a small band of enthusiasts while puzzling the hell out of everyone else. One of those enthusiasts, Dan Knight of United Mythologies Press, has made something of a quest of getting *More than Melchisedech* into print, and the publication of the second and third volumes, **Tales of Midnight** and **Argo**, finally permits us to see the novel as a whole. Apparently the three-volume format was the result of financial constraints at United Mythologies, because the book is in no sense a trilogy and the breaks between volumes seem abrupt and arbitrary.

Lafferty, of course, brings us back to the theme of religion. More than Melchisedech, it turns out, is something of a companion piece to his 1971 theological fantasy *The Devil is Dead*, and even includes some of the same characters. In telling the tale of the twentieth-century adventures of Melchisedech Duffy, Old Testament king of Salem, original shipmate with Jason on the Argo, contemporary magus and enemy of the devil, Lafferty clearly intends this novel to have an epic sweep, and by the time it's over we discover that most of the characters have enough multiple identities to subsume most of Greek and Celtic mythology as well as the Bible. Jason, for example, is also Finnegan, and the three "slant-face men" who have plagued Duffy since childhood are three wicked kings from the Book of Genesis. The main antagonist, however, is the devil himself, freed from a thousand years of bondage in 1946 and since then responsible for the systematic "trashing" of art, morals, politics, and everything else in the world. This is epic stuff, all right, and the novel is dense with incident, eventually taking us up through Armageddon, Duffy's own death, and back on board the Argo. It'll be a gold mine someday for some budding Joseph Campbell.

Lafferty's digressive and sometimes too-whimsical style, however, constantly derails the single-minded forward sweep needed for a good epic. He can't bring a character onstage without pausing for amusing and instructive anecdotes about the character, and the anecdotes themselves often give way to detailed explanations of what's wrong with our world and why it may not even be the real world in the first place. When he approaches something that looks like an SF concept — alternate worlds, for example — it turns out to be a theological concept (in this case, the various "rescensions" of the world God tried out before settling on this one — if he did settle on this one, which is also up for questioning). And the theology, if you take the time to sort it out, turns out to be fairly crabby and conservative. I don't think *More than Melchisedech* succeeds as the apocalyptic epic it tries to be, but like most of Lafferty it certainly succeeds at being unique. It's the only novel I can think of where you can get the flavor of S.J. Perelman and C.S. Lewis in the same place.

— February 1993, Locus #385 —

The Singularity Project ~~ F.M. Busby

Red Mars ~~ Kim Stanley Robinson

Beautiful Soup: A Novel for the 21st Century ~~ Harvey Jacobs

---

Every once in while, SF writers toy with an idea for a few years or even decades, and then — as if by spontaneous consensus that the idea may just be Too Dumb To Live — nearly abandon it. This is one of the reasons we don't see too many worlds-within-atoms stories anymore, and it may be one of the reasons we haven't heard much about matter transmitters lately. Once a convenient staple of superscience, matter transmission has figured in at least one verifiable classic — Algis Budrys's *Rogue Moon* — and given Larry Niven some cause for fun, but by and large it's been co-opted by movies like *The Fly* or TV shows like *Star Trek*, not noted for their aversion to silliness.

This may also be the reason that the matter transmitter in F.M. Busby's **The Singularity Project** is treated for most of the novel's length as little more than a macguffin in a murder mystery. There is, to be sure, a bit more speculative science than we would see in a standard mystery, but the question of whether the matter transmitter really works, or is merely an elaborate hoax, is far more important to the narrative than any science fictional implications of such a device. Busby seems to have gone out of his way to minimize the SF aspects of his plot, setting his tale in a near-future Seattle that is nearly indistinguishable from the present and populating it with characters straight out of hardboiled fiction. Mitch Banning, the narrator, is a telecommunications consultant who becomes involved with a crooked promoter acting as middleman in a scheme to build a working matter transmitter, using an eccentric financier's funds and a dope-addicted scientist's theory of man-made singularities. But a mysterious saboteur called the Hornet plagues the project, and the unmasking of the Hornet is what drives the plot for most of the novel.

Even though I consider myself a lousy mystery reader, I figured out the Hornet's identity fairly early on – there aren't really enough suspects – but even after the mystery gets resolved the novel is only two-thirds over. What should be wrap-up details keep the plot moving, but Busby's real purpose seems to be to try to turn *The Singularity Project* back into an SF novel before it ends. It doesn't quite come off, since the novel isn't really conceived or shaped as SF, but it's an intriguing approach to genre-mixing, and in an odd way the old-fashioned idea of the eccentric millionaire underwriting the brilliant lone inventor matches the slightly old-fashioned tough-guy prose. Busby writes good action scenes, his dialogue is sharp, several of his characters are memorable, and his opening sentence is a classic hardboiled hook. In this context, the matter transmitter is much more of a provocative notion than it would be in a straight SF novel. But why take a mystery with an unusual twist and disguise it as an SF novel without one?

Kim Stanley Robinson's **Red Mars** – the first novel in a projected trilogy – is indeed the full-featured, brilliantly complex Martian colonization novel that you've heard about, and it's also the most self-conscious treatment of Mars as a utopian frontier since Bradbury's *The Martian Chronicles*. One of the main characters, the semi-legendary first man on Mars, is named John Boone, and at one point he finds himself under investigation by a bureaucrat named Sam Houston. When Boone undertakes a long exploration of the emerging Martian colonies years after he first set foot on the planet, it carries echoes of the historical Boone's explorations of Kentucky. Martian colonization is pushed forward by a twenty-first-century version of trading companies called transnationals and by the pressure of growing population, exacerbated by the discovery (initially among the Martian colonists) of a technique to extend the human life span. Meanwhile, back east, the earth is rapidly sinking into economic and ecological chaos. Mars holds out the only hope for a new start, and in the speech that opens the novel, Boone sounds almost like de Tocqueville in his assertion that the new world is producing not merely an extension of the old, but an entirely new social order and a new kind of human.

He's wrong, of course, and in a daring structural trick Robinson kills him off shortly after this speech, leaving us to backtrack to discover how what started out as an unstable mix of utopianism and opportunism leads to the assassination which is one of the novel's two climaxes. During its first half-century of colonization – roughly the period covered by *Red Mars* – Mars becomes a welter of special interests and ideological subcolonies. The novel's centerpiece is that long odyssey of Boone's, in a section significantly titled "Falling into History." Boone's journey introduces us to colonies of Swiss, Australians, South Africans, Arabs, Japanese – even Sufis – all more or less intent on creating idealized versions of the earth societies from which they came. The most significant point of contention, not surprisingly, centers around the questions of terraforming and economic development, and the novel is not without its assortment of Greenpeace-style ecological terrorists. If all this sounds a bit Politically Correct, it's not surprising: unlike Ben Bova's Mars (reviewed here last August), in which a patina of PC was overlaid on what was essentially an engineering novel, Robinson builds his novel around these political and utopian questions, and derives his detailed and generally quite convincing scientific narrative from these same concerns. He seems to suggest that while terraforming may lead to more or less predictable results, human behavior is far less manipulable. His novel is a provocative epic of science versus history, with nature as the arbiter.

Robinson's main challenge, then, is keeping his scientific and utopian narratives from going off by themselves, and he handles it masterfully by focusing on character, and to a lesser extent on the stunningly realized setting. His major viewpoint characters are all members of the First Hundred colonists (it's always capitalized like that), and they include preservationists, technocrats, pioneers, and visionaries of all stripes. Boone's main rival, both sexually and ideologically, is Frank Chalmers, who tries to represent a *realpolitik* approach to the various factions, but who finds that even this approach isn't dependable when the forces set loose on Mars go out of control in a spectacular and cataclysmic finale that recalls, on a considerably larger scale, the ending of Gregory Benford's *Against Infinity*. Robinson may have built his emerging Martian social order on extensions of current geopolitics, but his ending suggests this may have been necessary to provide a kind of intellectual archaeology for his next two volumes. *Red Mars* is an impressive novel in its own right, but it's also a spectacular stage-setting for what's yet to come.

It isn't normally the policy of *Locus* to review self-published books, and when it became apparent that "Celadon Press" seems to be Harvey Jacobs himself, I began making plans for the time I would save by not having to finish **Beautiful Soup**. But Jacobs is no amateur out to satisfy an inflated ego; his 1969 story collection *The Egg of the Glak and Other Stories* earned him comparison with Bernard Malamud, and his infrequent short fiction first began showing up in SF anthologies as long ago as Judith Merril's 1966 "best of the year" volume. He's worked extensively in television (an experience that shows up in the way he writes dialogue), and boasts an impressive list of awards and fellowships, including a *Playboy* fiction award. The obvious next question is, did he just go off his noodle and produce a genuinely unpublishable novel, or is his claim valid that commercial publishers have become so constrained by market segments and last year's successes that they can't handle anything new?

Well, the novel is certainly not unpublishable, and in fact is far more original and enjoyable that much of what does make it to market. On the other hand, I can see how a beleaguered editor might remain unconvinced, after glancing at the opening chapters, that untold numbers of readers have been just waiting for the first novel about Universal Product Codes. In today's market, I could easily see a similar fate befalling Bernard Wolfe's *Limbo*, which is the only novel I can think of to which *Beautiful Soup* is remotely comparable. Both begin with an absurdist premise in which physical disfigurements provide the basis for peace and order in a dystopian future America — amputation in Wolfe's novel, mandatory human bar codes to determine social status in *Beautiful Soup* — both use their initial premise to launch a broad-based comic satire with a bewildering array of targets, both approach their SF premises as controlling metaphors for novels otherwise worked out as mainstream, both belong to that small but significant subgenre — sometimes visited by Vonnegut as well — that we might call the picaresque dystopia.

Jacobs's protagonist, James P. Wander, is born into the elite of a 21st-century America in which bar codes are imprinted on everyone's forehead at birth, their meaning and status controlled by a hidden master computer. Through a bizarre accident, his code is altered to that of a can of pea soup, and Wander immediately becomes a non-person. He appeals through the legal system and even to the inventor of the bar-code system, but to no avail: deliberate alteration of a code is the society's main taboo. Arrested for trying to alter the code at an art gallery, he is remanded first to a psychiatric facility whose holistic therapeutic techniques derive entirely from the works of a Norman Rockwell-style painter, and later to the Millhaus Correctional Facility. He eventually joins a mysterious circus which may or may not be a disguised missile-launching facility, suggesting that the vaunted accomplishment of world peace may be no more than an illusion. Along the way he meets a colorful variety of characters, and Jacobs gets in digs at everything from prepackaged newscasts to trendy art to wandering garbage barges.

The notion of humans as commodities may the oldest idea in dystopian fiction, many of Jacobs's targets are easy shots, and the slightly too-whimsical notion with which he sets his fable up tends to make it look like it's going to be a one-joke novel. But it unfolds with a richness of invention, character, and dialogue that more than overcome this initial premise, and that make *Beautiful Soup* a worthwhile addition to a small but significant tradition of dystopian fiction. In the end, it's not nearly as complex and philosophical as Limbo, but at the same time it lacks that novel's didacticism about psychoanalytic theory, and is almost as entertaining.

Hard Landing ~~ Algis Budrys

The Destiny Makers ~~ George Turner

Cold Allies ~~ Patricia Anthony

Back in the 1950s, Algis Budrys wrote a handful of haunting, understated stories about stranded aliens or anonymous supermen living unnoticed among us; tales like "Nightsound," "The Distant Sound of Engines," and most famously "Nobody Bothers Gus" come quickly to mind even though it's been years since I read them, and even though the basic premise of such stories was already hackneyed way back then. But Budrys — still one of the most underrated writers to emerge from that underrated decade — always managed to find a hard edge of real alienation in the theme, implying far more than he stated and sensing the metaphorical undercurrent of much of SF's stock currency — he was one of our first minimalists. (I always wondered if his acuteness in evoking alienation — and his fondness for plots involving crash landings of one sort or another — may have had something to do with his own situation as a stateless citizen of a then-nonexistent free Lithuania.) Now he has returned to this theme with a short novel as spare and tight as his best short fiction. **Hard Landing** — which in its very title brings his old crash landing motif right to the foreground — is a model of narrative compression, with a surprising array of techniques and points of view crammed into a short space. The only question is, can he still make this old chestnut seem new in the 1990s?

For me, the answer is a clear yes, but not necessarily because of Budrys's attempts to thematically update the material. The novel covers a long time span, from the late forties to the early seventies, and by the time it is over such timely issues as immune-deficiency diseases and political scandals come to play an important part in the fates of the alien spacemen stranded on earth after their survey ship crashes. Budrys's plot carries more than a hint of tabloid-style paranoia, and I'm not sure it would work at all if one regarded it as the main point of the novel, but it does serve to generate enough tension and mystery to keep the pages turning; other writers might keep you going for 800 pages with less incident than you get here. What seems more important, though, are Budrys's showroom-model narrative techniques (some of the multiple points of view are defiantly and cheerfully impossible), his deft snapshots of several aspects of American life during a period when the country was becoming more urbanized and less innocent, and his tough/sensitive portrayals of the survival choices and overwhelming isolation of his main characters. At times, especially in sequences set around the pine barrens of New Jersey, Budrys's evocation of loneliness and desperation calls to mind the best of Sturgeon, but without the sentimentality.

As I've already hinted — and as the mention of Sturgeon suggests — the novel is in some ways a throwback to the sf of the fifties. But the Budrys fifties was different from everyone else's. Much of the SF in a Budrys story has to be inferred by the reader – there's seldom a certifiable infodump in sight – and *Hard Landing* makes the most of this economy of scale. We learn fairly early on that five aliens were stranded on earth sometime in the 1940s, that one of them died shortly after the crash, and that the remaining four – interdicted from ever communicating with one another or revealing their existence – have forged very different lives for themselves according to their different natures. We learn that their civilization is involved in a vague commercial rivalry with other aliens called Methane-Breathers, and that the earth is approaching a stage of development making it worthy of contact. But we learn next to nothing about the details of their own society, the background of their mission, or the histories of the individual characters; their widely varying personalities are revealed almost entirely through their actions on earth – the casual brutality of the ship's captain Ravashan, the growing desperation of the unsophisticated Selven, the more successful attempt at integration of the navigator Arvan.

If a current trend in SF is to give us alien societies with the depth of exposition of a Victorian novel, Budrys is certainly out to buck it: he's as reticent about unnecessary detail as Albert Camus (whose name shows up on a minor character here – appropriately, a pathologist), and just as existential. The effect is to make this deceptively old-fashioned narrative – with its false documents, bogus "reconstructions" and author's notes, wild surmises and portentous implications – seem exciting and innovative. By the time you get toward the end, as the story's connections with real historical events grows more and more obvious, you may find yourself feeling just a bit lumbered – as though you've been on the receiving end of a whopper told with a perfectly straight face. (Budrys warns us up front that "everything that follows is a lie.") But then you realize you've read it all in one sitting, and that it all fits together like clockwork.

George Turner's **The Destiny Makers** also carries at least one echo of the 50s; the title sounds as if it belongs on an old Ace Double with a lurid Valigursky cover. But it's quite literal: these "destiny makers" are world leaders who, faced with massive overpopulation, declining resources, and ecological catastrophe in the middle of the next century, must seriously entertain notions of a kind of global triage in order to keep the whole social order from collapsing. Turner's most depressing point, which he makes at great length, is that the future politicians who may well face such monumental decisions are likely to be no less weak, indecisive, and bigoted than the politicians we have today. Unfortunately, they aren't much more interesting, either.

Beltane, the Australian premier who finds himself faced with casting the deciding vote among leaders of industrialized nations on a proposal which smacks loudly of the Final Solution, turns out to be little more than the puppet of his Joe Kennedy-like father, whom he has brought back from Alzheimer's disease by means of illegal rejuvenating treatments. Meanwhile, Beltane's unmarried daughter is also busily violating the draconian 21st-century population laws by getting herself pregnant by an "unsuitable" proletarian youth, and refusing to abort the baby. Into this political time bomb walks Harry Ostrov, a cop with an overdeveloped moral sense who is assigned to guard Beltane's father. Ostrov, his sidekick Gus, and the elder Beltane are presented as islands of competence in a world hopelessly unable to cope with itself — but they each also hide terrible personal secrets, some of which are revealed through an experimental drug which strips away all civilizing pretense. (The drug might have been an interesting idea, but Turner uses it in the narrative as little more than a super truth serum.)

Turner has taken on a lot of Big Issues here, and his attempt to draw parallels between failures of policy and failures of character is often insightful and provocative. But so much of the narrative is devoted to the machinations necessary to protect Beltane from the political and public relations consequences of his and his family's actions that the novel very nearly turns into a political thriller in which the well-realized setting — which ought to be the star of the book — recedes into the background. Turner provides us with enough convincing glimpses of life in a deteriorating world to show that he's thought it out carefully (although the division of society into Minders and Wardies — or wards of the state — carries familiar echoes of Orwell and even Kornbluth), but the intrigue gets in the way and finally has the odd effect of trivializing everything around it. I suppose it's deliberate that the characters aren't up to the magnitude of the decisions they must face, but that doesn't make them necessarily compelling as characters. By the time we come to what's supposed to be a startling revelation about Beltane and his father — a revelation that would work perfectly well in a mainstream novel — we're wondering what the hell it has to do with the fact that the whole world is going down the toilet.

Turner makes a valiant effort to bring his global catastrophe theme back into the foreground in the concluding chapters, and Beltane's final surprising decision leads to a genuinely ominous ending, with implications that seem especially timely given our current problems with "ethnic cleansing" ideologies. Unfortunately, by then it almost seems an afterthought, an attempt to lend apocalyptic weight to the personality flaws we've been awash in since chapter one. For the most part, the characters responsible for saving the world aren't themselves worth saving, and while this gives the title a nice, bitter irony, it doesn't quite make for a thematically unified or entirely satisfying novel.

Patricia Anthony's first novel, **Cold Allies**, is also set in an apocalyptic post-greenhouse future and features a cast of troubled characters whose personal preoccupations influence global events; in fact, there are no fewer than eight important viewpoint characters whose stories must be juggled in the novel's short, episodic chapter sections. Anthony complicates matters even further by casting this all as a future-war novel in which a united Arab army threatens to isolate a fuel-starved Europe by pincer-like invasions of Spain and the Ukraine. And then she complicates *that* by introducing some genuinely eerie aliens who manifest themselves as blue lights accompanied by vague sounds of rain or sleet in the back of your head. The aliens sometimes merely observe the war, sometimes make vampire-like raids on the dying, and sometimes abduct selected individuals into the light, where they are "interrogated" by being made to experience flawed reconstructions of their own memories in a manner reminiscent of Bradbury's "Mars Is Heaven!" Like Budrys, Anthony borrows some aspects of her aliens from cult UFOlogy, and she acknowledges this by making one of her viewpoint characters a popular author of several fraudulent UFO books.

So far, this sounds likes a recipe for chaos – a novel that wants to do too many things at once. But *Cold Allies* is brilliantly controlled and focused, and the various storylines unfold in an elegant series of parallels that converge in a satisfying and original conclusion. The novel is really about memory and desire, and how they serve to both trap and liberate a range of very different characters whose paths cross throughout the novel: an American sergeant whose remote-controlled robot vehicle offers him a sense of power and competence, a Ukrainian officer haunted by an earlier defeat, an Egyptian general who dutifully sends his son to his death, an Okie-like refugee from a devastated Texas, a pathologist who tries to understand the bizarre mutilations of the dead caused by the aliens, an American general who sees in the aliens – and eventually in the woman pathologist – the promise of love.

Somehow, Anthony keeps all this going without losing focus on her carefully thought-out scenario of future warfare. We understand clearly not only the economic and ecological backgrounds of the war, but the technology and tactics involved, the problems of fuel and supply lines, and the respective strengths and weaknesses of the opposing armies. (The Arabs have more manpower and better fuel supplies, the European/American allies have superior discipline and more advanced technology.) Even without the aliens, this is one of the best future-war novels I've seen in years, and its sympathetic Arab characters help it avoid any suggestion of an "Arab menace" novel without bending over too far in the direction of political correctness. But with the aliens – and with the well-realized human characters whose lives the aliens change – *Cold Allies* becomes more than a future war tale, and turns into a strikingly original tour de force, a first novel of truly unusual maturity and complexity.

Sandman, Sleep ~~ Herbert Lieberman

In the Electric Mist with Confederate Dead ~~ James Lee Burke

The Porcelain Dove, or Constancy's Reward ~~ Delia Sherman

The Drylands ~~ Mary Rosenblum

BUNCH! ~~ David R. Bunch

Whatever benefits it's supposed to offer from a marketing standpoint, and despite its worthwhile intentions in breaking down the barriers of formula, genre-mixing doesn't usually fool anybody. It's not easy to construct a situation that leads with equal logic in narrative directions that seem to be mutually exclusive and that rewards differing sets of reader expectations, and yet this may be the very reason we seem to be seeing a lot more of this sort of crossbreeding than we used to — it's become a kind of hat trick that writers often find difficult to resist. Usually, however, the result is like those flavored coffees; no one is fooled into thinking it isn't coffee, but it tastes vaguely like something else as well. Asimov's SF mysteries were SF novels with nominal mystery plots; F.M. Busby's *The Singularity Project* was a mystery with an SF macguffin; Dean Koontz sometimes uses detective work as a means of unfolding his horror plots, but I don't think anyone reads Koontz as a detective writer.

Cross-genre work has become so familiar to SF readers that it's even become problematical to think of a Dan Simmons or a Tim Powers as an SF writer — but what happens when writers from other precincts venture into this territory? Herbert Lieberman's *Sandman, Sleep* and James Lee Burke's *In the Electric Mist with Confederate Dead* are both novels by writers with substantial mainstream reputations, both are essentially detective stories, both introduce significant fantastic elements, and both come trailing clouds of promotional glory about the startling innovations they represent.

Of the two novels, Lieberman's is the more ambitious in the way it tries to subsume whole categories of pop fiction. **Sandman, Sleep** takes place in the latter half of the 21st century, but its geographical setting is so remote that we get no sense whatsoever of the future, and it eventually becomes apparent that the time frame is needed mainly to credibly work out some of the chronological details of Lieberman's plot. In a remote castle in northern Canada, surrounded by a bestial tribe of aborigines called Woodsmen, the six children of a mysterious billionaire named Jones are being raised in complete isolation from the outside world. The only change in their routine comes when their father pays his annual visit to the castle, interviewing each of them from behind a screen that keeps his appearance a mystery. Often, after one of these visits, one of the children disappears. Letters arrive from the absent siblings describing the inspiring humanitarian projects they are involved in, but the narrator Jonathan – one of the remaining children – grows suspicious when he notes that the style and typeface of all these letters seems oddly similar.

With its faint echoes of Mervyn Peake, this setting creates a compelling and beautifully realized fantasy atmosphere. But when Jones is murdered during one of his visits and a brilliant detective is brought in to investigate, things take a decided turn toward the Poirot. As the murder investigation unfolds, we learn who Jones really is, the nature of his strange relationship with the Woodsmen, and the real reasons for the disappearances of the children. It would be churlish to reveal more, but by the time the novel is over we've had tastes not only of Peake and Agatha Christie, but of *The Island of Dr. Moreau, The Boys from Brazil, The Wicker Man*, and even a few Doc Savage-style hairbreadth escapes. What we don't get is any real sense of SF, even though an SF premise drives the plot and even though it's set some eighty years from now. This leads to some disturbing lapses in a plot that is otherwise ingeniously worked out. In order to sustain the suspense in the novel's final chapters, for example, Lieberman has to convince us that a remote castle full of high-tech equipment in the 21st century depends on ground-laid telephone lines for its communication with the outside world, something that isn't even the case today. He also has to convince us that a more-or-less mad scientist, working alone but with substantial funding, can discover a wonderful serum unknown to science and keep it a secret for decades without any other researchers duplicating it. All this suggests a setting of around 1930, not 2070.

In short, Lieberman has constructed a wonderfully atmospheric suspense tale, with interesting characters and a provocative setting, that fails only at the conceptual level – which in this case means the SF level. With all of its mysteries, conspiracies, and high adventure, the novel moves along at an admirable clip, makes some good points about ethics and morality along the way, and gives us an exciting rollercoaster trip through the resources of pop – and pulp – fiction. But like much such fiction, it suffers from the Wile E. Coyote syndrome: if you pause to look down or think, you find you've run out of ground, and you're out over thin air.

James Lee Burke's **In the Electric Mist with Confederate Dead** is less ambitious in combining genres, and in fact the fantasy element here seems such an add-on that it would barely warrant consideration in Locus were it not so unusual. With his series of five novels featuring the Louisiana detective Dave Robicheaux, Burke has achieved an outstanding reputation as a mystery writer, a reputation warranted by a superb prose style and an unerring sense of place and character. Introducing an apparent supernatural element into so successful an ongoing series seems almost perverse (although hardboiled writers have played for years with the chivalric and Arthurian aspects of their heroes). Furthermore, the ghostly confederate general who takes on the role of Robicheaux's conscience isn't really necessary for working out the detective-story plot (although he's given a small but important role in finally doing in the bad guy).

In the Electric Mist with Confederate Dead is a detective story from beginning to end. A movie company has moved into the small Louisiana town where Robicheaux lives, bringing with it a ruthless gangster who was once Robicheaux's schoolmate. One of the film's actors discovers the body of a Black man whose murder Robicheaux had witnessed in 1957, and Dave begins to suspect a connection between that murder, a series of brutal killings of young girls, and the presence of his old school rival, who is an investor in the film. Working with a female FBI agent, Robicheaux starts putting it all together in good hardboiled fashion. But meanwhile the actor, Elrod Sykes, claims to see visions of confederate soldiers in the swamp. Soon Robicheaux also begins to see the phantom soldiers, and eventually he meets the ghost of Confederate General John Bell Hood, who offers hints about the investigation. By the end, there's more than enough physical evidence to convince us that this is more than an hallucination.

There have been real ghosts in detective stories before, of course, but it seems to me Burke is taking some interesting chances. It's one thing to suggest a ghostly presence on, say, the English moors, but quite another to introduce one into an ongoing series praised for its convincing realism. My own guess is that pursuing the chivalric motif in crime fiction has led Burke straight into the mythic dimension offered only by fantasy. His confederate general may not be much of a detective's helper, but he does provide a powerful avatar of one of hardboiled fiction's most enduring conventions – the honorable man forced by circumstance to fight on behalf of a dishonorable system. In any event, Burke makes it work, and does so without violating the essential form of his superior detective tale.

When most of us think of generic crossbreeds, of course, we tend to think along the detective story-horror-SF axis, but there are other animals out there as well, and at least one of them has gained a considerable degree of respect and acceptance: the historical fantasy. Perhaps it's because the historical novelist shares with the fantasy or SF writer the problem of creating a convincing world that lies outside the reader's experience, or perhaps it's because an archaic world-view is more amenable to the introduction of fantastic elements, but whatever the reason it seems a skilled novelist can get away with more in an historical setting. And, after reading **The Porcelain Dove**, there is little doubt that Delia Sherman is a skilled novelist. Sherman's earlier novel, *Through a Brazen Mirror*, made use of fantasy's all-purpose medieval setting, but here she takes on a far more specific historical period – France in the latter part of the 18th century. Taken simply as a fictional memoir of a chambermaid's adventures from 1745 until a few years after the Revolution, the novel works wonderfully as a detailed and convincing work of straight historical fiction. (In an historical note, Sherman gives credit to Ferdinand Braudel's school of revisionist annaliste historians, and her novel demonstrates what a treasure such microhistorical research can be to a conscientious novelist.)

Sherman introduces her fantasy elements in an ingenious manner. At the outset, we learn that the narrator, Berthe Duvet, and six other members of the household where she worked, a country estate called Beauxpres, have been trapped for two centuries in an unchanging "earthly paradise" which remains isolated from the world of historical time. Persuaded to write an account of the string of ancient crimes, spells, and curses which got them there, Berthe chooses to begin the narrative with her own birth in 1745 — and for much of the next couple of hundred pages the novel proceeds as a fascinating historical memoir, with frequent hints and portents of the fantastic events which eventually unfold. Berthe tells of her childhood, her love of Paris theatre, and her eventual employment as a maid to the aristocrat Adele du Fourchet, where she remains in service for the next several decades. When Adele marries the duc de Malvoeux, the action shifts to the rural estate of Beauxpres, where the duke's obsession with bird-collecting, and his general mean-spiritedness, eventually contribute to the family's ruin. Malvoeux, the descendant of a fourteenth-century child murderer clearly based on Gilles de Rais, unwittingly activates a sorceror's curse against his family when he thrice refuses alms to a beggar. The curse — which gives the novel its title — is that unless Malvoeux obtains for his aviary a fabulous bird called the porcelain dove, his family will suffer endless misfortune. The quest for the dove, which might have provided fodder for a whole numbing trilogy, wisely takes place entirely offstage.

As Sherman seamlessly weaves these threads of fantasy and horror into her narrative — and she does not stint on the fantasy when it comes — the novel grows in complexity and power, alternating among scenes of harrowing crimes, revolutionary violence, and fairy-tale enchantment. Underlying it all is a sophisticated understanding of storytelling as a kind of magical or mythic time which has the power of preserving events outside of history. *The Porcelain Dove* begins with the fairy-tale formula "Once upon a time" and ends with the seven survivors of Beauxpres preparing to act out one of the home-made plays with which they entertain themselves during their centuries of solitude. They've become actors in their own self-invented artifice, as if they've learned that becoming a story is the only way to escape history.

For the last couple of years, Mary Rosenblum's series of interlocking "Drylands" short stories, about survival in a drought-stricken world, have created some excitement among readers of Asimov's and seemed to portend a promising first novel. The Drylands admirably validates that promise, bringing together several of the characters from those short stories in a novel that builds on the events of the stories without reading at all like a fix-up. What it does read like is a vaguely old-fashioned ecological disaster adventure, in which a brilliantly detailed vision of a devastated landscape dominates the actions of a disparate group of characters who have to find their own strategies for survival. Rosenblum's blighted Oregon is the real star of the book, and it harks back more to novels like, say, Charles Eric Maine's *The Tide Went Out* than to such metaphoric, "psychic projection" landscapes as the one in Ballard's *The Drought*. Given what Rosenblum has set out to do, this isn't a bad thing at all: in the first place, there aren't as many SF drought novels as everyone thinks there are — so that the premise isn't as hackneyed as it at first seems — and in the second place, Ballard has done pretty much all that needs to be done in the psychic wasteland front of disaster fiction. In short, Rosenblum's is a classic SF landscape, defamiliarized by the removal of a single crucial element, water. She doesn't dwell much on the causes of the drought, and she doesn't need to.

Carter Voltaire is an Army major who, after a disastrous experience with a water-riot in Chicago, is assigned to protect a pumping station in Oregon which has been plagued by sabotage. He immediately begins to suspect a local leader named Dan Greely, but grows increasingly suspicious of his hostile second-in-command, Delgado. Meanwhile, a young mother named Nita Montoya is also making her way to Oregon with her daughter in search of her missing husband, and an alienated youth named Jeremy Barlow is traveling the villages of the Pacific northwest putting on magic shows. Both Nita and Jeremy have developed unusual psychic abilities, perhaps as a result of the environmental change: Nita is an empath who can read others' feelings, and Jeremy has the power to produce hallucinations in those around him (which is the real source of his "magic"). These three characters form an unlikely alliance to investigate the sources of the sabotage, the causes of the intense hostilities between local farmers and the Army, and the role of an almost all-powerful national governing agency called Water Policy in the whole affair. It all leads, of course, to Ever-Widening Revelations.

Rosenblum's plotting is efficient and brisk, and she manages to work in the psychic powers theme in ways that make it seem integral to the novel. Her characters are for the most part sympathetic and complex — although Delgado and another character whose name I shouldn't reveal both turn out to be rather cardboard villains — and she handles big set-piece mob scenes quite well. But the novel is driven by style and setting. In straightforward but evocative prose, Rosenblum builds a convincing picture of a disintegrating society in an increasingly barren landscape. Her scenario is so consistent, and so detailed, that when Jeremy conjures up a vision of a water-filled world of the past — our own world — we are as filled with wonder as are the characters in the novel. Although in many ways modest and unpretentious, *The Drylands* is a first-rate debut.

One of the true eccentric classics of modern SF is David R. Bunch's 1971 *Moderan*, a surrealist technological nightmare so unusual in form that it can't properly be called either a novel or a collection of stories. Relatively few contemporary readers know the book, and fewer still are aware that, since 1957, Bunch has published scores of stories unconnected with the *Moderan* world. It's not surprising that Broken Mirrors Press, which last year issued a collection of R.A. Lafferty — another of the field's great stylistic eccentrics — should be the first to give us an overview collection of Bunch's work. BUNCH! includes 32 stories, few of them more than three or four pages long, ranging from Bunch's first published SF story ("Routine Emergency") to the hitherto unpublished "Control." The fact that Bunch was able to sell the same kind of stories to commercial SF magazines and to small-press literary magazines says a great deal about how unusual and compelling his style is, and how little it resembles anything else in or out of SF. Whatever you think about Bunch's convoluted, mock-hysterical prose (he must use more hyphens, exclamation points, and capital letters per page than any living writer), you have to admit that he's remained true to his art, even at the cost of wider readership.

And that art, at its best, reveals a civilization bent on such psychotic dehumanization and mindless violence that some of these stories make Harlan Ellison (a Bunch admirer) sound like Alastair Cooke by comparison. A highway clean-up crew makes no distinction between scooping up metal and flesh ("Routine Emergency"), garbage collectors routinely toss living children into their trucks ("In the Time of Disposal of Infants"), a bored tinworker entertains himself by kicking severed heads around his apartment ("Any Heads at Home"), a college class inures students to atrocity through live immolations and machines that chop children to shreds ("The College of Acceptable Death"). Not all of the stories are quite so violent, but most of them share the same ironic tone of bland boosterism that made *Moderan* so chilling.

At the same time, it must be said that *Moderan* was easier going than this collection, if only because the vignettes in that book incrementally build toward a consistent, if harrowing, vision. Here the vision is fragmented, even though it's possible to see Bunch building toward coherent themes in stories that seem to fall into series based around common themes. Bunch is much concerned with how children are made to lose their innocence, for example, and four of the stories take the form of "training talks" in which Bunch's characteristic psycho narrator masquerades as a concerned father. (Children get an unexpected chance to escape in another story, "That High-Up Blue Day That Saw The Black Sky-Train Come Spinning," which is not only one of the book's best stories, but one of the more upbeat.) Several stories ("In the Complaints Service," "Breakout in Ecol 2," "In the Time of Disposal of Infants," "Routine Emergency") portray Kafkaesque public service bureaucrats seemingly unconcerned with the horrors their jobs entail. Although dark humor pervades all of Bunch's fiction, a few lighter stories offer twists on such conventional SF situations such as aliens, robots, or overpopulation. "Control" is about a crazed inventor who thinks his computerized "last-chance pants," which will permit governments to monitor all sexual activity, will solve overpopulation. "In the Jag-Whiffing Service" reveals that UFO aliens are here to steal our tires, which they sniff to get high. "Let Me Call Her Sweetcore" is a clever variation on del Rey's robot love story "Helen O'Loy".

Individually, almost any one of these stories would stand out as brilliantly inventive in the context of a magazine or anthology; even though many are 20 or more years old, almost none seem dated. Trying to read them all together, however, leaves one with the vague sensation of being pelted with razor-studded marshmallows

— of being pummeled with a brand of irony that begins to get wearing from its consistently coy shrillness. This doesn't mean the collection isn't long overdue and welcome — merely that it's probably best taken in small doses. Bunch is a poet as well as a fiction writer, and to some degree his fiction demands to be read as a kind of gonzo, sprung-rhythm poetry — as if Gerard Manley Hopkins had gotten himself reincarnated as William S. Burroughs.

— May 1993, Locus #388 —

Vultures of the Void:
A History of British Science Fiction Publishing, 1946-1956 ~
~ Philip Harbottle and Stephen Holland

Earthsea Revisioned ~~ Ursula K. Le Guin

SF and fantasy scholarship is almost unique among literary studies in its populist zeal for a kind of democratic debate that's all but died out in mainstream criticism. The mainstream of critical thought has its occasional "independent scholar" (formerly "gentleman scholar"; in either case often a euphemism for "unemployed scholar"), and a good number of novelists who occasionally turn to criticism, but by and large it's owned by the academy. But the academy came late to SF criticism, and still hasn't attained enough clout to be able to check ID's at the door; almost everyone can get in. There are SF writers with a genuine critical or scholarly bent, and those just obsessed with explaining themselves; academics who specialize in SF and make a lifelong study of it, and academics who don't know much about SF but are sure they can figure it out in a jiffy on the basis of whatever books their undergraduates recommend; fans who have amassed enormous original research on topics or writers that no one else yet cares much about, and fans who simply won't shut up. It's both frustrating and rewarding to realize that useful insights and valuable information can come from just about any of these camps, despite the mutual mistrust among them.

Philip Harbottle and Stephen Holland's **Vultures of the Void: A History of British Science Fiction Publishing, 1946-1956** is a first-rate example of the sort of thing dedicated fans can do better than anybody — in part because almost no one else would devote so much energy to exploring the kind of indefensibly awful writing that they describe, sometimes in such hilarious detail that it recalls Neil Gaiman and Kim Newman's *Ghastly Beyond Belief.* Except for those writers who made it in American magazines, postwar British SF has been notably invisible both in histories and anthologies, as though it were a dreadful family secret best left unexplored (and it pretty much is, as it turns out). Harbottle and Holland, with considerable help from interpolated short essays by Ted Carnell, Gordon Landsborough, E.C. Tubb, Kenneth Bulmer, and others directly involved in that period, do an excellent job of reconstructing a genuine nightmare of hackdom, far worse than most of us would imagine – and exactly the sort of "subliterary" topic that traditional scholarship shies away from. At first I thought the title *Vultures of the Void* seemed precious, but it turns out to be cannily appropriate on two counts: for one thing, it echoes the British pulp industry's inexplicable fondness for house pseudonyms beginning with "V," such as "Vargo Statten," "Volsted Gridban," or (my favorite) "Vector Magroon"; for another, it describes pretty accurately those opportunistic publishers who helped to fill the pop fiction "void" created by wartime paper rationing by issuing appallingly shoddy ripoffs of American gangster, western, or SF stories.

According to Harbottle and Holland, British SF publishing in the postwar decade was dominated by a single factor: the continuation of the paper rationing through 1953. After the war, this led to unscrupulous publishers – who obtained paper by buying others' rations or even tail-ends of newspaper rolls – commissioning cheap paperback novels full of sex and violence and written to order under impossible deadlines and at rates of about ten shillings per thousand words. SF became a natural part of this market, and while most of the fiction that resulted was astonishingly bad – Harbottle and Holland might have added considerably to the entertainment value of their book just by quoting more examples – a few genuine hack heroes emerged, most notably John Russell Fearn, whose millions of words of prose included most of the "Vargo Statten" and "Volsted Gridban" stories. But more characteristic is Gordon Landsborough's haunting memory of meeting an anonymous young "staff writer" who lived and slept in a publisher's cellar while working day and night against an impossible quota of ten thousand words per day. Such tales sound a lot like publishing folklore, but there seems little doubt that these were the original Publishers From Hell.

Meanwhile, of course, the most successful English writers, such as Clarke and later Brunner and Aldiss, were making far superior wages selling to American magazines, which could not be imported directly, but which gained popularity in the form of "British Reprint Editions." Given the sorry state of the domestic paperback industry and this considerable competition from abroad, Landsborough's successful attempt to launch *Authentic Science Fiction* from one of the more exploitative paperback houses seems quite an accomplishment – as does Carnell's launching of *New Worlds* or Peter Hamilton's of *Nebula*. Much of what we think of as the most important British SF of the 1950s and 1960s would emerge from these magazines, of course, and by the mid-1950s, with the end of paper rationing, more respectable paperback publishers began to re-enter the field as well. What came later is a pretty familiar part of SF history, detailed in such books as Colin Greenland's *The Entropy Exhibition*. But the shadowy history of Vargo Statten and his predecessors may never be told more fully than in Vultures of the Void. It's a useful and invaluable addition to SF history, even though it's not a cat you'd ever want to let out of the back yard.

Among writers who occasionally take it upon themselves to write about their own fiction, Ursula Le Guin is one of the most articulate – and she'd better be. No living SF or fantasy writer has more scholars and critics peering over her shoulder than Le Guin, and this became acutely apparent in 1990 when – 17 years after the *Earthsea* trilogy was "finished" and safely pigeonholed by a legion of scholarly letter-sorters – she published a fourth novel, *Tehanu*, which rather seriously seemed to undercut some of the assumptions of the first three novels. Why Le Guin couldn't leave well enough alone is the topic of a brief but very provocative talk she delivered at an Oxford conference last August and which she has now published under the title **Earthsea Revisioned.** What is provocative about the book is not just her reasons for rethinking Earthsea from a female point of view, but the issues she raises about "revisioning" texts (the term is Adrienne Rich's) after one's point of view has broadened and matured, about the political structures inherent in the heroic fantasy form, about representations of authority in fiction, about fictions of power versus fictions of freedom. Anyone who has enjoyed any of the Earthsea books – and particularly those who cynically suspected that *Tehanu* was merely an attempt to retrofit a classic work with a facade of political correctness – ought to seek out this classy little pamphlet, which offers insights not only into the making of Earthsea, but into Le Guin's wonderful story "Buffalo Gals, Won't You Come Out Tonight" as well.

– June 1993, Locus #389 –

The Encyclopedia of Science Fiction ~
~ edited by John Clute and Peter Nicholls; technical editor,
John Grant; contributing editor, Brian Stableford
The Hammer of God ~~ Arthur C. Clarke
Glory ~~ Alfred Coppel

The first and probably most inescapable thing to be said about the new edition of Peter Nicholls' and John Clute's **Encyclopedia of Science Fiction** is that it is even more monumental and imposing than the first edition, and competes with nothing but that earlier volume as the standard one-volume reference for the whole SF world. The dimensions alone are staggering: 1370 pages (vs 672 for the first edition), over three-fourths more words (1,300,00 vs. 730,000), more than half again as many entries (4360 vs. 2800), more than half again as many authors covered with individual entries (2900 vs. 1817), no fewer than 212 essay-type "theme" entries (including 169 updated from the earlier edition). Without wavering from its clear focus on SF – not fantasy or horror, although many relevant authors from those genres are covered – the book manages to weigh in at a length comparable to that of reference works with far larger purviews: it's much longer than Benet's *Reader's Encyclopedia*, which takes all of world literature as its scope, and almost outpaces the main text of *The Cambridge Encyclopedia*. In short, the new edition isn't just an update; it's an essentially new work, as indispensable at $75 as the first edition was at $12.95 (paperback) in 1979. Compared to other reference book prices, it's almost cheap.

It also looks and feels a lot more like a mature encyclopedia than the first edition did. Gone are the illustrations and the old magazine-style page layout of three lined columns, and in its place is a more staid and readable unillustrated two-column format. Gone also is the plethora of critical voices, which occasionally led to contradictory judgments of the same author or work in the same book. Although almost three times as many contributors are listed for this edition as compared to the first (101 vs. 34), the editors claim that some 85% of the present text is by Clute, Nicholls, and Stableford, with different authors specializing in particular kinds of entries. Clute, for example, wrote some 2300 of the 2900 or so author entries, while Stableford provided most of the theme entries. While this has the advantage of giving a more unified tone to the entries, especially since all three main contributors write with wit and grace, it also makes the book seem more like a critical juggernaut – a work which is at once more clearly opinionated and more seductively "definitive" than the earlier version.

Perhaps because they're aware of this, the editors have for the most part been generous – sometimes to a fault – in their treatment of various authors and topics, saving their juiciest invectives for such easy targets as "survivalist fiction" ("a nightmare at the bottom of the barrel of SF") or *The Starlost* ("it was dire"). In the entry on *Locus*, Nicholls gently chides this magazine for not featuring killer reviews, but the *Encyclopedia* seems to find something nice to say about almost everybody, often coding adverse judgments in the form of backhanded compliments (R.L. Fanthorpe gets credited with at least one "not-unsuccessful fantasy" out of his zillion or so published stories; Alan Dean Foster's output is "generally competent"), or confining an entry to historical description (as with Sax Rohmer). At times, the critical stance seems so cleverly even-handed that you begin to wonder if some judgments are imbedded in the odd ways certain authors get introduced at the beginning of their entries: why would M. John Harrison be described as a "UK writer and rock-climber" or Mike Resnick as a "US author and dog-breeder" if there isn't some sort of implied vocational counseling going on? (But then, even Asimov is introduced as "US writer whose second marriage, in 1973, was to fellow writer J.O. Jeppson." Maybe they just have trouble writing meaningful opening sentences.)

The author coverage, of course, is the core of the book, making up well over half its entries. These entries are principally critical and bibliographical rather than biographical, and in general the book is not a good source for biographical details. Even major authors get only a short paragraph of background, leading to their discovery of or involvement with SF, and for some subjects even basic information is missing. (No birth dates are given for Tom Maddox or Boris Vallejo, for example, even though neither seems to be particularly secretive about such things.)

Deciding which authors to include has obviously been a problem, what with the vast number of new writers on the scene since the 1979 edition, the generally improved scholarship of SF history, and the blurring of genre lines in the work of many writers. (In some of the topical entries, most notably those on "Fantasy" and "Mainstream Writers of SF," you can see Nicholls agonizing over this very question, as though he's sharing with us the hard decisions he faced in organizing the book.) Omitted on principle are writers who have not produced a book, authors whose books have not appeared in English translation (although several are mentioned in entries for individual countries), authors who are exclusively self-published, and fantasy authors who haven't had "enough impact" on SF. Omitted out of practical deadline considerations are most, but not all, authors who entered the SF book field in 1992 or later.

This, of course, is an invitation to nitpicking. Many early magazine authors, some of whom were included in the first edition (and none of whom are likely to be remembered in any reference book but this one), are now consigned to oblivion: G. Peyton Wertenbaker, Charles R. Tanner, Charles Willard Diffin, and Drury D. Sharp are examples. Recent authors who apparently didn't make the cutoff include Katherine Kerr, Neal Stephenson, and Charles Oberndorf. (Daniel Quinn is included, although his *Ishmael* arguably had considerably less impact last year than Stephenson's *Snow Crash*.) In general, fantasy writers seem to have a greater chance of being included if they have a mainstream reputation; thus we have entries for Mark Helprin and Robert Coover, but not Megan Lindholm or Peter Beagle (who was included in the first edition). [Of course, in retrospect, it is apparent that Clute and Grant's later Encyclopedia of Fantasy would absorb many of these lacunae among fantasy writers.] Nicholls and Clute make a good case for their decision to offer extensive coverage of mainstream writers (the rationale is expounded in "Mainstream Writers of SF" and "Genre SF," the latter of which gets a little prickly in its pointed contrast of principles with those of James Gunn's *New Encyclopedia of Science Fiction*), but the pattern by which mainstream writers are included is a bit vague. Some, like Kafka and Borges, are unavoidable, but others, like Jerzy Kosinski, seem shoehorned in on the argument that some aspects of some of their works seem vaguely SF-nal. Garcia Marquez is mentioned only in passing in an entry on "magic realism," and Beckett and Ionesco don't even show up in the entries for "absurdist SF" or "theatre." Perhaps too conveniently, Robert Scholes's "fabulation" − a catch-all term for a variety of postmodern fictions − is repeatedly invoked as a rationale for including other mainstream writers, and even gets its own entry (as does "Postmodernism and SF").

Coverage of major authors is almost always balanced and solid, with frank acknowledgment made of, for example, Asimov's undistinguished style or Van Vogt's psychotic plotting. But in every such case, there is a conscientious attempt made to discover the sources of a given author's appeal and his or her historical significance; the editors have studiously avoided exploiting their bully pulpit in order to reshuffle reputations or smash icons. In fact, an almost elegiac tone creeps into the accounts of old grand masters like Asimov, Heinlein, Herbert, and Simak, calling to mind how much the SF field has lost since the 1979 edition appeared. Balancing this, to some extent, is the advocacy shown for younger writers such as Greg Bear, Paul McAuley, Connie Willis, Karen Joy Fowler, and any number of others new to this edition. (Whether Fowler's *Sarah Canary* is "the finest First Contact novel yet written" – or whether John Fowles's *The Maggot* is a First Contact story at all – might seem to be judgments more appropriate for a critical essay than for an encyclopedia, and lead you to suspect that Clute has a First Contact essay inside him which he's chosen to distribute among various entries rather than publishing separately as an extended argument. There are several other examples of what we might call "distributed essays" throughout the book – arguments that only become apparent as a recurring pattern of observations.)

Next to the author entries, the 212 "theme" entries make up the largest single segment of the book – nearly a quarter of its length, according to the editors. These mini-essays – which would constitute a substantial book on their own – sometimes run into the thousands of words, and reveal even more clearly than the author entries the contours of the SF landscape as seen (primarily) by Clute, Nicholls, and Stableford. Most of them briefly introduce and define the topic, and then gallop chronologically through a discussion of relevant texts or subthemes. Probably less than half of the topics are ones that would demand to be covered in anything calling itself an SF encyclopedia; the rest represent judgment calls, curiosities, and occasional self-indulgence. Some, like "Crime and Punishment," seem designed to take advantage of Stableford's training as a sociologist as well as a critic.

Generally, the theme essays can be divided into two categories: things you would be likely to look up, and things you have to stumble across, sometimes with help from the generous system of cross-references. In the former category are generally accepted terms relating to kinds of SF or SF-type narratives (children's SF which unfortunately excludes books written for children under 11], cyberpunk, dystopia, hard SF); familiar icons of the genre (aliens, robots, monsters, computers); various individual sciences or social sciences (astronomy, anthropology, biology, economics, math, physics – curiously, there is no entry for chemistry); and historical terms (dime novel, boys' papers, fantastic voyages, pulp magazines). The historical pieces include a few terminological oddities: Stableford covers precursors of SF in an essay titled "Proto Science Fiction," a term that never widely caught on even after its repeated use in the 1979 edition; and Clute's essay on inventor-heroes is found under the heading "Edisonade," a word which, sounding as it does like some kind of electric soft drink, is unlikely to be deliberately looked up by anybody. (Fortunately, it gets cross-referenced from "Inventions.")

Such unusual terms make for great browsing, but also reflect the problems faced by any reference-book compiler in guiding users to the desired information. I tried to look up "alien artifacts," a common SF theme, but couldn't get anywhere (no entry on "artifacts," and "Aliens" just talks about aliens) until I stumbled across "Big Dumb Objects," a term apparently coined by Roz Kaveney to describe at least one sort of such artifact. It's not a self-evident term, but is probably better than "megalotropic SF," which Nicholls uses as a synonym in the entry. Other SF themes, such as generation starships, space travel, time travel, colonization of other worlds, and virtual reality, are pretty much where you'd expect to find them; but look up "microcosm" (in the Ray Cummings sense) and you get referred to "Great and Small" (another carryover from the first edition that hasn't exactly become a standard term). Some of these theme entries are so narrowly focused that they actually describe specific plots, and read like tabloid headlines: "Adam and Eve," "Hitler Wins," "Sleeper Awakes." The latter essay, by John Clute, is presumably distinguished from Brian Stableford's separate entry on "Suspended Animation" because one deals with a literary theme and the other with speculative science, but sometimes these lines get pretty faint.

Only a few of the theme entries seem self-indulgent or hobby-horsy. "Cliches," a carryover of a John Sladek essay updated by Peter Nicholls, is just a lot of fun, a kind of late-night bull session on SF embarrassments, as is the Nicholls/Sladek "Scientific Errors" and Nicholls' generally debunking essay on "Prediction." Some of Nicholls' other essays, though, take on a querulous Andy Rooney tone as he wonders aloud why so many SF writers have long careers ("Longevity [in Writers and Publications]") or how SF "Villains" have changed over the years. The most curious − and disappointing − of such essays is titled "Anti-Intellectualism in SF," which is not, as one might suspect, about the anti-intellectual attitudes which crop up from time to time in the SF community, but rather concerns SF works in which anti-intellectual attitudes are portrayed, as though it's somehow important to underline this (usually) politically correct stance in the genre. Lisa Tuttle's various essays on women in SF ("Feminism," "Women as Portrayed in Science Fiction," "Women SF Writers") also take on a vaguely self-congratulatory air, although they represent a significant advance over Nicholls' catch-all "Women" entry in the first edition. It's still very difficult to track down information on gay or Black SF writers, however; as a group, the latter are confined to a wide-ranging essay on "Politics" and the former are hardly visible at all.

In a sense, Nicholls' anti-intellectualism essay also belongs with what is probably the most important pattern of thematic essays in the book, at least in terms of revealing the *Encyclopedia's* general strategy for presenting SF to the world. In perhaps a dozen or so scattered entries, the editors reveal pretty clearly what they feel is important about SF, and their attitude doesn't at all reflect the alleged "New Wave" bias for which the earlier edition was often taken to task. Some of these key entries are "Definitions of SF," "Fantasy," "Genre SF," "Science Fantasy," "Conceptual Breakthrough," "Critical and Historical Works about SF," "History of SF," "Optimism and Pessimism," "Cultural Engineering," "Golden Age," and "Sense of Wonder." The latter term, despite its once being banished into limbo by Darko Suvin, is not only defended in its own entry, but repeatedly invoked throughout the book as a shorthand expression of one of SF's central effects (or affects). (It's interesting that "sense of wonder" had no entry in the first edition.) Roughly parallel to this is "Conceptual Breakthrough," a first-edition carryover which purports to describe one of the central *intellectual* strategies of SF. In their discussions of SF criticism and SF definitions, the editors seem to lean in the direction of critical approaches that try to take these notions into account (although in general their treatment of academic and critical work is surprisingly extensive and broad-minded). What finally emerges − reinforced by many individual author entries − is a view of SF that is at its core quite traditional, though open-minded toward experimental or non-genre works. The genre is prized for its protean energy, the quality and variety of its ideas, and its unique emotional resources; it gets chided for too-frequent provincialism, sloppiness, commercialism, and failure to live up to its own ideals.

In addition to authors and themes, Nicholls and Clute identify thirteen other kinds of entries: terms used in SF or fandom (65); national literatures (27, with all of Latin America covered in a single entry); films (544); filmmakers (34); television (96); magazines and journals (240, including professional fiction magazines and academic or professional journals); fanzines (36); comics and comic artists (59); illustrators (64, excluding mainstream artists unaffiliated with the SF community); book publishers (35); original anthologies (19, the only books with individual entries); awards (11, with a catch-all entry for those awards not listed separately); and "Miscellaneous" (30, including such things as "Conventions," "Collections," and "Futurians").

It isn't possible to comment on all these here, of course, but it's worth noting that among the terms listed, "Hard SF" has replaced "Hardcore SF" from the first edition, and the entry "Fixup" (referring to novels cobbled from previously published work) now contains a spirited defense of the term against attacks made by James Gunn and others when the first edition came out. Some other terms that the editors seem to want to cement into critical discourse include "Braid," "Tie," and "Sharecrop," all of which reflect the ongoing difficulty, in this field, of separating genuine literary or narrative innovations from publishing gimmicks.

The huge number of entries concerning film and TV (674, including films, filmmakers, and TV programs) demand mention, since they add up to a reference guide of well over 100,000 words in their own right. There seems little doubt that Clute and Nicholls are aware that a lot of second-rate films are getting comparatively generous coverage at the expense of some authors disappearing altogether, but it's also only realistic to admit that a good chunk of the potential readership is going to want to look up *The Creature Walks Among Us.* (At least they draw the line at *Queen of Outer Space.*) Film entries are written mostly by Nicholls and Kim Newman, and include revisions of John Brosnan's first-edition entries. Not surprisingly, the film criticism is considerably less polite − and thus often livelier − than the literary entries, although the somewhat different standards which must be applied and the mind-numbing quantity of films covered lead to a few punch-drunk judgments:

this has to be the only place you'll ever see *The Incredible Shrinking Man* compared to *King Lear*. Gerry and Sylvia Anderson, whose contributions to SF film and TV might well drive potential fans to a life of reading Proust, earn three-quarters of a page, while Peter Weir is out, presumably because his films are not explicity science-fictional enough. As the Anderson entry also suggests, TV coverage is one of the few areas that reveal a British perspective: the "Dr. Who" entry is so detailed that it includes a rather pointless list of cast members over the years, while Hanna and Barbera's *Flintstones* and *Jetsons*, which arguably had a greater impact on a generation of American kids than much of what's included, escape notice altogether. (Perhaps they're taken as falling under that "under-11" exclusion.)

There seems little doubt that a book as massive as this contains errors, but most of these will be apparent only to those intimately involved with specific entries (right off, I found myself credited with a book that my brother edited). Such is the book's careful attention to detail, however, that I found error-checking almost impossible; anything you'd check it against is probably *less* reliable or comprehensive than the *Encyclopedia* itself. This is perhaps the most telling index of the book's stature: even if it suffered from more evident sloppiness or glibness, it's still the only game in town. Nothing comes close to it, either for completeness or soundness of judgment. One might harp about a more usable, less truss-inducing format – it's very nearly at critical mass for a one-volume reference book, and would be easier to consult if, say, the author and film entries were separated into their own volumes – but given the contingencies of modern publishing (and modern library budgets), it's an achievement that it could be published at all at such a length. Clute and Nicholls and their accomplices deserve not only congratulations for an astonishing feat of scholarship, but respect for such dogged commitment to SF. *The Encyclopedia of Science Fiction* is not only a reference tool; it's a mission, a presentation piece for the whole SF world, and it reminds us that this great shambling mutual estate of ours is uniquely important.

Arthur C. Clarke's **The Hammer of God** is something of a presentation piece as well, and is in some ways even encyclopedic, even though it checks in at barely over two hundred pages and will never need a separate large-print edition. Expanded from the 1992 story of the same title published in *Time* magazine – only the second piece of fiction published in that magazine's history – it shares with *The Ghost of the Grand Banks* Clarke's newfound fondness for minimalist storytelling, with a few hastily-drawn characters acting out a classic problem-solving scenario in short, punchy chapters. What makes it seem encyclopedic is that the familiar plot – a spaceship crew is assigned to divert a rogue asteroid from colliding with Earth – is really little more than a scaffolding on which to hang a whole catalog of classic Clarkean inventions and digressions: virtual reality, the Alvarez theory of dinosaur extinction, the failure of capitalism as well as communism (and the attendant breakup of the U.S. into a "Commonweath"), the terraforming of Mars, Lunar Olympic competitions, automated "Fullerhomes," SETI, Disneyland on Mars (complete with tributes to Wells, Burroughs, and Bradbury), the rise of a new high-tech religion merging Christianity and Islam, and even the comparative joys of sex in various gravities. Every chance he gets, Clarke is off at right angles to the narrative, and almost every digression suggests an unwritten story.

This, of course, is what Clarke is best at: simply spinning ideas. And this is what makes the book a presentation piece in the manner of *Imperial Earth* – it's like a travelogue through a good speculative writer's mind. You can see why *Time* liked the original story (which is not much changed except for the ending); this is what you show to people when trying to convince them that SF can be both accessible and thought-provoking. Seasoned SF readers may be annoyed at the lack of development of these ideas in any significant narrative way – it's almost as though the infodump has taken over the whole novel – but it's worth keeping in mind that the story was written for what may have been the largest print audience ever to be exposed to a single SF story at one time. Yes, it's playful, but it's also fun – and none of the ideas are exactly throwaways.

On the other hand, this idea-blitz doesn't do much to help the novel move along as a novel. It's disarming, when we know the Earth is about to get creamed, to be treated to a leisurely account of a marathon race on the moon in what is the novel's longest sustained episode. The epic potential of his plot simply doesn't seem to interest Clarke. In an afterword, he acknowledges that the theme had been already exploited in earlier novels by Gregory Benford and William Rotsler, Larry Niven and Jerry Pournelle, and James Blish and Norman Knight (why does asteroid doom spark so many collaborations?), the first two of which aimed straight at the throat of the bestseller list with their multiple characters and special-effects setpieces. Clarke, whose book will do well anyway, takes the opposite tack, suggesting far more than he portrays and apparently trying to get as many ideas in print as time and his flimsy narrative will permit. It almost reminds you of Keats's "When I Have Fears," and suggests some of that poem's elegiac tone. This is nowhere more apparent than in the first chapter, which recalls the similar virtual-reality opening (before there was even such a term) of *The City and the Stars*. But whereas Alvin, in that novel, enjoyed a pulp fantasy adventure, the hero here relives long-lost moments with his son and a favorite pet.

Golden-sailed starships, an elite class of spacemen neurologically "wired" for interstellar flight, bionically altered space-cats and monkeys rebuilt to do maintenance work – so much of the furniture of Alfred Coppel's **Glory** seems leased from Cordwainer Smith that at first glance the novel looks like a deliberate pastiche. Later, it becomes clear that other influences are at work as well: Gene Wolfe is actually alluded to in the text, and the apparent format of the proposed "Goldenwing Cycle" which this novel inaugurates looks a lot like *Star Trek* – or perhaps more accurately, those numerous late-era space opera series in which a multicultural starship crew visits a variety of less-civilized colonies and solves their problems for them. In this first one, the interstellar sailing ship *Glory* is delivering to the strife-ridden planet Voerster a cargo of earthly animal embryos ordered centuries earlier "downtime".

The novel turns out to be much less derivative than it at first seems, however, because of Coppel's detailed working out of the society of Voerster, a transplanted Afrikaner colony which, after abandoning earth because of international sanctions against South Africa, has managed to maintain a repressive apartheid society for millennia. The idea of examining South African society through the laboratory lens of a distant planet is an intriguing one, even though it asks us to swallow the unlikely proposition that a viciously racist society fleeing sanctions on earth could somehow persuade thousands of Blacks to come along – the kind of set-up that works only as long as you don't ask, "What were they *thinking*?"

Almost inevitably, the racial tensions on Voerster led, generations earlier, to a catastrophic rebellion and war, which effectively destroyed the colony's technological infrastructure and reduced it to a repressive feudal society, complete with inherited monarchies and contentious warlords with ugly sons who want to marry the princess. Only in such a deteriorating society could *apartheid* be sustained, Coppel seems to argue, but that's about as far as he goes in the direction of real social criticism, and it's pretty much of a "so what?" Soon the plot begins to revolve more and more around the evil Voerster and his virtuous wife bent on protecting their even more virtuous daughter from marriage to a smelly person, and the suspicion grows that racism is really little more than a fairy-tale device to show us how wicked the wicked ruler is. We never really get a sense of the horrors of racism from the point of view of the kaffirs, who are pretty much kept in the background throughout. The main Black character isn't even a Voerster native, but a stranded spaceman, and he turns out to be something of a sacrificial lamb for the emerging melodrama.

Glory represents the return to SF of Alfred Coppel, a prolific and competent magazine writer of the 50s and the author of one of the field's most overlooked post-holocaust novels, *Dark December*, as well as an effective series of young-adult SF novels. In recent years, he's found success as a writer of international thrillers, some of which (like *The Burning Mountain*, about an invasion of Japan after the Bomb fails) use SF premises. He brings back with him a sureness of plotting, a talent for melodrama, and a lot of promise, which isn't quite fulfilled here, but which certainly makes me wonder what the next one will be like.

– July 1993, Locus #390 –

The Year's Best Fantasy and Horror: Sixth Annual Collection ~
~ edited by Ellen Datlow and Terri Windling

Nomansland ~~ D.G. Compton

The Children of Men ~~ P.D. James

PITFCS: Proceedings of the Institute for Twenty-First Century Studies ~
~ edited by Theodore R. Cogswell, introduction by Algis Budrys

Once Around the Bloch: An Unauthorized Autobiography ~
~ Robert Bloch

In a letter to Ted Cogswell's *Proceedings of the Institute for Twenty-First Century Studies* (reviewed below), Groff Conklin calls himself a "professional appreciator" of SF. It's a rather modest description for an anthologist whose work helped shape a whole generation's view of SF, and it reflects another era's attitude toward the role of the anthology. Today, as Ellen Datlow and Terri Windling's sixth annual **Year's Best Fantasy and Horror** illustrates, anthologists are more than good readers; they're literary theorists with clout, defining in real-time terms the growth and development of genres, ferreting out good stories from an impressive variety of sources and setting them up as if to challenge as well as reward both writers and readers. (Less than a quarter of Datlow and Windling's selections come from traditional genre magazines, more than half are from books or chapbooks, and a few are from sources as unexpected as *The New York Times*.) The issue with the Datlow/Windling annual is no longer whether it's the most consistently literate and unusual of the various "best of" anthologies – we've come to expect that of them – but what it does to the way we read the genres involved. They've taken Judith Merril's old practice of finding out-of-the-way stories and using them to deliberately question traditional wisdom, and raised it to an art form.

For example, Windling's introductory note to Brian Aldiss's provocative cross-genre tale "Ratbird" notes his reputation in SF and New Wave fiction and then offers the odd comment that this may lead people to "forget that he has written works in a fantastic vein." This implicit exclusion of SF from the realm of the fantastic is reflected in the selection of nearly four dozen stories and handful of poems that make up the anthology – almost none of them could be expected to show up in an SF collection – but it takes on added meaning when you realize that perhaps a sixth of the selections lack any supernatural or magical elements, and that many more use them only marginally. It's as though fantasy has become as much an attitude as a mode. Several of the stories – Jack Cady's "Tinker," Charlotte Watson Sherman's "Swimming Lesson," Midori Snyder's wonderful "Elfhouses," Graham Masterson's "Absence of Beast," Sue Ellen Sloca's "Candles on the Pond" – suggest that fantasy is as much a matter of childlike perspective as of world-building. And many of the horror stories gain their effects with few if any supernatural appurtenances: Ed Bryant explores our fascination with serial killers in "Human Remains"; Christopher Fowler realizes everyone's dental nightmare in the totally unpleasant "On Edge"; Joyce Carol Oates parallels the life of a rat with that of an abused woman in the almost equally unpleasant "Martyrdom"; Stephen Gallagher convincingly portrays a dying mental institution in "The Sluice"; Ed Gorman deals with child deformity in "The Ugly File"; Steve Rasnic Tem opposes an overprotective parent with a strange exterminator in "Rat Catcher" (rats seem to be big this year). Several of these stories are more grotesque than horrifying – like Faulkner or Flannery O'Connor pushed way over the edge.

Horror, of course, has never really depended on the supernatural for its effects, and stories like those just mentioned make some of the more traditional horror tales seem garish by comparison. Poppy Z. Brite's "Calcutta, Lord of Nerves," for example, is nothing more or less than *Night of the Living Dead* meets *Song of Kali*. (Kali is big this year too, showing up also in D.R. McBride's oddly touching tale of an Indian immigrant, "Puja.") And M.R. Scofidio's "Playing With" is pretty much your standard immolation-at-a-seance tale, dressed up with cynical yuppie urbanites. More effective are two Vietnam stories, Joe Haldeman's "Graves" and Peter Straub's "The Ghost Village," in which the suggestion of supernatural horror seems to derive naturally from the real horrors of that war.

But if horror can be neatly divided into natural vs. supernatural, where are the fantasy stories that are the equivalent of "non-supernatural" horror? Datlow and Windling seem determined to find them, and they succeed admirably – at least for readers who are willing to stretch their definitions of fantasy a bit (although they do lean heavily on the rubric "magic realism" to cover stories that don't fit easy expectations). Stories like Haruki Murakami's "The Second Bakery Attack," Diane de Avalle-Arce's "Bats," Nancy Farmer's "Origami Mountain," Harlan Ellison's phantasmagorical "The Man Who Rowed Christopher Columbus Ashore," and Angela Carter's literary pastiche "Alice in Prague, or the Curious Room" simply defy traditional categories, but all seem appropriate here.

Lest I've given the impression that the book lacks the traditional rewards of such salad-bar anthologies, I should offer some reassurance. To be sure, unicorns and vampires are nearly invisible here (despite Datlow dubbing 1992 "the Year of the Vampire"), but A.S. Byatt's "The Story of the Eldest Princess" is as elegant a modern fairy tale as you could ask for, and James Powell's "Ruby Laughter, Tears of Pearl" is a hilarious send-up of the same form. Nicholas Royle's "Glory" and Clive Barker's surprisingly delicate "Hermione and the Moon" are good ghost stories, and some very effective *Twilight Zone* spookiness is generated by Robert Silverberg's "It Comes and Goes" and Lisa Tuttle's subversively feminist "Replacements." Gene Wolfe's "The Sailor Who Sailed After the Sun" is a sophisticated and satisfying beast-fable. And perhaps the best overall story in the whole book – John Brunner's "In the Season of the Dressing of the Wells," from last year's Tolkien memorial anthology, is a stunning evocation of post-World War I English village life, complete with ancient rituals, that resembles Algernon Blackwood more than Tolkien. Such stories are treats for anybody.

In the 1960s and 1970s, D.G. Compton attained a deservedly formidable reputation for his often brilliant treatments of personal relationships in the face of catastrophic or technological changes in society – Brian Aldiss's "cosy catastrophe" elevated to the status of the mainstream novel of character. In **Nomansland**, he returns to this theme after a long silence, and it's a welcome return. *Nomansland* belongs squarely in the tradition of what scholar Kathryn Hume calls "subtractive worlds" – imaginary societies from which a familiar element has been removed, in this case male children. Something has caused a worldwide epidemic in which pregnant women reject male embryos, resulting in "The Attrition" – a world populated increasingly by women. Dr. Harriet Kahn-Ryder is a research physician who may have discovered a cure for the malady, but who is prevented from publishing it – and even terrorized – apparently by the very government agency which is funding her research. The main thrust of the narrative, set 40 years into the Attrition, is a mystery in which Kahn-Ryder tries to uncover the reasons for the censorship, while protecting her young daughter and trying to re-establish relationships with her disturbed brother and alienated mother.

Compton's plot provides for plenty of suspense and a whole array of unsavory characters, and as Kahn-Ryder discovers the source of the plague and the reasons for the coverup, it takes on a provocative relevance to major medical issues of today, not the least of which is AIDS. But the novel's rich texture derives from the alternating flashback chapters describing incidents from Kahn-Ryder's life, which not only trace the evolution of an increasingly male-less society over several decades, but reveal the sources of her and her family's strained relationships. The society which Compton portrays is for the most part one of the most believable female-dominated societies I've seen – not so radically displaced as the one portrayed in Elisabeth Vonarburg's *The Silent City or In the Mothers' Land*, and far less goofy than Charles Eric Maine's old potboiler *World Without Men* or Philip Wylie's *The Disappearance* (although it shares with the latter novel the conceit that such a society would put an end to war). The progress of the Attrition is portrayed not as a social experiment on the author's part, but as an ongoing catastrophe in the lives of several interesting characters. Like most of Compton's novels, the story is really about coping.

There are elements in the novel that don't seem entirely satisfactory. A subplot about a serial killer and terrorists who bomb birth clinics seems largely gratuitous, even though it finally becomes a key element in the dramatic conclusion. And the novel shares a hazard inherent in the form – namely, that a global catastrophe seems reduced to a crisis in the lives of a few individuals. How to treat such catastrophes is always a problem – whether to go for the big canvas multi-viewpoint epic (as in Frank Herbert's *The White Plague*), or keep the special effects in the background of a drama which follows its own internal logic. Compton chooses the latter route, and does a good job of reminding us that a novel has to be more than a Big Idea and some special effects – even though his ideas are pretty provocative in their own right, and ought to satisfy most SF readers on that level alone.

Compton's basic premise, of course, is a variation on Brian Aldiss's 1964 novel *Greybeard*, which presents us with an aging world some decades after near-universal sterility has resulted from nuclear testing damaging the Van Allen radiation belts. (Replace the Van Allen belts with the ozone layer, and Aldiss's novel is right up to date.) Unlike Compton and Aldiss, however, P.D. James doesn't offer any plausible explanation for her sterility plague in **The Children of Men**; she simply makes vague reference to a 1991 report on declining European birthrates, and almost suggests divine intervention by indicating that even sperm frozen before the catastrophe suddenly loses its potency. Her novel is set in the same 21st century decade as Aldiss's, and shares with *Greybeard* the premise that a declining population would give rise to fascist governments. But while Aldiss's novel turns this premise into one of SF's more disturbing post-catastrophe pastorals, James seems less certain of her direction.

This uncertainty is reflected in her narrative technique, which alternates between the diary entries of Theo Faron, an Oxford professor of Victorian history and cousin of the dictatorial "Warden of England," Xan Lypiatt; and third-person chapters which read much more like a P.D. James mystery, with convincing dialogue and James's characteristically evocative sense of place. The diary chapters give her the opportunity to fill in loads of exposition, while the narrative chapters detail an increasingly unconvincing underground-vs.-the-fascists plot, involving a group of youthful resisters calling themselves the Five Fishes and sounding like nothing so much as the White Rose of Nazi Germany. The resisters persuade Faron to talk to his cousin the Warden about various abuses of power, as though anyone thinks that would do any good, and as a result he ends up on the lam with them, culminating in a far too contrived and symbolic climax which asks us to believe, among other things, that dictators with virtually limitless powers take time off to personally participate in backwoods manhunts. James knows how to generate this excitement, and her vivid handling of violence – always startling in the civilized contexts of her mysteries – gives the novel an edge that belies its earlier self-consciously elegiac tone. But the logic of character and situation that makes those mysteries work well doesn't sustain the speculative social aspects of *The Children of Men*, and if you try to read it as SF you may come away thinking it's something of a mess.

Last year, in reviewing Charles Oberndorf's first novel *Sheltered Lives*, I wondered whether Oberndorf's next work would be SF or mainstream, since the novel seemed to depend very little on its science fictional setting. His new novella, **Testing**, doesn't really answer the question. This time the issue isn't AIDS and government spying; it's the question of whether morals can be objectively taught and tested for in schools. This is not an exciting premise. Again, his main character faces a moral dilemma, and again he tries to focus it by identifying with Raskolnikov in *Crime and Punishment* (which seems increasingly to be the novel that Oberndorf wants to write). And again the SF setting and machinery seems self-consciously interpolated into a story that doesn't really need it.

Following an unspecified economic collapse, 21st-century America has revamped its educational system. College is harder to get into, and admission depends not only on academic qualifications, but on "citizenship points" (gained through such activities as participating in political campaigns) and – most importantly – on the way a student handles various moral dilemmas presented in a virtual reality experience called the "dreamchair." The story opens with Karl, the young protagonist, canvassing for a political candidate as he prepares for his dreamchair testing. Out of frustration and impatience, he dumps most of the campaign material he's supposed to be distributing, and this action takes on a ridiculous weight of meaning, causing him to obsessively read Dostoevski and haunting him for years to come. Most of the rest of the story concerns Karl's and the other high school students' preparations for, and anxiety over, the dreamchair test, administered by a high school principal rather unsubtly named St. August. It's a setup not unlike that in Asimov's "Profession," the story with which *Testing* is most easily compared. But when we finally get to the test itself, it turns out to be a rather lame compilation of moral dilemmas, vaguely along the lines of Philip K. Dick's Voight-Kampff Empathy test, but a lot less interesting and not at all dependent on the elaborate virtual-reality setup. We even learn that the results of such tests aren't absolutely crucial to one's career. *Testing* offers believable teenagers in Judy Blume-type situations, and it might work reasonably well for a young-adult audience for whom the potential of VR-based SAT's seems life-threatening, but it offers remarkably little genuine speculation about the future of education or the real potential of educational technology.

Chicago's Advent: Publishers has probably done more to preserve important documents and memoirs from American SF history than any other publisher, and their latest undertaking is one of their most fascinating. In 1958, long before there was an SFWA, Theodore Cogswell conceived the idea of a fanzine for professional writers to exchange ideas – specifically, the idea (suggested originally by Reginald Bretnor) of forming an SF writers' organization to improve pay rates and deal with arrogant editors. Cogswell gave his fanzine the mock-pretentious title *Publications* (later *Proceedings) of the Institute of Twenty-First Century Studies* and gave the first issue the subtitle "Special Series No. 127A." (The jokes backfired in a wonderful way, and the publication gained inadvertent legitimacy by getting listed in directories of associations and periodical indexes.) *PITFCS*, as it came to be known, ran from April 1959 to December 1962, when Cogswell took time off to finish his doctoral dissertation. A long-delayed final issue, produced in the expectation that Gregg Press would sponsor the journal and reprint its early issues, appeared in June 1979. But the Gregg deal fell through, and now – some five years after Cogswell's death – Advent has collected the entire run of PITFCS, with the exception of an issue in which the invective apparently got too personal.

The book is huge, but absolutely engrossing, and is essential for anyone wanting to understand the development of American popular SF during a crucial period in its history, when the old editors were beginning to lose their absolute power and writers were beginning to sense the possibility of a literature defined by something other than available markets. Consisting almost entirely of letters from "members" (who included not only the predictable roster of 50s SF writers, but also Kingsley Amis, Kurt Vonnegut, Pierre Versins, and even Hugo Gernsback), the collection at times reads almost like a novel. Here is John W. Campbell, Jr., clearly losing his grip on the field as he obsessively defends the Dean Drive against taunts by Damon Knight and John R. Pierce. Here are writers grappling with unfamiliar issues of moral responsibility as they debate Heinlein's *Starship Troopers*. Here is a foreshadowing of the New Wave debate as writers take sides about Ward Moore's relatively experimental story "Transient" and Philip Jose Farmer responds to accusations that he's "sick" for dealing with sex. Here are provocative pieces by Fritz Leiber on SF and modern art and SF and the mainstream. Here are good critical essays by Gordon Dickson and Kingsley Amis on Budrys's *Rogue Moon*, Richard McKenna on Aldiss's *Hothouse*, and Leiber and Blish on *Stranger in a Strange Land*.

The key debate, however, concerns the possibility of writers organizing themselves into something which would eventually become the SFWA. The debate centers not only on pay rates, but on the author-editor relationship, with some authors adopting a hack-like attitude of resignation while others insist on something resembling intellectual and artistic freedom. The latter point brings a couple of startlingly nasty responses from Donald Wollheim, and a rather condescending one from Frederik Pohl. The least interesting letters are those which endlessly debate, sometimes with astonishing naivete, the possible structure and bylaws of an authors' organization (it's a wonder SFWA ever got formed at all). But it's the nascent SFWA that forms a kind of ongoing narrative line for the collection, and that gives the final issue – some 17 years late – a kind of poignancy. By then Cogswell had already served as editor of the SFWA Forum, and was complaining that it was so full of business matters that there was little room for the kind of freewheeling debate that had defined *PITFCS*. But something had ended, and several of the authors whose dusty letters of comment appear in that last issue – Richard McKenna, Miriam Allen de Ford, Groff Conklin, Rog Phillips, and Anthony Boucher – had already been dead for years.

Most authors know their lives aren't very interesting, but they write autobiographies anyway. The challenge seems to be to see how far you can get on style and attitude. Asimov, to whom nothing much seemed to have happened at all, managed to do this for some 1500 pages, so it's not too surprising that the equally waggish Robert

Bloch can bring it off for 400 pages in **Once Around the Bloch: An Unauthorized Autobiography**. The subtitle tells you all you need to know about Bloch's attitude, which will be familiar to anyone who has ever talked with him or heard one of his convention speeches. His book is liberally peppered with bad jokes and Rodney Dangerfield asides, and it's as charming as the man himself. It also has a lot more substance than you might expect, showing in detail how Lovecraft helped motivate younger writers, how Bloch's fondness for puns carries over in thematically important ways in novels like Psycho, how writers survived in the Hollywood studio environment of the 1950s and 1960s.

Once Around the Bloch is an entertainment, not an introspective self-examination – Bloch is clearly more delighted at meeting Boris Karloff or Buster Keaton than at winning a Hugo award – and it lacks an index, table of contents, or even chapter titles (though Bloch's opening paragraphs clearly lay out what each chapter is about, so that it's easy to find what you're looking for). Although his literary relation to the SF field is almost marginal, his involvement in fandom is legendary, and his accounts of conventions and various fan organizations are delightful – both witty and nostalgic, with none of the epic obsessiveness and high dander of most fan memoirs of the period. As in describing all aspects of his career – which, to be fair, is more interesting than that of most writers – Bloch never forgets the pulp writer's dictum to keep it interesting and keep it moving, and he does.

– August 1993, Locus #391 –

The Broken God ~~ David Zindell

Meridian Days ~~ Eric Brown

Vietnam and Other Alien Worlds ~~ Joe Haldeman

The Elephant Vanishes ~~ Haruki Murakami
(translated by Alfred Birnbaum and Jay Rubin)

There are all sorts of problems characteristic of first novels, but what about second novels? The most common problem here – at least if the second novel shares the same setting as the first – is the author's optimism about how many people actually read that first one. Such second novels inevitably have a dual audience with vastly differing expectations: continuing readers who want new inventions on top of the familiar, and new readers who have to be brought along patiently. (Trilogies and series are another matter, since packaging alone tells readers that subsequent novels aren't really meant to stand alone.) It's been more than five years since David Zindell's Neverness streaked across the firmament as one of the great romantic epics of modern SF, and readers of that novel should be delighted with **The Broken God**, which shares the same vivid setting, the same energetic style, the same flood of ideas, and some of the same characters. *The Broken God* is the story of Danlo the Wild, the son who Mallory Ringess abandoned late in that earlier epic, and of his continuation of his father's quest for what it means to be human. On the very first page, we learn that Ringess is again the narrator, and this knowledge takes on a haunting meaning as it becomes apparent that Ringess has long since disappeared from Neverness and perhaps become a god; we have no idea from what perspective he's narrating the story.

For readers of *Neverness*, then, this is a rich and rewarding sequel. But how does it work for new readers? The intellectual fireworks, the elements which gave that first novel a constantly renewed sense of wonder, are now part of the accepted furniture of this world, and even new revelations cannot quite recapture that space-opera pizzazz. Zindell's strategy for dealing with this problem seems to me especially ingenious: by casting his narrative as a coming-of-age story about a boy whose ignorance of his world is as great as that of the first-time reader, he's able to re-introduce his world through the eyes of Danlo, while keeping *Neverness* readers enthralled through Danlo's adventures. It's just as well that Zindell doesn't try to top his own earlier inventions, because having such a thoroughly realized setting in place provides him the opportunity to explore questions of character and character relationships much more fully.

We first meet Danlo as the adopted son of the Neanderthal-like Alaloi, a culture which long ago altered its genetic structure to survive in this cold world, and in short order the members of his tribe die out from a strange illness. This leads to the first of several marvelous set-pieces: Danlo's arduous journey across the ice to the fabled "unreal" city of Neverness, where he hopes to fulfill his destiny to become a Pilot. Rescued and educated by a kindly group of aliens called the Fravashi, Danlo undertakes the first of several trials to enter the Academy — which consists of sitting overnight in a bitterly cold plaza.

So far, for first-time readers, this promises to become an epic of frostbite. (Zindell's brutally icy world feels more like Jack London's arctic than Le Guin's Gethen.) But during his initiation trial Danlo meets — and saves the life of — Hanuman li Tosh, and their complex love-hate relationship grows into the central conflict of the novel. Hanuman eventually becomes the leader of a powerful religious cult built around the legend of Danlo's missing father, Mallory Ringess, and Danlo becomes the cult's chief opponent. This alienates him from his father's companion Bardo and — in one of those stunning examples of cruelty which only the best melodrama can bring off — costs him the love of his life. It also sets up a romantic revenge plot which Zindell resolves in an unexpected way — until you realize that the extensive philosophical asides that pepper the narrative are in fact crucial to understanding Danlo's character. In the end, it's not an epic of frostbite at all, but something you would think almost impossible to bring off in the heroic mode: an epic of nonviolence.

I haven't focused much here on the Big SF Ideas of the novel — the ancient race which may have implanted the secrets of godhood in human DNA, the strange cult bent on destroying the galaxy one star at a time, the dead god found floating in space – because most of this carries over from *Neverness* and remains backgrounded to the main action, which is confined to Neverness itself. Suffice to say that there are again enough novel concepts to satiate the hardest SF reader, and enough betrayals and reversals to feed anyone's romantic angst. (Sometimes the romantic melodrama almost gets out of hand, as when Danlo literally falls in love at first sight across a crowded room, or when Bardo too-conveniently transforms himself from a brutal taskmaster to a lovable drunk.) But Zindell always manages to rein in his goofier impulses, and he has a huge talent for juggling believable characters and settings with over-the-top SF conceits. In what may be an in-joke, one of the concepts that Danlo learns from the Fravashi is *ostrenenie*, "the art of making the familiar seem strange in order to reveal its essence." It's also the old Russian formalist term for the kind of estrangement that many believe is crucial to SF, and Zindell brings it off as well as any new writer of the last decade.

One of the key SF devices that Zindell uses to convince us of the cruelty of his villain occurs when a character we've been made to care about is effectively removed from the action by a kind of mind-surgery. It's SF's reinvention of the old *Random Harvest* amnesia ploy, and it also figures in a big way in Eric Brown's excellent first novel, **Meridian Days**. Like Zindell, Brown has created a convincingly forbidding world where part of the human population has reshaped itself through genetic alterations or computer implants; like Zindell, he combines romance with a tale of inhuman cruelty and secret conspiracies; like Zindell, he writes with unusual clarity and grace. But his scale is more modest, and his plot proceeds along the lines of a pretty good mystery. Bob Benedict, a burnt-out ex-pilot consumed with guilt over a spaceship accident he feels responsible for, lives in a drug-induced haze on Meridian, a planet inhabitable only on a vast archipelago between its Brightside and Darkside. Primarily an artists' colony, the world depends on supplies transmitted from Earth via a matter-transmitting device called a Telemass. When Benedict becomes involved with Fire Trevellion, the abused and imprisoned daughter of the planet's most powerful artist, he thinks he's found a means for his own redemption.

Brown has lived in Greece, and at times his evocation of a decadent group of cynical artists living in exile on remote islands calls to mind Lawrence Durrell more than any SF writer. Especially interesting is Brown's treatment of the artists and the art they produce. Obsessed with their own images, they remake themselves into odd amalgams based on animals (or, in the case of Fire's mother, a fish) and create works that seem neither particularly inspired nor innovative, except for the technological advances. We've talked about art-oriented SF in these pages before (Mark Geston's *Mirror to the Sky* is another recent example), but Brown's is one of the few novels on this theme to suggest directly that advances in artistic technology may do nothing more than expand the scale of ego-driven mediocrity; his artists here are anything but intellectual heroes.

But the SF element in *Meridian Days* isn't confined to imagining new forms of art (and new forms of artists, for that matter). When Benedict ventures into the sunbaked Brightside in search of drugs or on a mission to capture a ferocious "sand lion," the burning landscape is as convincingly detailed as that in Alan E. Nourse's "Brightside Crossing." While on one of these trips, he and a companion see a uniformed woman attacked by a sand lion, and find a shred of her clothing. Authorities seem reticent to investigate, and later the companion is kidnapped and eventually murdered. How all this connects to Benedict's growing love for Fire Trevellion, her unexplained memory lapses about the uniformed woman and her own sister's death, the obsessive need of her spiteful mother Tamara to create ever-more-spectacular artistic "events," and the fate of the planet itself, adds up to a deftly plotted and suspenseful adventure which never loses its strangely elegiac and haunting tone.

Not long ago, when Larry Heinemann, who won a National Book Award for his second Vietnam-related novel Paco's Story, told me he hoped that his third novel would help him break out of the "Vietnam author" category, it occurred to me that Joe Haldeman enjoys (or suffers) the distinction of being a multiple-ghetto author. Not only is he SF's semi-official Vietnam vet, but some fans, stubbornly misreading *The Forever War*, want to count him as a military-SF guru as well. **Vietnam and Other Alien Worlds**, a collection of four stories, five essays, and four poems, should help to clarify the various ways Vietnam has shaped his writing. What's most interesting is that only two essays and one poem directly concern Vietnam. (Despite the book's title, this is not a definitive collection of Vietnam writings; such stories as "Graves" and "The Monster" are not included.) The stories, only one of which ("Passages") has not appeared in a previous Haldeman collection, all take place in the Confederación universe that is the setting of *All My Sins Remembered* and *Starschool*, and all concern conflicts between cultures that don't understand each other. The best of the stories is the harrowing "Seasons," which ought to be recognized as some kind of classic among alien contact tales, and which suggests on a number of levels what went wrong in Vietnam.

The essays include the autobiographical title piece, originally delivered at California's Eaton Conference; a chillingly predictive personal account of the space program, "Confessions of a Space Junkie," written in 1981; a piece on the Challenger disaster; a review of several Vietnam books; and an insightful essay on a controversial Robert Mapplethorpe photo exhibit. In many ways, though, the core of the collection is the group of four "Story Poems" that conclude it. All have previously appeared in various books, but reading them together is enough to convince you of Haldeman's considerable gifts in this area and of the potential of SF poetry in general. "Saul's Death" is a rare linked sestina whose formal structure gives a kind of incantatory power to a violent tale, and "DX" is simply the most haunting evocation of Vietnam survivor guilt I have read. Of course, as Haldeman himself observes, nobody reads poems anymore and narrative poems are almost unheard of. Is he colonizing yet another ghetto?

Of the 17 stories in Haruki Murakami's **The Elephant Vanishes**, two have been chosen for Datlow and Windling's *Year's Best Fantasy and Horror* annuals (in 1991 and again this year), which alone is enough to suggest that Murakami, a Japanese novelist living in Rome, is worth the attention of the SF and fantasy community. In fact, only about a half dozen of the stories collected here directly involve the fantastic, although all of them have a surrealistic edge that at times recalls Donald Barthelme and at other times Raymond Carver (whom Murakami has translated into Japanese). What is most striking about them is Murakami's apparent obsession with American pop culture; although most of the stories are set in Japan, their world seems defined by American brand names and celebrities.

In "The Second Bakery Attack," for example, a married couple satisfies their late-night munchies by raiding a McDonald's and forcing the crew to cook up 30 Big Macs. (They insist they're not crooks, though; they don't take any money and even insist on paying for their Cokes.) The woman narrator of "Sleep" finds that after she loses the need for sleep, she can read Tolstoy and Dostoevsky with complete concentration. Another woman, in "The Little Green Monster," telepathically tortures and destroys the title beast, which has crawled out of her garden and into her house. A mysterious windstorm barely impinges on the consciousness of the narrator of "The Fall of the Roman Empire, The 1881 Indian Uprising, Hitler's Invasion of Poland, and the Realm of Raging Winds"; at the end of the day, he records in his diary only the random thoughts he has had that day, which give the story its title. In the title story, "The Elephant Vanishes," the narrator reveals that, before the mysterious disappearance of an elephant and its keeper, he had seen them changing in size, becoming more the same. Elephants also figure in the best of the book's fantasies, a surrealistic fairy tale called "The Dancing Dwarf," in which the narrator works on the assembly line of an elephant factory, and enlists the aid of a dwarf from his dreams to help him impress a girl. The plot is the most coherent and traditional in the book, but it doesn't lose the edge of sheer *weirdness* that make all Murakami's stories unique and challenging.

– September 1993, Locus #392 –

The Innkeeper's Song ~~ Peter S. Beagle

A Plague of Angels ~~ Sheri S. Tepper

Peter Beagle once said in a Locus interview that *The Last Unicorn* might well go on dominating his work, and he's probably right: it became an instant classic for its grace, wit, complexity, and accessibility. It's not surprising that many readers, including myself, found 1987's *The Folk of the Air* a little thin by comparison with what we'd hoped for after such a long wait. By now, Beagle must certainly be accustomed to readers wanting another *Unicorn*, just as Woody Allen has to live with fans who want him to do more funny movies. His new novel, **The Innkeeper's Song**, is likely to confound everyone's expectations. Its basic premise – a war between two nearly all-powerful wizards – seems the stuff of supermarket fantasy, but it's a fantasy in the same way that Clint Eastwood's *Unforgiven* is a western, and it draws the same kind of power from setting, character, and memory. *The Last Unicorn* may always be Beagle's best fantasy, but *The Innkeeper's Song*, based on an enigmatic song Beagle wrote some years ago, is his best *novel*.

If I seem to be invoking filmmakers to describe this novel, there's a reason: Beagle has been doing a lot of film work in recent years, and perhaps as a result this contains some of the most strikingly visual of his writing. The love of language is still evident, but it's no longer as playful, and his gritty, dark setting, lightly sketched in as it is, is among the most memorable worlds in recent fantasy. What is surprising is that Beagle achieves this with a minimum of self-conscious world-building, and without the aid of the omniscient narrative voice he has used in the past. Instead, he offers no fewer than six major narrators and four minor ones, each with a distinct voice and perspective, and each with his or her own story. This technique of describing a common crisis in the lives of several characters through a kind of volleyball point of view is difficult enough to bring off in mainstream fiction – Ernest Gaines's *A Gathering of Old Men is* an example – but in fantasy, where so much of the nature of the fictive world must be revealed by indirection, it's a positive *tour de force.*

All these characters' stories converge during one summer when three mysterious women arrive at a rural inn called the Gaff and Slasher, pursued by the forlorn lover of one of the women, Lukassa, who had earlier drowned and been resurrected by Lal, a swordswoman and sailor with some supernatural powers. The third woman is Nyateneri, who it turns out is also being pursued by some genuinely chilling assassins. (Nyateneri also provides us with an effectively startling surprise during a sexual escapade that is one of the book's several set-pieces of narrative technique.) Accompanying the women is a fox who can change into a jolly old man, and the chapters told in the fox's quirky voice at times call to mind the butterfly's speeches in *The Last Unicorn*. The innkeeper himself, the gruff and exasperated Karsh, is another wonderful voice, and one which serves to ground the narrative with periodic doses of no-nonsense realism.

Other characters include Karsh's stable boy Rosseth, who falls in love with all three of the women visitors; Tikat, Lukassa's devoted lover; and the two wizards, who are the only major characters who never narrate chapters. The older wizard, the former teacher of Lal and Nyateneri, is sheltered at the inn while the two women undertake a quest to find his enemy and former pupil Arshadin. The quest ends surprisingly badly – heroics don't always add up to much in Beagle's world, though they're impressively portrayed – and the final apocalyptic battle returns the action to the inn itself, and gives a surprising and satisfying role to the drowned woman Lukassa. By the end, all the pieces and voices fit together in a tapestry that is both rich and simple, filled with both genuine hope and genuine regrets. Unexpected though it is given his previous work, *The Innkeeper's Song* may be the novel that we've all been hoping Beagle will write, and it may be some sort of classic.

Science fantasy is one of those shadowy areas that drives some critics and literary theorists buggy. Despite the obvious relationships – and overlapping readership – between fantasy and SF, the minute you try to define one you start excluding the other. Fantasy, as everyone knows, is built upon impossibilities, and SF upon possibilities. You can't mix spaceships and robots with dragons and ogres; you can't have high-tech cities in the middle of medieval fairy-tale landscapes. Sheri S. Tepper does exactly this in A **Plague of Angels**, and it works beautifully. Tepper, whose *Grass* was criticized for using an SF setting to rationalize a fantasy adventure and whose *Beauty* placed her fairy-tale heroine into SF worlds as well as traditional milieux, adopts the same science fantasy strategy used by authors as diverse as Gene Wolfe and Anne McCaffrey: using SF concepts to generate what appears to be a fantasy environment, and then gradually leaking out the SF underpinnings so that the novel changes as we're reading it. Science fantasy of this type is so easy to do badly ("Golly! The oracle is a *computer!*") that when it works it's especially impressive; it becomes a way of asserting that the author and not the genre is in control of the material. *A Plague of Angels* plays with this issue of authorial control in ways unusual even for this unusual genre.

One of the first clues we get comes when we learn that a young girl named Orphan lives in an "archetypal village" where everyone fulfills a traditional fairy-tale role: hero, oracle, miser, etc. What's odd is that the characters *know* it's an archetypal village, and refer to it as such in the text. So do other characters, such as a farm boy named Abasio, who sets out hobbit-like to have an adventure and ends up in the violent and seedy city of Fantis. Dominated by youth gangs and plagued by drug abuse and immune-deficiency diseases, Fantis also helps to underline that this world is neither as innocent nor as pastoral as it seems. By the time we learn that the "witch" Ellel is seeking to dominate the world with the aid of an army of androids and weapons she hopes to retrieve from a long-abandoned space station, we're pretty sure we're in a disguised SF environment. Then Tepper introduces talking animals.

Much of the pleasure of *A Plague of Angels* comes from learning how and why this world came to be; much also comes from watching Tepper adroitly fit new pieces into her puzzle as the narrative progresses. But the story is also a first-rate epic on its own terms. We watch Abasio and Orphan grow from childhood to adulthood as their destinies gradually intertwine; we learn that neither is quite who they seem to be; and of course we learn from crucially placed clues that the world isn't what it seems to be, either. This rich background gives rise to a plot that on its surface is the simplest of fairy tales: the wicked witch pursuing the innocent orphan for nefarious purposes, while the farmer's son helps her evade capture and gradually enlists the aid of whole armies of allies, each with different strengths. The concluding confrontation is a truly epic battle, and even then we are still learning new and significant revelations about the world and the place of humans in it. Tepper weaves together themes of ecology, technology, psychology, and occasional feminism in a fine example of what science fantasy is good for.

— October 1993, Locus #393 —

The Norton Book of Science Fiction:
North American Science Fiction, 1960-1990 ~
~ edited by Ursula K. Le Guin & Brian Attebery;
Karen Joy Fowler, consultant

Chimera ~~ Mary Rosenblum

Core ~~ Paul Preuss

A Tupolev Too Far ~~ Brian Aldiss

Argyll: A Memoir ~~ Theodore Sturgeon

The Rediscovery of Man: The Complete Short Science Fiction
of Cordwainer Smith ~~ edited by James A. Mann

The more opinionated SF readers — those for whom an anthology is by definition a collection of the wrong stories — will find in **The Norton Book of Science Fiction** a target as big as a barn door. The authoritative combination of the names Norton (familiar to everyone who's ever taken an undergraduate literature survey) and Le Guin (familiar to everyone, period) give the book an unusually high profile both in and out of the SF community, as well as a good chance of staying in print and showing up in a lot of classrooms. You can already hear the litany of potshots to come: Writers Wrongfully Omitted, Writers Inexplicably Included, Writers Justly Included But Who Have Done Better Stories, Writers Included For the Sake of Political Correctness, Writers Included To Avoid The Appearance of Political Correctness,

Writers You Never Heard Of But Who Are Bumping Writers You Admire, Writers Included By Special But Unstated Privilege, etc., etc. So the first thing we should try to establish is what the book pretends to be and what it does not pretend to be.

It does not pretend to be a definitive historical or typological anthology of SF. Le Guin makes this clear in her long and very intelligent introduction, and the title underlines it. Those vast historical collections you read in school were Norton *anthologies*; this is only a Norton book, although the distinction will likely be lost on most readers. (A similar fine line characterized Tom Shippey's *Oxford Book of Science Fiction Stories* last year, which stopped short of calling itself the *Oxford Book of Science Fiction*.) The subtitle narrows the range even further: "North American Science Fiction, 1960-1990" (a half-dozen Canadian stories justify the "North American"). The putative reason for such restrictive coverage was simply to make the size of the book manageable, although 67 stories seems pretty roomy by most standards. Furthermore, more than half the stories date from 1981 or later, which suggests that the collection really is a generous overview of contemporary American literary SF. Taken in that more modest light, it's unarguably first-rate.

Ah, but there is that conditional "literary," which again carries the whisper of guns being drawn. Le Guin does not specifically characterize the selections as such in her introduction, but it's clear from the selection and from the editorial assumptions Le Guin outlines that she and her co-editors share a particular, more or less postmodern view of SF. SF is a literary tradition as broad as that of realism, Le Guin argues, but it draws on both realistic and fantastic narrative techniques to tell stories which refer, implicitly or explicitly, to the "mythos of science and technology." Quoting co-editor Brian Attebery's *Strategies of Fantasy*, she sees the scientific world-view as a "megatext" or "nourishing medium" in which SF stories take place.

This seems innocent enough, but it produces a radically different view of the field than you get from the Big Anthology from an earlier era, Healy and McComas's *Adventures in Time and Space*. That collection, drawn almost entirely from a single decade of *Astounding* when the short story was the principle medium of SF, showcased work in which the Idea came first, and the narrative followed – stories governed more by metonymy than by metaphor. Only a handful of stories in *The Norton Book* – perhaps those by Dick, Bear, James H. Schmitz, Poul Anderson, Octavia Butler, and Andrew Weiner – could remotely have made sense in that collection. Today, in a field in which novels and novellas very nearly outnumber short stories and from which consensus has long since evaporated, even the possibility of trying to represent SF in such a collection is problematical. Thus the cutoff date of 1960, when Le Guin tells us SF "changed" because both readers and writers gained new sophistication and new consciousness. In other words (mine not theirs), metaphor trumps metonymy.

If the Campbellian ethos is pretty much invisible in *The Norton Book*, then it seems entirely reasonable to ask what has replaced it. A handful of more-or-less traditionally canonical authors set the stage for the collection, and three of these – Cordwainer Smith, Philip K. Dick, and Fritz Leiber – are singled out for special praise in Le Guin's introduction. Smith (represented by "Alpha Ralpha Boulevard") pioneered the morality play in ultra-exotic settings, which shows up here in stories by Bunch, Lafferty, Gene Wolfe, Suzette Haden Elgin, Michael Coney, and a few others. Dick (represented by "Frozen Journey") may not have invented the notion of reality-slippage, but he certainly made it a convention, and it's featured in various ways in stories by Ellison, Gibson, Shiner, Crowley, and Eileen Gunn. Leiber, whose "The Winter Flies" stretches even the editors' generous notion of what SF includes, is rapidly emerging as one of the pioneers of the whole notion of literary SF. (Leiber's "Coming Attraction" — far too old to include — seems to haunt several of the grittier stories in the book, and Bruce Sterling's "We See Things Differently" reads almost like a 1980s revisioning of it.)

Other old masters seem to set certain tones, too. Theodore Sturgeon's alienated children and outcasts show up not only in his own "Tandy's Story," but haunt well over a dozen other stories, more if you include the various portrayals of women as outsiders by Tiptree, Russ, Elgin, and others. Pohl's "Day Million," though perhaps not particularly characteristic of his own fiction, heralds further explorations of media culture by Andrew Weiner, Malzberg, Sheckley, Gibson, Shiner, Michael Bishop, and Candace Jane Dorsey. Several other stories carry echoes of writers not present: Delany's "High Weir" suggests Bradbury's humans-as-Martians, and the alternate science history of Howard Waldrop's ". . . the World, as we Know 't" suggests Farmer's "Sail On, Sail On".

Recent SF's preoccupation with history is represented not only by Waldrop, but by Kim Stanley Robinson ("The Lucky Strike"), Connie Willis ("Schwarzchild Radius"), Paul Preuss ("Half-Life"), and John Kessel ("Invaders"). The Preuss and Willis stories also form a group with other stories which use science metaphors to illuminate character relationships, most notably Edward Bryant's "Precession" and Gregory Benford's "Exposures." A few other patterns emerge as well: feminism and sexual identity (which includes Michael Blumlein's "The Brains of Rats" as well as authors I've already mentioned); conflicts with native cultures (Kessel, Resnick's "Kirinyaga," Card's "America," Diane Glancy's "Aunt Parnetta's Electric Blisters"); even SF itself (in Kessel, Eleanor Arnason's "The Warlord of Saturn's Moons," and Gibson's "The Gernsback Continuum").

One nagging question is whether teachers assigning this book or their students (or any readers generally unfamiliar with the field's history) will be able to detect such patterns, or to discern any sort of meaningful context for what is essentially an ahistorical portrait of the field. Gone are the easy dichotomies that made the old SF seem manageable. There are no epics of technological optimism here — but nor are there any tales of nuclear doom. What was once a literature of heroes and villains here seems overrun with outcasts, victims, and invaders; it is, if anything, a literature of confrontation. Environments once ripe for eminent domain now fight back (ironically, the story that portrays this most directly is also one of the more traditional SF pieces in the book — James H. Schmitz's "Balanced Ecology"). If it's hard to find a center in all this, it may be simply that SF doesn't really have a center anymore, and doesn't seem to want one much.

One thing the editors deserve considerable credit for is a great deal of winnowing and a fiercely independent judgment. Out of 30 years of stories, they've included only two Hugo winners (Butler's "Speech Sounds" and Resnick's "Kirinyaga") and two Nebula winners (Silverberg's "Good News from the Vatican" and Kress's "Out of All Them Bright Stars"). I counted fewer than a dozen stories which had appeared in the Dozois annuals of the 1980s, none which overlap with his *Legend Book of Science Fiction* (which covers a similar period and includes many of the same authors), and only one (Blish's "How Beautiful with Banners") which is also in Shippey's *Oxford Book of Science Fiction Stories*. This selection of stories not often anthologized, together with Le Guin's useful and important introduction, are more than enough to suggest that the book probably ought to be on the bookshelf of every reader concerned with the shape of modern SF — it just shouldn't be the only SF book on that shelf.

Mary Rosenblum is one of the finest new writers to appear in the last several years, and one of the things that makes her work interesting is that it combines virtues of both the "old" and the "new" SF. Her first novel, *The Drylands*, was a finely realized eco-catastrophe tale with added surprises — including hypnagogic hallucinations suggestive of virtual reality. In **Chimera**, she takes on virtual reality full tilt, and the result is another suspenseful, well-plotted novel which gives Rosenblum a chance to show she can handle a lot more than droughts. Rosenblum's version of the Net, although handled with assurance and fine attention to detail, is nothing particularly new — VR fiction seems to have quickly established its own conventions — but it gives her added opportunities to exploit her greatest strength as a writer, which is building convincing relationships between character and landscape. The real-world settings of the novel — a high-tech Antarctica, the depressed "'burbs" of Seattle, the deserts of southeast Oregon — are as vivid and memorable as those of her *Drylands*, which was also mostly set in the Northwest. But the VR settings — particularly an ice cave which becomes a projection of the mind of one of the main characters — provides a nice internal counterpoint to these external landscapes.

Jewel Martina, who has escaped poverty to become a medical aide to a powerful Net broker in Antarctica's Erebus Complex, finds her own efforts to succeed as a deal-maker haunted by phantom images of a fox and a chimera. The fox turns out in real life to be Flander, an outlaw hacker who wants to help her track the chimera — but before he can, he's nearly murdered in Jewel's apartment. By saving his life, she becomes involved with his lover, a successful VR artist and designer named David Chen, who has his own problems as the prodigal son of a staid but wealthy Chinese family. Together, Jewel and David's investigation into Flander's attempted murder and the mystery of the chimera leads them back to Seattle, into Jewel's own twisted family history with her adoptive sister and her sister's daughter, and finally into a pretty standard Web of Conspiracy that pits them all against increasingly powerful operators in the Net. Some of the characters seem a bit too familiar – most notably Flander, Jewel's employer Harmon Alcourt, and her street-smart but spunky niece Susana – and the payoff is a little tame for readers who might be led to expect World-Shattering Revelations, but the novel's strengths far outweigh its weaknesses.

Rosenblum is interested less in the bells and whistles of VR than in its potential for revealing aspects of character – the images that people present to one another, the meaning in the details they surround themselves with, the landscapes that haunt their imaginations. The most striking examples are David Chen's ice cave and a holographic desert in her employer's office that stirs disturbing feelings in Jewel. Such images gain in power when contrasted with the real-world landscapes that are their sources – the Antarctic icefields that surround Erebus Complex, the desert where Jewel once lived as a child. Handled in this way, virtual reality becomes not just a series of power games, but a way of articulating the fancies and illusions that we all live by all the time. It's a brilliant treatment of a theme already in danger of overuse – but exactly the same could have been said of *Drylands*. Rosenblum is emerging as the kind of writer who startles you not with dazzling new inventions, but with haunting images carefully built up to reveal more than you expected. She could do a lot worse.

The economics of modern science has all but done in the old-fashioned engineering epic, in which enormous amounts of money could be raised at the drop of a hat by visionary industrialists bent on building spaceships or transatlantic tunnels. In the 19th century, Verne could optimistically assume that enough pocket change was floating around in America to enable a group of gun nuts to finance a moon shot as a club project; had he known the real cost, he'd have had to do some quick backing and filling. Modern writers know that in order to generate the necessary capital, such projects had better justify themselves – by promising great wealth, producing superweapons, or saving the planet from doom. Paul Preuss's **Core**, about efforts to drill into the earth's core, offers all three rationales, and in the process very nearly breaks into two separate novels. Like Preuss's *Broken Symmetries* or Gregory Benford's *Artifact*, it combines well-researched state-of-the-art scientific problem solving with international intrigue, and it ties the whole thing together through a complex love-hate relationship between a father and son. Whether the Michael Crichton crowd will sit still for the elaborate science, the zigzag chronology, and the complex character relationships seems doubtful, but the novel is far from a failure, and contains some bold strokes.

The first of these bold strokes is taking a near-future disaster scenario, setting it in the recent past, and very nearly convincing us that it's actually happened. In 1985, a dramatic shift in the earth's magnetic field exposes much of the world's population to unprotected radiation from solar flares. The only scientific fix available is to attempt to drill into the earth's core and discover what might be happening there. Spearheading the project are Leidy Hudder, a maverick geologist whose long-disappeared father had discovered a superhard crystal called hudderite – the only substance which could withstand the temperatures and pressures of the core – and Marta McDougal, an establishment scientist who has developed a way of producing hudderite in usable quantities. So far, the plot seems straightforward – a developing catastrophe, a set of engineering and political problems to solve, and a testy romantic relationship between the principals.

Preuss's second bold stroke involves chronology. Suddenly, we're back in the early 1940s at the University of Nevada, where Cyrus Hudder – Leidy's father – suffers a series of misfortunes. Abandoned by his mother shortly after his father's death and accused of cheating on a physics exam, he finds himself haunted by the single question on the make-up: what is the deepest hole that can be dug into the earth? Later, working on the Manhattan project, he discovers the "hudderite" which might make such a drilling project possible. The narrative begins jumping among several time frames, paralleling Cyrus's career with Leidy's and exploring with unusual insight the ways in which the lives of scientists determine their attitudes toward science and its institutions. The novel is at its strongest as it brings a whole half-century of scientific history to bear on its immediate crisis.

But then it gets weird. What promised to be an exceptional novel of character and science begins to turn into a James Bond thriller, as Cyrus's disappearance is linked to Middle Eastern terrorist governments bent on using the core-drilling technology to generate focused earthquakes against enemy nations. The world-saving research project of Leidy and Marta takes a back seat to the world-threatening superweapon created by the same technology. It's almost as though C.P. Snow developed a good idea and turned it over to – who, Frank R. Stockton? – in midstream. This second half of the novel is thrilling enough, as such things go, but by the time the bad guys are found out, the business of saving the world's magnetic fields seems almost an afterthought, and ideas that had been very carefully worked out give way to some vaguely sketched bells and whistles in the final chapter. On a scene by scene basis, everything in Core works vividly and convincingly, but it's hard to avoid the suspicion that, in the end, a truly excellent novel of science got ambushed by a pretty standard – and more marketable – suspense thriller.

Ask a successful novelist why he or she spends time and energy on far less lucrative short stories and you'll likely get a string of high-minded sentiments about how this is an opportunity to experiment, explore new techniques, and escape the constrictions of the mass market. Everybody says this, but Brian Aldiss actually does it. Readers who fear that Forgotten Life and Remembrance Day – both fine, shapely mainstream novels – represent a taming of Aldiss's legendary imagination should be pleased, if not actually taken aback, at the stories in A Tupolev Too Far. With the exception of a short piece from a 1967 Punch, all of the dozen stories in the book date from 1989 or later, and they take risks that a writer of Aldiss's stature clearly doesn't need to take – stories embedded in other stories, dreamlike stories that take off at right angles to themselves, stories in the form of glossaries or alphabets, *hommages* to other writers and texts. For the most part, these experiments work brilliantly if often mysteriously; Aldiss's narrative authority is such that he convinces you he knows exactly what he's doing, even when you don't.

Probably the closest thing to a traditional SF scenario in the book is the title story, in which a Russian airliner passes through a mysterious light and lands in an alternate timeline. But we soon recognize this alternate world as our own; it's the protagonist who comes from another history. With its multiple narrators and embedded tales, this is far more than a twist on a *Twilight Zone* plot, and instead turns into a haunting meditation on the randomness of history. "Ratbird," also with multiple narrators, is a similar meditation on alternate evolution. "FOAM" reveals a clever SF premise – the idea that someone else may steal your memory – but mostly uses this premise to mount a magnificent game of manipulating point of view. And "A Day in the Life of a Galactic Empire" sounds like it's going to be grand old space opera, but instead raises interesting philosophical questions about a the nature of human aggression.

Two stories are essentially literary *hommages*. "Better Morphosis," about a cockroach transformed into Franz Kafka, is an absolutely hilarious stand-up comedy routine that someone might have thought up years ago, if comedians were more literate. The more serious "Summertime Was Nearly Over" returns to Aldiss's beloved Frankenstein myth, and somehow makes the monster seem even more tragic and desperate than Shelley – or Aldiss himself – ever did before. "North of the Abyss" isn't a hommage to literature, but rather to Aldiss's travels in Egypt, which becomes a convincingly mythic landscape to contrast with the seedy domestic dispute that frames the tale.

This juxtaposition of the mundane with the exotic, in fact, may be the hallmark of the book. Aldiss repeatedly convinces us we're in a mainstream story, then sends us right over the edge. In "Three Degrees Over," an Oxford professor brings a crude American woman into her home and soon finds her garden – and her husband – given over to primitive pagan orgies. "A Life of Matter and Death," subtitled "A Novel in One Chapter," is exactly that – a convoluted tale of sibling rivalry and alien intervention covering several decades and several continents. In some of these tales, Aldiss seems to be showing off his mastery of technique – his ability to take a story wherever he wants to, despite our expectations, and to convince us that it ends up where it belongs. Not very many writers ought to try this, but Aldiss knows how, and never fails to provoke and enlighten.

Finding stories by Theodore Sturgeon's and Cordwainer Smith in *The Norton Book of Science Fiction* serves as a reminder that the highly personal, beautifully crafted work of these authors stands up to modern literary tastes as well as that of any pre-1960s writers. But unlike Bradbury and a handful of other stylists from that gilded ghetto, they've never quite found the broader readership they deserve, and both now seem in danger of disappearing from the memories of younger SF readers as well. As has been the case with authors from Lovecraft to Lafferty, small presses are trying, perhaps quixotically, to come to the rescue. In Sturgeon's case, his daughter Noel and Paul Williams are spearheading something called "The Sturgeon Project" with the long-range goal of bringing into print a multi-volume set of his complete stories. En route to this massive project, they've published **Argyll: A Memoir**, which consists of a long essay on his troubled relationship with his stepfather (written about 1965) together with a painful letter on the same topic he sent to his parents in 1952. As Samuel R. Delany notes in his afterword to this little book, the publication of this material invites comparison to Franz Kafka's similarly accusatory "Letter to His Father," and is valuable for exactly the same reasons.

Except for a brief episode detailing Sturgeon's discovery of SF and his stepfather's finding and destroying his carefully hidden collection of magazines, the memoir has virtually nothing to do with SF or the SF community. But that's like saying that Kafka's letter has nothing to do with *The Trial*. The key Sturgeon text that this memoir illuminates is *The Dreaming Jewels*, whose autobiographical elements become crystal clear; more importantly, it reveals many of the sources of the lifelong obsession with love, loneliness, and empowerment that permeates all his fiction. As with Kafka, the litany of festering injustices at times borders on carefully-reasoned whining (Nadine Gordimer once wrote a wonderful story-answer to Kafka's letter that underlines this), but the detail is so vivid, the emotion so raw, that the memoir gains enough power to be read simply as confessional autobiography, apart from its associational SF value. "I write *beautifully*," Sturgeon claims in a pathetic defense of himself in the 1952 letter, and this sad memoir is unexpected new evidence of how right he was. Anyone interested in Sturgeon should read it, and those not interested in Sturgeon should get interested.

The Cordwainer Smith rescue project is less ambitious and more straightforward. The NESFA Press edition of **The Rediscovery of Man: The Complete Short Science Fiction of Cordwainer Smith** contains little that is new for readers who own the Ballantine-Del Rey collections and reprints from 1975-1979, but is a very handsome hardbound volume with a useful introduction by John J. Pierce, who draws on recent Smith scholarship and suggests that the timeline he developed for those earlier collections may be all wrong. Of the 33 stories included, 27 deal with Smith's Instrumentality of Mankind and six are listed as "Other Stories." Four stories which both Ace and Ballantine had previously tried to palm off as a novel (*Quest of the Three Worlds*) are here reprinted under their original titles, but the two parts of Smith's only real SF novel (*Norstrilia*), originally published as novellas, are not.

Four items are of particular interest. Smith's most famous story, "Scanners Live in Vain," is here reprinted from the manuscript and corrects some relatively minor omissions and changes from all earlier published versions. "War No. 81-Q," written when Smith was in high school, is included along with a previously unpublished later revision which improves it and fits it into the Instrumentality scheme, but doesn't really save it. "Down to a Sunless Sea" is a Cordwainer Smith story entirely written by Genevieve Linebarger (Smith's widow, whose involvement in completing and revising his other work is still to be fully accounted for). Genevieve is also credited with "adapting" the most interesting new piece in the book, "Himself in Anachron," from a 1946 manuscript. Originally slated for Harlan Ellison's *Last Dangerous Visions*, the tale begins as a romantic Smithian take on "The Cold Equations," but gets better fast as the protagonist, separated from his spacecraft, is caught "between the Probabilities" where time accelerates faster than his consciousness can keep up. Several SF writers have portrayed similar situations, but only Cordwainer Smith would describe it with a line like "His thoughts became old memories while he thought them." Whether it's Genevieve or Paul Linebarger who wrote that, it's exactly why Cordwainer Smith should stay in print.

— November 1993, Locus #394 —

Rama Revealed ~~ Arthur C. Clarke & Gentry Lee

Moving Mars ~~ Greg Bear

Green Mars ~~ Kim Stanley Robinson

Growing Up Weightless ~~ John M. Ford

Brother Termite ~~ Patricia Anthony

The Ramans may do everything in threes, as Arthur C. Clarke tells us in the last sentence of his 1973 classic *Rendezvous with Rama*, but Clarke and Gentry Lee don't. **Rama Revealed** is the *fourth* entry in the Rama series, and the third in which Lee is a heavy — and at times heavy-handed — collaborator. Looking at the whole series, however, it quickly becomes apparent that the new novel does in fact conclude a "Rama" trilogy, and that the initial *Rendezvous with Rama* is no more a part of this trilogy than Tolkien's *The Hobbit* was part of *Lord of the Rings*. Clarke's original novel introduced one of the most famous of what *The Encyclopedia of Science Fiction* calls SF's Big Dumb Objects, then proceeded to reveal enigma after enigma in classic Clarkean style. Like Clarke's most famous earlier work, it constantly opened outward, and finally left us with the haunting notion that some mysteries may remain unanswered, and that the makers of those mysteries couldn't care less about our efforts to understand them. The Rama trilogy proper — *Rama II, The Garden of Rama*, and now *Rama Revealed* — tends instead to narrow its focus, to deal more with an increasingly limited cast of characters in a small corner of the Rama spacecraft, and to offer answers where Clarke's original novel offered questions. Essentially, the trilogy tells the life story of Nicole des Jardins, a member of the exploratory team in Rama II who was trapped aboard the spacecraft in that novel and who was slated for execution by a despotic government of colonists at the end of *The Garden of Rama*. *Rama Revealed* picks up literally where the last sentence of that novel left off.

It's a safe bet that much of the Rama trilogy is the work of Gentry Lee, who is as much of a romantic as Clarke, but whose romanticism is focused more on character and family relationships than on startling shifts of perspective. At times, especially in *The Garden of Rama* and the present novel, you get the clear impression that you're reading a sentimental family saga for which Rama is little more than a backdrop; even the ominous alien "octospiders" become friendly allies to the small group of honorable humans who seek to escape the aggressive dictatorship that has taken over the human colony on Rama. Freed from prison with the aid of her husband Richard and some Tinkerbell-size robots, Nicole manages to assemble most of her family around her in a kind of colony in exile, which eventually forms an alliance with the octospiders and sets out to overthrow the dictatorship of the main human colony, while at the same time earning the respect of the mysterious Ramans themselves and discovering their purpose in constructing such huge habitats. But for most of the novel, the Ramans and their secrets remain in the background, and much of the imaginative invention is devoted to the society of octospiders, who communicate (like Blish's VOR) through color and whose advanced science is based on genetic engineering (like that of the dinosaurs in Harrison's *West of Eden* trilogy).

Partway through the novel, the characters discover a mysterious subway which leads to unknown destinations. It's a great image of the sense of wonder, and it calls to mind a similar subway that the young Alvin finds in Clarke's *The City and the Stars*. It also points up a major contrast between the early Clarke and Clarke working with Lee: whereas Alvin's subway is a simple icon of mystery, leading to unimaginable dangers and discoveries, Alvin didn't feel compelled to talk to anyone about it – he just climbed aboard. Here the subway becomes a topic for endless debate among the various characters. Clarke was never strong on dialogue, and he always had a keen sense of when some good haunting poetic prose was called for. Lee, who has learned much from Clarke during their several collaborations, doesn't seem to have developed this sense, and he wants his characters to discuss everything. But most of the dialogue is so wooden you could carve figurines with it, and to some extent that's exactly what the authors have done: some of the characters, such as the hard-headed Arkansas farmer Max or the wistful Eponine (lifted name and all from *Les Miserables*) are so formulaic you could write their lines for them, and even when major characters such as Richard try to explain (for example) octospider science, they sound like Richard Carlson lecturing Julia Adams in a 50s Jack Arnold flick. All the characters are repeatedly astonished, awe-struck, dumbfounded, and amazed by revelations that ought to be allowed to stand for themselves.

But in the end, for all its excesses and occasional embarrassments, *Rama Revealed* is surprisingly effective, and provides persuasive evidence of Lee's continuing maturation as an author with his own voice and concerns. By the time the aging Nicole is reunited with her family for one last time, trying desperately to learn as much as she can of the Ramans' near-universal store of knowledge before her heart fails, we begin to feel a sense of genuine epic power, of a full-scale romance with a larger-than-life heroine brought to a satisfying, sentimental conclusion. Like Marianne O'Hara in Joe Haldeman's *Worlds* trilogy, Nicole emerges as a strong enough character to unify the whole series and give it a distinctive sensibility and point of view. Like O'Hara, she becomes a legendary figure representing the best of what humanity has to offer, even as humanity itself – as seen by the Ramans – turns out to be a pretty questionable idea for an intelligent species. Rama Revealed doesn't reveal as much in the way of Clarkean wonders as we might hope for, but – and here Lee probably deserves much credit – it reveals far more of the human heart than we expect.

At the end of *Rama Revealed*, the problem of human evil is literally given a send-off that only SF could manage: through a kind of high-tech Calvinism, the elect are allowed to develop their own society under superhuman guidance, while the rest are condemned to sterility and sent off to fend for themselves. Maybe there's a trend developing here, because much the same solution is offered in Greg Bear's **Moving Mars**: if you can't beat the bad guys, take your planet and leave. Nothing less than such unabashed superscience is at the heart of this complex and ambitious novel – the title turns out to mean exactly what you think it means – and Bear manages his space-time bells and whistles with enough panache that the idea seems at least as convincing as Le Guin's ansible or any number of soft-shoe rationales for faster-than-light travel. So right off the bat we have to give him credit for a breathtaking concept boldly presented – the kind of Stapledonian vision that few writers seem willing to commit to, but that Bear threatens to make his stock in trade.

But even if such a Big Concept is at the conceptual heart of the novel, it isn't really at its narrative center. For that, we have to look somewhere between the Mars of Ray Bradbury (to whom the novel is dedicated) and the Earth of Bear's own *Queen of Angels*. In fact, *Moving Mars* may be read as a companion piece (one tastefully avoids the word "trilogy" if only because there isn't a continuous narrative as there is with the Rama books) to both *Queen of Angels* and *Heads*, which introduced us to a prosperous 22nd century dominated by supranational economic entities, a growing class division between the "therapied" and the "untherapied," and colonies on the Moon (the setting of Heads) and Mars. But whereas *Queen of Angels* portrayed what appeared to be a nanotech version of an old-fashioned rationalist utopia on Earth, *Moving Mars* shows us what that same society looks like from the outside, from the point of view of the more revolutionary pioneer society of the Mars colony, which comes to be viewed as a threat to earth's hegemony.

Casseia Majumdar, a daughter of one of the Binding Multiples, the extended families which direct Mars's economy, gets her first taste of revolution as a young university protester. There she meets and develops a romantic relationship with Charles Franklin, a brilliant young physicist working on a theory of the universe as a kind of computational system — probability theory carried to macro levels you wouldn't *believe*. Casseia breaks off the affair and loses touch with Charles. A few years later, she is given the rare opportunity to visit earth as an apprentice to a distinguished Martian diplomat, and the account of her visit — more than a fifth of the novel — gives us a somewhat jaundiced view of this bioengineered utopia. Casseia's mission fails, but she learns that the research Charles is engaged in seems of supreme importance to Earth. More years pass, Casseia continues to advance in government, marries (not Charles), and eventually is elected vice-president of a newly unified Mars. It quickly becomes apparent that a unified Martian government equipped with the technology made possible by Charles's physics is too much for Earth to tolerate, and the novel rapidly accelerates toward the stunning conclusion implied in the title.

Whether or not Bear's political-thriller plot actually supports the radical technological solution he concocts for it is up for debate, even among the novel's own characters. But the richness of texture with which he brings all this off — the continued exploration of his favorite nanotech themes, the insightful sketch of Earth society during Casseia's sojourn there, the complexity of characters and relationships as they are affected by "enhancements" of various kinds, the imaginary physics of Charles's research — make *Moving Mars* far more than just another entry in the news Mars sweepstakes, although it should be noted that Bear's depiction of Martian life and landscapes stands up to the best of them. It's another Mars novel, all right, but it's one that only Greg Bear, among contemporary SF writers, would dare to take on.

It's clear from the outset that Bear's high-concept physics has no place in Kim Stanley Robinson's Mars trilogy, although Robinson isn't afraid to push the limits of big-budget technology: moholes, space elevators, "soletta" satellites focusing the sun's rays to burn giant trenches in the Martian landscape to release gases. Robinson is an enormously intelligent writer who does his homework well and never lets his technology overwhelm his characters, but his real passion seems to be not science or engineering, but philosophies of history. One of the key sections in *Red Mars* was titled "Falling into History," and that might well serve as a subtitle for the second novel in the trilogy, **Green Mars**. Beginning about a quarter-century after the end of *Red Mars* and featuring many of the same characters (who benefit from life-extending gerontological treatments), the novel covers the next four decades of Martian history, ending with a war for independence which conveniently coincides with a massive ecological catastrophe back on Earth. But those readers of *Red Mars* who enjoyed Robinson's complex evocation of pioneering exploration and society-building had better be ready for a novel in which the central dramatic event is a constitutional convention. *Green Mars* falls into history with a vengeance.

One could make the argument that historical processes are at least as much a part of the fabric of SF as scientific or technological speculation, and deserve to be treated with as much rigor. Asimov's recycled Victorian readings of imperial Roman history produced the genre's first action-free classic, and even Bradbury's Mars seemed imbued with a kind of pop-psychology version of the Turner thesis. But neither author really grappled with the questions of how the nature of history itself might change over time: the future was simply the past on a grander scale, and to a great extent this has become the accepted historicism of most SF. Robinson sincerely wants to question this received wisdom, and several of his speculations – such as the notion of an Earth society destabilized by a growing disparity between those populations receiving the gerontological treatments and those remaining "mortal" – are persuasive and intriguing. (Greg Bear's distinction between the "therapied" and the "untherapied" is a similar sort of rethinking class structures.) But the central narrative line of *Green Mars* is the forging of Mars's various fiercely independent colonies into a central government, independent both of Earth governments and of the transnational corporations who have long dominated both Earth and Mars. At its most provocative, the novel questions the need for government at all, but such questions are notoriously difficult to dramatize, and Robinson seems forced to lean back on American history for much of his template – only this time it's not the pioneer America of de Tocqueville and Daniel Boone, but the early democracy of Jefferson and Franklin.

Unfortunately, there's a reason why American literature has developed such a rich tradition of pioneer tales and only a limited range of fiction about forming governments: pioneer tales are simply more exciting. Some of this excitement is captured in Robinson's opening chapters, describing the coming of age of the young Nirgal in a colony established under the south polar Martian ice cap by the renegade ecologist Hiroko toward the end of *Red Mars* (the setting echoes, perhaps deliberately, the scenes set in an Antarctic training facility early in that first novel). But the colony proves dangerously fragile, and soon Nirgal sets off on an exploratory journey with Coyote, the mysterious and semilegendary stowaway of the first settlement expedition. It's the first of several such journeys depicted in the novel, and it quickly becomes apparent that the journey motif is Robinson's way of trying to recapture some of the density of invention in that earlier novel. Soon we're reintroduced to Sax Russell, Maya Toitovna, Ann Clayborne, Michel Duval, and a host of other characters from the First Hundred of *Red Mars*, together with a few wild-card characters, most notably the industrial spy Art Randolph, who comes to figure in important ways in the Martian move for independence. There are enough kidnappings, murders, rescues, disasters, and acts of sabotage to keep it all exciting, but the tale is driven by the problems of gaining independence from both earthly governments and the giant corporations who continually seek ways of exploiting the Martian colony. This leads to long passages of political and economic debate that slow down Robinson's momentum, and that are likely to make the novel puzzling

— if not downright sluggish — to anyone who hasn't read *Red Mars*. In the midst of these debates, we're often told of the ways in which Earth is falling apart both economically and ecologically, and it's ironic that the offstage tale of 22nd century Earth at times seems more compelling than the problems facing the Martians. *Green Mars* suffers from some of the inevitable problems of being the second book in a trilogy, and it may look different once *Blue Mars* is out and we can see what seeds have been planted here. The most obvious thing to expect, given the pattern of the first two-thirds of the trilogy, is a civil war novel.

John M. Ford's **Growing Up Weightless** is also a novel of a post-pioneer society, set in a fully developed and industrialized moon colony late in the 21st century. Like Robinson, Ford is aware that the problems of an established and economically viable society are a bit different from those of an outpost, and his detailed rendering of the problems faced by second and third generation settlers makes this one of the most convincing moon novels in recent SF. Before hard-SF purists start complaining about the title — after all, people on the moon aren't quite weightless — I should point out that the "weightlessness" to which Ford alludes is not so much matter of gravity as of spirit. Essentially, the novel is a coming-of-age tale about a brilliant teenager, Matt Ronay, who along with his equally brilliant companions finds himself growing up without challenges and responsibilities, thoroughly at loose ends about what to do with his life in a society in which the most difficult problems have already been solved (partly with the aid some bells and whistles involving matter-transmission and interstellar travel). Although his father is an influential politician involved in plans to bring water to the moon, and his mother is a successful surgeon, Matt feels that his own options are limited.

Right away, then, it becomes apparent that Ford is doing something unusual with his lunar setting. In some ways, it seems like an alien world, its language liberally sprinked with doses of Russian and Japanese and metaphors drawn from space and computer technology, its complex subterranean (or sublunar) settings veritable mazes of tubes and gardens. In other ways, Ford might as well be writing about 19th century New England, or the 1920s midwest, or any setting in which young people feel frustrated and unfulfilled by what their society has to offer them. New England comes to mind in particular because the interstellar starships which periodically visit the moon, and represent the next phase of real frontier exploration, are viewed by Matt in much the same way that some of Melville's young heroes viewed the sailing ships which always seemed to be returning from unknown worlds.

Partly to ease their frustrations, Matt and his friends devote much of their time to elaborate virtual-reality games with a vaguely Robin Hood-like setting. Even though Ford does a pretty good job of relating these fantasy adventures to the main themes of the novel, they still tend to interrupt the narrative excessively (is it part of the standard SF novel contract now that everyone has to put in VR sequences?) Much more satisfying are the passages dealing with the theater, which Ford seems to know a lot about and which serves as a kind of real-world counterpoint to the VR sequences.

Matt and a few of his friends are hoping to be selected to join a theater company which offers the promise of fame, fulfillment and — most important of all — travel. In the novel's best sequence, Matt and his friends sneak off for a train ride to the far side of the moon, where Matt helps solve a conspiracy-puzzle involving his father's water negotiations and rescues a starship crew from a barroom brawl in a way that will eventually determine his destiny. At its heart, *Growing Up Weightless* belongs to the great American tradition of running-away-with-the-circus novels, but it brings this tradition seamlessly into a carefully realized and convincing SF milieu.

Patricia Anthony's first novel, *Cold Allies*, introduced us to some of the most unusual aliens in recent SF; her new one, **Brother Termite**, goes to the opposite extreme of offering up the most familiar aliens of all: those humanoid stars of supermarket tabloids who've been secretly controlling the White House for generations, and even mating with humans on occasion. The novel begins a half-century after the aliens have come out of the closet — the main character, Reen, is chief of staff to a president who's served that whole period thanks to an extended-term amendment to the Constitution — but it's clear that their involvement in human affairs is a secret going back at least to the Eisenhower administration. This sounds like a promising set-up for a rapid-fire satirical romp, and Anthony doesn't lack in comic invention: the President, Jeff Womack, has gone goofy in his old age, urinating on treaties, declaring himself on strike, appointing a psychic who channels John F. Kennedy as his vice-president. The human population is declining precipitously, although the fact is kept secret until the German government discovers that most of the peas shipped to Gerber for baby food are disappearing (Gerber, now also controlled by aliens, is desperately trying to hold on to its market share by recycling its excess inventory into such things as strained-pea flavored pop tarts for adults). One especially deft scene involves Reen trying to fire the White House Educational Counsel using Reaganesque football metaphors given him by the President, and getting it so garbled the employee doesn't know what he's talking about.

Anthony's near-future international politics isn't nearly as well worked out as her future war scenario in *Cold Allies*, but it doesn't have to be given the very different tone of this novel. At the same time, the tone isn't all that consistent; beneath the satirical jabs, Anthony strives to construct in Reen a sympathetic and sensitive observer, equally appalled at the irrationality of human politics and his own race's penchant for genocide in the guise of love. Love, in fact, turns out to be one of the central concerns of the novel, just as it was in Cold Allies. Reen is concerned with maintaining and learning to understand his relationships with his half-human daughter Angela, her mother Marian, President Womack, and his various hive-like alien Brothers, with whom he needs to be together in order to sleep. The novel's most affecting scenes occur when Reen is exiled from communal sleep by the Sleep Master, and seeks to redeem himself both in the eyes of his brothers and of the humans who distrust him.

While this unexpected sentimentality undercuts *Brother Termite's* satirical edge, it also gives the novel an added gravity, and helps to make Reen one of the more ingratiating alien characters in recent SF. Like Karellen in Clarke's *Childhood's End*, he finds himself learning to love humans even as he knows his real mission is to assist in bringing the human race to an end (not nearly as transcendently as in the Clarke novel, although Reen's occasional contacts with the mysterious "Old Ones" hint at such transcendence). In the end, I don't think *Brother Termite* hangs together quite as effectively as *Cold Allies*, but Anthony's strength in portraying an unusual cast of characters and her generally quirky imagination give her a highly individual voice, and she has a genuine talent for the unexpected.

— December 1993, Locus #395 —

Antiquities: Seven Stories ~~ John Crowley

Rivers of Time ~~ L Sprague de Camp

Out of Time ~~ James P. Hogan

Passion Play ~~ Sean Stewart

John Crowley's **Antiquities** is a collection of seven beautifully crafted tales, mostly from literary or mythological sources, that comes as close as anything I've read in years to capturing the peculiar mix of erudition, wonder, and longing that you feel when first stumbling upon Borges. Crowley has long been lauded for the elegance of his style, and these mostly short tales display that style at its purest, unencumbered by the sometimes convoluted plotting of his novels. The opening story, "The Green Child," is based upon the same medieval legend as Herbert Read's 1935 novel of that title, but whereas Read moved the tale to the early 19th century and used it as a basis for utopian musings, Crowley retains the medieval setting and the chronicler's voice, speculating that if such wondrous children ever did exist, their magic is long since gone from the world, or at least hopelessly diluted in the bloodlines of their descendants. It's an appropriate opening, for the theme of lost magical worlds permeates the rest of the stories in the book.

Two of the stories cast this theme in specifically literary terms. "Missolonghi 1824" has a dissolute Byron telling a Greek boy whom he has almost seduced about his earlier encounter with a satyr, and in "The Reason for the Visit," a narrator who is in the habit of summoning literary figures from the past visits with Virginia Woolf and tries to learn her narrative secret of compressing time into an instant of near-infinite meaning; it's a touching commentary on the relationship of writers with their forebears and on what Harold Bloom called "the anxiety of influence." Another story with literary overtones, "Her Bounty to the Dead," draws its title, setting, elegiac tone, and some of its imagery from Wallace Stevens's poetry, especially "Sunday Morning".

The only real SF story in the book is also probably the best known: "Snow" (already semi-canonized by its inclusion in *The Norton Book of Science Fiction*) imagines flying microtransmitters called "wasps" which can record thousands of hours of a person's life to create a kind of living video memorial. After losing his wife, the narrator obsessively views the footage, trying to recapture meaningful moments. But the only access available is purely random — specific moments can't be summoned up — and gradually the images themselves begin to deteriorate, and inexplicably to edit out all but wintry, snow-filled moments. It's one of Crowley's most achingly beautiful stories, and one of SF's most powerful metaphors for the ways in which memory works, and the ways in which it fails us.

L. Sprague de Camp's **Rivers of Time** is about as far removed from the Crowley collection as you can get and still be in the same review column. At first glance it looks like an old warhorse is cashing in on what David Letterman keeps calling "dino-mania," and if so, more power to him — I'd rather see bucks flowing toward de Camp than toward Barney any day. But even though it's not a major book, it has an interesting history. In an afterword, de Camp tells of reading a dinosaur-hunting story published in the early 1950s — undoubtedly Bradbury's "A Sound of Thunder" — and being appalled at the author's scientific errors. His response was the 1956 *Galaxy* story "A Gun for Dinosaur," which would be a better title for this collection had not de Camp already used it for a 1963 collection of mostly non-dinosaur tales. The story not only corrects some of Bradbury's coloring-book science, but rethinks the premise in such macho terms that it goes right past Hemingway into Robert Ruark territory. Rivers, the Australian narrator, is explaining to a client why he won't take on his time-safaris anyone too small to handle a .600 caliber weapon. In the tale that follows, a trigger-happy Great White Hunter gets his comeuppance, but de Camp obviously relishes all the talk of guns and rampaging beasts.

The story also establishes a formula that is almost never varied in the rest of the collection — all published since 1991, when "Crocamander Quest" was commissioned for Robert Silverberg's *The Ultimate Dinosaur*. Every story begins with Rivers regaling an off-stage client with an adventure — why he won't take women along, why he doesn't use powered vehicles in the past, how he outsmarted a fundamentalist, who his strangest client was. Every story reintroduces Rivers's partner Raja in the same way; every story features a minor initial encounter with a prehistoric beast followed by a more dramatic encounter with a larger beast. Someone is always messing with his camera or the local flora just long enough to make the return trip a split-second escape. It's consummate recipe-fiction, and you quickly get the sense that de Camp could spin one of these off the top of his head if you bought him a drink. Only occasionally does a story try to evoke a real sense of wonder — most notably "The Big Splash," about a visit to view the cataclysm that killed off the dinosaurs.

Some of de Camp's satirical targets misfire or seem churlish — he takes on animal-rights activists, environmentalists, disengaged scientists, religious fanatics, feminists, and almost anyone the narrator perceives as a wimp. Nor do all the stories successfully dramatize the "morals" the narrator is trying to illustrate. But on the whole, for all its political incorrectness and repetitiveness, the book makes for an enjoyable light read, and echoes an era in which competent, off-the-cuff formula fiction was a pleasant staple of the SF magazines.

James P. Hogan isn't nearly as much a veteran as de Camp (come to think of it, nobody is), but his new novella, **Out of Time**, seems even more determinedly retro than de Camp's barroom dinosaur tales. It takes us right back to an era in which a profoundly goofy premise could be handled with a perfectly straight face, a lot of fast action, and a cast of characters who actually seem to resemble those old interior pulp illustrations. By the second chapter, Hogan has hauled onstage a vaudeville German physicist with an accent egregious enough to threaten diplomatic relations, and a few pages later he gives us a hard-drinking Irish priest who talks just like Barry Fitzgerald. The long-limbed female lead is actually named "Deena." Those readers who have been hoping that Hogan would someday return from his libertarian sermons to the kind of old-fashioned hard SF that he used to do well are going to get more than they bargained for here. Those who are still waiting for the early Murray Leinster to return will be thrilled.

Still, there are undeniable pleasures to be gotten from this kind of fiction, if one takes it – as Hogan presumably intends – as a lark. Hogan's basic premise – clocks all over New York begin keeping time at different rates – is a genuine puzzler, the kind of bizarre problem that pulp writers regularly used to think up before they had any idea what they were going to do with it. Joe Kopeksky, the criminal investigator assigned to find the source of the problem (and why this is seen as a law-enforcement problem is anybody's guess), begins by testing the German physicist's hypothesis that aliens from another dimension are stealing our time. With the kind of logic shared only by characters in such stories, Kopeksky begins interviewing philosophers and psychics, finally settling on the Irish priest – who by fortunate coincidence is also an amateur epidemiologist. It's the priest who notices that the time distortions seem to follow an infectious pattern, with areas of high electrical or computer activity as the centers of infection. Sure enough, these centers are experiencing the greatest time losses, and are even beginning to be surrounded by a red haze caused by the shift in wavelengths of light. The culprits, it appears, may not be intelligent alternate-dimension aliens *a la* Asimov's *The Gods Themselves*, but rather – well, time-termites. Or maybe time-rats.

What makes such silliness enjoyable is not only Hogan's poker-faced treatment of it as a credible problem-solving tale, but his brief and unobtrusive asides about various theories on the nature of time; his soft-shoe accounts of space-time physics, used in exactly the same way superscientific gobbledygook was used in the pulps, are intelligent if not persuasive. And for all the tale's flat-out pulpishness, one could make the argument that it also fits into an emerging tradition of what, for lack of a better term, we might call "viral SF" – SF driven by metaphors of infestation rather than exploration or confrontation. The last several years have given us novels in which microorganisms eat plastic, transmit religious beliefs, turn people into slime, and transform whole landscapes. Maybe, sooner or later, a time-space bug was inevitable.

One of the early reviews of Sean Stewart's **Passion Play** — originally published in Canada last year — hailed it as the best work of Canadian SF since Margaret Atwood's *The Handmaid's Tale*, and this got me to wondering if there's some lurking fascination up north with the whole idea of fundamentalist dystopias. In Stewart's novel, a near-future "Redemptionist Presidency" — the Reds, for short — has turned America into a fear-ridden, anti-technology, anti-foreign, anti-sex hierarchy of unforgiving moral codes and enforced worship. Diane Fletcher is a Shaper, or empath, who uses her special talent to work for the police as a criminal investigator, and we first meet her as she puts away a fanatical fundamentalist deacon who has led his flock in stoning a woman to death for adultery. This opening quickly establishes the noir-punk sensibility of Stewart's world, where executions are media events and seedy poverty still permeates the city's barrios. Soon Fletcher is called in on another case: the apparent suicide of Jonathan Mask, the country's most famous actor, who's been electrocuted by his special-effects-laden Mephistopheles costume designed for a high-tech production of *Faust*. The rest of the plot unfolds as a straightforward theater murder mystery, with Fletcher offering some nifty deductions based on close observation of the suspects and occasionally quoting her role model, Sherlock Holmes. Except for the setting and Fletcher's psionic talent, much of this follows the pattern of those non-SF mysteries in which the detective works under the restrictions and political pressures imposed by a regressive regime and grapples with the attendant ethical dilemmas (for example, the Soviet mysteries of Martin Cruz Smith or Stuart Kaminsky).

The question, then, is what do the psychic abilities and the Redemptionist background add to such a tale? After all, we've seen esp-toting detectives as far back as Bester's *The Demolished Man*, and fundamentalist autocracies in Atwood and others. What knits this altogether — and gives the novel a surprising texture and substance — is the theatrical setting. The actors and directors who are the prime suspects are professionals at faking emotions, the most accomplished being Mask himself, a brutal and manipulative hypocrite who became chief spokesman for the Redemptionists while secretly holding their entire philosophy in contempt. While the irony of his being done in by his own costume is perhaps a bit leaden, the whole theatrical milieu, together with the Faust theme, becomes increasingly entangled with the larger dynamics of Stewart's imaginary society and Fletcher's own problems of guilt and responsibility until the novel takes on a denseness that you wouldn't at first suspect. But the strongest point of Passion Play is Fletcher herself, both tougher and more violent than any of the popular mainstream women detectives, but equally as complex and vulnerable. She'd be a memorable character in any setting, and is more convincing than the world she inhabits.

1994 – Overview: The Year in Review
~ originally published in Locus #409 (Feb 1995) ~

A year ago in this space, under the impression I was supposed to identify trends, I arrived at the rather infelicitous phrase "creeping mainstreamism" to describe a growing tendency to publish and market mainstream works as though they were SF or fantasy. Apparently, a few people regarded this as a complaint against the corruption of the purity of the genre through importation of mainstream values, but that wasn't really my intention at all. Essentially mainstream novels such as Geoff Ryman's *Was* or Jane Yolen's *Briar Rose* are still rare (although the trend is still healthy in short fiction, as witnessed by the dozen or more mainstream stories in Datlow and Windling's *The Year's Best Fantasy and Horror: Seventh Annual Collection*), but novels which combine both mainstream and genre values are becoming increasingly common. It wasn't so long ago that the SF community embraced, say, Benford's *Timescape* or Le Guin's *The Dispossessed* as rarities – novels whose characters and situations were as compelling as their SF themes – but now we can expect to see three or four such novels a year. (I realize this implies an unarticulated distinction between "SF values" and "mainstream values," but in the interests of saving you from theory, let's adopt the convivial premise that everyone knows what these distinctions are.)

This year, for example, we have Elizabeth Hand's *Waking the Moon* – to my mind the best fantasy novel of the year, which is fundamentally a thoroughly realized novel of a group of college friends and what happens to them – even though one of them turns out to be the apocalyptic reincarnation of the Goddess. Michael Bishop's *Brittle Innings*, which could be classed as fantasy or SF depending on how you view his take on the Frankenstein theme, is an equally satisfying Southern coming-of-age tale set in baseball's minor leagues during World War II – and it succeeds on this level long before Old Bolt-Neck even makes his appearance. Brian Aldiss's *Somewhere East of Life* is a little different – the concluding volume of a mainstream quartet, which, like Doris Lessing's *Children of Violence*, simply moves the narrative a little beyond the present; its major SF device, a technology for recording memories, serves the novel's main themes of memory and betrayal, set in a convincing post-Soviet Europe and Turkmenistan. I was a little less satisfied with my fourth example, James Morrow's *Towing Jehovah*, a sixties-style apocalyptic satire on the literal death of God, but the novel gained a good deal of mainstream attention, as did William Hjortsberg's historical frolic *Nevermore*, which pits Houdini against Arthur Conan Doyle in a murder mystery involving spiritualism. Meanwhile, Stanislaw Lem returned to familiar satiric territory with *Peace on Earth*, a delightful overview of his earlier themes and characters.

Despite this continuing trend toward the literary, both SF and fantasy reasserted their core identities during the year, led by a couple of important anthologies. David Hartwell and Kathryn Cramer's *The Ascent of Wonder: The Evolution of Hard Science Fiction* generated some controversy with its generous and somewhat fuzzy view of the nature of hard SF, but succeeded in reinvigorating debate over this exact question. A better-focused but less widely discussed anthology, Tom Shippey's *Oxford Book of Fantasy Stories*, set out to do much the same thing for fantasy, reinvestigating its pulp traditions almost in defiance of the post-Tolkien view of the genre as purely a literature of trilogies. Datlow and Windling's seventh annual *Year's Best Fantasy and Horror* continued their ongoing project to redefine fantasy in a more literary way. Among SF anthologies, I found the hard SF debate – the question of what SF could and ought to be doing these days – most tellingly reflected in a couple of Australian titles Paul Collins *Metaworlds* and Terry Dowling and Van Ikin's *Mortal Fire*.

Interestingly, this exploration of hard SF seems to have taken hold more in England and Australia than in the states. Stephen Baxter, one of the most interesting younger English writers, was all over the SF map with three novels: the almost impenetrable super-hard SF *Flux*, with its submicroscopic tin-nuclei humans cavorting inside a neutron star, the alternate-Victorian *Anti-Ice*, and his best work so far, the Stapledonian cosmic epic *Ring*. The Australian Greg Egan, with *Permutation City*, produced what may be the most convincing and rigorous hard-SF scenario about information processing to date. If I were to name one SF theme that seemed to emerge as dominant during the year, it would have to be nanotech, a concept so appealing that SF writers have already taken it light-years beyond any rational connection to published research. Paul McAuley's *Red Dust* used it to give a unique thrust to his contribution to the ongoing Mars trend, and to permit him to re-examine many of the ways SF has handled Mars. But the overall nanotech championship has to go to an American, Kathleen Ann Goonan, whose remarkable *Queen City Jazz*, with its surrealistic vision of an "enlivened" Cincinnati transformed into a pop-culture inferno, gets my vote as the best first novel of the year. (An almost equally surrealistic city, achieved without the SF/nanotech trope, can be found in Simon Ings's compelling *City of the Iron Fish*.)

A theme made explicit in Ing's novel, but reflected in various ways in those of Goonan, Egan, and others, seems to be turning into a favorite philosophical preoccupation of SF and fantasy writers, and one uniquely suited to these genres. Stated perhaps too simply, the theme is this: "reality must be sustained." This isn't simply the old question of energy vs. entropy, although that's a part of it, but a much broader question involving the role of imagination and consciousness in defining the world. This can be presented in terms of computer code (as in the Egan novel), of nanotech (as in the Goonan) or in terms of narrative itself, as in the key stories in Ursula Le Guin's *A Fisherman of the Inland Sea*, a collection which seemed to mark her conscious reassertion of herself as an SF writer. This theme also shows up in other major story collections of the year, including Connie Willis's *Impossible Things* (also notable for gathering together some of Willis's funniest stories) and Lisa Goldstein's

Travellers in Magic (notable for three of her stories about the mythical country of Amaz, as well as for a couple of haunting Holocaust tales). It even shows up in the title story of Gregory Benford's *Matter's End*, another noteworthy collection (and one which gains added value by revealing Benford's ongoing dialogue with genre SF.)

The year's nonfiction was generally unremarkable except for one astonishing fluke of publishing: *every single nonfiction book published in America during 1994 contained new revelations about Star Trek!* As cast members desperately tried to head off each other's memoirs with versions of their own, Gene Roddenberry himself became the subject of biographies in the opposing traditions of Walter Winchell and Parson Weems. Even self-help and instant-management books got into the act. While almost none of these individually are worth serious attention, collectively they may constitute the most extended body of insight-free prose published during the year. By contrast, Samuel R. Delany's collection of written or rewritten *Silent Interviews* was full of provocative notions, and Isaac Asimov's posthumous "personal" autobiography (as opposed to his purely reportorial earlier volumes) *I, Asimov* revealed a more opinionated and emotional Asimov – who turned out to be pretty much exactly who we had all thought he was.

In looking over the year's list, it's possible to see a revisiting of origins as a frequent, if far from universal, theme: Le Guin deliberately subtitling her new collection "science fiction stories" and even returning to the Gethen of *The Left Hand of Darkness* in other short fiction; Lem offering another seriocomic adventure of Ijon Tichy; McAulcy cvoking antecedents in the literary history of Mars in *Red Dust*; Stephen Baxter using current cosmological theory to bring a Stapledonian vision down to dramatic size in *Ring*. In a year that saw no less an icon than De Niro take on Frankenstein in the movies, it's significant that Underwood/Miller reprinted Berni Wrightson's sumptuously illustrated version of Mary Shelley's novel, and that Michael Bishop drafted the famous monster for minor league ball. SF and fantasy may be scattered to the winds in terms of any real notion of genre coherence, but we're apparently not too proud for the occasional family reunion.

– January 1994, Locus #396 –

Impossible Things ~~ Connie Willis

Xanadu 2 ~~ edited by Jane Yolen

The Oxford Book of Modern Fairy Tales ~~ edited by Alison Lurie

The Willows in Winter ~~ William Horwood

The Art of Michael Whelan ~~ Michael Whelan

In his introduction to Connie Willis's **Impossible Things**, Gardner Dozois – in whose magazine nine of these eleven stories first appeared – claims that Willis is "one of the funniest modern writers since Thurber," and, exaggerated as that sounds, he may have a point. Willis the humorist is at work in more than half the stories, which set the tone for the book despite the inclusion of such relatively somber tales as "Chance" and "Schwarzchild Radius." (It's nice that the author who depressed the hell out of everybody with *Doomsday Book* also sees fit to give us a good time.) What's more interesting, though, is that Dozois should choose Thurber as his point of comparison. SF, after all, does have its own long tradition of funny writing (by which I mean *intentionally* funny writing), and you don't need to go all the way back to Thurber to find antecedents. But Willis, even though she may deserve anointing as the genre's premier modern humorist, doesn't really draw on those earlier traditions, and her approach to comic writing raises some interesting questions about humor and SF in general.

Humor is alway difficult to talk about as a valid mode of storytelling; even the word "humor" itself is, in campus jargon, a major buzzkill. Given SF's sometimes neurotic concerns with its own importance, humor becomes a doubly sensitive issue. Perhaps because of this, most SF humor has been pretty much internalized to the genre — self-referential parodies like you get in "Lewis Padgett," Arthur C. Clarke, or Harry Harrison; bad puns and shaggy dog stories of the sort Fredric Brown and Reginald Bretnor used to write as short-shorts (but which have since been expanded to novels of breathtaking triviality by the likes of Robert Asprin). There have been some genuinely sharp-edged satirists from Robert Sheckley to Eileen Gunn, and some very funny post-Pynchon gonzo-absurdist comic epics like Neal Stephenson's *Snow Crash*, but even here the humor tends to derive from the SF premise more than from close observation of actual human behavior. Thurber-type comedy — the kind that sees people as inherently funny — is still rare in the genre.

Willis is such a rarity. Her comedy comes from the same sources not only as that of Thurber, but of Peter de Vries or — perhaps more to the point — of Shirley Jackson (whose comic novels of suburban life are almost forgotten, and whose wild manic-depressive shifts from the ominous to the hilarious seems most to anticipate Willis). For me, the funniest stories in *Impossible Things* are those that belie the book's title (from Lewis Carroll) by not seeming impossible at all: in "Ado," Shakespeare gets eviscerated by political correctness; "In the Late Cretaceous" shows how semiliterate educational "consultants" can wreak havoc on university teaching; "At the Rialto" places a quantum physics convention in that most indeterminate of all environments, Hollywood. Only the first of these is even slightly SF; the others draw their effects from comic situations paralleled with enough scientific rhetoric to make them look like SF. Another story, "Time Out," involves time travel (or time displacement, at least), but the witty portrayal of parents, kids, and teachers would be just as sharp without it. For me, the least successful comic story in the book — which is still plenty enjoyable — is also the one most dependent on its SF setting. "Spice Pogrom," written as a tribute to old screwball-comedy movies, makes as much use of awful wordplay as those films and is just as contrived. (Screwball comedy almost never works as well in print as on screen.) "Even the Queen," which also draws from this tradition, gains added zing from its outrageous premise and its not-so-subtle parodies of feminism and dietary trends.

Of the remaining five stories, the most familiar are "The Last of the Winnebagos," with its oddly moving evocation of a dogless world, and "Schwarzchild Radius," a complex and multilayered tale of war, science, and memory which combines these various discourses as subtly as any postmodernist could want. "Winter's Tale" is a clever take on the Shakespeare-authorship controversy seen through the eyes of Anne Hathaway, and "Jack" returns to the London blitz setting of Willis's "Firewatch," but with supernatural events replacing the SF elements of the earlier story. "Chance," about a wife who sees her life disintegrating around her, is the best-constructed and most deeply-felt tale in the collection, despite its minimal fantastic content. For a writer who publicly eschews doctrinaire feminism, Willis handles women's lives with acute sensitivity, and peoples those lives with some of the most unpleasant – and unpleasantly believable – husbands and other assorted male creeps in contemporary fiction.

One of the healthier trends in fantasy of the last couple of decades is its growing multiculturalism, and Jane Yolen has been a major influence in this direction both in her own fiction and in her work as editor. **Xanadu** 2, the second in her annual state-of-the-art anthologies of original fiction and poetry, reaches far beyond the familiar Anglo-German traditions that still dominate so much commercial fantasy, and finds a wealth of material in traditions ranging from China to Norway to Native America. While I found a couple of the tales a little too winsome for my tastes, I'm happy to report that there isn't a single verifiable Tolkien dropping in the book. There is, however, a consistent sense of storytelling returning to its roots, of new writers harking back to oral traditions rather than to other literary fantasies, and this is the main source of the book's considerable energy.

At first, I thought there were going to be too many cats in the book. (Before I hear about this, I get along with cats just fine, but I do question their apparently unchallenged hegemony over the bookselling industry.) But it turns out the only really cute cat-story is Tappan King's "A Most Obedient Cat"; the cats in Megan Lindholm's "The Fifth Squashed Cat" are all dead, and the title creature of Diane Duane's "The Dovrefell Cat" turns out to be a bear. Both of these latter tales are among the more memorable in the anthology, anyway. Nor are there too many dragons: Vivian Vande Velde's "Just Another Dragon-Slaying" is more about the economics of such an enterprise than its heroic potential. There is one frog-prince – in Milbre Burch's "Metamorphosis," which works a reversal on the familiar tale – and one mermaid of sorts in "Bloodtide" by Mary A. Turzillo. Weavers and spinners figure in Martha Soukup's "The Spinner" and Terri Windling's poem "Weaver's Cottage," but in all these cases shifts in point of view or emphasis give the tales a twist of originality. The most dramatic such twist may be in Barbara Hambly's "The Little Tailor and the Elves," which turns the familiar material into a tale of wife abuse and poetic justice – a fairy tale as Stanley Ellin might have told it.

The other stories I found most memorable include Delia Sherman's "Young Woman in a Garden," which portrays with convincing detail the search for the secrets of a minor Impressionist painter; Ursula K. Le Guin's elliptical "In the Drought," which conveys the alienation of the gay community through a striking central metaphor; Richard Kearns's "Raven," a darkly poetic creation myth from Native American sources; and Patricia McKillip's "Transmutations," a kind of meditation on unity and diversity not only in alchemy, but in language as well. The Chinese setting of Jessica Amanda Salmonson's "The Hell Gamblers" lends it an exotic texture, but it's still a night-in-a-haunted-house deal-with-the-devil story. Finally, some note should be made of the nine poems Yolen has interspersed among the 17 stories. Too often, in anthologies such as this, poems seem little more than fillers, but Yolen has gotten at least one major American poet – Marvin Bell – to contribute the chilling "The Book of the Dead Man," and the pieces by Barbara Van Noord, T. Winter-Damon and Thomas Wiloch, Carol Edelstein, and Yolen herself are all well worth spending time with. Yolen's astute combination of familiar and lesser-known writers makes *Xanadu 2* a fine snapshot of what modern fantasy can do when it doesn't have to come in trilogies.

On the other hand, Alison Lurie's **Oxford Book of Modern Fairy Tales** provides ample evidence that many of the "contemporary issues" that modern fantasists often graft onto this old form were really there all along. Lurie's definition of "modern" is pretty loose; the oldest of the 40 tales in this fine collection, Catherine Sinclair's "Uncle David's Nonsensical Story About Giants and Fairies," dates from 1839, and 15 of the stories are from 1898 or earlier. (For the record, 11 stories fall between 1900 and 1941, and 14 between 1953 and 1989. If Lurie's chronology intends to be representative, there seems to have been an interruption in fairy tale production during World War II and after, which is probably something that ought to be looked into.) Perhaps Lurie is after stories that reflect a more modern sensibility; Ruskin's classic "The King of the Golden River" is described in her introduction as an "ecological fable," while the hero of Laurence Housman's "The Rooted Lover is described as a "post-feminist man" and Kenneth Grahame's "The Reluctant Dragon" is "possibly the first overtly pacifist fairy tale." This may sound as though Lurie is swaying heavily in the wind of political correctness, but in fact she is an acute reader of fairy tales, as evidenced not only by her earlier *Once Upon a Time* but by her insightful introduction and selection of tales here.

Although she draws entirely from Anglo-American sources, Lurie's representation of the evolution of the modern fairy tale seems both fair and judicious. There are a few widely reprinted classics (the Ruskin and the Grahame, George MacDonald's "The Light Princess," Oscar Wilde's "The Selfish Giant"), but there is also a good selection of more or less revisionist 19th-century women writers like Mary de Morgan, Lucy Lane Clifford, and Juliana Horatia Ewing, as well as once-familiar but now lesser known tales by Dickens, Hawthorne, and Robert Louis Stevenson. Nor does she overlook the influence of American democratic populism, represented in works by L. Frank Baum, Carl Sandburg, and (surprisingly) Philip K. Dick. Sometimes you wonder what Lurie's definition of a fairy tale is, and if there's any distinction to be made between fairy tales and other short forms of fantasy. H.G. Wells's "The Magic Shop," for example, seems to me a classic treatment of the disappearing-shop fantasy, while John Collier's "The Chaser," Thurber's "The Unicorn in the Garden," and Malamud's "The Jewbird" are all sly satires – but are they fairy tales?

Such questions aside, there are almost no disappointments in this collection, and it provides a wonderful opportunity to see the fairy tale change over time, growing more urban and technological. Mythical kingdoms and fabulous beasts prevail in the earlier stories, but by the time we get to Naomi Mitchison's "In the Family" (one of Lurie's real discoveries), the magic is about buses and highway accidents, and Donald Barthelme's "The Glass Mountain" appears to be a skyscraper in Manhattan. While there's a feminist tone to several of the Victorian pieces, the feminist viewpoint becomes more overt in Tanith Lee's "Prince Amilec," Jay Williams's "Petronella," and Jeanne Desy's "The Princess Who Stood on Her Own Two Feet." The growing multiculturalism that seems so evident in *Xanadu 2* is less well represented: apart from Malamud's "Jewbird" and Isaac Bashevic Singer's "Menaseh's Dream" (and perhaps the lone Sandburg Rootabaga story), the only selection to represent a clearly independent cultural tradition is Louise Erdrich's "Old Man Potchikoo," a version of a Native American trickster story. Apart from such relatively academic matters, one of the tests of an anthology such as this is that it should contain powerful stories that you think you should have read before but haven't. For me, these included T.H. White's chilling "The Troll," Richard Hughes's disturbing "Gertrude's Child" (in which toys own children, and treat them pretty much the way children treat toys), the Tanith Lee story, Angela Carter's "The Courtship of Mr. Lyon," and Jane Yolen's "The River Maid." I've told enough people about these and other stories that I'm going to have to start loaning the book out, and I'm going to have a hard time getting it back.

One of Lurie's selections, Kenneth Grahame's "The Reluctant Dragon," serves as a reminder of the quirky wit and odd charm of *The Wind in the Willows*, which is one of those books that consistently seems a favorite of people you'd never expect to fall for such coziness. (At times, Grahame's riverbank is so comforting that it makes Tolkien's shire look like Calcutta at high noon.) I suspect that part of what redeems Grahame for unsentimental readers is the irrepressible and genuinely irresponsible Toad, and perhaps the fact that Toad gets involved with high-speed motorcars, which brings an edge of technology into an otherwise archetypal animal-story idyll. It's a very delicate mix, and it takes a certain amount of *hubris* for William Horwood to try to recapture it in a new sequel, **The Willows in Winter**. But Horwood handles it surprisingly well. Having already established himself as one of the few modern masters of the animal story with his *Duncton Wood* series about moles, Horwood seems exactly the right person to take on the most famous mole in literature (and thus to lay claim to the dubious mantle of the century's leading author of mole fiction). *The Willows in Winter* opens with the reliable, Hobbit-like Mole relaxing by the fire when he receives what appears to be a summons for help from his friends Water Rat and Otter. The opening immediately recaptures Grahame's famous sense of warmth and comfort, and the stormy wintry setting immediately established Horwood's own claim to originality. (Even though part of Grahame's original took place around Christmas, you remember it as always spring.)

Mole disappears in an icy river, and when Water Rat and Badger set out to find him they are interrupted by Toad, who now is learning to fly a Bleriot airplane in place of his old motorcar. They attempt to enlist the aid of the plane in their search, but Mole's ambition and ego lead to a series of disasters culminating in his own near-execution and the apocalyptic destruction of everything he values. As with Grahame, much of the book splits into two separate narratives, one tracing the adventures of Mole in the Wide World, the other following his more modest friends in the Wild Wood. Although Horwood tends to anthropomorphize his characters a bit more than Grahame did (he refers to "hands" where Grahame said "paws," for example), he does a marvelous job of recapturing their personalities and recycling the familiar themes of friendship and loyalty.

But Horwood's best stroke lies in realizing that the reformed Toad at the end of *The Wind in the Willows* wasn't really reformed at all. Like many other readers, he felt that the taming of Toad meant sapping the book of its main source of energy, and that Toad's main appeal was that of the archetypal trickster — who can be frustrated and defeated, but never undone. Horwood's Toad is as outrageously selfish and insensitive as Grahame's, and Horwood wisely avoids the temptation to sentimentalize the characters and setting or to treat them as immovable icons. His use of an airplane may seem to be merely a convenient updating of Toad's motorcar, but he makes good use of it, and it even leads at one point to a moment of transcendent epiphany when Rat, falling from the plane, catches a glimpse of "Beyond," the vast world outside his own, including a distant city. It's a dramatic image of the fragility of the world of the willows, and a moving tribute to Grahame's own sense of endangered innocence.

As everyone knows, no other literary field comes close to science fiction and fantasy in making a fetish of its own illustrations. What is sometimes called "western art" — the work of Remington and others — was never really an offspring of western genre fiction, and the healthy tradition of fantastic painting and book illustration in the 19th century antedated the notion of modern genre literature altogether. Neither case represented the kind of cross-fertilization of writing and illustration that still puzzles people unfamiliar with the SF and fantasy field — where else would you find artists and illustrators honored with such ostensibly literary awards as the Hugo, or made major guests at conventions of readers? The usual reason given is that SF grew up in pulp magazines at a time when garish covers were needed to sell magazines, but SF isn't the only genre with such a history, and you don't see gift books and calendars celebrating the work of "hardboiled" artists or true romance illustrators. Nor does the impulse to illustrate seem so compelling in other genres; amateur convention art shows are still peppered with crude renderings of Mr. Spock (or, to be more current, Data), but I don't think I've ever seen an amateur painting of Philip Marlowe or even Columbo. There's something more going on here, and maybe we can get some clues from some of those art books that seem unique to the genre.

The Art of Michael Whelan, for example, is a beautifully produced, full-scale coffee table book from a brilliant artist who's clearly begun to transcend the category of "illustrator" (and whose works are often far more accomplished than the novels they decorate). About 100 color and numerous black-and-white plates are supplemented by Whelan's comments on each work and by three separate interviews (with Anne McCaffey on illustration, Terry Booth on Whelan's "personal" art, and David Cherry on techniques and materials); it's the sort of lavish volume one associates with popular mainstream artists like Dali or O'Keeffe. The people who buy those books have probably never heard of Whelan, but Bantam thinks there's a sizable market for this book, and there is — a market developed almost entirely among people who first learned of Whelan through their involvement with fiction rather than with art. For Whelan, it's a golden opportunity to lead his illustration-bred audience into his more personal artistic visions, such as his "Passage" series, and he makes the most of it.

The book is divided into two major sections. The first, which will be most familiar to Whelan fans, consists of the lush romantic images developed for book covers — a gallery of dragons developed for Anne McCaffrey and other commissions, Joan Vinge's Snow Queen and Summer Queen, several covers for horror anthologies or Stephen King books, C.J. Cherryh's catlike Hani and H. Beam Piper's Fuzzies (which, as Whelan admits, are "supposed to be irresistably cute," but which are so overboard they make Bambi look positively gimlet-eyed). In this section, Whelan shows a distinct preference for fantasy over high-tech hardware, and a great deal of sophistication in devising visual symbols for what he takes as major themes of the fiction, which he obviously reads thoroughly and sensitively (on occasion worrying over minor discrepancies with the text which few readers would likely notice). Two aspects of the appeal of SF art are evident here: Whelan can give convincing anatomical form to the bodies of imaginary creatures, and he can create the kind of vast, receding landscapes that are among the most stirring emblems of the sense of wonder (or, in its earlier incarnation, the sublime). Some of the works, such as his cover for Larry Niven's Destiny's Road, suggest the work of such earlier landscape visionaries as the Victorian John Martin, but with SF concepts replacing religious conceits.

The central image in the book, however — reproduced on the dust-jacket, in a color detail, and again in a color plate — is not an illustration, but rather "The Avatar," the first of Whelan's series of "Passage" paintings (the evocative series title, it turns out, has more to do with his determination to work more in oils than to any mystical enlightenment). This striking image of vaulting fluted columns surrounded by what appear to be flames in floating crystal spheres recalls the ruined cathedrals of Caspar David Friedrich (one of the handful of artists who provide epigraphs for the various sections of the book, giving us a hint of Whelan's interests if not of direct influences). It also suggests much about the possibilities of an SF art, because – like all the other "Passage" paintings – it seems to imply an unwritten SF or fantasy text. Those crystal spheres show up in several other paintings, and their counterpoint seems to be aging stonework, sometimes streaked with rust stains, that suggest a monumental but oppressive past. It isn't quite narrative art, but it isn't exactly free of narrative, either: one could almost tease an evolutionary fable out of these images of consciousness freed from architecture and (in a couple of later paintings) drawn toward green trees and lawns. In short, whether it has to do with his genre origins or the nature of his visual imagination, Whelan seems to be an SF artist even when he's not painting to a specific text and not using specifically SF iconography.

– February 1994, Locus #397 –

Brittle Innings: A Southern Gothic World War II Baseball Novel ~
~ Michael Bishop

Hot Sky at Midnight ~~ Robert Silverberg

Interface ~~ Stephen Bury

A Work of Art and Other Stories ~
~ James Blish, edited by Francis Lyall

Although I confess I haven't been keeping up with such things, I think it's a likely bet that some university, somewhere, has already offered a full-credit undergraduate course on baseball literature. There's certainly enough of it around, ranging from the formidable journalism of Roger Kahn to fiction by novelists as unexpected as Bernard Malamud. (I think there were even one or two pulps devoted to baseball stories.) There are all kinds of theories to account for this – the season makes a nice dramatic arc, the game alternates moments of high drama with stretches of inaction that can be filled by the writers' own preoccupations, the pitcher-batter confrontation seems much more a one-on-one test of character than most other sports permit. Some have even argued that the nature of the game itself is novelistic – it's the only major sport without a clock, and in theory can go on as long as it needs to play out the drama.

Less often noted is how often baseball fiction veers into the fantastic, from *Damn Yankees* to more recent novels and stories by James McManus, W.P. Kinsella, and even Nancy Willard. By 1981, there were already more than enough baseball SF stories to fill an anthology called *Baseball 3000*, and although few took advantage of the literary potential of the game, it provided solid evidence that SF writers are as fascinated as everyone else with what it all means. The problem, though, is that baseball writing tends toward nostalgia and pastoral, while SF tends in the opposite direction (what Tom Shippey calls "fabril" in *The Oxford Book of Science Fiction Stories*). You can't get a decent feel of the game just by introducing robot pitchers and low-gravity home runs.

So it was with considerable interest that I began **Brittle Innings**, Michael Bishop's self-styled "Southern Gothic World War II Baseball Novel." For one thing, it's by far the biggest baseball fantasy to date, and in many ways the most ambitious. For another, its subtitle is irresistible; it sounds like a looped-out screenwriter's desperate attempt to pitch a "concept" to a bored producer, and in fact (Bishop tells us in an afterword) there's already a finished screenplay based on an earlier unpublished novella version of the story. But the novel doesn't turn out to be nearly as wacky as all this sounds — it's not quite Flannery O'Connor meets Joe DiMaggio, but it isn't that far from it, either. For the most part, it's a brilliantly realized and often deeply moving mainstream coming-of-age novel about minor league ball in Georgia during the war years, and may be one of the best baseball novels I've ever read. The narrator, Danny Boles (who as a famous baseball talent scout is telling his tale to a reporter) learns about sex (including sexual abuse, which renders him speechless for much of the story), brutality, racism, and finally trust during his single season as a teenage rookie with a third-string minor league team in the Chattahoochee Valley League. Bishop takes full advantage of all the dramatic possibilities of the baseball novel that I mentioned above, but without resorting to easy nostalgia or celebrity-mongering (there are no ghosts of Shoeless Joe Jackson here, although FDR does get a cameo). This alone is a considerable achievement.

And it's also a sequel to *Frankenstein*. (After all, we're dealing with Michael *Bishop* here, the man who put Bob Dylan in the software business; did you expect something *normal*?) I trust I'm not giving anything away (I haven't seen how the novel is being publicized), but most SF readers will get suspicious as soon as they learn that the hulking and strangely literate first baseman who is Danny's roommate goes by the name of "Henry Clerval," one of the monster's first victims in Mary Shelley's classic. (Another minor joke is an umpire named Polidori.) The revelation comes less than halfway through the novel — which hardly makes it a surprise ending — and it demands attention, not only because it justifies reviewing this novel here at all, but because it gives rise to a narrative stroke so bold it borders on the nutty.

While Henry (more often called "Jumbo" for his size) is away, Danny rummages through his belongings and finds his journal. This journal, which we are treated to in great gobs, picks up the narrative of Frankenstein's monster exactly where Shelley's novel leaves him, in the arctic in the late 18th century. Suddenly, the folksy tone of the elderly Boles narrator is replaced by an uncanny replication of Shelley's relatively ornate style, as we learn how the monster survived, lived among the Inuit, altered his appearance, and eventually learned how to play baseball. We also learn — as if we didn't already know — why Danny's friendship is so important to him.

This shift in narrative is a ferociously creative and undoubtedly risky stroke, as Bishop now has to bring us back into the main narrative of Danny's own alienation, which (begging your pardon) seems decidedly minor league after what Henry has been through. He does this through a series of dramatic and at times gruesome incidents, culminating in an act of supreme if misguided friendship that effectively climaxes both Danny's and Henry's stories. *Brittle Innings* – the title refers to those innings in which a baseball game could go either way – doesn't really extend the SF premise of Shelley's novel, and at times it even seems to owe as much to the Karloff movies as to Shelley. Drawing equally on America's past and the past of SF, it's a masterpiece of its own kind, and its own kind, surprisingly, is exactly what the subtitle says it is.

Robert Silverberg's 1990 *Playboy* story "Hot Sky" ended up in Gardner Dozois's *Year's Best* anthology for that year, probably for its unremittingly bleak portrayal of a world ruined by pollution and greenhouse warming. There's as much bleakness in the novel **Hot Sky at Midnight,** and they are its main strengths – vivid descriptions of North American landscapes in an ecologically doomed 23rd century, when the main topic of debate among scientists is no longer how to reverse the greenhouse effect, but how to adapt to it. One school of thought argues that humanity should be re-bioengineered from the ground up – Silverberg makes the good point that the planet isn't being destroyed, it's only being rendered uninhabitable by oxygen-breathers like us – while the other holds that we might as well give up and go find a new planet. Already, the sky is peppered with L-5 colonies – which, like those in Joe Haldeman's *Worlds*, represent different societal models and affect contempt for the "dinkos" from earth.

The plot concerns two close friends, Nick Rhodes and Paul Carpenter, who hold very different positions in the same megacorporation, Samurai Industries. Rhodes is a geneticist struggling with the ethics of his project to redesign humanity, while Carpenter is a career-track executive who takes on the odd assignment of captaining an iceberg-retrieval ship. Both eventually become involved with an eyeless (but not really blind) corporate agent working secretly on an interstellar travel project, a possibly treacherous Latin seductress, an Israeli spy, and a group of California-based terrorists intent on taking over one of the L-5 colonies. Along the way, Carpenter ruins his career with an impulsive seafaring decision that very nearly turns him into Lord Jim (is Silverberg – who's already reimagined "Heart of Darkness" and "The Secret Sharer" – going to work his way through *all* of Conrad?), and Rhodes is torn between the temptations of corporate headhunters and the misgivings of his lover about his whole profession.

Silverberg knows how to keep his various plot lines moving crisply and quickly enough that you don't ask too many questions. But neither of his main characters are very interesting, and his treatment of women (as harpies and seducers) and future Israelis (as cynical paranoid spies) seems facile and stereotypical. The most arresting character, Farkas, is an eyeless product of genetic experiments who seems to have walked in from another novel entirely; his odd perceptions of the world are well matched by his oddly distorted moral sense. Silverberg generally seems more at home in his apocalyptic descriptions of a wasted earth, but even this material seems strangely passionless; Silverberg knows the scenarios of ecological doom so well that they become for him little more than technique. His major premise − that the earth may one day become unsalvageable for humans − is an important one, but by framing this premise in a tale of terrorist plots and bad career moves, he seems to have written a novel whose real theme, in terms of both ecology and the possibility of moral action in general, is giving up.

Interface is a near-future political thriller that isn't nearly as cyberpunkish as you would expect from the title − or from the fact that the "Stephen Bury" pseudonym is reportedly a collaborative effort between Neal Stephenson of Snow Crash fame and his uncle. There's little of the zonked-out Pynchonesque inventiveness of Snow Crash, and the SF elements, though crucial, involve minimal extrapolation: the development of a biochip that can replace damaged parts of the brain, and supersophisticated polling techniques involving wrist-TV monitors. What does seem familiar is the richness of convincing detail, the notion that the United States as a political and economic force is expendable, and the influence of a vast secret global conspiracy that would put the Illuminati crowd to shame. Interface is constructed as a bestseller in the Richard Condon tradition, but it's thought out as an SF novel.

Two simultaneous events set the plot in motion. At the very moment that the incumbent president announces a policy of capping payments on the national debt − in effect, forgiving the debt − William Cozzano, the governor of Illinois and a potential candidate, suffers a disabling stroke. The aforementioned worldwide conspiracy, which stands to lose trillions in lost debt payments, decides it's time to take over the world once and for all. Finding an Indian neurosurgeon working on the biochip implants and a young computer whiz trying to market the wristwatch polling device, they start putting together a heinous plot that is exciting in part because of its very predictability. Cozzano will become the first perfectly media-managed candidate: fitted out with the biochip, he can receive signals that program his responses to keep them instantaneously in synch with the reactions of a demographic sample outfitted with the wrist-TV monitors. Campaigning from his home in Tuscola, Illinois, Cozzano is a mixture of Michael Crichton's The Terminal Man and Ronald Reagan (unless Ronald Reagan was already such a mixture).

Needless to say, things begin to go wrong almost at once. Cozzano's neurologist daughter and his former legal adviser, aided by some conscience-stricken techies, get suspicious at the changes in her father's personality. An articulate Black woman, mistakenly chosen as a running mate because of an unpredictable error in the polling sample, proves a far stronger moral force than anyone expected. And one of the key polling subjects gets loony and begins to act out paranoid fantasies that, ironically, are almost exactly right. Much of the fun of the novel comes from watching how the authors have worked out in convincing detail the kind of high-tech presidential campaign that both the Republican and Democratic National Committees must be dreaming of right now – but there's some fun in spotting glitches as well. A key plot point, for example, depends on our believing that the technicians monitoring sensitive bioelectrical signals from their polling sample can't even tell when one of the wrist devices is suddenly being worn by another person entirely. Still, the vivid settings, fast action, and technical ingenuity of the novel make it an enjoyable thriller with largely unarticulated comic undertones.

One of the more encouraging minor trends I noted in last year's "year in review" column is the effort, usually on the part of small publishers, to keep in print the work of SF writers such as Sturgeon, Lafferty, and Cordwainer Smith. Occasionally, though – as with Lafferty – the focus has been on getting unpublished works in print, while the stories that made the author's reputation get more and more inaccessible. In selecting the nine stories and one short essay for **A Work of Art and Other Stories**, Francis Lyall has made little or no attempt to uncover the obscure or "lost" works of James Blish; all but one of the selections ("Statistician's Day") have been included in previous Blish collections, and one ("Common Time") has been anthologized at least a dozen other times. The intent seems to be to provide a sampler – or perhaps a primer for new readers – of Blish's short fiction, primarily from the 50s and 60s. It's a worthwhile endeavor, and a good book, even though the two best stories are likely to be the most familiar – "Common Time" and "How Beautiful with Banners," both of which deal in symbolic and poetic terms with alien encounters.

Blish's well-known love of music is evident in the title story, "A Work of Art," which plops a reconstituted Richard Strauss into the degraded musical world of the 22nd century; Strauss labors to complete a new work, only to realize that it lacks inspiration and that in fact he *himself* is the work of art of the title – the product of a "mind sculptor" who has reconstructed Strauss's mind and implanted it in a new body. Unfortunately, the story is dated by Blish's lamely imagined future musical technology and his prissy musical-modernist bias. "Testament of Andros," an experiment in multiple narrations of the same story that must have seemed startling in *Future Science Fiction* in 1953, also seems dated, in part because the parodies of SF styles are now barely recognizable. Nor does the alien group mind of "This Earth of Hours" seem as fascinating now as it did to Blish in 1959, although he handles the theme well. "There Shall Be No Darkness" is a pretty good werewolf story (which made a pretty good werewolf film, *The Beast Must Die*, in 1974), notable now mostly for its viral explanation of lycanthropy. "Statistician's Day," the only piece likely to be new to most Blish readers, is an ironic little satire on controlling population by killing off members of selected professions (not a bad idea, really), and "Who's In Charge Here," better known as "None So Blind," is an equally ironic treatment of blindness. The collection is rounded out with the two-page parody of program notes, "The Art of the Sneeze." This isn't a "best of" collection, and it doesn't fairly demonstrate Blish's range, but it's valuable for anyone who doesn't have much Blish short fiction, and it's in print.

– March 1994, Locus #398 –

Mortal Fire: Best Australian Science Fiction ~
~ edited by Terry Dowling and Van Ikin

Proud Man ~~ Katharine Burdekin ("Murray Constantine")

The Mushroom Jungle: A History of Postwar Paperback Publishing ~
~ Steve Holland

There was a time when for most North American readers the thought of Australian SF conjured up little more than *On the Beach*, A. Bertram Chandler, and perhaps vague thoughts about mutant koala bears. Then, beginning in the late sixties, a number of eye-opening anthologies began to appear from John Baxter, Damien Broderick, and others, coinciding roughly with the worldwide success of visionary filmmakers like Peter Weir and George Miller and the uniquely Anglo-Australian magic realism of Peter Carey. With the work of Donald Tuck and later Peter Nicholls, Australia also seemed to get an early hammerlock on the serious study of SF, and it's possible that this tradition of critical acuity has helped catalyze the fiction. For whatever reasons, Australia has managed to develop a home-grown New Wave that won't quit, and "Australian SF" now seems more like a movement than a sub-branch of a national literature. So we'd better pay attention when something like Terry Dowling and Van Ikin's **Mortal Fire: Best Australian SF** comes along, even if it means going out our way to look for it, because there's no telling what to expect.

Actually, that's not quite true; there are some things we have every right to expect. Those familiar with Terry Dowling's Rynosseros stories, such as in Twilight Beach, will find here the lead story from that collection, "Shatterwrack at Breaklight." Readers familiar with George Turner's convincingly bleak portrait of world economic collapse in his 1987 novel *The Sea and Summer* will recognize "The Fittest" as the bitter and powerful source story for that novel. Peter Carey's surrealistic "Report on the Shadow Industry" is from his famous collection *The Fat Man in History*, although the story was not included in the American edition of that book (which was actually culled from Carey's first two collections). And A. Bertram Chandler's "All Laced Up" (by far the book's oldest story, from 1961) is a cheerful but pretty standard visitor-from-the-future tale, its familiar mainstream SF flavor almost jarring in this context.

The rest of the book is mostly pleasant surprises. There are clearly a number of first-rate women writers in Australia, for example, best represented here by Lucy Sussex's "My Lady Tongue," which manages at once to embody a strongly feminist utopia and a subtle critique of doctrinaire feminism. Philippa Maddern's Ballardesque "Inhabiting the Interspaces," while less overtly concerned with feminism, nevertheless conveys a powerful sense of alienation in a tale of a woman living secretly in the recesses of an office building where she once worked. Rosaleen Love's "Trickster," a kind of joke on anthropologists, and Leanne Frahm's "A Way Back," about a plague of dinosaur sightings, are also original in both conception and execution. Cherry Wilder's "The Ark of James Carlyle" offers a more conventional SF setting, but as the protagonist defies orders to save his alien neighbors ("of no ethnological value") from a flood, he learns exactly the kind of lesson Le Guin would have him learn.

There are relatively few variations of standard SF plots. Two of the tales, Greg Egan's "Axiomatic" and David Ireland's "Death of a Thousand Cuts," offer ingenious futuristic murder plots; Egan manages a genuinely appropriate plot twist in a tale of a man who buys a temporary personality implant to enable him to commit a revenge killing, while Ireland's gory SF horror tale suffers from an unconvincing medical premise. David Lake's "Creator" is an enjoyable but predictable microcosmic-god tale, and much the same might be said of Damien Broderick's time-loop story "Coming Back" (which nevertheless is a clear anticipation of the film *Groundhog Day*) and Van Ikin's first-contact story "The Juronka Validation".

The remaining selections seem to me to be genuine originals. Sean McMullen's "The Colours of the Masters" is a rare SF story about music, which would probably have delighted James Blish, who was always on the lookout for such things. The title character of Michael Wilding's "The Man of Slow Feeling" finds his nervous system slowed down following an accident, so that sensations take hours to reach his brain — a kind of neurological "Slow Glass." And John Baxter's "Apple" — the most overt piece of surrealism in the book — is about miners threatened by giant moths as they excavate a mountain-sized apple. Whether memorable images such as this have anything in particular to do with Australia seems unlikely — in fact, Dowling's tale is the only one in the collection that makes full use of imaginary Australia-scapes — but it does suggest that there's something about being large and underpopulated that leads to a disproportionate amount of first-rate SF.

Katharine Burdekin, who died in 1963, has remained all but invisible in critical and historical works about SF; even Sarah Lefanu's generally well-informed *Feminism and Science Fiction* misidentifies her 1934 novel **Proud Man** as a "future dystopia," and most readers who have heard of Burdekin know her only through the spookily prescient *Swastika Night* (1937), which — published two years before the invasion of Poland — depicted a Europe some seven centuries after Hitler's conquest, and remains Burdekin's best work. Both of these novels were published under the name "Murray Constantine," not so much to gain the added leverage of a male name but — according to Daphne Patai in her afterword to the new Feminist Press edition of *Proud Man* – to protect Burdekin's family from possible repercussions against such strongly antifascist work. This alone tells us something of the atmosphere in which Burdekin was writing, and of her perceptive understanding of the appeal of fascism. (Burdekin had already published two time-travel fantasies under her own name in the 1920s.)

The Feminist Press has already reprinted *Swastika Night* and, in 1989, published for the first time Burdekin's far-future feminist utopia *The End of This Day's Business*. Now, with *Proud Man* once again available, it's becoming clear that Burdekin deserves recognition as the leading feminist utopian writer of her era, as well as one of the most thoughtful and provocative SF writers of the 1930s – and possibly as one of the more influential as well. Olaf Stapledon knew her work, and Daphne Patai has provided suggestive evidence that *Swastika Night* may have been one of the unacknowledged influences on Orwell's 1984. *Proud Man*, about a visitor from a far-future hermaphroditic utopia to 1930s England, seems in many ways to anticipate Doris Lessing's *Canopus in Argos* series, with its long expository passages and coolly analytical questioning of the more irrational aspects of human behavior. And the notion of exploring the role of sex in human affairs from the perspective of a character from a society without sexes prefigures Le Guin by three and a half decades.

For me (as I suspect for many readers), exposition is the sugar in the gas of utopian fiction: no matter how profound these great gouts of social analysis, they tend to bring narratives chugging to an ungainly halt, and to reduce characters to the status of spokespersons. Burdekin isn't entirely free of this, but her strategy is interesting. The first 50 pages of *Proud Man* – the section titled "The Person" – is virtually nothing but an account of "subhuman" society (us) as seen by a distant-future "Person" (the narrator), focusing largely but by no means exclusively on the role of sex in human personal and social development. It's clear that Burdekin was familiar with Freud, and her narrator's disingenuous comments include ingenious reworkings of such concepts as penis envy. It can be rough going, though, if you're expecting something to happen.

But then things *do* start to happen. Upon arriving in the 20th century, the narrator is taken in by a kindly but spiritually confused priest, who suspects – partly because of the narrator's telepathic powers – that an angel has come into his life. Disguised as a woman, the narrator lives with the priest until local gossips force them both to leave the village. He gives "her" enough money to set up a life in London, where "she" befriends and lives with an aspiring woman novelist still mourning the death of her child. "She" helps the novelist gain confidence and come to terms with her loss, and then sets off to explore the "other" half of society – the male world – disguised as a man. The plot takes a decidedly odd turn as "he" now takes up the case of a guilt-ridden child-murderer, who turns out to have been traumatized at a young age by his mother's death. The rigorous analytical tone of Burdekin's narrator (whom Patai compares to *Star Trek's* Mr. Spock) is tested by what seems to be a sympathetic portrayal of a child-killer, until we remember that the narrator is truly without sympathies, and that we cannot help reading "human" motivations into "his" actions.

The novel's ending seems decidedly abrupt, and the often contrived manner in which the mysterious stranger's ingenuous probings help various characters solve their problems seems at times like so much facile psychoanalysis. We get very little information about the narrator's own society, and the strongest SF-narrative aspect of the book is the way it explores the interpersonal effects of telepathy. But Burdekin's real strength is her relentless and unsentimental analysis of a startling range of human behaviors, from war and economics to homosexuality and hair and clothing styles. During her time in London, the narrator has occasion to read and comment on Huxley's *Brave New World* and *Point Counter Point*. This not only gives us a sense that Burdekin knew quite well the tradition in which she was writing, but that she viewed that tradition with a kind of critical insight we would not see again until the feminist writers of the 1970s and 1980s. The fact that she has all but disappeared from that tradition ought to be an embarrassment to SF history, and The Feminist Press deserves much credit for giving her a second chance.

Last May I reviewed Philip Harbottle and Stephen Holland's *Vultures of the Void: A History of British Science Fiction Publishing 1946-1955*, an entertaining if piecemeal chronicle of a justly-ignored era of British SF, when publishers of truly Dickensian sleaziness would sometimes lock writers in the basement to hack out reams of junk fiction, under appalling deadlines (reportedly 70,000 words per week in the particular case in question), for a pulp paperback industry that even Rupert Murdoch would find embarrassing. That writer-locked-in-the-basement story, which sounds suspiciously like a colorful bit of publishing folklore, is repeated in Holland's **The Mushroom Jungle: A History of Postwar Paperback Publishing**, but with the additional testimony of a corroborating witness. It's a small example of the greater discipline and thoroughness of this full-fledged study of the postwar British paperback industry (the title refers to the fly-by-night publishers who proliferated in vast numbers during this time) as compared to the anecdotal nature of *Vultures of the Void*. Holland apparently knows more about what's under this rock than anyone, and his detailed accounts of print runs and buyouts can get a bit monotonous, but for scholars of this sort of thing (if there are any), it's likely to be the standard resource for some time to come.

If the hero of *Vultures of the Void* was John Russell Fearn, who as Vargo Statten sold some five million copies of SF books in the early 1950s, the hero on this broader canvas is the even more forgotten Stephen Frances, whose ridiculously tough "Hank Janson" gangster stories sold more than twenty million, stayed in print into the 1970s, and even got reprinted in America. (Near the end of his career, Frances wrote a well-received Spanish Civil War epic, *La Guerra*, but he died in obscurity in 1989.) It becomes clear that the pseudo-American gangster epic was the basic model for other genres as well, leading to such SF titles as *The Human Bat v. the Robot Gangster* and to endless fake tough-guy dialogue drawn from American B-movies. An exception might be the Westerns, which were often written in an impenetrable version of American cowboy slang and bore equally impenetrable titles such as *Owlhoot Triggers for the Law*. You can't help wonder what kind of writing lies behind such titles, and Holland gives you about as much as you can stand by way of examples; nor can you help but wonder how they came up with those wonderful house names (two of my favorites from the SF lists are "Vektis Brack" and "Bengo Mistral," the latter of whom is credited by Holland as the author of "the worst single piece of fiction ever published," *Pirates of Cerberus*). Holland describes how all the major genres of pop fiction got trashed by these small-time sleazelords, discusses the major authors and cover artists of the period, and offers some supplementary material on censorship trials and the anti-horror comics campaign in Britain. Several publishers and writers actually spent substantial time in jail under a Victorian obscenity law, which would seem outrageous if you didn't suspect they deserved it on the basis of sentence structure alone. While Holland's focus is not exclusively on SF, he offers enough insights into the British pulp world to provide convincing evidence that Americans never again need apologize for Hugo Gernsback or Ray Palmer or even Mickey Spillane. On the other hand, who might be the American Vektis Brack?

— April 1994, Locus #399 —

Mysterium ~~ Robert Charles Wilson

Flux ~~ Stephen Baxter

Anti-Ice ~~ Stephen Baxter

Parable of the Sower ~~ Octavia E. Butler

Robert Charles Wilson has a talent for depicting communities under stress and a predilection for alternate worlds, so it's not surprising that he would eventually try his hand at the old saw of the community mysteriously cut off from its familiar surroundings. Following an explosion at a secret government research facility, the entire town of Two Rivers, Michigan finds itself surrounded by dense forest, its roads and power lines neatly cut off in all directions. We've seen this sort of business handled by everyone from Rod Serling to Stephen King to Karen Joy Fowler, and we know just what questions to ask: is it an alien experiment? A time displacement? A mad scientist's experiment? An alternate world? This being a Wilson novel, of course it's the latter: Two Rivers has been plopped into a world in which the Roman empire was never Christianized and gnostic Christianity was permitted to flourish. That's a fairly distant point of divergence, but the repressive wilderness midwest which results isn't a lot different from, say, Phyllis Eisenstein's alternate Illinois in her *Shadow of*

Earth, which posited a world derived from a victorious Spanish Armada. There's also a mad scientist of sorts in the book, keeping in mind that in post-paranoid SF, a mad scientist is anyone in charge of a secret government project. (If it weren't secret, the logic seems to go, they wouldn't have to hire a goofball to run it.)

The secret government project in Two Rivers is established to investigate a strange and deadly alien artifact originally discovered in Turkey in 1989. Wilson does a fine job of convincing us that this thing is really alien, with just enough hard SF to permit the mad scientist in question, Alan Stern, to draw loopy connections between his own brand of gnosticism and quantum reality. These ideas are handled deftly enough, but they aren't really the focus of the book. The main character, Dex Graham, is one of Wilson's decent, conscientious, but basically ordinary characters who find hidden resources when faced with the unknown. And the characters who surround Dex – his sometime lover Evelyn Woodward, 12-year-old Clifford Graham, the young physicist Howard Poole, the alternate-world anthropologist Linneth Stone – are for the most part also decent and sympathetic. On the other hand, the Nazi-like alternate-America Proctors and the military overlords they send to occupy Two Rivers are as ruthless and one-dimensional as you'd expect – and their plans for Two Rivers are just as brutal.

Obviously, Wilson has a lot of balls to juggle in a relatively short narrative, and I haven't even mentioned the atomic bomb which provides the major suspense-hook. The fact that he's able to bring it all off without significantly slowing the tightening spiral of the adventure-story plot, with its hairbreadth rescues and heartless betrayals, is strong evidence of Wilson's economy in both plot and style. For all its weird gnostic physics and alternate world-building, the novel leaves you with the same odd mixture of sentiment and nostalgia that has been Wilson's trademark ever since *A Hidden Place*. It's not a bad trademark to have, even though it does mean everyone compares him to Sturgeon. With last year's *The Harvest* and now **Mysterium**, maybe it's time we permit Wilson to graduate from this imposed apprenticeship, and to recognize that much of what he does is entirely his own.

Now here are two novels by Stephen Baxter, one of the most interesting newer hard-SF writers, and like it or not I'm going to have to use the word "tropes" in discussing them. One of the most popular tropes of hard SF is what we might call (borrowing a phrase from George Eliot) the Lifted Veil – the rediscovery of immensity from the perspective of a closed or limited environment. It's central to Asimov's "Nightfall," Heinlein's "Universe," Clarke's *The City and the Stars*, and most of their myriad descendants, and it's clearly attractive to Baxter as well. **Flux** offers one of the most radically circumscribed environments I've seen in quite a while, and even getting into the narrative proper involves slogging through such a soup of speculative physics that all but the most devoted hard-SF readers may be put off. Despite this, the plot begins like a pastoral fantasy: A small band of hardy country folk lose most of their herd of pigs in a bad storm. To replenish the herd, a boy, his sister, and an older man venture into the forest where the old man is seriously wounded by a renegade boar. Rescued by the inhabitants of a nearby city, the boy and girl are forced into indentured servitude to pay for the older man's medical expenses. She's sent to work on a farm while he becomes a fisherman. Another storm, which may be caused by an alien spacecraft, damages the city so severely that the old man, whose folk-knowledge of the aliens may offer clues on how to fight them, is called upon to advise the city fathers. But the needed weapons may be buried far beneath the sea, so plans are made to build a submarine to search for them.

This is roughly the first half of the novel, and even in summary it's a textbook case of the kind of language-referent problems that Samuel Delany has argued are central to SF – and that are especially problematical in the kinds of circumscribed hard-SF environments I mentioned earlier. Words like "man," "pig," "forest," "city," "fisherman," "storm," "sea," and hundreds of others demand to be read metaphorically – as convenient images to make the narrative comprehensible – because the spectacular setting of all this is inside the mantle of a neutron star. Baxter's humans are only some ten microns tall and composed of tin nuclei; they live in a chaos of synesthesia in which they see sound waves, smell photons, and hear temperature variations. "Pigs" (actually "Air-pigs") are primitive life forms that inhabit the mantle, a "storm" is a disturbance in the star's magnetic field, the "sea" is the "quantum sea" of the star's core, even the "air" is a superfluid-charged neutron gas. Baxter doesn't tell you this in anything so simple as a second-chapter infodump; instead he thrusts you *in medias res* during that first storm, leaving you to sort out dense speculative physics and the natives' own odd terms for these phenomena ("Glitch," "Magfield," "upflux," etc.). This is defamiliarization with a vengeance.

Baxter can obviously work out superhard-SF environments with the best of them, but as is often the case – and here I think of Larry Niven, Robert Forward, Hal Clement, and perhaps James Blish's "pantropy" series – the question arises as to whether the payoff, the lifting of the veil, is going to be worth it. In the case of *Flux*, Baxter's revelations involve bringing back the Xeelee, the mysterious race of super-aliens from his earlier work, uncovering some dark secrets about ancient wars and the real reasons that these submicro-humans were created, and – almost inevitably – revealing to a viewpoint character (in this case the girl Dura) the True Nature of the Universe. Baxter has a stunning talent for conceptualization, but at times seems so infatuated with it that he asks it to carry too much weight. His big revelation scene works intellectually, and opens up the novel in a classically satiSFying way, but it's underlined with hokey, portentous dialogue that might have come out of a Harry Harrison parody. When we're having the stars and galaxies revealed to us as if for the first time, it's best not to be reminded that our heroes are, literally, made of tin.

Baxter's other new novel – actually published before *Flux* – shows less spectacle but more grace and humor, and is far more accessible to the general reader. Anti-Ice also explores an increasingly familiar trope: Victorian England retrofitted in high-tech. SF of the last few years has given us Victorian computers, Victorian spaceships, and Victorian megaweapons, but *Anti-Ice* is almost certainly the first novel to give us Victorian superconductors. In 1720, a new "Little Moon" appears over Europe, and a fireball crashes into Antarctica, where British explorers later discover a lode of what comes to be called Anti-Ice. An efficient superconductor at low temperatures, Anti-Ice is unstable and highly explosive when allowed to warm up. The brilliant engineer Josiah Traveller – a kind of amalgam of I.K. Brunel and Wells's Cavor – dramatically demonstrates the destructive power of Anti-Ice at the siege of Sebastopol in 1855, and by 1870, the time of the main narrative, English technology has come to thoroughly dominate Europe with anti-ice driven monorails, mining machines, ocean liners, a giant land leviathan, and even an experimental aircraft which is now Traveller's principal means of transportation. The analogies with nuclear power and the cold war are obvious.

But Baxter isn't averse to having fun with this premise. The narrator, Ned Vicars – Bedford to Traveller's Cavor – contrives to attend the launching ceremony of the massive landship *Prince Albert*, hoping to catch sight of a French girl he's fallen in love with. The *Prince Albert* is so huge that Traveller's airship *Phaeton* can land comfortably on its garden-like promenade deck, and Vicars, together with a journalist named Holden, is being shown around the *Phaeton* by Traveller and his servant when French saboteurs simultaneously hijack the airship and sabotage the land liner. Suddenly we're in a fast-moving and ingenious pastiche of a Victorian space opera, as the *Phaeton* rises uncontrollably beyond earth's atmosphere, using up its precious fuel supply of water and heading toward the moon. Baxter evokes wonderfully the cozy drawing-room atmosphere that writers like Serviss once imagined space travel would be like, and whips up some genuinely unexpected surprises on the far side of the moon.

Unfortunately, this neat adventure ends with more than a fifth of the novel to go, with Baxter not only tying up various loose ends, but staging an almost gratuitous battle spectacle and offering too much speculation on the emerging balance of power in Europe. Anti-Ice is a wonderful concept, but isn't it a bit much to go on about what Bismarck might have done with it, or what its effect might be on the eventual election of Lloyd George? None of this is so intrusive as to fatally slow down the narrative, but it does demonstrate one of the hazards of writing alternate history – namely, the temptation to work it out in more detail than the plot warrants, as though you were really writing history. It's a minor cavil in what is generally a thoroughly enjoyable novel and a provocative contribution to one of SF's more colorful emerging subgenres – pseudo-Victoriana.

Even people who suspect that Octavia Butler's near-unique status – a major SF writer who is also a Black woman – gives her an exceptional degree of mainstream visibility have to admit that, all other considerations aside, she is one of the field's treasures. She has staked out a clearly identifiable region of important concerns, generally clustered around the complex dynamics of genetics, social decay, and enslavement, and within this region she has consistently demonstrated an ability to combine large-scale SF concepts with gritty, at times almost savage portrayals of believable settings and events. Her celebrity hasn't seemed to affect her fiction much, although it apparently has given leave to Four Walls Eight Windows, the small-press publisher of her new novel **Parable of the Sower**, to treat it more or less like a mainstream novel even though it's pure SF from beginning to end. (*Kindred* was much closer to mainstream with its deliberate de-emphasis of its time-travel motif.) And the novel itself, which is for the most part a harrowing tale of survival in a 21st century U.S. devastated by environmental and economic collapse, may show the beginning signs of guru-ism. Whether this is intentional on Butler's part I can't say, but in a strange way the novel's antecedents are as diverse as *Stranger in a Strange Land, Dune*, and *Always Coming Home* – all works which described belief systems that proved attractive to readers quite apart from their fictional contexts.

In Butler's case, this system is a non-revelatory, non-supernatural religion called "Earthseed," which is developed in the notebooks of the novel's teenage narrator, Lauren Oya Olamina, as her society collapses around her. The daughter of a minister, Lauren is increasingly dissatisfied with the inability of existing religious beliefs to provide a usable model for moral choices in a world that seems out of control. "God is Change" is the motto of Earthseed, which emphasizes adaptability, diversity, and – as its only transcendental goal – the eventual colonization of other worlds. This goal is especially interesting in light of Butler's portrayal of a society that can't even afford to hold itself together, much less mount a space program; you begin to wonder if Butler hasn't thought this up after having repeatedly been confronted with the old "how can you support space programs when people are starving?" argument. And except for being called a religion and expressed through portentous verses that head each chapter, Earthseed isn't a lot different from what SF writers and scientific humanists have been saying for decades. There are echoes in it of Julian Huxley, of Carl Sagan, even of what Donald Wollheim called the "consensus cosmonogy" of golden age SF: manifest destiny among the stars, and muddling through until we get there.

I've spent too much time talking about Earthseed partly because Butler draws so much attention to it that I suspect that we haven't heard the last of it. But in terms of the larger novel, Lauren's musings don't really interfere all that much with Butler's driving narrative skill. The main story, told through Lauren's journal entries between 2024 and 2027, depicts in prose of persuasive and painful directness the collapse of the embattled enclaves which try to hold on to a semblance of civilization, the dangers Lauren faces as she takes to a road filled with thousands of other displaced persons, and the tentative growth of a community around her. Drug-induced arson, murder, rape, even cannibalism are presented with an hallucinatory clarity which is multiplied by Lauren's hypersensitive empathy: she can't even shoot someone without also feeling the pain. (We've seen empaths before in SF, but I can't recall anyone putting them in an environment this brutal.) Butler makes us empaths, too: we feel the fear and pain of all the little catastrophes, even though the details of the larger catastrophe are never fully worked through. (The flight from urban centers and the implication that the rest of the world hasn't been as hard hit as the U.S. suggest that Butler has simply adapted the model of a post-nuclear wasteland; we're never sure how ecology and economics have led to all this.) Lauren, her lover Bankole, and the other characters who accompany them on their quest for safe ground are convincing enough, and the quest itself is so detailed you could follow it on a map. But if the world depicted in *Parable of the Sower* ever comes to pass, it's hard to believe that a gentle philosophy like Earthseed is going to make much difference.

– May 1994, Locus #400 –

I. Asimov ~~ Isaac Asimov

White Shark ~~ Peter Benchley

Terminal Games ~~ Cole Perriman

Gun, with Occasional Music ~~ Jonathan Lethem

Unconquered Countries: Four Novellas ~~ Geoff Ryman

Mind Fields: The Art of Jacek Yerka / The Fiction of Harlan Ellison

---

A frustrated creative writing teacher once told me about a student who turned in a draft of a story, apologizing that he still had to go back over it to "put in the symbols." Isaac Asimov, who thankfully never worried much about putting in the symbols, seems to have written *I. Asimov* with the express intent of putting in the opinions that were largely invisible in his first two thick volumes of autobiography. Both *In Memory Yet Green* and *In Joy Still Felt* – titles taken from a fake "anonymous" poem that Asimov wrote expressly to yield up such titles – were strict chronological accounts of Asimov's life and career, offering few real insights but standing as monuments to the pure power of anecdote. You found yourself reading page after page of details about a life at least as uneventful as your own, captivated in part by the very mundanity that ought to be putting you to sleep.

Near the end of *I. Asimov*, when Asimov is describing how his wife Janet persuaded him to undertake this new autobiography (although Janet insists in an afterward that he really wanted to do it), he offers the disarmingly simple observation that "I have a pleasant writing style and can keep people reading, whatever I write." Short of a complex stylistic analysis, that's about all you can say about what makes Asimov's prose so engaging. He was our era's great artist of explanation, a master of the declarative sentence and the lockstep paragraph, and both his fiction and his nonfiction conspire to convince you that the world makes more sense than you thought it did. *I. Asimov* – Asimov himself preferred the title *Scenes from Life*, another line from that same poem, but Doubleday has opted for the pun on *I, Robot* – is no exception.

For all his 470-odd books and his legendary contributions to the development of SF, Asimov may well earn belated recognition as one of the premier short essayists of our time. *I. Asimov* takes full advantage of this, consisting of 166 short chapters on a variety of topics and people that were important to him. More than a quarter of these chapters, not surprisingly, concern Asimov's own writings, and another quarter are sketches of specific people, mostly family members and SF personalities. The latter is a who's who of four decades of SF: Pohl, Kornbluth, Wollheim, Campbell, Heinlein, de Camp, Simak, Williamson, del Rey, Sturgeon, Clarke, Gold, Boucher, Garrett, Ellison, Bova, Clement, Silverberg, Martin H. Greenberg.

For the most part, Asimov's true feelings about these people, revealed at last, are hardly the stuff of lid-blowing; the man seems to have been almost pathologically affable. But whereas the earlier volumes reduced almost everyone to walk-on roles in Asimov's galloping chronology, here they become real, and even the most familiar stories take on a new light. The split with Campbell over dianetics, for example, is treated gingerly in *In Memory Yet Green*, but what Asimov politely called "mysticism" in that earlier book is here treated as what we all know it was – a fatal romance with pseudo-science that critically weakened *Astounding* and turned Campbell into a "diminishing shadow of what he had once been." (Elsewhere, Asimov misses the boat when he suggests that only his own writings have kept Campbell's name alive – an indirect expression of the fear that his own name may fade. Fat chance.) Similarly, Heinlein's occasional mean-spiritedness and growing right-wing militance (which Asimov seems to ascribe, Reagan-like, to a change of wives) is treated candidly, as are Sturgeon's growing financial problems late in life. But for the most part, Asimov is generous with his fellow writers and friends. He is less forgiving of his first wife Gertrude, but even here he seeks to find some logical external cause for their growing incompatibility (mainly, it seems, she smoked – even though it took more than 30 years for this and other factors to lead to divorce).

Anyone hoping for insights into the Asimovian creative process – exactly where the Foundation stories or the robot stories came from and how they were shaped – won't find much more help here than in the earlier autobiographies. To the end (and much of *I. Asimov* was written from the hospital bed when he knew his days were numbered), Asimov seems genuinely mystified by his own talent. He recounts again the famous story of how Campbell gave him the assignment for "Nightfall," but he hasn't a clue as to why the story was so popular. Nor did he seem to think there was much special about the Foundation series when he turned it over to Gnome Press in 1951. When he tries to explain the dynamics of his straight-ahead, no-nonsense narrative style, he ends up throwing up his hands. When he achieves unexpected emotional impact – which seems to be how he gauges his own favorite stories ("The

Last Question," "The Bicentennial Man," "The Ugly Little Boy") — he simply ascribes it to "writing over my head" and can't figure out how he did it. For a man who seemed almost as egotistical as he says he is, he is constantly amazed at his own successes — the most artless of major artists.

For all its congeniality, however, *I. Asimov* is inescapably the work of a dying man. In a three-page chapter titled "Gathering Shadows," he obsessively details the deaths of no fewer than 26 friends, and the chapters dealing with his own heart attack, triple bypass, and later hospitalizations reveal an odd mixture of clinical detail, resignation, and embarrassment at his own mortality. By the very end of the book, detailing his activities in May of 1990, Asimov returns to the simple catalog-of-events style of his earlier autobiographies, almost as if to show us that he was simply too busy to die. The very reserve and lack of sentimentality with which Asimov treats his progressive physical decline give these chapters an almost heartbreaking quality, but he never ceases from explanation — even when it's his own leaking mitral valve in question. I couldn't help suspect that the fabled Asimovian wit must have seen in this final confrontation with mortality the seeds of the greatest explanatory challenge of all — *Asimov's Guide to Death*. *I. Asimov* is a sad book, and in some ways a tired one, and it does nothing to modify the classic Asimovian view of himself as a convivial genius — no grumbles from the grave here. But if Asimov wants to be charmingly opaque until the end, what's to complain about? A man is entitled to his own myth.

Sometimes we get asked why we don't pay more attention to "bestsellers," meaning, presumably, novels (almost never story collections) whose principal defining characteristic is the number of people expected to buy them. "Bestsellers" in this sense doesn't mean the same thing as bestselling books; we're talking here not just about books that sell well, but that are *designed* to sell well. Nor is it the same thing as popularity; as movie distributors know, you can frontload ticket sales so effectively that even the mangiest film opens like a hit — at least until everybody realizes they hate it. (For much the same reason, advance review copies of surefire bestsellers are sometimes not even sent out.) In cases like this, a high concept may be popular enough to jumpstart sales, but the end product — the movie or novel — can cheat you a thousand ways from Sunday and almost get away with it. The point is, such a work doesn't have to be *liked*, it only has to be *bought*.

To test this notion, I loaned Peter Benchley's monster-movie book **White Shark** to a friend who enjoys such things (actually, I didn't even have to loan it — he just grabbed it from me), and he dived in with the enthusiasm I imagine characteristic of the kick-back summer beach readers who are going to make sure this thing sells a zillion copies from airport newsstands alone. (Airport newsstands may have more to do with the aesthetics of bestsellers than we'd like to admit, since all an airport novel really has to do is be marginally more interesting than the dog-eared Sharper Image catalog in the seatback in front of you.) Within a couple of hours, my friend began asking me, "Is this going to get any better?" and later, "Why did you get me into this?" But had he been an actual summer reader, he wouldn't have had me to blame.

White Shark, like Benchley's much better *Jaws*, is about people getting eaten. But while the people-eater of that earlier book was an elemental force of nature, only slightly exaggerated from actual case histories, Benchley's new monster is clearly science fictional. Those who remember the "Saturday Night Live" TV parodies of *Jaws* − about a "land shark" − will catch on all too quickly to what Benchley is wreaking with his own formula, and may have to be reminded that this really is Peter Benchley and not Robert. But there's more: this is not just a land shark, but a *Nazi* land shark. (I said this was high concept.) At the end of World War II, a mad Nazi scientist (not Mengele; the not-quite-Mengele scientist has become almost as much a staple of Nazi thrillers as the Holocaust survivor with a decades-long vendetta − who also shows up on cue here) escapes in a U-boat with a prototype of a genetically altered amphibious warrior. The U-boat sinks, but the monster, sealed in a metal coffin, spends the next 50 years developing an appetite. When he's inadvertently freed, he acts just like a shark in water but then (literally) pukes his guts out and begins breathing air. Up against him are a marine biologist, a child, and a Native American too tough even to be played by Robert Shaw. Of course, the local authorities refuse to cancel the summer festival despite mounting evidence that something is treating their tourists like potato salad.

So what do we have here − "The Jaws from Brazil"? More important, what can you say about this in terms of SF? Is it even necessary to point out that the limited tactical value of such an uncontrollable Pac-man would be evident to the most lame-brained Nazi commander? Or that Benchley works out his speculative biology with about as much attention to detail as *The Creature from the Black Lagoon*? What makes it fundamentally useless to try to review a novel such as this − apart from the fact that reviews will not make a whit of difference to the book's readership − is that, in SF terms, it has nothing to say. In fact, like many monster movies and monster-movie novels, it turns SF against itself. Whereas the best SF expands the imagination by opening up possibilities − by setting loose ideas that grow even after the plot has wrapped up − novels like *White Shark* work to close down the imagination by literalizing paranoia and reducing moral issues to questions of who and what ought to get killed. Perhaps the best example of Benchley's ambiguous integrity is this: like *Jaws*, *White Shark* is filled with little lectures on how more people are killed by lightning (or by pigs!) than by sharks, which are really only the misunderstood targets of irrational fears. Then he uses his narrative skills to whip these same irrational fears to a frenzy − he's probably done more than any other writer to create the very paranoia he ostensibly condemns. Don't be afraid of the monster under your bed, but this is what he looks like while he's eating you.

Now here's another one. **Terminal Games,** by "Cole Perriman" (Wim Coleman and Pat Perrin, according to the copyright page) also takes a limited SF concept – interactive computer environments – and hammers it back into a bestseller mode. A woman discovers that simulated murders in a popular on-line network are re-enactments of real murders, and the question is who among the thousands of subscribers might be a killer. This is a passable premise for a murder mystery, and it might open out in all sorts of ways. The authors seem familiar with the kind of surrogate sex and power games that are increasingly characteristic of these nets, and they set up the promise of a clever computer detective story. There's no reason for the novel to be anything more than that, and no reason for it to move in the direction of SF, but it does because it needs a gimmick to push it out of the mystery genre and into bestsellerdom. (The differences between bestsellers and genre fiction are a topic for another column altogether.) As a computer-SF-mystery, the novel can't hold a candle to say, Gibson's *Virtual Light*, but the concepts there are far too complicated for the audience Perriman is after – an audience who suspects that all those people at their PCs are doing something vaguely unhealthy, but that isn't sure how it all works. So we get a detective whose understanding of computers rivals that of Sheriff Andy of Mayberry, and lots of primer-style explanations designed to bring him (and us) up to snuff. I'm not all that familiar with the architecture of existing networks or just how speculative all this is, but the most unnerving single aspect of the novel's publicity release is a claim that it's written "with the scientific probability of *Jurassic Park*".

The main SF element involves a renegade artificial intelligence loose in the net. It's not a big concept by SF standards, and it's certainly not as goofy as a non-Mengelian Nazi land shark, but it's interesting because of the way in which it co-opts the developing detective story. This time, it's not a matter of using SF against itself, but using SF against mysteries. What seems like a perfectly serviceable whodunit metastasizes, at the end, into the beginning of a rather low-concept SF novel, and I can't imagine either mystery or SF readers being very satisfied with it. As with *White Shark*, the SF ideas, which ought to open things up, instead are used to shut things down – because the issue once again is not where the ideas lead, but who's going to get it. The trick used to defeat the AI won't come as much of a surprise to anyone who's read an Asimov robot story – or for that matter to anyone who's seen the film *War Games.*

Both of these novels are more or less readable, and both pace their narratives briskly enough to keep you intrigued until the cabin attendant shows up with the peanuts. Each is careful to sketch in enough background about the principal characters to create the illusion that a novel is actually happening, but each begins slamming doors in your face as soon as you begin to get interested in either the characters or the central concepts. This doesn't mean that you can't successfully adapt SF concepts to the thriller format – that's been done often and well – but here the exigencies of the bestseller recipe conspire to trivialize both genres. These are novels meant to be consumed, not read, and reviewing them is about as useful as a restaurant critic taking on the new McDonald's that just opened. That Sharper Image catalog is beginning to look pretty intriguing.

Jonathan Lethem's oddball **Gun, with Occasional Music** is another attempt to blend mystery and SF, and to my mind a much more interesting one than *Terminal Games*. I don't think it entirely succeeds, but it takes some crazy chances and never compromises its quirky vision, which contains elements of *Fahrenheit 451*, Cordwainer Smith, and *Who Censored Roger Rabbit?* Conrad Metcalf, a hardboiled private eye whose first-person narrative is a parody of Raymond Chandler wisecrackery, lives in a 21st century world following some unspecified "Inquisition" which has rendered social intercourse circumspect – no one asks questions of anyone else – and in which memory itself is becoming increasingly illegal. Free drugs with names like Forgettol, Avoidol, and Regrettol keep the population in check, and something called "evolution therapy" has transformed animals into an intelligent underclass and replaced children with rapidly-maturing "babyheads." Print is obsolete; newspapers consist only of pictures and even radio reports give only musical impressions of the news. Citizens are assigned "karmic points," which are deducted from their cards at the discretion of "inquisitors"; run out of points and you end up in a deepfreeze or on a slave farm. Metcalf's client is about to suffer such a fate after being falsely accused of murder, and he hires Metcalf to find the real culprit.

Despite the complexities of this world – and we're never told how or why it came about – Lethem manages to keep his focus firmly on the murder mystery, and works it out with enough conspiracies and betrayals – and enough tough-guy dialogue – that it might well stand on its own. But he never really connects it with the SF elements, and his future dystopia never adds up to anything very consistent. We never get a clear picture of what makes the babyheads or evolved animals or free drugs socially necessary; there's not an infodump in sight, and the solution to the mystery doesn't help explain the SF context in any significant way. It's as though Lethem simply took his opening epigraph from Chandler – "the subject was as easy to spot as a kangaroo in a dinner jacket" – and jerry-built a world for the purpose of literalizing Chandler's metaphor (evolved kangaroos indeed show up as low-level gunsels). The Chandleresque prose doesn't work too well in this context, either; we can't imagine where this narrator or his 1940s-L.A. sensibility comes from in this world, and the story is full of anachronistic details: smoke-filled rooms, seedy bars, and gin-and-tonics seem jarring in a drugged-out dystopia.

Nevertheless, Lethem gets credit for trying something different. If the SF side of his narrative is far less worked out than the mystery side, at least he's produced enough bizarre images and ideas to make his novel a memorable sport. In its own way, *Gun, with Occasional Music* is unique, a genuine experiment that tries in good faith to stretch its genre in new directions. If Lethem doesn't use his SF scenario particularly well, he doesn't deliberately misuse it either. Whatever he's shooting for, it's not a formula bestseller. I don't think we'll see another novel like this anytime soon, but with *Terminal Games* and *White Shark* I *know* we will.

"Never give a hundred per cent" is the Bob Dylan credo quoted by Geoff Ryman in his afterword to **Unconquered Countries**, a collection of four novellas originally written between 1976 and 1989, but with two ("A Fall of Angels, or On the Possibility of Life Under Extreme Conditions" and "Fan") published here for the first time. Ryman says when he first heard this he thought it a "terrible credo for an artist," but it may turn out to be the best advice for the kind of fiction Ryman is drawn to. Unashamed to move toward extremes of sentimentality and brutality, his greatest hazard may lie in trying too hard, in investing too much of himself in his work, perhaps in showing off. Even his much-praised World Fantasy Award winning "The Unconquered Country," which anchors this collection, comes close to calling too much attention to its own special effects; when we learn of the young protagonist renting her womb to grow organic weapons or offering to sell her eye on the black market, the shock is mitigated by the dazzle of the concept. It's a horror, but it's a neat thing to have thought of, as are the living houses and the various other imaginative transformations worked upon what is essentially the Cambodia of the 1970s. The story works wonderfully, but you can see why Ryman later thought it a good idea to constrain himself by realism in *Was*.

Samuel R. Delany, in his introduction to the collection, says that all four stories concern characters trapped in circumscribed worlds, but seeking the freedom and power of what is outside (that also could apply to *Was*). The most extreme such contrast is in the first novella, "A Fall of Angels," which Ryman describes as his own favorite among his stories. Set in a far future society determined to control entropy, the narrative is presented as various excerpts from documents and memoirs – the logs of "angels" (humans stripped of their bodies to survive anywhere), letters of a colonist on a distant world, old textbooks, memoirs of one of the angels. The angels live in a world of transcendent consciousness, and meet an alien who sounds just as Joycean as the alien in Blish's "Common Time," while the colonist faces much less glamorous versions of similar problems and the textbook passages are exactly what Ryman in his Afterword says they are – expository lumps. The story very nearly achieves the splendor it reaches for, but is just as nearly weighed down by its own technique.

For me, the most consistent novellas in the book are "Fan" and "O Happy Day." "Fan," about a working class Englishwoman who shapes her life around her feelings for a mysterious pop star, offers a modest and predictable SF premise (although Ryman's notion of celebrities being turned into interactive computer icons seems both ingenious and inevitable), and one that doesn't overwhelm the emerging portrait of a dreary and increasingly hopeless life. "O Happy Day," which draws its imagery from the Holocaust even more directly than "The Unconquered Country" draws from Cambodia, could be misread as an antifeminist parable – men are being rounded up and exterminated in an effort to breed male violence out of the human race – until you realize its real focus is on the gay men who guard the camps, and who survive in an uncomfortable shadow world between warring genders; it's essentially an odd (and more sophisticated) reversal on Margaret Atwood's *The Handmaid's Tale*, and it's as seamless and courageous as any story in the book.

Earlier, I mentioned what might become an incipient trend (does that hedge enough?) toward fantastic fiction based on fantastic paintings, rather than the other way around. This isn't new in literature, of course; Auden's poem "Museé des Beaux Arts," from a Brueghel painting, is one of the more familiar examples. It isn't exactly new in the SF world, either, as Harlan Ellison well knows: he was one of those who suffered the indignities of trying to write stories to match prepurchased magazine cover illustrations back in the fifties. **Mind Fields** provides Ellison with a much more promising springboard: 34 paintings by the Polish artist Jacek Yerka, whose imagination seems as fertile and unpredictable as Ellison's own. Originally asked to write an introduction to a collection of Yerka's work, Ellison found the paintings – all acrylic on canvas, and all painted since 1981 – so compelling that he chose to write short fictions for each one.

I use the term "fictions" because it would be a stretch to call each of these 33 prose pieces a story; some might better be termed prose poems or vignettes or meditations. Usually, Ellison seems to begin with a general emotional tenor suggested by his response to the painting, imagine a scenario of his own that reflects this tenor, and then return to the painting to find points of congruity with Yerka's images. It works more often than you'd suspect, especially given the different sensibilities of the two artists. Most of Yerka's images derive from the fields and cottages of his native rural Poland, upon which he works delightful surrealist transformations: the wall of a stone cottage becomes a cave wall, which becomes waves of water; a thatched-roof barn soars above the countryside on dragonfly wings; fields of grain hide whole villages or collections of strange objects. Ellison, on the other hand, has been accused of many things, but pastoralism isn't one of them. How can his sharp-edged, satirical imagination blend with Yerka's ominous but essentially gentle visions?

In some cases, startlingly well. A painting called "Fever" (all the titles are Yerka's except two pieces called "Susan" and "Ellison Wonderland") shows a bedridden figure, only hands showing, cowering under ominous clouds. Ellison turns this into a Borgesian parable of Icarus after the fall (faintly echoing that Auden poem I mentioned earlier). A crowded cupboard with hands peeking out of a drawer becomes an image of the afterlife of a Holocaust resistance fighter. In a few cases, Ellison reveals the old nonmetaphorical SF sensibility: "Shed of Rebellion" constructs a dystopian future to account for Yerka's image of a printing press in a ramshackle shed; and Yerka's two visions of fantasy-cities, "Eruption" and "Ammonite," become tales of the lost civilizations that might have built such structures. "Ellison Wonderland" is vintage Ellison paranoia, made oddly appropriate to Yerka's Gaudi-like buildings rising from muddy waters. Less successful is "Amok Time," a deliberately politically incorrect fable of Africans and teleportation spun out of an image of a cottage in a tree. One of Ellison's best pieces in the collection, "Base," has virtually nothing to do with Yerka's painting beyond the title; and another, "Attack at Dawn," completely abandons any attempt to explain why a Volkswagen which is also half-lizard is being attacked by what appear to be biomechanical planes.

Perhaps the best way to approach a work such as this is to regard it as three books in one. Yerka's paintings, like those of Bosch or the surrealists, present their own mysteries and preoccupations quite well on their own terms, and this is a first-rate portfolio quite apart from Ellison's contributions. Most of Ellison's fictions can also stand on their own, and often don't need the paintings to make sense. But in a few cases, a real synergy sets in, and the painting-plus-text becomes something entirely apart from either work individually. "Susan" is a sensitive and understated little romance of mortality which matches perfectly Yerka's equally understated image of a bed and lamp in a wooded landscape. But the best example may be the final piece, "Please Don't Slam the Door." It's not really Yerka's most original painting – by now we've grown used to his floating landscapes, rural cottages, and volcanic structures – and it's not Ellison's best prose, verging on too-delicate sentimentality. But the combination becomes a moving elegy to the son Yerka lost during the preparation of the book, and to the child's sense of wonder.

– June 1994, Locus #401 –

The Ascent of Wonder: The Evolution of Hard Science Fiction ~
~ edited by David G. Hartwell and Kathryn Cramer

New Legends ~~ edited by Greg Bear with Martin Greenberg

Permutation City ~~ Greg Egan

Towing Jehovah ~~ James Morrow

Uncharted Territory ~~ Connie Willis

The debate over what is and isn't hard SF probably dates back at least to Jules Verne's famous put-down of H.G. Wells ("he invents"), but in recent years – with SF seeming to drift all over the literary map – it's become the focus for arguments over the nature of SF in general. Neither the 1983 Eaton conference on hard SF (and the 1986 critical book derived from it) nor the special hard-SF issue of *Science-Fiction Studies* in 1993 seemed able to arrive at any sort of consensus definition, and yet most science fiction readers would still argue that they know hard SF when they see it. The latest and most ambitious contribution to the conceptual wars is David

G. Hartwell and Kathryn Cramer's forklift-sized anthology **The Ascent of Wonder**, which comes complete with some 67 stories, three introductions (by Hartwell, Cramer, and Gregory Benford), and extensive story notes. It's a very readable collection, and it contains a high proportion of stories that go flat-out for the old-fashioned (and equally undefined) "sense of wonder," but it's inevitably going to confuse the issue more than it clarifies it.

One of the more useful concepts imported from the realm of logic into SF and fantasy criticism (by Brian Attebery in his 1992 *Strategies of Fantasy*) is that of "fuzzy sets" – categories with identifiable centers but indeterminate boundaries. Attebery argued that fantasy is a fuzzy set; hard SF may be an even better example, since it exists within the framework of a larger, equally ill-defined genre. Both Hartwell and Cramer, in their introductions, agree that hard SF is widely perceived by readers and writers as somehow being at the core of the SF enterprise, but beyond that they never quite let themselves get pinned down to a usable definition. It's up to the reader to weasel one out of their various comments, story introductions, and – above all – the selection of stories included. Most SF readers are likely to come away, as I did, convinced more than ever that hard SF is a fuzzy set – but that it's not *this* fuzzy.

Those who believe that hard SF can be defined historically by the period of John W. Campbell, Jr.'s editorship of *Astounding* will find that *Ascent of Wonder* contains a pretty good selection of classically Campbell-era stories and authors, not all of them overly familiar. From Campbell's *Astounding* we get Hal Clement's "Proof," Henry Kuttner and C.L. Moore's "Mimsy Were the Borogoves," Philip Latham's "The Xi Effect," Tom Godwin's "The Cold Equations," Gordon Dickson's "Dolphin's Way," Clifford Simak's "Desertion," Raymond F. Jones's "The Person from Porlock," Theodore Thomas's "The Weather Man," and Vernor Vinge's "Bookworm, Run." Add to these some predictable classics from Heinlein ("It's Great to Be Back"), Asimov ("The Last Question," "The Life and Times of Multivac," "Waterclap"), Clarke ("Transit of Earth," "The Star," "The Longest Science Fiction Story Ever Written"), Poul Anderson ("Kyrie"), James Blish ("Surface Tension"), Bob Shaw ("Light of Other Days"), and representative works by more recent heirs of this tradition such as Robert L. Forward ("The Singing Diamond"), Dean Ing ("Down and Out on Ellfive Prime"), Gregory Benford ("Exposures," "Relativistic Effects"), Donald M. Kingsbury ("To Bring in the Steel"), Larry Niven ("The Hole Man"), James P. Hogan ("Making Light"), Greg Bear ("Tangents"), and David Brin ("What Continues, What Fails . . . ") – and you've got a pretty healthy selection of stories of the sort you would expect in an anthology of this scope. The editors may have shortchanged some interesting newer writers, such as Paul J. McAuley or Greg Egan, but few would argue that most of these tales belong within the general range of hard SF.

Now the fuzziness sets in. The stories mentioned above constitute about two-fifths of the contents of *Ascent of Wonder*. The remainder including a handful of historical precedents (Verne, Wells, Kipling, Poe, Hawthorne), a few run-of-the-mill magazine stories that are exemplars of their type (Miles Breuer's "The Hungry Guinea

Pig," Randall Garrett's "Time Fuze") – and no fewer than two stories each by Le Guin, Ballard, and Gene Wolfe, plus such unlikely candidates as Richard Grant, C.M. Kornbluth, Anne McCaffrey, John Sladek, John M. Ford, Theodore Sturgeon, James Tiptree, Jr., Cordwainer Smith, and Philip K. Dick. To find out what they're all doing here, you have to read carefully the introductions and story notes – more than most anthologies, this one lives in its story introductions – and what gradually emerges is that *Ascent of Wonder* is not quite as advertised. It becomes clear, for example, that the editors do have some notion of a center for hard SF – Poul Anderson's 1970 novel *Tau Zero* is repeatedly cited – but that their real intention is a much more ambitious examination of, in Hartwell's words, "the way science functions in science fiction." The problem with this, of course, is that if science doesn't function in *some* way, it's not science fiction in the first place. Hence, we're left with a fuzzy set with a clear center and no boundaries at all – there's no principle of exclusion, no acknowledgment that any subset of SF exists *other* than hard SF. In other words, there's a fair amount of fudging going on here.

That fudging doesn't extend to Gregory Benford's introductory essay, in which he takes a fairly hard line toward what he calls "playing with the net up." Cramer, however, starts off by arguing that SF writers play with science the way M.C. Escher plays with geometry – to give form to "impossible imaginative content." Already, the "impossible" is getting sneaked into the ranks of SF from fantasy, where it traditionally belongs. Hartwell immediately contradicts this by arguing that hard SF is "about the emotional experience of describing and confronting what is scientifically true" – a much more conservative description, but one that would seem to admit all sorts of mainstream works from Hardy to Bellow. He comes closer to defining hard SF when he argues that, in hard SF, the moment of revelation for the reader involves "the functioning of the laws of nature" rather than of "the inner life" – thus excluding (his example) Daniel Keyes's *Flowers for Algernon*. Then he offers us – as the very first story in the collection – Le Guin's "Nine Lives," which reveals far more about confronting the "inner life" of our own uniqueness than it does about the laws of nature governing cloning. Perhaps the key claim in Hartwell's introduction is that the anthology tries to present stories "both in the center and on the edges of the argument" – but that isn't what the subtitle "the evolution of hard science fiction" says.

The soft-shoe routines really go into high gear in the story introductions, which seem to contain the real keys to the editorial process but which are much less clearly focused than the straightforward informative comments which helped to make Hartwell's horror anthologies so valuable. At times rambling and pedantic – as though it's necessary to reassert the editors' authority at every opportunity – the notes sometimes seem directed toward the general reader, sometimes toward the aficionado, and sometimes toward no one at all. They often invite comparisons to stories and authors not in the collection (such as John Varley, who is summarily dismissed as "innocent of hard science"). This might be helpful if some sort of bibliography were attached, listing the numerous novels and stories mentioned throughout; as is, it sounds smug, and is almost certain to leave the non-fan feeling like an outsider. Sometimes the notes take off at right angles to the story under discussion, and end up discussing another author altogether. They persistently refer to the "affect" or "attitude" of hard SF, as though these had been described clearly in the introductions, and they defend stories that seem way off base (such as Ballard's) as being "in dialog" with hard SF – though this "dialog" hasn't been described anywhere either, save in Benford's essay (which clearly would exclude Ballard from it). Sometimes they refer to "Modern SF" in a way apparently derived from Algis Budrys's use of that term, but they don't explain how that differs (radically) from "Modernism" when it's used to refer to Benford's debt to Faulkner.

Hawthorne's "Rappaccini's Daughter" is here because it has a heartless scientist in it, but it's described as representing a gothic strain "antithetical" to hard SF. Gene Wolfe is fair game because he uses science and technology "metaphorically" but "without stating the tenors" of his metaphors. (Richard Grant's "Drode's Equations," to which this note about Wolfe is inexplicably appended, gets away without even stating the vehicle, since we never get to see the equations that are at the story's Borgesian center.) The longest story in the book, Anne McCaffrey's "Weyr Search," is included because she worked out an SF world for her dragons early in the Pern series, even though that working out is barely in evidence in the story itself ("intentions count," the editors remind us).

In one of the more circuitous arguments, John T. Sladek's creationism-as-surrealism parable "Stop Evolution in its Tracks!" is included because his parody of irrationalism affirms his "allegiance to reason and science" – which seems to imply that anyone who favors reason over pseudoscience is a kind of hard SF writer. Similarly, John M. Ford, in "Heat of Fusion," is "importing the Kafkaesque" into hard SF; Bruce Sterling's "The Beautiful and the Sublime" is "a challenge to hard SF"; Frederik Pohl's "Day Million" is ok because its "attitude is right"; Tiptree represents a recent movement "away from the hard SF affect into the fantastic"; and Michael Flynn's "Mammy Morgan Played the Organ; Her Daddy Beat the Drum" – a *ghost story*, for heaven's sake! – gets in because physics is "the privileged science" in Flynn's trumped-up "explanation" for the ghosts. Theodore Sturgeon's "Occam's Scalpel" – arguably not even an SF story (and the editors admit strict "Constructionists" would exclude it) – is claimed to be "about scientists," but it isn't. Greg Bear's "Tangents" is hard SF, but not, as its introduction says, because the characters "solve problems, go places, do things." But isn't that also what characters do on Sesame Street?

The fudging is equally apparent when we look at how certain themes develop. Giantism, for example, shows up in Hilbert Schenk's "Send Me a Kiss by Wire," Miles J. Breuer's "The Hungry Guinea Pig," and Edward Bryant's "giANTS." The Schenk is a giant-squid adventure story with a minimum of extrapolation – hard SF because it barely plays with biology at all. In the introduction to Breuer, the editors tell us that a hard-SF giantism story is one which doesn't violate the cube-square law of size in relationship to mass (otherwise it's satirical SF, one of the few alternate categories for SF mentioned anywhere in the book). But Breuer's pulp giant-lab-animal-on-the-loose tale, which cheerfully violates the square-cube law, presumably qualifies because it's old, while Bryant's story — which owes as much to fifties monster movies as to hard extrapolation — qualifies because it *uses* the cube-square law as its gimmick. Both Breuer and Bryant are heavily satiric, and might well fit in another big anthology of "satiric SF." On the other hand, it's hard to think of a giantism story anywhere in SF that wouldn't fit under one of the editors' rubrics.

The pleasures of reading hard SF, to be sure, are much in evidence in *The Ascent of Wonder*, and most of my quibbles come directly from the book's ambitious and misleading subtitle. (With all the special exceptions and counter-examples, the book's argument is less a theory of SF "evolution" than a kind of literary creationism.) Viewed from another angle, the collection might be seen as a deliberate response to such other recent forklift anthologies as Le Guin, Attebery, and Fowler's *Norton Book of Science Fiction*, designed with the intention of putting hard SF back in the center of the table while acknowledging the impact of more metaphorical and "literary" texts. (Nearly two-thirds of Hartwell and Cramer's contents date from 1960 or later — the same period covered in the Norton book.) And it's almost certainly true that a more credible subtitle — say, "the way science functions in science fiction," as Hartwell puts it in his introduction — would lack the marketing pizzazz of a buzzword like "hard SF." As both a reading and a teaching anthology, *The Ascent of Wonder* has much to offer that *The Norton Book* doesn't, and many readers will prefer its inclusive approach to that earlier anthology's implied reinvention of the field. And certainly the arguments likely to be engendered by the book's odder selections may help to enliven critical debate. But SF readers who hope to clarify their understanding of hard SF aren't likely to find much illumination coming from the very fuzzy set of stories included here.

Given all these problems in nailing down hard SF, it's revealing that Greg Bear, in assembling his first anthology with Martin Greenberg, should state in his introduction that he deliberately avoids the term because it's been so "abused and misused." Nevertheless, New Legends covers much of the same kind of territory as *The Ascent of Wonder*, omitting fantasy and "in-between" stories and focusing heavily on the ways in which writers today make use of science and SF tropes. The fifteen original stories and one essay (by Gregory Benford, who's also represented by a story under his own name and a "Sterling Blake" story, giving him nearly a fifth of the book) cover a surprising amount of territory, some of it newsworthy to all SF readers. The two most newsworthy items are a new Ursula Le Guin story set in the Karhide society of *The Left Hand of Darkness* and a new story by Carter Scholz, from whom we've heard little in recent years. There are also a couple of high-concept hard SF pieces by Benford and Greg Egan; a genuinely haunting portrait of a distant future society in disruption by Paul J. McAuley; effective future war stories by Greg

Abraham, Geoffrey A. Landis, and Scholz; and fine examples of type by Robert Sheckley and Poul Anderson.

Bear has organized the stories into five sections, according to fairly traditional themes: ecology stories, stories of maturation, aliens, war, "redemption," and "ciphers." But, as with the Hartwell-Cramer anthology, other patterns of arrangement suggest themselves as well. Marriage or marriage-like relationships, for example, show up with surprising frequency as subthemes in stories ostensibly focused elsewhere. "Sterling Blake's" "A Desperate Calculus" sets up a sure-to-be-controversial near-future scenario about disease and population control, made more convincing by the devotion of the husband-wife team whose parallel stories converge to reveal their real mission. James Stevens-Arce's "Scenes from a Future Marriage" addresses the theme more directly, but unfortunately suffers from overwriting and self-conscious literariness. Le Guin's "Coming of Age in Karhide" answers questions many *Left Hand of Darkness* readers may have had about how stable relationships evolve in an ambisexual society, and even Poul Anderson's "Scarecrow" locates its classic SF technopuzzle in the context of a married couple trying to save each other. The most touching portrait of a marriage, however, is George Alec Effinger's "One," a haunting story that surprisingly went unsold for years, perhaps because (as Bear suggests) it challenges SF's principle of plenitude by suggesting that the universe may indeed be lifeless except for us. A couple explores lifeless worlds for decades until the wife dies and the husband, now so far from Earth that he can't return, has to come to terms with his newfound cosmic isolation. Even Sheckley's delightfully funny tale of an earth overrun with friendly but unremittingly gauche aliens features a human-alien marriage at its center.

There are also, in good hard SF tradition, a number of thoughtful portraits of scientists at work. Mary Rosenblum's "Elegy" concerns the possibility of using squid cells to repair damaged brains, but focuses as much on the main character's troubled relationship with her dead mother, a kind of Rosalyn Yalow figure. Robert Silverberg offers a portrait of an archeologist who discovers his life's work is built around a hoax, and then offers him an unlikely convenient way out. In "Wang's Carpets," Greg Egan has scientists investigating a huge, carpet-like alien ocean-dweller – made up of a single immense molecule! – and deducing that the molecule may function as a supercomputer with a kind of virtual intelligent life buried in its "circuitry" and totally unaware of the external environment (an idea explored more fully in Egan's *Permutation City*, reviewed below). An even more bizarre concept is at the heart of Benford's "High Abyss," a "Nightfall"-style tale of a visionary scientist discovering the true nature of the universe despite accepted dogma – and the fact that his home environment is nothing more than a cosmic string.

Of the future war stories, Geoffrey Landis's "Rorvik's War" stands out as what may be the first post-Zhirinovsky war-with-the-Russians scenario, combined with speculation on the role virtual reality might play in such a conflict. Scholz's "Radiance" is a much closer-to-home account of the ethical dilemmas faced by a scientist working on a Strategic Defense Initiative-type project, and Benford, in an essay titled "Old Legends," offers an account of the SDI debate among SF writers, coupled with a brief history of the relations between SF and defense science since the days of Cleve Cartmill and the famous *Astounding* security raid. Greg' Abrahams "Gnota" also strikes close to home with its depiction of near-future Eastern European conflicts, then takes off in a strange direction involving a wounded soldier's relationship with the pig who is growing his new heart and the woman who is raising it.

To my mind, though, the outstanding piece in the collection is Paul J. McAuley's "Recording Angel." Set in a far future space colony, it describes the radical change this society undergoes when visited by travelers who have spent millions of years in space. Like the Effinger and Egan stories, it suggests that life is rare in the universe, and accordingly more precious, but what gives the story its haunting tone is best described in Bear's introduction, which presents it as an amalgam of E.M. Forster and Cordwainer Smith. It's a complete and convincing world, sketched with poetic economy and yet retaining the large-scale perspective of the best hard SF. Like several of the other works in this superior anthology, it demonstrates clearly what Hartwell and Cramer tried to do on a broader canvas, and what Benford has almost made a career of — it shows that the conceptual rigor of hard SF need not be sacrificed to gain metaphorical power and literary depth.

One author included in Bear's anthology who is trying to do genuinely new things with hard SF is Greg Egan, whose first novel, *Quarantine* (1992) combined a Stapledonian-sized cosmic vision with elements of contemporary quantum theory. In **Permutation City**, Egan brings a similarly large-scale concept to information theory in what is probably the most thoroughly worked-out exploration so far of what it might be like to be self-aware software in a software environment. The basic conceit isn't entirely new; the notion of variable evolutionary rates in a controlled environment dates back to such pre-information-age texts as Sturgeon's "Microcosmic God," and Charles Platt's 1991 *The Silicon Man* explored in a thriller format what it might be like to become information. Stanislaw Lem's "Non Serviam," one of his "perfect reviews of nonexistent books," even came close to reviewing this novel fifteen years before it was written, and touched upon many of the philosophical issues Egan treats. But Egan works out the feelings and experiences of what Lem called "personoids" in convincing, and endlessly fascinating, novelistic detail — even to the point of providing programmed environments for the characters to function in. (Wander too far from your programmed "home," for example, and the world starts to disintegrate as you approach regions of unwritten code.)

The novel begins by parallelling two stories: in 2045, Paul Durham begins experimenting with computer "Copies" of himself, accelerating and slowing down the Copy's time sense, manipulating the environment, and generally toying with its consciousness in ways that often seem brutal. Six years later, in 2051, he (or possibly a Copy that has somehow become flesh-and-blood) commissions Maria Deluca to design the seeds of a software universe in a broad-based environment called the "Autoverse." Deluca soon learns that Durham is also selling a kind of "immortality insurance" to wealthy Copies, promising indefinite life free of hardware constraints inside a "cellular automaton" called TVC (after Turing, Von Neumann, and Chang). She, and the government, are suspicious of how he's going to find the computing power to do this, and his answer turns out to be one of those outrageous leaps of superscience that makes literal the notion of the universe as self-organizing information. Before you know it, the action shifts to the cellular universe, billions of years have passed in Deluca's seeded cosmos, and Deluca herself awakens as a Copy some seven thousand years after the TVC universe is "launched." A couple of subplots involve other inhabitants of the cellular automaton and what happens to them when the controlling program begins to decay.

It occurs to me that this looks nearly incomprehensible in summary, but Egan writes convincing action sequences that effectively dramatize, for example, what it might feel like if your mind could be slowed to a few billion instructions per second — or per minute, or per year. What he fails to convey is any real sense of the alienness of such a state of being — his Copies cling tenaciously to useless human traits, cooking and eating meals, defecating, copulating, long after they've left behind the bodies that would generate such imperatives. Even after 7,000 years, they still seem trapped in a kind of virtual reality game, showing little imagination and having little to look forward to other than what's already been programmed for them — namely, meeting the alien beings in the universe evolved from Deluca's original seed program. Perhaps Egan is trying to convey something of the boredom of immortality — and in one or two well-conceived scenes, he does this quite effectively. But for the most part, his novel makes the case that downloaded people are if anything less interesting than their originals. Where we expect something of the evolutionary strangeness of Cordwainer Smith or Olaf Stapledon or even Sturgeon's neoterics, we get a bunch of aging neurotics who seem to have no idea at all what to do with an almost infinitely malleable universe. *Permutation City* (the title itself gets subjected to endless anagrammatical permutations throughout the text) is filled with wonderful set-pieces and vaulting leaps of imagination — it's a real trip — but it stops short of the kind of transcendence that seems promised by its striking premise.

God is dead — no, he's *really* dead this time, and his corpse is floating in the Atlantic near the equator, and the angels have hired a disgraced supertanker captain to tow the two-mile-long body to a prepared tomb inside an arctic iceberg. This is not only the premise, but pretty much the entire plot of James Morrow's **Towing Jehovah**, an entertaining mock-adventure comedy which strains to be an outrageous satire of modern morality. Its characters include the aforementioned captain, Anthony Van Horne, his career ruined by an *Exxon Valdez*-type oil spill; a Jesuit quantum physicist named Thomas Ockham; a militant feminist playwright; a fabulously wealthy condom-industry heir involved in an anti-fundamentalist "Enlightenment League"; a disillusioned former rabbinical student; an anti-Semitic Evangelical Christian; a couple of manic impresarios who stage full-scale reenactments of World War II battles; a horny nun; and various officious Vatican bureaucrats (since it's the Vatican who pays for the towing project). It's a lot of fun, but the fun is more in the conception than the execution, because Morrow tries to work out this extended Lenny Bruce routine as though it were a real novel.

Towing Jehovah may be Morrow's most Vonnegutian book to date, and while that comparison has been made before, it seems especially apt here. Robert Scholes described the work of Vonnegut and other 1960s black humorists as "fabulations," and this is a classic fabulation right down to its oddly 60s flavor. As Morrow piles on the absurdities, it begins to look as though he wants to skewer just about every sort of modern belief system, but most of these belief systems have pretty well skewered themselves in the last 30 years, and it's frankly harder to shock us these days. Sometimes, Morrow cheats a little: by making almost every character an irrational obsessive, he reduces their positions to easy targets. His feminist, for example, wants to sabotage the mission because to acknowledge the existence of a male god would reinforce centuries of patriarchical oppression. His "Enlightenment League" sets out to sink the corpse for similar reasons; its existence would interfere with their antireligious dogma. In other cases, he runs a joke into the ground: when a mutinous crew is lured back by Quarter Pounders and Filet-o-Fish sandwiches fashioned from the Divine Cadaver, he keeps reminding us of it until you want to let him know we got the point the first time.

One can argue that the goal of satire is not to be fair, and that the goal of black humor is not even to be corrective. But both kinds of fiction are essentially philosophical, even when that philosophy reduces itself to the later Vonnegut's increasingly annoying aphorisms. Morrow doesn't offer that much; his central image is little more than a litmus test for competing belief systems – no one even attempts to examine it or find rational explanations – and the fundamentalists, oddly enough, come closest to getting their position validated. In some ways the novel is reminiscent of Ballard's far more enigmatic "The Drowned Giant," and it some ways it recalls another recent god-as-cargo novel, Charles Johnson's *Middle Passage* (whose fantasy elements have been overlooked by almost everyone). But while those stories seriously questioned the way we believe things, Morrow turns beliefs into cartoons. The result is often hilarious, and Morrow is a talented enough storyteller to almost keep it all under control, but he never really gets under your skin.

Connie Willis's fondness for old movies and impatience with trendy political correctness were much in evidence in her recent collection *Impossible Things*, and both feature strongly in her new comic novella **Uncharted Territory**. With only five characters and a minimalist setting, it calls to mind those old John Wayne-Maureen O'Hara westerns as much as any earlier SF stories, and even comes complete with a comic native sidekick and an effete Easterner (or at least someone unfamiliar with the frontier, which amounts to the same thing). The narrator, Sarah Findriddy, and her partner Carson are surveyors trying to map an alien planet with the assistance of a sex-starved housekeeper named C.J. and a recalcitrant native guide, Bult, who delights in imposing fines for every perceived slight to the planet's ecology or to himself. Joining them on "loan" is a "socioexozoologist" named Evelyn Parker, whose name even suggests Leslie Howard. Willis makes obvious jokes over misunderstandings involving the male Parker's first name, and this question of sexual identity becomes a major theme (she keeps Findriddy's sex and first name from the reader for a good while into the narrative).

As the slight plot develops, the parallels with Westerns grow more apparent. Parker has developed inflated romantic notions of the "legendary" Carson and Findriddy by watching holographic entertainments called "pop-ups" – sort of high-tech dime novels, all written by a "Captain Jake Trailblazer." He also finds himself attracted to Findriddy, and courts her by recounting bizarre mating rituals of a variety of alien species. She's flattered by the attention, but of course what she really wants is for Carson to see her as a woman, and her frustration also shows itself as catty sarcasm about C.J. Will the relationships fall into place in time for a ride into the sunset? Will growing jealousy combined with an appropriately timed crisis – and perhaps a moment of sublime revelation – finally open the dimwitted Carson's eyes? Willis handles all this with the high spirits and cheerful insensitivity of a Howard Hawks, and gets off some genuinely funny lines along the way.

– July 1994, Locus #402 –

Summer of Love ~~ Lisa Mason

Aggressor Six ~~ Wil McCarthy

Beyond the Veil of Stars ~~ Robert Reed

Is there anything more debilitating than discovering that your youth has become the stuff of historical fiction? Lisa Mason's **Summer of Love**, set in Haight-Ashbury in the summer of 1967, is not only a paean to the love-and-peace generation, but seems to be a serious attempt, using an old SF cliché, to present that legendary time and place as some sort of turning point for five centuries of future history. The cliché involves a 25th century time traveller sent back to protect the life of a teenage girl whose offspring may prevent a catastrophic future; it seems some sort of "dim spot" in the historical record – discovered, apparently, when lyrics of 60s rock songs begin disappearing – creates the potential for "demons" from an alternate time stream to disrupt the flow of history by causing the girl's death. The girl, Susan Stein, is a dropout from a middle class midwestern family who reconstitutes herself as a budding hippie-chick named Starbright and flees to Haight-Ashbury to partake in the lovefest. She is taken in by a black shop owner named Ruby T. Maverick, a veteran of the earlier Beat era, and there she meets the time traveler, whose name is Chiron Cat's Eye in Draco.

Mason does a pretty good job with her central characters, especially Ruby, who represents a kind of historical consciousness missing from much of the rest of the novel (Maverick reminds us how close in time the Beat and Hippie movements actually were). There seems little doubt that Mason has done extensive research on the Summer of Love and that her portrait of Haight-Ashbury is correct in the essential details – she even has a couple of brief walk-ons by Janis Jopin and Lew Gottlieb of the Limelighters – and one wonders why all this couldn't have simply been presented as a mainstream nostalgia piece. But while Mason gets the surfaces right, and offers some glimpses of the darker side of the era – such as the second-class status of women and the long-term effects of the inauguration of the drug culture – she never offers any clear analysis of how and why this moment in time came to be, or what it represented to its participants. For historical perspective, we're pretty much left with the accounts of Chiron, whose preoccupation is the next five centuries, not the decade before, when the seeds of the hippy movement are sown (the only glimpse we get of this is through the memories and ruminations of Ruby). And what the next five centuries show us is that the Summer of Love, if not quite the dawning of the Age of Aquarius, is at least a kind of primitive age of innocence, the Edenic source of Chiron's world. It's a scenario familiar even to non-SF readers from the *Terminator* and *Back to the Future* films, and it doesn't seem much more convincing to me here than it did there. (In an odd way, it's also reminiscent of Joe Haldeman's *The Hemingway Hoax*, another case of an SF writer taking a time and place close to his heart and investing it with cosmic meaning.)

I've commented before on the growing tendency of SF writers to incorporate the devices of historical fiction into future or alternate-world histories, and Mason seems to clarify one reason why this is so. Good historical fiction, it seems to me, is at some level always about cause and effect – it makes us understand how people came to think and behave in a certain way in a certain place and time. With *Summer of Love*, the usual cause-effect relationship is inverted: the Haight in 1967 is not seen as the result of anything in particular, but rather as a distant cause for a fully imaginary future history. This isn't too far removed from the kind of transcendental utopianism that Theodore Roszak and others saw aborning at the time – the Aquarian age projected science-fictionally. The key to making something like this work, it would seem, is the way such a narrative might make the last quarter-century of history "fit" into the larger scheme being proposed, but except for some references to ozone depletion and environmental degradation, there's little of our own time accounted for in Chiron's future scenario. (This is probably why Mason has to set Chiron's "now" so far in the future – so that she doesn't have to work out all the details.)

As a portrait of a time and place, *Summer of Love* works with a kind of easy nostalgia, offering few surprises and reinforcing much of what we want to believe about the 60s. With her strong sense of character and mastery of telling detail, she makes Haight-Ashbury come alive in a way few recent works of fiction have done. But as SF, the novel grows increasingly contrived and conventional, and in the end the SF elements don't add much that's convincing to a somewhat idealized, but genuinely affectionate portrait of an era that in many ways has begun to seem as remote from us as Chiron's own.

Last month, I speculated that David Hartwell and Kathryn Cramer's *Ascent of Wonder* seemed likely to spark debates about the nature of hard SF; at least it set me to thinking. One of the problems that has been nagging me was Hartwell's claim in his introduction that the moment of recognition in a hard SF story has to do with some new perception of the laws of nature (as opposed to some insight about "the inner life"). This seemed to exclude not only several of the more debatable stories in that anthology, but also a large number of stories traditionally thought of as hard SF. The traditional technological problem-solving story – most of Asimov's robot stories, for example – doesn't reveal much about science or nature at all; new scientific advances are more likely to be treated as initial conditions rather than narrative revelations. At the same time, Hartwell was on to something: there is indeed a certain kind of hard SF that tries to show us the whole universe in a new light, that moves far beyond the "normal science" of technological SF.

I'm borrowing the phrase "normal science" from Thomas Kuhn's classic 1962 *The Structure of Scientific Revolutions*, still one of the most useful essays on the history of science, despite the fact that its concept of paradigms has since been co-opted to rationalize everything from alternate universes to holistic health fads. Much of hard SF – including the problem-solving story – seems based in the widely accepted paradigms that Kuhn calls "normal science" (Kuhn even identifies problem-solving as a defining activity of normal science). Other hard SF texts (Greg Bear's *Moving Mars* is a good recent example) share more in common with Kuhn's notion of "scientific revolutions," even though in reality such revolutions never occur with the kind of thundering fanfare they're apt to get in an SF story.

In other words, some hard SF is about normal science, and some is about revolutionary science. A good example of the former is Wil McCarthy's **Aggressor Six**, and a flawed example of the latter is Robert Reed's *Beyond the Veil of Stars*. *Aggressor Six* is a neat, action-filled first novel about interstellar war in the 34th century. McCarthy offers all the appurtenances of hard SF, including charts and diagrams, but his SF-nal innovations are for the most part derived from existing SF concepts – Le Guin's ansible, "enhanced" animals, beam weapons, etc. – and he never really strays from normal science. Nor is his premise very original: a ferocious and seemingly invincible alien race, the Waisters, is systematically invading and destroying human colonies throughout the galaxy. Ken Jonson, a Marine corporal who survived a disastrous encounter with the Waisters, is assigned to a tactical forecasting team called Aggressor Six, whose mission is to learn to think like the enemy and predict their likely actions. But his team has barely begun to function before the Waisters arrive in the solar system and threaten Earth itself.

So far, this sounds like a standard military-SF adventure, with members of a dedicated unit trying to outwit both the aliens and their own bureaucrats. There's also a healthy dose of old-time space opera: giant spaceships blow up in spectacular space battles, ugly aliens get splattered by "wireguns," whole planetary colonies with millions of inhabitants get wiped out in a single engagement. What sets the novel apart is its resolution, which turns not on some ingenious technological or scientific fix, but on understanding alien behavior – which, it turns out, fits neatly within the range of normal ethology. What starts out as Heinlein ends up looking a lot more like Haldeman. McCarthy's conclusion suffers from some of the flaws you might expect of a first novel – saving the world comes down to a too-contrived guerilla action with a very abrupt resolution, and he actually signals a happy ending by having a friendly dog slobber over everyone's face. Despite such cloying touches, several derivative set-pieces, and the overall sense that this is really an inflated short story of the sort that might have appeared in *Analog* some years back, *Aggressor Six* is a satisfying debut, and a good example of a large-scale hard SF adventure which doesn't play too many games with normal science.

Robert Reed's sixth novel, **Beyond the Veil of Stars**, plays all sorts of games with normal science, and constantly promises to break out of accepted paradigms and into a radical re-imagining of the nature of the universe. His title is a classic lifting-of-the-veil image that would do justice to Arthur Clarke, but Reed is no Clarke (at least not yet). By nature, Reed doesn't even seem to be a hard SF writer – he works out marvelous images and situations, but when it comes time to make some kind of rational sense out of it all, he is apt simply to have the narrator told that the scientific details are "classified." He plays with information theory as a way of rationalizing his most dramatic image – a night sky in which the stars are replaced by the reflected image of Earth itself – but the explanation seems only half-hearted (and half-baked). He concocts something called "quantum intrusions," but it quickly becomes apparent that this isn't really based on any recognizable quantum theory, but rather is a convenient device for having characters "projected" into alien lifeforms on distant planets – an effect reminiscent of Clifford Simak's "Desertion".

The first part of Reed's novel is the sensitive and insightful coming-of-age tale of Cornell Novak and his troubled relationship with his UFO-hunting father, an amateur scientist fascinated by rings of black glass-like substances that have begun appearing in various rural locations. Cornell shares his father's quest in part because he believes his mother was kidnapped by a UFO. Reed draws convincing characters and relationships, and evokes the growing embarrassment Cornell feels as he realizes his father is something of a crackpot. In this first section's climax, Cornell's relation with his father reaches a crisis when he realizes what really happened with his mother. But the big dramatic image — paralleling Cornell's personal discovery — is the sudden "eversion" of the night sky as it changes permanently into a reflection of earth.

In the second part of the novel, Cornell is an adult recruited by a secret government agency to participate in the exploration of other worlds via the "quantum intrusions." He finds himself assigned to a planet called High Desert, where he takes on the form of a creature with six bodies and a separate, egg-like brain which controls them telepathically. He begins to develop relationships with fellow-workers, especially a woman named Porsche, and eventually begins to suspect that Porsche may herself be an alien. By the end of the novel, Reed has to tie all this together — the glass disks from UFO landings, the quantum intrusions, the alien planet, the everted sky, and Porsche — and he just barely manages it. The novel is supposed to end on a note of revolutionary transcendence, but there's so much on the plate by then that it doesn't seem like a clean ending. What began as a provocative character study in pseudoscientific obsessiveness with Cornell's father ends in a kind of muddle which tries to rationalize the pseudoscience with still more pseudoscience. That's the problem with transcendence — it's only a few doors down the street from incoherence, and it's easy to get the wrong address.

— August 1994, Locus #403 —

The Year's Best Fantasy and Horror: Seventh Annual Collection ~
~ edited by Ellen Datlow and Terri Windling

The Oxford Book of Fantasy Stories ~~ edited by Tom Shippey

Somewhere East of Life ~~ Brian Aldiss

Metaworlds: Best Australian Science Fiction ~~ edited by Paul Collins

— Lunar Memoirs —

Moon Shot: The Inside Story of America's Race to the Moon ~
~ Alan Shepard & Deke Slayton with Jay Barbree & Howard Benedict

Deke! US Manned Space from Mercury to the Shuttle ~
~ Donald K. "Deke" Slayton with Michael Cassutt

— Star Trek Lit —

Star Trek Creator: The Authorized Biography of Gene Roddenberry ~
~ David Alexander

Gene Roddenberry: The Myth and the Man Behind "Star Trek" ~~ Joel Engel

Star Trek Memories ~~ William Shatner with Chris Kreski

Gene Roddenberry: The Last Conversation ~~ Yvonne Fern

All I Really Need to Know I Learned from Watching Star Trek ~
~ Dave Marinaccio

Fantasy is evaporating. I don't mean that it's disappearing altogether – quite the opposite – but that it's growing more diffuse, leaching out into the air around it, imparting a strange smell to the literary atmosphere, probably even getting into our clothes. There's still a murky pool of hardcore fantasy down there – Tom Shippey's *Oxford Book of Fantasy Stories* is evidence of that, as we shall see in a moment – but the lesson I'm learning from Ellen Datlow and Terri Windling's seventh annual **Year's Best Fantasy and Horror** is that fantasy, along with its allied genre of horror, is no longer really separable from the grotesque, the gothic, the surreal, the absurd, or the plain old romance. Windling says as much in her introduction, arguing that fantasy includes "all forms of magical, surrealist, myth- and fairy tale-based stories, novels, and poems" and that all such works need have in common are "narrative roots in forms of storytelling much older than the twentieth-century novel of social realism." But since there's plenty of social realism in these pages, too – everything from wife and child abuse to the exploitation of third-world countries – it's not clear that that's a very useful distinction, either. What it all seems to come down to, in practice, is a question of tone and voice – a question that Shippey also raises in his much more traditional anthology.

As has been their practice in the past, Datlow and Windling include a substantial number of stories that more conservative genre readers would object to as mainstream; of the fifty stories included (along with four poems), I count fifteen in which the supernatural plays no role at all, or at best a marginal one. Horror, of course, has no particular need for the supernatural; it's always been a genre identified by its affect more than by its narrative conventions (in fact, it's the only genre I can think of actually *named* for the feeling it tries to evoke). Thus, Nancy Collins can build a pretty effective foreboding atmosphere around a central grotesque image – a Civil War-era prosthetic jaw – in "The Sunday-Go-To-Meeting Jaw," John Coyne can get an equally ominous tone out from the alienation of Americans in Africa in his two stories set in Ethiopia, and Dennis Etchison can find horror in the way Hollywood uses its public spaces in "The Dog Park." None of these involve the kind of graphic sex and violence so often associated with modern horror fiction, but even when such elements are present, as in A.R. Moylan's "Tattoo," Nancy Holder's "Crash Cart," Steve Rasnic Tem's "Doodles," or Thomas Tessier's "The Last Crossing," the authors can get along just fine without resorting to the supernatural. In a few cases, such as Holder's especially unpleasant story about a respected doctor who tortures his wife to death as a sexual game, the horror arises precisely because of the author's refusal to give us a supernatural escape route.

Fantasy, however, is another matter: you can't really tell what a fantasy is by the way you respond to it. Or can you? This is where the question of tone becomes more problematical, and where Windling's introductory comment about the older narrative roots of such fiction becomes important. If there's a single trend in this year's anthology (and there isn't – there are two, but I'll get to the other one in a minute), it's a trend toward fiction *about* fiction – stories rooted in other stories, or in myths and superstitions that suggest a fantasy pedigree even though the tales themselves may not always be fantastic. The most obvious examples are those stories that refer to particular antecedents – Ursula Le Guin's "The Poacher" (a moving take on Sleeping Beauty), Thomas Disch's "One Night, Or Scheherezade's Bare Minimum," Elizabeth Hand's "The Erl-King" (which imaginatively updates the Goethe tale to the era of Andy Warhol's Factory – the same focus as her novel Black Light), Bruce McAllister's Santa Claus tale "Cottage," Patricia McKillip's urbanized version of "The Snow Queen," Neil Gaiman's "Troll Bridge" (from "Three Billy-Goats Gruff"), Daniel Hood's "The Wealth of Kingdoms" (a clever but somewhat overdone parody of the economics of Jack and the Beanstalk), Graham Masterson's "The Taking of Mr. Bill" (which malignly reinterprets Peter Pan as a zombie child-killer). Other stories are cast specifically in the form of fairy tales: "The Chrysanthemum Spirit," by Osama Dazai (a Japanese writer who died in 1948 and who the editors deserve much credit for introducing to us); Rafik Schami's Syrian parable of the lure of storytelling itself, "The Storyteller"; Rosario Ferré's Puerto Rican tale "Rice and Milk"; Will Shetterly's "The Princess Who Kicked Butt" (which covers some of the same ground as the Disch story, but with a joke that never really goes beyond the title); O.V. de L. Milosz's

Lithuanian fairy tale "Alvyta"; Patricia McKillip's excellent "Lady of the Skulls"; Jane Yolen's George MacDonald-like fantasia on a tombstone inscription, "Inscription." (The disproportionate number of non-English titles in that list is interesting, and makes you wonder if Yolen and a handful of other American writers might be almost alone in keeping alive a tradition still rich everywhere else.)

Still other stories use literature or literary interpretation as significant plot elements. Two of the funniest stories in the book, Fred Chappell's "The Lodger" and Sara Paretsky's "Freud at Thirty Paces" (which is a delight even as it seems way out of place here) satirize bad writers and trendy critics. Miriam Grace Monfredo's "The Apprentice" uses literary texts as a way of uncovering a child's troubling secret. Both the Paretsky and Monfredo stories are structured essentially like mysteries, yet another literary form that is also echoed in Charles de Lint's "Dead Man's Shoes"; Robert Devereaux's bizarre tale of a clown world, "Ridi Bobo"; and Robert Westall's haunting (but very mainstream) story of tracking down the figures in old photographs, "In Camera".

The second trend that seems to me apparent in this annual is a tendency toward romance — perhaps not a trend at all, but simply a hint that Datlow and Windling may themselves be closet romantics. At least a fifth of the stories prominently concern children — a sure source of sentiment — and one is even a love paean to a faithful dog (Mary Ellis's "Angel"). Pre-Raphaelite-like obsession is at the heart of Lisa Goldstein's "The Woman in the Painting"; love entering the lives of two maiden sisters is the focus of Carol Emshwiller's "Mrs. Jones"; and dead lovers return in Michael Marshall Smith's "Later," Nicholas Royle's "The Crucian Pit," and Caila Rossi's "Small Adjustments" (in which the dead husband never really goes away, but keeps getting reincarnated on the fringes of his wife's life). Love redeems nearly-lost souls in Adam Corbin Fusco's "Breath" and Harlan Ellison's "Susan," as well as the tales by Dazai, Ellis, and McAllister. Even Dan Simmons's "Dying in Bangkok," the best of the book's gruelling gross-out stories, turns out to be a tragic tale of unrequited love and revenge.

As long as I've mentioned the gross-out stories, I should mention that the prize for sheer unpleasantness goes to Roberta Lannes's medical *vagina dentata* nightmare, "Precious." In general, though, splatter-horror doesn't get a lot of coverage, nor do traditional horror icons. To be sure, zombies seem to be making a comeback (as is their wont, I guess) thanks to three stories from last year's *Mammoth Book of Zombies*, and Ian McDonald offers an intelligent rethinking of incubi and succubi in "Some Strange Desire," but for the most part the editors have avoided the predictable vampires and elder gods. Many of the most memorable stories don't fit easily in any of the categories I've mentioned. Terry Bisson's "England Underway" bizarrely combines the strange voyage of the title with problems of reading Trollope. Gabriel Garcia Marquez's hilarious "The Saint," with its hiccuping Pope and incorruptible dead child, seems a perfect one-story definition of magic realism. Terry Dowling's "The Daemon Street Ghost Trap" rethinks the ghost story in an entirely new way.

Sherman Alexie's "Distances" investigates Native American lore in a convincingly authentic voice that is at the same time quite modern. John Crowley creates his own mysterious mythography in "Exogamy," and Danith McPherson creates a seductive mythical Africa in "Roar at the Heart of the World".

If, like me, you've never heard of many of the writers represented here, that isn't even half the story. Nearly a hundred pages of introductory essays cover enough additional material — from novels to comics and music — to convince you that you haven't the faintest clue as to what's *really* going on out there, and that the editors really know what they're talking about (as do their guest summarizers Will Shetterly, Emma Bull, and Edward Bryant). We can niggle over the appropriateness of individual selections, and debate their generous definitions of fantasy and horror, but it's hard to deny they've produced another first-rate collection of riches. Far from a best-of-type anthology (as some earlier horror and fantasy annuals were), *The Year's Best* is becoming more and more a broad-based literary annual, but with a particular tone and a particular audience — sort of a *Best American Short Stories* with an attitude (and with a far more international cast).

Still, for all their focus on mainstream virtues, the Datlow and Windling annuals are largely bought and read by genre readers. What, then, might we expect from a decidedly upscale Oxford University Press anthology with the potential of reaching a much broader mainstream audience? Tom Shippey's **The Oxford Book of Fantasy Stories** has already received enthusiastic reviews in the mainstream press, and seems well-positioned to become one of those texts that will provide a kind of baseline definition of modern fantasy for some time to come. Is it, then, another mainstream reclamation project, a kind of sanitary landfill bent on establishing a pedigree for a despised genre by hauling out the familiar litany of Forster, Henry James, Kafka, Singer, and such, with perhaps a polite nod in the direction of Tolkien and Lewis and a smattering of safely postmodern literary icons like Barthelme and Barth?

Not even close. There's not an inkling of an Inkling here, and the closest we get to a literary *doyenne* is Angela Carter ("The Erl-King"), who somehow managed to write both in genre and out at the same time. Shippey, a distinguished academic with plenty of pedigrees of his own, has chosen a radically different strategy; hoping to "rescue a powerful living tradition from academic marginalization," he argues vigorously for what he calls "common usage and current practice" in fantasy literature — in other words, the kinds of popular fantasy likely to be familiar to genre readers, but hitherto almost invisible in anthologies of this sort. Shippey isn't out to show that respectable writers have written fantasy; he wants to show that fantasy writers can write respectable fiction. By his own count, about a third of his selections are variations on sword-and-sorcery tales — perhaps the single most maligned subgenre of modern fantastic writing. Is Shippey just being perverse, or is he up to something?

I think he's up to something important. More than any other anthology in recent memory, *The Oxford Book of Fantasy Stories* succeeds in recreating for both new and veteran readers the experience of discovering modern genre fantasy, an experience that normally takes years of reading, of gradually coming to realize that each new writer represents whole new worlds, as well as characteristic styles and techniques – but with a common heritage. I found myself remembering my own discovery of Lovecraft, and how that led backward to Dunsany and forward to Clark Ashton Smith – a pattern that can also be followed in this collection. The connections between these and other authors are implicit throughout the book, and by the time you're through, you have no doubt that fantasy, as Shippey presents it, is not simply a matter of technique or mode, but a conscious dialogue – as he says, a "living tradition".

The main strategy he uses to convey this sense of tradition is his consistent and deliberate use of what some critics would call "megatexts": nearly half the selections come from story sequences with imaginary worlds or characters that extend far beyond the specific tales included. Thus, we are introduced to Dunsany's mythology through "The Forest Unvanquishable, Save for Sacnoth," to Lovecraft's through "The Nameless City." We learn of Clark Ashton Smith's Zothique through "Xeethra," Jack Vance's Dying Earth through "Liane the Wayfarer," Thomas Burnett Swann's Greece through "The Sudden Wings," James Tiptree, Jr.'s Quintana Roo through "Beyond the Dead Reef." We meet C.L. Moore's Jirel of Joiry, Fritz Leiber's Fafhrd and the Gray Mouser, Henry Kuttner's Hogben family and Ray Bradbury's "Homecoming" family, Keith Roberts's Anita, Manly Wade Wellman's Silver John, John Brunner's Traveller in Black, Sterling Lanier's Brigadier Ffellowes, even Robert E. Howard's Conan (showing uncharacteristic restraint in a tale of surprising sensitivity, "The Tower of the Elephant"). Science fictional treatments of magic are represented with stories from Poul Anderson's "Operation Chaos" series and Larry Niven's "Magic Goes Away" series. Even many of the non-series selections, such as Phyllis Eisenstein's "Subworld" (about mice-people in the subway) or Jane Yolen's "Johanna" (about a were-deer) present worlds that might yield additional narratives, further reinforcing the theme that fantasy is as much about world-views as about stories.

But – and this is where Shippey's volume may connect to Datlow and Windling's – as Shippey suggests in his provocative introduction, fantasy is also about tone. He argues that modern fantasy, under the influence of archeological discoveries and the privileging of scientific attitudes, moved from the earlier "genteel" tradition of unexplained phenomena politely shrugged off (represented here by Richard Garnett's "The Demon Pope" and a few more recent selections) toward a growing need to interrogate the fantasy worlds, to locate their geography and uncover the rules by which they work. This leads not only to the science fictional treatments of Anderson and Niven – to what David Hartwell in a different context has called "sword-and-sorcery procedurals" – but to psychologically sophisticated, self-interpreting stories such as those by Angela Carter and Tanith Lee ("Bite-Me-Not or Fleur de Fur") and to stories with contemporary settings, such as those by Eisenstein, Avram Davidson ("The Singular Events Which Occurred in the Hovel on the Alley off of Eye Street"), Mervyn Peake ("Same Time, Same Place") and Peter Beagle ("Lila the Werewolf"). Toward the end of the collection, this tone becomes by turns comic and elegiac, as Brunner's "The Wager Lost by Winning" shows the forces of Chaos at bay in a changing world and Terry Pratchett's "The Troll Bridge" shows a debased "Cohen the Barbarian" facing down an equally underemployed troll. Like the heroic worlds it portrays, the fantasy tradition Shippey outlines in *The Oxford Book of Fantasy Stories* may be on the wane, giving way to parodies of itself and to the far more diffuse fictions represented by Datlow and Windling. But it was fun while it lasted, and Shippey has done us all a service by giving it a respectable home.

Here's a thought: SF has often promoted itself with the phrase "literature of ideas," but the similar phrase "novel of ideas" is more likely to connote heavy-duty mainstream intellectual fictions about as far from SF as you can get — Thomas Mann or Saul Bellow, say. Why is that? Why does SF, for all its willingness to tackle enormous cosmic questions, seem so often to shy away from genuine intellectual fictions? For that matter, why does intellectual fiction shy away from SF, even when its premises seem to lead in that direction? (Plenty of exceptions come to mind on both sides, of course; Doris Lessing cheerfully moved her "Children of Violence" series into SF territory when her larger narrative called for it, and Kim Stanley Robinson shows intelligent characters debating the nature of government in his Mars novels.)

One writer with substantial credentials in both camps is Brian Aldiss, whose 1980 *Life in the West* inaugurated a series that Aldiss now calls "the Squire Quartet" after that novel's protagonist Thomas Squire, who also appears briefly in Aldiss's new **Somewhere East of Life**. Like *Life in the West*, the two intermediate novels in the quartet are mainstream, but of interest to SF readers. SF itself gets discussed at length in *Life*, and the role of fantasy in making life bearable is a central topic in *Forgotten Life*, and plays something of a role in *Remembrance Day* as well. *Somewhere East of Life*, parts of which have been published as straight SF (in *New Worlds* and *Universe*) starts with a clear SF premise: through a process called "e-mnemonicvision" or EMV, parts of people's memories can be recorded and sold as entertainment. The only problem is that the original memory is lost, and some unscrupulous producers steal the memories of unsuspecting victims. This is what happens to Aldiss's protagonist, Roy Burnell, a professional cataloguer of architectural treasures for an organization called World Antiquities and Cultural Heritage (WACH).

In contrast to the relatively domestic settings of his last two novels, Aldiss leads us on a series of often hair-raising and sometimes violent adventures through a near-future Europe as Burnell tries to carry on with his work while searching for the EMV "bullets" that contain his lost ten years of memory. From a mysterious clinic in Budapest, the action shifts to the English village of Bishops Linctus (where

Burnell narrowly escapes slaughter by a mass-murderer), then back to Budapest and Frankfurt, then to the remains of Soviet Georgia (where he becomes involved with – and eventually assassinates – a brutal local strongman), next to Turkmenistan, and finally to his family home in Norfolk. Throughout, reminders of the novel's near-future setting – wristwatches that are also AIDS indicators, a nuclear meltdown in a former Soviet republic – are subtly backgrounded; the most memorable images are those evocative of Burnell's plight, such as a lost medieval ikon called "The Madonna of Futurity" and a half-finished bridge once meant to unite the Muslim peoples of Turkmenistan and Iran. Through such images, we become aware of the odd parallels between Burnell's search for his personal past and his efforts to catalog the rapidly disappearing past of Europe and the former Soviet empire.

The risk in such an enterprise as *Somewhere East of Life* is evident in its publisher's own categorization of it as "Fiction/Science Fiction," as though two different bases need to be covered. Mainstream readers, while impressed at Aldiss's broad grasp of the current muddy state of civilization and his perceptive handling of themes of memory and identity, might view the SF elements as little more than convenient set-ups or plot gimmicks. SF readers might want a more cyberpunkish focus on EMV technology, wondering why (for example) memories would have to be destroyed in order to be recorded, and what all this stuff about central Asia is for (despite the fact that Aldiss, a seasoned travel writer, seems to have found in these remote locales exactly the kind of ruined landscapes and neomedieval societies that other writers build whole planets for). It's not quite a case of holding two contradictory ideas in mind at once, because it seems to me that *Somewhere East of Life* really is conceived as both mainstream and SF at the same time – a tour-de-force that evokes Kosinski as well as Dick, that is consistent both with Aldiss's recent SF and with the three mainstream novels that preceded it. In short, it aspires to be a "novel of ideas" within the framework of SF's "literature of ideas," and it succeeds on both counts – with the added bonus of more flat-out adventure than we've seen from Aldiss in quite a while.

Now Aldiss has me thinking about writers who seem to saddle SF and the mainstream, at least in terms of thematic content. One such writer is Australia's George Turner, whose sad story "I Still Call Australia Home" is one of the high points of Paul Collins's anthology **Metaworlds**. Back in March, we looked at Terry Dowling and Van Ikin's *Mortal Fire: Best Australian Science Fiction*; Collins's book is also subtitled "Best Australian Science Fiction," and more than half its contributors also appeared in the earlier anthology. Is there so much "best" stuff coming out of Australia that multiple volumes are needed? Of course there is, especially since Australians still conform to the old-fashioned practice of producing convenient, hand-held volumes of only a dozen or so stories each (whereas American anthologies, by contrast, seem increasingly designed to fit into workout programs). I have no way of determining if the stories collected in *Metaworlds* are significantly better than the stories not collected here, but they make up another provocative overview of a lively and energetic tradition of SF writing.

In his introduction, Collins notes the tendency toward "birth/rebirth and transmutation themes" among the stories included, and indeed the collection starts off strong with Greg Egan's "Learning to Be Me," another of Egan's ingenious explorations of alternative modes of consciousness (note his *Permutation City*, reviewed in June). In this case, people have learned to achieve a kind of immortality by implanting indestructible "jewels" in their brains which duplicate the brain's learning and memory; at a key point — before the jewel begins duplicating the brain's decay and loss of memory — control of the body is switched over to the jewel. Characteristically, though, Egan asks what it might be like to be the jewel. Rebirth also figures in Dirk Strasser's "Waiting for the Rain" (one of four stories in the collection originally published in America), in which a colonist gradually assumes the form of one of the intelligent plants unthinkingly annihilated during colonization. In Damien Broderick's "A Tooth for Every Child," a man carrying his dead wife's child in an artificial implanted womb watches his mother die giving birth to a strange mutation; he takes vengeance on the infant before tragically realizing what such mutations really are. In Leanne Frahm's "Reichelman's Relics," a space miner on a remote asteroid tries to nurse alien eggs to life. The whole notion of nurturing and motherhood is given a bitterly satiric treatment in Rosaleen Love's "The Total Devotion Machine." And far-future post-technological societies are the focus of David Lake's "Re-deem the Time" (in which a future society decides to run time backwards, eliminating certain technical advances at predetermined points and thus rendering history fully deterministic) and Turner's "I Still Call Australia Home," a moving version of the familiar scenario of a spacecraft crew returning to earth after several centuries and finding itself not welcome.

Several of these stories — Lake, Strasser, Turner — also deal with the ecological themes that seem so pervasive in Australian SF, and that are made even more explicit in two complementary tales — Terry Dowling's "The Last Elephant" and Jack Wodhams's "The Token Pole." Dowling's story — which along with Turner's may generate the strongest emotional power in the collection — describes the rituals that develop as humans systematically watch the extinction of other species, after trying too late to keep the last specimens alive. Wodhams chooses a different strategy, portraying a world in which rampant *reforestation* itself threatens to become an ecological hazard. In one of the book's most original conceptions, Sean McMullen combines history and evolutionary biology in a strange but hypnotic tale concerning — well, concerning intelligent electrosensitive possums. The remaining two stories explore aspects of dehumanization. Paul Collins's "The Wired Kid" portrays a future in which terminally ill patients are used as cannon fodder for violent tv programs, and Stephen Dedman's "But Smile No More" concerns the effects of a drug which shuts down the pleasure centers of the brain — "a cure for happiness," as one character aptly puts it. Few of the stories try for radical narrative techniques — Dedman's is even cast in the familiar form of the barroom confession – but all of them play with good ideas, and treat those ideas with the sense of discovery and excitement that has become more characteristic of Australian writing than of any other kind.

Lunar Memoirs

J.G. Ballard may have been the one who was right all along. With his abandoned gantries and launch pads, aging and regretful astronauts, and titles like *Memories of the Space Age*, he seems in retrospect to have captured more presciently than anyone else the odd kind of technopolitical nostalgia that's already beginning to envelope our memories of the space race. Now, 25 years after the moon landing and nearly 22 years after the abandonment of the moon, it seems more clear than ever that older SF's doggedly rationalistic vision of the birth of space exploration was a textbook case of premature extrapolation. The sense of awe and wonder that you can still get even from old films like *Destination: Moon* is almost invisible in two memoirs published to coincide with the anniversary of the moon landing, Alan Shepard and Deke Slayton's **Moon Shot** and Slayton's autobiography, **Deke!**. Whereas SF writers and readers viewed going to the moon as a stirring, almost evolutionary challenge to humanity, the people who actually went into space saw it – and still see it – as a set of engineering problems to be solved in the service of a political and ideological public relations program.

Not that these detailed memoirs fail to capture the suspense and excitement of those years – they do, and they each offer a great many anecdotes that were previously unfamiliar to me, although much of the ground covered was handled in higher style in Tom Wolfe's 1979 *The Right Stuff*. (Slayton, in his autobiography, admits that he liked that book more than the other astronauts, although he complains about what he regards as Wolfe's unfair treatment of Gus Grissom.) But in reading about these real-life adventures, I kept trying to remember what it was like to read SF versions of the same thing at about the same time, and what eventually came to mind was a now-forgotten *Astounding* story from 1958 called "Murphy's Law" (I have no idea who the author, "Hugh B. Brous, Jr." was, or if the story was ever reprinted; I suspect the only reason I remember it is that it's where I first learned of Murphy's Law.) The story described launch pad blowups, incompatible rocket stages built by different contractors, control panel indicators that didn't work, shipboard clocks out of sync, arguments over getting a window in the spacecraft, endless launch postponements – all snafus that are recounted in real life by Shepard and Slayton. The story was supposed to be a joke – a parody of how spaceflight could go wrong – but it looks in retrospect as though Brous, whoever he was, was on the right track. As much as anything, it's the litany of real-life screwups that help to make both of these memoirs almost comically entertaining – Shepard desperately needing to urinate in a Mercury spacesuit that had no provision for it, an enraged chimp named Ham emerging from a 1961 test flight and biting everyone in sight after having been inadvertently subjected to 15 Gs, Slayton himself shattering the windows in his neighborhood when he decides to fly over his house and say hi to his son by kicking in the afterburner of his F-106.

But there are more serious ways in which these accounts of the space program reflect earlier SF visions. Slayton, who died of cancer last year, emerges as the hero not only of his own autobiography but of Moon Shot, which is structured around his grounding at the beginning of the Mercury program (due to an occasional heart fibrillation), his subsequent management of the astronaut corps, and his finally making it into space on the Apollo-Soyuz mission; this reads like nothing so much as the plot of Heinlein's "Requiem." And Slayton, along with the other astronauts, seem to represent the fruition of another Heinleinian dogma – the myth of the competent engineer. The justifiable pride with which Shepard and Slayton describe the split-second problem-solving skills of the pilot-astronauts – such as Gordon Cooper's stick-and-rudder re-entry of the last Mercury capsule when the automatic navigational system failed – reflect the value they place on the kind of practical technical skills that Heinlein had so long valorized. This is reflected further in the vague distrust in which the earliest scientist-astronauts were held, and the more open distrust of politicians, bureaucrats, and contractors, who emerge as clear villains in such episodes as the Apollo fire that killed Grissom, White, and Chaffee. Ironically, it is this tragedy and the near-tragedy of the ill-fated Apollo 13 mission that provide the dramatic high points of both books – that most nearly capture a science fictional sense of wonder. The 1969 landing itself, while presented with as much fanfare as Slayton, Shepard, and their co-writers can muster, seems almost anticlimactic.

Moon Shot offers a more complete and balanced account of the space race, but Deke! is by far the better book. Working with TV writer and space journalist Michael Cassutt, the famously taciturn Slayton comes across as blunt, opinionated, conversational – in other words, with a distinctly human voice. He succinctly sums up his reactions to the death of his close friend Gus Grissom with "It was a bad day. Worst I ever had." He recounts, perhaps a bit too often, what his favorite planes were as a test pilot, what it felt like to fly in both the Italian and Pacific campaigns in World War II, what it was like to train and briefly share a spacecraft with his Soviet counterparts. He admits he started out uninterested in space flight, and his account never strives for fake poetic effects. Collaborator Cassutt deserves credit for letting Slayton's voice and personality come through so clearly. While much of the same material is covered in Moon Shot, the aerospace journalists Jay Barbree and Howard Benedict never let us hear either Shepard or Slayton clearly; both putative authors are referred to in the third person throughout, and the book itself constantly works at building a portentous and dramatic narrative. Perhaps that's what's needed for a new generation born after the last man left the moon, but Slayton's sometimes grumbly voice seems more authentic.

Star Trek Lit

Ironically, only 47 days before the moon landing, network television broadcast the last original episode of Star Trek. Heinlein's "Requiem" comes to mind here, too

– it's well-known that thanks to a sympathetic astronaut, Gene Roddenberry finally got his ashes hauled, posthumously, on a space-shuttle mission – but I'm having a hard time getting it through my skull that Roddenberry qualifies as a Heinlein hero, let alone one of the great cultural innovators of the 20th century, a spiritual guru, and the inventor of most SF concepts and ideas that I had previously thought had been around for generations. I realize that this may partly be due to my own obtuseness, but it seems to me that both David Alexander's massive "authorized" hagiography, **Star Trek Creator**, and Joel Engel's scandal-mongering demonization, **Gene Roddenberry: The Myth and the Man Behind "Star Trek"**, lead pretty much to the same conclusions. Engel's shoddy book is actually more entertaining, if only because of its relentless mean-spiritedness, but it shares with Alexander's 600-page press release a kind of awe-struck naivete about the ways in which the TV and movie industries work. Engel wants to shock us with his portrayal of Roddenberry as an alcoholic, womanizing, attention-grabbing egomaniac with limited talent and a penchant for stealing other people's ideas – in other words, a TV producer. What else is new? Alexander wants us to swallow the myth of a war hero ex-cop who fought valiantly to bring to the screen a humanistic philosophy of a better tomorrow – even though all *Star Trek* showed us of this vision was a militaristic spaceship armed to the teeth with defensive shields and photon torpedos. (Even the much-vaunted "first interracial kiss on TV" – between Kirk and Uhura – was the result not of affection but of evil alien coercion.)

The Roddenberry myth, in its purest form, is expressed in the opening pages of William Shatner's **Star Trek Memories** – for the most part, a collection of amusing but trivial anecdotes about production and casting problems. Shatner sets his dramatic account of the origin of *Star Trek* in El Paso in the mid-1920s, where a sickly child escapes to a makeshift cardboard-box spaceship to read his copies of *Astounding* and dream of a better tomorrow. Never mind that, according to Alexander, Roddenberry left El Paso when he was nineteen months old, or that *Astounding* didn't appear until six years after that – what we're dealing with here is *Hollywood bio*, a peculiar genre whose main imperatives are to give the audience what it expects, to validate gossip and trivia as cultural history, and to make the offhand remarks of famous people sound like philosophy.

No better example of this attitude can be found than in Alexander's memorable sentence, "Nineteen thirty-nine was a good year for films and a bad year for Europe," which he follows with a list of a dozen hit movies and an almost offhand mention that "Adolph" Hitler invaded Poland. In the Hollywood mythos, new releases always get top billing. (Almost as if to acknowledge this, Alexander offers explanatory footnotes and bonehead-history background on everything from who Greta Garbo and John W. Campbell were to what SNAFU meant; he seems to be targeting readers who can only get their historical bearings through mentions of actors and movies, and need explanations for everything else. Is this the *Star Trek* generation?) Engel and Shatner aren't any better; for them the world of *Star Trek* might as well have existed in a social and cultural vacuum, the product solely of contract negotiations and studio politics.

None of these books offer much useful insight into how *Star Trek* evolved or what it represented; Alexander and Engel both note that someone loaned Roddenberry a copy of *Last and First Men* when he was trying to figure out what SF was, and both credit him with trying to get professional SF writers involved (including one whom Alexander repeatedly calls "Pohl Anderson"). The most famous *Star Trek* script story, concerning Roddenberry's rewrite of Harlan Ellison's "City on the Edge of Forever," is recounted in all three books; none of them note how Roddenberry introduced an ideological subtext critical of the then-budding antiwar movement. Alexander notes that Don Ingalls was similarly so outraged at Roddenberry's rewrite of an anti-Vietnam script that he invoked his Writer's Guild pseudonym – but fails to note that the rewrite, far from being antiwar, clearly supports the "balance-of-power" argument that was then official U.S. policy. (Both of these episodes are analyzed tellingly in Bruce Franklin's essay "*Star Trek* in the Vietnam Era" in the March 1993 *Science-Fiction Studies*.) Alexander consistently argues that such rewrites preserved Roddenberry's pristine vision, while Engel argues that they reduced many episodes to a level of mediocrity or even incompetence. It's entirely possible they're both right. But both seem to miss the point that *Star Trek* may have had something to do with SF, and something to do with the 1960s. That book – one that simply looks at the actual *Star Trek* episodes in the context of its time and its antecedents – has yet to be written, which is pretty amazing when you consider that the publishing industry has begun to spew out *Star Trek*-related books with a degree of incontinence hitherto reserved for cats and celebrity workouts.

Shatner, for his part, cheerfully recounts one anecdote after another, and then professes astonishment when he comes to realize, at the end of the book, that some of the other cast members hated him for his arrogance and screen-hogging. In some ways, his book seems the most honest of the three, because it begins and ends with the classic Hollywood bio premise that history is made up of egos rather than events. Roddenberry's ego is what haunts all three books, but none of them are able to back off far enough to suggest any substantial new insights on what Roddenberry actually accomplished; instead of cultural history, what we get is marketing strategy; even as Roddenberry withdrew (or was pushed) from involvement in the later movies and successor TV series, the studios continued to be wary of him for fear that he somehow controlled a huge mass of fans crucial to the ongoing success of the franchise and committed to his personal "vision." (I doubt that the fans were ever that zombie-like, but in a perverse way it must have been comforting for Hollywood to think so.)

Perhaps, in the end, marketing is the key to most of what Roddenberry actually did accomplish: he found a way of packaging familiar SF concepts for a brutally simple-minded TV environment, and he empowered fans in a manner beyond their wildest dreams. *Star Trek* may have only sporadically achieved coherence as dramatic art, but it achieved something even more seductive: the mass marketing of that most classically dull of ideologies, utopian humanism. Just how seductive this was is apparent in the ways in which Roddenberry was able to enlist figures such as Clarke, Asimov and Bradbury – and even Ellison, for a time – to his cause. Just how much it can destabilize your brain is apparent in John W. Campbell, Jr.'s lone contribution to the marketing blitz: in a letter to Roddenberry (quoted in Alexander), he enthusiastically offers up the idea of fuzzy Spock hats for kids, complete with pink felt Vulcan ears. (Why didn't he ever suggest *that* to Hubbard?)

We get a much clearer idea of how Roddenberry's mind worked in Yvonne Fern's **Gene Roddenberry: The Last Conversation**, an extremely odd book from the University of California Press, part of a series called "Portraits in American Genius" which, to give us some bearings, also includes a study of cartoonist Chuck Jones. What this book reveals is that, whether or not Roddenberry had a thoroughly thought-out *Star Trek* philosophy when he began, he certainly developed one once he realized how many people were listening to him. Fern spent several months with Roddenberry and his wife – as it turned out, the last months of Roddenberry's life – and the book is an account of the extended conversations that took place during that period. And it is indeed a conversation rather than an interview; Fern makes herself as much the center of attention as Roddenberry, leaping on every opportunity to show how delighted and amazed he was at her softball "philosophical" questions ("What is the difference between truth and integrity?" "What would you not want to lose?"). The main point of the book seems to be to chronicle the developing spiritual bond between Fern and Roddenberry – she seems to want to portray herself as Joy Davidman to Roddenberry's C.S. Lewis, and she isn't averse to grasping at mystical straws to find evidence of this. Since Fern was born near Pearl Harbor after the war, and since Roddenberry flew in the Pacific theater, Fern writes, "I am certain that my existence on this planet is related to his – that we shared a direct connection".

Fern's relentlessly enlightened New Age attitude permeates the book, but syrupy as it is, it may provide some of the clearest evidence yet of how Star Trek's appeal has transcended SF's traditionally rationalistic base to become a pop philosophy

(Fern uses the term Star Trek – unitalicized – to distinguish this philosophy from the *Star Trek* shows and movies.) It may annoy some SF readers to see how she uncritically credits Roddenberry with ideas that predate *Star Trek* by decades – "first contact" is defined not as a traditional SF plot, but as the *Enterprise* crew meeting up with aliens, and such familiar chestnuts as society-organisms, humanity as an adolescent species, and dumping minds into computers are all presented as startling Roddenberry insights. In fact, it's hard to find an original idea anywhere in the book, and many of those that do crop up seem confused. Both Fern and Roddenberry refer to androids as machines, and when she gets around to asking him what the difference between an android and a robot is, his response is "'I don't know, exactly. I don't remember'".

If Roddenberry's general grasp of SF seems slight, one book emerges as the most likely source for the *Star Trek* concept itself, and not surprisingly, it's a boys' book.

Roddenberry describes Heinlein's *Space Cadet* as "one of the most significant books in my life," and indeed Heinlein's multinational crew and code of honor seems reflected in the *Enterprise*. But precious little other SF gets mentioned in the book, and even other *Star Trek* writers get little credit. "'I *am* Star Trek," Roddenberry repeatedly insists – a claim that takes on a certain pathos when we realize that by now he had pretty much lost creative control of his franchise – and he also insists on his identity as a writer rather than a producer. "I couldn't write a bad script if I tried," he boasts, momentarily forgetting *Pretty Maids All in a Row*. And if there's any doubt remaining about his emerging self-conscious guru-dom, note his response to Fern's question about whether others will remember him as a "pleasant person": "No. Some persons have been attracted to false paths." Not Fern, however: she comes away from her encounter with Roddenberry with a beatific glow, and her book is the testament of a disciple.

Another disciple is Dave Marinaccio, an ad executive whose **All I Really Need to Know I Learned from Watching Star Trek** pushes the notion of *Star Trek* as philosophy right into the feelgood territory of such pop gurus as Robert Fulghum, whose bestselling title Marinaccio deliberately rips off. His book offers about as much substance as those Star Trek greeting cards and lapel buttons that have been around the past few years, and that's likely to be the secret of its success – taking already simplified ideas and simplifying them even further (I can see the same trendy computer-store managers who three years ago were xeroxing pages from *Leadership Secrets of Attila the Hun* for their hapless employees doing the same with this paltry volume). At first, Marinaccio gets off some good, breezy lines ("I live in Washington, D.C. We have all your money"), and he openly admits his observations are simplistic ("These are lessons culled from a television show, not the library at Alexandria"), but it quickly becomes apparent that he's at least half serious, mixing throwaway jokes (Kirk shows us it's ok to have a potbelly) with familiar bromides (every organization should have a mission statement like the Enterprise's) and genuinely lame-brained epiphanies (a car is today's version of a transporter pad).

What is interesting about Marinaccio's book, other than the fact that its title is self-evidently wrong, is that it demonstrates two things about the Star Trek phenomenon that none of the other books quite make clear. The first is that Star Trek no longer has anything to do with SF; Marinaccio claims to be inspired and motivated by the provocative ideas on the show, but it seems never to have occurred to him to turn the set off and go find a book that might extend or deepen these ideas. The second is that, freed of references to anything but itself, Star Trek has gotten loose in the culture in a way far beyond its earlier cult status. Marinaccio makes it clear that he himself is not a Trekkie, and he's pretty sure there are many more like himself – people who don't go to conventions, don't know about the fanzines, don't read even Star Trek fiction, but who find their conversations and thoughts peppered with references to tribbles and transporter beams. At the end of the book, Marinaccio invites these people to send him examples of how Star Trek has changed their lives.

(Clearly, he isn't done with us yet.) If this book and *Gene Roddenberry: The Last Conversation* are any indication, *Star Trek* may just turn out to be the first genuine TV-bred religion, and the producers may have missed the boat by not just going ahead and titling the sequel series *Star Trek: The New Testament.*

— September 1994, Locus #404 —

Future Primitive: The New Ecotopias ~~ ed. by Kim Stanley Robinson

Future Quartet ~~ ed. by Charles Sheffield

Peace on Earth ~~ Stanislaw Lem
(trans. by Elinor Ford with Michael Kandel)

This Side of Judgment ~~ J. R. Dunn

Martians and Misplaced Clues: The Life and Work of Fredric Brown ~
~ Jack Seabrook

As Brian Aldiss noted in "Utopia: Dream or Pipe Dream" in the May 1993 *Locus*, "the zeitgeist has turned its phantasmal back on utopianism." Still, this persistent subtheme of SF survives, even though it seems to be undergoing a kind of metamorphosis in the post-cold war era. For decades — perhaps centuries — this subgenre was fueled by a kind of paranoia bred from competing ideologies. Writers warned us of forces at large that would either prevent this wonderful society from coming about, or that would lead directly to this other, terribly depressing society, or both. As narratives, dystopias clearly had the advantage, if for no other reason than that they provided their characters with something interesting to do beyond listening to lectures. This either/or approach had already begun to change in the 1970s, when writers such as Le Guin, Russ, and Delany began investigating what critic Tom Moylan has called "critical utopias" — imaginative societies that interrogate the whole notion of the utopian tradition and that are, in Le Guin's word, "ambiguous." But even the key utopian work of the past couple of decades — Le Guin's *The Dispossessed* — focused on a bipolar opposition, as though we really only had two futures to choose from, neither of them perfect. With the decline of the major totalitarian states, SF writers seemed freed to explore more multivalent futures — in effect, to start over from scratch in asking what kinds of societies we might want to live in, or to avoid. (Is it too farfetched to wonder if the fall of communism had something to do with the sudden proliferation of Mars colonization novels in the last couple of years?) Kim Stanley Robinson, at least, has deliberately used his Mars novels to reinvigorate utopian-style debates, and now he's set out to do much the same thing in an unusual anthology titled **Future Primitive**.

Clues to what *Future Primitive* is all about are already there in Robinson's Mars novels, in which the major conflict is terraforming versus preservation. The central utopian debate, he suggests, has already shifted from ideological to ecological grounds, and ecological utopias — or "ecotopias," in Ernest Callenbach's term — are at the center of this anthology. What makes the anthology unusual is that only a couple of the thirteen stories and two poems would be regarded by most readers as having anything at all to do with utopian or dystopian writing. (And Robinson acknowledges that few of the authors likely had it in mind, either.) A more accurate term for these fictions might be "utopist," in the sense that David Fausett uses it to describe symbolic rather than prescriptive or extrapolative societies (see below). Framing the collection with two ecological anthems by Gary Snyder and Robinson Jeffers, Robinson sets out to offer a selection of visions of future "primitive" societies as models of potentially healthier relationships with nature. He sees in much SF a need to re-establish some kind of unity with the natural world, and begins with a section called "Statements of Desire," including Terry Bisson's "Bears Discover Fire," Pat Murphy's "In the Abode of Snows," and R.A. Lafferty's "Boomer Flats." The latter two stories both deal with the abominable snowman legend — almost certainly the first time this figure has been presented as any kind of utopian ideal.

Robinson's sole representative of the "dystopian" tradition is equally odd: Garry Kilworth's "Hogfoot Right and Bird-hands," about an isolated old woman who has parts of her body amputated and refashioned into pets for companionship. Since we see almost nothing of this woman's society except for references to the "welfare machine" that authorizes the amputations, we're clearly meant to focus on the alienation from the body that the story portrays. Robert Silverberg's "House of Bones" offers a revisionist view of Cro-Magnons as humane and artistic, and this sets the stage for the central section of the book, titled "And Might We Ever Be Like That Again?" This leads off promisingly with Gene Wolfe's "'A Story,' by John V. Marsch," portraying the doomed aboriginal society of his *The Fifth Head of Cerberus*, and continues with Rachel Pollack's "The Bead Woman," about the inability of a near-future society to handle psychic visions. The narrative energy set up by these stories goes as flat as an emergency-room heart monitor in the next story, Ernest Callenbach's "Chocco," promoted as his first short story and one of his few works of fiction since *Ecotopia*. Set in a tribal society some thousand years from now, Callenbach's is the only piece in the collection that harks back to the deadly old utopian lecture-motif, as two competing students are asked to describe what went wrong with the "Machine People" (us) to cause their society to collapse. The ecological message is familiar, and Callenbach is clearly intended as the centerpiece of the book, but his ham-fisted talkfest isn't a story. Nor does it seem a particularly good idea to excerpt one of the more didactic passages from Frederick Turner's long poem *The New World*, which is a much more interesting work than this selection indicates.

The anthology comes alive again with Howard Waldrop's characteristically loony tale of a tractor-pull in a neoprimitive society, "Mary Margaret Road-Grader," and with the longest story in the collection, Paul Park's "Rang River Fell," set in the same dying world as his "Starbridge Chronicles" novels. The book ends with two "parables for our time," Carol Emshwiller's "Looking Down" and Ursula Le Guin's "Newton's Sleep." Robinson almost apologizes for not including a more predictable Le Guin selection – *Always Coming Home* haunts the whole anthology – but her tale of the re-emergence of nature in a squeaky-clean orbital colony seems to represent the main thrust of the collection (and its relation to more traditional SF) better than any other selection. Robinson himself notes that not many of the "primitive" environments portrayed in *Future Primitive* seem very attractive places to live, but if he means to expand the scope of utopian debate, to suggest a new way of reading much modern SF, and to convince us that we can't ever really escape the world, he does a credible and provocative job. He also provides us with endnotes and a substantial bibliography of both non-fiction and fiction related to his theme. It's a very interesting book, if you save the Callenbach for last.

If Robinson wants to present us with alternatives to traditional technological futurism, Charles Sheffield's anthology **Future Quartet** is probably exactly the sort of thing he's trying to answer. In 1990, Sheffield was commissioned by the magazine *The World & I* – kind of a crypto-Moonie-libertarian *National Geographic*, as I recall, and about the size of a Sears catalog – to create scenarios for the year 2042. Sheffield hit upon the idea of writing a scenario based on expert forecasts and asking Ben Bova, Frederik Pohl, and Jerry Pournelle to do the same. Then each writer would produce a story set in the future scenario they described. The result is four pretty dull essays and four uneven but interesting stories that not only provide us with a kind of state-of-the-art picture of traditional futurology, but offer an object lesson on how the imagination works differently in stories than in essays about the future. In every case, the story reveals far more about the nature of the authors' imaginations, and about the assumptions and anxieties that underlie their rational-sounding scenarios. Surprisingly, all but one of the stories involve education.

Ben Bova's "cautiously optimistic" scenario identifies global warming and population growth as continuing problems, but that technology might address these problems if it were more equitably available among rich and poor nations. The main enemies, of course, are politicians. But the first thing you notice in Bova's story, "Thy Kingdom Come," is that working-class people in 2042 talk and act just like small-time hoods from 1950s crime magazines. The narrator, Vic, is blackmailed into joining a terrorist plot to kidnap the Chairman of the World Council; during the resulting standoff, the Chairman patiently lectures Vic on why the world is the way it is, and offers him a nice scholarship. This is about all Bova can do to connect his large-scale scenario with the class divisions implicit in his story. Much the same is true of Pournelle and Sheffield's story "Higher Education" (in which working-class *teenagers* in 2042 talk just like juvenile delinquents in 1950s crime magazines). This is based on another "cautiously optimistic" scenario in which Pournelle tells us that global warming and acid rain aren't even problems, but that tenure for teachers may do us all in. After being expelled from school for a prank, Rick Luban goes to work on an asteroid-mining station, where he learns first-hand the value of literacy and computational skills and gets offered a nice scholarship – if he agrees to go teach. (Is Avon hoping to market this book to financial aid officers?)

Interestingly, Sheffield's own "The Price of Civilization" is one of the darker stories in the book, even though it's derived from the most "optimistic" scenario. Rather than offer everyone nice scholarships, he suggests that an era of peace and plenty may come about partly as a result of giving up on the ideal of universal education and creating a lower class of "Exempt Literacy Employees" – ironically dubbed "ElitE." When a gifted, self-taught ElitE teenager begins to fall in love with the daughter of a prosperous family significantly named Veblen, class separation gets enforced with surprising viciousness – undercutting much of Sheffield's "optimistic" scenario without actually contradicting it.

Like Sheffield, Pohl shows his characters reacting in a believable way to the conditions described in his scenario, which is the most gloomy of all (and which is by far the most readable, being itself cast as a kind of story). Pohl's "What Dreams Remain" is the best, most complex, and most cynical tale in the collection – and the only one that doesn't focus on adolescents or education. In a decaying future Florida, an unemployed engineer-turned-drifter named Jake Bailey is betrayed by a girlfriend, arrested for looting, and imprisoned. Released to the service of a reclusive millionaire (as in the Sheffield story, the wealthy live in armed enclaves), he bizarrely finds himself involved with the underground remnants of the L.-5 society – and responds in a way perfectly in keeping with his character and situation. Pohl's story may not reflect his scenario as didactically as the others, but it tells us a lot about the effects of disaster on the possibility of hope.

Stanislaw Lem is a writer who has consistently invited us to rethink utopian and dystopian assumptions, and his ironically titled **Peace on Earth** presents a future in which disarmament has been achieved on earth by simply moving the arms race to the moon, where it is carried out by intelligent, self-evolving systems in sectors assigned to different nations. In order to wage war, a nation would have to apply to the Lunar Agency for permission to use its moon weapons, but the Agency clearly doesn't plan to give anyone permission, and without it all information about the moon weapons is embargoed. In other words, no one on earth really knows what is happening on the moon or what new weapons systems have been developed by the autonomous intelligences there. Responding to rising anxiety that the moon may be evolving some kind of machine civilization, Lem's redoubtable space hero Ijon Tichy is sent to investigate, using a series of increasingly sophisticated "remotes" which are destroyed one by one under increasingly bizarre and comic circumstances. While on the moon, Tichy is subjected to a "remote callotomy," separating the two halves of his brain, so that his right hand literally doesn't know what his left hand is doing. It's a nice image of the crazed weapons race itself, and Lem makes much of its comic possibilities, offering up a number of *Dr. Strangelove*-like scenes of Tichy doing battle with his own left hand.

Apart from a slightly dated quality in the references to arms races and superpowers (the novel was published in Poland in 1987), *Peace on Earth* is a fine and very funny late work that recapitulates many of Lem's favorite themes, as well as those of other SF writers. Most notably, Tichy's repeated "deaths" as his remotes are systematically destroyed recalls Budrys's *Rogue Moon*. The remotes are also accompanied by swarms of surveillance "micropes" – mechanical insects reminiscent of Lem's own *The Invincible* – and his final remote, an intelligent molecular cloud, carries this idea of dispersed mind even further. A kind of liquid-mercury robot that forms itself in his hospital room after his return to earth seems a remarkable anticipation of exactly the same thing in *Terminator 2* (which the novel predates by four years). Images cast up from Tichy's own unconscious – either by his enemies on earth, who try to seduce him with a simulacrum of Marilyn Monroe, or by the moon intelligence – recall Solaris, as does the ineluctable nature of the moon itself. "Phantomatics," the artificial reality systems from *The Futurological Congress*, show up here as "fants," and the background of the disarmament scheme is presented in a book Tichy reads – and which is summarized at considerable length – called *The Unhumanization of Weapons Systems in the Twenty-First Century, or Upside-Down Evolution*; Lem readers will recognize it as one of his own earlier "historicophilosophical papers," working out SF ideas in essay form.

If all this sounds a bit retrospective, none of it interferes with the novel's pacing, its relentless comic inventiveness, or its exuberant style (readers familiar with Lem only through earlier, more stilted translations and retranslations may be surprised at his playfulness). A paleobotanist wants to rewrite the history of science in terms of vegetables; the right-to-life movement develops to the point that a "Probacteria" party wins seats in the German Bundestag; the use of remotes as sex-surrogates leads to a wave of complicated divorces, and eventually the sex surrogates themselves are replaced by an "Orgaz" machine straight out of Woody Allen; the prosperity resulting from the end of the arms race leads to mass illiteracy and an anti-education movement (shades of Bova and Sheffield!) For a short novel, *Peace on Earth* is packed with provocative ideas; its very digressiveness becomes a virtue. Lem's heavyweight reputation sometimes overshadows his skills at both humor and believable extrapolation – he knows how to do SF as well as satire – and this may turn out to be one of the best introductions to his work for first-time readers.

Thanks largely to A.E. Van Vogt, utopian thinking has even become a staple of another familiar SF subgenre, the superman novel, within which there has developed a sub-*sub*-genre that we might call the "slan novel." Slan novels contend that a better world can be achieved once we replace everyone in power with people as weird as ourselves. Whereas superman stories as a whole involve fairly universal wish-fulfillment fantasies, slan novels deal with the specific wish-fulfillment fantasies of

SF readers; they emphasize intellectual and psychic gifts over speed and strength, and focus on groups rather than individuals. Needless to say, these superior groups are put-upon, alienated, and socially dysfunctional, and they have to disguise their true identities and seek each other out clandestinely until they're ready to take over the world and turn it into a giant con. The old slogan "fans are slans" wasn't kidding.

J. R. Dunn's **This Side of Judgment** updates the slan mythology in a way that was probably inevitable. In place of mutations – atomic age SF's almost universal emblem of transformation – he gives us "chipheads," the subjects of a well-meaning experiment to wed humans with technology through computerized brain implants. The experiment goes awry, however; the massive data influx overwhelms the subject's mind, resulting in a progressive psychosis called Pelton's Syndrome. A group of chipheads had tried to take over the country during a destructive war with a Latin American dictator, and most were supposedly killed. But a brutal murder in a small Montana town bears the marks of a chiphead, and Ross Bohlen, agent for the federal Computer Subversion Strike Force, is called in to investigate. Bohlen is a hardboiled, cynical veteran of the war (which in flashbacks looks a lot like Vietnam), and his testy relationship with the local police and a local vigilante group get the novel off to a good start as a near-future tough-guy mystery. Unfortunately, Dunn's idea of a hardboiled style often seems derived from old John Wayne movies; Bohlen tells a vigilante, "that's not law, Nast, that's vengeance – and it's not good enough"; and elsewhere we're told of a burned-out chiphead, "You didn't hate people like that. Not where Bohlen came from you didn't." (A press release for the book describes Bohlen as wielding "a computer in one hand and a Colt Python in the other," and while Dunn can't be blamed for that memorable image, he often comes close.)

While Bohlen gets on the track of a renegade chiphead named Page, other surviving chipheads, or "imps," make their way to the same Montana town to help protect innocent chipheads from both Page and the law, and the novel begins to take on something of the form as well as the language of a western. Stories about groups of people converging on a particular place for a showdown can get pretty monotonous unless they lead to broader themes, and the theme Dunn wants to explore is the tragedy of the chipheads themselves. This is developed through his best-written and most moving subplot, in which a chiphead named Telford leaves his deteriorating lover on the East Coast to try to help out. Through Telford, we glimpse the kind of Frankensteinian plight in which the chipheads find themselves, and the plot comes close to achieving the kind of inevitability that tragedy demands. But in the end, Dunn never really follows through. Instead, we get an extended slam-bang action sequence and a couple of obligatory "surprises" that had been signalled since page one. As always, slans can't really be killed off – they only get day jobs.

Not counting books from specialty presses, there are apparently only two ways for SF writers to become the subjects of full-length critical biographies. One is to be Isaac Asimov. The other is to have established a sufficient reputation outside the

SF field to catch the attention of a wider audience. Jack Seabrook's **Martians and Misplaced Clues: The Life and Work of Fredric Brown**, would almost certainly never have been published on the strength of Brown's SF reputation alone, which rests on a few classic stories, a talent for humor rare in the genre before he arrived, and a brilliant facility for short-short stories. As a mystery writer, however, Brown has had the good fortune to be caught up in the rediscovery of 50s genre writers. His classic, tightly plotted mysteries – *The Fabulous Clipjoint, The Screaming Mimi, Night of the Jabberwock* – still get reprinted, and from 1984 to 1991 Dennis McMillan published an astonishing 19 volumes of Brown's detective pulp fiction in limited editions. These mysteries, along with Brown's almost-forgotten mainstream novel *The Office*, are the main focus of Seabrook's study, which devotes only two chapters to Brown's SF.

Like many writers trying to make a living from the pulps, Brown tried his hand at different genres even while establishing a substantial reputation as a mystery writer. He wrote a handful of western stories, and began writing SF as early as 1938, producing some of his best-known stories ("Etaoin Shrdlu," "The Waveries," "Arena") by the early 1940s. After moving to Taos in 1949 and meeting Mack Reynolds, Brown responded to the boom in SF magazines by substantially increasing his output and trying his hand at SF novels, starting with *What Mad Universe* (based on a 1948 *Startling Stories* novelette). This, together with the later *Martians, Go Home* established Brown's reputation as an SF humorist, but Seabrook also calls attention to the surprisingly moving *The Lights in the Sky are Stars*, with its almost uniquely prescient view of a 1997 in which space travel is all but abandoned. Seabrook – whose book generally tends to depend a bit too mechanically on his sources, including Brown's own logbook – lacks the sense of context for Brown's SF that he provides for the mysteries, and without the aid of Philip Klass's introduction to a 1978 reprint of *What Mad Universe*, he'd be pretty much at sea untangling the fannish in-jokes of that novel. He's quite accurate, however, in noting that Brown's later SF novels are nothing to write home about, and his portrayal of the apparent burnout that affected Brown's last decade makes for a moving elegy to a whole generation of genre writers who very nearly wrote themselves to death. Even with its lack of critical depth and tendency toward plot synopses, *Martians and Misplaced Clues* is a valuable source text, and is likely to be the most complete account of Brown's career that we'll ever see.

— October 1994, Locus #405 —

Shadow's End ~~ Sheri S. Tepper

Dark Rivers of the Heart ~~ Dean Koontz

Death Dream ~~ Ben Bova

Rim: A Novel of Virtual Reality ~~ Alexander Besher

Half the Day is Night ~~ Maureen F. McHugh

Nevermore ~~ William Hjortsberg

The Best from Fantasy & Science Fiction: A 45th Anniversary Anthology ~~ ed. by Kristine Kathryn Rusch and Edward L. Ferman

Nebula Award-Winning Novellas ~~ ed. by Martin H. Greenberg

Washed by a Wave of Wind: Science Fiction from the Corridor ~ ~ ed. by M. Shayne Bell

Lovelock ~~ Orson Scott Card and Kathryn Kidd

In little more than a decade, Sheri S. Tepper has built a fiercely loyal following, not only among feminists and not only because of her substantial skills at building complex worlds and characters. It almost certainly isn't due to the originality of her plots, which tend to follow a pretty familiar quest pattern: characters set out on journeys which gradually reveal the true nature of their world (or worlds), and along the way discover hidden strengths and often hidden identities as well. But the richness with which she endows her inventions, and the clear and strong passions which inform them, have enabled her to do wonders within this fairly narrow formula; more than any other writer, she has given coherent meaning to a term usually invoked in a mania of political correctness: ecofeminism. Shadow's End, her new novel, wears its ecofeminist didactic more openly than most of Tepper's fiction, but again the complexity of the imagination at work here lifts the novel from easy classification as a feminist novel or ecological parable.

Shadow's End takes place on a series of worlds: Earth, or "Alliance Prime," which like many planets in Tepper's Alliance has been completely "homo-normed," its native species destroyed and their DNA patterns kept in storage; Dinadh, which reflects Tepper's own southwestern landscapes and is home to a patriarchal tribal society; Kamir, an almost completely homo-normed world whose idealistic king is powerless to stop the destruction of the remaining natural environment; and Perdur Alas, an outpost for colonization which has yet to feel the destructive hand of humanity. These worlds represent various stages of the transformation of the cosmos under the influence of the "Firster" philosophy which maintains that the universe was made for man, and should be reshaped to fit his needs. (And that isn't a generic use of "man," either; Tepper makes it plain that the same impulses lie behind the marginalization of women in this future.)

A century earlier, a mysterious force wiped out the populations of several colony worlds, and now that force is back. The novel's narrator, Saluez, a girl mutilated by one of Dinadh's more unpleasant rituals involving the mysterious ghost-like Kachis, finds herself serving as maid and hostess to Lutha Tallstaff, who has arrived from Earth to try to track down clues about the threat which may have been discovered by her ex-husband's grandfather. With Lutha is her apparently retarded son Leely and a faithful companion named Trompe. Meanwhile, a rebellious young girl named Snark − ostracized into "shadowhood" for her antisocial behavior − is sent to Perdur Alas as a kind of guinea pig, since this planet seems a likely the next candidate for the mysterious exterminations. Soon, Lutha's missing husband appears, along with a pair of assassins and the King of Kamir, and much of the novel consists of this group's journey to the mythical source of Dinadh's human population. From there they are transported to Perdur Alas, where Snark has already begun to discover the true nature of the destructive force. The novel's original title, "Behold Now Behemoth," with all that suggests about the Book of Job, giant animal presences, and God's mysterious intentions, is literally realized in a visionary conclusion full of revelations, spectacular imagery, and some very Old-Testament rhetoric about the limits of human hegemony, man's disobedience, and the purpose of creation.

Tepper can bring off these big-canvas epic conclusions about as well as anyone in the SF field, and generally can convince you that her whole narrative leads inevitably toward this moment. But in *Shadow's End*, the didactic almost threatens to undermine the complexity of the worlds she has constructed. The large-scale sins represented by the Firster philosophy and the Alliance's cold-blooded despoilation of planets seem to warrant the harsh Old-Testament judgment of the conclusion, and the novel works well on this galactic scale. But some of Tepper's most interesting subplots nearly get lost in the climactic shuffle of Big Ideas. Saluez's Amerindian-like society, for example, becomes merely another illustration of patriarchal mismanagement, while the Foundation-like Alliance is only vaguely sketched in, as though SF readers should already know it (and they will). Tepper's most humanly moving story − that of Lutha's relationship with her semi-retarded son Leely − is also resolved by an expedient SF device, as Leely turns out to be far more than he seems. This may be meant as a kind of after-the-fact validation of Lutha's faith in Leely, but does such a relationship even need validation? (Just once, I'd like to see a "special" child remain special in an SF work, without the cop-out of hidden purposes or secret powers.) Tepper can handle themes of pain and loyalty as convincingly as anyone writing SF today, but at times, her writing at the human level seems almost too good to be subsumed by her ambitious agendas.

Dean Koontz's first novel for Knopf, **Dark Rivers of the Heart**, seems to mark a deliberate move from genre horror into the realm of the Ludlumesque thriller, and makes less overt use of SF than many of his bestsellers, but it brings together two issues that I've been wondering about in recent columns. One is the general relationship of SF to bestselling paranoid thrillers, and the other is the tendency of such thrillers to incorporate more and more of the characteristics of dystopian fiction. A recent bibliography of dystopias included a number of works set in the present, suggesting that some form of dystopia may have already arrived, and we're too dense to see it. This, it turns out, is a key theme in *Dark Rivers of the Heart*, in which Koontz sets out to demonstrate with his usual over-the-top excess that modern information technology, together with government's increasing lack of accountability and infringement of civil liberties, may have already created a fascistic shadow-state. In short, we're all at risk of having our property seized and being hunted down by high-tech crazed psycho serial killers operating under the auspices of black budgets. (I knew that.) In case we miss the message, Koontz phones it in with an afterword that calls for voiding all asset-forfeiture laws (which he says have become a major source of law-enforcement funding), eliminating congressional exemptions from prosecution, and repealing laws that "criminalize beliefs" (his example is that of a white separatist whose family, along with the family dog, were gunned down by the FBI in 1992).

So much for the message — which, for the most part, is given to us in bite-size chunks as the two principals speed through the desert at 80 miles per hour while talking like libertarians at a cookout. The plot, on the other hand, is a non-stop chase adventure of undeniable power, one of the most purely paranoid adventure stories I've ever read, and one that draws in equal measure on Ludlum, Hitchcock, and even Philip K. Dick (who gets cited by a minor character as a kind of paradigm for what the world has become). Former computer cop Spencer Grant gets enthralled with a cocktail waitress named Valerie Keene, who disappears the next day. Breaking into her house to investigate, he narrowly escapes a SWAT team attack and finds himself pursued by the same shadowy government agents that are after her. The leader of these agents is Roy Miro, an almost comically overbaked nut-case who sees in his job — with a renegade government agency under a power-hungry deputy attorney general — the opportunity to create a utopia through weeding the population; Miro casuallly murders people who are disabled, imperfect, or just a little depressed. With computer access to all the information systems in the world, Miro seems an unbeatable foe — until he falls in love with another, equally loony operative named Eve Jammer, a stunning ex-showgirl-turned-superspy with whom he shares a fear of bodily fluids. (Did I mention that *Dr. Strangelove* gets worked in, too?) As Grant himself comments, "'There's enough paranoia in this concept for half dozen Oliver Stone movies'." Fortunately, both he and Keene are also computer whizzes, capable of creating new identities at the drop of a hat and disabling enemy satellites with handy laptops.

Needless to say, none of these people are quite who they seem, and by the time all the hidden identities and secret pasts are sorted out, we've also gotten doses of *The*

Manchurian Candidate and *The Silence of the Lambs*, not to mention David Koresh and Lassie (yes, there's a faithful dog, no doubt in memory of that white separatist mutt that got shot. And even the dog has a hidden past.) Koontz keeps up a breakneck pace, and provides a few spectacular set-pieces (most notably a hair-raising flood sequence), but he also requires a suspension of disbelief that many readers will be able to achieve only with the aid of medication. And despite his relatively ambitious moral agenda – he wants to show us that seeking a perfect world by surrendering liberties leads instead to dystopia – the chaotic action and some gruesome details (particularly involving Grant's father) blow any messages right out of the water.

What does any of this have to do with SF, since Koontz argues that all the technologies he describes are already possible? Well, for one thing there's that dystopian element. For another, this novel might well be studied by anyone who wonders why SF writers don't sell as well as Koontz (or for that matter, as well as Peter Benchley, whose *White Shark* we looked at back in May). Toward the end of the novel, Koontz hauls out one unarguable SF special effect involving satellite-based laser weapons. By now, his readers are pretty much willing to accept anything, as long as it fits in with the general conspiratorial mood – but they might not have accepted it had it been foregrounded as a premise of the novel. In other words, SF is permissible in a paranoid thriller as long as it's presented as revelation, but not if it's introduced so early that it seems to thrust us into an SF world. SF works by estrangement, and the key to the paranoid thriller is almost the opposite of estrangement; it lies in trying to convince the reader that this could be happening to you any minute; the psycho is at the door, and if he has strange technologies at his disposal, they're not imaginary – you just haven't been reading the right magazines. SF writers have an unfortunate tendency to want to explain things, and to make the world seem rational (see, for example, the Ben Bova novel reviewed below). Thriller readers don't want a rational world; they want to confirm their worst suspicions about the irrational one they live in, and Koontz's epic of paranoia gives them their money's worth with a vengeance. With the haul he's going to make from this book alone, no wonder he's in a panic about those asset-forfeiture laws.

Unlike Koontz, whose earlier SF already veered toward the paranoid end of the genre (remember, he gave us the first computer rape in *Demon Seed*), Ben Bova has developed a solid career within the rationalist hard-SF tradition, and his bid for moving into mainstream thrillerdom, **Death Dream**, comes across as downright plodding when compared to Koontz's gonzo chase-fest. High-level computer hacking also plays an important role in Bova's novel, but his real concern is the possible near-future application of virtual reality, and his subplots methodically show how VR may be used in schools, in recreational theme parks, in military training, in government policy decisions, and in plots to take over the world. Like Koontz, he offers up a psycho computer whiz (along with a psycho computer *executive*), a spunky woman hacker, a sexy but power-crazed female employee who knows everyone's secrets, and a shadowy government agency. But Bova's own clear thinking sabotages his potential thriller in a couple of key ways. For one thing, he tries to make these characters credible by filling in background to explain their motivations, which often slows the narrative to a crawl; and for another, he really wants us to understand the implications of VR technology, and how it works. Like a good SF writer, he wants to explain things, but — as I said above — the only thing the thriller reader needs to have explained about VR is how and when it's going to get him. By the time Bova gets around to developing a measure of paranoid suspense at the end of the novel, it's too little and too late.

Dan Santorini is a VR specialist developing training simulations for the Air Force until his brilliant former partner, Jason Lowrey, lures him away to work for ParaReality, Inc., which is developing a VR theme park in central Florida. Santorini soon finds that the corporation is not only in financial trouble and facing draconian deadlines, but that his boss is a creep who mysteriously shows up in the ParaReality-developed educational programs that Santorini's daughter uses at a local school. Santorini is approached to work on a secret government contract unknown to the company's investors, and is summoned by the Air Force to return to Dayton when one of his VR training programs starts killing people. Meanwhile, someone is trying to sabotage the opening of the planned theme park.

Gradually, it becomes apparent that both Santorini's boss and his former partner are seriously unhinged; that the company's personnel director is plotting her own power fantasies; and that his daughter Angela may be in real danger. Bova's descriptions of how a VR theme park might work is convincing (although in practice not a lot different from Michael Crichton's *Westworld*, with VR helmets instead of robots), as are his descriptions of flight-training simulators and educational programs. His argument that VR technology could be used to influence presidents and congressmen — by showing them the results of possible courses of action — is far less persuasive, and depends on our willingness to believe that politicians are even denser than they are.

Bova raises worthwhile issues about VR technology in the short-run future, and like Koontz, he keeps his technology within the range of what is almost possible today, saving his SF set-piece — a battle to the death in a series of VR environments — for late in the novel. (Even this set-piece, for all its VR bells and whistles, reads like one of the old telepath battles out of Frank Robinson or Alfred Bester, making me wonder — as did J.R. Dunn's *This Side of Judgment* last month — if modern computer technology isn't simply giving SF writers a way of rebottling old wine.) But Bova can't muster the lapel-grabbing hysteria that might turn this material into a good thriller, and his efforts to develop character depth are undermined by a parade of stereotypes — the disheveled computer genius in slogan-ridden tee shirts, the faithful and patient wife whose own computer skills help save the day, the executive with a secret obsession. Lacking the killer instinct of a Koontz or the SF adventurousness of a Gibson, *Death Dream* isn't likely to provide much excitement for either SF or thriller readers, although it may appeal to that apparently sizable segment of the technothriller audience who actually finish novels by Tom Clancy.

It wouldn't be fair to claim that the lame simulations in *Death Dream* represent all that Bova can do with the virtual reality theme, since he's obviously lowballing his extrapolations for a wide audience. But they do raise the question of why SF's treatment of VR – the most relentlessly hyped arena for tech-speculation in recent memory, and already on a par with space travel and other major SF themes – hasn't, in more than a decade, moved significantly beyond Gibson's original "cyberspace." One reason is that VR technology is no more a new development in SF than the moon landing was in 1969; we can find VR games described in detail in Clarke's *The City and the Stars* and earlier. All SF writers have really had to do was move a far-future technology up to a near-future one. But how might non-SF writers coming in at a different angle, but fairly sophisticated about the software, handle the possibilities? This is what makes Alexander Besher's **Rim: A Novel of Virtual Reality** of particular interest. Besher, whose earliest marginal connection to the genre consisted of bringing two unpublished David Lindsay novels into print for his Chicago Review Press, now is a columnist and "consulting futurist" in San Francisco. Parts of Rim have appeared in periodicals in Japan, which Besher seems to know well, and the novel as a whole calls to mind Japanese writers like Haruki Murakami as much as the American cyberpunks.

In no sense is Besher's novel aimed at the broad audience of Koontz or even the middle audience of Bova. Its plot is that of a noir thriller, but its ambition is to be the first post-VR novel, and its sources are as varied as California New-Age psychic fads and – especially – the *Tibetan Book of the Dead*. In the 21st century, a global "virtuopolis" managed by the giant Satori Corporation mysteriously crashes, stranding several thousand participants in the net. Frank Gobi, a retired "consciousness detective" whose son is among those trapped, is hired to track down the company's CEO, who disappeared at the time of the crash and who possesses the lines of code needed to bring the system back on-line. His adventures in corporate espionage lead him to a space-station resort and finally to Neo-Tokyo – a city which disappears entirely for twelve hours each day as the result of a recent earthquake. The secret of what causes the city to disappear is, of course, closely related to the crash of the system, and involves a notion of reality that Philip K. Dick would have understood in a minute.

Besher drops in a wealth of comic detail that shows a solid imagination at work – Ray-Ban sunglasses equipped with artificial intelligence to record key events, "interactive sushi," faxes that transmit whole people, "fuzzy-logic" panties and evening gowns that compliment the wearer, living origami, toxic waste dumps for "discarded software karmas," hot tubs in space, intelligent Earth-shoes, even "Doc Dalais" – "boots with a firm grip on the afterlife." As the last example may indicate, not all of this is entirely under control, and Besher at times seems willing to go after the Douglas Adams crowd. His narrative's cavalier acceptance of every New Age psychic belief, from auras to reincarnation, adds still more confusion to the role of virtual reality in the story; between the various psychic manifestations and the VR illusions (which are eventually shown not to be illusions at all, but simply "digitized reality"), the reader has no real home base. Dick was able to bring this off because of the very controlled and deliberate ways he deconstructed reality before your eyes; Besher, spinning off in several directions at once, barely keeps his headlong narrative on track. But it's an inventive and energetic first novel, and it features the most convincing and original VR environment I've seen since Greg Egan's *Permutation City* (reviewed last June).

Maureen F. McHugh made one of the more stellar debuts in recent years with her 1992 novel *China Mountain Zhang*, and much of the praise accorded that novel had to do with McHugh's ability to create a realistic and seemingly inevitable future society populated by convincing characters. These virtues are also evident in her second novel, **Half the Day is Night**, set in a third-world undersea Caribbean city called Julia. There's little of the technological adventurousness of underwater tales like Clarke's The Deep Range or Asimov's "Waterclap," however; McHugh imagines that such a setting will retain many of the characteristics of today's third-world tropical nations – overt class distinctions, the almost anomalous rise of a banking industry, an oppressive but inept government. McHugh doesn't waste time describing the wonders of the undersea world – the exterior is all blackness – and she doesn't give us lectures about the need for mining the sea in order to feed burgeoning world populations; she doesn't even explain how such a society came about, or offer many details on the geopolitical arrangements of the surface world. What she does do is offer us a convincing portrait of two characters caught in a web of believable political intrigue, with the claustrophobic setting functioning principally as a metaphor for a society with increasingly limited options.

David Dai, a French-Vietnamese veteran of a recent war in South Africa, arrives in the underwater nation of Caribe to work as a driver and security guard for Mayla Ling, heir to a Chinese banking dynasty. Dai soon learns that his predecessor, Bennett, is being released because of an unsatisfactory personal relationship with Ling, and that Ling herself may be the target of a Catholic terrorist group – as well as of a banking syndicate bent on forcing her into bankruptcy. It doesn't take Dai long to realize that his new job is more than he bargained for, and soon he and Ling find themselves in hiding both from the government – which suspects Dai of being involved in the bombing of Ling's house – and from the terrorists themselves. McHugh's fairly simple plot tends to disguise the subtle richness of the novel, with its detailed descriptions of a world in which even the air quality is a reflection of class distinctions, in which "fish jockeys" risk their lives in hazardous low-paying jobs, and in which the international financiers exploit poverty to construct ever more complex networks of power and control. *Half the Day is Night* is a modest novel that lacks the surprisingly original impact of *China Mountain Zhang*, but it reinforces McHugh's promise as a novelist with an uncanny talent for developing a realistic and tellingly detailed future.

The celebrity/historical mystery is a fairly old tradition (Lillian de la Torre began writing her Samuel Johnson mysteries back in the 1940s), and has provided Stuart Kaminsky and Nicholas Meyer with a good portion of their careers. E.L. Doctorow upped the ante in 1975 with *Ragtime*, which wasn't exactly a mystery, but which brazenly hypothesized an early twentieth century in which almost every walk-on character was a famous historical figure. The current success of Caleb Carr's bestselling *The Alienist* is keeping the tradition profitable, so the timing couldn't be better for William Hjortsberg's *Nevermore*, in which Harry Houdini (also a main character in the Doctorow novel) and Sir Arthur Conan Doyle team up in 1923 New York to track a murderer whose crimes replicate the stories of Edgar Allan Poe. Assisting Doyle is the apparition of Poe himself, who appears by means of some sort of time displacement; Poe thinks Doyle is a visitor from the future in 1849, while Doyle initially thinks Poe is a ghost. Houdini, meanwhile, is dogged by Opal Crosby Fletcher, a spiritualist who seems intent on seducing him for her own mysterious purposes. Both Doyle and Houdini are irritated by the press coverage given the case by none other than Damon Runyon. Before the novel is over, we've encountered Jack Dempsey, Babe Ruth, Casey Stengel, Paul Whiteman, King Oliver, Gene Fowler, Ring Lardner, Buster Keaton, Charlie Chaplin, Hamlin Garland, Louis B. Mayer, Douglas Fairbanks and Mary Pickford, the Ku Klux Klan, and just about everyone else you can think of who was around in 1923. Part of the appeal of novels like this is the creation of a rich fantasy past in which almost everyone was someone.

Hjortsberg is a versatile, underrated novelist best known for the film version of his grim *Fallen Angel* and the screenplay for Ridley Scott's *Legend*, but also remembered by many SF readers for his 1971 *Gray Matters*. Here he seems in a more playful mood, cheerfully juggling occasional anachronisms but backing up his scenario with enough solid research to make the settings and characters both convincing and appealing. He makes much of the tension between Doyle, on a lecture tour to promote his growing interest in spiritualism, and Houdini, who devoted a good part of his career to exposing spiritualists. He effectively captures the changing world of the twenties, as Houdini worries about the death of vaudeville and Doyle, visiting Hollywood, sees in the vast crumbling set of Griffith's *Intolerance* a metaphor for what America is becoming.

At the same time, he keeps the action moving at a pulp-adventure level, complete with a hazardous barnstorming flight from Chicago to New York and a series of gruesome crimes ending in a rooftop confrontation. His mystery plot is competent if not outstanding, but the supernatural aspect of the story — the appearance of Poe — is never convincingly integrated into the mystery. Poe makes suggestions to help Doyle solve the crime, but his presence isn't really needed and he provides no crucial insights. Thematically, of course, the ghost of Poe does hover over the careers of both Doyle and Houdini, but this isn't a novel that moves by literary themes. Instead, it's a carnival ride through a history that should have been, and it's almost irresistible.

The **Best from Fantasy and Science Fiction** anthologies, which began appearing annually when the magazine was less than three years old, have become increasingly infrequent of late; Kristine Kathryn Rusch and Edward Ferman's 45th anniversary volume is the 26th in the series (let's keep these numbers straight), but only the second to appear in the last decade. It's a good solid volume, offering a concise portrait of the transition that took place in the magazine in the last $2^1/_2$ years of Ferman's editorship and the first $2^1/_2$ years of Rusch's, which began with the July 1991 issue. But there's no sudden, dramatic break as the torch was passed; I didn't even try to figure out who bought which story, and noted several that might even have appeared comfortably in the old Boucher and McComas version of the magazine.

F&SF has always been the classiest-*looking* of the SF magazines, and was bending traditional genre boundaries decades before Dozois, Datlow, and others broadened the scope of the competition. That eclectic, style-sensitive reputation shows up well in the selection of stories here, which range from the sophisticated horror of Thomas Ligotti's "The Last Feast of Harlequin" to the high-concept SF of Ray Vukcevich's "Mom's Little Friends," about trying to negotiate a truce with nervous "nanopeople" inhabiting a scientist's body. There are few trends about which to generalize, although I note that *F&SF's* longstanding attraction to rural settings as opposed to high-tech urban futures is still very much alive. In addition to the Ligotti story (written in that quaint, slightly stuffy diction that horror narrators seem so fond of), both Dale Bailey's "Touched" and Gene Wolfe's "The Friendship Light" are set in remote areas. The Bailey concerns a young retarded man with a special gift, and Wolfe reveals his darker side in a chilling, if somewhat gnomic, tale of retribution. Carolyn Ives Gilman's "The Honeycrafters," which I admit to having saved for last out of a personal conviction that I didn't ever want to read a story about a honey-blending contest, even builds a whole society around the arts of beekeeping.

Another noteworthy trend is the use of Vietnam as a setting for supernatural horror. Karen Joy Fowler's "The Dark" ambitiously folds disappearing campers, feral children, and plagues into what eventually becomes a Vietnam nightmare, and both Joe Haldeman's World Fantasy Award-winning "Graves" and Alan Brennert's Nebula-winning "Ma Qui" make use of local Vietnamese ghost legends as a means of conveying the essential alienness of that time and place, and of exploring how the war could be viewed as an aspect of Vietnamese, and not just American, culture. Mike Resnick's African story "Kirinyaga" – quite possibly his best single piece of work – also investigates an alternate culture's viewpoint with an unusual combination of macho and sensitivity, and the juxtaposition of clashing worldviews is a main feature of both Marcos Donnelly's "The Resurrection of Alonso Quijana" (which bitingly contrasts the chivalric code of Don Quixote with the Gulf War) and James Morrow's

"Abe Lincoln in McDonald's," whose title doesn't quite say it all, since the version of the present that Lincoln visits is one in which slavery was never eradicated.

Despite the major names represented in the anthology – Haldeman, Fowler, Morrow, Wolfe, Terry Bisson (whose "Next" is a provocative comment on race relations done entirely in dialogue), and Harlan Ellison (whose evocative "Susan" is already becoming a minor classic of its kind) – much of the pleasure of such an anthology comes from the newer or less well-known names. In addition to Bailey, Vukcevich, Donnelly, and Gilman, there is a witty, Connie Willis-like take on Frankenstein by Madeline E. Robins ("Willie"); an imaginative tale of role-playing robots on a deserted resort world by Ray Aldridge ("Steel Dogs"); a chilling hardboiled tale by Richard Bowes ("On Death and the Deuce"); and Mike Conner's Nebula-winning tale of art, communication, and slavery ("Guide Dog"). Two writers most closely associated with the recent *F&SF*, R. Garcia y Robertson and Robert Reed, are represented by stories which show that the magazine – despite its increasing proportion of horror stories – has not abandoned fairly traditional and well-thought-out SF adventures. In all, this latest addition to a distinguished series honors both the magazine's rich tradition and its interesting new directions.

A more traditional overview of SF of the last couple of decades can be found in Martin H. Greenberg's SWFA-sponsored **Nebula Award-Winning Novellas**, published by Barnes & Noble as an "exclusive" to bookstores in their chains. It ought to be a fairly risk-free enterprise for Barnes & Noble, since it brings together a number of well-known stories of reputable provenance in a very reasonably-priced package. Although most of the stories have already been reprinted in various Nebula Awards annuals, the idea of bringing them together in an omnibus seems to me a good one, especially for readers interested in exploring the ways in which the craft of the SF novella differs from that of the novel or short story. Years ago, Groff Conklin argued that the novella was a form unusually well-suited to SF, since it gave the authors room to develop unfamiliar worlds or concepts while keeping the narrative focused on a single series of events. There are also historical reasons for the SF writer's affinity for the novella: during the quarter-century or so between the advent of *Amazing Stories* and the development of a book-length novel market, the novella and the serialized novel were just about the only chances most SF writers had to develop narratives at any length. As a result, a disproportionate number of classic SF stories fall into this length (defined by the Nebula Awards as from 17,500 to 39,999 words). Perhaps this tradition helps explain why, even in today's novel-driven market, writers consistently produce outstanding stories that pay far less than novels but require more work than short stories.

Greenberg's anthology includes exactly half the Nebula-winning novellas from the 1970s and 1980s, leaving open the possibility of two future volumes to cover the remaining and missing years. Given Greenberg's limited field of selection, one of the first questions that comes to mind is why these particular stories were selected (this is one of the few anthologies where you can quickly check to see what's been *excluded*). Is there, for example, a tendency to go for big names? Certainly, the authors included are big enough – Leiber, Clarke, Zelazny, Varley, Longyear, Anderson, Bear, Silverberg, Willis, Bujold – but the authors excluded are almost as big (from the two decades covered, they are MacLean, Wolfe, Tiptree, Spider and Jeanne Robinson, Charnas, Kessel, Shepard, and Kim Stanley Robinson; Willis, Silverberg, and Varley each won two Nebulas during this period). The only lesson to be learned here seems to be that Nebula novella awards don't go to unknown writers. Has Greenberg then gone for the more accessible, mainstream SF stories, omitting Wolfe and Tiptree, for example, because they're too challenging? There may be some evidence of this, but that would hardly account for the presence of Greg Bear's bleak and challenging anti-war epic "Hardfought" or Fritz Leiber's "Ill Met in Lankhmar," one of the darkest of his Fafhrd and the Gray Mouser series. No, suspicious as we may be of an anthology published by a bookselling chain, there's simply no evidence to suggest that Greenberg has undertaken to make SF look anything like Danielle Steele. It's a good anthology, and a valuable service on the part of Barnes & Noble.

Thus reassured, what does this volume tell us about the state of SF from 1970 to 1989, or about the novella as a vehicle for SF? For one thing, it clearly gives the impression that for much of the 70s, SF was principally concerned with alienation. Leiber's dark tale of heroic thieves who lose *both* their lovers in an especially brutal way undermines much of the sword-and-sorcery tradition Leiber helped invent, and portrays Lankhmar as a violent, dirty city than in odd ways looks forward to the bleak cityscapes of cyberpunk. Zelazny's "Home is the Hangman" is a study in guilt and responsibility that ultimately focuses on the alienation of an artificial intelligence from its makers, while Varley's "The Persistence of Vision" portrays a character so isolated and a future so uninviting that joining a utopian deaf-and-blind colony seems his best hope. Even the indefatigably wonder-struck Clarke ends his spectacular tale of Jupiter exploration, "A Meeting with Medusa," with the main character realizing he is neither human nor alien, but at best a mediator with no society of his own.

Things begin to soften a bit as we move into the 1980s. Neither Longyear's "Enemy Mine" nor Bujold's "The Mountains of Mourning" really need their SF settings at all, but both are moving novellas simply in terms of plot and sentiment. Longyear's tale of a stranded space pilot who befriends an enemy alien and later raises its child is a classic plea for brotherhood that could easily have been set in World Wars I or II, and Bujold's account of a wise and judicious nobleman investigating a child murder – from her Miles Vorkosigan series – carries a distinctly medieval tone, with the whole Vorkosigan saga firmly backgrounded. Both stories are self-consciously uplifting, and even Robert Silverberg's ingenious "Sailing to Byznatium," with its ancient cities constructed by 50th-century tourists, ends by resolving its narrator's well-developed alienation with a couple of twists leading to a literal riding-off-in-the-sunset ending.

The remaining three stories, however, remind us that SF didn't go all mushy in the 1980s after all. Poul Anderson's "The Saturn Game," which debates the virtues and dangers of fantasy gaming in a hostile SF setting, offers no easy solutions at all, and Greg Bear's "Hardfought" is a much tougher-minded and more ambitious treatment of the near-impossibility of human-alienation communication than is Longyear's. Finally, for all its doggy sentiment, Connie Willis's "The Last of the Winnebagos" is almost too convincing in its wan portrait of a bleak and decaying future. None of these stories – indeed, none of the stories in the whole collection – contain enough plot complexity to need novel-length treatment, yet they all require length sufficient to build convincing settings and to develop a narrative arc of characters acting within such settings. All of which is what Groff Conklin said about SF novellas back in 1954, and he was right.

With Sheri Tepper playing with imagery from the *Book of Job* and Alexander Besher from the *Tibetan Book of the Dead*, we are reminded once again of the rich sources available for SF in religious mythography, which is not quite the same thing as religion itself. Given SF's occasional affinities with frontier literature, it's not too surprising that Mormonism – America's home-grown frontier religion – should also provide a rich source of stories and ideas. Certainly, much of Orson Scott Card's fiction shows its Mormon origins, and now it's apparent that the desert is full of budding Mormon or Mormon-related SF writers. Most of the contributors to M. Shayne Bell's **Washed by a Wave of Wind: Science Fiction from the Corridor** are graduates of Brigham Young University living in Utah, and the "corridor" of the book's subtitle refers to the area of Mormon settlement in Utah and southeastern Idaho. Is there some natural connection between Mormonism, with its revelatory history and extraterrestrial messengers, and SF? Barbara Hume, whose prologue to the book provides an interesting footnote to the history of fandom, notes the long-running cons and fanzines in Utah, the appearance of an earlier Mormon SF anthology, and the disproportionate number of Mormon winners of Writers of the Future contests (M. Shayne Bell, Virginia Ellen Baker, and Dave Wolverton, all included here).

Well, several of the contributions do reflect an apocalyptic tone. The two best stories in the collection, Wolverton's "Wheatfields Beyond" and Card's "Pageant Wagon," feature post-catastrophe settings and suggest the importance of Mormonism's community identity in surviving such catastrophes. (Card's story also includes a fascinating defense of manipulative schlock art in a tale of a wandering band of actors in a future wasteland). In Charlene C. Harmon's "Pueblo de Sión," a more limited catastrophe leads to the recolonization of ancient Pueblo villages, while Pat Bezzant's "Finale" concerns fears of apocalypse at the turn of the millenium in 1999 and Michaelene Pendleton's "Dealer" portrays a *Fahrenheit 451*-like society in which the title character deals in bootleg music. Aliens are seen as portents in James Cummings's "Space People" and Kathleen Dalton-Woodbury's "Signs and Wonders," but play more conventional roles in Elizabeth Boyer's "A Foreigner

Comes to Reddyville" and Carolyn Nicita's "Solitude," the latter of which is strongly reminiscent of Sturgeon's "A Saucer of Loneliness".

If there's one thing the book makes clear, it's that Mormonism is as much a culture as a religion, and one much imbued with a sense of place, family, and history. The natural background of the region is central to Glenn Anderson's "Shannon's Flight," with its ghost horses and dinosaurs, and the Native American heritage is the focus of Diann Thornley's "Thunderbird's Egg." The collection's two virtual reality stories, M.W. Worthen's "You Can't Go Back" (about an asteroid miner's efforts to recreate in the computer the Utah of his past) and M. Shayne Bell's "The Shining Dream Road Out" (about VR controlled cars and an abused wife) suggest the role of such technology in recreating or restoring community.

Too many of the stories, however, go nowhere with their ideas, and sometimes the ideas seem pretty lame as well. B.J. Fogg's "Outside the Tabernacle" imagines the Mormon elders permitting temporary marriages – perhaps an interesting issue for Mormons to debate, but hardly an awe-inspiring extrapolation for the rest of us. Diana Lofgran Hoffman's "Other Time" uses the old saw of a device that stops time (or actually speeds it up, a la Wells's "The New Accelerator") to explore the unrealistic expectations faced by women who try to combine careers and homemaking. D. William Shunn's "Rise Up, Ye Women that Are at Ease," also critical of the treatment of women, has them simply abandon the world en masse. David Doering's "Snooze" concerns a drug that makes babies sleep all night, and Lyn Worthen's "Rumors of my Death" is about a person exiled by his reported death; none of these stories offer much more than their initial premise. Melva Gifford's "Scrap Pile," about a jinxed spaceship that gets fixed only to find its crew unable to get along without crises, features the kind of stupid, predictable ending you used to see in filler stories in the 50s digests. There are enough clunky first efforts in the collection to give it the distinct flavor of a Mormon *Writers of the Future* volume, but there's also enough authentic atmosphere to make it a creditable contribution to the small but growing number of regional SF anthologies. Still, it's the pros – Card and Wolverton – who make it worth the price of admission.

It would take some kind of bigot, of course, to assume that all SF by Mormon writers necessarily concerns Mormonism or Mormons, but many of the same themes mentioned above – family, community, the frontier, even the role of the church – figure in important ways in **Lovelock**, the first volume in Orson Scott Card and Kathryn H. Kidd's "Mayflower" trilogy about life aboard a giant interstellar spaceship. (Mormonism itself is hardly mentioned at all). In his introduction, Card describes how he persuaded Kidd to write a Mormon novel for his Hatrack River Publications, and that her success led him to view her as an ideal collaborator. He may be right; while Card's trademark moral earnestness is much in evidence, it's leavened by an incisive and at times brittle humor that brings a noticeably harder edge to the characters. I've always suspected that part of Card's success lies in writing young adult novels for adults, focusing on intra-family competitiveness, the problems of gaining acceptance in a new community, the dilemmas of facing your first big moral choices – with plenty of kids and melodramatic primary-color emotions thrown in to resolve any ambiguity. All that is here, but with a few more teeth and a good deal of wit which I assume is mostly Kidd's.

Actually, the novel *literally* has more teeth: its narrator is an enhanced capuchin monkey named Lovelock (after the originator of the Gaia hypothesis, who probably never suspected it would lead him to monkey-immortality), still sufficiently instinct-driven that he bites people who seem threatening. Lovelock is a "Witness" whose task is to record vast chunks of the life of Carol Jeanne Cocciolone, an eminent "gaiologist" who has signed on – along with her extended family – to the Ark, a vast colony ship about to embark in search of a habitable planet. As in a number of fictional generation-ships, social stability aboard the Ark is maintained by organizing its population into replicas of small villages. Cocciolone and her family are assigned to a New England-style village apparently modeled on Peyton Place, and much of the novel's action concerns the gossip, backbiting, and social climbing of the villagers and Cocciolone's own family – especially her insufferable mother-in-law Mamie and her manipulative and unfaithful husband Red.

This aspect of the novel hardly needs to be SF at all, and doesn't work very well as SF; it's hard to imagine any sort of screening process that would allow such a gaggle of dysfunctional neurotics to populate the first starship, and the whole notion of a church-centered Presbyterian village as a stable futuristic social unit is almost worthy of a *Starlost* episode. But the novel's second major plot – about Lovelock himself – is more rewarding, and fortunately promises to be the main narrative arc of the trilogy (this novel ends just before the Ark is launched). Those expecting (or dreading) a heartwarming tale of a cute monkey in space may be surprised to find that far from being sentimentalized, Lovelock is a complex character, highly intelligent and articulate but never quite freed of primate instincts (such as defecating and biting) and increasingly tormented by the slave-like status of the enhanced and conditioned animals used as Witnesses. His battles with his instincts and conditioning, his growing need for sexual and moral freedom, and his increasingly ambivalent attitude toward his "master" Cocciolone, suggest that Card and Kidd want to deal with questions of freedom and responsibility that will make their little human soap opera seem as trivial as it is. If Lovelock's story fulfills the promise of this first volume, the "Mayflower Trilogy" may turn out to be quite an impressive work – and one for which Kidd will deserve a full measure of credit.

Queen City Jazz ~~ Kathleen Ann Goonan

Travellers in Magic ~~ Lisa Goldstein

A Fisherman of the Inland Sea: Science Fiction Stories ~
~ Ursula K. Le Guin

Wrath of God ~~ Robert Gleason

Red Dust ~~ Paul J. McAuley

I Robot: The Illustrated Screenplay ~
~ Harlan Ellison & Isaac Asimov, illustrations by Mark Zug

Post-catastrophe tales, for all their admonitory gloom about nuclear devastation, ecological disaster, and resurgent tribalism, tend to have one thing in common: they usually deal in some way with the collapse of information and information systems. The reconstruction of this lost information has been a staple of SF plots as varied as Heinlein's "Universe," Clarke's *The City and the Stars*, and Brackett's *The Long Tomorrow*, and it's the latter novel that comes most readily to mind in the opening chapters of Kathleen Ann Goonan's spectacular first novel, **Queen City Jazz**. Like Brackett, Goonan sets these chapters in a rural Ohio community which has rejected new technology in favor of fundamentalist religious dogma (in Goonan's case, Shakers; in Brackett's, Mennonites). Goonan's protagonist, Verity, resembles Brackett's young Len Colter in her yearning to know more about the forbidden cities; like Colter, she reads forbidden texts and listens to a contraband radio (in the form of a crystal). And like Colter, she eventually makes her way into the realm of forbidden technology, where she must struggle to overcome her long-conditioned fears.

But from here on, *Queen City Jazz* is very much its own story, and pretty much unlike anything else in SF. The forbidden technology in question turns out not to be computers or nuclear energy (as in Brackett), but a very sophisticated form of nanotechnology (called "nan") which has converted whole cities into living organic environments. And the catastrophe — the original information collapse — was not a nuclear war, but the appearance of a nearby quasar, disrupting electromagnetic radiation and virtually ending all radio and TV communications. As a means of maintaining information transfer in the "enlivened" nanotech cities, giant bioengineered bees roam among flower-crowned buildings. A second catastrophe, nanotech "plagues" which alter not only the human carriers but the environment itself, soon follows.

When her boyfriend Blaze and her telepathic dog Cairo are shot by a fanatical Shaker, Verity makes her way toward the enlivened city of Cincinnati in hopes that the technology there can restore them. Accompanied by a jazz freak named Sphere (presumably from Thelonius Monk's middle name), she finds the city transformed into an ever-regenerating wonderland which she compares at one point to the "completely alive paranoid informational world of Pynchon, Dick, and every religious mystic who ever lived." The human population has lost control to the bees themselves, which have become addicted to the emotional chaos generated by pop culture fantasies brought to life through nanotech. At one point, we are in Paris in the twenties with Hemingway and Stein; later, we're in Krazy Kat's Cocomino County. Scott Joplin and Coleman Hawkins perform nightly, and Billie Holiday and Charlie Parker are drafted to play baseball for the Reds. Goonan's text is peppered with quotations from and allusions to everybody from Pound and Flannery O'Connor to Judy Collins, but as the title of the book implies, jazz is the controlling metaphor for this wildly improvisational environment. As Sphere reminds Verity more than once, human creativity — like jazz — depends not on perfect recreations of what has gone before, but on assimilating that and then moving beyond it. This is what nanotech has subverted in Cincinnati, and what holds its residents hostage in a kind of pop-culture hell. In a brilliant reversal of the information-collapse scenario, Goonan has constructed a disaster out of information excess.

Aided by the implanted memories of Abe Durancy, Cincinnati's legendary nanotech designer, Verity discovers that her own role in the destiny of the city is far greater than she had originally suspected, and to some extent the narrative returns to SF form as Verity discovers her true identity and sets about challenging the city itself. But the nature of the challenge is so complex, and the issues it raises are so compelling, that *Queen City Jazz* never reverts to a comfortable formula, and never quite lets you get your balance. The most obvious comparison is with SF's earlier nanotech masterpiece, Greg Bear's *Blood Music*, but Goonan moves far beyond Bear's horror-story scenario and shows that the possibilities of this theme are at least as powerful as those of SF's more popular current preoccupation, virtual reality. *Queen City Jazz* is a first novel of startling virtuosity and complexity, and almost certainly the most important debut novel I've seen this year.

The most important short-story collection debut I've seen this year, on the other hand, is Lisa Goldstein's **Travellers in Magic**, which displays an imposing array of talents from a writer who never seems to earn the attention she deserves, possibly because (as she herself says) she doesn't seem to fit into any comfortable niches. Technically, I suppose this collection of fifteen stories isn't a debut, since five of them were collected in 1989 in one of Pulphouse's "Author's Choice" volumes called *Daily Voices*, but this is the first time Goldstein's rather sparse body of short fiction has had a fair chance to find an audience on the open market. Ideally, I suppose, that audience might consist of readers who enjoy some Borges, some Ballard, and some Crowley, but it's not likely to be the SF genre audience. In fact, it's something of a testament to Goldstein's craft that the only easily certifiable SF story in the bunch, "Midnight News," has already been canonized in *The Norton Book of Science Fiction*.

Goldstein is fascinated with hapless protagonists drawn into shifting realities, and she manages to portray these shifts with such understated subtlety that it takes a beat after the story's over before the reader realizes what's really happened – her voice is strongest in its echoes. The clearest example of these shifting realities is the enigmatic third-world country of Amaz, the setting for her novel *Tourists* and featured in three of the stories here. Sometimes in the far east, sometimes in Latin America, Amaz is vaguely reminiscent of Borges's Tlön, with its odd language, nameless streets, mysterious ruins, and ubiquitous decks of cards which serve as newspapers. In "Tourists," an American who gets lost trying to make his way to the airport is gradually absorbed into this strange culture. A journalist in "Death is Different" finds herself interviewing a dead Communist leader and thereby discovers a means of handling an unexpected tragedy back home. In "A Game of Cards," a deck of cards imported from Amaz becomes a kind of yuppy parlor game, while the Amaz-born maid looks on and sees what the cards actually reveal about the players. Similar to the Amaz stories is "Preliminary Notes on the Jang," in which a family of gypsy-like immigrants from an unknown culture seduce an anthropology student.

Occasionally, Goldstein deliberately plays with specific source materials. In "Infinite Riches," Sir Walter Raleigh actually finds El Dorado, along with other mythical regions from early travellers' tales. "Ever After" explores with delicious irony the likely aftermath of Cinderella's marriage to the prince. "Rites of Spring" is a contemporary version of the Demeter and Persephone myth, "The Woman in the Painting" an exploration of Pre-Raphaelite obsessiveness (also included in the current *Year's Best Fantasy and Horror*), and "Split Light" (published here for the first time) an imaginative but pretty unconvincing speculation on why the 17th-century Jewish false messiah Shabbetai Zevi agreed, in prison, to convert to Islam.

Of the remaining stories, "Cassandra's Photographs" is a haunting meditation on free will, using the classically simple idea of a camera that photographs the future. "Daily Voices" might qualify as the book's sole horror story, with its chilling portrait of a woman controlled by voices that may be her own or may be the work of aliens. "Midnight News" is a telling satire about a neglected old woman given the power to save or destroy the world, and "A Traveller at Passover" has the simplicity and conviction of a Jewish folktale or a Singer story. As a rule, Goldstein does not trade heavily on her Jewish heritage, although her Holocaust fantasy *The Red Magician* broke important ground in dealing with that difficult subject in fantasy. Still, she is the child of survivors, and the two most memorable and important stories in the collection derive directly from this. In "Alfred," a teenage girl in 1967 befriends a strange old man in the park, and later finds that his name and appearance match those of her grandfather, who died in the camps. The inspired stroke that sets the story apart is the quiet subtheme involving the girl's younger brother, who is afraid of everything. "Breadcrumbs and Stones," which is fantasy only by virtue of its use of the Hansel and Gretel fairy tale, is one of the best short stories yet written about the ambiguous plight of survivors' children. It will remind some readers of Jane

Yolen's *Briar Rose*, which also recasts Holocaust memories in fairy tale form, but the intensely personal voice, with its real sense of anguish and loss, makes the story uniquely powerful. Goldstein says it's her favorite of all her stories, and it should be.

Unlike Goldstein, Ursula K. Le Guin is almost too well-known for her own good, and seems to be struggling to maintain her ties to the SF world despite persistent attempts by critics and academics to move her uptown where the big parties are. Perhaps this is one reason she appended the subtitle "Science Fiction Stories" to her new collection **A Fisherman of the Inland Sea** — as though she wants to co-opt the inevitable mainstream reviews that will claim this stuff isn't SF at all, but sophisticated postmodern storytelling. Of course, it's both, and it's the most complete overview of Le Guin's recent SF since *The Compass Rose* back in 1982 (1987's *Buffalo Gals and Other Animal Presences* was sophisticated postmodern storytelling). As such, it amply demonstrates how Le Guin both draws upon and subverts traditional SF material.

Her use of imaginary science, for example, is central to a triptych of Hainish stories included here — "Another Story, or A Fisherman of the Inland Sea," "The Shobies' Story," and "Dancing to Ganam." The science in question is what she calls "churten technology," a means of instantaneous transportation or "transilience" that does for people and objects what her ansible did for communications. As Le Guin cheerfully acknowledges in her introduction, this technology is "pure hokum," and she makes it sound no more convincing than one of A.E. Van Vogt's concoctions. But while Van Vogt and others saw in such gimmicks a simple means of bypassing story logic, Le Guin milks them for all the metaphoric denseness they're worth. "Another Story" sets up an alternate world time-travel scenario which turns out to be a way of exploring the protagonist Hideo's apparent need to be two people at the same time. The story concerns the experiments that lead to the development of churten technology, but also offers a well-textured portrait of Hideo's group-marriage oriented society on the planet O. "The Shobies' Story," which concerns the first churten "expedition," finds in the technology an apt metaphor for narration itself; the story almost becomes the machine it describes. And "Dancing to Ganam," with its glass spaceships and self-consciously legendary hero, seems in part to be an exploration of what Cordwainer Smith might have made of Le Guin's Hainish universe.

In addition to these Hainish stories, Le Guin also offers a range of her other styles, not least of which is her often overlooked talent as a humorist. "The First Contact with the Gorgonids" is a Thurberesque tale of an American tourist couple who encounter Space Aliens in the Australian outback; the SF is little more than a backdrop for her hilarious and incisive characterization of the churlish husband and his apparently dimwitted wife. "The Ascent of the North Face," a short joke about climbing high-rises with the aid of "Sherbet" guides, vaguely recalls Donald Barthleme's treatment of the same idea in "The Glass Mountain." The collection is rounded out with two parable-like stories, "The Rock that Changed Things" and "The Kerastion," both of which weave whole societies around the central metaphors of stonelaying and a musical instrument that can't be heard, and "Newton's Sleep," about the re-emergence of parts of earth's environment in a sterile space colony.

Although it lacks the richness and subtlety of "Another Story," "Newton's Sleep" may provide the best single illustration of what Le Guin is really up to these days: a kind of magic realism worked out in a convincingly detailed extrapolative environment. As dirt and poverty mysteriously reassert themselves in this sparkling high-tech world, it's tempting to read the story as a comment on modern SF itself, with Le Guin out to show us that the technological imagination provides no real escape. Ike, the main character, is a familiar Le Guin figure – a rationalist confronted with events beyond his expectations, caught in a story he can't fully understand. If there's a consistent theme in this collection, that's probably it – that stories are more than the sum of their rational parts, and that SF can provide the means of liberating metaphors, and not just rationalizing them.

Now here's another post-catastrophe scenario: after most of the population of the world has been wiped out, an archetypal confrontration between Good and Evil is shaping up out in the American desert. Decent folks gather around a charismatic old woman, and the bloodthirsty antagonist seems to be the latest incarnation of an ancient nemesis. In case you're thinking you've seen this before, maybe even on TV, you're wrong. This is Robert Gleason's **Wrath of God**, and it's different from what you're thinking of in a lot of important ways. In the first place, it has *guest celebrities.* These are no ordinary schmucks gathering around the old woman; they include George Patton, Stonewall Jackson, and Amelia Earhart, snatched out the past by a time machine which seems to work only with the aid of an Apache shaman. And the nemesis isn't just some creepy guy dressed in black (although he does favor that occasionally), but *Tamerlane himself,* or at least someone who believes himself Tamerlane's reincarnation (Gleason doesn't make it clear how he makes it into the 21st century on his own, while the good guys need the aid of a time machine.)

The catastrophe in this case isn't a plague, but a nuclear war, started by some fanatical middle eastern nation. (Fanatical middle eastern janizaries also make up the core of Tamerlane's shock troops, and they're kept in line partly by his Lilith-like companion Legion, because – we are told – Muslims are afraid of women. If there's a note of racism here, Gleason apparently thinks he makes up for it by making his Apaches more noble than Lassie.) Also, the book you may be thinking of doesn't have an extended cowpunching sequence, it doesn't have an eagle named Betsy Ross, and it *certainly* doesn't have a triceratops falling in love with Amelia Earhart. (The triceratops is another time-travel abductee.) In other words, this novel has *features.*

I sometimes suspect that the guiding world-views, if not the actual plots, of most contemporary thrillers can be found in the American Psychiatric Association's *Diagnostic and Statistical Manual of Mental Disorders.* Last month, we saw how

Dean Koontz distilled the paranoid thriller in his *Dark Rivers of the Heart*, but there's nothing paranoid about Gleason's equally ambitious shot at an epic. He's not really worrying about ancient warlords returning to life or about the dangers of nuclear war, and he even admits in an introduction that this cataclysm is introduced simply to level the playing field for Tamerlane's horse-mounted army. His real concern, it seems, is to ask if Tamerlane could be defeated today, without the aid of modern weapons (although he does allow us a couple of planes). Drawing on westerns (of which Gleason has written several), science fiction, fantasy, history, war stories, and survivalist adventures, Gleason has distilled the hysterical dimension of modern pop fiction almost as purely as Koontz distilled the paranoid dimension. His version of Tamerlane is as relentlessly rotten as Christopher Marlowe's, and Legion is even worse.

Underlining all this is a portentous, let-the-other-shoe-drop style that drives every small irony home with a battering ram, and a breakneck, episodic pace that keeps you dumbstruck, if not exactly riveted with suspense. As Niven and Pournelle's former editor, Gleason learned well how to fashion genre materials into bestsellers, and he raids genres with abandon for anything that looks like it might work. Mostly, what seems to work for him are pitched battles and horrendous tortures (performed by an underling of Tamerlane's coyly called "the Cuddler"). It is this violence, not the breadth of the story or the depth of its characters, that finally gives the novel its bogus epic tone; surprisingly, it's not really a very long book, and it's not for a moment convincing. (The only real rationale given for selecting Jackson, Patton, and Earhart is that books about them are lying around when the time machine becomes operational.) Still, it's a lot different from most formula bestsellers, and when Gleason finally gets down to describing the battles and tortures themselves, he does a more than creditable job. In the age of Oliver Stone, it's oddly reassuring that there's still some room left for Kit Marlowe – or Cecil B. DeMille.

At first, Paul J. McAuley's **Red Dust** looks like it's going to be just another novel about Elvis-worshipping Chinese Martians. Some centuries after Martian colonization (first by Americans, later by Chinese with the aid of Tibetan labor), terraforming has led to a breathable atmosphere, a certain amount of free water, and a variety of genetically-engineered native species. But now the terraforming project has been abandoned, under the influence of a shadowy but powerful government called Earth's Consensus, which has pretty much grown hostile toward organic life in general, which it views as all but obsolete in the new age of artificial intelligences and computer-encoded personalities. Opposing this decision are "Sky Roaders" and asteroid-based anarchists, who would like to wrest control of Mars from its aging Chinese rulers, the Ten Thousand Years, and restore the terraforming process.

Wei Lee works as an agronomist at a rural settlement called Bitter Waters, where he passes time listening to mysterious broadcasts from the region of Jupiter from someone claiming to be the King of rock 'n' roll. Although fearful of his powerful great-grandfather, he hopes to eventually learn from him what happened to his parents, who disappeared in some sort of political disgrace; his only aid is an AI "librarian" who appears to him in his dreams. But an opportunity seems to present itself when he rescues a crashed anarchist, Miriam Makepeace Mbele, who turns out to be a clone harboring various "fullerene viruses" that give the host all sorts of powers, from enhanced vision to super-acceleration to the possibility of surviving in other bodies. Convinced to escape with Mbele, Lee embarks on a series of adventures that take full advantage not only of the utopian and technological potential of this subgenre, but also of the flat-out adventurousness of Edgar Rice Burroughs and the playful inventiveness of Stanley Weinbaum. Captured by mad computer-controlled monks in an abandoned Tibetan lamasery, Lee barely escapes with his life – and with that of Mbele, partially transferred to him by the viruses when she gives him a kiss before dying. He takes up with a band of yak-herding cowboys (making this the second novel this month to feature a trail drive; have to keep that in mind when it comes time to sum up the year's trends) and makes his way to Xin Beijing, the sprawling capital – where he is received as a god by a group of fisherfolk who get their nanoviruses from dolphin-like creatures. After fomenting a revolution there, Lee sets out for the highest mountain on Mars, called here Tiger Mountain, where he meets his final destiny – and finds out who Elvis really is – in a conclusion that almost reads like an intelligent version of the ending of *Total Recall*.

McAuley draws on a wide variety of SF sources – Mars adventures, nanotechnology, artificial intelligence, virtual reality, terraforming – while maintaining firm control of both his narrative and the consistency of his complex environment. While the political intrigues, the debates over terraforming, and the historical background invite us to consider the book in light of other recent Mars novels by Robinson, Bear, Bisson, Bova, and others, it's clear that McAuley is up to something quite different from any of these. His Mars is not only a convincing hard-SF environment, but the kind of playground for adventure and imagination that it was for the writers who first discovered it (in fact, McAuley's nanotech, VR, genetic engineering, and artificial intelligence would be enough to rationalize even Burroughs' more farfetched daydreams, and in her own way McAuley's Miriam Makepeace Mbele is a distant descendant of Dejah Thoris.) A small example: while on the run in the desert, Lee hides out from a storm in the eyesocket of a gigantic skull, the remains of an ancient failed effort to introduce genetically engineered "archiosaurs" to Mars. Burroughs would have been proud of the sheer wonder invested in such a detail, but in McAuley, it makes sense.

Among his many other records, Harlan Ellison may well hold the title for the most published-but-unproduced or published-and-messed-up-in-production TV and movie scripts; he almost certainly holds the title for most *awards* won this way, with Writer's Guild honors for original versions *Star Trek* and *Starlost* episodes that never quite made it to the screen intact, and a special Reader's Award for *I, Robot: The Movie* when it appeared in *Asimov's* in 1987. Now that screenplay has become a book, retitled **I, Robot: The Illustrated Screenplay**. Asimov's original introduction from the magazine appearance is retained – which lets us know he would have been thrilled to see the movie made – as is Ellison's longer account of the project's history, updated to include the 1991 results of a lawsuit and, of course, Asimov's death. Ellison is still one of our best chroniclers of Hollywood bone-headedness, and even as you suspect that there may be other points of view on the matter, you can't help sharing the outrage, and the introduction is no small part of the book's appeal.

As a "film-novel," *I, Robot* turns out to be as much a *hommage* to Orson Welles as to Asimov. Deliberately choosing *Citizen Kane* as his model, Ellison weaves a handful of Asimov's original stories into a narrative about a determined reporter trying to track down the reclusive, 82-year-old Susan Calvin after the death of her reputed lover, Stephen Byerly. Asimov readers will recognize Byerly as the politician who may or may not be a robot from "Evidence" and "The Evitable Conflict," the two stories that provide the general background of the frame – although you can bet that Ellison isn't about to let stand Asimov's conclusion that we'd be just as well off letting our lives be ruled by machines. By talking to people who knew Calvin, the reporter, Robert Bratenahl, reconstructs the stories "Robbie" (in which the little girl Gloria is turned into the child Susan), "Runaround," "Liar!" and "Lenny," all of which are presented as flashbacks. Ellison makes this work much more effectively than you'd suspect; each of the stories he's chosen adds another clue to our understanding of Calvin, and each makes sense in terms of the overall plot. Toward the end, however, in an epic special-effects confrontation between Byerly and a hostile machine intelligence, Ellison draws less on Asimov than on his own "I Have No Mouth, and I Must Scream," undercutting the Asimovian technophilia that ends the actual book.

Common sense would seem to tell us that, for all the legendary status this screenplay has already attained, *I, Robot* was probably never a very good idea for a movie. Most of the stories were intellectual puzzles based on permutations of the laws of robotics, and it apparently wasn't until Asimov was fairly well along in the series that he realized Susan Calvin was turning into an interesting and complex character in her own right. Furthermore, the idea of humanoid robots helping us to explore the solar system now seems like a dated, 1940s vision of the future. None of this seems to add up to very compelling movie material, and even if it did, Ellison would seem to be the last person likely to turn it into a screenplay; when he himself tried a robot-puzzle (with his second published story, "Life Hutch"), the robot already had turned into a crazed killer, a distant ancestor of the nightmare computer of "I Have No Mouth." How could writer take half-century-old material with no continuous plot and a world-view strongly at odds with his own and turn it into anything coherent? Part of Ellison's strategy, of course, is using a half-century-old movie as his model; some of the dialogue even seems to have a deliberately dated ring to it, as if trying to convey some of the nostagia for a lost future that is now part of the experience of reading early Asimov.

Much has been made of the film's unproduceability, and to be sure Ellison fills the tale with spectacle, not all of which is crucial to the plot. Is it really necessary to have a full-scale hidden city in the Brazilian rainforest for Calvin's hideaway, or immense *Forbidden Planet*-style caverns for the crypts where one of the "witnesses" is in cryonic sleep? Probably not. Nor is it likely that many directors would let Ellison's screenplay tell them what music to use *and* which recording of that music *and* when the recording was made, or that the principals ought to look like Martin Sheen and Joanne Woodward. Ellison is no Pinteresque minimalist when it comes to screenplays; what we get is not a dialogue outline of a movie, but the exact movie that's in Ellison's head. As a reader, I wouldn't want to miss a single detail, even as the faint specter of line producers having coronaries rises over every page. As a potential moviegoer, there's nothing here to convince me that this relatively simple story about a lonely woman in a lost future is impossible to film.

[In 2004, a film titled I, Robot was finally released, with little relationship to Asimov's stories and even less relationship to Ellison's earlier screenplay.]

— December 1994, Locus #407 —

Ring ~~ Stephen Baxter

Matter's End ~~ Gregory Benford

The Stone Garden ~~ Mary Rosenblum

City of the Iron Fish ~~ Simon Ings

Something Rich and Strange ~~ Patricia A. McKillip

Although his work is only gradually percolating its way into the American SF consciousness, Stephen Baxter may turn out to be the most intellectually ambitious of the new breed of English hard SF writers. The first two novels in his "Xeelee sequence," *Raft* and *Timelike Infinity*, appeared in the U.S. as paperbacks in 1992 and 1993, and the third, *Flux* (reviewed in April 1993), is scheduled for spring 1995. All of these portray wonderfully weird worlds (a universe of supergravity, the interior of a neutron star) worked out in the context of dense speculative physics, and all are peppered with tantalizing references to an ancient and nearly omnipotent alien race called the Xeelee, who seemed to have some unimaginably vast plan in mind for restructuring the entire universe. None of these novels, however, quite prepare us for the wildly ambitious finale to the sequence, **Ring**, which ought to immediately thrust Baxter into the front rank of hard SF writers — and which, surprisingly, is the most accessible novel of the series.

One of the standard defenses for hard SF is that it may help bridge the gap between C.P. Snow's "two cultures" of literature and science. In practice, that defense hardly ever works, and I can't imagine any Matthew Arnold freaks getting off on Baxter's cosmological epic, even though it partakes heavily of what W. Warren Wagar aptly termed the "entropic romance" and gloomily portrays the demise of the sun, planets, galaxies, life, the universe, and everything. Although his characters are less wooden than in earlier works, he still expects us to believe that a woman can spend five million years roaming around the interior of the sun and come out talking like she's just seen a good flick. Nor has he quite figured out how to stylistically integrate his complex science with his romantic narrative; he often resorts to textbook lectures complete with italicized key terms, and has a tendency to give his alien races cute, Weinbaum-like names (Qax, Squeem, Xeelee), as if a profound sense of strangeness could be conveyed by rare consonants alone.

None of this really matters, though, because the real strength of novels like Ring is not connecting science with literature, but science with imagination, of which literature is only one aspect. Stylistic infelicities and shaky character motivations aside, Ring is a mind-boggling experience that at times recalls the most visionary moments of Wells, Clarke, and even William Hope Hodgson, and takes on the classic hard-SF task of trying to construct a human-scale drama out of the most far-reaching implications of current cosmological theory. Some two thousand years from now, an organization called the Holy Superet Light Church, determined to ensure the long-term survival of humanity, sets two projects in motion. One involves Lieserl, born human but subjected to a nanotech-induced accelerated growth cycle which turns her into an old woman by the age of three months and eventually into a disembodied consciousness. Something has been rapidly accelerating the sun's life cycle, and Lieserl is sent into the sun's interior to find out what. Meanwhile, Louise Ye Armonk is persuaded to take her massive starship the *Great Northern* – named after Brunel's Victorian steamship, which is preserved on board – on a five-million year quest into the future to establish a wormhole interface linking the time periods and to find out why, according to earlier explorer Michael Poole (the protagonist of *Timelike Infinity*, who disappeared into the far future), the entire universe seems fated to a similar premature death. Ye Armonk's mission, which takes a thousand years of subjective time, soon turns into a kind of generation-starship tale, with the shipboard society breaking down into several subcultures, each with partial memories of the original mission. Through a variety of mishaps, Ye Armonk and her surviving crew find themselves trapped at the end of time; stars are dying and galaxies are drawn to a "Great Attractor" – presumably the same one actually hypothesized by a group of astronomers in 1986 – that may be a construct of the Xeelee (who are tactfully kept offstage even in this final volume). The crew returns to a dead solar system and a red-giant sun, from which they rescue Lieserl, who in her megayear exile has learned of "photino birds," dark matter beings who have eaten away at the core of the sun, and perhaps of most other stars as well. When they all finally make their way to the Great Attractor – the Ring of the title – they discover it is indeed an alien construct, the only way the all-powerful Xeelee could find to meet the threat of the photino birds, and very possibly the most colossal of all of SF's Big Dumb Objects. It would be churlish to give away exactly what this is, or its exact size and purpose, but by now we've already seen neutron stars used as torpedoes and whole galaxies shipped across the universe, and it's irresistible to report that Baxter can still top himself this late in the novel. While *Ring's* best emotional moments come as his characters explore a dead and lifeless universe – and as one finds himself alone at the end of time – he's also constructed a history of transgalactic warfare bold enough to make Doc Smith look like a minimalist, and Stapledon like a regular guy.

In the eight years or so since the publication of his first story collection, *In Alien Flesh*, Gregory Benford has so solidified his reputation as a literary hard SF novelist (with occasional forays into thrillers) that it's easy to overlook both his versatility and his roots in the general SF community. His new collection, **Matter's End**, contains several stories which predate that earlier collection (including his first published story, "Stand-In"), and the book generally provides a more revealing overview of Benford's career, demonstrating his facility not only with science and character, but with humor, dystopian satire, and experimental modes of writing. The fact that the stories aren't all really first-rate adds to the fascination of the collection.

One thing that emerges immediately is a portrait of a writer engaged in intense dialogue with SF themes, modes, and even individual works. The title story, for example, concerns an American scientist investigating a proton-decay experiment in a nightmarish future India devastated by well-meaning biotech projects gone awry. The results of the experiment seem to validate an Eastern mystical worldview strongly at odds with the author's own, and by the time the cataclysmic conclusion comes around we can't help but feel we're reading a take on Clarke's "The Nine Billion Names of God," dressed up in real physics and strengthened by its vivid, unsentimental setting. Similarly, as its title suggests, "Centigrade 233" rethinks Bradbury's assumptions in *Fahrenheit 451* of what might actually lead to book-burning (and is replete with references to SF works and writers). The fear of McCarthyism that supposedly prompted Bradbury to writer that novel is made manifest in the scary alternate world of "We Could Do Worse," in which old Joe actually is President. "Shakers of the Earth" explores the reconstructed-dinosaur theme later used in Crichton's *Jurassic Park* (although Benford finds a different source for his DNA). And "Touches" is a fantasy-gaming update of Julio Cortázar's famous self-reflexive story "The Continuity of Parks." The setting of Benford's own *Against Infinity* provides the backdrop for the future-war story (also self-reflexive, in that it turns on itself) "Sleepstory".

Apart from SF itself, the most noticeable recurring theme in the collection is individual mortality. Perhaps the best piece in the collection is "Mozart on Morphine," a highly autobiographical treatment of a scientist facing an appendectomy and ruminating on the meaning of a life's work so far removed from such human concerns; it actually attains more immediacy than his more famous "Exposures."

"Cadenza" describes a dying woman's attempt to take control of her death in the face of a medical profession even more technified than our own. Two stories, "Knowing Her" and "Immortal Night," suggest the possible consequences of immortality for the wealthy; the stronger former story covers some of the same issues as Haldeman's *Buying Time.*

Benford the humorist is a little more uneven. "Freezeframe" has to be a realization of every new parent's fantasy, while "Proselytes" offers a refreshingly off-the-wall view of aliens as door-to-door evangelists (even though it ends on a slightly ugly joke). Aliens also take on unexpected personalities in "Stand-In" (Benford's first published story, from 1965). "Side Effect," however, is little more than a very lame Feghoot, and "Leviathan," despite some interesting ideas, also leads to a clunky punchline. "Time Guide" offers an on-target catalog of various contemporary lifestyles and affectations, and its non-narrative structure is but one of several examples of Benford's interest in playing with different kinds of narrative forms. "Calibrations and Exercises" is the most successful of these experiments, with its neatly numbered sections, nameless characters, and frequent questions to the reader. One story, "The Bigger One," is even in the form of a radio play about the seismic destruction of California – and its unexpected impact on real estate values. Of the remaining stories, "Nobody Lives on Burton Street" is an unnerving possible answer to urban violence, and "Dark Sanctuary" is a good, hard-SF alien contact tale. As whole, *Matter's End* is far from a "best of Gregory Benford," but it's an enjoyable collection that provides a roadmap to the work of one of the field's major authors, and that contains at least three of his finest stories – "Mozart on Morphine," "Cadenza," and "Matter's End".

Is there a radically different aesthetic between SF and fantasy? One way to approach this question is to look at the ways in which art and artists are portrayed in each genre, and some of this month's novels give us a useful opportunity to do just that. Historically, the arts seem to play a more central role in fantasy novels than in SF, perhaps because the "other worlds" of fantasy are more clearly aesthetic constructs, unconstrained by the limitations of extrapolation. In fantasy, art is often connected with magic, and can sometimes provide a direct portal to another world. Without magic to play with, SF seems limited to portraying art as a means of responding to an imaginary world arrived at through other, more cognitive means. What is the role of the artist in such a world?

Mary Rosenblum has been circling around this question for some time – first with a hypnagogic "magician" in *The Drylands* and later with a VR artist in *Chimera* – so it's not entirely surprising that her new novel, **The Stone Garden**, takes on the problems of artists as its central theme. In this case the artist is Michael Tryon, and the art is an unlikely kind of sculpture extrapolated from nothing we know; using rare stones from the asteroid belt which are somehow capable of storing human sensations and emotions, Tryon is one of a select group of artists capable of investing these stones with complex psychic patterns – drawn from his own emotional life and those of hired "models" – which then resonate to the viewer. In effect, this doesn't differ a lot from the "psycho-sculpture" of Robert Silverberg's *The Second Trip* (1972) – except that there's no technology involved, save the problem of getting the raw materials in the first place, and that soon becomes an important element of the plot. Rosenblum's non-extrapolative art form may tell us nothing at all about the likely future of art, but it provides a marvelous metaphor of what all artists do – pour feelings into objects in an ordered way, and hope the objects pay off for the viewer (or reader, or listener).

Tryon, however, is haunted by a message he has received from a girl claiming to be his daughter by an old lover, Xia Quehaches. This awakens him to his own growing sense of burnout and eventually prompts him to leave his sheltered, historically-preserved enclave of Old Taos and search for her among the modernistic arcologies of Albuquerque. As always, Rosenblum's sense of place serves her well in these visions of a future southwest, but her plotting suddenly shifts to a hardboiled mystery mode. Tryon learns that, by refusing to sell a sculpture to a vengeful multimillionaire named Archenwald-Shen, he has collected himself a nemesis, and soon he finds himself beaten unconscious and suspected of the murder of a fellow sculptor. Enlisting the aid of the dead sculptor's lover Andy Rodriguez, and eventually his own missing daughter, his ex-lover Xia, and Archenwald-Shen's "boy," Zed, Tryon begins investigating what turns out to be a pattern of suicides; the path leads him to an orbiting colony and finally to the asteroid mining station that is the source of the mysterious stones. What he finds alters the very assumptions on which his art is based.

As Rosenblum said in a *Locus* interview in April 1993, *The Stone Garden* is a direct extension of her *Asimov's* story of the same title. This may account for the sudden shift in tone after the first chapter and some raggedness of structure – such as an abrupt shift in point of view to Tryon's daughter Margarita to introduce a subplot involving her and her lover Katrina, and an equally abrupt shift later on back to Tryon. (Logically, these would seem to be parallel plot lines, but Rosenblum can't keep them untangled for more than a chapter.) Thematically, Margarita's role seems to be that of the struggling young artist still unsure of her abilities (she works in a multimedia form called "holoture") as a kind of counterpoint to Tryon's aging cynicism, but it takes some fortuitous coincidences to bring her and her lover under the threat of the same archvillain. And although Archenwald-Shen smacks far too much of Sydney Greenstreet, most of the rest of the characters and their relationships are convincingly drawn – especially Margarita's testy relationship with her mother and the thwarted aesthetic ambitions of Archenwald-Shen's assistant Zed. It's tempting to say that *The Stone Garden* shows both the strengths and weaknesses of a novel written in mid-early career – more ambitious plotting, but still not quite seamless, and more fully realized characters – but the various portraits of artists that make up the core of the novel give it a resonance that transcends its technical problems, and makes it something unusual in recent SF.

Simon Ings's second novel, **City of the Iron Fish,** uses the arts in a much more radical way, and perhaps in a way only available to fantasy. The publication a couple of years ago of Ings's first novel, *Hot Head*, led many to regard him as another promising young post-Gibsonite staking out a career in the skidmarks of cyberpunk, but *Fish* is, well, a different kettle altogether. In this surrealist world of artists, artisans, and actors, even the environment is sustained by artifice: the city of the title is a strange, haunting and haunted place — a port city anomalously in the middle of a desert wasteland which renews and sometimes reinvents itself through ancient rituals re-enacted every twenty years. No one knows why the city is the way it is, or why the world ends only a few miles beyond its borders, although scholars devote their lives to these mysteries.

In the novel's very first sentence, the twelve-year-old Thomas Kemp asks his father a disarmingly simple question which leads him inexorably into these mysteries: 'Why must we feed the gulls?' In other words, why do all the elements of the "natural" world need to be sustained by human action? Why is nothing in this world a "given," and is there a "given" world somewhere outside? Thomas's father puts him off, and the family prepares for the Ceremonies of Stuffing and Hanging, the twenty-year ritual whose central element is the construction and dissolution of a giant iron fish, prepared by a different artist each time and loaded with scraps of poetry. Thomas witnesses a suicide, plants a supposedly magical doll in a bridge high above the city, meets a mysterious gypsy woman with limited news of the world beyond, and experiences his first Ceremony.

Six years later, after his father's death, Thomas enters the Academy, which trains the city's poets, artists, and historians. Over the next several years, he forms a lasting friendship with the artist Blythe Maravell (with whom he tries to explore the world beyond the city), is initiated into gay sex after a night at the opera (later becoming the live-in lover of a famous professor), and finally is reduced to performing in a low-class erotic theater. All this is leading, of course, to the next twenty-year Ceremony. But by then, the City has been overrun by murderous black-garbed gypsy women, violently opposed to all forms of art and artifice and determined to see the ritual fail and the city die. Complicating matters further is one of Thomas's old Academy professors, convinced he can restore the ritual to its ancient potency through barbarous acts of sacrifice.

Although not a particularly long novel, *City of the Iron Fish* is dense with imagery and incident, and is a far cry from the traditional fantasy *bildungsroman*. Ings has a genuinely original visual imagination — at times, the novel almost cries for illustration, and his explorations of how the various arts of painting, drawing, poetry, sculpture, opera, drama, and even sex theater try to invest meaning in a world that sustains none of its own are provocative and intelligent. Readers impatient for a timely SF-nal infodump showing how, say, this whole world is a VR construct or a far future Last Redoubt will find that Ings hands them nothing on a platter, but is generous with hints and mysteries: a main character whose name suggests Thomas à

Kempis and whose friend is named Christ, a central image evoking the Cosmic Fish of mythology, landscapes with human forms suggesting similar images in surrealist paintings. For readers willing to enjoy mysteries of artifice and meaning, *City of the Iron Fish* is a rare treat.

A more traditional use of art-as-portal-to-another-world can be found in Patricia McKillip's **Something Rich and Strange**, the second novel in a series called *Brian Froud's Faerielands*, based on a series of paintings and drawings by Froud. I haven't seen the color plates that accompany the text, but based on the black-and-white illustrations in the proofs, McKillip has gone off entirely in her own direction, conjuring up a variety of delicate seascapes that are nowhere reflected in Froud's brooding Celtic imagery. Not that it matters much: the novel stands very much on its own as a lyrical fantasia based almost literally on the famous quotation from *The Tempest* that provides the title. McKillip's protagonist Megan is a west-coast artist who, with her husband Jonah, operates a seaside arts-and-crafts shop. Megan spends her mornings making sketches of the flotsam-polluted shore, and things begin to turn weird when she finds things appearing in her drawings that she hadn't been aware of. At the same time, a mysterious stranger named Adam Fin shows up to sell his odd jewelry through their shop. Megan finds herself drawn to Adam, and, more catastrophically, Jonah is drawn to Adam's equally mysterious sister Nereis, who first appears as a singer in a local rock band. A third stranger, an old woman named Dory, appears to be the mother of both Adam and Nereis.

It doesn't take long before we realize we're dealing with mermaids and undersea kingdoms, and it doesn't take long after that before we get the message that this fabulous world is endangered by human action – namely, pollution. (This is, according to Froud's introduction, a central theme of the whole *Faerielands* series.) McKillip makes it clear that our access to this world is through art – Megan's drawings, Adam's jewelry, Nereis's singing – and this is especially apparent in a key scene when Megan, determined to rescue Jonah from the undersea world, is told that she can enter it by drawing a staircase and then descending it. At the center of this undersea world is a powerful image that encapsulates the book's ecological message – a shining tower surrounded by an intractable wasteland, the result of humanity's damage to the oceans. All this is presented in prose of such lyrical beauty that it sometimes overwhelms the characters; whenever *anyone* talks about the sea – even a taciturn bookshop owner – their sentences take on the same lilting and formal cadences of McKillip's narration. I suppose this sort of thing is ok in a parable, and the prose is so attractive it's hard to complain; maybe McKillip is saying the sea makes everyone a poet. If that's the case, it just underlines what I was saying about the relationship of art and fantasy: the fantastic makes us all artists, and the art we make is the core of the fantastic.

1995 - Overview: The Year in Review

~ originally published in Locus #421 (Feb 1996) ~

In the latter part of the year, a London conference celebrated the 100th anniversary of the publication of Wells's *The Time Machine*, with more than 90 critical and academic papers devoted to that one book! I wasn't at the conference, but what impressed me about it was not only that it might have set a new SF standard for obsessing over a single text, but that the centennial it recognized was indeed a kind of milestone. As far as I know, no one has argued that 1995 was the centennial of science fiction itself — people argue for inception dates as varied as 1818 and 1926 — but there's a case to be made that Wells's novel set in motion a kind of continuous dialogue that can be traced more or less unbroken, through a community more or less definable, down to the present day. Time travel was only a small part of this dialogue, which really has to do with the interactions of mind, time, and nature, principally as expressed in notions of progress and evolution. Wells took Victorian pride and *fin de siècle* anxiety and sent it reeling into a century of unimaginable chaos, and we're still dealing with it as that century draws to a close. It may be no accident that several of the most notable novels of this past year return to the major themes of Wells's first novel.

Stephen Baxter's *The Time Ships* is, of course, a direct sequel to *The Time Machine* — the "authorized sequel," as the blurb rather spookily has it — but it is also a Stapledonian extension of Wells's basic notions, and the most purely enjoyable SF adventure I read all year. A similarly grand perspective is achieved by Gregory Benford in *Sailing Bright Eternity*, a satisfyingly ambitious conclusion to his Nigel Walmsley/Galactic Center series of novels. As in Wells, predation and evolution — organic, machine, and hybrid — are at the heart of Benford's far future universe. On a somewhat narrower stage, both Greg Bear's *Legacy* and Ian McDonald's *Evolution's Shore* (or *Chaga*) imagine complete different models for evolutionary change, Bear's on a distant planet called Lamarckia, McDonald's in a magically transformed, and transfiguring, Africa. By now we're getting pretty far away from our putative source, but I'd still argue that the issues raised by these novels are issues at least implicit in Wells.

What about the *fin de siècle* aspect of Wells's work? Are we beginning to see a fascination with decadence in SF as our century begins to fade? Of course we are. Look at the ritualized neo-Victorians of Neal Stephenson's *The Diamond Age*, easily the year's richest melodrama; or the nihilistic terrorist-run tomorrow of John Barnes's *Kaleidoscope Century*, which actually tries to envision a 21st century worse than this one in terms of plagues, wars, and politics. What about the haunted, decaying urban centers of Nicola Griffith's *Slow River*, Paul McAuley's *Fairyland* (with its highly suggestive image of a nanotech revolution being run out of the ruins of EuroDisney), or Walter Jon Williams' *Metropolitan*? Richard Calder's *Dead Girls* trilogy – of which only the first volume saw print in the U.S. during the year – is the sort of science fiction Rimbaud might have enjoyed, even though there's hardly a word in it he would have understood. Lisa Mason's The *Golden Nineties* even paid direct homage to the end of the last century. And of the few fantasy novels I had a chance to read, the most impressive was Elizabeth Hand's *Waking the Moon*, which carries distinctly eschatological overtones in its tale of a reborn apocalyptic goddess-cult.

Among new writers, there seems to be a tendency to get started fast. In addition to Richard Calder, several writers began with two novels in less than a year. Linda Nagata followed her nanotechy *The Bohr Maker* – another pretty decadent future – with the remarkable future chronicle *Tech Heaven*. Valerie Freireich introduced her "Polite Harmony of Worlds" in *Becoming Human* and then made it really convincing in *Testament*. Tricia Sullivan gave us a skillful tale of a gene-war ravaged earth, *Lethe*, and published her first short story in one of the year's best original anthologies, *Full Spectrum 5*, edited by Jennifer Hershey, Tom Dupree, and Janna Silverstein. Other important second novels appearing in 1995 included Griffith's *Slow River* – surely one of the genre's best novels of character during the year – and Jonathan Lethem's unpredictable *Amnesia Moon*, a more ambitious follow-up to his one-joke *Gun, with Occasional Music*.

Several important author collections appeared during the year, the briefest of which was Octavia Butler's *Bloodchild and Other Stories*, which came out just in time to provide a convenient – and powerful – sampler for all those people wondering what kind of an SF writer gets a MacArthur Foundation genius grant. Those wondering what kind of SF writer has enough clout to recommend people for the genius grants can find out in Ursula K. Le Guin's *Four Ways to Forgiveness*, which represented even more of a return to her Hainish universe than the previous year's *Fisherman of the Inland Sea*. Le Guin's interconnected stories formed a kind of thematic cycle, and this was also the case with Brian Aldiss's ingeniously linked collection *The Secret of this Book* and with Paul Di Filippo's manic variations on 19th century cultural history *The Steampunk Trilogy* – probably the single most unalloyed delight of the year. A somewhat more traditional SF collection of the "let's throw out some ideas and see what we can do with them" school was Charles Sheffield's *Georgia on my Mind and Other Places*. One of the more encouraging signs during the year was a number of reprint anthologies of authors no longer with us – not only new recyclings of Lovecraft and Clark Ashton Smith, whose tales seem to reappear as each new generation discovers purple prose, but collected stories from Angela Carter, collected "people" stories from Zenna Henderson, and a mixed bag of early Sturgeon called *The Ultimate Egoist*, a title which might seem better suited to any number of writers, but which comes from a Sturgeon story, not from his reputation.

Another welcome sign during the year was a slight renascence in what might be termed the serious-minded original theme anthology, once a staple of the SF short fiction market but in recent years eclipsed by gimmickry. Looking over the preceding two years' *Locus* recommended lists, I find plenty of original horror theme anthologies (mostly having to do with lovestruck vampires) and a handful of alternate history "concept" anthologies (the SF equivalent of microwave popcorn), but nothing quite like this past year's *New Legends*, edited by Greg Bear; *Far Futures*, edited by Gregory Benford; or *How to Save the World*, edited by Charles Sheffield. Although the contents of these anthologies are inevitably uneven (the Benford is probably the best overall collection), each of the editors set out in good faith to find new directions and explore new possibilities for SF, in particular hard SF. Terri Windling's *The Armless Maiden and Other Tales for Childhood's Survivors* did something of the same for fantasy, with its combination of original and reprint material focused on the need for society to assume responsibility for its children. Among reissues of earlier anthologies, two highlights were Pamela Sargent's *Women of Wonder*, revised and repackaged in a new two-volume format (the first volume contained authors from the classic 1970s series of this title, while the second was a brand-new anthology updating the first); and H. Bruce Franklin's critical/historical *Future Perfect: American Science Fiction of the Nineteenth Century*, still the definitive collection of its kind, also somewhat revised.

In the world of SF criticism and scholarship, Liverpool University Press emerged as the most significant new player with several important books appearing in its "Liverpool Science Fiction Texts and Studies," under the general editorship of David Seed. Seed himself gathered together an impressive variety of scholars and topics in *Anticipations: Essays on Early Science Fiction and its Precursors* (No. 2 in the series), while Brian Aldiss collected many of his own shrewd and entertaining essays in *The Detached Retina: Aspects of SF and Fantasy* (No. 4) and John Clute offered a new and substantial collection of various reviews and essays in *Look at the Evidence* (No. 10). Clute also wrote the year's prettiest SF coffee-table book, the misleadingly titled *Science Fiction: The Illustrated Encyclopedia* from Dorling Kindersley. While it amused some to watch the idiosyncratic Clute rein himself in for the sake of visual soundbites, it also should be noted that the book is probably the bestselling nonfiction work about SF in several years. Other critical books of note during the year included Damien Broderick's rather densely theoretical *Reading by Starlight: Postmodern Science Fiction*; a long-overdue assemblage of some (but not all) of Joanna Russ's SF criticism and theory, *To Write Like a Woman: Essays in Feminism and Science Fiction*; and a first posthumous collection of Dick's essays, *The Shifting Realities of Philip K. Dick: Selected Literary and Philosophical Writings*, which like his fiction alternates between startling brilliance and scary goofiness.

Sometimes, looking over all this stuff, I'm amazed at the breadth of the field, and sometimes I'm amazed by its narrowness. On the one hand, this genre — or group of genres — has gotten so diffuse, so tangled in cultural and market forces, so peopled by quirky individualists and risk-averse corporate sheep, that the idea of trying to keep track of it in any meaningful way seems quixotic. On the other, talking about trends in SF, as though it were completely separate from the culture at large, seems insular and self-defeating. Was 1995 the official beginning of the *nouveau fin de siècle* in

SF, or in general? There's some evidence to suggest that. But since we're not just on the downhill side of the last decade of the century, but also hot on the heels of the millenium, maybe we'll just bypass the decadence altogether and head straight for apocalypse.

— January 1995, Locus #408 —

The Diamond Age ~~ Neal Stephenson

Remake ~~ Connie Willis

Science Fiction in the 20th Century ~~ Edward James

Silent Interviews: On Language, Race, Sex, Science Fiction, and Some Comics ~~ Samuel R. Delany

---

Following the huge success of his 1992 *Snow Crash* — a rare first SF novel (*The Big U* was a mainstream novel of academia) whose literary inventiveness kept pace with its science fictional extrapolation, and vice versa — it wasn't surprising that Stephenson's next novel, *Interface*, should appear under the collaborative pseudonym "Stephen Bury." After all, this competent and well-crafted near-future political thriller seemed decidedly low-key to be presented as the "next novel by the author of *Snow Crash*," even though word quickly got around and the novel seems to have done pretty well. There's little doubt, though, that Bantam is treating **The Diamond Age** as the more-or-less official followup to Stephenson's resounding debut. Set in a worldwide futurescape as densely imagined as that of *Snow Crash* and similarly organized around a new technology — in this case nanotech instead of virtual reality — it's positioned to be the novel Stephenson readers have been waiting for. Only it isn't — at least if they're waiting for another frolic.

At first, it looks like it's going to be. We're immediately introduced to Bud, a leather-clad punk on high-speed skates on his way to get a new weapon implanted in his skull in a suburb of a future Shanghai dominated by special-interest enclaves reminiscent of those in *Snow Crash*. Bud is so annoying that we don't really mind when he meets a horrible death a few chapters later, but it quickly becomes apparent that his role in the novel is so marginal that Stephenson uses him primarily as a kind of transition device between what *Snow Crash* readers expect and what they're going to get. And what they're going to get — already signaled by the subtitle "A Young Lady's Illustrated Primer" and the running narrative gloss used as chapter headings — is something very close to a Victorian novel, stretched out over decades and depicting, in one of its central plot lines, the growth and eventual flowering of a lower-class little girl named Nell. Stephenson even provides a pseudo-Victorian culture as background; one of the most powerful groups in this retribalized future is the neo-Victorians, who travel in exotic airships, maintain a kind of smug repression in interpersonal relations, and concern themselves (among other things) with the proper education of the young.

The novel's other major plot-line concerns one of these neo-Victorians, unsubtly named John Percival Hackworth, a successful nanotech designer commissioned to devise an interactive educational "primer" for the daughter of a peer named Lord Finkle-McGraw. Hackworth makes an illegal copy for his own daughter, but loses it in a mugging, and it eventually finds its way into Nell's hands. Over the next several years, Nell grows to maturity guided by the book (and by Miranda, an interactive performer who remotely provides the book's "voice" and serves as surrogate mother, even though she can never find who or where Nell is), while Hackworth sets off on another assignment to find a mysterious hacker known as the Alchemist. Eventually, all these threads intertwine, along with several others involving a hedonistic underwater tribe called the Drummers, a group of terrorists out to sabotage the molecular "Feed" lines that supply Shanghai's nanotech "matter compilers," and Miranda's supervisor Carl Hollywood. In terms of sheer complexity, *The Diamond Age* outdoes even *Snow Crash*, and as a novel of character and history it's in many ways superior.

In SF terms, however, it seems almost oddly restrained compared to *Snow Crash's* wild inventiveness. Stephenson's version of a nanotech-transformed world doesn't go nearly as far as, say, Kathleen Ann Goonan's *Queen City Jazz*. He describes almost convincingly how nanotech "feeds" might work and offers a spectacular set-piece involving nanotech-induced coral growth, but his "matter compilers" don't seem a lot different from the old molecular synthesizers which date back to the SF of the thirties, and many of the mundane applications he imagines – sheets of paper that function like display terminals and fold themselves into letters – seem downright trivial in SF terms, while at the same time providing the kind of detailed texture that makes Stephenson's world convincing. The most significant example is the primer itself, which is heavily text-driven and at times seems to illustrate the possibilities of hypertext more than of nanotechnology. Considerable parts of the narrative are given over to extracts from the primer, which recasts Nell's life in terms of an heroic fairy tale; in the most interesting of these extracts, the "Princess" Nell finds herself in "Castle Turing," where she is given a quick course in computer architecture and must successfully pass a Turing test (as the human subject, not the machine) in order to escape. The passage reads like nothing so much as one of those didactic philosophical fables from Lem's *The Cyberiad* or a Douglas Hofstadter book.

In the end, *The Diamond Age* is not the "nanotech" novel to match Stephenson's earlier "VR" novel. Nor, despite some considerable touches of humor, is it nearly as funny as *Snow Crash*. But so what? Novelists whose first major book is such a hoot are always faced with this dilemma: give them more of what they want or try to stretch out into new territory, deepening characterization and broadening the range of themes. (No one today argues that Pynchon should have written another *V*.) Had

The Diamond Age appeared as Stephenson's first novel, it might very well have knocked people's socks off, and it still might. Never mind that the attempt to more fully develop characters leads to touches of sentimentality, or that the multivalent Victorian narrative structure leads to occasional melodramatic plot contrivances (such as assiduously keeping Miranda and Nell apart to build a kind of pathos), or that at times the pacing seems to slow to a crawl in order to bring the various threads up to speed. *The Diamond Age* is the work of a serious novelist reaching into new territory, and if it's not perfect, it's still well worth the trip.

Last year, I noted that Connie Willis's *Uncharted Territory*, like some of the stories in her collection *Impossible Things*, seemed in part to be a celebration of her love for old movies. Anyone who wants to argue with that should take a look at her new short novel, **Remake**, which is indisputably the work of a novelist with a VCR. The plot of *Remake* is even slighter than that of *Uncharted Territory*, and in fact is little more than a short story of the sort we used to expect from, say, Richard Matheson or Jack Finney. In a 21st century Hollywood in which live actors have virtually been replaced by computer-generated simulacra, a young woman named Alis arrives from Illinois with the dream of becoming a dancer in the movies. The narrator, Tom, whose current assignment is going through the entire classic movie library of a conglomerate called "Viamount" to remove any references to substance abuse, offers to help her, even as he warns her that no musicals have been made in decades and that live actors are equally obsolete. Soon Alis disappears, and Tom begins to think he sees her in minor roles in the old movies he's censoring – as a chorus dancer in *Seven Brides for Seven Brothers*, for example. At first, he assumes she's simply gotten herself digitally inserted into the prints, but later finds this isn't possible, and he begins to suspect that time travel may be the solution to the mystery. Willis is aware that this situation sounds a lot like that in Woody Allen's *The Purple Rose of Cairo*, and has her narrator make that explicit comparison, but she's careful to keep the reader looking for a science-fictional explanation rather than a purely fantastic one.

Remake isn't as consistently funny as the best of Willis's humorous stories, although she makes much of Tom's hopeless task of trying to logically remove drinking and drunkenness from films like *The Philadelphia Story* or *Casablanca*. She also has fun depicting a future film industry given over entirely to self-cannibalization, with nearly all movies remakes or sequels using digital technology to insert new actors into old roles (Marilyn Monroe in *Pretty Woman*, Sylvester Stallone in *Ben-Hur*), and "warmbody" actors making themselves over into images of Monroe or James Dean. The images of dead actors are copyrighted, resulting in endless litigations over rights and sometimes making movies available for viewing for only hours at a time before the next injunction is filed. In many ways, this is all too believable to work well as purely wacky comedy; in fact, Willis's future film industry seems downright likely. What gives the book much of its charm, however, isn't the story at all, but Willis's own random opinions and observations about the movies she loves – why Astaire was a better dancer than Kelly, or why Busby Berkley wasn't a choreographer at all. *Remake* is far from great sf — it's more like a good cocktail-party debate about old movies — and for that reason alone film buffs should love it.

Whatever else academic and nonfiction publishers may think about SF, they seem to agree that it belongs firmly in the class of Things That People Need Concise Introductions To. Over the years, we've seen such handy guidebooks from Basil Davenport, Kingsley Amis, Sam Lundwall, Eric Rabkin and Robert Scholes, David Hartwell, Sam Moskowitz, Patrick Parrinder, Thomas Clareson, and others, and this doesn't include more ambitious histories or theoretical works. There aren't nearly as many "concise introductions" to other genres such as mysteries or fantasy, and it's never been entirely clear to me exactly who the audience for such things is supposed to be. Edward James's new **Science Fiction in the 20th Century** is a case in point. Published as part of Oxford University Press series called Opus Books ("concise, original, and authoritative introductions to a wide range of subjects"), it's clearly organized and written, generally free from cant and soapboxing, and displays the kind of broad-based international perspective we might expect from the editor of *Foundation*, the most consistently readable and provocative of the field's critical journals. It's in no way meant to demean James's temperate and good-natured effort when I find myself asking, who needs it?

Who *does* need it? I find it hard to believe that there are thousands of readers poised on the brink of diving headfirst into the sea of SF, holding back only until a nice guidebook comes along to direct their reading. Fans, on the other hand, are notoriously fickle about such projects, often ready to take umbrage at perceived slights such as, say (in the present case) the omission of any mention of Mike Resnick. Academics will likely feel they've moved beyond the general introduction stage and are ready for more focused theoretical works; a few of them might find this useful as a supplementary classroom text (which is certainly is, although most SF teachers I know find it hard enough to get students to plow through actual *fiction*, let alone historical material). This leaves us with an imaginary reader, not quite a fan, familiar enough with SF to be curious about its origins and dynamics but not quite ready to launch into Aldiss's *Trillion Year Spree*. For such readers (both of them), James's book is first-rate.

James begins with an acute discussion of labels and categories, and moves on to two chapters of historical survey beginning in 1895 and taking us roughly through the end of the Campbell period in 1960. He makes the persuasive point that American and British SF diverged following the radically different experiences of the two nations in the First World War, and details what he calls the "victory" of American SF under Campbell. Using Clarke and Wyndham as examples, he shows how British SF of the fifties managed to respond to, and yet remain separate from, the American tradition. (James's treatment of British and Australian SF is predictably excellent, but in tracing its development in other national literatures he falls into the trap of hunting for genre magazines on the American model; the modern Japanese tradition, for example, gets reduced to a single mention of *Godzilla*.)

Before continuing his historical survey through the New Wave and the cyberpunks, James pauses to add two chapters on "Reading Science Fiction" and "The SF Community." The first of these is potentially the most interesting chapter in the book; James takes on contrasts with the mainstream, accusations of escapism, the sense of wonder, the satirical and romantic poles of SF, and reading strategies (using Asimov's "Nightfall," Vance's "The Moon Moth," and Shaw's "Light of Other Days" as sample texts). But his theoretical base here consists largely of citing the approaches of Robert Scholes and Darko Suvin, and his example of SF's syntactical uniqueness is the oldest saw in the book, the Heinlein-by-way-of-Ellison-by-way-of-Delany sentence "The door dilated." (Am I the only one who doesn't swoon at that sentence, who wonders what real purpose such a door serves other than as a future-marker, who worries about getting caught in it?) James does a perceptive job explaining the kind of anxiety that reading such sentences can engender in the uninitiated reader, but he stops short of showing us how this consistently leads to a different kind of aesthetic for SF.

Following a penultimate chapter on SF fandom and its fringes (such as Shaver, von Däniken, and of course Hubbard), James concludes with a discussion of the 1960s and after. Taking issue with some of his fellow British critics, he argues that while neither the American nor British New Waves constituted real movements, the American version had a much more lasting effect on the field, expanding both its readership and its stylistic variety. He treats the rise of subgenres such as hard SF (which had always been around, but had to define itself more militantly following the New Waves), fantasy (which had also obviously been around, but diverged as a marketing category), feminist SF, and of course cyberpunk. A final section on current trends notes the recent popularity of alternative histories and the recent spate of Mars novels. James is consistently even-tempered and reasonable, to the point where you begin to hunger for some hidden agenda or secret mania, like a belief that John Russell Fearn secretly moved to the U.S. and became H.L. Gold. But no such luck; you can't really argue with much of what James says — although at times you'll wish you could.

Samuel R. Delany, on the other hand, never shies away from contestable positions or provocative opinions. In his fiction, Delany can write like quicksilver, and in lectures or on panel discussions, he is easily SF's most articulate spokesperson in academia. But, so the complaint goes, in his critical writing the quicksilver often turns to molasses, and the articulate voice takes on a tone of studied pedantry — the voice of someone who, from the point of view of many SF fans and writers, has spent too long sleeping with the enemy. For such readers, **Silent Interviews**, a collection of ten written interviews (that is, written responses to written questions) plus one interview *by* Delany of composer Anthony Davis, might seem the ideal pathway into

Delany's critical philosophy and thought. And in many ways it is, although arguably as much is lost in the process as is gained.

In his introduction, Delany justifiably complains about garbled transcriptions of past oral interviews ("*récit*, dialogue, and action" into "racy dialogue in action") and argues that since his thoughts and feelings are formed by the act of writing, writing is the appropriate way for him to be interviewed. Any writer might say as much, and certainly the frustrations attendant upon reading an interview in which the subject half-remembers a text or quotation are ameliorated by a form that gives him time to look them up properly. What is potentially lost, however, is spontaneous observation of Delany in action, the inherent drama of conversation. The result could easily be a series of portraits retouched by the subject into self-portraits, until the interviewer fades away (or disappears altogether, in the case of the "K. Leslie Steiner" interview, "conducted" by Delany's own critical alter ego).

This turns out not to be so much a problem as it might seem, for two reasons. In the first place, half of the interviews were not "written interviews" at all to begin with, but have simply been reworked from transcripts, and Delany has too good a dramatic sense to dampen the feel of a living dialogue. Furthermore, when the interviewer is a perceptive critic familiar with Delany's work, such as Takayuki Tatsumi (who has two interviews) or Larry McCaffrey and Sinda Gregory, there is a sense of real intellectual engagement. When Delany starts talking about "paraspaces" in the work of Budrys and Bester, Tatsumi seems to surprise him by identifying much the same thing in several Delany novels.

What may be more frustrating for anyone seeking to get a clear angle on Delany's recent thought (the interviews cover the decade 1983-1993), is the inevitable backtracking and repitition. When an interview is focused on a particular topic, such as a *Comics Journal* piece that deals largely with *Empire*, this isn't a problem, but elsewhere in the book we're told more than once how a visit to the Port Authority bus terminal resulted in passages in two different stories, and given several versions of Delany's familiar argument that SF is a way of reading rather than a genre in the traditional sense. But there are also enough unique insights and comments about SF, race, sexuality, language, criticism, and individual writers to make the book invaluable despite its random pattern of coverage. Delany offers a cutting critique of "true" vs. "academic" versions of SF history, for example, and argues persuasively that SF criticism — both by academics and writers — has too easily been sidetracked into debates over unattainable definitions or catalogues of generic conventions. He makes trenchant observations about the New Wave (which he regards as "anti-theoretical" and in many ways conservative), noting that its principal "islands" were *New Worlds*, the *Orbit* series, and the *Dangerous Visions* anthologies. Unlike most historians (including James) who see feminist SF largely as a kind of demographic broadening of the field in the 1970s, he argues convincingly that it represented a crucial change in the genre between the New Wave and cyberpunk, even claiming that without the feminist writers there would be no cyberpunk. And he offers up some telling personal reminiscences: how a nightlamp he had as a child helped teach him about the multiplex meanings of objects, how he discovered SF, how he found his way into postrstructuralist and deconstructionist theory (many will be relieved to find he was as confused as anybody at first), how he has dealt with issues of race and sexual orientation. In short, there is much here that is not covered in Delany's critical or autobiographical writings, and much that anyone seriously interested in SF — or many of Delany's other favorite topics — ought to consider.

— February 1995, Locus #409 —

Waking the Moon ~~ Elizabeth Hand

Georgia on My Mind, and Other Places ~~ Charles Sheffield

Earthfall: Homecoming, Volume 4 ~~ Orson Scott Card

Becoming Human ~~ Valerie J. Freireich

The survival and validation of ancient beliefs constitute one of the most common motifs in fantasy and horror fiction, and for the most part fantasy and horror writers don't do much with it. It's a Faustian temptation for novelists to simply install a powerful myth in their narratives and let it take over, leaving characters and setting on cruise control as the myth works itself out with a kind of authorless inevitability. In other words, the cautionary note implicit in nearly all such stories — be careful about taking these ancient beliefs too lightly — might well apply to the writers themselves, who often seem to end up with more than they can handle. Since this challenge is exactly what Elizabeth Hand has set for herself in **Waking the Moon**, it's all the more remarkable that she has managed to keep such firm control of her materials that we almost feel we're reading it all for the first time. *Waking the Moon* takes on one of the most fundamental of all mythologies — the pre-Minoan cult of the Goddess — and, without substantially violating the evidence of archeology and anthropology, makes it her own in one of the most powerful and affecting fantasy novels in recent years.

I use the term "fantasy novel" deliberately — even though some would argue that fantasies and novels aren't quite the same thing — because *Waking the Moon* works brilliantly on both levels. There's plenty of apocalyptic furniture spaced throughout the novel to keep the thrill-crazed on the edge of their seats — angelic apparitions, meteorological portents, magic amulets, secret societies, mysterious archeological digs, murders-by-possession, murders-by-remote-control-of-animals, portals into terrifying otherworldly wastelands — but somehow it never seems excessive, never seems to be reaching for effects (with the possible exception of a *de rigeur* set-piece at the end, which is strained by its need to top an even better-written set-piece hundreds of pages earlier). The reason it doesn't, I think, is that all this lightning is grounded in a romantic and attractive novel of character, and Hand does an amazing job of keeping her believable and sympathetic characters from being overwhelmed by special effects. She is one of the few recent writers to make full use of what used to be called (by Freud and others) "the uncanny."

The key character is the narrator, Sweeney Cassidy, whom we first meet as an awe-struck undergraduate at the spectacular campus of the University of the Archangels and Saint John the Divine in D.C., a campus so convincingly and eerily detailed it functions virtually as a character in these opening chapters. (Hand's evocation of campus life is worthy of Evelyn Waugh, whom she invokes at one point.) Sweeney befriends two beautiful and brilliant classmates, Oliver Wilde Crawford and Angelica di Rienzi, both recipients of esoteric scholarships sponsored by an ancient secret society called the *Benandanti*. Meanwhile (temporarily abandoning Sweeney's viewpoint), we learn that the *Benandanti* have received word of a "sign" appearing on campus, and that one of the society's few female members, a distinguished anthropologist, is quietly plotting to betray them. All this secrecy and betrayal has to do with the prophesied reincarnation of the Goddess, an event which the *Benandanti* have been trying to forestall for millennia. Inevitably, Sweeney, Oliver, and Angelica – already forming a love triangle – are swept into the center of this epic battle, with Angelica seeming to represent the restoration of the Goddess after centuries of oppressive male hierarchies.

So far, the novel seems headed toward a fairly uncritical feminist rendering of goddess-hood as empowerment, underlined by a variety of strong female characters – Sweeney, Angelica, Angelica's gay roommate Annie, the anthropologist Magda Kurtz – and the relatively one-dimensional brutality of the male *Benandanti* leaders, who dispatch Magda in a particularly unpleasant way. As Angelica comes to realize her destiny, this first part of the novel rushes toward a violent and sexy climax involving a pagan ritual which leads to Sweeney's expulsion, Oliver's suicide, and Angelica's disappearance. Suddenly we're in Part Two, it's eighteen years later, and we find things are only beginning. In a bold stroke that immensely deepens the novel's thematic complexity, Part Two turns out to be very nearly an inverted mirror image of Part One.

Sweeney is now a museum archivist, Angelica is a bestselling author and talk-show guest promoting female empowerment (and what better modern emblem of the historical marginalization of women's power than talk shows?), and Annie is a performance artist who's growing suspicious at the number mysterious deaths among the old college gang. The horror-story devices earlier associated with the *Benandanti* now shift to Angelica, and the idea of restoring the Goddess begins to seem like it may not be such a good thing after all. With the aid of Annie, Angelica's and Oliver's son Dylan, and a mysterious phantom figure in yellow, Sweeney finds herself once again in love, and once again at the center of the epic, only this time with even more at stake. Can Hand mount a final climax spectacular enough to unload all the baggage her narrative has by now accrued? I think she has a few problems, but I can't imagine many readers seriously complaining after such a marvelous ride. (Meeting Sweeney alone was worth the trip.) *Waking the Moon* is one of the most thoughtful treatments of the White Goddess myth I've seen in fiction, covering much of the same thematic material David Lindsay wanted to cover in his unfinished (and klutzily written) *The Witch* — but carried off with the sure hand of a writer who knows how to weave her own spells, and who has now given us her first masterpiece.

H.G. Wells once argued that the key to a successful fantastic story lay in restricting the tale to a single marvel — invisibility, alien invasion, time travel, etc. Charles Sheffield, who might well be regarded as one of Wells's most direct heirs among modern hard SF writers, seems to have developed his own formula for generating compelling SF stories, and — at least to judge from his new collection, **Georgia on My Mind, and Other Places** — it involves guaranteeing not one, but two marvels per story. The best example of this, and the best piece in the collection, is his Nebula-winning title story "Georgia on My Mind," which involves a fascinating mystery concerning evidence that Babbage's Analytical Engine may actually have been built in a remote part of New Zealand in the 1850s — and then tacks on a subplot with strong implications of alien visitors. The subplot works only because of Sheffield's carefully understated treatment of the aliens, and it's easy to see how Wells might object that this secondary marvel very nearly undercuts the wonder of the first.

Bad SF writers do this all the time, of course; it's the entire basis of what Moorcock called "shaggy god stories," with aliens or time-travelers or post-holocaust scenarios invoked at the last minute to salvage plots that otherwise resemble kamikazes. But Sheffield is far from a bad SF writer, and his mix-and-match scenarios almost always succeed in keeping us a little off-center, uncertain of where the story is really going. At their best, they are fascinating exercises in technique, and a good deal of fun besides. (I found that, even while I was in the middle of reading other things, I kept picking up this collection just to see what Sheffield would do next.) Sometimes he sets the story up as a mystery, as with the title story or "Destroyer of Worlds," in which a puzzle in philately leads to the discovery of a potentially catastrophic experiment in artificial biospheres. In "Trapalanda," he turns an explorer's adventure in Patagonia into a hard SF scenario complete with gravity wells and time distortions. But on occasion, such as with "The Feynman Saltation," the combination of unexpected themes (in this case brain surgery and paleontology) seems strained and too dependent on convenient plot set-ups (the patient, who begins dreaming scenes from millions of years in the past, just happens to have a sister who's a paleontologist). And in "Fifteen-Love on the Dead Man's Chest," the attempt at a slapstick combination of tennis and mortuary science on the moon is just silly. (Sheffield reports that it's one of a series of stories written to appease his children's taste for gross-out subjects, and it reveals its origins.) Generally, Sheffield does better with humor in a couple of short-shorts ending in clever jokes, or in his take on SF writers' egos in "Obsolete Skill".

In a few cases, real-life pathologies are joined with SF themes to yield surprisingly apt results. "The Bee's Kiss" shows how compulsive voyeurism can be a useful skill in understanding alien behavior. In "Health Care System," a wealthy woman's obsession with survival at all costs leads to a horror story about computer brain implants (a less successful treatment of a similar theme, "The Fifteenth Station of the Cross," invokes Jesus in something dangerously close to a shaggy god story). An experienced hunter who leads safaris in virtual-reality microworlds finds his skills useful in nanosurgery in "Deep Safari," and − in what is perhaps the most original SF conceit in the book − a servant of the papacy helps introduce Arab numeration to the court of Kublai Khan in "Beyond the Golden Road".

Given such a consistently novel way of developing stories, it's almost disappointing when Sheffield offers what is in most ways a perfectly competent treatment of a traditional SF scenario in "Humanity Test." Combining genetically enhanced chimps with space exploration has become virtually an SF convention − the nonhuman companion who must earn its humanity (it's probably SF's version of the nonwhite sidekick who's been a staple of American storytelling from Queequeg to Tonto). Sheffield wrings as much sentiment out of this as you'd expect, but along the way you realize that he's also writing a response to the problem posed in Tom Godwin's "The Cold Equations" − a recombinant trick of a different sort. Unlike the more literary-minded Benford, Sheffield seldom tries for stylistic innovation or significant depth of character, and is generally content to play within the rules of conventional SF. But when he does try to evoke the romance of computer history and the isolation of an exiled mathematician in "Georgia on My Mind," he can succeed brilliantly.

A few chapters into **Earthfall**, the fourth volume in Orson Scott Card's ongoing epic about a godlike, *angst*-ridden, and malfunctioning computer trying to bring colonists back home to Earth after 40 million years, it becomes apparent that the squabbling adolescents who have taken over the series aren't going to change and aren't going to disappear. What started out promisingly with the scale and sensibility of Arthur Clarke, overlaid with Card's trademark concern with moral behavior, seems instead to given way to a simplistic contest of good and evil, as if the Hardy Boys had wandered into *Against the Fall of Night*. Every motivation is highlighted in neon, and the characters pummel each other with lines like "You don't know everything" and insults like "snotnose." By now, I'm beginning to side with that poor computer − called the Oversoul − whose only real malfunction seems to be that it didn't drown the whole litter of them a couple of volumes back.

By now, it's become fairly common knowledge that Card is basing the series on the *Book of Mormon* (primarily the first and second books of Nephi, whose name is echoed in Card's hero Nafai), and Patrick L. McGuire did a pretty good analysis of parallels in the first two novels in the fanzine *Fosfax* in April 1994. Basilica, the home city from which the adventurers are warned to flee, is Jerusalem; the Index which enables access to the Oversoul's memory corresponds to the golden plates containing genealogy; Earth is the Promised Land (the Americas); Nafai's wicked brother Elemak, who establishes an opposing sect, is Nephi's wicked brother Laman; and so on. Although interesting, this hardly seems crucial as long as the source doesn't distort the series' shape as an SF epic; SF writers have a long history of modeling stories on everything from Edenic myths to Roman history. And it seems like we're home free (so to speak) when, in the current novel, the travelers arrive on Earth to find a bifurcated society that seems drawn more from Wells's *The Time Machine* than from Mormon texts: Diggers, idol-worshiping subterranean creatures evolved from rats, and Angels, weaker and more spiritual flying creatures evolved from bats. Then I found a reference in *The Book of Mormon* to idols being left "to the moles and to the bats," "to go into the clefts of the rocks, and into the tops of the ragged rocks," and I began to suspect the source was asserting itself with increasingly less subtlety. By the time Nafai's tribe (having literally joined with the Angels) is driven into the wilderness by his wicked brothers – exactly what happens to Nephi in the Promised Land – and especially when Nafai decides to engrave the history of his people on golden plates, I'd pretty much abandoned any hope that the narrative could ever make sense as SF, independent of its source.

Apart from the questionable rhetorical strategy of demonstrating that one's own religion works pretty well as SF (even C.S. Lewis quickly turned his SF-like *apologias* into allegorical fantasies), and the more complex questions raised by casting a buggy computer in the role of God, one has to ask if the return to Earth – the central promise that the series has held out for four volumes – works in purely narrative terms. And I can't see how it does. Despite some ingenious evolutionary theorizing and the one remaining wild card – an intelligence even more mysterious than the Oversoul, called the Keeper of Earth – Card's future Earth is no evocative Gene Wolfe construct, but just another alien planet with colorful primitives ready to worship us. In earlier volumes, Card tempered his religious mythologizing with fascinating inventions of his own – the unpredictable General Moozh, for example, or the matriarchal society of Basilica. Now, when such inventions seem called for more than ever, they get very nearly shunted aside to make room for the religious narrative. Maybe Card's final volume will brilliantly resolve these tensions – he's an extremely clever storyteller – but *Earthfall* comes dangerously close to turning an epic into a pamphlet.

One of the more interesting questions raised by Card's Diggers and Angels is the classic SF puzzle of what is a human. As its title implies, Valerie Freireich's first novel **Becoming Human** takes this puzzle as its central focus, and approaches it from a number of interesting angles. Freireich lacks the considerable story-shaping abilities of Card, however, and the novel quickly reveals its origins as a long story originally published in *Tomorrow*. Like Mary Rosenblum in *The Stone Garden*, Freireich chooses to turn the story into a novel by simply extending it, and she comes up against some of the same problems (more, actually, since her central character was killed off at the end of the story). The main problem, of course, lies in what makes a good short story in the first place: it raises problems of sufficient complexity, and resolves them with sufficient ambiguity, that it *suggests* a whole novel. Actually writing that novel risks dissipating all the qualities that made the story powerful in the first place.

In the story – the novel's first three chapters – a loyal "toolman," or genetically created servant not unlike a classic android, appears to betray his beloved master Sanda Brauna by creating a political scandal concerning the proposed admission of the planet Neuland into an alliance called the Polite Harmony of Worlds. The problem is that the Neulanders have altered themselves genetically to be free of pain, and in the eyes of the Harmony this makes them also less than human. The toolman, Alexander, is accused of having made a deal with them to gain added life beyond the preprogrammed mortality common to all toolmen – an accusation he admits to as he reveals the Neulanders' staging of a false alien attack on a Harmony world, killing millions in hopes that the fear of this common enemy will help them gain admittance to the Harmony.

Freireich chooses the rather clumsy device of having Alexander's clone, August, carry the rest of the story. Feeling a pariah because of his identification with a famous traitor, August mutilates himself in an effort to achieve a separate identity in the eyes of Sanda. He also becomes involved in the politics of Neuland and the Harmony, and like his predecessor yearns for full human status – something never granted for toolmen. This plight is hardly different from that suffered by androids and robots as far back as Capek's *R.U.R.*, and it involves "becoming human" only in the sense of gaining simple human rights (there's little biological inventiveness in the novel). But as we learn more about the Neulanders and the worlds of the Harmony, it becomes apparent that *Becoming Human* is indeed an apt title, as Freireich raises the questions of the role of pain in defining human feeling, and of the Harmony's own humanness, compromised by its unquestioned acceptance of a slave class. Such questions are provocative, as are the glimpses we are given of the "Jonist" philosophy which guides the Harmony's thinking, but Freireich's only technique for dramatizing them is to have characters talk endlessly as events plod along. Freireich is easily thoughtful enough to be regarded as a promising writer, but she hasn't learned to shape a novel yet.

Nobody's Son ~~ Sean Stewart

Resurrection Man ~~ Sean Stewart

Glory's War ~~ Alfred Coppel

The Bohr Maker ~~ Linda Nagata

A recent editorial in *The New York Review of Science Fiction* takes a host of unnamed SF reviewers to task for privileging traditional literary values such as characterization over more "traditional" SF values as setting, plot, and exposition – and thus presumably allowing a whole gaggle of well-written but imaginatively deficient works to escape into the marketplace unscathed by stern reviews. Whether this is actually the case or not, it does raise the old issue of SF and fantasy aesthetics, and whether these aesthetics differ significantly from those of the mainstream. The editorial seems to subscribe to the more-or-less traditional SF view that setting, plot, and exposition can make up for thin characters and pedestrian style, while stronger characters and style can't make up for "SF-nal" weaknesses. (The traditional mainstream view, of course, is exactly the opposite.) But SF has grown so diverse, and overlaps so often with related genres and the mainstream, that such a principle seems pretty narrow. To be sure, a hard SF setting makes demands on the author quite apart from what the characters do or say – but in dystopian and utopian literature, the setting is largely a function of the work's overall rhetoric, and in fantasy setting can be almost entirely an outgrowth of character or character relationships. Peter Beagle's *The Innkeeper's Song*, for example, demonstrates that a thoroughly rewarding fantasy can be evoked in a minimalist setting, and I don't know if that is as possible with SF.

In any event, these questions seem especially relevant in regard to some of this month's novels. In Alfred Coppel's *Glory's War*, the SF setting is very nearly everything, and it's almost as crucial in Linda Nagata's *The Bohr Maker*. On the other hand, two fantasy novels by Sean Stewart keep the settings clearly backgrounded to more "traditional" concerns of character and style. Stewart is a Texas-born Canadian whose first novel, *Passion Play*, was an SF murder mystery set in a repressive fundamentalist future. The novel's main strength was its convincing central character, and the setting seemed to function more as a way of placing constraints on that character than as a fully-realized SF world; because of the implicit rhetorical power of an imaginary pro-life autocracy, we wanted to know more about this world than the author seemed ready to tell us. With his next two novels (both appearing in the U.S. this year), Stewart moves emphatically in the direction of fantasy, and it seems much better suited to his strengths as a writer.

The setting of **Nobody's Son** (first published in a small edition in Canada in 1993) is thoroughly undistinguished – a vanilla fantasy world in which the title character, a commoner named Shielder's Mark, successfully exorcises the haunted "Ghostwood," which had foiled his society's greatest heroes, and then returns to claim as his prize the hand of the king's daughter. Mark's heroic quest, however, occupies only the novel's first chapter; the main action has to do with the question Mark finds himself repeatedly asking: *"Whatever happened to happily-ever-after?"* Unlike the fairy-tale world in which social class seems to evaporate once heroism is proven, Mark confronts a court ridden with political intrigue and clearly annoyed by this upstart interloper. He finds his real quest has yet to begin – overcoming his own intimidation and lack of education, and winning the respect of the court, the tomboyish Princess Gail, and her elegant lady-in-waiting Lissa. When he is awarded a dukedom, he finds himself thoroughly inept at managing affairs, and increasingly dependent on the politically savvy Lissa. Even his new bride refuses to sleep with him, because she wants to put off having children.

For most of the novel, it would seem that the fantasy setting is little more than a convenient backdrop for a coming-of-age tale with vivid, likeable characters, and indeed these characters are the novel's major strength. But then the fantasy reasserts itself as it becomes apparent that Mark's initial heroic act has had the unforeseen consequence of releasing magic back into the world. Mark finds himself returning to the Ghostwood on a more terrifying quest, which involves uncovering an ancient patricide and a generations-long curse. The generic fantasy world begins to take on a depth of meaning with clear overtones of Oedipus, but now Mark's quest isn't a simple adventure, but an outgrowth of the character-based issues that have been developing throughout the novel: Mark finds that his ambiguous identity as "nobody's son," which has plagued him throughout the story, can also be a source of strength. Written in straightforward yet often lyrical prose, *Nobody's Son* is a fine example of how character and setting can enrich each other in a fantasy narrative.

The return of magic to the world, and the loss of a father (fathers are important in all of Stewart's novels), are also central elements in **Resurrection Man**, a more ambitious and far more original novel that is likely to be the one that establishes Stewart's reputation as a new and highly individual voice. For reasons that are never fully explored, magic began to reassert itself in the Western world (there are strong suggestions it never really left China) following World War II, when Golems began to appear in the Nazi death camps. By the 1990s, minotaurs bred of collective fear roam city streets, psychically sensitive "angels" assist police investigations, and ghosts and dead bodies materialize out of nowhere. The magic has had an effect on history, too: although JFK was assassinated, a psychic helped avert the murder of Robert Kennedy, who became President. But not everything is changed; poverty and street gangs still haunt the cities, and in a cleverly written conversation which succinctly interrogates the whole notion of alternate worlds, several characters wonder if the film *Star Wars* could ever have been made without the return of magic.

If the alternate-world setting evokes SF, the novel's opening scene evokes horror:

Dante Ratkay, returned to his family home for Thanksgiving, is preparing to perform an autopsy on what appears to be his own dead body, which somehow materialized on his bedroom dresser. Dante, who possesses some of the powers of an angel (and whose name will prove to be no accident), is assisted by his spectral foster-brother Jet and his stand-up comic sister Sarah. Although the autopsy fails to clearly reveal the meaning of the corpse, it serves as a striking metaphor for the process of self-examination that is the novel's real theme. Dante views it as an omen of his own impending death, and as the action unfolds during the following week – presumably Dante's last – he and his siblings uncover a series of dark secrets about their Hungarian-American family, Jet's birth, and a daughter which Sarah miscarried years earlier. Meanwhile Laura Chen, a Chinese-American architect with whom Dante is secretly in love, becomes involved with the family after she discovers a break-in at Dante's apartment back in the city.

Nearly all these characters have interesting problems of their own, and nearly all of their problems get symbolized through different aspects of the re-emergent magic of Stewart's world. Stewart's controlled yet hauntingly poetic style (at its most haunting in a series of interpolated comments by Jet on family photos he has taken) gives this unusual plot something of the flavor of a mainstream family saga. Although his narrative weaves together threads of mystery, horror, and fantasy, Stewart's remarkable understated setting does a good job of showing us how both magic and altered history can serve as focusing lenses for the very real hopes and anxieties of believable people trying to learn to live with each other.

Glory's War is the second novel in Alfred Coppel's "Goldenwing Cycle," about the interplanetary adventures of a spectacular golden-sailed starship called *Gloria Coelis*. As I noted in reviewing the first novel, *Glory*, in 1993, the concept owes much to Cordwainer Smith – wired spacemen, telepathic cats, golden sails – and the new novel even features a prominent appearance by something closely resembling the subspace "dragons" from "The Game of Rat and Dragon" (as in Smith's story, this strange entity is perceived differently by the cats and the human telepaths). *Glory* is one of the last of the legendary interstellar "seed" ships, now reduced to running a kind of UPS service to colony worlds, and as in the earlier novel, Coppel divides the action between intrigues on the planets being visited and the ship itself. This also tends to divide the novel thematically, as it did the first one; if Coppel's spacefaring sequences pay homage to classic SF, his repressive planetary societies seem to owe as much to Amnesty International. In this case, the political scheming centers on the warring twin worlds of Nineveh and Nimrud, the former being the site of a colony of Sharia Christians from Russia, the latter a ferociously inhospitable world settled by an ill-fated second wave of settlers dominated by fundamentalist Muslims. The "Nimmies" want to share – or conquer – the limited habitable land on Nineveh, while the unfortunately nicknamed "Ninnies" want to protect their sinecure. The resulting war has flared up periodically for generations.

Coppel brings these planets vividly alive, but we barely have time to notice them because we're busy learning about the complicated intrigues on both sides as each schemes to capture the approaching starship for their own purposes. The novel is so front-loaded with exposition that it's two-thirds done before the *Gloria* even makes contact with the planets, and most of the exposition consists of outlining the history and strategies of the latest "Recurrence" of the war; the only character developed with any sympathy and depth is Katerina Volkov, a Ninnie military leader who worries about compromising her principles by enlisting in the plot to overtake the starship, which carries an almost religious significance to both colonies. Meanwhile, the chapters set aboard the Glory seem to mostly be marking time, although one adventure when the captain is nearly lost serves to introduce the idea of the mysterious faster-than-light entities who seem to thrive on human fear and hatred (and who seem to derive in equal measure from Cordwainer Smith and Colin Wilson).

In terms of those "SF-nal" virtues we were discussing earlier, then, *Glory's War* delivers a good deal – the settings are vivid (the most vivid is *Glory* herself, which Coppel is clearly enthralled with), and the societies he has worked out comment intelligently on the futile politics of *jihad* – just as his earlier novel in this series commented on *apartheid*. But he introduces so many characters and so many conspiracies during the book's first half that the central action of the plot – the meeting with *Glory* – is almost fatally postponed. When it finally does happen, and the war is taken aboard the starship itself, Coppel offers a series of slam-bang space war sequences worthy of A.E. Van Vogt. Suddenly, *Glory* – which has spent most of the novel hanging around striking awe in everyone – emerges as the central actor as well as the central image. The novel ends almost exactly as you know it has to from page one – that's the curse of a series novel with a continuing cast of crew members – but not before Coppel offers a healthy taste of the kind of grand space opera which this series continually promises – but which sometimes seems postponed by Coppel's equally valid (if less exciting) human rights agenda.

Impressive, fully-imagined settings also help to make Linda Nagata's **The Bohr Maker** an unusual and very promising first novel, one which deserves more attention than it's likely to get given its enigmatic title, which has nothing to do with Niels Bohr or what made him. A "Maker" is a nanotech program, it turns out, and the most powerful such program is one designed by a brilliant molecular engineer named Leander Bohr. The program is so powerful, in fact – adaptive, intelligent, capable of altering its environment – that it violates the legal restrictions on nanotech development imposed by the repressive Commonwealth, Nagata's term for the industrialized future society dominated by orbiting cities linked to the Earth through space elevators. Outside the Commonwealth, particularly in the third-world nation of Sunda, squalid poverty and overpopulation have run unchecked. Nagata shines in her unflinching portrayal of life among the homeless in Sunda, and it almost overshadows her equally ambitious vision of corrupt, high-tech future – until she shows us the very original nanotech-drenched space colony of Summer House in a spectacular conclusion.

Nikko Jiang-Tibayan is an experimental artificial human facing the fast-approaching termination date which was mandated at his inception by the Commonwealth. He wants to get his hands on the Bohr Maker in hopes it will help him illegally extend his life, but his sometime lover Kirstin Adair, the Commonwealth Chief of Police, has no intention of letting such a dangerous Maker loose. When Nikko's accomplice successfully steals the Maker and is murdered while trying to hide out in Sunda, the Maker ends up in the body of an illiterate prostitute named Phousita. What follows is essentially a chase plot, but one of increasing complexity and rewarding surprises. Nikko's brother Sandor is arrested because of suspected complicity, and escapes to fall in love with Phousita, who grows ever more powerful. (To her and her brother, the nanotech-induced powers are evidence of witchcraft and sorcery.) Kirstin obsessively tries to track down the maker, and this quickly turns into a vendetta against Nikko. People die horrible deaths, get resurrected as "ghosts" in the system, send electronic copies of themselves all over, inhabit each other's "atriums" (special organs developed to accommodate software) and generally pop up in so many guises and locations that it becomes hard to tell who's really where at any time. But this is part of the fun, and Nagata has worked it out in such careful detail that her plot folds neatly in upon itself at the end.

Although *The Bohr Maker* earns itself a place on the growing list of nanotech novels worth reading, Nagata doesn't really attempt to explore the actual mechanics of the science more than anyone else has. (In fact, Phousita's growing awareness of her powers calls to mind nothing so much as Theodore Sturgeon's "Tandy's Story," which has nothing at all to do with nanotech.) She does, however, recognize a number of issues that seem to be emerging as important aspects of nanotech fiction. For one thing, she sees that such apparently unlimited possibilities give writers the chance to rationalize all sorts of what would otherwise be supernatural occurrences (spells, transformations, resurrections). She also insightfully suggests that legal restrictions on the development of such technology might create a fermenting frontier of illegal research, and that such self-governing systems might pose a particular threat if made available to the poor or disenfranchised (Nagata – for the most part an undistiguished stylist – uses the wonderful phrase "feral technology"). The notion that new technology might be used to increase the distance between rich and poor is of course one of the oldest themes in SF, but Nagata makes it convincing in the particular terms of nanotech, and shows a passionate sympathy for those left behind by technology.

The Steampunk Trilogy ~~ Paul Di Filippo

Metropolitan ~~ Walter Jon Williams

Nebula Awards 29: SFWA's Choices for the Best Science Fiction and Fantasy of the Year ~~ ed. Pamela Sargent

The Ultimate Egoist: Volume I: The Complete Stories of Theodore Sturgeon ~~ ed. Paul Williams, forewords by Ray Bradbury, Arthur C. Clarke, and Gene Wolfe

The Ultimate Guide to Science Fiction: An A-Z of Science Fiction Books by Title, 2nd ed. ~~ David Pringle

It's no news that medieval Europe provides a major paradigm for fantasy writers, and that the pre-medieval period serves a similar role for sword-and-sorcery epics, but who would have thought that SF — a genre usually characterized by what critic Marc Angenot once called the "absent paradigm" — should so enthusiastically lay claim to the 19th century that it's become the baseline for virtually a whole subgenre? Moorcock, Aldiss, Jeter, Gibson and Sterling, Blaylock, Powers, Resnick, Card, Baxter, Stableford, Greenland — the list keeps growing, and doesn't even include such neo-Victorian futures as Neal Stephenson's recent *The Diamond Age*. Angenot was right in that the future — and the far future in particular — provides no paradigm at all in any historical sense, forcing writers to turn back to the familiar simply to maintain a measure of comprehensibility. History (or alternate history) is another matter: with the broad outlines already in the reader's mind, the author can focus on the interplay of imagination and reality, on the specific variations that set the created world apart from the received world. Instead of a world that probably won't be, we get a world that certifiably wasn't.

But why the 19th century in particular? Well, the issues that tend to show up in "steampunk" fiction may provide clues: the imminent collapse of great empires, the subjugation of women, racism, urbanization, crime, media-made celebrities, the explosive growth of new technologies and information systems, challenging new discoveries in the biological sciences — not to mention the early development of SF itself, partially as a response to all these issues. So in some sense this may be a sign of a genre mature enough to look back at its roots without embarrassment, and in some sense it may simply be a case of SF doing what it's always done — only extrapolating backwards instead of forwards.

I'm not sure that "steampunk" is the best name for this, if it has to have a name — it's the most widespread of a growing number of excessively cute back-formations from "cyberpunk" (which is annoying enough by itself) — but I am sure that it isn't the best name for Paul Di Filippo's **The Steampunk Trilogy**, which rethinks the movement in brilliantly original ways. "Steampunk" clearly implies technology, and technology isn't at all what Di Filippo is concerned with in this collection of three vaguely connected novellas, which deserves wider attention than it's likely going to get. (I emphasize the latter point because novella collections are about as close as you can get to the kiss of death according to traditional marketing wisdom, and Four Walls Eight Windows — which had good luck with Octavia Butler's *The Parable of the Sower* — deserves at least as much success here, as well as considerable credit for putting this forth as a major book. Maybe the title is forgiven after all.)

Di Filippo is, however, concerned with are some of those very issues I mentioned above. His lead novella, "Victoria," explores Victorian sexuality and the treatment of women in the guise of a detective story with a twist: the young Victoria has disappeared prior to her coronation, and the naturalist Cosmo Cowperthwaite is drawn into the investigation when he is asked to provide a figurehead replacement in the form of one of his biologically altered — and quite promiscuous — humanoid newts. With the aid of his American assistant Nails McGroaty — a figure borrowed full-scale from the American tall-tale tradition — Cowperthwaite uncovers the secret to the disappearance, while foiling a couple of deliciously melodramatic villains. Di Filippo is not above providing the celebrity walk-ons that seem endemic to such alternate histories (and that can be part of their charm) by giving roles to Viscount Melbourne and I.K. Brunel.

As delightful and funny as this story is, it's only a prelude to the more elaborate and longer tales that follow. It soon becomes apparent that Di Filippo isn't just messing with historical figures and events — he's messing with the meaning of imagination, in guises that range from pulp adventure to pseudoscience to confessional poetry. He in fact suggests what postmodernism really means in fiction, and what it means is this: *you can do anything you damn well please, as long as it adds up*. His second story, "Hottentots," centers on Louis Agassiz, the Harvard naturalist, opponent of Darwinism, and — in Di Filippo's world, at least — crypto-Nazi racist and eugenicist. The plot again involves a mystery — in this case, the theft of a magical Hottentot fetish (whose exact nature you can find out for yourself) by a sorceror bent on releasing its powers by taking it to a magical place somewhere in Massachusetts. Again, there are comic villains, as well as an outrageous vaudeville-Dutchman who enlists Agassiz's help, and again there are explorations of 19th-century assumptions about sexuality. The walk-ons include William Lloyd Garrison, Sojourner Truth, Thoreau, Emerson, Melville, Webster, and Ticknor & Fields — but now the allusiveness grows more complex. Melville is accompanied by Queequeg; Mark Twain's Captain Stormfield shows up; one of the villains offers his picture of the future by quoting an uncredited Orwell; another character speaks with the unmistakeable voice of Foghorn Leghorn; and the whole thing ends in a thinly-disguised version of Lovecraft's Innsmouth (complete with a character named Howard Phillips). For all its mannerisms, the story is still a pretty good adventure tale.

These techniques are equally in evidence in the third novella, "Walt and Emily," which concerns, of all things, the origins of modern American poetry. Emily Dickinson, described through a *tour-de-force* melange of her own words and phrases, meets about the most unlikely lover you could imagine – Walt Whitman (who talks mostly in phrases from his poetry). The two of them get involved in a seance to physically visit the spirit world so that Emily's brother can meet the two children his wife secretly had aborted. (In another in-joke, the seance is conducted by a Madame Hrose Selavy, a name best known as one of Marcel Duchamp's Dadaist pseudonyms.) While in the other world – an apparently infinite grassy plain – Emily and Walt make love, and soon the grass begins to yield up children – first Allen Ginsburg, then "Sylvia, Hart, Delmore, Anne and Adrienne." Put off by her discovery of Whitman's bisexuality, Dickinson returns to face a haunting vision of her remaining years as a lonely spinster.

It seems to me that what Di Filippo reveals about the emerging steampunk tradition is that SF writers can no more write about the real past than they can write about the real future – they can only write about our *ideas* of the past or future. History thus becomes a source text, no more privileged than other source texts (even the American Historical Association, I understand, now has its own band of deconstructionists). So when we encounter fictional characters alongside historical figures in these stories, or anachronistic allusions to Orwell or Lovecraft or Allen Ginsberg, the effect is less jarring than slyly reassuring – a reminder of who we are and when we are reading this. For all its lighthearted funkiness and melodramatic set-ups, *The Steampunk Trilogy* is a serious work touching on serious themes, as well as a delight and an astonishment.

SF and surrealism have long maintained an uneasy alliance, with surrealism celebrating the very irrationality of its dream images while SF wants to have those images and make sense out of them, too. Sometimes this creates exactly the sort of problem that Walter Jon Williams faces in **Metropolitan**, which opens with an image of such surrealistic intensity that you wonder if Williams will ever be able to concoct a story to match it without draining it of its power. A naked, burning woman ten stories tall stalks a city street, incinerating people and buildings as she passes. Williams knows he has dynamite stuff here, and he lets the image haunt the rest of the narrative – but he never quite matches it again. We learn we are in a far future metropolis called Jaspeer whose sole power source is a kind of all-purpose psychic stuff called "plasm" and whose chief technology for extracting and managing the plasm is geomancy (a kind of magic which plays a similar role in Sean Stewart's *Resurrection Man*, reviewed here last month. Got to keep this in mind for next year's trends list ...) "Plasm" is a wonderfully ambiguous word, suggesting both spiritualism and physics, and I can't think of a better one to convey the kind of punk science fantasy world that Williams wants us to believe in here.

Soon Williams introduces a second striking image, one more familiar to SF readers: at some time in the past, apparently to contain humanity's ambition, a shield appeared around the world, isolating it from the rest of the universe. (There may be another trend here, since both Greg Egan and Robert Reed have made use of similar shields in the last year or so.) Like Chekhov's pistol, we know that if a barrier such as this is introduced in the first act of an SF story, it had better be breached by the third act. The fact that it isn't is our first clue that *Metropolitan* isn't the end of the story, and the plot bears this out. The protagonist, Aiah, is a functionary with the city's Plasma Control Authority assigned to trace the illegal plasma source that gave energy to the burning woman. She locates the source, but instead of reporting it decides to offer it to Constantine, a powerful but controversial "Metropolitan" whose utopian schemes for restoring social justice to the oppressive, class-ridden society have gone awry in the past. Constantine trains her in the use of plasm energies, they become lovers, and she becomes his secret agent inside the Plasm Authority while he plans to use the new power source to mount a coup in another country. Will Aiah successfully avoid detection by her superiors? Will Constantine's new order prove to be salvation, or just a new dictatorship? Will Aiah choose to abandon her long-time lover Gil to join the romantic revolutionary? And what about that damned barrier? Williams leaves a lot hanging.

What he does offer – in addition to that stunning opening – is an eerily convincing portrait of a very odd and curiously low-tech future. Once he establishes the principles of geomancy that govern the world, he works out the implications of such a magical technology, and such a single-commodity economy, with admirable logic and a kind of hard-SF rigor; his plasm might as well be (and could even turn out to be) a mythologized kind of nanotech – a universal source of transformational energy that nevertheless fails to improve the lives of most of the city's inhabitants. The ancient, layered city of Jaspeer, with its abandoned tunnels, creepy streets, and vaulting skyscrapers, may show its cyberpunk origins, but it's enough to make us want to see more of this world, and to wonder about its unresolved mysteries.

If J.G. Ballard had written "Heart of Darkness," he probably would have set it at a Club Med. Judging from several earlier stories, he's clearly suspicious of tropical islands, and these suspicions come to the fore in his new novel, **Rushing to Paradise**, about the attempts of an inept crusader to establish a haven for endangered species on a French-owned atoll earmarked for nuclear tests. Like much recent Ballard fiction, it is neither SF nor fantasy, but it does investigate utopian impulses (in the same elliptical way that Conrad or Golding did), and it gradually transforms itself from a satirical comedy of manners into something approaching a horror novel, complete with overtones of Jim Jones and Guyana. It's full of the kind of trademark Ballard images – abandoned airstrips and observation towers, a sunken bomber, the architecture of nuclear test sites – that tend to make his fiction seem like SF even when it isn't, but it also boasts an uncharacteristically large cast of characters and takes on a variety of contemporary issues, chief among them the animal-rights movement, the power of the media, and feminist separatism.

An American teenager named Neil, still coming to grips with the suicide of his father, first encounters Dr. Barbara Rafferty as "the bag lady of the animal rights movement" – a shabby, almost unnoticed crusader trying to raise support for a project to save the albatross on Saint-Esprit, a Pacific atoll where France plans to resume nuclear tests. When he joins her protest mission to Saint-Esprit, he is shot in the foot by a French soldier, generating international attention. Later, another protest leads to a full-scale media circus. Dr. Barbara succeeds in taking over the island, hoping to create a refuge for endangered species from all over the world. Supplies and new recruits arrive in abundance – a Hawaiian nationalist, a married couple of Japanese botanists, an assortment of wealthy American idealists, a gaggle of European hippies. Even Club Med sends a representative. Seeing her pristine vision spoiled by abundance, Dr. Barbara first convinces Neil to bulldoze the supplies into the sea, and later begins to behave in increasingly ominous ways. Several mysterious deaths and disappearances occur, and she begins speaking of women as the most endangered species of all. Her vision transforms itself into a utopian refuge for women, and her means for achieving it are chilling.

Despite considerable touches of humor in the early chapters, *Rushing to Paradise* is finally a pretty grim novel which, like much of Ballard, relies more on carefully measured exaggeration than on SF-style extrapolation. (Put another way, ever since the "Concrete Island" trilogy he's been fascinated with exploring extremes of behavior without crossing the line into SF, as though he wants us to see our own world as a kind of SF construct.) In the case of *Rushing to Paradise*, which continually seems as though it could cross into SF at any moment, the payoff comes instead in the form of a thriller, in which the ecological and feminist themes give way to a characteristically Ballardian study in weird obsessiveness. Dr. Barbara earns a memorable place in the gallery of Ballard's obsessives, but in stealing the show she also shifts the focus away from the very issues she comes to represent. Like Frankenstein or Mr. Kurtz, she makes a better monster than symbol.

The main problem with the annual Nebula Awards anthologies is timeliness: Pamela Sargent's **Nebula Awards 29** appears nearly a year after the 1994 awards banquet rewarding stories from 1993, and most of those included have already appeared in "year's best" anthologies or single-author collections, leaving little room for undiscovered treasures. Like most Nebula editors, Sargent seems to be aware of this and tries to make up for it by adding all sorts of options: overview essays by no fewer than eight writers; memorials to Avram Davidson, Lester del Rey, and Chad Oliver; two Rhysling Award-winning poems; an overview of 1993 films by Kathi Maio. While this adds texture to the anthology, in some instances it also dates it even further; Kathi Maio is a fine film critic, but do we need to be reminded of *Carnosaur* or *Super Mario Bros.* at this late date? Much the same can be said of the various short essays on 1993 trends, the most interesting of which is a piece by Robert J. Sawyer in which he notes how many excellent writers are being co-opted by production-line series based on movies, TV series, games, or sharecrops. That's a trend worth worrying about, and it's not confined to 1993.

As I've already noted, much of the fiction will already be familiar to regular SF readers. Nebula winners include Joe Haldeman's excellent "Graves" (his best Vietnam story in years), Charles Sheffield's haunting "Georgia on My Mind," Jack Cady's paean to rural America "The Night We Buried Road Dog" (although his style is quite different, Cady seems to be staking out much of the territory once occupied by Theodore Sturgeon), and – in a fairly unusual choice – an excerpt from the winning novel, Kim Stanley Robinson's *Red Mars*. In choosing from among the nominees, the editor has considerably more leeway in deciding how to represent the year's SF – and the reader plenty of opportunities for second-guessing. Perhaps because of space, none of the nominated novellas are included (except, of course, Cady's winner). This leaves room for three additional novelettes and two more short stories, and for the most part Sargent has gone with the obvious choices. The novelettes include Terry Bisson's quirky and wonderful "England Underway" and Connie Willis's funny-creepy "Death on the Nile"; the only real discovery (for me) is John Kessel's alternate-world "The Franchise," in which baseball players George Bush and Fidel Castro face off in the 1959 World Series. It's a lark, but Kessel's political acuity makes it a demonstration piece of what alternate histories are really good for.

The two short stories included (along with "Graves") are Harlan Ellison's "The Man Who Rowed Christopher Columbus Ashore," a *tour-de-force* of time travel and narrative fragmentation which made it into *The Best American Short Stories*, and Lisa Goldstein's "Alfred" (also already anthologized in her own *Travellers in Magic* collection), a tender exploration of Holocaust survival unto the second generation. The general level of excellence of all these stories makes Sargent's editing hard to argue with, and the Nebula anthologies always have the advantage of offering a much more concise overview of the year than the increasingly encyclopedic "year's best" collections. Over time, the series may turn out to be the best record we have of how SF writers have wanted to represent their craft to the world.

Within the SF world, the terrors and wonders of childhood have long been recognized as largely the province of Theodore Sturgeon, a writer whose complex craftsmanship and brilliantly original transformations of SF materials have been overshadowed by his one-note reputation as a stylist in markets that generally had no use for style. Ironically, that reputation may be doing more harm than good to Sturgeon's memory: if he was merely a writer who delivered superior prose when every one else was just trying to keep Campbell from jumping on their equations, what use is he now that SF writers have learned how to write? The argument that he was ahead of his time – that he was doing things with SF in the 1940s that we wouldn't see anyone else doing until the 1970s, that he opened up possibilities for a whole generation of new writers – doesn't seem to help much, and most younger readers now know him for a handful of stories, if at all. Thus, I can't think of a more worthwhile project than bringing all his short fiction back into print, of which the first volume is The Ultimate Egoist. At the same time, I can't help but wonder if Paul Williams has chosen the best strategy for doing this, because the present volume frankly isn't likely to convert many new readers to Sturgeon's cause.

There are essentially three ways of packaging a multivolume "complete stories" collection: frontloading the best stories in the first volume to maximize impact, distributing these same stories throughout the series to avoid a "dregs" volume, or following the more academic practice of simple chronology. Williams has chosen the latter practice, as though this were some variorum edition of Hawthorne, and the result is likely to be of interest mostly to scholars. (Unfortunately, there are a lot more Hawthorne than Sturgeon scholars.) *The Ultimate Egoist* contains some 46 stories written between 1937 and 1940, including several found in a trunk in Staten Island and never before published. Many of those which *were* published are romantic little vignettes, often with lame "surprise" endings, written for the McClure Newspaper Syndicate which was Sturgeon's first regular professional market. So the first thing that must be said is that there are no undiscovered SF masterpieces lurking in this collection, and that the best stories have appeared in earlier collections ("It," "The Ultimate Egoist," "Ether Breather," "Butyl and the Breather" in *Without Sorcery*; "Bianca's Hands," "Fluffy," and "Cellmate" in *E Pluribus Unicorn*; "The Heart" in *Sturgeon in Orbit*). But seeing such stories in the context of Sturgeon's other writing during this period sometimes casts a whole new light on them; that disturbing little classic of obsessiveness "Bianca's Hands," for example, is even more startling when set alongside the insipid romances he was producing for the newspapers at the same time. (Williams's excellent story notes tell us that this tale was so disturbing to some editors that it nearly damaged Sturgeon's career.)

We also can learn from this collection much about how Sturgeon came to be Sturgeon. Like many journeymen of the pulp era, he apparently never set out to be an SF writer, but simply found those markets more amenable to his better work. This becomes apparent when we look at his first published newspaper-syndicate story, "Heavy Insurance" – a clever but trivial tale of an insurance scam involving dry ice – and then note that his next three stories ("The Heart," "Cellmate," "Fluffy") didn't find markets for years, when they were picked up by *Weird Tales* and *Other Worlds*. These are followed in the collection by six unpublished stories and eight more short-shorts sold to the McClure syndicate, before we get to "A God in a Garden," Sturgeon's first sale to Campbell's *Unknown*. It's the first example of the kind of ironic wish-fulfillment fantasy that Sturgeon would later handle better in "He Shuttles" and "The Ultimate Egoist" (both also included). Then we get another pile of McClure stories and trunk stories until Sturgeon breaks into *Astounding* with "Ether Breather" and "Helix the Cat." The overall impression of these early stories, taken together, is clearly one of a writer at odds with his main markets – like Norman Rockwell doing Francis Bacon-style canvases on the side.

The break comes with "Bianca's Hands," which beat out a Graham Greene story in a British *Argosy* competition. Not only is this Sturgeon's first masterpiece (and stands up remarkably well today), but it must have given him some hope of finding a place for his most personal voice. It's followed by two more *Unknown* stories ("Derm Fool," about a man who can shed his skin, and "He Shuttles," which uses an unusual narrative trick to give life to the old "three wishes" routine) – and then by a bunch more McClure tales (which by now are getting trying). The volume concludes with three stories that finally begin to look like the Sturgeon we know: "The Ultimate Egoist," still one of the best treatments of solipsism as an SF trope; "It," still one of the great monster stories; and "Butyl and the Breather," which like "Ether Breather" might still work as a satire of TV if the SF aspects weren't so badly dated.

As a portrait of an artist struggling to emerge through the demands of his available markets, *The Ultimate Egoist* – together with those valuable story notes – is a document of considerable value. For students of the craft of the short story, it's almost equally valuable; even the silliest of the McClure stories are exercises in concise construction. For Sturgeon readers, it is a reminder of what has been lost. But for a reader who has heard about Sturgeon and wonders what the fuss is, subsequent volumes are likely to be more informative than this one. With the exception of "Bianca's Hands" and "It," there's not much here to explain exactly why Sturgeon was as important as he was, and why SF – and a good segment of the domain of the short story – is different because he was there.

For all its virtues, Nicholls and Clute's *Encyclopedia of Science Fiction* can be frustrating for readers trying to track down a title when they can't remember an author, or looking for commentary on minor novels which may rate no more than a mention in author entries. David Pringle, whose ambitiously titled **Ultimate Guide to Science Fiction** first appeared in 1990, has now produced an updated and expanded second edition, alphabetically listing some 3500 SF titles in what may be the best single choice for a title-based companion volume to Clute and Nicholls. By comparison, Neil Barron's *Anatomy of Wonder* – just out in its fourth edition – selectively lists about 2100 titles (although with longer annotations and a great deal of supplementary material on criticism, library collections, general history, and magazines not in Pringle), and the massive five-volume Salem Press *Survey of Science Fiction Literature* (1979, and also in the throes of a new edition) covers only about 500 (although with longer essays by a variety of critics). This leaves Pringle almost alone in the field of near-comprehensive annotated bibliographies, and his book resembles nothing so much as those massive movie guides (some of which now top 20,000 entries), complete with a quirky and questionable zero-to-five-star rating system. Fortunately, though Pringle's critical judgments show some clear biases and a certain degree of discomfort with American SF of the fifties, they are for the most part about as clearly reasoned as you can expect in entries that often run no more than 50 or 60 words (often supplemented by quotations from reviews, especially those in *Interzone*). In other words, there's not much point in arguing with Pringle about his opinions — that's the perk of being a critic — and this is an enormously impressive critical undertaking, even as it takes a lot of effort to find out what he thinks about a particular author. But as with any reference book, you can raise plenty of questions about what he includes and omits.

In his introduction, Pringle identifies six categories to be excluded: fantasies, children's books, non-English language SF, "slipstream" titles by mainstream authors, older "ephemeral" paperbacks, and minor works by minor writers. In each of these categories, he admits, there are plenty of exceptions: fantasies by David Lindsay and C.S. Lewis which happen to be set on other planets; juveniles by Heinlein, Norton, and others; plenty of Verne, Lem, and the Strugatsys; titles by Burgess, Amis, and Lessing; a few *very* "ephemeral" titles (such as James Grazier's *Runts of 61 Cygni C*) included apparently as jokes; and far too many "minor works by minor writers." The bulk of this latter category results from what is undoubtedly Pringle's strangest new editorial decision: the inclusion in this second volume of many media novelizations, on the rather specious grounds that these titles are familiar to younger readers who may ask librarians or veteran SF readers about them. Librarians are constrained by professional training, but most SF readers I know, if approached by youngsters wanting to know if there's a "book" of *Honey, I Shrunk the Kids*, would kill them.

And here's the curse of selectivity: I wouldn't object to all these novelizations if I weren't aware that something had to go to make room for them. Without trying very hard, I noted omissions of clearly SF titles by Gene Wolfe, Joan Slonzcewski, James Gunn, David Duncan, Rod Serling (with all the tie-ins how did *The Twilight Zone* get stiffed?), Dean Koontz, Hugo Gernsback, Murray Leinster, and John Christopher. Even if *Operation ARES* is by far the least of Wolfe's books, you can't convince me it's less important than something called *C.H.O.M.P.S.*, based on a movie about a cute robot dog. Nor are all the excluded anthologies less important; in fact, this is the area where Pringle seems most inconsistent. Among anthology series, *Spectrum* and *Universe* are listed, but not *Star Science Fiction*, *New Dimensions*, or *Clarion*. Among the various "year's bests," Dozois is listed along with Merril and Harrison and Aldiss — but not Bleiler and Dikty (the very first of them) or Wollheim (no Wollheim titles or anthologies are included at all, which leads you to suspect that Pringle has pretty much decided Ace is the American equivalent of Panther, which it isn't). Among magazine-based anthologies, the *Interzone* and *New Worlds* titles make it, along with several *Astounding* collections — but not Campbell's original *Astounding Science Fiction Anthology*, any of the *Galaxy Reader* series or other *Galaxy* anthologies, or any of the *Best from Fantasy and Science Fiction* series.

By emphasizing books that were in print after 1970, Pringle underrepresents historical SF as well, although most of the expected classics are here. The book's real strength is in its post-1970 coverage and its currency. And realistically, this is where the book is likely to get its heaviest use; the huge mass of SF published over the last couple of decades is much harder to keep a handle on than more historical material, and Pringle seems to recognize this in the almost *pro forma* discussions of acknowledged classics from Wells to Le Guin. The not-quite-remembered book, the generic-sounding title that could belong to a dozen authors, the novel your friend who used to read SF wants you to identify for her – these are what *The Ultimate Guide to Science Fiction* is best at, and it also makes for fabulous browsing for all those SF fans who periodically wonder what books may have caused their lives to turn out this way, and where all those years went.

– May 1995, Locus #412 –

Dead Girls ~~ Richard Calder

Bright Messengers ~~ Gentry Lee

Ganwold's Child ~~ Diann Thornley

The Shifting Realities of Philip K. Dick:
Selected Literary and Philosophical Writings ~
~ edited and with introduction by Lawrence Sutin

All right, I know we're supposed to review books here, and not the way books are presented, but the novels reviewed immediately below – radically different from one another in form and substance – share one trait in common, and it's a trait that involves publishing more than novel-writing, and it's getting a bit unnerving. What it is, is that none of these novels are really *complete*. They are incomplete in different ways, but in each case the publisher seems to be presenting the novel (at least in the advance copies) in a way that implies a kind of stand-alone closure that isn't really there. I'm not talking about simple first volumes of trilogies or series that are clearly labeled as such, like Gene Wolfe's *Book of the New Sun* or Orson Scott Card's *Homecoming*; in such cases we know up front what we are getting into. I'm talking about an increasing trend toward something that might be called the "tentative trilogy" or the "conditional series" – novels which may or may not be followed by an indeterminate number of successors, perhaps based on sales, perhaps based on the vagaries of the authors' evolving vision of the narrative, perhaps even based on corporate and editorial musical chairs. In any case, I can't help but wonder what this trend is doing to the art of plotting.

There are of course many ways for a novel to be incomplete. Alfred Coppel's *Glory* series, for example, completes a narrative arc within each volume, but implies that there is a larger narrative arc involving the title starship which we only glimpse fragmentarily in each novel. Of this month's titles, Richard Calder's *Dead Girls* is labeled as the start of a trilogy, but it's not clear if "trilogy" is meant in the sense of a continuous narrative or three complementary narratives set in the same world (the novel itself permits either reading). Gentry Lee's *Bright Messengers* is labeled a first solo novel, somehow connected to the Rama series that Lee wrote with Clarke, but it ends in midstream, and its open-ended narrative could be finished in one more book or a dozen more books. Dianne Thornley's *Ganwold's Child* is identified as the first volume of an "epic," but the only clue we have as to the shape of this epic is the novel's coming-of-age structure, which suggests an extended hero-biography that could stretch on indefinitely. By itself, this lack of closure doesn't doom any of these novels, but it distorts each of their plots in different ways – and, if carried not too much further, could raise questions about truth in packaging on the part of the publishers.

Of the three novels at hand, Richard Calder's **Dead Girls**, first published in England a couple of years ago, seems to promise a more traditional literary trilogy. It completes the narrative of one character, but raises enough issues to sustain subsequent volumes with or without a continuous plot. One such issue is the idea that the pornography industry might benefit enormously from new kinds of illicit biotechnologies, a hypothesis often suggested but never pushed quite this far. Calder, who lives in Thailand, seems to have a clear notion of the scope of this "pornocracy" has already reached in the Far East, and his dazzling evocation of the brutally corrupt 21st-century Bangkok and Nongkhai is perhaps the greatest strength of this disturbing novel. Described through prose that is alternately breakneck and overripe, the cities seem as convincing and terrifying as the Calcutta of Dan Simmons's *Song of Kali* – and what we learn of a depopulated London seems even worse. Jaded tourists enjoy live torture shows and politely ask for new girls when the one on their table dies; teenage girls are impaled on stakes, while others commit murder in the name of industrial espionage.

What helps to make the novel disturbing is that – for a tale which revolves around carnality and desire – there are virtually no human women anywhere in sight. The few grown women are automata, nanoengineered through "fractal programming" down to the quantum level; the girls are "lilim" – born normal, but infected by a nanotech plague, transmitted through their fathers, which gradually transforms them into mechanical nymphets facing an early death, but already biologically "dead." If one believes that the sex industries dehumanize women, Calder offers the most dramatic metaphor yet to show just how this works: his lilim partake of every aspect of the woman-as-alien from Lolita to dominatrix to vampire. The protagonist, Ignatz Zwakh, has been infatuated with one of them, Primavera, since he met her in school while she was still human. Now he has escaped with her from a plague-quarantined London and works as her decoy to help set up targets for murder. Captured by American intelligence agents who want to know how they escaped quarantined London, they become pawns in an international game whose stakes seem to be the very survival of humanity as a biological species.

But the plot is not what gives *Dead Girls* its considerable power; in fact, Calder relies a bit too heavily on chases and escapes, and gives us only tantalizing glimpses of what England has become or of the real strategies involved in containing the plague. (Perhaps this is something that will become clearer in subsequent volumes). Instead, he focuses on Ignatz's almost obsessive love for the already-dead Primavera (the name even suggests Ignatz the mouse's irrational love for Krazy Kat, and the novel is not without echoes of Cocomino County as it might have been imagined by Henry Miller), and on Primavera's own tragic understanding of her situation, and her vague memories of being human. All the connections between nanoviruses and sexually transmitted diseases, between sexually transmitted diseases and vampirism, between vampirism and desire – all these themes that have haunted so much recent horror fiction and nanotech fiction – come together in Calder's exotic and brutal world, in which women are aliens and men carry the disease that makes them that way. If he can keep this up, Calder may be on to something here.

Gentry Lee also portrays a degraded future in his first solo-credited novel **Bright Messengers**, but it's a much softer vision, and at the first opportunity Lee whisks us away from earthbound problems, first to Mars and then to a vast interstellar starship that comes to look more and more like Rama. Lee's career has moved in a decidedly countercylical direction to that of most scientist-authors. He first came to fame with real hard science credentials, as Mission Planning Director on the Viking project, but his romantic tendencies quickly became apparent when he worked with Carl Sagan on the *Cosmos* TV series. His hugely successful collaboration with Arthur C. Clarke seemed at first to derive from their shared technological optimism and fascination with hardware, but as Lee took over the writing of more and more of the Rama trilogy (Clarke's original novel was really a separate work), the focus began to shift further away from the marvelous alien hardware to the relations of increasingly romanticized characters. With the new novel, it has become clear that technology isn't what Lee is interested in at all – he really wants to write romances.

Bright Messengers details the parallel stories of Sister Beatrice, a young priestess in the vaguely Catholic, vaguely New Age Order of St. Michael, and Johann Eberhardt, an angst-ridden German engineer. Each of them is visited by mysterious clouds of glowing particles, but Beatrice regards them as evidence of angelic presences while Johann sees evidence of alien intelligence. (Already we hear echoes of Clarke, as the angel-aliens counterpoint the devil-aliens of *Childhood's End*). Because of Beatrice's brilliant organizational work in helping feed London's burgeoning homeless population, Beatrice is named Bishop of Mars, and arrives there at about the same time as Johann, who has taken a position managing a water distribution facility. Now the glowing clouds start appearing to them on Mars, and while investigating the disappearance of four scientists Johann finds what appears to be a huge alien structure underneath the Martian surface. Convinced of the divine origins of the artifact, Beatrice joins an exploratory team which soon finds itself aboard an alien spaceship, and soon after that Johann and Beatrice are plucked from the group and left alone aboard an even more immense starship, complete with a lake, mountains, and forests. Here, Johann and Beatrice are treated to nightmare pageants of human inhumanity — Nazism, Hiroshima, boat people — while Johann falls madly in love with Beatrice, who is a knockout as well as a priestess. She responds by singing to him most of the score of *Phantom of the Opera*. The author, meanwhile, is rapidly losing control of things.

The main problem I have with *Bright Messengers* isn't just that it's half a novel (or less), or that Lee introduces conflict in the form of a cartoon-Muslim villain, or that Beatrice seems far too thoughtful to doggedly hold on to her fundamentalist interpretation of events long after the alien presence seems unarguable, or that so much of the imagery and setting seem deliberately to reconstitute Rama (which is mentioned almost in passing), or that Lee has failed to think through a past for his future (we're supposed to be in the middle of the 22nd century, but all historical and cultural references date from before 1995). The main problem is that Lee himself has fallen hopelessly in love with his heroine, and it leads him to write dialogue that would gag the Hallmark Corporation. (Beatrice is clearly meant to invoke Dante's Beatrice, and the section aboard the starship is even titled "The Divine Comedy.") This in turn slows the pacing to a crawl during the novel's second half, and nearly causes us to forget the aliens — who remain at the end the novel's one great mystery. Lee's mentor Clarke was never especially strong on character or dialogue either, but he knew when to rip away another veil and expand the stage a hundredfold. Here, Beatrice just launches into another rendition of "All I Ask of You."

Sooner or later, I keep telling myself, you're going to have to deal with military SF. It's arguably one of the oldest of the subgenres (dating back at least to *The Battle of Dorking*); it became the center of one of the field's historic debates after Heinlein valorized it in the 1950s (and was rebuked by the first great wave of anti-war SF); it commanded the attention of millions who knew of no other kind of SF following the success of George Lucas's *Star Wars* movies; and it has given birth to whole nations of fandom whose interest in any other type of SF is at best perfunctory, but whom you feel strangely reluctant to argue with (especially given the way they tend to decorate themselves at conventions). In recent years, it has disproportionately dominated Hugo voting, thanks in part to the development of a kinder, gentler brand of militarism in the work of novelists like Orson Scott Card and Lois McMaster Bujold. Unlike the Heinlein-Pournelle heroes, these protagonists suffer regrets and ambivalence about zapping whole civilizations, but they're still the fastest genocides in the west.

Diann Thornley, whose **Ganwold's Child** inaugurates a series of novels set in a universe contested by warring alliances called the Unified Worlds and the Dominion, follows in the Card-Bujold tradition. This is not a tradition noted for startling new SF concepts, and Thornley offers none. It does place a strong emphasis on character and family relationships, and Thornley offers these in abundance: fleeing the evil Dominion armies and the even more evil masuki slavers, Darcie Dartmouth (we've got a problem here already) and her son Tristan escape to the noble yet primitive society of Ganwold, where the native ganan accept Tristan as a brother. Years later, when his mother grows ill, Tristan sets out with his native companion Pulou to track down his father. They are captured by the scheming Dominion General Renier, who plans to use them as pawns to draw out his father, Lujan Serege, now an influential Unified Worlds admiral. But Tristan is determined to escape and find his father on his own terms.

Thornley's plot not only antedates earlier military SF; it tracks right back to early Westerns. Tristan is a distant descendant of Natty Bumppo, complete with a trusty companion who speaks (as does Tristan in the early chapters) in Tontoese. "'They have things that fly to stars,'" says Tristan when trying to explain to Pulou why he wants to infiltrate the Dominion encampment on Ganwold. "'No other way to find my father.'" "'Hunter who goes alone,'" Pulou replies, "'can't watch for jous all ways at once.'" As usual, the high-tech galactic empires may lack the simple dignity of backwoods aliens, but they control all the indefinite articles. Thornley's use of language seldom gets much more sophisticated than this. A Masuk slaver shows his contempt for Tristan by calling him a "pup," so Tristan calls him a "slime-sucking swamp worm." In short, Thornley isn't much more comfortable with dialogue than Gentry Lee, but by this point I'd be glad to hear another number from *Phantom*.

Nor does Thornley's plot develop with exactly iron-fisted logic. When General Renier captures Tristan, his idea of strategically using him consists of enrolling him in flight school against his will. When Tristan refuses to go without Pulou, this supposedly brutal militarist — who has never before approved the admission of an alien to military training — caves in with hardly an argument. For later plot purposes, Thornley has to have a way for Tristan to learn how to pilot a spacecraft, but this is a klutzy way to do it. Similarly, when a fake death certificate for Tristan makes its way to his father, the father's personal physician sees through it at once — even though it has conveniently fooled the Dominion doctors, who are supposedly on the lookout for such tricks. When Tristan nearly falls in love with the evil Renier's daughter, she gets dispatched in a scene so contrived that Victorian melodramatists would have considered a rewrite. Surely one of the first rules of military SF ought to be that the opposition shouldn't behave so consistently like idiots that you wonder how they got their power in the first place.

And yet it seems a safe bet that *Ganwold's Child* and the series which will follow will turn out to be popular. Its very lack of resonance can be a virtue for readers who prize old tales in new packages, and it makes no science fictional demands on them beyond what they may have learned from movies and TV. More important, it promises sequels which will likely permit Tristan's competence to rise to near-epic levels, while the galactic wars grow more complex and introduce neat new kinds of weapons and strategies. *Ganwold's Child* is certainly no worse than much popular military SF, and is better than much of it. It's hardly a convincing picture of its world, but it is a vivid picture, and it's suitable for gaming.

In 1992, the journal *Science-Fiction Studies* published a compendium of reviews and essays on Philip K. Dick which began with the kind of bold critical pronouncement rare among usually cautious academics. One of the editors, Istvan Csicsery-Ronay, Jr., claimed that "Philip K. Dick is the single writer most responsible for the acceptance of SF as a dominant genre of literature in the second half of the 20th century." Of course the statement is contestable (acceptance by whom?), but it underlines the remarkable ballistic arc of Dick's posthumous reputation as a guru of paranoid hipness. In his introduction to The Shifting Realities of Philip K. Dick, Dick's biographer Lawrence Sutin, rounds up a procession of even more delirious plaudits from the likes of Art Spiegelman, Ursula Le Guin, Timothy Leary, Jean Baudrillard, and "New Age thinker" (an oxymoron if ever there was one) Terrence McKenna, concluding with a slick headline from the *L.A. Weekly*, "The Novelist of the '90s Has Been Dead Eight Years".

I have no problem in acknowledging that Dick warrants such belated acclaim; those of us who bought those cheesy Ace paperbacks when you could still get them for thirty-five cents can't help but feel a bit smug, and the whole SF enterprise (not to mention the paperback industry itself, as celebrated by the Philip K. Dick award) seems validated by this late discovery of oil in the ghetto. What we're seeing now is the construction of the rigs and towers. But that *L.A. Weekly* headline rankles a bit, as does this whole business of abducting Dick into the canon of postmodernism, because the bulk of the evidence presented in Lawrence Sutin's *The Shifting Realities of Philip K. Dick* seems to suggest that Dick was quintessentially a writer of the 1950s, and that there is precious little in the work which followed his celebrated 1974 "event" that wasn't already there in some form in stories of the early fifties. In fact, Sutin deserves credit for bringing together a wide variety of Dick's nonfiction prose (along with a few fiction passages) from throughout his career, since Sutin's earlier *In Pursuit of VALIS: Selections from the Exegesis* (Underwood-Miller, 1991) may have given some readers the impression that all of Dick's philosophical and literary writing was just as incomprehensible as much of what has been written about him.

Shifting Realities offers, among other things, a portrait of Dick as a working SF writer and craftsman, widely read in the genre and sophisticated in his understanding of how tropes might be manipulated in a commercial marketplace. It is divided into six sections: autobiographical writings, pieces on SF, material related to *The Man in the High Castle*, plot proposals and outlines, general essays and speeches, and a few selections from the *Exegesis*. Many of these are generally inaccessible pieces written for fanzines or old SF magazines, and a good many are published here for the first time. The earliest are fragments of a 1949 mainstream novel, *Gather Yourselves Together*, the most recent from 1981. Sutin provides an intelligent introduction and headnotes for each section, explaining where the material first appeared and what is known of the circumstances of its composition.

The "autobiographical" writings, as you might suspect, are not especially revealing about the details of Dick's life, but they do reveal an early and consistent obsession with death and separation – the agony of separating from his characters when he finishes a novel; the untimely death of Anthony Boucher, whom Dick regarded as his first mentor in the SF field (and about whom he writes, "Tony got bad advice from everyone who could talk"); the fears resulting from his own 1976 heart attack; his worries about his reclusive downstairs neighbor. The section on SF is considerably more substantial and intriguing. In a 1966 piece for Terry Carr's fanzine, Dick offers the opinions that Vonnegut's *Player Piano* was the best SF novel he had read, that "Heinlein has done more to harm SF than has any other writer," that Lovecraft's visions may have been real, that religion has no place in SF except as sociology (a particularly ironic comment, in retrospect). The other most substantial piece here is an essay titled "Who is an SF Writer," which demonstrates an insightful understanding of the importance of the SF community to its writers.

The next section of the book includes a rather testy statement of Dick's own liberalism in defense of *The Man in the High Castle*, some working notes on a character in that novel, and two chapters from the proposed sequel. The selection of plot proposals and outlines contains the outline of what might have been a very interesting novel titled "Joe Protagoras is Alive and Living on Earth," ideas from 1967 for an episode of *Mission: Impossible* and a proposed new TV series about guardian angels (Sutin speculates that Dick may have envied writers such as Ellison, who were doing well in TV by this time), and notes on *Do Androids Dream of Electric Sheep?* written for the filmmaker who took the first option on the novel. The longest section, "Essays and Speeches," finds Dick speculating on some of his major themes: drugs, schizophrenia, the *I Ching*, androids and the question of how you know you're human, and – finally – cosmological and ontological questions. The longest pieces here are a sometimes ill-tempered foray into social ethics titled "The Android and the Human" and a rambling (and rather sad) attempt to make some kind of sense out of Dick's own *Exegesis* in a piece called "Cosmogony and Cosmology." As a philosopher, Dick reveals himself to be more confused than rigorous; this becomes even more apparent in the selections from the *Exegesis* that conclude the book. Like a less-assured William Blake (whose philosophical writings are just as intractable, but add up to something for those willing to do the work), Dick struggled to make himself the center of a vision that incorporated all he knew of science and religion into the framework of his own anxieties. No wonder academics can't resist this.

– June 1995, Locus #413 –

Slow River ~~ Nicola Griffith

Gaia's Toys ~~ Rebecca Ore

Ill Wind ~~ Kevin J. Anderson & Doug Beason

Kaleidoscope Century ~~ John Barnes

Dead Boys ~~ Richard Calder

In a brief afterword to her elegantly constructed new novel **Slow River**, Nicola Griffith complains that readers often assume that women writers who deal with themes of abuse inevitably must be drawing on their own experience. It's a valid complaint (and one that notably haunted Susan Palwick following the publication of her incest-abuse fantasy *Flying in Place*). But *Slow River* raises so many other issues about an author's relationship to her work that I'm surprised the complaint stopped there. Largely on the basis of her Lambda Award-winning first novel *Ammonite*, Griffith was instantly bemantled as the leading young lesbian SF writer, and it seems to me that's almost an equal burden, tempting readers to look for agendas where there may be none and to filter the author's vision through a distorting lens of preconceptions. The label "SF writer" is tough enough to deal with without adding further qualifiers.

So we might as well get this out of the way up front: lesbian relationships are important to the main character in *Slow River*, and they are handled both sensually and matter-of-factly, but they aren't what the novel is about. Nor is the novel really about the considerable variety of abuse that Griffith puts her protagonist, Lore Van Oesterling, through during the course of three separate but converging narrative timelines. No, the theme that gives the novel its major SF content – and that I confess had me wondering where Griffith got her sophisticated industrial information from – is *waste management*, and specifically the treatment of wastewater through proprietary industrially-engineered microbes. This may be the best novel ever written about the processing of contaminated water, and if that sounds like a bad joke sprung on the folks in marketing ("does for raw sewage what *Moby Dick* did for whales"), then we have to turn back to those themes of sexuality and abuse to see how the novel builds its oddly full and rewarding texture.

As SF, *Slow River* makes few demands and offers little in the way of startling speculation. What it does offer is still fairly rare in the genre: a near future made convincing through selective details that render it subtly different from our own, but still easily recognizable – like walking down familiar streets but finding new buildings and the ruins of expected ones. Lore Van Oesterling is the heir of a fabulously affluent family whose wealth derives from patented microorganisms used in waste treatment and the nutrients needed by those organisms. Kidnapped, tortured, and humiliated for reasons that remain unclear until almost the end of the novel, she is rescued and soon becomes the lover of a shadowy underground figure named Spanner. Later, under an assumed identity, she takes a laborer's job at a water treatment facility, where her unusual expertise brings her under suspicion. Interspersed with these chapters are brief episodes from her privileged childhood, leading up to the kidnapping. Could all of this have been handled in a Dreiseresque mainstream novel of family intrigues, workplace rivalries, and class oppression? Probably, but that's hardly the point (similar complaints were made about Dick from time to time). The point is that Griffith's carefully imagined future urban ecology, and the societal decay that derives from it, become all the more disturbing for their familiarity, their lack of radical displacement from our own world. Major industrial disasters, computer-chip IDs imbedded in flesh, hijacked net transmissions – so many of the speculative elements are subtly backgrounded that it comes as something of a surprise to realize how much SF there really is in the novel. But the major ecological catastrophe that always seems just around the corner – and that could have turned the novel into a more familiar disaster epic – is kept precariously in check. Such a technique can only be pulled off through very careful writing, and Griffith's prose here is just as evocative but more controlled than in *Ammonite* (some of her passages describing the river that runs through the city and the narrative are hauntingly powerful, invoking the whole archetypal tradition of river literature without abandoning the claustrophobic urban setting). With its persuasive characters trying to form identities in an unstable society, its midnight streets and shabby apartments, and its vast industrial engines, *Slow River* is a powerful prose poem on issues that are already with us, but that other writers might deem too mundane for this kind of quiet, character-based SF. It's a worthy, and radically different, successor to its author's acclaimed debut.

Betrayal is a recurring theme in *Slow River*, and it's very nearly the dominant theme in Rebecca Ore's equally original new novel, **Gaia's Toys**. It's so dominant, in fact, that I found myself irrationally thinking of John Le Carré, even though all the novel has in common with his work is its complicated web of deceit and betrayal, both by governments and the terrorists that oppose them. Ore has long been interested in the question of what it means to be human, and here she casts that question in frankly ecological terms. The "alien" in this novel – or perhaps more appropriately the "other" – is nothing less than nature itself, and the novel raises the very provocative question of whether nature should be altered to protect itself from human depredations, to level the playing field a bit. The novel begins in a world in which nature has been thoroughly subjugated to human needs – the few remaining wilderness areas are sustained for their entertainment value, and even camping trips become tawdry VR experiences in giant indoor malls – and ends with resistance fighters seeding the world with bioengineered insects designed to control human aggressiveness.

But this is only a part of Ore's complex and consistent future, in which members of the vastly increased welfare class become "drode heads," renting out parts of their brains for computer processing time while government scientists debate the merits of achieving immortality through abandoning nature altogether in favor of life among the software. Allison Dodge, orphaned in childhood and later subjected to bizarre forms of voyeuristic mechanical sexual abuse (in a society terrified of real sexual contact), finds herself working as a saboteur for a band of eco-terrorists; unaware that the bomb she is delivering to a refinery is a "baby nuke" and that her mission was meant to be suicidal, she is rescued, captured, and interrogated by the government. The long, harrowing interrogation sequence is by itself a *tour-de-force* of psychological horror. Allison accepts an offer to be rejuvenated through nanotechnology, and offers to help track down a rogue scientist who has been releasing genetically altered insects into the environment – mainly giant praying mantises whose venom acts as an addictive tranquilizer and is widely used by the drode heads.

During a training exercise, Allison apparently escapes and sets up a new life in hiding, working as a nanny. She is almost tracked by a drode head named Willie Hunsucker, but after being tricked and raped by a band of adolescent hackers, she turns herself in and is assigned to infiltrate the laboratory of the scientist in question, Dorcas Rae. Rae has become concerned that the environment no longer offers any effective controls on human behavior, and has decided to design some herself, in the form of customized insects. Once she discovers this, Allison is faced with the question of whether Dorcas represents the most serious ecological threat so far, or if she is simply trying to restore a needed balance.

Ore's nightmarish imagery – giant mantises and wasps, squid-like brain probes, recreational mountain-climbing malls, orgasm machines (described in Allison's memories of her earlier life), infection-prone brain sockets among the drode heads – is held together both by narrative logic and by a group of sympathetic and fully-realized characters, not the least of whom is Allison herself. We see Allison as an orphan rejected by her parents, as a sex performer in an age fearful of sexual contact, as an aging terrorist almost ashamed of her body, and finally as a rejuvenated double agent, still unsure of her own loyalties. She is complemented by the scientist Dorcas Rae, half idealist and half goofball, and by Willie Hunsucker, whose story embodies a terrifying Swiftian vision of the poor as raw materials for the computer age. What emerges from all these elements is a satisfying and often brilliant SF scenario, which makes use of all the trendiest themes from nanotech to human software to bioengineering, but which never loses sight of its central concerns, and which never itself seems trendy. For all her nightmare images of friendly bugs gnawing on our knees, Ore is a sly and subtle writer, and one who deserves recognition as one of the genre's truly original newer voices.

Way back in 1971, British authors Kit Pedler and Gerry Davis published a novel called *Mutant 59: The Plastic Eater,* based in part on an episode of their own *Doomwatch* TV series, which as I recall dealt with a virus designed to consume oil, but which mutated into something that attacked all petroleum-based plastics, resulting in a whole catalog of civilization-threatening disasters. It was pretty standard early-seventies catastrophe fiction, but I've always thought the idea was kind of neat, given the very real attempts being made to develop biotech solutions to oil spills. Now here come Kevin J. Anderson and Doug Beason with *Ill Wind,* which is pretty much the same story only slightly updated, but which at least has the courage to follow through on its premise. *Ill Wind* begins with a rogue seaman inadvertently creating a massive supertanker spill in San Francisco bay while trying to cover up his own crimes, and ends in a decimated world trying to piece together a post-petroleum civilization. It's mostly just dumb fun, with a cast of characters designed for a miniseries and an obligatory subplot about the need for solar power (ensuring that we have good-guy scientists as well as nutcases), but it generates a kind of homiletic immediacy which is absent from better-written recent disaster novels like David Brin's *Earth* or John Barnes's *Mother of Storms.* Here's an Awful Warning, the authors want us to think, that we can actually do something about. More federal funding for microwave solar satellites! No tankers in the bay!

Once the supertanker breaks up, and once the oil company responsible rushes through approval of an experimental oil-eating microbe to help clean up the spill, the plot unfolds with almost no surprises but with admirable pacing and a succession of wonderfully surrealistic images, from massive traffic jams as cars stall out to melted computers and disappearing buttons. There's a great potential for both satirical and slapstick humor in this material, which the authors for the most part studiously avoid. Instead, we get predictable scenarios of romance (the Stanford biologist who initially approves use of the microbe falls for the gruff petroleum engineer who knows how to survive in the new world), guilt (the supertanker captain becomes a haunted stranger who resurrects a locomotive using animal fat as a lubricant), idealism (a White Sands physicist brilliantly mounts his solar satellite experiment against all odds; a pair of environmentalists start an agricultural commune), totalitarianism (a power-mad general takes his martial law authority to heart), and politics (a randy Speaker of the House becomes a powerless President). The authors do a good job of keeping the pacing hysterical while juggling this huge cardboard cast, and they barely pause long enough to tell us anything useful about either biotechnology or oil tankers (they do a slightly better job on solar power), but that isn't the point. The point is that the high-tech, fast-paced, Prozac-inducing civilization that we've made finally gets it, and we can all go back to the farm. There's a wonderful innocence in all this, even as the authors want us to get gimlet-eyed.

I've about concluded that the two passages of 20th-century poetry most abused by SF and fantasy writers are from Yeats's "The Second Coming" (the business about the rough beast) and Eliot's "Gerontion" (the business about not ceasing from exploration). Both are relevant to John Barnes's **Kaleidoscope Century** and Richard Calder's *Dead Boys*, and Barnes even chops up the famous Yeats line to make chapter headings for his apocalyptic view of the 21st century. Neither author quotes Eliot directly, but both make use of the "eternal return" motif implied by it (or *l'Éternel retour*, to give it the properly decadent spin that Calder uses). In quantum terms, Eliot's spiritual notion becomes a "closed timelike curve" (abbreviated CTC in both novels), and both Barnes and Calder find in this little anomaly of theoretical physics a convenient way to layer their narratives with ever more startling degrees of nastiness, as their protagonists make repeated "passes" through the timespace of the narrative. The result is a unique kind of quantum dystopianism, a way of constructing futures so unnerving that they can't reasonably be extrapolated from a single starting point.

In Barnes's novel, the first clue we get that something like this is going on is when the narrator, who was born in 1968, watches on TV the assassination of Yeltsin during the 1990 siege of the Russian parliament. It's a bold stroke (is Barnes creating an alternate future which diverges about now, and if so what's the point?), and it sets the stage for a nightmare world controlled by warring "memes" (self-replicating AIs capable of taking over human personalities) and terrorist organizations, and plagued by oil wars and mutant varieties of AIDS. Joshua Ali Quare, Barnes's narrator, is one of the most thoroughly repugnant protagonists in recent SF — a terrorist assassin, torturer, and rapist (raping is called "serbing") who is recruited by a shadowy organization which first appears as the KGB and which reappears in various guises throughout the narrative. The organization infects Quare with a virus which enables him to regenerate his body every 15 years, but the catch is that he becomes violently ill during the regeneration and wakes with almost no memories of his previous life. As the narrative begins, he awakens on Mars in 2109, and sets about reconstructing, with the aid of his computer-like "werp," his lives during the previous century. His only continuing relationships are with a fellow terrorist named Sadi, a woman named Alice, and the Organization.

Despite a title that sounds like a kids' public TV series, Barnes has constructed a brutal vision of a history that might have been, and very nearly is, designed by terrorists and assassins (his last line is absolutely chilling). And while the business of losing memory every fifteen years serves a convenient purpose as a narrative gimmick, permitting Barnes to alternate chapters from the present and the past, it also makes a telling point about the relationship of history and memory: in effect, Quare (who doesn't show much affect to begin with) is cut loose from history every fifteen years, and comes to regard it increasingly as a kind of playground for his baser impulses. His friend Sadi, we eventually learn, has found that the CTCs mentioned above provide a mechanism for making it exactly such a playground — and one in which the bullies are in charge. If some of the SF ideas here seem familiar (Joe Haldeman's *Buying Time* meets Gene Wolfe's *Soldier of the Mist* meets Anthony

Burgess's *Clockwork Orange*), Barnes combines them in a way that seem frighteningly apt, given our own accelerating loss of historical consciousness. *Kaleidoscope Century* is an unpleasant book full of unpleasant characters, but in a world in which even Oklahoma City is no longer safe, it can scare you in ways that a conventional disaster epic like *Ill Wind* can't even touch.

Last month, I concluded my review of Richard Calder's *Dead Girls*, the first volume in a projected trilogy involving nanotechnology and sexual violence in a baroquely decadent future, by suggesting that Calder may be really onto something. Well, he's onto something, all right, and he may need counseling to get off it. **Dead Boys** continues the tale of Ignatz Zwakh after the death of his "dead girl" lover Primavera, and it piles on even more of the detailed, brutal tortures and murders of the nanotech-induced sex dolls called Lilim which already were disturbing in his first novel. That novel portrayed a worldwide plague, carried by men, which turned girls into inhuman Lolitas by the time they reached puberty. Among its chief virtues was the dense, coruscating prose in which Calder revealed this world through the eyes of his besotted narrator.

In *Dead Boys*, Calder has cranked up the style yet another notch. When his fevered prose slows down enough for events actually to occur, we learn that the nanoplague is connected to something called Meta, which turns out to be another self-replicating "meme" just like those in Barnes's novel (only Meta, with its philosophy of sex and death, has apparently existed for centuries). While Meta threatens to supplant human life on earth – and is beginning to produce "dead boys" (called Elohim) as well as "dead girls," a Martian pleasure colony called Paris has begun to offer sanctuary to the threatened lilim from earth. New characters with names like Vanity and Lord Dagon are introduced (and turn out to be more than they seem), but the set pieces still involve sex-tortures, and by the time we get to Calder's key SF idea – again involving closed timelike curves and repeated passes through alternate histories – it's almost too late; what works so well as a fever dream hardly seems to need quantum physics to rationalize it. At one point Calder refers to something called the Doll, the presumed endpoint of Meta's transformation of the universe, and describes it as "a redemptive fiction wherein cruelty and death have been eroticized, converted, to turn, through millennia, aeons, through all eternity about love's green superluminous sun." I think Calder wants *Dead Boys* to be such a redemptive fiction itself. But while he's reaching for J.-K. Huysmans, he sometimes only makes it to Bret Easton Ellis.

Sailing Bright Eternity ~~ Gregory Benford

Lethe ~~ Tricia Sullivan

Full Spectrum 5 ~~ edited by Jennifer Hershey,
Tom Dupree, and Janna Silverstein

Amnesia Moon ~~ Jonathan Lethem

In a recent essay Brian Aldiss makes a telling point about Olaf Stapledon, the acknowledged granddaddy of cosmic-visionary SF. "Stapledon's grand theme was communication," he writes. "Yet we have to admit that — the world being what it is — he has largely failed to communicate." Anyone who has tried to teach Stapledon to a class of undergraduates can vouch for this; my own students, taking on *Star Maker*, quickly got confused as to whether they were reading fiction at all, let alone science fiction. Even among seasoned SF readers, Stapledon's reputation is largely that of the Great Unexamined Wellspring, kept on a nearby shelf for occasional dips but seldom read straight through (I'm referring, of course, to *Last and First Men* and *Star Maker*, not *Odd John* or *Sirius*).

But by the standards of modern hard SF, Stapledon had a relatively easy time of it: he could construct his sentient stars and billion-year perspectives armed with little more than an understanding of basic evolution and astronomy and a mystical commitment to notions of the sublime. He didn't have to deal with Big Bangs, quarks, proton decay, information theory, cosmic strings, black holes, and all the other paraphernalia that modern science brings to the table when cosmological questions are raised. So when a writer like Gregory Benford — one of whose grand themes may also said to be communication — wants to attain a Stapledonian perspective within the context of hard SF, the potential problems of getting any point at all across are immense. Not only is the science likely to be daunting for the lay reader, but there's the classic "Stapledonian problem" — the one that so soundly defeated my students, and yet that haunts much of SF — of how to maintain the scale of a human drama while moving the action across vast distances of space and time and introducing fundamental questions about the nature of the universe. And yet this is exactly the problem Benford has raised for himself in the series of six novels which now concludes with **Sailing Bright Eternity**. (By way of context, the series began with two novels about astronaut Nigel Walmsley, *In the Ocean of Night* [1977] and *Across the Sea of Suns* [1984]; and continued with three novels about the Family Bishop, *Great Sky River* [1987], *Tides of Light* [1989], and *Furious Gulf* [1994]. When you realize that part of *In the Ocean of Night* originally appeared as early as 1969, the whole project begins to take on the aspect of a life's work).

Taken as a unified work (which requires a bit of gerrymandering of the earlier novels, which Benford has done), the "Galactic center" series raises so many questions about the nature and problems of SF that it has to be regarded as one of the major accomplishments in the recent history of the field, even if you question the success of some of its parts. It suggests, for example, that Stapledon indeed had a firm handle on SF's grand theme, although in looking beyond Stapledon I'd modify Aldiss's claim that this theme could be identified simply as communication. No, the grand theme of SF, as revealed by Benford out of Stapledon (with Clarke as intermediary), is nothing less than the relationship of mind and nature. It's a theme which not only haunts the work of all three writers, but which subsumes nearly every favorite subtheme of the genre, from space travel to alien intelligence to technology – all of which are important to Benford's series as well. By taking up such a vast theme, Benford is also forced to devise strategies to address the main problems inherent in it: namely, how do you get characters meaningfully involved in such questions in such a way that their actions have consequences at the cosmic level – as Walmsley himself asks at the end of *Sailing Bright Eternity*, "Does human action have any meaning?" – and how do you devise a kind of rhetoric that seem stylistically consistent while accommodating complex scientific notions, abstract philosophical questions, and intimate character relationships? These are problems that every SF writer faces in part, but Benford takes them all on at once.

Anyone who has tried to get non-SF readers involved with the genre is aware that some novels are good entry points and others are not. Much of the popularity of Clarke and Asimov derives from their skill at consistently producing such entry-level texts, and Benford has often, but not always, done the same thing; *In the Ocean of Night* is a pretty good SF entry point, but *Sailing Bright Eternity* is not; from its opening prose poem on black holes, "photovores," and "metallovores" to the strange space-time continuum or "esty" in which much of the action takes place, the novel demands some awareness of the "protocols" that Samuel R. Delany says we need to fully appreciate SF aesthetics. (The entire six-volume sequence might even be read as a course in how to understand SF.) This doesn't mean that Benford asks too much of the reader; throughout the novel are enough passages of scientific exposition to make sense of everything (curiously, some of the most basic explanations of organic vs. machine evolution are saved for the final pages), and the challenge to the reader is to make the connections between these large-scale speculations and the environments through which the characters move.

This is the classic problem of hard SF, of course: a rhetoric of action and human drama must be juggled with a rhetoric of science and philosophy in a way that must be made to appear seamless. Benford presently does this better than anyone else. While other writers either give us cardboard characters against a spectacular backdrop, or fudge the science in order to make the plot work out, Benford (as he puts it) plays with the net up – and not only the net of scientific consistency, but the net of character as well. His style is at its best when he tries to construct a kind of poetics of scientific speculation; such passages in *Sailing Bright Eternity* work perfectly well quite apart from the narrative (as Benford himself shows in his science column on "The Far Future" in the July 1995 *Fantasy and Science Fiction*, which weaves in several word-for-word passages from the novel without mentioning it). He is less successful when he insists on such unlikely neologisms as "TwenCen" (for twentieth century) or "Darwinnowing" (for natural selection), or when he sometimes strains to valorize and sentimentalize the "outward-seeking" urge that he views as making humanity almost unique among organic intelligences.

But by and large the rhetoric of the novel works, and it works as a kind of summative statement of Benford's career to date. Nigel Walmsley, the Cambridge-educated astronaut whose encounter with the Snark in *In the Ocean of Night* began to reveal the nature of the universal war between mechs and organic life, arrives near the galaxy's core some 30,000 years in the future and meets the survivors of the Family Bishop, whose pursuit by the mechs was recounted in the most recent three novels in the series. Somewhat protected by an artificial "esty" constructed by higher intelligences and consisting of different "lanes" and timelines, they brace for a final confrontation and discover that the key to defeating the mechs may lie in a "trigger code" embedded in the human genome. What this key is turns out to be so bold it's almost comic – galactic warfare reduced to a parody of addictive self-destructiveness. But – and this is where Benford differs from almost every other hard SF writer – the literary side of the equation get almost equal time. Walmsley, a 30,000-year-old savior of the universe, aspires only to become like Eliot's J. Alfred Prufrock, while members of the family Bishop embark on a classic river journey deliberately evoking Twain. (Benford is not only among the most rigorous of hard SF writers; he's also among the most quintessentially American in terms of literary models.) Toward the end of the novel, Toby Bishop (whose ambivalence at inheriting his father's leadership role was made clear in *Furious Gulf*) undertakes a hunt for the wounded Mantis, the brutal artist-mech who has haunted the Family Bishop from the beginning, and the hunt echoes not only Benford's own *Against Infinity* but that novel's source in Faulkner's "The Bear." Another strategy Benford uses for keeping the human scale in focus is purely physiological – gruesome descriptions of the bodies of mech victims, or convincing sensory details.

Throughout the Galactic Center series, Benford's basic strategy has been to focus on small groups of individuals acting against spectacular backdrops, while introducing his epic themes through a variety of dramatic devices – conversations with mechs or cyborgs, occasional trips into the far future, flat-out narrative exposition. The result is that his Stapledonian perspective emerges only as a function of the ways in which he has constructed the novels themselves – the novels control our perspective, not the other way round as it was with Stapledon. This has to be counted as a major achievement in realizing the potential of hard SF not only as speculation, but as literature, and it suggests that *Sailing Bright Eternity*, even though it might have some problems as a stand-alone novel (which it clearly isn't intended as), is Benford's most important single work to date, and the series as a whole is his masterpiece.

If you're willing to accept my hypothesis that mind and nature constitute a central theme of SF — especially hard SF — then a logical corollary is that the past decade or so has seen an increasing presence of hard SF women writers, who often treat this theme, and that their contribution to this aspect of the field has gone largely unnoticed. Fewer than a half-dozen women made it into last year's massive *Ascent of Wonder* anthology by David Hartwell and Kathryn Cramer, which was widely regarded has having been pretty generous in defining the scope of hard SF. Perhaps one problem is that women don't always privilege the science (Le Guin could make speculative physics the center of *The Dispossessed* and even make a physicist the hero, but everyone still focuses on the political-philosophical aspect of the novel); perhaps it's because many women writers seem to drift toward the biological sciences rather than "harder" physics and astronomy; perhaps it's because the scope of their novels is sometimes more intimate — but even among the considerable number of feminist studies of the genre published in the last few years, I've seen little discussion of how women have helped to shape this aspect of SF.

Here, for example, is a brand-new writer, Tricia Sullivan, who has taken the unusual step of publishing her first short story (in *Full Spectrum 5*, reviewed below) and her first novel (**Lethe**) in the same month. Both take on the mind/nature problem full tilt, and with interesting results. *Lethe* is a smart, confident first novel complete with the postscripted timeline so characteristic of hard SF (*Sailing Bright Eternity* has one, too) showing us that the future depicted has been thought through in greater detail than the text itself reveals. This particular timeline leads us to a 22nd century earth devastated by a series of 21st century "gene wars." With earth's ecology rapidly evolving away from a human-friendly environment and most of the normal population confined to protected urban "reservations," humanity finds some hope in a mysterious object on the edge of the solar system — possibly an alien artifact — called "Underkohling," which contains a series of "gates," one of which may lead to a habitable world. An expedition to explore this gate is abandoned in mid-mission, leaving explorer Daire Morales stranded on the strange planet Dilarang, dominated by a sentient forest called the lywyn and inhabited by children who never seem to reach maturity, and who may be descendants of an earlier spacecraft containing the worst criminals of the Gene Wars.

Meanwhile, on an earth dominated by a tribunal of disembodied heads who control all information systems, a young woman named Jenae Kim — herself the product of a gene-altering virus that permits aquatic adaptation and communication with dolphins — is assigned by the Heads to use her skill to convey newly discovered information about the Gene Wars to the dolphins, whose telepathic network is used for processing vast amounts of data. With the aid first of the dolphins, later of mutated humans called One Eyes, and finally of the scientist who supervised Daire's ill-fated mission to Underkohling, she begins to uncover secrets about the true nature of the Gene Wars, the criminals who escaped punishment, and even the Heads themselves.

It takes some 300 pages for Sullivan to bring these two narratives to their inevitable convergence, and along the way she relies a bit too heavily on convenient dreams to foreshadow the action and foreground her themes, but she also constructs believable and complex character relationships, particularly between Jenae and her troubled sister Yi Ling.

But the real strength of the novel is Sullivan's convincing portrayal of two radically different worlds, both revealing aspects of the relationship of mind and nature, each calling to mind scores of SF antecedents. Her future earth may in part be a compilation of familiar ecological disasters – radiation, viruses, mutations – and her alien lywyn may belong to an even older tradition of psychic trees (dating back at least to Stapledon, but perhaps with a nod to Le Guin as well), but when Daire's erstwhile lover Tsering (the leader of the children on Dilarang) argues with him that humanity is only that part of nature that changes the other parts, she puts her finger right on one of the central questions of mind/nature SF. If *Lethe* is any indication, Sullivan is on her way to becoming one of the field's major new talents.

In an era when the original-anthology market seems largely given over to sharecrops and contrived pseudohistorical theme anthologies (can *Alternate O.J.s* be far off?), the *Full Spectrum* series begun by Lou Aronica and Shawna McCarthy in 1988 has done a more than respectable job of keeping alive one of SF's more important and unusual traditions. Original anthologies became a significant factor in SF markets in the early fifties, partly as an alternative to the more formula-bound magazines which had begun to proliferate wildly in this period (more than 60 new magazines appeared between 1950 and 1955 alone, according to Tymn and Ashley's very useful *Science Fiction, Fantasy, and Weird Fiction Magazines*). With editors such as Pohl, Carnell, Knight, Silverberg, Ellison, and Carr, the series anthology not only helped guide reader tastes toward more literary and experimental SF, but helped sustain the short fiction market in general as the magazines began to die off in the 60s and 70s. The short fiction market still needs to be sustained, of course, but with the editors of the major surviving magazines showing much more catholic taste (and with the annual "best" editors showing a decidedly literary bent), the question arises as to what purpose a huge collection such as **Full Spectrum 5** is supposed to serve, at least in helping to shape and define the field. We can't help but expect that such an anthology should be different from what we get in the magazines, but how should it be different?

A cynical answer – as least in regard to a clearly publisher-based anthology such as this one – is that it can help maintain that publisher's image as a leader in the field, and perhaps even to burnish that image a bit. With Bantam offering us a whole crop of *Star Wars*, *Star Trek*, and *Batman* spinoffs this year, a literate, thoughtful collection such as this one certainly helps keep the corporate karma in balance. Perhaps, too, the editors want to show us that their view of the field isn't necessarily what the novel market dictates. These are, after all, people who live on the boiling edge between art and commerce, and their opportunities to show us what they value in art are considerably more limited than their opportunities to show us how well they can sell books.

And perhaps, in turn, that's one reason that so much of *Full Spectrum 5* seems to be about art − and not only the art of SF, but the functions of art in general. Nearly a third of the stories deal directly or indirectly with this theme, and the very first two introduce it in quite different ways. Michael Bishop's "Simply Indispensable" concerns a popular talk show invaded by an alien intelligence who, believing in its own "indispensability," may or may not be God. This is Bishop's familiar trademark of building a whole complex of philosophical questions around what in other hands would be a simple one-liner, but when the alien intelligence withdraws from our world, the narrator notices that "overhead, without any fuss," the stars are going out. The allusion to Clarke is no accident, and notches up the story another level to the more general question of how sf treats the ineffable. That question also becomes central in Jonathan Lethem's "The Insipid Profession of Jonathan Hornebom," which as its title suggests is a takeoff on Heinlein's "The Unpleasant Profession of Jonathan Hoag," complete with an art critic who threatens the fabric of reality and hyperreal "birds" which threaten to invade that reality (but with TVs replacing the mirrors of Heinlein's story). Lethem ingeniously connects Heinlein's birds with those which supposedly obsessed Max Ernst, and constructs a mysterious and funny tale of a mediocre commercial painter who finds his insipid paintings altered by Ernst's visions. Is there a suggestion here of the invasion of commercial fiction (say, SF) by the liberating forces of surrealism?

Surrealism also plays an important role in Lisa Mason's "The Sixty-Third Anniversary of Hysteria," which draws intelligent connections between it, Freud, and many of the plagues of the 20th century. In S.A.Stolnack's "Evita, Among the Wild Beasts," the "wild beasts" turn out to be the Fauves, the loosely-knit group of French painters who exhibited together in 1905, and the SF element is a virtual-reality technique which allows viewers to enter the world of a painting; the dilettante narrator becomes involved with a girl obsessed with the world of a Derain painting. Michael Gust's "A Belly Full of Stars" features a painter determined to definitively portray the Annunciation. Howard Hendrix's "The Music of What Happens" invokes both Hokusai and Ansel Adams in a tale of a billionaire who commissions a perfect VR replica of Yosemite, while scheming to destroy the original.

Time-traveling actors test their art against historical reality in Mark Bourne's "What Dreams are Made On" and Patricia McKillip's "Wonders of the Invisible World." Video artists, monitored by floating cameras, compete for audiences with increasing stridency in Jean-Claude Dunyach's "The Dead Eye of the Camera." Pregnancy becomes a punk-style statement in Pat York's "Cool Zone" and a political statement (protesting the loss of deaf culture in a genetically-"improved" world) in Karawynn Long's "Of Silence and Slow Time." And the archetype of all artists, Orpheus, gets re-imagined in terms of artificial intelligence mythology in Jean Mark Gawron's "Tale of the Blue Spruce Dreaming (Or, How to Be Flesh)" – a story which also calls to mind Roger Zelazny's "For a Breath I Tarry" with its dialogues on the nature of creativity.

Not only is the nature of art under serious debate in this anthology, but the nature of sf and fantasy as well – and this despite the fact that only one story (Doug Beason's "Homecoming," about a psycho astronaut) even comes close to a traditional hard-sf scenario. Just as Bishop invokes Clarke, Lethem Heinlein, and Gawron Zelazny, Beason's story suggests yet another critique of Tom Godwin's "The Cold Equations" (which by now must share with Heinlein's *Starship Troopers* the distinction of most responded-to story in SF). Beason's narrator realizes that if his Mars landing fails, a life-support system designed to keep six alive for one year could keep one alive for six years – with predictable results. Tricia Sullivan's "The Question Eaters" belongs in that long tradition of stories, from Weinbaum to Lem, about strange planets that seem to communicate with human visitors in bizarre ways – a theme we already saw echoed in her first novel, *Lethe*. Lawrence Watt-Evans's "Hearts and Flowers" – the most darky funny piece in the book – weaves a broadly satirical scenario around the basic premise of John Collier's small classic "The Chaser." Even the major story in the collection – not surprisingly by Gene Wolfe – could be read in counterpoint to James Tiptree's "The Women Men Don't See." Following a painful divorce, Wolfe's protagonist finds himself snowbound with his ex-wife and children – and apparently hunted by alien women. The story evolves masterfully from a thriller to a family drama to a profound speculation on the alienation of the sexes.

If the nature of art is one of the anthology's recurring themes, another is equally unusual in light of SF's general optimism. This is the theme of personal loss, which is much in evidence in stories already mentioned – the loss of a whole culture of deaf people in Long, of the natural beauty of Yosemite in Hendrix, of one's children in Wolfe. Loss is also central to Paul Park's heartbreaking story of an autistic child, "The Breakthrough"; Richard Bowes's haunting tale of lost childhood innocence "Fountains in Summer"; Lauren Fitzgerald's tale of plants grown from dead family members "A Fruitful Harvest"; and Karen Joy Fowler's historical-mythic saga of 17th-century Japan, "Shimabara" (which is also a thinly disguised meditation on the losses entailed in motherhood). The unending legacy of Vietnam is the theme of Pat MacEwen's "Where the Shadows Rise and Fall," a story somewhat marred by its affected use of dialect, and the end of Native American societies underlies John M. Lansberg's "Which Darkness Will Come Upon Us?," in which aliens visit an Indian tribe. William Barton's "When a Man's an Empty Kettle" asks what ought to be an obvious question about people being downloaded into machines – namely, how do they handle the loss of sexual contact?

To get back to our original question, *Full Spectrum 5* does indeed seem to serve a useful and very particular purpose in helping to characterize the current state of SF and fantasy – mainly by showing us how SF and fantasy writers are striving to incorporate a broader cultural vocabulary without entirely abandoning the intertextual dialogue which has for so long helped to define the field internally. Lethem's "The Insipid Profession of Jonathan Hornebom" may be the clearest example of this, with its unlikely force-mating of Max Ernst and Robert Heinlein, but the general strategy is apparent throughout the volume. With only a handful of familiar Big Names – Bishop, Wolfe, Fowler, McKillip, Park, Mason, Stephenson – the anthology is also a fair bellwether of new and emerging writers. It's hardly the "full spectrum" of SF and fantasy that its title implies (I suppose nearly all series anthologies have to have such generic-sounding titles), but it's an interesting spectrum, and it revels in the diversity of the field. As it should.

If Jonathan Lethem's story in *Full Spectrum 5* blends surrealist irrationality with science fictional paranoia, so does his new novel **Amnesia Moon**. Lethem has already gained something of a reputation for exuberant genre-mixing, and when his first novel *Gun, with Occasional Music* won the International Association for the Fantastic's Crawford Fantasy Award (and was nominated for a Nebula), there was some debate about whether it ought to be read as SF, as fantasy, or simply as a kind of transgeneric hardboiled pastiche. That novel was so dominated by style and attitude that it was sometimes hard to get a handle on the exact nature of Lethem's imaginary world, but at least that world seemed consistently and – given its own bizarre rules – relatively stable. Instead of Raymond Chandler, Amnesia Moon takes as its model the countercultural road novel – you can sense echoes of everyone from L. Frank Baum to Roger Zelazny to Tom Robbins, and characters bear names like Edge, Chaos, Crash, and Fault – but the world it portrays is anything but stable.

The novel begins in Hatfork, Wyoming, where an apparent nuclear war has left the town populated by mutants and a young man named Chaos has moved into the abandoned local cineplex. The area is tyrannized by Kellogg, who lives in nearby Little America and whose dreams seem to have a controlling effect on everyone. When Chaos challenges Kellogg and escapes with a fur-covered girl named Melinda Self, he learns that whatever happened to the world, it wasn't as simple as a nuclear war. Instead, as a hippie named Boyd explains to him, "'Things got all broken up, *localized*'." Each region has its own version of the disaster, and its own bizarre alterations. First, Chaos and Melinda arrive at the White Walnut, where the air has turned an opaque green and where Chaos finds himself in the role of a character named Moon who is trying to get Melinda (now Linda) into a private school. Again, the region has a dominant dreamer, named Elaine. Escaping again, they meet up with Boyd, who takes them to visit the McDonaldonians, ritually serving up burgers in an abandoned town because that's all they remember how to do. Finally they make their way to Vacaville, California, where everyone exchanges residences every week, where government functionaries star in all the TV shows, and where citizens can issue tickets for rudeness (an echo of the "karma points" of Lethem's earlier novel). Here they meet a family being harassed by a government agent who wants the mother, Edie. Now chaos learns his name is Everett, and he seems to have had some connection with characters named Billy Fault and Cale Hotchkiss, a childhood friend who now survives only as a drug. Trying to trace his own past and the nature of "the break," as it comes to be called, Everett moves on to a San Francisco peppered with robot street evangelists and still more power dreamers. Before the novel is over, he learns that he, too, shares the power of changing reality through dreams, and that the "break" may have had something to do with an alien invasion.

All these inventive metamorphoses provide Lethem with opportunities for tour-de-force surrealism (Everett even spends one chapter as a clock, as the result of another world-altering dream). From the bizarre but tightly-controlled world of *Gun, with Occasional Music*, Lethem has moved to an equally bizarre series of fragmented worlds that finally come together in an ambiguous but oddly moving conclusion. *Amnesia Moon* belongs in that small but powerful tradition of novels which include Le Guin's *The Lathe of Heaven* (which also dealt with world-altering dreams, but with a considerably more moralistic edge), Fredric Brown's *What Mad Universe?* and a fair amount of Philip K. Dick. It's a worthwhile and entertaining addition to that tradition, though its wealth of transformations make it occasionally maddening.

— August 1995, Locus #415 —

The Year's Best Fantasy and Horror: Eighth Annual Collection ~
~ edited by Ellen Datlow and Terri Windling

Four Ways to Forgiveness ~~ Ursula K. Le Guin

Fairyland ~~ Paul J. McAuley

Legacy ~~ Greg Bear

Journals of the Plague Years ~~ Norman Spinrad

When Terri Windling complains, in her introduction to the eighth compilation of **The Year's Best Fantasy and Horror**, that some critics have worried about mixing genre materials and literary fiction in these volumes, she of course wants us to respond "But no! That's the best part!" and she's right. Ideally, these annuals can serve to enlarge the reading horizons of both mainstream and genre readers by bringing to light stories that would otherwise be virtually untraceable, and this current volume — as usual — offers an impressive and broadly eclectic sampling of the uses which modern writers can make of the fantastic. The word "sampling" is key here, and Windling uses it herself in acknowledging that a more complete volume of the year's best would be twice the size (or even larger, given the 800-odd "honorable mentions" at the back of the book).

So we're invited to treat "sampling" as something of a disclaimer in a volume otherwise titled "best"; it's a way of co-opting the obvious question of whether *every one* of these 47 stories, five poems, and one essay (not counting the introductions) is "better" than all of the honorable mentions, let alone items the editors may have missed (although it's hard to imagine they missed much, given the comprehensive nature of the introductory essays). But it raises an even more fundamental question, which is "sampling of what?" Here Windling hedges her bets, noting that the question of defining fantasy and horror is more problematical than ever, and falling back on such weasely terms as "magical, mythical, memorable" and "sense of wonder" – terms that certainly could include a lot of SF (excluded at one end of their editorial spectrum) and straight mainstream work (excluded at the other end). Windling seems to be referring more to the fantasy than to the horror selections, since such a thoroughly unpleasant piece as Kevin Roice's "Is That Them?" hardly seems to fit in with the "magical mythical" business. On the other hand, Roice's story is immediately followed by Geoffrey Landis's airy fairy tale "The Kingdom of Cats and Birds," an almost textbook example of the kind of life-affirming fantasy that Windling describes.

Such unnerving juxtapositions have become common in the last several Datlow/ Windling annuals, giving you an odd lady-or-the-tiger feel as you begin each new story (and this interstitial experience – moving from story to story – is what makes reading any good anthology more than just reading a bunch of stories). Are we going to get charming talking cats and birds, or razors in the mouth (in the case of the two stories mentioned above)? While there are a few stories that hover somewhere between fantasy and horror (Charles Grant's poetic ghost story "Sometimes, in the Rain," for example), there are many more that nestle uncomfortably close to one another, like Tweety and Sylvester, or perhaps more like Alice in Wonderland and Ted Bundy. Is there any longer a convincing reason – beyond sheer marketing – to lump together fantasy and horror? Is it possible that it's time for Datlow and Windling to consider separate anthologies? Even the editors' introductions seem to be heading in opposite directions that suggest their different interests: Windling's a celebration of hidden treasures and magical discoveries, Datlow's a no-nonsense account of corporate and editorial politics in the publishing world (which itself almost reads like a horror story). And the tension shows up in the selection of stories, as well: two tales of dystopian futures, by Nicholas Royle and Kelley Eskridge, generate some horror from the societies they portray, but seem out of place because they're closer to SF than fantasy. A separate horror volume might permit the inclusion of more such quasi-SF pieces without forgoing the more mainstream horrors of a Joyce Carol Oates, while a separate fantasy volume might permit the inclusion of more genre materials without ruling out magic realism.

This eighth volume also begins to reveal a slight sense of *déjà vu* in its selections. Nearly a third of the authors represented also had stories in one of the two previous annuals, and a half dozen (Jane Yolen, Charles de Lint, Steve Rasnic Tem, Neil

Gaiman, Nicholas Royle, and Harlan Ellison) had stories in both – making this their third consecutive appearance. There's nothing inherently wrong with this – it may be the beginnings of a canon for the nineties – but one has to feel a bit sorry for an author such as Lucy Taylor, who has amassed an impressive 24 honorable mentions in three years without once making it into the volume. There are also odd thematic repetitions: last year saw a 19th-century-painter story from Lisa Goldstein, this year there's one from Delia Sherman; last year had a photography story from Robert Westall, this year it's Jonathan Carroll; last year's ugly-stuff-in-India tale was by Dan Simmons, this year's is by Douglas Clegg. And the weirdest of all: last year saw a *vagina dentata* story by Roberta Lannes, and this year there's one by A.R. Morlan (who seems to be one of Datlow's favorite writers, with two stories here and regular appearances in earlier volumes). More disturbing is the tendency to honor graphically violent tales of sexual or child mutilation and rationalize them because it's an "issue": last year the main example was by Nancy Holder; this time it's by Kevin Royce, whose "Is That Them?" is far more repugnant than enlightening.

But such evidence of ruts starting to form doesn't detract from the general excellence of the anthology, and anyone starting out with this eighth volume will not fail to be impressed by the breadth and variety of coverage. If a third of the stories are by the aforementioned regulars, another third are from mainstream sources as varied as *The New Yorker* (which yields what may be the first potato-horror story, Nicholson Baker's oddly funny "Subsoil," as well as Stephen King's haunting and subdued "The Man in the Black Suit"), *Harper's* (Steven Millhauser's parable of teenage alienation "The Sisterhood of the Night"), *Playboy* (Ray Bradbury's somewhat too-antic take on therapists, "Unterseeboot Doktor"), and *The Village Voice* (Pagan Kennedy's punk-voodoo Elvis fantasia "Elvis's Bathroom"). Interestingly, more than half the stories are reprinted not from magazines, but from books – mostly genre anthologies or author collections or chapbooks. Mainstream SF or fantasy magazines yield fewer stories than literary journals (such as *The Iowa Review*, which provided a very postmodern fairy tale redaction by Leonora Champagne), and genre horror magazines yield fewer still (only four stories, by my count).

Despite the eclecticism which this variety of sources dictates, the *Year's Best* seems clearly organized around two poles, with a lot of stories floating around the edges. One pole is the fairy tale, represented in satirical contemporary versions (A.R. Moylan's "Yet Another Poisoned Apple for the Princess," Leonora Champagne's "The Best Things in Life"), point-of-view revisions of traditional tales (Neil Gaiman's "Snow, Glass, Apples," which convincingly makes the evil queen the sympathetic protagonist of "Snow White"; Nancy Kress's "Words Like Pale Stones," from "Rumpelstiltskin"), and originals (Patricia McKillip's beautifully written alchemical tale "Transmutations," Jane Yolen's original – and suprisingly violent – unicorn tale "De Natura Unicorni," Judith Tarr's poor cobbler-meets-the-devil "Mending Souls," Geoffrey Landis's "The Kingdom of Cats and Birds"). The related genre of the folktale provides inspiration for Emily Newland's "Who Will Love the River God?," based on rural legends of waterbabies, and Charles de Lint's delightful updating of coyote legends in "Coyote Stories." (Native American folklore also figures significantly in Kristin Kathryn Rusch's "Monuments to the Dead," about the sudden disappearance of the Mt. Rushmore memorial. Steve Rasnic Tem's "Angel Combs" takes basic fairy tale material − a poor mother and daughter − to weave an odd story that is part magic realism, part horror. And Margarita Engle's "Buenaventura and the Fifteen Sisters" takes fairy tale material purely into magic realism.

The other pole, of course, is horror, and in Datlow's hands this is more likely to mean aberrant behavior than the supernatural. There are virtually no vampires or Elder Gods here, and only one certifiable werewolf (in Michael Marshall Smith's "Rain Falls," although it's described only as a big dog). There is, however, enough obsessive behavior to make you want to put Prozac in the water supply. In a sex-reversal enchantment tale ("The Sloan Men"), David Nickle describes a family of ugly and stupid men who are irresistable to women. In M. John Harrison's affecting "Isobel Avens Returns to Stepney in the Spring," a disturbed woman so rejects her life she tries to become a bird through bioengineering. An Indian holy man is obsessed with making (literally) the perfect wife in Brian Mooney's "Chandira," and a psychiatric patient's phobia about dead things invades the therapist's life in Andrew Klavan's "A Fear of Dead Things." Obsessive kinky sex gets disguised as literary theory (and how did I miss *that* in school?) in Jack Womack's "That Old School Tie," while obsessively shaving a woman's body is virtually the entirety of Noy Holland's "Winter Bodies." As might be expected, the very creepiest stories are those that work from inside out. Joyce Carol Oates's "The Brothers" begins with a composer's obsessive dreams about two childhood friends who never really existed, but who come to control his present life. David Garnett's even more understated "A Friend Indeed" also brings a childhood figure back into the protagonist's life − in this case a bully with strange powers. And the unseen contents of the title object in Jack Ketchum's very mysterious "The Box" destroys a man's family in a kind of updated Kafkaesque version of the old Phil Harris song "The Thing".

Last year, I noted that a number of the stories seemed recursive, in that they concerned or referred to other texts or were concerned with the nature of art or storytelling. This trend certainly continues in the several fairy tale redactions mentioned above, as well as in several stories about the power or nature of art. Some of these pay direct homage to art or artists − Elizabethan playwright John Fletcher in Gregory Feeley's "Aweary in the Sun," music in the Oates and Kelley Eskridge stories, impressionist painters in Delia Sherman's "Young Woman in a Garden," Anais Nin in Carme Riera's "Report," a Paul Delvaux painting in John Bradley's poem "The Village of the Mermaids." Two of the most original such stories are B. Brandon Barker's "Superman's Diary" − exactly what its title says − and Ian McDonald's "Blue Motel," a thoroughly inventive and delightful romp through a landscape of Hitchcock films, complete with music by Bernard Herrman. These two large themes of the anthology − art and obsessiveness − come together dramatically in Bradley Denton's almost primal story of art as life, "The Conflagration Artist." I should also note that the art of fantasy comes under insightful scrutiny in Michael Swanwick's essay "In the Tradition ..." and the art of fairy tales in Jane Yolen's short poem "Märchen".

As always, the editors' own introductory surveys of the year past are dauntingly thorough and knowledgeable, as are the summaries of media by Edward Bryant and comics by Will Shetterly and Emma Bull. These introductory essays are a considerable part of the value of the Datlow/Windling annuals, and what they reveal is that the short fiction assembled hear is only the tip of the iceberg. So much material is cited (films, TV, comics, music, magazines, videos, art) that you begin to wonder if this might someday metamorphose into a kind of multimedia package with virtually nothing excluded – a year's best that would actually take a year to get through. (It'll probably happen, once the CD-ROM people swoop down out of the hills.) In the meantime, we should enjoy the Datlow/Windling annual while we can. It may be showing a little wear on the treads, but it's still the best vehicle we've got.

By now, it should go without saying that Ursula K. Le Guin seems incapable of writing an inelegant story, and every one of the four stories that make up **Four Ways to Forgiveness** is a model of craft and intelligent sensibility. Furthermore, all the stories are connected to each other in various intricate ways – primarily through theme and character – and to the larger Hainish sequence which has served as backdrop for much of Le Guin's major SF of the last three decades. By now, this cozy galaxy teeming with various cultures and linked by "nearly-as-fast-as-light" ships and ansible communications has become as familiar to many SF readers as Asimov's Foundation or Niven's Known Space, but Le Guin isn't about to do with it what Asimov and Niven did with theirs. She's still very much the anthropologist, and every world she creates has a point. Her main challenge is in introducing enough texture into her stories so that the imagined worlds don't seem like set-ups, contrived specifically to drive home that point.

In the current case, we're introduced to the contrasting societies on the planets Werel, where centuries ago black-skinned people from the southern hemisphere invaded and enslaved the lighter-skinned people of the north; and Yeowe, a neighboring planet operated as a slave colony by Werelian industries until a war of liberation established it as an independent state. As if that isn't enough to perk up our message-finding antennae, we learn that the uprising began with a deadly battle in a town called Soyeso (which of course echoes Soweto, sight of a similar insurrection in 1976). Throughout, these stories carry echoes not only of South Africa, but of the American civil rights movement and even Vietnam. Not since "The Word for World is Forest" has Le Guin seemed so overtly political in connecting her imaginary Hainish worlds with real-life correlates.

And yet the key word there is "seemed," because virtually all the background information above is concisely relegated to an afterword following the stories, which introduce us to these worlds much more elliptically, fully developing the political themes only in the last two stories. By then, we have learned to focus on Le Guin's complex characters and the ways in which their various interactions illustrate the "forgiveness" of the book's title, and the kinds of betrayals that make that forgiveness necessary. The revolution, when it finally comes (in the final story) seems less like a set-up than a way of providing a context for the character relationships that propel each individual narrative. And when we look at these specific relationships, the politically astute and usual unsentimental Le Guin reveals herself to be much the closet romantic, bringing together unlikely pairs of lovers under turbulent circumstances.

The characteristic recurring scene in *Four Ways of Forgiveness*, in fact, is one taken straight from the pages of any number of historical romances: a lonely but competent woman nurses back to health a decent but uncommunicative man, as we learn the circumstances that brought each of them to this moment. In the first story, "Betrayals," it's a retired teacher and school administrator living in a the remote marshes of Yeowe, who helps a disgraced revolutionary leader named Abbarkam come to terms with his betrayals of his ideals. In the second, "Forgiveness Day," it's the young and decidedly liberated envoy of the Ekumen worlds to the Werel kingdom of Gatay who helps nurse her assigned guard Teyeo back to health when both are imprisoned during an uprising. The third and fourth stories form a pair, each constituting a kind of mini-novel which narrates the life of its protagonist, with the two protagonists brought together in the book's ending. In "A Man of the People," a native of the planet Stse named Havzhiva grows up to become a student of history and eventually a diplomat assigned to Yeowe, where he promptly gets hit on the head by revolutionaries resentful of the Ekumen presence (and of course nursed back to health by a medicine woman named Yeron, although in this case she isn't the love interest). Later, Havzhiv becomes instrumental in promoting equality for women in the still-misogynistic revolutionary society. The last and longest story is called "A Woman's Liberation," a kind of pun which refers not only to the individual coming-of-age of the narrator Radosse Rakam, but to the liberation movement begun on Yeowe by tribal women protesting legal rape and sexual enslavement. As a child, Radosse experiences exactly this kind of sexual enslavement as the "pet" of a Werelian lady. Freed with other slaves when the master's idealistic son inherits the estate, she is captured by another estate, and escapes to the city and eventually to Yeowe, where she becomes a teacher. Dr. Yeron (from the previous story) asks her to join an educational society, and there she meets Havzhiva, providing a happy ending to both stories at once.

Individually, some of these stories need not be SF at all; "Betrayals" could as easily have been set in any postrevolutionary society or in Orsinia. Collectively, however, they weave together a picture of two unstable societies uncomfortably trying to find a place in a larger community of worlds, trying to find ways of changing their more abhorrent customs without abandoning their deepest beliefs. If there's an anthropological point to all this, it's what Havzhiva learns and subsequently teaches in "A Man of the People" — that "All knowledge is local, all truth is partial. ... No truth can make another truth untrue." The goal of a civilized society, then, is to discover the larger pattern of truth of which its local belief system is only a part — not to reject the past so much as to incorporate it in an unfolding future. That seems to me to be exactly the sort of broad theme that is perfectly suited to SF, and by approaching it through the strategy of four linked novellas, Le Guin achieves the feel of a major novel stripped of its baggage but not of its depth.

One of the more high-sounding literary rationalizations for SF — reiterated at some length by Ursula K. Le Guin in her introduction to *The Norton Book of Science Fiction* — is that it provides a means for "literalization of metaphor"; that is, blurring the line between figurative and literal images. "He was absorbed in the landscape" is one of Le Guin's examples. Such a notion does wonders for SF's pedigree, providing evidence that here's a genre dedicated to reviving and "re-embodying" otherwise dead language (again I'm using Le Guin's terms). The only problem is that this theory works so much better in hypothetical than in real examples. The kind of sentences that Le Guin (and Delany before her) celebrate are actually pretty rare in SF narratives, and when they do occur they're likely to be highlighted in neon, like bad puns. To find a whole narrative which explores in some detail a particular metaphor made literal is even less common, and that's only one of the reasons that Paul McAuley's new novel **Fairyland** is an important book. During the course of its three-part narrative, we watch the "fairyland" of the title transformed from pure metaphor — a mother's description to her son of the lights of a city — into a literal construction of nanotech and virtual reality, with the middle section offering us the ruins of France's Magic Kingdom as a kind of intermediary step. (And indeed, who has done more to actually literalize metaphor than the Disney corporation?)

A couple of months ago, I complained that Gentry Lee's *Bright Messenger* failed to provide a lived-in past for its future characters; virtually all the cultural allusions came from our own time or earlier. McAuley is guilty of the same thing, peppering his 21st century with references to Gary Larson, Mortal Kombat, Snoop Doggy Dogg, "The Killing Fields," Elvis, "The Day the Earth Stood Still," and even Whitley Streiber (who in a neat joke gets his name attached to a virus-like "fembot" which provides the host with a UFO-abduction experience). But in McAuley's case it seems more deliberate, and more in keeping with the memories of his main character, Alex Sharkey, who grew up in our era. More important, McAuley wants to establish a clear cultural context against which to show us the transformation of a world very much like our own (the novel begins in the early 21st century) into the literalized "fairyland" of the title.

In a world rapidly being transformed by nanotech and virtual reality on the one hand and growing civil disturbances and economic inequity on the other, Sharkey is a renegade "nanoware" designer whose most successful products are used as semi-legal hallucinogens. Sidestepping both the police and a powerful criminal family, he is enlisted as a gene-hacker by a dimwitted mob boss who wants him to find a way to enable the bioengineered "dolls" – used mostly for pets, or for violent cockfight-like entertainments – to reproduce themselves biologically. He also meets a strange, superintelligent little girl named Milena, herself the product of a genetic experiment, who has her own agenda for the future. She uses his expertise to convert a doll into a "fairy," then disappears.

Twelve years later, in a decadent world already transformed by nanotech and gene therapy, with dolls used for cheap labor and hunting sports, the fairies have mounted their own liberation movement, using the ruins of the Magic Kingdom as their headquarters. Sharkey, still trying to track down Milena, has moved from London to Paris, where he enlists the aid of a paramedic named Morag Gray. The Magic Kingdom is overthrown and the fairies dispersed, but Sharkey still fails to find Milena, now known as the "Fairy Queen." In the novel's third section, the action shifts to Albania, where a "Children's Crusade" has been mounted with the aid of a self-replicating viral "meme" that convinces the victims that they will find their own way to "fairyland," described by Milena as a "hyperevolutionary potential" where "we can dream ourselves into being." One of the sponsors of the crusade is an American named Glass, who has constructed a legendary virtual environment called the Library of Dreams. One of Glass's goals – perhaps shared by Milena – is the "Ultimate Hack" of gaining immortality by crossing the barrier between organic and software existence.

Many of the central features of McAuley's novel – dolls, memes, VR, nanotech, a disintegrating society – call to mind Richard Calder's more obsessive *Dead Girls* and *Dead Boys* (reviewed here in May and June). But while Calder was concerned mostly with what life might be like for sexually exploited pseudowomen, McAuley makes this only one aspect of a much more thoroughly imagined future, clearly connected to our own world and yet radically transformed through nanotech and VR. It is a rich, complex novel, on occasionally slowed down by jargon-ridden explanations of how various aspects of gene-hacking and nanotech design might work (McAuley seems more interested in actually working out the science of such things than almost any other writer). In what is rapidly appearing to become the year of the meme in SF, he has given us a thoughtful look at how such concepts might actually change our world, how our most powerful metaphors can be made real.

In **Legacy**, Greg Bear returns to the Way, the asteroid-starship setting of his earlier novels *Eon* and *Eternity*, and given the large-scale cosmological sweep of those epics, the new novel seems almost modest in scope. Like many SF writers who have imagined a setting with almost infinite possibilities, Bear can't resist exploring some of the potential byways of his invention, although a reader unfamiliar with the earlier novels might well wonder why such a huge concept – an infinite corridor dotted with openings to alternate realities – needs to be invoked in order to set up what turns out to be, for most of its length, a rousing sea adventure. For more than seven hundred years, the inhabitants of the hollowed-out asteroid called Thistledown have been journeying to a distant star while evolving a complex society of pro-technology Geshels and more conservative Naderites. Some years before Legacy begins, a radical Naderite named Lenk disappeared along with four thousand followers into the Way, through an illegal gate that led to an earthlike world called Lamarckia, where they proposed to set up a utopia. Now a young Naderite named Olmy is recruited to investigate what happened to the colony and to retrieve a stolen "clavicle," which permits travel through the gateways of the Way.

The real star of the novel is the world of Lamarckia, so named because evolution there seems to have taken an inexplicable turn permitting the inheritance of acquired characteristics. It soon becomes apparent, however, that evolution there has been different in far more radical ways: the entire planet consists of only a hundred or so separate genetic organisms, called ecoi, grown to such complexity that they resemble entire forests or even storms, and capable of sending out "scions" and "samplers" – organisms which at first appear to be independent, but which cannot reproduce and serve as information gatherers and processors for the larger beings, which thus can steal each others' organic designs. Olny learns that the ecoi have been neither particular hostile nor receptive to human colonists, but that the colonists themselve have split into warring groups, one led by Lenk and another by a dissident named Brion. His first encounter on the planet is with a woman who survived the massacre of her village by militant Brionists.

Making his way to the city of Calcutta, Olmy signs aboard a sailing ship, the Vigilant, setting out to circumnavigate Lamarckia and catalog its life forms. Much of the rest of the narrative is a marvelously inventive exploration of what kinds of beings such a radically different evolutionary system might produce, cast in the form of a frankly romantic adventure tale reminiscent alternately of *Two Years Before the Mast*, "The Rime of the Ancient Mariner," and of course Conrad (who is subtly alluded to from time to time). Olmy meets and eventually falls in love with a junior research named Shirla, and together they witness a parade of unique and bizarre lifeforms and landscapes, the most spectacular of which is a massive storm which appears to be an ecoi unto itself. The storm eventually destroys the Vigilant in a long and spectacular set-piece, and in its aftermath Olmy finds in himself the kind of heroic leadership qualities which enable him both to resolve the political disputes among the humans and to discover further remarkable secrets about Lamarckia and its potential for human habitation.

Although Bear's worlds-within-worlds scenario seems a bit confusing at first – it takes nearly a third of the novel for Olmy to even get aboard the ship – the result is rewarding in a way quite different from, and yet related to, Bear's earlier novels. By focusing on the development of Olmy from a rather rootless youth to a courageous leader (and eventually an old man looking back on all this), Bear has managed to build a novel solidly around engaging characters who are never quite overwhelmed by the spectacle of the setting. Only occasionally do these characters seem to bow to plot convenience – as when the evil General Beys, who was responsible for a series of massacres, walks away with a whimper near the end. Despite such occasional lapses and the overall question of why this story needs to be set in the universe of *Eon*, the novel is a rewarding and often thrilling adventure, whose most important consequences remain focused at the human level rather than the cosmological.

When Norman Spinrad's novella **Journals of the Plague Years** first appeared as part of the inaugural volume of the *Full Spectrum* series in September 1988, Mark Kelly commented in these pages that the only problem with this "generally excellent and worthwhile story" was that it read like a novel outline. Now, in an afterword to its first freestanding book publication, Spinrad tells us that that's exactly what it was – a very detailed and ambitious outline for a full-length novel which Lou Aronica and Shawna McCarthy rejected as a book, but wanted to include *as an outline* in *Full Spectrum*. Since then, as Spinrad aptly notes, times have changed, AIDS hasn't gone away, and in fact a novel that might have made publishers skittish in 1988 would be readily acceptable today. Only now Spinrad doesn't want to write the novel. So what we get instead is a slightly fleshed-out version of the same 1988 novella, complete with its not-too-subtle references to an unnamed plague that apparently originated somewhere in Africa and "spread first to male homosexuals and intravenous drug users." It's still a powerful novella, and in many ways is even more disturbing in the Age of Newt than it was in the Age of Reagan.

AIDS has long been a problem for writers of speculative fiction, like a haunting medieval curse that somehow survives the assaults of high-tech medicine and that changes society and behavior in still unpredictable ways. Within months of the isolation of the HIV virus, Samuel Delany published his "Tales of Plagues and Carnivals" as part of his Nevèryon series, and that remains one of the most evocative treatments of the theme (Delany understood even in 1984 that straightforward accounts of the disease's spread already seemed like SF). Since then, SF writers have tended to use variants of AIDS to construct *1984*-like dystopias (as in Charles Oberndorf's 1992 *Sheltered Lives*, to provide a historical discontinuity to set off their imagined futures (as in Rebecca Ore's *Gaia's Toys*, reviewed in June), or as part of the nightmarish fabric of any number of decadent-punk futures. Spinrad comes closest to the first strategy – his near-future U.S. features a goofball fundamentalist senator directing quarantine policy and all of San Francisco turned into an off-limits Quarantine Zone – but he shares with Delany the realization that not a great deal of extrapolation is called for in order to get at the real social and political issues that AIDS unmasks.

Spinrad tells his story in very short chapters, alternating among four narrators – John David, a volunteer soldier in the "Army of the Living Dead," which offers medical treatment and pleny of sex to plague victims; Walter T. Bigelow, the fundamentalist senator whose own repressed gay urges drive him to manic homophobia; Linda Lewin, an upper-class kid from Berkeley who becomes a prostitute and eventually a prophet after getting infected; and Dr. Richard Bruno, a genetic scientist who, to save himself, discovers a cure for the plague. None of these characters are developed in any depth, and Bigelow is treated with all the subtlety of Walt Kelly's Simple J. Malarkey. Nor does Spinrad offer much unexpected in his grim prognostications of mandatory testing (your card turns up black and you get zapped away), "meatsex" parlors, elaborate contraceptives, and sex machines. In fact, there are several questions he simply avoids, such as why simple condoms no longer work or how the health system is financed in such a way as to make billionaires out of pharmaceutical barons who offer temporary cures until the plague mutates again.

Those pharmaceutical barons, by the way, provide the book with its one true horror, which has more to do with capitalist greed than with disease. What really sets *Journals of the Plague Years* apart from most other SF about AIDS is Spinrad's focus on what might happen if a cure were found, and what that might do to the sex and drug industries that have by then become dependent on the continuation of the disease. There's enough paranoid hysteria in this notion to turn the novel into a fast-moving adventure tale, with echoes of *Fail-Safe* and *Escape from New York*, and to suggest that had Spinrad opted for a full novelization he might have had a snazzy bestseller on his hands. Unfortunately, in what is otherwise a good and tight novel, these very elements are the ones that strain credibility; one can almost see the film already, probably with Ronny Cox or Dan O'Herlihy playing the conscienceless villains. Spinrad is sensitive and intelligent enough to construct four separate narratives that begin to explore the human side of a real and present tragedy, but by the time he brings them together, we're uncomfortably close to Robocop and Indiana Jones. Somehow, I don't think that's how the problem will be solved.

— September 1995, Locus #416 —

The Time Ships ~~ Stephen Baxter

Bloodchild: Novellas and Stories, ~~ Octavia E. Butler

Superstitious -and- *The Horror at Camp Jellyjam* ~~ R.L. Stine

The Dream Cycle of H.P. Lovecraft: Dreams of Terror and Death ~ ~ H.P. Lovecraft

---

Wells's *The Time Machine* is of course one of SF's seminal works, and it seems to have had an influence on the field far out of proportion to Wells's other work. Its central device, rationalized through philosophical doubletalk rather than any imaginable technology, has come to be regarded as the most blatantly pseudoscientific of all Well's inventions — and yet time travel is so narratively seductive that it's become one of SF's major themes, surviving the skepticism of physicists and cheerfully exploited even by hard-SF writers (such as Asimov and Poul Anderson) who probably never believed in it for a minute. Mechanical time travel has remained part of SF by courtesy and convention, but mostly because it's an irresistable story-generator – perhaps the most purely literary theme that Wells gave us.

Wells's open-ended tale has inevitably proven irresistible to sequel-writers, from K.W. Jeter's 1979 *Morlock Night* to David J. Lake's 1981 *The Man Who Loved Morlocks* and even Nicholas Meyer's 1979 film *Time After Time*. Now Stephen Baxter, whose initial romp into mock-Victorian SF was last year's *Anti-Ice*, has produced what is certainly the most ambitious *Time Machine* sequel, **The Time Ships**. Like Jeter and Lake, Baxter initially focuses on the Morlocks, who are more fascinating and more ripe with narrative possibilities than the Eloi (who are, after all, essentially a bunch of dumb suburban teenagers). Baxter's strategy is to rehabilitate the Morlocks from their traditional degraded role, while at the same time bringing Wells's notions of time travel up to date with the many-worlds interpretation of quantum mechanics and making every effort to turn it all into the definitive time-travel novel. Baxter's narrative is so ambitious, in fact, that you wonder if he hasn't constrained himself unnecessarily by linking it to Wells, even if it does give him a prepared audience.

In *The Time Ships*, the narrator (whose first name we learn is Moses), haunted by guilt at having abandoned Weena to the Morlocks, sets out to return to the future and set things right. Watching the centuries pass, he realizes he is travelling into a different future from the one he remembers, and he lands in the year 657,208 inside a Dyson sphere constructed by disarmingly civilized Morlocks. His guide and eventual sidekick, Nebogipfel, is a Morlock historian explains that by returning to 1895 and telling his story the narrator set in motion a different timeline – in effect obliterating Weena and her world. Determined to return to the past and prevent his own invention of the time machine, he flees to 1876 – now accompanied by Nebogipfel – and confronts his own younger self. A huge war machine appears – a nod to Wells's "The Land Ironclads" – commanded by a woman who explains that her mission is to protect the invention of the time machine, since it has become a necessary weapon in the war with Germany in her year of 1938. She whisks the narrator, his younger self, and Nebogipfel into a war-torn 1938 (where he meets Kurt Gödel, among others), from which they eventually escape again, this time millions of years into the paleocene past. Again they are tracked down by time patrols, including one from Germany which A-bombs their settlement. Fleeing again into a future of orbital cities and an abandoned earth dotted with pyramids (reminiscent of Hodgson's *The Night Land*), they confront an advanced machine civilization which has mastered the technique of crossing timelines. Finally, the narrator sees a chance to re-enter the timeline which contains Weena – and to re-enter the original world of Wells's novel.

As a set of ingenious variations on Wells's original idea, *The Time Ships* is a spectacular and exhilarating ride. As a novel, it doesn't make much of an effort to give its characters convincing motivations; the narrator's obsession with the vapid Weena seems an ironic reason for rewriting the whole nature of the universe (although

Asimov did pretty much the same thing in *The End of Eternity*), and the secondary characters, especially Negobipfel, serve the familiar expository roles of Victorian SF. The dramatic flourishes with which Baxter introduces some of the historical characters — Barnes Wallis or Guy Gibson, for example — are likely to be lost on American readers, as is much of the alternate World War II Britain. But Baxter's aim isn't to redeem the novelistic virtues of Wells's romance so much as to redeem its SF content and reaffirm its cosmic sweep, and he does this with considerable panache and style.

Four Walls Eight Windows must be thinking they've lucked out beyond their wildest dreams by signing Octavia Butler, and I hope they have. Not only did last year's *Parable of the Sower* gain considerable attention outside the genre, but now Butler's much-publicized MacArthur Foundation grant (reported in the July *Locus*) stands a good chance of vaulting her to a level of recognition comparable to that of Le Guin and a handful of other SF writers. (What may be more important for the field as a whole is that the MacArthur citation didn't shy away from using the term "science fiction" to describe Butler's work, and that Butler herself has never hedged her identity as an SF writer.) **Blood Child** collects all of Butler's short fiction, and it has to be the tiniest volume of collected fiction in recent memory: five stories, only three of them SF, buttressed by a preface, story notes, and two short essays on writing. Butler obviously writes little short fiction, but it's a testament to her skill that of the three SF stories, one ("Bloodchild") received a Nebula and another ("Speech Sounds") a Hugo. The third, "The Evening and the Morning and the Night," is equally powerful, and appeared as a separate chapbook in 1991 after its original 1987 appearance in *Omni*.

What this means, of course, is that the SF in *Bloodchild* is likely to be already familiar to most SF readers, and thus the main interest in this collection would seem to be the nonfiction pieces and the non-SF stories. But that's not the case; in fact Butler seems to be the kind of writer who's uncomfortable in talking about her own work, and one of the essays ("Furor Scribendi," from a *Writers of the Future* volume) consists of bland advice for aspiring writers. The other, a short piece from *Essence* on the beginnings of Butler's own career, is far more interesting. Nor are the non-SF pieces particularly revelatory. "Crossover," Butler's first published story, shows a woman coping with the hopelessness of her life and job, while "Near of Kin" approaches the theme of incest in a novel and sympathetic way. Both are finely crafted if slight stories.

Which brings us back to the familiar territory of the SF stories. As widely reprinted as they've been, having these stories together in one volume does seem to make a difference. Given Butler's tendency toward complex large-scale series, it's likely that *Blood Child* may join *Kindred* as the book most likely to attract new readers wanting to check Butler out, and I can't think of a better introduction to her strengths as a writer. The visceral power of "Bloodchild," with its disturbing yet convincing portrayal of a genuine bond of love between an alien and the human male whose body will serve as host for her grub-like offspring, remains startling on successive readings (and in her afterword, Butler reminds us that this is not a story of slavery, but a "pregnant man" story). "The Evening and the Morning and the Night," about a terrifying genetic disease that causes self-mutilation (and that is derived from elements of several real diseases) recapitulates the theme of alienation from the body, and how commitment and responsibility can become survival techniques. "Speech Sounds," about a world devastated by the loss of spoken language, reminds us that communication keeps us civilized, and serves to highlight this theme in the other two stories as well. In other words, these stories tend to echo each other's themes in synergistic ways, creating reverberations that give the whole collection a sense of depth and power that belies its brevity, and enhances its considerable power. It also makes you wish Butler would offer us more of these gems.

This past summer, Kristine Kathryn Rusch wrote a number of intriguing editorials in *The Magazine of Fantasy & Science Fiction* on the question of where SF's young readers might come from. The August issue — with its rather awestruck tribute to the enormous success of R.L. Stine — arrived just as I'd finished reading Stine's first adult novel, **Superstitious**, and was starting in on a couple of his *Goosebumps* series, hoping to get a handle on the sources of his appeal. Preteen kids, it seems, buy the books in this series by the armload. At 33 titles and counting, *Goosebumps* has sold upward of a half million copies *per title*, making Stine reportedly the bestselling ·writer in the world by a comfortable margin. Rusch sees all these young readers as potential recruits for the adult SF and fantasy market and wonders how she and other editors might eventually capture them — but if I were her, I wouldn't hold my breath. The "Stine kids" seem far more likely to gravitate to genre horror or paranoid thrillers than to *F&SF*. (The most important unasked question in Rusch's editorial is not whether young readers can be engaged by modern SF, but whether horror readers can be; more about that in a moment.)

The Stine phenomenon is interesting in several ways. In the first place, the age groups involved — 9-to-12 year-olds for the *Goosebumps* series, a little older for the series called *Fear Street* — are the same age groups that are traditionally cited for beginning SF readers (remember David Hartwell's dictum that the golden age of SF is twelve; Hartwell even cites old *Locus* polls indicating that readers of the magazine began their involvement with SF between the ages of 10 and 14). But by and large those young SF readers of a generation ago didn't wean themselves for long on young adult fiction (unless it was Heinlein, Andre Norton, and a handful of others); they leapt quickly into the adult market and either stayed there or (worse!) grew up. Is Stine (along with Christopher Pike and other leviathans of this huge market segment) co-opting these readers, or delaying their entry into adult markets? Or — perhaps more important — is horror the new genre of choice for that group of kids who persist in choosing their own reading over what their parents and teachers foist upon them?

I don't have much patience with those critics and teachers who argue that Stine doesn't teach anything worthwhile or that he lacks literary value; I agree with Rusch that almost anything that gets kids reading on their own steam and using their imaginations to confront their anxieties ought to be celebrated rather than condemned. (I'd even be encouraged if some of my adult college students were *Goosebumps* addicts.) But I am curious about what kind of expectations *Goosebumps* sets up for its readers. Both in *Superstitious* and in the two *Goosebumps* novels I read, Stine shows himself to be a master of the kind of irrationality that can sometimes give horror its most visceral effects. As a writer, he is sometimes given to Swiss-cheese plots, horror-movie set-ups, and conclusions so swift that you barely notice nothing much has been explained. What he is very, very good at, however, is identifying and exploiting sources of anxiety in his readers. He doesn't restrain himself from confronting head-on the sorts of things kids are nervous about, and good enough at it to scare adults as well.

The classic paranoid thriller takes some of your worst fears and tries to convince you that you don't even know the half of it. Kids have different anxieties – moving to a new town (the topic of the first *Goosebumps* novel, *Welcome to Dead House*), going to summer camp (the topic of **The Horror at Camp Jellyjam**, the latest) – and traditional kiddylit wisdom says that responsible young adult authors should address these anxieties in order to alleviate them. Alleviating them is the farthest thing from Stine's mind, however; as far as he's concerned, the residents of the new town really *are* all zombies, and the gung-ho camp counselors are mindless slaves of a purple blob-monster. He validates kids' fears in exactly the same way horror writers validate adult fears, and it's no wonder the kids love it. Adults don't want to be told to shut up and stop worrying, and neither do kids. And thus it isn't enough to say that Stine's appeal rests solely with his gross-out effects (although he supplies plenty); he's a master of tone as well, and can generate a genuinely creepy atmosphere simply from the affectless dialogue of the new kids in *Welcome to Dead House* or the gung-ho rhetoric of the campers in *The Horror at Camp Jellyjam*.

Stine also knows the uses of irrationality. Irrationality seems to be almost as important to horror fiction as rationality does to SF; where SF tries to open up new narrative spaces, horror deliberately constricts them, narrowing the possibilities until rational behavior is all but eliminated from the arena of effective action. With *Superstitious,* Stine exploits this pattern to the hilt. If he makes a misstep as an adult horror writer, it's that he still focuses on childhood anxieties rather than adult fears – in this case, the suspicion that superstitions may actually protect us against something. His two main techniques for rendering this as grown-up material are sweaty sex and hyped-up violence. If the opening scene of post-coital depression isn't clue enough that this isn't the *Goosebumps* world, the end of that first chapter – when the girl gets her scalp ripped off, her eyeballs pried out, and her spine snapped – ought to do the trick. Over the next several chapters, we witness an increasingly brutal string of murders (one character is literally picked apart), setting up what appears to be a serial-killer thriller – although most such thrillers involve sophisticated investigations, while Stine gives us a police officer so dim he seems never to have heard of interviews, let alone forensics.

Apart from the violence, the novel's most striking feature is its exploration of obsessive-compulsive behavior. Liam O'Connor, a charismatic visiting professor of folklore at a small college in Pennsylvania, woos and marries graduate student Sara Morgan – who soon finds that her new husband's superstitious behavior is more than a charming eccentricity. O'Connor is a fascinating character, apparently paralyzed by his own irrational fears. But part of horror's aesthetic is that irrational fears are valid, and as secondary characters (all of them with connections to O'Connor that would be obvious even to Inspector Clouseau) turn up in pieces about the campus, O'Connor's compulsions take on a still darker edge. There's a climactic monster-spectacle that *Goosebumps* readers would find familiar, and a closing flourish – purely out of left field – that sets up room for a sequel.

Several elements in this novel seem to derive directly from the *Goosebumps* series. A bright girl in a strange new environment also figures in both *Welcome to Dead House* and *The Horror at Camp Jellyjam*, and in each of those novels the girl's initial problem is understanding the odd behavior of her new companions. In *The Horror at Camp Jellyjam*, the setting is a remote sports camp for kids, where young Wendy and her brother end up after the house trailer in which they were riding becomes detached from the family car. The camp counselors and all the kids seem unnaturally obsessed with competing in the nonstop string of sports events. No one but Wendy notices that whoever appears in the nightly "Winners Circle" disappears the next day, and when she investigates, she discovers a vast underground cavern where a foul-smelling purple lump – King Jellyjam himself – enslaves the winning kids, who wash down his disgusting body so that he doesn't choke on his own stench. Is Jellyjam is supposed to be a demon or an alien? Who cares? – he's really gross. For kids, this is fine – Stine promises effects, and he delivers. But when several relatives of King Jellyjam crawl onstage at the end of *Superstitious*, adult readers who feel they have a right to ask some questions get the same brushoff: who cares?

To return to our original question, where will Stine's readers end up once they outgrow Stine? Ballantine would like them to discover Lovecraft, apparently, and they could do far worse. **The Dream Cycle of H.P. Lovecraft: Dreams of Terror and Death** is the second of three volumes collecting Lovecraft's work for the mass market (this seems to happen periodically, and the new collections bear more than a passing resemblance to the Ballantine/Beagle reprints of a quarter century ago). Lovecraft is of course the chief lurker at the threshold of the modern horror boom, and he commands an adult readership as loyal as Stine's kids. But is a reader raised on the quick payoffs and easy-to-find "good parts" of a Stine novel likely to find Lovecraft even approachable?

Stylistically, there's good and bad news with Lovecraft. The good news is that he avoided dialogue as much as possible, since he seemed to sense he wasn't having much luck with it. (Stine, on the other hand, can use dialogue to great effect.) In "The Statement of Randolph Carter," one of the key works in the current collection (which includes the entire Carter cycle of this story, "The Dream-Quest of Unknown Kadath," "The Silver Key," and "At the Gates of the Silver Key"), an explorer enters an ancient tomb while his companion – Carter – remains above in telephone contact. When the companion hears the explorer's screams and asks for more information, another voice comes on the line – "deep; hollow; gelatinous; remote; unearthly; inhuman; disembodied" – announcing "'You fool, Warren is DEAD!'" Part of me wants to say this is the voice of the impatient reader, as usual one step ahead of Lovecraft's thick-brained explorers, but part of me recognizes that Lovecraft knew something sophisticated about the value of offstage action in horror.

The bad news about Lovecraft, of course – at least in terms of gaining new readers – is all those words. As in the sentence quoted earlier, no adjective is permitted where seven will do just as well. And he has an almost self-destructive fondness for words like "gibbering," "hysterical," "feverish" – words which, like cheap handguns, are too easily turned against those who wield them. When he tries for a patina of pseudoscience, he often misses entirely; in "From Beyond," the narrator is shown a machine which generates a "pale, outré" color which is explained as ultra-violet. But Lovecraft's infelicities as a stylist have been fodder for critics as far back as Edmund Wilson, and it must be admitted that his style seems to attract as many readers as it repels. In the end, it probably isn't style at all that makes Lovecraft unique, and that keeps him being reprinted for each new generation since his death.

What more likely keeps Lovecraft alive is the undeniable seductiveness of his imagination, and this is where the new Ballantine volume shows him to be far more compelling than many more modern horror writers. *The Dream Cycle* collects twenty-five stories that are supposed to make up Lovecraft's "dream cycle," as opposed to his more familiar "Cthulhu mythos." It's never been entirely clear to me what Lovecraft actually had in mind by connecting so many of his stories in various ways, but it lends a kind of unusual authority and power to the individual stories by implying an underlying consistency. The stories here range from early fragments to substantial novellas like "The Dream Quest of Unknown Kadath" and "The Case of Charles Dexter Ward" – still one of the most compelling and best-plotted of Lovecraft's tales – and what they have in common is a sense of real conviction, a worldview which gives a kind of moral substance to horrors which otherwise might seem irredeemably goofy. Such a worldview – a kind of deterministic paranoia – seems crucial to the effectiveness of much early horror fiction, in which the special effects made an eerie kind of sense, deriving from some unholy system of which we could gain only occasional glimpses. In a crazy way, Lovecraft was reaching for the sublime, and not just for the gross-out.

The First Century After Beatrice ~~ Amin Maalouf

Blade Runner 2: The Edge of Human ~~ K.W. Jeter

Reading by Starlight: Postmodern Science Fiction ~
~ Damien Broderick

Highcastle ~~ Stanislaw Lem

When does an SF idea become a mainstream idea? More precisely, when does an SF concept get close enough to home to start attracting the attention of non-SF writers, and how does it change in the hands of such writers? We've seen plenty of examples over the years, from Marge Piercy's fairly astute use of SF tropes to Paul Theroux's clunky *O-Zone*, and now we have **The First Century After Beatrice**, by the French-Lebanese writer Amin Maalouf, whose previous novel received the Prix Goncourt. For the most part the response of SF writers and readers to such "outsiders" has been a kind of supercilious envy, as tales whose basic outlines would have been rejected by John Campbell get reviewed by big-gun media and sometimes even climb the bestseller lists. At the same time, there's often a covert smugness, a sense of validation, as though an SF idea or plot which breaks out of the ghetto is almost as good as a writer breaking out. Either case is likely to be taken as a hopeful sign that the long exile is about to be over, that SF may finally assume its rightful place as the postmodern literature, that — as most critical histories of SF have claimed — the day nears when SF can vote and sit at lunch counters with anyone.

It's a nice thought, but it tends to ignore both economic realities on one end and literary realities on the other. The economic realities are the most obvious: as long as SF is a leading market category, few publishers or booksellers are going to want to let it assimilate completely (even though they're more than willing to stretch it out of any coherent shape, like a string of taffy with *Star Wars* novels at one end and Le Guin at the other). The literary realities may be a little more complicated, and raise some fundamental questions about what SF is good for. The fact is, for every mainstream writer who klutzily recycles old SF clichés, there's another who seems to actually *treasure* the speculative novum, treating it with a degree of care and wonder that is increasingly rare in the idea-glutted genre itself. Maalouf belongs in the latter category, a writer genuinely fascinated with the implications of a single SF idea: What if a drug were available that guaranteed the birth of male children?

This premise will seem very familiar to readers of two SF anthologies reviewed just last month: Pamela Sargent's "Fears" appeared in her *Women of Wonder*, and Lawrence Watt-Evans's "Choice" in Charles Sheffield's *How to Save the World*. All three authors agree that such a development would lead to societal breakdown, as fewer girls are born, birth rates plummet, and surviving women are commodified beyond feminism's worst nightmares. Both Watt-Evans and Maalouf also show how such a development would have a disproportionate effect on those Third-World cultures which inordinately prize male children, and might even come to be viewed as a kind of self-selecting genocide of the disadvantaged. But here the parallels pretty much end, for both SF writers tend to see the idea itself as fairly unremarkable concept, tame by SF standards, to be redeemed by technique. Sargent's tale opens in a nightmarish future where the few surviving women hide out in terror; the sex-choice technology is revealed only as how we got from here to there, and the story itself gains power as an exaggerated metaphor of what is already a reality in many women's lives. Watt-Evans's bitter satire takes the familiar didactic-SF form of an outsider visiting an experimental society, in this case a male-dominated nation on the verge of chaos, and explains how the sex-choice drug became a conspiratorial instrument for population control; the conspiracy is the real thematic center of the tale.

Maalouf seems much more fascinated with the possibilities of the sex-selection premise as way into a generalized parable of technology, political oppression, and the idea of parenthood. He may be vague with the biochemical details of what he calls simply "the substance," but he is far from an amateur in thinking through the social implications, and his strategy for telling the story – an historian's voice mixed with a doting father's personal memoir – permits him to explore a range of ancillary issues, from the responsibility of scientists to endemic sex- and racism. The Beatrice of the title is the long-hoped-for daughter of the narrator, a reclusive entomologist whose journalist wife singlehandedly breaks a story about unexplained increases in male births in several third world countries. At first, no one believes the phenomenon to be anything other than a statistical fluke; for centuries, folk medicines like "scarab beans" had been sold to guarantee male children with little effect. Later, a sinister scientist is found to have used such folk medicines as vectors to introduce his real "male-only" chemical into these societies, and the resulting "gynosterilization" soon pits the industrialized northern nations against the southern hemisphere, with violent upheavals, trafficking in female babies, and accusations of genocidal plots.

In SF terms, Maalouf's 21st century resembles that of John Barnes's *Kaleidoscope Century* more than the scenarios of Sargent or Watt-Evans. He does fall into Philip Wylie-style lecturing from time to time, and his narrator helps found an unlikely "Network of Sages" to promote wiser use of science and technology, but the novel attains a haunting, parable-like quality that gives it substance far beyond its initial premise. Although Beatrice herself hardly comes alive as a character, she survives as an emblem of the kind of hope fathers inevitably invest in their children, and thus in the promise of future generations.

As you've probably noticed, we don't normally review novels based on movie or TV franchises, but K.W. Jeter's **Blade Runner 2: The Edge of Human** is particularly interesting in a number of ways. For one thing, I didn't realize that *Blade Runner* had become a merchandisable property until I saw the little trademark symbol and notice of a licensing agreement on Jeter's novel. For another, there's Jeter himself, returning to one of the important iconographic sources of the cyberpunk movement in a kind of full-circle poetic justice. Jeter was arguably one of the important precursors of cyberpunk, and his novel *Dr. Adder* sat unpublished for more than a decade until after *Blade Runner's* release, finally appearing the same year as Gibson's *Neuromancer.* Those familiar with Jeter's work will also note the irony of his constraining himself to work in the drizzly Ridley Scott vision of 21st century L.A., when Jeter's own versions of future L.A. in both *Dr. Adder* and the later *Madlands* are so bleak as to make *Blade Runner* look like a Merchant/Ivory film. And it's not the only constraint he faces: he's also set out to clear up some plot inconsistencies in the film and to resolve some of the many differences between the film and Philip K. Dick's *Do Androids Dream of Electric Sheep?* And then there's the nagging question of whether this is a sequel to the Dick novel, to the original 1982 film, or to the "director's cut" issued a decade later. Clearly, *Blade Runner 2* comes to us with so many assignments to complete that you wonder if there's even room for a new novel to get off the ground.

The answer to one of those questions is easy: this is not a sequel to *Do Androids Dream of Electric Sheep?* Jeter successfully introduces Dickian questions of the moral status of being human into the narrative, but he doesn't address the many themes and subplots that the movie completely ignored (except for a few scenes with the underground veterinarian Isidore). The question of whether blade runner Rick Deckard himself may be a "replicant," only hinted at in the original film, moves closer to center stage, as does the broader question of whether any such bounty hunters can claim to be more human than their prey. Deckard is called back from Oregon, where he keeps his beloved Rachael in suspended animation to prolong her four-year life span, to investigate an apparent plot to destroy all the blade runners. His employer, Sarah, is not only the new president of the replicant-manufacturing Tyrell Corporation, but also happens to be the human "templant" for Rachael – and she's every bit as mean as Rachael was sweet. Meanwhile, Holden (the blade runner blown away in the opening scene of the movie) is abducted from his hospital bed by a man claiming to be the original Roy Batty – the templant for the superhuman villain of the movie. Add to this such complications as the discovery of another renegade replicant in addition to those killed in the movie; the revelation that one of those killed, Pris, was actually human; and some dark secrets about the Tyrell corporation's ill-fated space mission decades earlier, and there's plenty of material for a decent adventure novel, and that's about pretty much what we've got here.

But it's clear that Jeter's main focus is not to significantly expand the scope of the original film, or to introduce many significant new ideas, but to recreate as directly as possible the visual *mise en scène* that has become the film's trademark. Almost every key image in the film is worked into the novel somewhere – the advertising blimps, the cavernous Tyrell offices, the gouting flames, the decaying buildings – and on a few occasions Jeter even gives Deckard gestures taken from Harrison Ford's performance (his habit of wiping his mouth, for instance). He gives us a few new settings, such as a region of earthquake-toppled buildings called the "sideways world," and he offers some ingenious interpolations such as a reasonable etymology for the term "blade runner," but for the most part he doesn't stray very far from the original production design, and he doesn't venture very far into Philip K. Dick territory – or even into K.W. Jeter territory. Dick never authorized a novelization of the film, and the tie-in edition of *Do Androids Dream of Electric Sheep?* must have puzzled the hell out of fans who only wanted to recreate the buzz of movie moments. *Blade Runner 2* isn't a bad adventure novel on its own terms, but it exists to give you that buzz. All it needs is some Vangelis music.

Several of the chapters in Damien Broderick's **Reading by Starlight: Postmodern Science Fiction** have appeared as essays in journals such as *Foundation* and *The New York Review of Science Fiction*, and readers of those publications will already know that Broderick seems to be assuming the mantle of an Australian Samuel R. Delany. Like Delany, Broderick is a succesful SF writer who is equally at home in the sometimes torpid atmosphere of postmodern literary theory, and like Delany he seems driven to find great cultural and linguistic tidal forces at work in the genre where he makes his home. Not surprisingly, a good deal of the criticism and fiction he discusses is Delany's, although he finds compelling arguments in the work of other scholars as well, particularly Frederick Jameson. When Broderick reveals in a footnote that his cat was named Darko Suvin, we need no further evidence of the depth of his involvement in the gimlet-eyed and sonorous-voiced school of poststructuralist SF studies. Although Broderick arranges his various arguments about SF to lead toward a complex and provocative definition of the genre articulated at the end of the book, getting there isn't half the fun. In prose that is by turns lucid and fatally sclerotic, Broderick takes us on a detailed tour, not of SF, but of SF theory; on those too-rare occasions when he insightfully focuses on exemplary texts, such as Aldiss's *Helliconia* trilogy or Delany's *Stars in My Pockets Like Grains of Sand*, we feel almost as if we've been let up for air before being slammed beneath the surface again.

Most of Broderick's arguments are unexceptionable. He begins with a brief discussion of SF history and early definitions, then quickly turns to theoretical attempts to delimit SF first as a genre, then as a mode, and finally as a kind of megatext or modal system. The latter, of course, leads us into Delany territory, which is the primary focus of the second part of the book. Broderick offers informed critiques of Delany's sometimes shifty theoretical positions, and connects these in interesting ways with Delany's multileveled fictions, but much of the rest of SF gets lost in these final chapters. The big payoff, of course, is that definition, which cleverly incorporates elements from many of the critics and theorists Broderick has been discussing, but which turns out to be no less weasely a definition than anyone else's.

SF is not a genre, we learn, but a "species of storytelling native to a culture undergoing the epistemic changes implicated in the rise and supersession of technical-industrial modes of production, distribution, consumption and disposal." This is not the kind of definition likely to engender widespread forehead-slapping. Right off, we can see that it's taxonomic rather than structural – SF as a kind of weed in a problem-ridden culture. (It's a little like trying to define a rat by talking about urban sanitation.) The more useful part of Broderick's definition comes as a list of SF characteristics – "metaphoric strategies" and "metonymic tactics" (which actually makes sense as he explains it), the foregrounding of objects and icons from a communal "mega-text," de-emphasis on "fine writing" and subjectivity. Much of what he says here is true, but it's more true of traditional science fiction than of the "postmodern science fiction" that is Broderick's alleged topic, and his own prime paradigm, Delany, escapes the definition in all sorts of ways. It's a clear sign of SF's fabled slipperiness that when Broderick finishes his tour of the sophisticated SF and SF theory of the 1980s and 1990s, he derives from it a definition of the SF of the 1950s.

One of Broderick's most interesting and defensible points in his list of SF characteristics is the SF writer's tendency to privilege the object over the subject, resulting in a decreased emphasis on character and subjectivity and the foregrounding of a kind of shared iconography. This has been noted by other critics as well – even Bruno Bettelheim commented on SF's overemphasis on objectification – but usually it's brought up to show how out-of-step SF has been with the mainstream of modernist fiction by holding on to straightforward storytelling values in the face of trendy obfuscation. But reading Stanislaw Lem's **Highcastle**, a brief memoir of the author's childhood which has nothing whatever to do with SF, is enough to make you wonder if that emphasis on objects over people isn't something far more than a narrative strategy, and if in fact it may be a fundamental characteristic of the science fiction imagination.

In Lem's elegant and evocative memoir of Poland in the 1920s and 1930s, we learn virtually nothing about the formation of Lem the satirist and SF writer – a little about childhood reading, an early passion for Dumas, his discovery of Verne, Wells, and Karl May – but we learn a great deal about the young Lem's preference for objects over human relationships. The first few chapters of the book read like an autobiography of home furnishings, and early on he confesses that despite his detailed memories of such objects, he can't remember the face of a single child he knew. We also learn a good deal about Lem's mad childhood passion for destroying things, his self-consciousness as a pudgy, bespectacled kid, his discomfort with plants, and his fascination, even as a student, with the self-sufficient subculture of the Polish gymnasium (one is tempted to see here the origins of Lem's biting satires of bureaucracy). What emerges seems, in retrospect, to be an early portrait of a brilliant and sensitive SF nerd, only without the SF. But it is his oddly close relationship with things rather than people that is most consistently striking, and that seems to distantly prefigure his approach to science fiction, both as author and critic. I wonder if that passion for objects, which seems connected to Broderick's notions of SF privileging the object, is common among other SF writers as well?

Science Fiction: The Illustrated Encyclopedia ~~ John Clute

Look at the Evidence ~~ John Clute

Chaga ~~ Ian McDonald

Testament ~~ Valerie J Freireich

Quasar ~~ Jamil Nasir

Science fiction dresses differently, and talks more politely, when it goes out to meet people. Internally, the SF community prides itself on rambunctious eccentricity, but when an opportunity comes along such as that offered by John Clute's **Science Fiction: The Illustrated Encyclopedia**, the crazy obsessions and bad clothes tend to get left behind, and what gets presented is bright, thoughtful, and more than a little innocent. As one of the field's most volatile and provocative critics, Clute is certainly aware of this; in his other new book, a collection of reviews titled *Look at the Evidence*, he champions what he calls the "Protocol of Excessive Candor," which is essentially a complaint that too many reviewers in the field demur from tough criticism out of consideration for their friends and colleagues. "Truth is all we've got," he says more than once, and "reviewers who will not tell the truth are like cholesterol." Clute's own reviews are the best argument for the kind of criticism he advocates. But what candor makes it through to *The Illustrated Encyclopedia* is anything but excessive. Nothing the book says is likely to start any arguments (although a few might start over what it doesn't say — see below); it's a work of celebration, not criticism or scholarship.

Clute may be the closest thing the SF world has to a homegrown Edmund Wilson — each a sometime fiction writer far better known for criticism, each having earned a daunting scholarly reputation without benefit of academic sinecure, each associated with the most prestigious literary magazines in their field (Clute with *Interzone*, Wilson with *The New Yorker*), each given to occasional fits of proclamation-making, each sufficiently compelling as critics to sustain whole books consisting of little more than previously published reviews (sometimes of books that don't survive as long as the reviews). And what Alfred Kazin once said of Wilson is equally true of Clute: "some critics are boring even when they are original; he fascinates even when he is wrong." Above all, Clute is like Wilson in that he is principally an intelligent and engaged reader. Other prolific SF critics have usually been academics, SF writers on part-time duty, or fans in pig heaven. Clute is the real thing.

This is not to say, however, that his spirited enjoinders necessarily translate well to book form, let alone to snippet form, and snippets are essentially what make up the text of *The Illustrated Encyclopedia*. The *Encyclopedia* comes to us from Dorling Kindersley, a London-based publisher best known for their sumptuous coffee-table "chronicles," and like those volumes it is gorgeous to leaf through. Anyone unwilling to so leaf, however, will be punished, because the book's pattern of organization – everything has to fit into a two-page spread – make it maddening to try to look anything up, or to find an extended argument. (There is an index, but it's not totally reliable.) Each of Clute's eight chapters is organized chronologically, which means we're constantly revisiting the same eras from different perspectives, as though trapped in a bizarre time-loop. The opening chapters, "Future Visions" and "Historical Context," each take us decade-by-decade through the century – the first in terms of general cultural obsessions, the second more specifically in terms of SF history, presented in multilevel charts. A third chapter on magazines takes us back to the pre-pulp era and forward, a fourth on major authors returns to the decade-by-decade charts (this time followed by individual author entries), and a fifth starts the damn charts all *over* again in a chronological treatment of "classic titles." Clute has done an heroic job of making sure the literature remains the central focus of the book, and his final three chapters treat graphic works, film, and television – the latter two returning again to the strict chronological format. If you want to get a sense of SF in the fifties, then, you have to look in eight different places; the book is one of the best arguments for hypertext I've seen.

It should be clear by now that this book is not an encyclopedia at all, at least not in the sense of *The Encyclopedia of Science Fiction* (and Clute reportedly argued against the use of this term). Instead, it properly belongs in the company of other such presentation pieces as James Gunn's *Alternate Worlds*, Franz Rottensteiner's *The Science Fiction Book*, or Brian Ash's monumentally incomprehensible *Visual Encyclopedia of Science Fiction*. Hands down, Clute's is the best book of this type. But as with those earlier books (except for Gunn's which was one of the first usable histories we had), you have to ask exactly what the SF reader or scholar is supposed to do with it, beyond opening it on Christmas (a good chunk of its market is likely to be people who aren't themselves interested in SF, but know someone who is and who already has a tie). Clute's prose is vivid and his judgments usually defensible (if at times spiffed up considerably from what we know of his other criticism). On a spread-by-spread basis, it's both stunning to look at and fun to wallow in, but it's not any kind of a reference book, and it's sometimes confusing.

For example, in a section charting the future histories of various authors (arbitrarily inserted between the "historical context" chapters on the 1940s and the 1950s), Stapledon's *Last and First Men* is summarized in a neat flow chart – but the title isn't mentioned, and the book pictured is *Star Maker*. (Only one book is mentioned for each of the other writers here, too – Baxter, Niven, Anderson, and Heinlein – sending you off to the author entries for more information.) The entry for 1951 (again in "historical context" makes a cryptic reference to a movie serial of *Mysterious Island* which "adds an alien from Mercury," but the accompanying illustration is a poster (in French) for the 1961 American feature, and when you leap over to the film chronology to find out more about the serial, there's nothing there.

The chronology of authors is also sometimes confusing; Clute may be making a point about the decade in which an author made the greatest impact, but would anyone really think of looking for Clifford Simak among "authors of the 1960s," or Pohl and Silverberg among "authors of the 1970s"?

Probably the biggest howls Clute is going to get will be over the omissions and elisions. Fandom is completely ignored, and even awards like the Hugo and Nebula are mentioned only in passing. Perceived genre liabilities like L. Ron Hubbard or 1950s monster movies are very nearly swept under the rug, and instances of high goofiness such as Richard Shaver are wisely omitted. All discussion of SF art (except comics) is relegated to a single two-page spread, and there's virtually no mention of music or theatre. But the real arguments may come with the "major authors" and "classic title" lists. The former includes not only almost everyone you would expect, but Vinge (both), Priest, Sladek, Bujold, Harry Harrison, James White, Primo Levi, George R.R. Martin, Paul McAuley, and James Blaylock. Astonishingly, however, there are no "major author" entries for Benford, Bester, Spinrad, Taine, or Brackett, despite the fact that Bester is credited with *two* "classic titles" and Benford's *Timescape* is described (under "classic titles" again) as "the best time-travel-backward tale ever written." None of these authors are even given the "notable author" designation, apparently a lesser rubric which shows up in sidebars on Alan Dean Foster, M. John Harrison, and Franz Kafka(!). And the Australian George Turner, described in *The Encyclopedia of Science Fiction* as "his country's most distinguished sf writer" (in an entry by Nicholls), doesn't even make the index.

I have to assume these are oversights rather than messages, and the argument can be made that a very pretty book need not be held to quite the same standards as a very scholarly one; it simply would not be fair to expect this illustrated companion to SF (which seems to be what Clute initially conceived) to recapitulate all of the Clute-Nicholls *Encyclopedia*. At the same time, pretty books are seductive, and often end up on the same library shelves as the dense gray ones. *The Illustrated Encyclopedia*, with its colorful author photos (complete with reproduced autographs), book and magazine covers, and movie stills, makes a fine companion to the unillustrated *Encyclopedia*, but it's in no sense a replacement for it.

Nor, for that matter, is it a replacement for the almost infinitely more schleppy review collection **Look at the Evidence**, which is where you have to go if you want to know what Clute really writes like. At nearly three times the length of Clute's earlier collection *Strokes*, which covered twenty years of criticism, *Look at the Evidence* covers only the five years 1987-1992. It appears to include nearly all of Clute's critical writing of this period, virtually unedited except for occasional chronological rearrangements and later interpolations (some of which seem intended to retrofit the reviews to match the terminology of fantasy outlined in his July *Locus* interview – thus "rubberized ruritanias" gets translated into "pastorals" [at some loss, if you ask me]).

Although Clute organizes the book plainly enough on a year-by-year basis, each year starting with a roundup essay followed by reviews from venues as various as *Interzone*, the *Washington Post*, the *New York Review of Science Fiction*, and the *Times Literary Supplement*, the book can't really be approached as a simple chronicle of the years in SF. For one thing, Clute often doesn't review the books you expect him too, and often reviews at some length books that many SF readers would regard as odd or marginal. To me, this is a major part of the book's value. Even more important are the insights about SF buried in individual columns, which often cry for a more fully developed argument that never comes. Clute claims, for example, that as the old confrontational model of the SF future has been replaced by more propritiatory attitudes in "post-genre" writers, "Sf has been transformed into fables of exogamy." This obviously means a great deal to Clute, since he even sneaks it into his *Illustrated Encyclopedia* with a bizarre glossary entry on "Marrying Out" (who would ever look *that* up?), but to piece out the argument with examples, you have to ramble through his whole book.

On other occasions, Clute seeks to simply domesticate some of the mystique of SF, as when he argues (in a review of Paul J. McAuley) that the "sense of wonder" is simply a variety of dramatic irony – "the pleasure we feel when the hero learns something we already knew." I don't think this is entirely persuasive, but it's at least partially true, and it does what good criticism should always do – it makes you think seriously about what you've read and how you've read it and whether or not you can come up with enough counterexamples to punch him out. When Clute does build a sustained argument – as in his longish review of the Panshins' *The World Beyond the Hill*, which he describes as a "Whig history" of SF (referring to the tendency to interpret the past soley as preparation for the present – or in the Panshins' case, for the Campbell era) – he does so methodically and elegantly, surgically dismantling the book's callowness while recognizing its value as raw scholarship on important texts.

Clute's comments on individual novels are often equally flamboyant and provocative, as when he says that *Sarah Canary* is "the best First Contact novel ever written," or that Neal Barrett's *The Hereafter Gang* is "one of the great American novels." I don't think his intent is to be perverse in such judgments – perverseness would require him to trash many of the more traditional SF texts he approves, and he is generally quite sympathetic to authors' aims while cataloguing what are often technical failures or fizzled plots. For all the overpacked sentences, extended conceits, and wonky metaphors, Clute is transparently in love with what he reads, and sometimes almost sentimental about it. In many ways, the most telling pieces in the collection are his Pilgrim Award acceptance speech, where he talks of his own adolescence, and a tribute to Walter de la Mare written for the Washington *Post*. Of de la Mare's magic, he says "No child should ever be denied a chance to join that world," and you suspect he means the whole of what he loves.

Ian McDonald is a highly talented writer who combines a distinctly Northern Irish sense of bitter dispossession with a tendency to echo themes and images from earlier SF texts. This has led a number of critics to regard McDonald as a more derivative writer than he really is; no one seems to mind much if a whole generation of writers appropriate futures from Heinlein or Asimov, but if your models are more stylistically quirky writers like Bradbury or Geoff Ryman, eyebrows start elevating. McDonald's new novel, **Chaga**, is a first-rate piece of work, but it isn't going to help this situation much. The Chaga of the title is a kind of environmental plague that is transforming the African landscape into an alien wonderland, which of course calls to mind Ballard's *The Crystal World*. Add to this the mysterious disappearance of a couple of Saturn's moons, apparently through alien intervention, and you start thinking of Clarke. More alien things seem to be seeding the oceans – let's see, maybe Wyndham's *Out of the Deeps* or Benford's *Across the Sea of Suns*. And the text itself makes direct reference to Bester, Tolkien, Sagan, *Close Encounters of the Third Kind*, and *The Encyclopedia of Science Fiction* (whose entry on "Big Dumb Objects" provides the popular name for an alien artifact heading toward earth). The spaceships sent out to meet it are all named after SF writers. Even the more mainstream elements of McDonald's novel – his lovably aggressive protagonist Gaby McAslan or his steamy, oversexed version of a magic realist Africa – call to mind novels like Norman Rush's *Mating* (itself an almost SF-nal vision of Africa as a mystical place of idealism and transformation).

So what? The question is not whether parts of the novel resonate familiar tones, but whether the whole package works. I think it does, and I think those resonances add to its effect – it's the sort of novel Ballard might have written if he liked to explain things as much as Clarke does, or that Clarke might have written were he as genuinely passionate about metaphysical images as Ballard is. It's an expansion, with some significant alterations, of a scenario originally laid out in McDonald's 1990 story "Toward Kilimanjaro" (reprinted in his *Speaking in Tongues*), and McDonald has found ways to open up the story in several directions without losing the power of its central image, the Chaga (named after the Kenyan tribe to first be engulfed by the growing environment). McAslan is an ambitious and resourceful journalist, working for a futuristic CNN, who arrives in Kenya determined to investigate the "Kilimanjaro event," as the Chaga is sometimes called after the meteor strike that apparently brought it to earth. She quickly garners an interview with Peter Werther, one of the few humans to emerge from the Chaga, and soon is getting scoop after scoop about what is going on in the Chaga, what the U.N. is doing to cover it up, and how the whole thing relates to both the African AIDS epidemic and the events in outer space.

For all its SF invention and its adroit handling of *Childhood's End*-type themes of transformation, what really propels McDonald's narrative is a large cast of unusually vivid and full characters – McAslan's boss T.P. Costello, her mysterious benefactor Haran, her lover Shepard, the Russian woman AIDS doctor Oksana. Only McAslan herself seems at times to be spunky and adorable beyond belief, an unlikely amalgam of Margaret Bourke-White and Meg Ryan. By grounding his tale with such interesting characters, McDonald permits himself – and us – to rediscover the sense of wonder inherent in the SF to which he repeatedly refers. At one point, McAslan refers to this directly; remembering the movie *Close Encounters*, she complains that the appearance of the aliens at the end "killed the movie." "If they ever penetrate the mystery up there, I hope there is another behind it, Gaby thought. And another beyond that, and beyond that, so that we never dispel the Cloud of Unknowing." Gaby knows what SF is good for, and so does McDonald.

And so does Linda Nagata, a very talented newer writer with an unfortunate penchant for clumsy titles. Her first novel, *The Bohr Maker* (reviewed here in March), was a thoughtful and complex nanotech thriller whose title was absolutely devoid of both poetry and information. Her second novel carries the less cryptic title **Tech-Heaven**, but it's a title that implies a kind of flippant irony that is nowhere borne out by her narrative, which is essentially shaped like an historical romance. In *The Bohr Maker*, Nagata introduced us to a future earth in which technological development is rigidly controlled by the Commonwealth, an amalgam of national governments and orbiting colonies linked to earth by space elevators. *Tech-Heaven* seems to be taking us back to that universe, but in a near-future setting that eventually shows how the Commonwealth develops and how the first space elevators get built. Again, Nagata's theme is both ambitious and important: the attempted political regulation of new technologies, especially as they relate to human rights. But this time the technology in question isn't superintelligent nanomachines, but something much closer to home: cryonic suspension. (The nanomachines begin to show up later in the novel, but are handled with surprising restraint – a relief from the growing flood of "anything-can-happen" nanofiction of the last couple of years.)

Nagata unfolds her plot with great precision and control. When Katie Kishida's husband Tom is about to die from injuries sustained in a helicopter crash, she reveals that the two of them had arranged to have his body cryonically frozen for later repair and revival. To her surprise this seems an outrage to Tom's coworker (and Katie's best friend) Roxanne, and especially to Tom's sister Ilene, a U.S. senator. Soon Ilene's opposition becomes the platform for a new political movement to ban all life-extension technologies, and Katie and her children find themselves embroiled in a hot media war – clearly reminiscent of current abortion debates – on the question of whether the older generation has an obligation to make room for the younger in an increasingly deteriorating and overpopulated world. The debate plays out with growing violence over the next three decades, as Katie marries (and is deserted by) a new husband, new political alliances emerge around issues of technology and environment, the first space colonies are built, and abortive attempts are made to colonize Mars. Meanwhile, gradual advances in nanotechnology lead toward the day when Tom – now hidden for safekeeping in a cryonic vault in the Andes – might be revived.

The model for most cryonic suspension tales is, of course, "Rip Van Winkle," and most are thinly disguised time-travel narratives in which the sleeper wakes into a sanitized world of wonders — the "tech-heaven" of Nagata's title. Nagata takes the opposite tack of showing what happens to those the sleeper leaves behind, and how the world is headed toward anything but a sanitized utopia. Her future is depressingly believable, especially in such details as the abandonment of Mars by five hundred colonists when politicians fail to fund the next phase, or the takeover of national policy debates by sensational talk show hosts. Some aspects of the novel don't work as well as others — chapters detailing the frozen Tom's psychic experiences in a world of ice-demons awkwardly parallel the debates going on in the world of the living, too many characters talk in position papers, and the eventual solution proposed for the immortality-vs.-overpopulation debate is no surprise to any SF reader — but none of this seriously derails a serious and thoughtful book. Nagata has had the good sense to ground her unfolding future in the lives of unusually believable characters, and the undying link between Tom and Katie over three decades of turbulent change give *Tech-Heaven* the sentimental charge of a good romance as well. And Nagata's main concern — whether the vast changes that technology may offer us very soon will result in a kind of Luddite backlash in the political arena — is one we ought to be thinking about right now.

As Nagata demonstrates, second novels are usually more interesting than first novels in SF, if only because there is less desperation to pack everything in; it's like a gymnast doing free-form exercises after the compulsories. An even better example is Valerie Freireich, whose *Becoming Human* (reviewed here in February) introduced us to the Polite Harmony of Worlds, a somewhat priggish planetary federation whose guiding principles of rationalist "Jonism" always come up against their intolerance for any form of genetic alteration. Freirich's second novel, **Testament** (another title that could mean anything), avoids the wearying Harmony politics of her first, but has its own share of complex schemes. The novel is set at the same point in Harmony history, and one of its main characters, Martin Penn, is a holdover from the earlier novel. But *Testament* isn't really a sequel so much as an alternate take, and it's a much better plotted and more thematically focused novel.

Penn is an emissary to the planet Testament, a protectorate of the Harmony denied full membership because of a genetic alteration — its women are born with the memories of their matriarchal ancestors. Penn hopes to explore these memories to discover new information about Jon Hsu, founder of Jonism and the Harmony's spiritual godfather. He hires as guide Gray Bridger, a young man who seeks desperately to get off Testament, where he feels alienated as a "singleton" — one born without past memories. But Gray's grandmother Reed has arranged a marriage which will prevent his leaving. Even worse, the marriage is to an "alia" (a term borrowed from Frank Herbert), a woman so dominated by ancestral personalities that she has no identity. As Gray tries to find out what his grandmother is up to, his sister

Mead seduces Penn to advance her own agenda, and Penn has to deal with a brutal Harmony governor who'd just as soon wipe out everyone on Testament. As these conspiracies and counterconspiracies unfold, Gray finds that his new wife, Dancer, is dominated by the personality of Janet Bridger, the line's founder, who apparently knew Jon Hsu on earth way back in the early 21st century, and thus holds the key to the information Penn is trying to locate. All these complications are woven into a complex web of ironies and betrayals which consistently return to the themes of memory and identity that are the novel's real focus.

By confining the action to one city on Testament, Freirich is able to develop a vivid picture of a matriarchal society swamped by its own past, and its effect on a variety of characters. Interestingly, the male characters emerge as more convincing than the women; Penn and Gray are the ones who have to sort everything out, while grandma Reed sometimes looks a little too much like a Bene Gesserit and sister Mead is vixen enough to show up on a prime-time soap. The most touching character, handled with great skill, is Gray's wife Dancer, whose personality throughout (except for one brief glimpse) is completely dominated by ancestors – usually Janet Bridger, who falls in love with Gray and who is appalled at what her heritage has become. The least convincing aspect of the novel, if you regard it as anything more than a philosophical macguffin, is Jonism itself. As Freirich describes it, Jon Hsu's revered philosophy is a lame kind of rational liberalism compromised with bigotry – Hubert Humphrey as Hari Seldon. It's hard to imagine this taking over the whole galaxy for centuries, when it can't even get a Senate chairmanship today.

As long as I'm complaining about titles, I might as well mention that I have little patience for titles that use an SF-sounding word or phrase as play money; what does "Quantum Leap" have to do with anything quantum, for example? The title of Jamil Nasir's first novel, **Quasar**, turns out to refer to a character's name, and only by a stretch can you find any metaphorical connection between her mercurial, disturbed personality and a real quasar. As it turns out, *Quasar* is a fairly tight adventure story which also turns into be a First Contact novel, but not before it spends most of its time as a women's gothic with confused trappings of med-tech fiction, post-holocaust urban nightmares, and grunge horror.

Theodore Karmade is a down-on-his-luck psychiatric technician in a vast City, one of the last earthbound redoubts of humanity in a world devastated by biological wars and pollution. When he is summoned to the fabulous ZantCorp Complex, he finds that his patient is none other than Quasar Zant, orphaned heiress of the City's most powerful family, and supposedly suffering from multiple personality disorder. After rescuing her from a VR "transducer" which has nearly poached her brain, he begins to develop a strange symbiotic relationship with her – and to discover the secrets of the nightmarish gothic castle where she may be trapped). There is Quasar's vicious psychoneurologist Dr. Ziller, the mysterious security director Rothe, and hovering above it all – literally – Quasar's all-powerful guardian aunt Nelda, deranged by too many revitalization treatments. But is Quasar really insane? Are her parents really dead? What really happened to them before her birth, when they met as astronauts exploring Neptune? Why is Quasar drawn mysteriously toward the Warrens, the foul underworld inhabited by the City's exiled mutant population?

These are classic gothic cliffhanger questions, and Nasir lets us know it by periodically stopping midstream to ask them for us. But his puzzles are intriguing enough to survive both his own often amateurish handling of them and the novel's wildly uneven tone. At first, Nasir adopts a resolutely hard-SF approach to mental disease; no twitch is allowed to pass without its neurochemical source being explained, and when Quasar's eyes roll up in her head, it "looked like sudden-onset kainate and quisqualate ion channel saturation." By the time we get to the Warrens sections, however, the rhetoric has shifted to B-movie horror, with giant hairless mutants and aunt Nelda devising gruesome tortures for those who cross her. What remains constant is the claustrophobic sense of despair crucial to all such young-woman-trapped-in-a-big-house-with-evil-attendants tales. When the secrets are revealed, and the narrative tries to bring off another shift – this time into an SF myth of transformation, it doesn't quite work because it vitiates the simple romance structure that has been almost holding the whole thing together. Nasir's pacing is tight, his plotting ingenious, and his characters vivid enough to keep you turning pages, but the overall effect of his novel is something like sudden-onset quisqualate ion channel saturation.

– December 1995, Locus #419 –

Endymion ~~ Dan Simmons

Far Futures ~~ edited by Gregory Benford

The Ganymede Club ~~ Charles Sheffield

In one of the most famous hatchet jobs in the history of reviewing, Keats's rambling "poetic romance" *Endymion* was described by a contemporary reviewer in *Blackwood's Magazine* as "imperturbable drivelling idiocy," a phrase so colorful that modern paperback publishers might even entertain the thought of using it as a blurb (probably would sell books, too). Byron and Shelley apparently wanted people to think that this sort of thing led to Keats's premature death, and one suspects that writers ever since have wished it true that bad reviews might actually cause tuberculosis, and that reviewers should be informed of this. But the fact is that Keats himself was fairly apologetic about the poem, and it's since become one of those unread "classics" from which everyone remembers the first line ("A thing of beauty is a joy forever") and no one remembers anything else. In short, it's hardly an auspicious jumping-off point for Dan Simmon's new sequel to his highly successful diptych *Hyperion* and

The Fall of Hyperion (which drew their titles from *really good* Keats poems). That earlier work is a modern SF masterpiece which ingeniously deconstructed itself in the second volume, and which played sophisticated thematic games with English romantics transplanted to a space-opera environment. As a novelist, Simmons has persistently (dare we say imperturbably?) tried to find ways to draw on the resources of both literary and scientific culture without doing excessive violence to either; his *The Hollow Man* somehow combined Dante and Eliot with quantum physics and still made a kind of sense.

Endymion shows little of such ambition, though. Like the title figure of Keats's poem, his protagonist has been a kind of rural shepherd-swain, but it's clear that the real reason for the choice of title is simply to signal the connection to the *Hyperion* series (well, what else could he have called it? "The Eve of St. Agnes"?) In fact, there's less of Keats in this than there is of George Lucas or James Cameron, or even Frank Lloyd Wright (who seems to be lurking just offstage as the novel closes). Set two and a half centuries after *The Fall of Hyperion*, *Endymion* is essentially a fast-moving space opera on a grand scale, driven by a simple pursuit plot and so far offering only tantalizing hints of the kind of broad dramatic reversals that made the first two books so satisfying. I say "so far" because it becomes clear before you're halfway through the novel that it's not going to end in this volume (and if foreshadowing tells us anything, it's a good guess that Keats's "Lamia" looks like the likely source for the next sequel).

Endymion isn't a bad novel (or half-novel) at all, but it's not a thematically ambitious one either. Simmon's strong visual imagination, his direct and impassioned narrative voice (perhaps given over a bit much to the "had I but known" school of foreshadowing), and his horror writer's skill at handling sudden violence, are all much in evidence. But from the opening scenes, what we hear in the background echoes not so much the quest for ideal beauty (which was the subject of Keats's poem) as the stirring strains of a John Williams score. See if the opening sounds familiar: Raul Endymion is an unsophisticated youth from a backwater planet (Endymion) sent by a wise and somewhat mystical old man on a seemingly impossible mission to rescue a princess (well, not quite a princess, but she's Keats's daughter, which is close enough) from a stronghold of the galactic empire (here called the Pax, a kind of reconstituted Catholic theocracy). All he has to help him is a magical talisman (in this case a flying carpet) and a faithful if diffident android (there are actually two robots, if you count the chatty and petulant spaceship they escape in). He gets the girl, and the two of them are pursued from planet to planet by an obsessive high priest who never gets relieved of duty even though he royally screws up every chance at capture.

OK, now let's assume that this only coincidentally resembles a familiar movie series, because it's drawing on the same hero-myth sources. Certainly the dialogue is more sophisticated, the growing relationship between Raul and the eleven-year-old girl Aenea more touching, the landscapes of the various planets more richly detailed as the fugitives visit planet after planet in their effort to escape through the succession of "farcasters" or stargates that are collectively called the River Tethys. It becomes a wonderful grand tour, and even the villainy of their pursuer, Father Captain de Soya, is increasingly mitigated by complexities of character. It's not a movie. But then there's the shrike, the mysterious razor-monster from the Hyperion novels and as much of a special effect as prose is capable of. The shrike is as fast and unpredictable as a Ridley Scott Alien, as relentless and indestructible as the Terminator. Simmons has written enough horror fiction to know that you can't bring a shrike onstage unless you're going to have a set-piece shrike battle down the line, and this comes courtesy of a new nemesis, introduced late in the novel (I'm trying not to give too much away here), capable of moving in superfast mode and looking just like a figure made of liquid mercury when in battle. Yes — it's *Terminator II*! — and it's one hell of a fight, but that's when I lost it.

And yet I'm looking forward to the second *Endymion* novel. The various hints Simmons has sprinkled through this novel — some of them subtly insinuated, some dropped like a load of bricks on the livingroom floor — suggest that the real substance of the tale has yet to emerge. The mysterious powers that make Aenea such a threat to both the Pax and the mysterious TechnoCore (once thought defunct), the grand and tragic romance that lies ahead for Raul and Aenea, the mystery of how Earth (once thought destroyed) has been preserved, or moved, or reconstituted — all are left hanging, and all point toward some huge imaginative shift that could yet make the tale as compelling as its predecessors. There could be a great meal on its way, but meanwhile, well, the popcorn is quite tasty.

Gregory Benford's introduction to his new anthology **Far Futures** (which originally appeared as an essay in *Fantasy and Science Fiction* and parts of which showed up in Benford's *Sailing Bright Eternity*) is an odd kind of manifesto which begins by arguing that too little recent SF has tackled the truly grand perspectives offered by modern cosmology, suggests that most SF writers may simply find the demands of such fiction too daunting, then segues into the kind of hard-science elegy on universal entropy which is rapidly becoming Benford's stylistic trademark. What's odd about this is that the scientific portion of Benford's essay tends to argue against its initial thesis about modern SF. If anything, Benford shows that far-future scenarios represent just about the only aspect of extrapolation that SF writers can count on as likely; current physics is pretty useless at telling us what life will be like in Cleveland in fifty years, but it paints a fairly confident picture of what the sun will look like in five billion years. Narratives that stretch out into such perspectives already have a good deal of their work done for them, at least in terms of establishing setting and background, and it doesn't seem likely that simple laziness is what keeps SF writers from exploring such far futures.

Benford's real concern, I suspect, is that he doesn't feel enough hard SF writers have taken on the big cosmological questions. Hard SF often seems content to settle into a middle-distant future, far enough away enough to avoid detailed questions of how we got from here to there, but not so far as to invoke quasi-religious questions of eschatology. The far futures of Jack Vance and Gene Wolfe are clearly not what concerns Benford (as convincingly detailed as they may be). Nor is he calling for updated versions of Stapledon (who pretty nearly dispensed with human-scale narrative altogether) or Wells (for whom evolution provided a neat set of metaphors). I suspect what Benford is really after is that kind of narrative, admittedly rare in SF, which tackles cosmological problems with the kind of engineering gusto that has long been hard SF's stock in trade – the sort of thrill you get from a novel like Poul Anderson's *Tau Zero* (1970). Not surprisingly, two of the five novellas included in *Far Futures* address essentially the same question as Anderson's novel – namely, how do you preserve some aspect of human intelligence "at the eschaton" (to quote the title of Charles Sheffield's contribution)?

What *is* surprising – and not at all to the book's detriment – is that none of the authors represented have opted for clever engineering solutions to the questions they raise. Two of them, in fact, are essentially love stories. The best piece of fiction in the book in terms of unity of style, character, and setting is Joe Haldeman's "For White Hill," which concerns two artists who meet on an earth devastated by an earlier war with seemingly omnipotent aliens. When the war returns, all humanity seems doomed. Against this bleak backdrop, the growing relationship between the narrator and the woman White Hill, and their contrasting styles of artistic expression, Haldeman weaves one of SF's most telling meditations on the nature of art and survival. Sheffield's "At the Eschaton" is a more conventional tale of obsessive love, as his protagonist's determination to keep his dying wife cryogenically preserved until she can be revived leads him from the near future into a succession of increasing distant tomorrows and finally to the collapse of the universe. The sentimentality of the premise is more than redeemed by Sheffield's handling of the time perspectives, and his tale is the only one in the collection that actually carries through a Stapledonian succession of distant futures.

Greg Bear's "Judgment Engine" also casts the end of time in the perspective of a failed love relationship, in a manner more hard-edged than that of Sheffield. Bear's protagonist, Vasily, is revived some twelve billion years in the future into a society of disembodied "social=minds" because his primitive understanding of "argument, rebellion, desperation" may enable him to become a "judgment engine" for the confused superminds who are facing both internal rebellion and universal collapse. The notion of dragging a more-or-less contemporary personality into the far future as a way of lending some human scale to the setting is of course older even than Stapledon, and Benford himself did it with Nigel Walmsley in his Galactic Center series. It's one of the few strategies far-future writers have available to make their scenarios anything more than speculative essays, and it's not surprising that Poul Anderson uses it here along with Bear and Sheffield. But Anderson couples it with at least two other strategies – a primitive society of "new" humans evolving on a dying earth, and a set of machine intelligences given rather unlikely human personalities, reminiscent of the supercomputers in Zelazny's "For a Breath I Tarry." In "Genesis," Anderson resurrects the personality of an engineer named Christian Brannock to help the machine intelligences investigate the question of whether earth, nearing its demise, might be worth saving. Together with another resurrectee named Laurinda (hints of yet another love story here), Brannock explores not only earth's history, but a succession of possible alternate histories concocted by the earth's AI-overseer, Gaia. The result is a complex and intriguing meditation on history and meaning.

The oddest selection in the book also takes on the question of history and its meaning, but does so in the familiar context of Asimov's Foundation universe. Donald Kingsbury's "Historical Crisis" uses the tale of a gifted young psychohistorian named Eron Osa to question the fundamental tenets of Asimovian psychohistory by pointing out that any possible predictive equations would have to project a huge number of alternative futures, while psychohistory in practice focused only on protecting a single low-probability future. The point is well taken, I suppose, but does it need to be made at all at this late date? After all, psychohistory isn't *real*, and even Asimov knew that it was only the failures in the system that could generate stories. Kingsbury's rather flat style and flatter characters aren't enough to raise the story much beyond its basic idea, and that idea is more about SF than about history. Anderson's story does a much better idea of dramatizing the notion of alternate histories, but the notion of real "far futures" as revealed by Haldeman, Bear, and Sheffield offers us a much richer perspective. By offering some sensible speculations on the nature of prediction, Kingsbury covers issues that probably ought to be covered in a collection such as this, but the other authors brutally remind us that it's all going to hell anyway, and all we've got in the end is each other.

Charles Sheffield's **The Ganymede Club** returns us to the post-apocalyptic-war solar system of his 1992 novel *Cold as Ice*, but the novel's main virtue is that it does much to revive the best features of the SF juvenile and the SF mystery. This doesn't mean that it should be shunted aside into those black-hole subghettoes, however; it's a competent and compelling novel in its own right, and Tor doesn't seem to be promoting either the juvenile or the mystery elements. But they're unmistakeable, and not only because of the teenage heroes or the murderous conspiracy that drives the plot. The best juveniles demand a kind of clarity in both style and plotting too easily overlooked in many space operas, and only a handful of writers maintain this clarity in their adult fiction — Clarke, Haldeman, and Card come at once to mind as authors of such precisely tuned prose, and Sheffield makes a good bid to join their ranks. As far as the mystery element is concerned, it often shows up in juveniles as a surface plot that drives the novel toward more awe-inspiring revelations — and Sheffield makes good use of that, too.

He begins with a series of seemingly disconnected episodes each ending in a cliffhanger: a mysterious discovery on a tiny moon of Saturn in 2032, a strange proposal made to a fugitive on Mars in 2063, a conspiratorial discussion on Ganymede in 2066, an escape from an earth under attack in the "Great War" of 2067. Finally, we settle on Ganymede in 2072, where the two escapees from earth, the fifteen-year-old Spook Belman and his older sister Lola, have settled. Spook plays puzzle games on the computer net while Lola is in practice as a "haldane," a kind of supertherapist. Lola's new patient, Bryce Sonnenberg, is plagued by memories which we recognize as relating to the novel's opening episodes, but which could not possibly be his own. Lola reluctantly enlists the aid of Spook and his puzzle-master colleague Bat to investigate this mystery, and soon all of them are caught up in murderous intrigue involving the mysterious "Ganymede Club," whose origins go back to that first Saturnian exploration of 2032. Some of the adventures reach Saturday matinee levels of credibility strain – at one point Lola finds herself trapped incommunicado aboard a spaceship remotely controlled by the murderer – but the whole is narrated with such good humor and genuine ingenuity that you can hardly object, and the characters are sorted out in classic juvenile typecasting, with really cold bad guys and likeable good guys. The character of Bat in particular – a kind of black teenage Nero Wolfe, uncomfortable around people but a genius on the net – is alone worth the price of admission.

1996 - Overview: The Year in Review

~ originally published in Locus #433 (Feb 1997) ~

Any year has to be counted a success that began with the concluding volume of Kim Stanley Robinson's monumental *Mars* trilogy, saw the conclusion of an important four-volume novel by Gene Wolfe, and included major new works by Dan Simmons, Bruce Sterling, William Gibson, Stephen Baxter, Paul J. McAuley, Jack Vance, and Damon Knight. While most of these novelists were busy refining and extending ideas and forms at which they were already acknowledged masters, some — notably Baxter — set off in interesting new directions. Baxter, who began his career with hard-SF novels and stories characterized by ingeniously worked-out but radically alienating environments, has lately been domesticating his imagination in the service of such mock-Victorian SF as *The Time Ships*, his astonishing sequel to Wells's *Time Machine*, but *Voyage* takes this domestication several steps further. Essentially an alternate history of the last three decades of NASA, ending in a successful manned Mars landing in 1986, *Voyage* also represents one of the more interesting identifiable trends of the year. Together with Allen Steele's The Tranquillity Alternative and a number of stories and articles by a whole gaggle of hard-SF writers, Baxter's novel seems to reveal an emerging tragic nostalgia for a space program gone awry, and a desire to set history right through a kind of retro-corrective fiction.

Whether it represents a continuing trend or whether it's just another example of steam-engine time, this re-examination of recent technological history departs from its source modes in a couple of significant ways: unlike most alternate histories (which tend toward more playful "what if?" scenarios, it shapes itself as a specific kind of policy critique; and unlike most space exploration fiction, it shifts focus from technological and natural wonders to issues of management. Questions of management and governance increasingly came to preoccupy the characters in Robinson's Mars trilogy as well, and novels such as Michael Flynn's *Firestar* and Charles Sheffield and Jerry Pournelle's *Higher Education* even returned to decades-old fantasies of the privatization of both space exploration and public education, in novels that made up in homiletics what they lacked in inventiveness. Does all this mean that hard SF, having long since laid out its basic scenarios of cosmological romance, has decided that what is needed to get there is a stern critique of public will and a series of novelized management seminars? (Not that SF hasn't visited this territory earlier and often; most readers who only remember those wonderful walkways in Heinlein's "The Roads Must Roll" forget that the story was principally an argument about labor relations.)

Or is it simply that hard SF, like SF in general, is continuing to re-examine some of its own basic assumptions? One of the other trends of 1996 seemed to be a return to sources, to familiar themes and tropes revisited with new kinds of sophistication.

Surely, nobody believed there was much life left in the old generation starship motif until Gene Wolfe came along and showed that it gave room for his full measure of Proustian density in the *Long Sun* series. William Gibson's *Idoru* did not add much imaginatively to his earlier cyberworlds of the *Neuromancer* trilogy, but its newfound maturity of voice enriched the setting and characters substantially. Orson Scott Card returned to the morally earnest world of Ender Wiggin in *Children of the Mind*, Larry Niven to Ringworld in *The Ringworld Throne*, and Dan Simmons to the world of his *Hyperion* novels with *Endymion* (a two-part narrative whose conclusion will appear this year). Earlier nanotech fiction may have offered wilder and woollier worlds than the future Europe described in Paul McAuley's *Fairyland* and several stories in *The Invisible Country*, but none offered a richer or more internally consistent *mise en scène* or a keener sense of history.

McAuley also suggests another incipient trend in the introduction to one of the stories in *The Invisible Country*. Noting that in the last decade Europe has undergone social transformations of almost SF-nal proportions, he complains that this volatile and provocative environment remains all but ignored even by English SF writers. His own *Fairyland* is partly a corrective to this, but 1996 also gave us fresh views of an evolving Europe in Bruce Sterling's *Holy Fire* (which also offers his most fully-realized characters to date) and in Brian W. Aldiss's collection *Common Clay* (originally published in England in 1995, but included here because I want to).

But Europe is not the only notable new setting in last year's fiction; the broader trend may simply be to get away from the genre's traditional habit of viewing the future earth almost solely in terms of New York or L.A. Bangkok thus became the focus of *fin de siècle* techno-viral-eroticism in Richard Calder's Dead Stuff series (*Dead Girls*, *Dead Boys*, and last year's *Dead Things*), while a claustrophobic Tokyo gave a rich and convincing texture to Gibson's *Idoru*. Greg Egan's *Distress* (also originally published at the end of 1995 in England, but included here just because), offers a brief grand tour of an anxiety-ridden 21st century, finally choosing for its setting an artificial island called Stateless. Even some novels set largely in the U.S., such as Damon Knight's *Humpty Dumpty* or Kathleen Goonan's *The Bones of Time*, take on distinct regional flavors, with Goonan's novel and interesting combination of high-tech cloning and Hawaiian mythology. Perhaps the old manifest destiny myth of planetary Americanization has finally been knocked out of the pantheon of SF assumptions (along with that myth of competent management in the space program). Perhaps all we can hope for, like the battered space ranger of Terry Bisson's *Pirates of the Universe*, is the peaceful predictability of life in a Disney theme park.

One trend I keep half-expecting to show up, in pop media as well as SF, is millenial apocalypticism. The only such book from a major writer this year was Sheri Tepper's *Gibbon's Decline and Fall*, in which a real war of the sexes threatens catastrophe in the year 2000. Perhaps it's too earlier for such a trend to be apparent, but my prediction – based almost solely on the Tepper novel and on the Chris Carter TV series *Millennium* (which so far seems only to be about a somewhat psychic investigator solving creepy crimes, but constantly threatens to weave everything together into some kind of pattern) — is that such fiction, when it gets here, is more likely to be of the signs-and-portents variety than full-blown Book of Revelations circuses (I exclude tabloid newspapers, New Age bestsellers, and fiction of the Christian right from this prediction.)

1996 also was an encouraging year for short story collections. In *None So Blind*, Joe Haldeman demonstrated that his real signature theme over the past few years has not been war, but art and artists. Ursula Le Guin's "mainstream" collection *Unlocking the Air* only served to demonstrate that the line between mainstream and fantasy in her work is often an arbitrary one — and she, too, revealed that the nature of story and storytelling has become her characteristic theme. Michael Bishop, on the other hand, seemed as eclectic as ever in *At the City Limits of Fate*, which ranged from a sharply envisioned tale of snake-handling to the usual Bishop oddities. The richness of Paul McAuley's settings, including those of the novels *Fairyland* and *Pasquale's Angel*, was further demonstrated in his collection *The Invisible Country*. Important first collections came from Jonathan Lethem, whose *The Wall of the Sky, the Wall of the Eye* contains what is probably the best SF basketball story ever (although offhand I can't think of the competition); and Mary Rosenblum, whose *Synthesis and Other Virtual Realities* showed mastery of both environmental and VR fiction; and Jack McDevitt, whose *Standard Candles* showed a good deal more substance and originality than his much more successful novel, *Ancient Shores*.

But it was also encouraging to see new collections from old masters, and even reprint collections from masters in danger of oblivion. Ray Bradbury's *Quicker than the Eye* shows that the old poet's voice is still in fine fettle, even if his plots are not (have they ever been?), and Richard Lupoff's *Before 12:01 . . . and After* suggested that the SF field has all but ignored one of its more entertaining craftsmen of short fiction. Poul Anderson, whose short fiction is often overshadowed by his novel, also produced a collection, All One Universe (which I've not seen). White Wolf began a program of reprinting Harlan Ellison's stories and essays in a series of handsome volumes beginning with *Edgeworks*. The Sturgeon Project managed to keep alive with the publication of a second beautifully produced volume of early short fiction, *Microcosmic God*, and a small press named Tachyon brought back into print several of Clifford Simak's memorable tales in *Across the River and Through the Trees*. It is worth noting that not only did the Simak and Sturgeon collections come from small presses, but so did those of Lupoff, McDevitt, Rosenblum, and Bishop. This is becoming an important niche for the small presses to develop, and an important service they provide to readers.

The annual anthologies continued their reigns of excellence, although both the Dozois and the Datlow/Windling are beginning to look a little predictable from year to year, and it was good to see a new competitor enter the field in the form of David G. Hartwell's *Year's Best SF*. Hartwell, along with Milton Wolf, also produced the year's most ambitious anthology, *Visions of Wonder*, ostensibly a teaching text for members of the Science Fiction Research Association, but actually a provocative attempt to limn the whole field of SF in the 1990s. The most disheartening news is in the field of original anthologies and anthology series; with the end of Bantam's *Full Spectrum* series and Jane Yolen's *Xanadu* fantasy anthologies, the only ongoing series is the new *Starlight*, edited by Patrick Nielsen Hayden in a debut volume that is far more promising in terms of literary content than likely sales.

There is, of course, a good deal that I didn't see during the year, and probably a fair amount that I saw and have forgotten. But there seems to be a solid enough base of important works by talented writers that the overall state of SF is healthy, and healthily diverse; past years may have seemed like the Year of Nanotech or the Year of Cyberspace, but no such bandwagons seemed to dominate in 1996, as writers turned toward consolidating what they have learned from these new themes. Such years of consolidation usually produce better fiction, because what initially seemed like a toy (golly, nanotech lets us do *anything!*) loses some of its novelty and becomes a narrative tool, adding to the panoply of SF resources and subject to the same rules as all the other tools. Whether or not a feared shakeout in the industry would leave such literate and imaginative SF untouched, or whether a year from now you'll be reading year-in-review summaries of Trek, droid, and X-files books, I wouldn't hazard a guess.

– January 1996, Locus #420 –

The Dechronization of Sam Magruder ~
~ George Gaylord Simpson

Pastwatch: The Redemption of Christopher Columbus ~
~ Orson Scott Card

An Exaltation of Larks ~~ Robert Reed

Animal Planet ~~ Scott Bradfield

The Humanoids ~~ Jack Williamson

Last year's centennial of the publication of H.G. Wells's *The Time Machine* gave us a small number of informative conferences and symposia, a spectacular sequel to Wells's novel (Stephen Baxter's *The Time Ships*), and a good reason to ruminate on the nature of the time travel tale as a subspecies of SF. Despite being the most patently unlikely of SF's favorite themes (and one of the most overworked), time travel continues to flourish and has spun off enough overlapping subtypes to warrant a motif index: one-way travel to the future (the Rip Van Winkle motif) or to the past (the *Lest Darkness Fall* motif), travel to the future and back (as in Wells's original novel) or to the past and back (including stories about future time travelers visiting us), travelling back and forth all over to fix history or wage war, creating and exploring alternate histories, etc. Time travel is a convenient way to get at dinosaur tales, logical puzzles, historical settings, and weighty eschatological questions. In short, it's just so damn useful to writers that it doesn't really matter whether it makes much sense.

Take, for example, **The Dechronization of Sam Magruder**, a newly discovered novella by the great paleontologist George Gaylord Simpson, who died in 1984. Found by his daughter among a small group of family papers which Simpson's widow had apparently not thought worth sending to the American Philosophical Society along with other Simpson manuscripts, this rather modest tale now comes dressed up with an introduction by Arthur C. Clarke, afterwords by Stephen Jay Gould and Joan Simpson Burns, and an enthusiastic endorsement from Brian Aldiss. The supplementary material alone is almost worth the price: Clarke's essay is a fine little treatment of the problems of visiting the past, while Gould's is a useful discussion of the scientific and philosophical underpinnings of the story. All these bells and whistles might reasonably raise a caution flag, a suspicion that this may be no more than a minor curiosity dressed up as a real discovery. But despite such suspicions, and despite a title that sounds like it belongs on a Robert W. Service poem, *The Dechronization of Sam Magruder* is a first-rate survival tale, written not only to dramatize Simpson's ideas about dinosaurs and life in the Cretaceous, but also to offer a kind of personal credo about how life ought to be lived, and why one stays alive at all. The question that opens the book – in a kind of clubby, men's-club setting with characters identified only by their roles (the Common Man, the Pragmatist, the Universal Historian) – is not a question of paleontology or time travel, but one of existential speculation: "'What would you do if you knew you were going to be utterly alone for the rest of your life?'" It's a question worthy of Camus, and it turns out to be as important in the narrative that follows as all of Simpson's dramatized speculations about prehistoric life.

As in Wells, there is plenty of philosophical doubletalk to rationalize the notion of time-travel, but according to the theory outlined by Simpson, travel is only possible backward, since only the past has already come into existence. Hence, even though it might be possible to experience a "time-slip" or "dechronization" into the past, it would never be possible to return because the future you would return to hasn't happened yet, and therefore doesn't exist. This is what happens to Sam Magruder, a 22nd-century "chronologist" who disappears in a laboratory accident while experimenting with the quantum nature of time. Sometime later, a geologist in the American southwest discovers a set of incised quartzite tablets buried in layers of shale some 80 million years old – and the inscriptions turn out to be a narrative painstakingly kept by Magruder during his years alone in the Cretaceous. Magruder's narrative, which makes up most of the rest of the story, alternates between observations of dinosaur life and despairing questions of why survive at all, and comes to resemble *Robinson Crusoe* rather than most time-travel stories. It is remarkably unsentimental, sometimes brutal, and often bleak – no cute, cuddly dinosaur friends, no lost civilizations, no fellow time travelers with which to share discoveries. Only the laborious task of incising the stone messages, which Magruder has no reason to believe will ever be discovered, lend some focus to his life, some connection to a humanity he will never see again. As a dramatization of paleontological theory, Simpson's story may be a bit dated, but as a straightforward tale of pure time travel and almost unbearable isolation, it's a small masterpiece.

Orson Scott Card's **Pastwatch: The Redemption of Christopher Columbus** also uses time travel, also with certain built-in restrictions, but with a very different agenda. Apparently, this was originally supposed to be a Columbus quincentennial novel, delivered too late for the anniversary. It's just as well, since it hardly constitutes a celebration of the historical Columbus's legacy; in fact, the central feature of Card's tale is an elaborate project to undo that very legacy, along with the past five centuries of Western history. Along the way, Columbus himself – despite a well-researched and probably historically defensible scenario of his life – comes across looking more and more like Ender Wiggins, and the novel turns out to be another of Card's recurrent explorations of the nature of genocide, which provided the focus not only for the Wiggins novels, but for a good part of the Alvin Maker series as well. But while in those works the notion of genocide – of an alien civilization and Native American populations, respectively – provides the background for epic tales of guilt and redemption, here the idea of wiping out the entire population of the world doesn't seem to bother Card very much at all, as long as Columbus learns his lesson.

In a future devoted to restoring and reclaiming the natural environment, a "Tempoview" machine is invented which permits researchers to view the past, but not to travel there or intercede in any way. (Oddly, such a device seems even more unlikely than a faull-scale time machine; I kept wondering about camera angles and microphone placement in these scenes of the past.) What the machine reveals is a panorama of war, slavery, extinctions, and disasters, punctuated by enormous stretches of nothing happening at all – in other words, history. This is inordinately disturbing to Tagiri, a researcher with the Pastwatch project, who comes up with the idea that history needs fixing, that "we don't justify the suffering of people in the past because everything turned out well enough by the time we came along." There are only two problems with Tagiri's idea (not counting the fact, unnoticed by everyone else in the story, that it's hopelessly wacky and immature): the Tempoview machine permits no intercession in the past, and even if it did, changing the past would obliterate the entire modern world and everyone in it. Card rejects the "many worlds" view which has become almost standard in time travel tales of the past several years, and instead sets up a straightforward us-or-them dilemma: we can possibly eliminate 500 years of human misery, but at the certain cost of eliminating our own world.

Tagiri never gets to realize her dream of fixing history, but her daughter Diko continues her research on the life of Columbus, and is eventually joined by a young Turk (really) named Kemal, who made his reputation by tracking the origins of the

Atlantis and Noah myths; and by Hunahpu, a Mexican whose goal is to discover how Mesoamerican cultures might have developed had Columbus never arrived. (Card's little side stories about Kemal's and Hunahpu's discoveries suggest that his Tempoview machine might have generated an enjoyable series of clever short stories about origins of myths and legends.) When evidence is found indicating that Columbus's decision to sail west was influenced by time travelers from another future (suggesting that alternate time tracks may exist after all – although Card doesn't deal with this inconsistency), it becomes apparent that the past can be altered, and in almost no time the three adventurers are climbing into one-way time machines on a mission to pre-empt all the bad stuff of the last half-millenium. Astonishingly, no one back home seems seriously bothered by the fact that their entire world is about to be retroactively obliterated. Diko's task is to change Columbus's racism and imperialism, Kemal's is to prevent his ships from being able to return to Spain, and Hunahpu's is to reform the Zapotec cultures away from blood sacrifice and teach them metallurgy to even the playing field against the Europeans. This is not your standard Hardy Boys assignment. If the plan goes well, these plucky chums will bring into being a far, far better place than we've ever seen – although why they are so convinced that their hypothetical world will actually come to pass is never quite clear. The view of history here is so deterministic that it makes Asimov's psychohistory look like random violence.

That kind of determinism can be disturbing in the hands of a skilled storyteller like Card, whose works have come increasingly to reflect an absolute moral certainty and absolute faith in the results of actions based on that certainty. As might be expected, Pastwatch is readable and engaging, full of likeable heroes and unmistakeable villains, but at center it's an epic of self-justification, an oddball critique of America as a failed utopia that seems to draw on many of the same ideas as Card's better story "America." The idea that the right idea, the right machine, and a total lack of self-doubt will enable you to replace the world with one more to your liking seems to me a far more chilling disaster than the maimed history Card's self-appointed gods set out to replace.

What's wrong with Robert Reed? Here is a talented author with a reputation for never doing the same thing twice (which by itself may have cost him the brand-name identity that publishers cherish and many readers crave) and with a sense of place and time almost unequalled among modern SF writers, but who always seems just on the verge of fulfilling his considerable promise. There are enough similarities between his new novel **An Exaltation of Larks** and his previous one, *Beyond the Veil of Stars*, to suggest that he's following a coherent line of thought: both novels excel at vividly convincing settings and characters; both use these settings as springboards into huge perspectives of space and time; both turn into spaghetti just when they should be turning into dynamite. Reed may be one of only a handful of SF writers (Clifford Simak is perhaps the most notable) who can consistently write believable backyards — domestic settings that are more than stage flats for the big adventures to come (no one really cares about the backyard where Richard Seaton builds his spaceship, since it's only a cursory emblem of the here and now, but in Simak and Reed we know it has its own dignity). Reed evokes his Carter-era campus town with a realistic sensibility worthy of a Joyce Carol Oates, but when the turtles arrive from the far future to reinvent the cosmos, there's a sense that we're losing more than we're gaining; Reed's here and now is more interesting and compelling than his unfolding cosmic battleground.

Much the same was true of Reed's *Beyond the Veil of Stars*, another novel which thrust complex and sympathetic characters unwittingly into a cosmic spectacle. That novel very nearly broke in half under the strain, with the two halves divided by a distractingly spectacular image of an inverted sky. *An Exaltation of Larks* handles the transition much more smoothly and successfully. As the novel opens, Jesse Aylesworth is distributing copies of the college newspaper he edits containing an expose that will almost certainly lead to the college president's resignation. He is aided by Sully Faulkner, a fellow senior whom he has barely noticed before but who seems passionately attracted to him, and who will soon emerge as far more than she at first seems. Odd incidents begin to mount up: an aging turtle is stolen from the college's science lab, a mysterious Indian appears with surprisingly intimate knowledge of Jesse's life, communications with the outside world are virtually cut off by what everyone unquestioningly accepts as sunspot activity.

Finally, the old Indian, who calls himself the Turtle, "a sophisticated post-organic life form," begins to offer explanations which at first sound as cryptic as those of Alice's mock turtle. Certain select vertebrates, Jesse among them, have been chosen by travelers from the end of time for a kind of mystical transformation, which will not only grant them a kind of immortality but will make them players in an ongoing struggle to redefine the very nature of time through selective alterations in the past. The awakening to this new, fuller life — suggested by the novel's title and by allusions to a sentimental French painting called "The Song of the Lark" — affects animals as well as people, and moral purity has nothing to do with being selected; even the corrupt college president is among the elect. As all these characters learn they have only a few days to live in "our" history, and as Jesse comes to terms with the implications of his new role as a budding Calvinistic time-lord, he finds he must deal with his real past and real relationships as well, and Reed handles these scenes with insight and acute observation. The cosmic promises held out by the "turtles" and their battles for control of destiny never quite take on the dramatic immediacy of, for example, Jesse's final meeting with his parents, or even of such small but elegant set-pieces as Jesse following Sully *into* the painted landscape of "The Song of the Lark." Reed is wonderful at nuances and miniatures, and he's sincerely interested in developing large-scale SF ideas, but he's basically a first-rate observer trying too hard to be a visionary. If you're setting out to knock us for a Stapledonian loop, you'd better produce something more than Turtle Men from the End of Time.

Scott Bradfield deserves a lot of credit for simply undertaking a satirical fantasy about a revolt of the animals; Orwell's *Animal Farm* is one of the most widely read of all fantasy satires – it's even made it into high schools – and is many people's idea of just how such fantasy ought to be done. But a case could be made that Orwell's work is far from seminal, and that in fact it represents a very late entry in a very old tradition of animal fables. His satirical focus is political rather than cultural, and the traits he ascribes to his barnyard characters are based solidly in longstanding literary tradition – the sheep as conformists, for example, or the horse as steadfast and dependable. Both satires and animal tales have come a long way since Orwell; the former have grown more diffuse, more bleak, and less corrective, while the latter have begun to pay at least some attention to real-life ethology. Richard Adams's rabbits or William Horwood's moles are genuine alien societies compared to Orwell's denatured emblems, and have helped elevate the stakes for modern animal tales.

So what can Bradfield add to this tradition? His use of animals is probably closer to Orwell than to Adams or Horwood, but his wisecracking crows and penguins, love-starved gorilla, and rabble-rousing wildebeest are more likely to call to mind the hip neo-Disney cartoon figures from *Aladdin* or *The Lion King* than any literary precedents. But despite their sarcastic tongues, the animals remain charmingly innocent, giving the overall novel the odd flavor of a hardboiled Kenneth Grahame. Bradfield's satire, on the other hand, is far less pointed than Orwell's, and too often strives for the manic shotgun effects of Mark Leyner or T. Corragheson Boyle: talk shows, pop therapists, the military, image consultants, Princess Di – the usual round of easy targets. What makes it all almost work is Bradfield's episodic but rapid-fire narrative, which opens with an animal revolt at London Zoo incited by Charlie the Crow and follows the subsequent spread of the revolution and the various adventures of zoo escapees. One of the most entertaining plot lines involves Wanda the Gorilla, who gets work as an underpaid (and sexually exploited) au pair in Manhattan while trying to sustain the life of a Cosmo girl, despite her obvious shortcomings. Bradfield, who animal stories have appeared in volumes of *The Year's Best Fantasy and Horror* and whose first novel was the impressive *History of Luminous Motion*, is a fiercely entertaining writer, and **Animal Planet** is never dull and is often hilarious, even as it leaves an aftertaste of trendy slickness and facile cynicism.

The blurb on the new Orb edition of Jack Williamson's **The Humanoids** describes it as a "Golden Age classic, back in print after many years." No argument that it's a classic, and "Golden Age" can mean anything you want it to, but what I'm curious about is the "after many years" part. I don't know how many years are meant – there was a fancy Easton Press edition not too long ago – but it certainly seems like Williamson's most famous novel is less frequently available these days, and that this is a fate common to many SF classics. Checking an old Williamson bibliography, I find that *The Humanoids* went through more than a dozen English-language editions in the first twenty-five years of its history. Almost anyone who began reading SF during those years would sooner or later come across it in a new edition, and it was these regular reprints almost as much as the influence and quality of the works themselves that helped create the informal canon of classics that all of us of a certain age grew up with. Unlike mainstream classics, which usually get segregated into "literature" sections so that no one can accidentally mistake them for Sidney Sheldon, SF classics have always had to compete with the latest titles, earning their right to stay in print on the open market. Needless to say, some classics get lost in the shuffle.

All of which is a roundabout way to congratulate Orb on bringing *The Humanoids* back into print, no matter how many years it's been. The next, and probably more pertinent question, is how well the 1949 novel, and the earlier story "With Folded Hands," hold up after nearly half a century. For the most part, I think they both still work surprisingly well, although I continue to prefer the story over the novel. "With Folded Hands" seems to be an almost perfect realization of its premise, which has less to do with machines taking over than with the conflicting imperatives of freedom and civilization; the humanoid motto is "To Serve and Obey, and Guard Men from Harm," but it's soon clear that they interpret this to mean something like "to insure domestic tranquillity," and they're willing to lobotomize people to do it. It's a nightmare parable that doesn't lose its punch or its timeliness: when it first appeared it reflected the dark side of postwar suburban prosperity; today it reads like the latest Newt Gingrich welfare proposal.

The Humanoids is another matter, and has been the subject of a good deal of debate, particularly regarding its ending. As is well known by now, John W. Campbell was largely responsible for persuading Williamson to write a sequel to "With Folded Hands," and this happened at the same time Campbell was getting mired down in various forms of "psi" phenomena (he was only a year or so away from dianetics). The result is a novel that recapitulates much of the basic situation of the story (although with a different setting and characters), but that takes an oddball turn toward the psychic — the idea being that if people are saved from all physical work, they can develop powers of mind into something called "psychophysics." It's this sort of thing that dates the work, along with the equally bogus science of "rhodomagnetics" and some deliciously overripe Jimmy Stewart dialogue: "I'm going to fight the machines for a better deal — to give every man, everywhere, the same freedom a few of you have sold us out to get".

But it's that very Capraesque innocence that has led many readers of *The Humanoids* to overlook Williamson's sly sense of irony, which informs the novel at several levels and, far from dating it, often shows it to be ahead of its time. Even lines like the one above may turn out to have an unexpected spin; when Williamson writes "She yielded then, as gracefully as she could, to his more urgent passion," he knows it's twaddle — but in this case "his more urgent passion" is getting back to the observatory to watch a supernova, scrapping a romantic picnic in the process.

The irony works at more complex levels as well: Clay Forester is certainly a moody and ambiguous hero, just as Frank Ironside is a puzzling and often sympathetic antagonist. The boldest stroke is the novel's ending, which (and here I warn those who haven't read the novel that I'm giving something away) has either seemed a failed attempt at a reversal in which the humanoids turn out not so bad after all, or a subtle portrayal of a bleak "utopia" of brainwashed victims. Williamson finally made it clear in his 1984 autobiography which interpretation of the ending is the intended one, and in retrospect it's hard to see how we could read it any other way. Now we can see how the novel anticipates the paranoid universes of Philip K. Dick, and undermines the assignment given to Williamson by Campbell. *The Humanoids* may well represent one of the crucial turning points in SF, as Campbell's faith in problem-solving began to give way to more darkly visionary works that recognized genuine human dilemmas.

– February 1996, Locus #421 –

Blue Mars ~~ Kim Stanley Robinson

The Bones of Time ~~ Kathleen Ann Goonan

A Case of Conscience ~~ James Blish

A bit more than halfway through Kim Stanley Robinson's **Blue Mars**, the third and presumably final volume in his stunningly ambitious series on the colonial and postcolonial future history of the Red Planet, we find Sax Russell – one of our old acquaintances from the first two novels – reading a "dense multi-volumed analytical metahistory" by a Martian historian seeking to establish a "master narrative" to explain the sudden wholesale expansion of human colonies throughout the solar system. By this point, we are well into the second century of Martian settlement; Mars has hammered out a constitution and elected its first president (another old friend, Nadia), and major tensions are emerging not only between Mars and an overpopulated and ecologically devastated earth, but between the younger Mars-born nissei and the older issei – which includes the surviving members of the First Hundred settlers, whose tale has been the basis of Robinson's entire epic. There are plenty of episodes in *Blue Mars* that are far more dramatic than a character reading a theory of history, but in many ways this brief passage seems to encapsulate Robinson's own larger agenda – not only in his Mars novels, but in his earlier "Orange County" trilogy and much of his short fiction as well. Unlike the future histories of Asimov or Heinlein, Robinson's master narrative is neither a recapitulation of past imperialisms nor an extension of the industrial revolution; unlike the trendy post-cyberpunk vision of a future spiraling downward into unmanageable terrorist-ridden chaos (as in John Barnes's *Kaleidoscope Century*), Robinson's vision is at heart genuinely utopian. He may be one of SF's last believers in liberal rationalism as the road toward a society which, if not ideal, is at least pretty good.

On the other hand, he's no George McGovern. Even though he describes in some detail an attractive-sounding government in which economic policy is subordinate to ecological management, it quickly becomes clear that any government is to some degree ineffectual, and that the terraforming process set in motion by earlier capitalist interests is not quite reversible. For all his interest in government and politics, Robinson turns into a pure hard-SF writer when it comes to such issues as soil chemistry or meteorology, and his sophisticated handling of these areological issues underlines the theme – perhaps the dominant one in his entire trilogy – that living in a world entails compromises between adapting to it and changing it. Mars may have achieved a stable government by the end of the trilogy – an approach to the era of "general good will" that Robinson's fictional historian describes – but the rest of humanity is ambitiously seeking to find ways of living on Mercury, Venus, satellites of the outer planets, and even nearby star systems. This diaspora (sometimes called "accelerando," in what could become a textbook example of why musical metaphors don't work) carries clear echoes of the "consensus cosmogony" that Donald Wollheim once described as the master narrative of golden age SF, but in Robinson's hands it is far more dialectical and less linear, and as tragic as it is heroic.

The third volume of a continuous narrative always raises the question of whether the overall series is a single enormous novel (as in Wolfe's *Book of the New Sun*) or a trilogy (as in Robinson's own Orange County series). The plot of *Blue Mars* is both more ambitious and more episodic than those of the first two novels, and it tends to dissipate rather than conclude – as though what Robinson has been up to all along is less a tightly structured fiction than a grand meditation on world-building, enhanced by drama (utopian writing has always had trouble with the form of the novel, since it needs spokespersons more than characters). Once again the major viewpoint characters are Ann Clayborne, Sax Russell, Michel Duval, Maya Toitovna, and other survivors from that militantly multicultural First Hundred, all now entering their second or third centuries of extended life, all finding themselves turning into the stuff of legend as Martian history enters its mythmaking phase. (John Boone, the leader from Red Mars, is already a near-mythical figure, and the elusive Hiroko is fast becoming one.) With this many characters and such an ambitious agenda, Robinson might well have been tempted to extend the Mars series into half a dozen novels, exploring different aspects of the evolving society. Before *Blue Mars* is over, he comes pretty close to doing that anyway.

Each of the fourteen chapters follows a major character through a major plot sequence; like an historical text, the novel builds through the cumulative weight of these sequences rather than through a single narrative arc. Ann dissuades "ecoteurs" from trying to destroy the space elevator that brings earthlings to Mars (it had already been destroyed once, earlier in the series) and negotiates the shutdown of the "soletta" that brings magnified sunlight to the planet, resulting in a mini ice age that places limits on development. Michel and Hirgal visit an earth devastated by a rise in ocean levels (some of the sequences here recall Robinson's story "Venice Drowned"), where Michel falls in love again with his native Provence and Nirgal tracks down rumors of sightings of his elusive mother Hiroko. Nadia becomes the first president of Mars and faces problems ranging from currency design to criminal justice systems to soil policy. Meanwhile, the newer generation is represented largely by John Boone's descendant Zoya Boone, who visits settlements on Mercury and the Uranian moon Miranda on political missions for her mother Jackie (who eventually takes her political ambitions on an interstellar mission to Aldebaran). Sax, noting his own failing memory and that of Maya, undertakes extended research into brain chemistry to find out if there are mental limits built into the life extension treatments. And of course eventually, inevitably, some of the oldtimers who have carried us through all three volumes begin to die off, in episodes that will be especially moving for readers who have followed the whole series.

Robinson is one of the most conscientious SF writers alive, and every one of these episodes is developed as thoroughly as if it were the whole of the novel, both in terms of the science and engineering problems and of character development. For some readers, this degree of thoroughness may come across as obsessive-compulsive storytelling, as Robinson is willing to let everything else grind to a halt while he explains the possible mechanics of Venusian terraforming or the neurobiology of memory. He is as much an explainer as Asimov, and is equally charming in his unequivocal fascination with what he is explaining – and his own brilliance at getting it right. This may not do much for tightness of structure or traditional suspense, and may put something of a strain on the assiduous credibility that has been the hallmark of the series – it's frankly hard to accept a Mars this thoroughly transformed after only a couple of centuries – but it makes for an entertaining grand tour of a 22nd century solar system as busy and industrious as anything from Campbell's *Astounding*. *Blue Mars* not only extends the most important work of Mars fiction in recent years, but also offers a pretty good Mercury story, an Earth-based ecological catastrophe tale, and a believable saga of the colonization of the other planets. It's a wonderful showpiece epic for Robinson's fertile imagination, even if at times it reads more like a subscription than a novel.

In keeping with my unproven theory that a writer's second novel always tells us more than the first about what their career will eventually look like, Kathleen Ann Goonan has produced a somewhat more subdued followup to the nanotech fireworks of 1994's *Queen City Jazz*. *The Bones of Time* (an unfortunate title that suggests a young-adult archeology text) includes a bit of biological nanotech (called "bionan"), but for the most part heads off into new directions. Instead of a transmogrified Cincinnati, we get a near future Hawaii which has been virtually taken over by a corrupt metanational corporation called Interspace, which is involved in a vast multifaceted project to build a generation starship. Lynn Oshima, whose family is deeply involved with Interspace's shady deals, comes to suspect that the whole starship business is a cruel and even inhuman hoax, and comes in contact with the organization's only real opposition, the Homeland Movement. A powerful symbolic figure for this movement is the Hawaiian King Kamehameha, and Lynn is convinced she's seen a young man who is Kamehameha's clone – even though human cloning is illegal.

In a parallel story set 27 years earlier, a young Honolulu street tough named Cen Kalakaua – who turns out to be a mathematical prodigy of enormous importance – also thinks he sees a figure from the past, a girl claiming to be Kaiulani, the last heir to the Hawaiian throne who had died in 1899. The more Cen becomes convinced that this is the real Kaiulani, somehow shifted in time to his own world of 2007, the more he becomes intrigued by the cosmological equations that might make such a shift possible. Sponsored by a University of Hawaii professor, he begins to develop a set of mathematical proofs which not only demonstrate, but actually enable, a direct interface between mind and quantum reality. With its echoes of a Richard Matheson time-bending romance, Cen's story is a touching fable of personal redemption and the at least symbolic reclamation of Hawaii's past.

Meanwhile, back up in 2034, Cen's equations, along with the bones of Kamehameha himself – not only the source of the illegal clones, but a symbol of mystic power to the native Hawaiians – become key elements in the growing struggle between Interspace and the Homeland Movement, with Lynn more or less caught in the middle. Although Goonan introduces some large-scale ideas about quantum reality, her special effects here are restrained, and the novel finally stands or falls on how well we accept the characters, particularly Lynn's struggles with her heritage and Cen's lovesick brilliance, and the distinctive Hawaiian setting. I think she succeeds on both counts, and offers a quietly moving novel that touches upon both history and hard science, even though some fans of *Queen City Jazz* will find this relatively muted and reflective.

Last month, we had a chance to look at a reissue of Jack Williamson's classic *The Humanoids*, in part to see how well it stands up today (pretty well) and in part to give deserved recognition to those publishers who are willing to make such works available to a newer audience. I don't know how long James Blish's **A Case of Conscience** had been out of print prior to the current Del Rey reissue, but I have the impression that Blish – who died in 1975 – has not been having a particularly stellar posthumous career. His criticism is still required reading for critics and historians of the field, and a handful of his stories (most notably "Common Time") still show up with some regularity, but even his galactic epic *Cities in Flight* – with its Spenglerian answer to Asimov's Gibbon and its wonderfully cataclysmic finale – seems to fade from discussions of the genre's masterworks. *A Case of Conscience*, which seemed downright controversial when it first appeared in book form in 1958, well on its way to becoming an instant classic, has faded even more. Has it dated badly, or was it just a weaker novel than it seemed?

Neither, although the particular *ways* in which the novel has become dated may confuse some modern readers. I'm not referring so much to the handful of 1950s absurdities scattered through the book — an earth civilization driven underground by the mania for bomb shelters is the most glaring — but to the character of Blish's protagonist, a Peruvian priest named Father Ruiz-Sanchez. Sanchez is a scientist-priest perhaps loosely modeled on Teilhard de Chardin, but with the monochromatic theology of William Peter Blatty's Exorcist. With simple-minded ease, he concludes that the edenic society of the lizard-people of the planet Lithia — no crime, no art, no religion, no stress — must be a work of Satan, tempting earthlings away from Christ and undermining the authority of the church. Part of the problem isn't Blish's fault; just about all pre-Vatican II portrayals of a future Catholic Church saw it as a convenient emblem of medieval ritual to set against scientific progress, and Blish's tortured priest is a far cry from the kindly old padres who came to represent unblemished morality in much 50s SF. Part of it might have been thought through a bit better: Lithia may be a utopia, but hey, they're all *lizards* down there, and who ever saw a stressed-out lizard anyway? But as a whole, the novel is brilliantly structured, counterpointing Ruiz-Sanchez's ethical dilemma not only with that of a militarist who wants to turn the whole planet into a nuclear storage facility, but with his own struggles to make sense of Joyce's *Finnegans Wake*, and with the struggles of a Lithian who becomes a revolutionary leader on earth. If you have not read *A Case of Conscience*, I assure you that it is not at all what you expect; it is not The *Thorn Birds* in space; and it is not at all like anything by C.S. Lewis.

– March 1996, Locus #422 –

Bellwether ~~ Connie Willis

The Secret of this Book ~~ Brian Aldiss

Nebula Awards 30: SFWA's Choices for the Best Science Fiction and Fantasy of the Year ~~ edited by Pamela Sargent

Richter 10 ~~ Arthur C. Clarke and Mike McQuay

Shadow of Ashland ~~ Terence M. Green

Wildside ~~ Steven Gould

Microcosmic God: The Complete Stories of Theodore Sturgeon, Vol II ~~ edited by Paul Williams, foreword by Samuel R. Delany

I've recently begun wondering exactly what the thinking was back in 1960 when John W. Campbell, Jr. changed the title of *Astounding Science Fiction* to *Analog Science Fact/Science Fiction* (actually, instead of a slashmark, he originally used an unpronounceable little glyph he had invented, supposedly meaning "is analogous to" and incidentally anticipating The Artist Formerly Known as Prince by some three decades; who says Campbell wasn't ahead of his time?) Two things have bothered me about this title change. One is the awkward and redundant back-formation "science fact," a phrase which surely would never have come into common usage if it hadn't been for the term "science fiction" and the perceived need on someone's (possibly Campbell's) part for an unambiguous signpost to aid those readers otherwise unable to distinguish the writings of Sir Isaac Newton from, say, those of Doc Smith. The other problem, more to the point here, is the term "analog" itself, and the implied argument that science fact is analogous to science fiction, a fuzzy proposition if I ever heard one, and one that may have helped fatally weaken the magazine as readers were confronted with stories which, once astounding, were now merely analogous. A further problem is that the stories, for the most part, weren't analogous to science fact or anything else; the kinds of nuts-and-bolts fiction historically championed by ASF simply used scientific notions as background or plot elements in otherwise conventional, if often ingenious, stories. The relationship of science and fiction was one of content to form, not of one form to another, as "analog" would imply.

But that doesn't mean the term ought to be thrown out altogether. There really is a kind of analog science fiction, and it has nothing to do with Campbell at all. It has to do with Connie Willis.

Unlikely as it may seem, what started this whole line of thought was Willis's rather modest but very funny novella **Bellwether**, the third in a series of novellas-as-books that began with *Uncharted Territory* (1994) and continued with *Remake* (1995). As with those stories, Willis seems to take her main inspiration from romantic screwball comedies – her diamond-in-the-rough scientist Bennett O'Reilly here is virtually Cary Grant's character from *Bringing up Baby* – but here she also makes a point of foregrounding the conceptual vocabulary of science, from the history of scientific discoveries to modern chaos theory. The model here is Willis's 1989 story "At the Rialto," which gained much of its humor from the collision of frames of reference (to use Arthur Koestler's terms) from theoretical physics and Hollywood glitz. Like that story, and like much of Willis's best humor, *Bellwether* juxtaposes unlikely worlds – a trend-crazed corporate culture, research into the origins of fads, and communication and chaos theories. When she succeeds, she not only gets good jokes out of her material, but builds a sustained conceit that all these worlds actually exist in analogous relations with one another.

And this brings us back to the notion of analog science fiction – fiction that works not by traditional SF means, but by setting up fictional analogs of "science fact." By the standards of Campbell's magazine, "At the Rialto" isn't SF at all, and neither is *Bellwether* (although it might just make it, thanks to its ending). Neither, for that matter is Pamela Zoline's "Heat Death of the Universe," one of the archetypes of this kind of science-fiction-by-analog, or Willis's dense "Schwarzchild Radius," or much of the short fiction of Kim Stanley Robinson and other current writers. In the case of *Bellwether*, Willis concocts an ingenious system of analogs in the tale of Sandra Foster, a statistician employed by the HiTek Corporation to study fads (such as hair-bobbing in the 1920s). The idea is that if Foster can discover what triggers a fad, the corporation can not only anticipate new fads, but create them. Foster is plagued by an incompetent and fatally trendy office assistant named Flip, and increasingly fascinated with an apparently trend-immune chaos scientist named O'Reilly, who's studying information diffusion in animal groups. Meanwhile, management shanghais employees for one sensitivity seminar after another, Foster's colleagues debate this week's dogma in child-rearing or dating, and Foster herself fights with the local library over its policy of removing books that aren't checked out often enough (such as Browning, whose "Pied Piper" and "Pippa Passes" serve as leitmotifs).

Simply as a lark, or as a compendium of trivia (each chapter begins with a brief account of a different fad), *Bellwether* is a lot of fun, and doesn't demand a great deal of the reader; her use of chaos theory is attractively oversimplified in the same way entropy or indeterminacy have been by other writers for decades. But by pointing out (or inventing) structural parallels between everything from library policies to social trends to information diffusion theory, she's undertaking something much more particular than the simple metaphorical use of scientific concepts. All this may be a lot of baggage to load on a story which in many ways seems a piece of fluff, but that's exactly what makes it significant: Willis is among SF's most popular and accessible writers, and when she adapts one of SF's more interesting literary techniques to lighthearted comedy, we can see the possibilities expanding before our eyes.

Brian Aldiss is an author who has made a career of showing us such expanding possibilities, and in his recent work it has become almost impossible, if not pointless, to find the lines that separate fable, memoir, fantasy, and science fiction. It's equally pointless to discuss **The Secret of this Book** solely in terms of SF or fantasy or mainstream fiction, since to do so would lead to the worst sort of backseat driving ("Stay in your lane, Brian, you drifted into SF again there") and would miss the whole point of what Aldiss seems to be up to. Earlier in his career, we had no trouble telling Aldiss mainstream from Aldiss SF, except for a few oddities like *Report on Probability A* and some strange short pieces called "enigmas." Then important discussions of the role of fantasy and SF began to show up in mainstream novels like the "Squire Quartet," and contemporary political and social observation began to appear in novels with SF elements, like 1994's *Somewhere East of Life. The Secret of this Book*, subtitled "20-Odd Stories," is a collection of stories, playlets, "enigmas," memoirs, and commentary, sometimes connected in surprising ways, and veering with disarming ease all over the literary map.

It's a commonplace that great writers at a certain stage in their careers turn their passions into fables – Shakespeare's *The Tempest*, Faulkner's *A Fable*, etc. – and Aldiss's passions are everywhere in evidence here. Art and drama show up repeatedly, for example. In "Common Clay," a defiantly unsuccessful painter in Geneva loses his one chance at romance when she suggests he turn to popular art. An equally defiant Gauguin, visited in the Hereafter by a man "of common clay" in "That Particular Green of Obsequies," insists he has become a Neanderthal. "A Swedish Birthday Present" turns out to be a set of watercolors purchased by an unhappy husband for an elegant woman he's infatuated with, in hope that she will recognize a kindred spirit. An artist in a decadent media-drenched future performs – once – by decapitating himself in "Headless." Aldiss rethinks Shakespeare's Caliban in a short play, and Hamlet in the hilarious "If Hamlet's Uncle Had Been a Nicer Guy," in which we learn, among other things, that much of Hamlet's bad mood had to do with the fact that he was dieting. Sophocles also gets reconsidered in "A Dream of Antigone," in which a condemned prisoner dreams he enters her tale (this also has moments of humor, as when the prisoner, Joe Moone – who has only had Freud to read in his cell – explains to Creon that he is "acting out the inflexible male principle").

"A Dream of Antigone" (one of the best pieces in the book) also shows the various ways in which Aldiss has wired up these pieces to create something more than a story collection. The condemned dreamer, Joe Moone, is first introduced in the preceding story, "On the Inland Sea," which in turn is one of three "enigmas" about characters named Moon (the first two, which are SF stories, also take place on moons). The wife in "A Swedish Birthday Present" is reading a book of stories about Bosnia, and "The Mistakes, Miseries, and Misfortunes of Mankind" might well be one of the stories she's reading. It also is one of two stories that reflect the harrowing degradations of collapsing societies; the other, "Horse Meat," may be one of the most brutal stories Aldiss has written. Elsewhere, Aldiss describes a contest he invented for

50-word stories, then takes one of his own examples and expands it into "How the Gates Opened and Closed," which also becomes a commentary on stories in which not much happens, which leads to — well, you get the idea. The overall effect is a little like a mythological tapestry of modern Europe, from the invented (and quite contemporary) Greek legend "The God Who Slept with Women" to the Scandinavian fairy tale "Traveller, Traveller, Seek Your Wife in the Forests of This Life," from the horrors of Bosnia to a moving anecdote of dying parents. Fantasy and science fiction fit so comfortably into this mixture that it's hardly worth asking which of these tales belong in the genre and which don't, and it seems to me that this is exactly where Aldiss ought to be in his career. It's where SF ought to be in *its* career, too, only it isn't.

So where *is* SF in its career? One of the standard bellwethers is the annual *Nebula Awards* anthology, this year edited by Pamela Sargent, whose considerable editing skills also gave us last year's updated *Women of Wonder* collections. Despite some inevitable overlap with Dozois (three stories appear in both **Nebula Awards 30** and Dozois's 12th annual *Year's Best Science Fiction*), the Nebula volumes offer a somewhat less personal, but not quite official representation of the state of science fiction during the year (which in this case is 1994). Guided but not entirely limited by the Nebula Awards ballots, Sargent has included all the nominated short stories (plus one from 1994 Grand Master Damon Knight), two of the six nominated novelettes, and one of six nominated novellas. To this mix she has added a novelette-length excerpt from Greg Bear's winning novel *Moving Mars*, a tribute to Robert Bloch by Frank M. Robinson, a selection of Rhysling Award-winning poems, a survey of 1994 films by Kathi Maio, and a "symposium" (which means a bunch of short essays) with contributions by John Kessel, Nicola Griffith, Paul Di Filippo, Jack Dann, Sheila Finch, Pat Murphy, and James Gunn. Intended as an overview of the year in SF, the symposium also demonstrates, better even than our annual *Locus* wrapups, the principle that no two blind men can step in the same elephant twice (or whatever). Although it provides a more coherent overview, Kathi Maio's review of 1994 films seems the most dated piece in the book, and only underlines how different the world of fantasy and SF film is from the world of fantasy and SF.

Generally, I'm opposed to novel excerpts in anthologies such as this — people ought to either read the novel or not — but the excerpt from *Moving Mars* is sufficiently independent to have been published originally as a separate novella, and conveys a good deal of the odd power of Bear's novel without leaving you hanging. Of the other addenda, the three excellent Rhysling Award-winning poems — by W. Gregory Stewart and Robert Frazier, Jeff Vandermeer, and Bruce Boston — will come as a pleasant surprise to readers whose experience with SF poetry is limited to Asimov limericks and horrible Robert W. Service-style space ditties. The Robinson tribute to Bloch seems to me an entirely appropriate sort of piece for a book such as this, a reminder of what is lost as well as what is gained in the year being celebrated.

The short fiction is highlighted by familiar names, most of them showing considerable mastery of technique but breaking little new ground conceptually. "Seven Views of Olduvai Gorge" may be Mike Resnick's best story to date, but it returns to the familiar alien-excavation-of-earth-theme and ends with a direct echo of A.E. Van Vogt's "The Monster." Joe Haldeman acknowledges that his "None So Blind" was a story waiting to be written – with so much of their brain capacity freed up from visual processing, why don't blind people become geniuses? – but his handling of it in a tale of a brilliant nerd and a blind musical prodigy raises far more complex questions than the simple premise implies (has anyone noticed that Haldeman, despite his reputation as SF's official vet, has become its most eloquent explorer of the artistic impulse?) Damon Knight's "Fortyday" also explores one of those waiting-to-be-written ideas: what if growth reversed at age forty? Kate Wilhelm's "I Know What You're Thinking," the best-crafted tale in the book, takes one of the genre's oldest saws, the alienation of the lone telepath, and makes it new in a thoroughly convincing portrait of a crumbling marriage. Le Guin's "The Matter of Seggri" revisits gender roles in a way that makes her own pioneering *The Left Hand of Darkness* seem almost tentative. And Barry Malzberg's "Understanding Entropy" – the purest example in the book of what I earlier called "analog science fiction" – is a classic Malzberg parable of fate and entrapment.

Those stories that address more recent trends in SF include Ben Bova's "Inspiration," a rearranged-history tale which contrives to bring Einstein, Wells, and Lord Kelvin together, alkong with a twist ending which changes the whole spin of the story. Maureen McHugh handles the almost obligatory VR tale well enough in "Virtual Love," but the imaginative conservatism of the story reflects its origins as a piece conceived for a non-SF audience. Martha Soukup's "A Defense of the Social Contracts" reflects the utopian themes that SF has returned to recently (led perhaps by Kim Stanley Robinson), but seems uncomfortably close to *Nineteen Eighty-Four* in its resolution. Finally, David Gerrold's "The Martian Child" is about the most personal tale we've seen from Gerrold, a moving exploration of parenthood that nearly erases the distance between author and narrator, as well as between mainstream and SF. It's a fitting capstone to a collection distinguished more by the variety and excellence of its writing than by literary innovation.

I suppose if Arthur C. Clarke decided to write a novel about the future of automobile airbags, folks would snap it up, because everyone knows that Clarke has all the inside dope on the future. Because of his iconic status, his scenarios carry a kind of authority matched by no other writer, and even though he may have a visionary soul, it's the nuts-and-bolts credibility of his futures that get him syndicated TV shows and commissions from *Time* magazine. So if Clarke says, as he seems to in **Richter 10**, that California really is going to fall into the ocean, you can bet that some readers will start seriously thinking about cornering the surfboard markets in Phoenix. But in fact Clarke's contribution to *Richter 10* was no more than a thousand-word outline, which was developed into a novel by Mike McQuay shortly before his premature death last May. (Clarke had announced that his original outline would appear as an appendix to the book, but it doesn't show up in the bound proofs.) Despite Bantam's sales pitch that this is "vintage Arthur C. Clarke," it isn't, and it would be a shame if McQuay's final work — ironically marking his return to SF after nearly a decade of mixed success in other areas — should be eclipsed by Bantam's easy marketing strategy. McQuay deserves better, and his novel, though flawed, is far more interesting than the Irwin Allen disaster epic you might expect from the title.

Richter 10 is essentially *Magnificent Obsession* with magma. Its protagonist, Lewis Crane, is orphaned by the 1994 Norridge, California quake. A little like Batman, he decides to devote his life to fighting the forces that took his parents (in this case tectonic subduction rather than thuggery), and by 2024 he is already a near-legendary figure in seismology, famed not only for his skill in predicting quakes but for his foolhardy habit of sitting them out near ground zero to get better observations. With the aid of a brilliant colleague named Dan Newcombe, Newcombe's girlfriend Lanie, a trusty sidekick named Burt, and a svelte Japanese woman who, disguised as a man, becomes Vice-President of the U.S. (don't ask too many questions here; suffice to say that McQuay's version of the 21st century doesn't add up), Crane is able to gain more and more precise knowledge of where earthquakes will happen, and how they might be stopped. McQuay's way of symbolizing the speculative center of the novel is deliciously old-fashioned (and unlikely in the age of VR): a room-sized globe, modeling the earth's crust and lit up like a Christmas tree by computer feeds measuring tectonic activity. (All it needs is a Hubert Rogers illustration to complete the pulp effect.) Crane's long-range plan is to use thermo-nuclear explosions to spot-weld the tectonic plates back together, thus preventing subduction, thus preventing quakes. Needless to say, everyone thinks he's nuts.

There would seem to be a couple of inherent problems with earthquake novels. On the one hand, you've got the *Bridge of San Luis Rey* approach, in which a bunch of characters are followed through a single major disaster, with loving descriptions of ruined cities and spectacular deaths. On the other — and this is McQuay's choice — you can opt for more than one quake, and make the quakes themselves a kind of adversary. The problem here is that you have to keep topping yourself, and that strains credibility; during the four decades of the novel's main action, it seems like several centuries' worth of extraordinary earthquakes follow one another like clockwork: a giant tsunami in Japan, a New Madrid quake which rearranges the entire midwestern U.S., and of course the Big One On the Coast — all with concomitant geographical, social, and economic reorganizations. And Crane is there for every big event, a regular seismic Forrest Gump, but with the sensibility of an Ayn Rand hero.

Somehow, this unlikely tale begins to ingratiate itself in strange ways. McQuay never dwells on the sensational aspects of death and destruction, and sometimes even keeps them offstage altogether, preferring to describe their aftereffects. And as the disaster scenarios recede, the characters move to the foreground. McQuay has an unfortunate tendency to write dialogue the way Charlton Heston delivers it, but once you get past this the relationships of the principals begin to take on the dimensions of a real saga. The central struggle that emerges in the second half of the book is a moral contest between Crane and Newcombe, who has joined a Muslim breakaway state (formed in the southeastern U.S. after the New Madrid quake) and has inadvertently killed Crane's wife and child in a terrorist raid. The shifting fortunes of these two antagonists, including a Mandela-style imprisonment for one, begin to give the novel an unexpected resonance, and a surprisingly effective – and restrained – conclusion. *Richter 10* may not be at all an Arthur C. Clarke novel, it may be based on a premise that is almost doomed from the start, it may be plagued by wooden dialogue – but it has the heart of an SF epic, and holds a sad bright promise of what McQuay might have done.

Forge is so persistently flogging Terence M. Green's **Shadow of Ashland** as being "in the tradition of Jack Finney's *Time and Again*" that it got me to wondering exactly what that tradition is. Finney didn't invent the time-travel nostalgia fantasy, but he did give it bestseller (and later cult) status, and legitimized the most lame-brained mechanism of time travel yet: namely, if you act like you're in the past, and you're in the right place, you get whisked away, like Dorothy chanting "There's no place like home" or the Little Engine chanting "I think I can." Finney got away with this in several early short stories ("The Third Level," "Second Chance") and made it the centerpiece of his most famous novel, Time and Again. It also is the mechanism used by Green in *Shadow of Ashland*, which owes a debt to Finney in other ways as well – notably the haunted narrative voice that periodically interrupts the action with depressing little ruminations about how we make and unmake our own pasts, how memory works in odd ways, etc. (I suspect Finney got a lot of this, in turn, from Robert Nathan and Thornton Wilder, so maybe there's a tradition there after all.)

If Terence Green owes much to Finney, it's more likely the early Finney of the short stories than the latter-day tour guide to lost New York. There is a dark edge to the nostalgia of *Shadow of Ashland*, as Green evokes not only the past of a small-to-middling Kentucky town, but also the bitterness and desperation of footloose men trying to make ends meet during the Depression. The narrator, Leo Nolan, does not actively seek to return to the past. The action begins in Toronto, where Nolan's dying mother claims to have been visited in the hospital by her brother Jack, missing for more than fifty years. Nolan begins trying to track down his uncle, aided by nothing more than 50-year-old letters from the States. After more letters from Jack begin appearing – all mailed in 1934 but only arriving in 1984 (with no one in the post office seeming to notice) – Leo decides to trace the path that Jack had followed through depression-era America, leading eventually to Ashland, Kentucky.

By the time the novel's central time-travel episode begins, it's clear that Green is not after something as simple as warm nostalgia. Like Geoff Ryman in *Was*, he seems to share a kind of Canadian fascination with the ways in which America can dramatically fail its own citizens. Nolan finds a retired hotel owner named Stanley who not only knew his uncle Jack, but participated with him in a desperate scheme born of unemployment and bitter class resentment; even in the present, Stanley talks resentfully about the inherited wealth of Betty Hutton and the unfairnesses of capitalism. And when Leo finally manages to follow Jack back to 1934, what he finds there is far from a Finney-style glow of nostalgia, but a gloomy, angry community of unemployed workers who listen to Father Coughlin on the radio and eat twice daily at the soup kitchen. It's this edge of despair that finally sets *Shadow of Ashland* apart and gives it a distinctive power, as well as a formal elegance that more often recalls Paul Auster than Finney. Even though Green sometimes can't resist slapping you in the face with sepia-colored prose, and even though sizable chunks of his plot make no sense at all, his novel overall has to be counted a success – it works where it's supposed to, and it's genuinely evocative in the way it wants to be.

Tor has been offering some interesting young-adult titles in its general SF line (Charles Sheffield's *The Ganymede Club* was reviewed in December), and part of what makes it interesting is figuring out whether the author is working a YA angle into an SF text or vice versa. Sheffield pretty clearly followed in the hard-SF tradition of Heinlein and Benford by starting with a perfectly respectable SF scenario and then casting it into a young-adult framework. Steven Gould, whose first YA/SF novel *Jumper* won acclaim in both areas, seems more comfortable as a YA writer, at least on the basis of his second novel, **Wildside**. *Wildside* concerns a group of Texas high school graduates, complete with mixed-up romances and ill-defined ambitions, who control a gateway to an alternate world (a version of their own Texas, but unspoiled by humans), exploit it for considerable wealth (initially by selling passenger pigeons captured there, later by prospecting for gold), and get in trouble with the government, which in stories of this sort always seems to represent the dark side of the adult world.

The narrator, Charlie, is the kind of outsider who drives other kids to the prom but sits it out himself – studying his FAA manuals so he can be a pilot like his too-often-absent father. The secret that will win Charlie acceptance (not to mention sex, which Gould handles with intelligent understatement) and eventually make him a leader of his group is that his Uncle Max, who disappeared years earlier, left behind a farm which houses the gateway to the "wildside," or the other Texas. As soon as graduation is over, Charlie reveals his elaborate moneymaking plan to four schoolmates (one of whom he's secretly in love with), and introduces them to the world through the gateway. The idea of a group of kids who find a portal to another world is anything but new, and Gould even acknowledges this in a sly reference to C.S. Lewis's *Narnia* stories. But whereas Lewis – or most other SF and fantasy writers who've used this icon, including Le Guin – couldn't wait to explore the marvels of the new landscape, Gould is content to just let it sit there. The thrill of wonder at discovering the portal is quickly flattened by the realization that most of the middle part of the book is going to be a succession of mundane aviation lessons and camping problems. Occasional appearances by sabertooth tigers or dire wolves fail to make the alternate universe much more exciting than a backpack hike in Yosemite, and the ecological lesson that eventually emerges – Charlie and his pals are determined to protect this pristine world from exploitation by the government – is clouded by Charlie's own initial scheme to mine the world's resources for profit. Is the idea that it's OK for a handful of small-time entrepreneurs to exploit natural resources, but not grown-up governments?

This is why I begin to suspect that Gould is a young-adult writer playing with SF concepts. The novel opens up SF possibilities in a number of directions – particularly in terms of the alternate-world theme and the ecology theme – but by the last third, when the action finally picks up again after all those damned aviation lessons, it's turned into another black-budget paranoid fantasy, with the poor kids involved in a Waco-style standoff against renegade government agencies trying to kill them and take over. Gould's development of the changing relationships among the kids themselves is handled masterfully, and his fascination with explaining things works well at the nuts-and-bolts educational level. But the gateway itself – one of the great, can't-lose icons of wonder in the genre – is turned into little more than a macguffin. Only at the very end, when Charlie's mother reveals another family secret, does the wonder return, at least for a moment.

Last April, in reviewing the first volume in Paul Williams's ambitious effort to bring into print all of Theodore Sturgeon's short fiction, I had my doubts about the wisdom of organizing such a project chronologically; that first volume gave us some 46 stories written between 1937 and 1940, most of them undistinguished, many previously unpublished, none very likely to win new fans for Sturgeon. That opinion is unchanged by **Microcosmic God,** the second volume in the series, which includes 17 stories written between April 1940 and June 1941 and published between 1940 and 1942. This is the period of Sturgeon's emergence as a dependable Campbell writer, and all the stories appeared originally in *Unknown* or *Astounding,* except for two which were previously unpublished. Again, there are only a couple of genuine classics – the title story, "Shottle Bop," maybe "Poker Face" – but there's a great deal more vintage Sturgeon than in the first volume, and we can begin to discern the sources of his appeal, and his considerable contributions to *Unknown's* unarticulated project to invent the modern American adult fantasy genre. One of the best examples of this is "Yesterday Was Monday" (familiar to non-Sturgeon readers from its TV adaptation on the *New Twilight Zone*), in which a typically hapless Sturgeon protagonist slips out of the time stream and discovers that the world is literally a stage, rebuilt day by day. It's the kind of fantasy which establishes Sturgeon as the author, long before Philip K. Dick, who first successfully brought the ambience of Kafka into the traditions of American vernacular pulp fiction.

As quixotic a project as the Sturgeon series seems from the viewpoint of both marketing and resuscitating Sturgeon's fading reputation – a single good paperback collection would do more to bring new readers to his camp – I can't help but feel appreciative to both Paul Williams and North Atlantic Books for giving us such a chance to watch an entire career unfold. If the series survives, it will be something unique in SF publishing, as well as a valuable resource for any future Sturgeon scholars. Williams's notes on the stories are again excellent, and this second volume adds a substantial introduction by Samuel R. Delany which isolates the sources of Sturgeon's genius and locates him in an historical framework so compellingly presented that it constitutes not only one of the best pieces on Sturgeon, but one of Delany's best (and most accessible) recent critical essays. This piece alone is worth a substantial part of the cost of the volume. Of the remaining stories, a few hold up very well as examples of Sturgeon's favorite themes of transformation ("Biddiver") and alien intervention ("The Golden Egg," "Poker Face"), while others are badly dated tech-puzzles of the sort that served as *Astounding's* fillers ("The Purple Light," "Completely Automatic"). Sturgeon's overripe efforts at vernacular dialogue also date badly, and seem even more awkward in contrast with the beauty and precision of his best narrative prose. Even "Microcosmic God" itself, which remains SF's standard treatment of its theme, begins to look more and more like a tall tale as its characters and dialogue recede into cartoonishness. It's clear, even with such a masterpiece under his belt, Sturgeon was still growing as a writer, still held out the promise for greater things.

– April 1996, Locus #423 –

Pirates of the Universe ~~ Terry Bisson

None So Blind ~~ Joe Haldeman

Distress ~~ Greg Egan

Starborne ~~ Robert Silverberg

It takes a unique combination of style and substance to achieve genuine eccentricity in SF. In one sense, of course, the field is populated by almost nothing but eccentrics, and to many outsiders even an interest in SF seems an eccentricity, but there's a higher level of quirkiness that makes a handful of writers (not all of them necessarily of major importance) stand out even in a field of oddballs. Cordwainer Smith was perhaps the granddaddy of this tradition, which includes talents as diverse as David R. Bunch and R.A. Lafferty – and Terry Bisson. Bisson's unique storyteller's voice became unmistakeable a decade ago with the publication of his second novel, *Talking Man*, and really seemed to take shape with the series of short stories he began publishing in the 1990s. His last novel, *Voyage to the Red Planet*, appeared in 1990

– just as his short story career was getting underway – and the new one, **Pirates of the Universe**, echoes several of its themes, suggesting that the novel may have gotten started some time ago. As before, the action takes place in a solar system largely dominated by corporations ("Disney-Windows" here, "Disney-Gerber" in *Voyage to the Red Planet*); as before, the tale combines elements of pulpish space adventure with the distinctly elegiac tone and satirical flourishes we have come to expect in the short fiction. But it is also a work of cunning subtlety and complexity.

Sometime in the next century, following a devastating world war, mysterious alien objects called "Peteys" begin floating through the solar system, always in groups of three (shades of the Ramans!). Although no one understands their nature – they could be anything from alien beings to entire pocket universes – the highly-prized "skins" of these objects become the standard for a new economy. Gunther Ryder is a hapless Disney-Windows Ranger whose entire education seems to come from his father's collection of old National Geographics (assiduously annotated throughout the novel) and whose only goal is to qualify for residence in a live-in theme park called "Pirates of the Universe" Ryder is on a mission to harvest skins when a colleague's spacecraft disappears into a Petey. Shaken, Ryder tries to relax at Overworld, an 80-kilometer-long orbiting theme park built by Disney-Windows but largely abandoned during the war and now partly overgrown with the Tangle, a bewildering nanotech growth (originally designed as a defense during the war) with properties that distort space and time. Ryder finds that he cannot collect his e-mail or his paycheck because of something called "administrative hold," and sets out to find why. He travels to Heaven (a zero-g sector of Overworld), to Orlando on earth (with its buildings shaped like Disney figures), and finally to his family home in Morgan's Ferry, "K-T" (a disincorporated part of the U.S. where Kentucky and Tennessee once were). Here he meets his family, his girlfriend Donna, and his brother Gordon, recently escaped from prison. And he begins to learn that his life is more complicated than he had thought.

Throughout all these adventures runs a Dickian subcurrent of reality-testing involving a drug called Vitazine and the repeated mantra "It was like waking from a dream," which opens no fewer than five chapters and recurs in other variations throughout. It's clear that Bisson's surface narrative, with all its rich detail and wonderful set-piece images (such as a spaceman enlarged to a hundred feet and forever trapped in the moment of his death), is meant to be interrogated by the reader. Nearly everything in the novel is given an ironic spin, not least Ryder's own dream of living in "Pirates of the Universe" (a term which itself takes on two or three additional meanings before the novel is over). As the pulp adventure tale that the its might suggest, *Pirates of the Universe* is barely even coherent; as a multileveled commentary on how pulp dreams survive in a disintegrating reality, it's brilliant.

Joe Haldeman's new collection, **None So Blind**, his first since the NESFA Press *Vietnam and Other Alien Worlds* in 1993, is surprising both for what it includes and what it doesn't. Haldeman's beautiful recent novelette "For White Hill" isn't here, presumably because its original appearance in Gregory Benford's *Far Futures* anthology is still too current. Nor is the narrative poem "Saul's Death," which always seemed to me something of a piece with the "story poems" which are included here, especially "The Homecoming" and "DX." On the other hand, Haldeman has chosen to include the short version of "The Hemingway Hoax" (the version that won the Hugo and Nebula) even though the full novel appeared only some six years ago. Many readers preferred this somewhat tighter Asimov's version, although I was never able to detect really dramatic differences between the two. Still, it's good to have the award-winning version of a small modern SF classic in permanent form, just as it's always good to have a new collection from Haldeman, whose short fiction seems to garner awards the way Hemingway caught fish.

What interests me about *None So Blind* is that it clearly illustrates something I've been noticing about Haldeman for some time now: namely, that he seems increasingly fascinated by questions of aesthetics and artistic processes. His classic theme, Vietnam, is well represented in the collection, with the powerful horror stories "The Monster" and "Graves" ; the more SF-nal "Beachhead" and "The Cure"; and the poem "DX," which Haldeman aptly describes as one of the few pieces which can be described as both SF and autobiography at the same time (it's also probably Haldeman's most straightforward account of his own wounding in Vietnam). But it's his recurrent examination of the artist as mediator that very nearly defines the collection. The Hugo-winning title story is nominally a fictive answer to a good old-fashioned speculative query: why aren't all blind people geniuses, since they don't need to process visual information and thus should have more available brain space? But the story is also an examination of the mysteries of musical genius, as expressed through the talent of the protagonist's girlfriend Amy. Music is not the only art form Haldeman explores. "The Hemingway Hoax" is not only a complex and ingenious time-travel tale, but a deliberate *hommage* to the power of writing. Painting, and specifically watercolors, provide the basis for "Feedback," a tale which directly literalizes the artist-as-mediator by having professional artists hook their brains into those of amateurs who want to realize their own often lame visions – but who sometimes turn violent in the process. The world of theater provides the setting for "Images," a Budrys-flavored story of a shape-changing alien hiding out where shape-changing (of a sort) is what's expected. And the poem "Time Lapse" captures the humiliation and rage that might result from a young woman whose father digitizes and packages her whole youth as a 3-D video. Haldeman has a strong talent for getting near the center of artistic creation without sentimentalizing it, and without losing his hard edge. As we've a right to expect in a Haldeman collection, the stories here are tough, insightful, and crystal clear in thought and style.

The astute reviewer Russell Letson claims that **Distress** is strong evidence that Australia's Greg Egan is "one of the very best science fiction writers working today."

If Letson is right – and he is – then why, after more than a decade of provocative stories and two strong SF novels (*Quarantine* and *Permutation City*), is Egan still widely regarded in this country as an "emerging writer" whose own American publishers don't quite seem to know what to do with him. Egan's problem isn't lack of exposure – he was the first writer to have two stories in the Dozois annual for two years running – and it isn't that is work is particularly difficult or inaccessible; if anything, his science tends to be a bit oversimplified even as it's brilliantly dramatized. There is, however, a kind of grand looniness arching over all his novels, as though the young Van Vogt had gotten hold of a Benford manuscript and decided to spiff it up a bit. And there's the problem that his plots never seem to quite match his speculative set-pieces. *Distress*, in fact, is one of the few novels I've read that actually seems to lose momentum as the plot takes off. Egan has such a talent for playing with ideas that it's almost a shame he has to tell a story.

Distress begins with a horror-story episode: a murder victim's body is being temporarily revived in order that the police may interrogate it regarding the crime. The process is both painful and tragic for the disoriented victim, who at first doesn't realize he's dead; it's a textbook example of what the narrator, a video journalist named Andrew Worth, calls "frankenscience." Worth, whose body is packed with information storage and retrieval devices (he records a scene by simply looking at it) is making a documentary called "Junk DNA," which also features segments on an eccentric billionaire replacing his own and his family's DNA with an artificial analogue to guarantee their resistance to new diseases (and to starvation – he plans to snack on tires after the apocalypse); insurance companies designing "actuarial implants" that constantly monitor the wearer's activities and constantly recompute longevity; and people with slight neurological defects who seek surgery to make themselves fully autistic. While all this "frankenscience" becomes thematically important later in the plot, this opening segment also serves as a kind of Eganized version of a familiar set-piece: the grand tour, in which a naive narrator witnesses the variety and wonder of the future, in this case a mid-21st century which can achieve biomedical miracles but shows about as much common sense as Swift's Laputans.

Worth is the sort of detached observer-journalist who marriage always falls apart, and his does. Under the stress of personal crises and his work, he passes up an assignment to investigate a new plague called Distress, whose symptoms are extreme and hysterical anxiety, and instead co-opts a younger reporter's story on an international physics conference on the subject of TOES, Theories of Everything, which is being held on an artificial island called Stateless (shades of Laputa again). There he hopes to interview Violet Mosala, a brilliant young African Nobel prizewinner, but he is soon warned of what may be a plot to kill her. Who is behind it? A worldwide guerilla group called "technoliberation"? The assortment of Ignorance Cults, who range from neo-Luddites to new age airheads to militant humanists? Or an even more bizarre and cryptic organization, the Anthrocosmologists, who believe that the first person to describe a complete TOE will in fact bring the entire universe into existence, past, present, and future? And is someone trying to kill Worth himself, or at least give him a bad case of the runs?

As the action shifts to Stateless, the focus of scientific speculation shifts from biomedicine to physics, and eventually to that part of information theory that overlaps with physics. Egan rather cleverly cops a plea regarding the details of the various TOES presented by having his narrator mathematically unsophisticated, but he still presents a dazzling succession of intriguing ideas, and the real source of suspense is not so much Who's Killing the Great Physicists of Europe (or Africa) as which of these ideas Egan is going to latch onto for his resolution. The resolution, when it comes, isn't really very convincing; as in *Permutation City*, Egan gives us a glimpse of a world that we ought to find almost incomprehensible, but instead just seems bland and anticlimactic. It hardly matters. Along the way we've had enough intellectual entertainment for half a dozen novels. Egan is one of the few SF novelists who can actually make you sit still while his characters lecture one another, and one scene – a press conference in which Mosala confronts a New Age journalist – provides one of the most concise and coherent explanations of scientific rationalism I've ever read. Egan may have a bit of a problem containing his ideas within the boundaries of his plots, but he's as exciting to read as any other SF novelist around.

Robert Silverberg is another novelist who can get you to read just about anything, and he's been doing it since before Egan was born. I don't think I've ever been bored by a Silverberg story, not even those monster-movie potboilers he turned out for *Super Science Fiction*), not even by "Calvin M. Knox" and "Ivar Jorgensen." Probably the worst thing you can say about Silverberg's career since is that, even though he spectacularly transcended those early potboilers, he never entirely got rid of the pot. There are clear echoes of Ivar Jorgensen in **Starborne**, a pristinely realized *Planet Stories*-style adventure whose most intriguing mystery is why it got written in this time, in this place.

Much as I'd like to believe that there's some metatextual game going on over my head, I suspect that a major clue to the novel's attitude lies in its offstage portrayal of the jaded Earth civilization that sponsors an interstellar voyage out of sheer boredom. The population of this fat utopia is dwindling literally from lack of interest (no one wants to bother with kids, and virtual sex is far more rewarding than the sloppy kind). The hope of the race rests with fifty crewmembers and a shipload of gametes, sent forth to find new a planet where humanity can survive after Earth's population dies out. It's boredom as catastrophe – not a new idea in SF by a long shot, but one that seems increasingly to resonate with Silverberg, who's been just about everywhere and done everything in SF. Here, his ongoing re-examination of older styles (*vide* his novelizations of Asimov stories) takes him right back to the 50s. As in Heinlein's *Time for the Stars*, the ship keeps in contact with earth by means of telepathic twins (although the effects of relativity are erased in Silverberg's "nospace"). As in any number of stories from Weinbaum to Ellison, a strange psychic terror grips anyone who sets foot on the first planet they find. As in any number of other stories, the next planet is nothing but vegetation and burrowing monster. Throughout, the novel carries with it a strong sense of *déjà vu* which, to be honest, isn't all that unpleasant.

Silverberg knows enough about character by now to keep the relationships interesting even when the surface action cries out for an Emsh illustration. The "year-captain" of the starship *Wotan* (crew members are elected captain for one-year terms) reluctantly allows himself to be re-elected, develops a deep attachment to the blind telepath Noelle who serves as communication link with earth, and survives minor conspiracies (there is no villain, and little real conflict). The real crisis emerges not when the first two planets explored turn out to be unusable, but when Noelle and her sister begin to lose contact, the only link to earth. Even this is hard to get too worried about – the ship isn't returning home anyway – and the whole thing ends with what amounts to a Stapledonian smiley-face button. Silverberg handles this material about as well as anyone could, and for a handful of new readers *Starborne* might serve as a convenient introduction to the conventions of space adventure. For the rest of us, it's Silverberg Lite, colored in a faint wash of nostalgia.

– May 1996, Locus #424 –

Gibbon's Decline and Fall ~~ Sheri S. Tepper

Firestar ~~ Michael F. Flynn

Higher Education ~~ Charles Sheffield & Jerry Pournelle

War of the Worlds: Global Dispatches ~~ ed. Kevin J. Anderson

---

Time is running out. The calendar shows only a handful of years until the Big Rollover, and so far the anticipated wave of millennialist hysteria has failed to throw up anything much more entertaining than Pat Buchanan. You'd think that by now we'd be seeing some truly loony bad fiction in the tradition of Hal Lindsey's fundamentalist bestseller *The Late Great Planet Earth* (ostensibly nonfiction, I know, but in this area the distinction is hardly worth making), or at least a few eschatological horror novels involving the book of revelations and/or the Swiss banking industry. [I may have spoken too soon here; just as this column was being written, in April 1996, the religious publisher Tyndale House published Left Behind, the first volume in what would prove to be a series of more than a dozen bestsellers based on fundamentalist readings of the Book of Revelation.] But who would have thought that the first SF writer of note to tap into these apocalyptic anxieties would turn out to be Sheri S. Tepper, a novelist hardly known for hitchhiking on trends? And even upon learning that, who would suspect that Tepper's transfiguring tale of good vs. evil, set right in the middle of the year 2000, should turn out to be the first genuine cosmological epic of Planned Parenthood? And upon learning that, who would believe that it could possibly work as well as it does?

In many ways, though, **Gibbon's Decline and Fall** makes perfect sense in terms of Tepper's earlier work and career, both in and out of literature. By turns ferocious and lyrical, domestic and visionary, political and religious, the novel features the familiar Tepper band of mutually supportive women, not all of them strong but collectively almost unbeatable. Their opponents are nightmares of sexism who make normal Alpha males look like Muppets; they verge so close to cartoons that you have to keep reminding yourself that, well, Pat Buchanan really *is* out there. There are warm southwestern landscapes and a bone-chilling right-wing hideaway called the Redoubt. There are several stop-the-music lectures, most of them pretty interesting, and most having to do with what is trendily called gender construction, or with questions of excess population. These lectures may be largely set-pieces, but they make it chillingly clear that Tepper – a former executive with Planned Parenthood – knows exactly what's she's talking about, and how far we've already come along the path she plots for us.

The story begins modestly enough in 1959, when a group of college friends help one of their number avoid unwanted male attention by disguising her beauty and having her tote around a copy of Gibbon's famous treatise about civilization in crisis. From this, they take to calling themselves the Decline and Fall Club (Tepper's title later takes on an added pun concerning primate behavior), and meet almost annually for the next forty years. As preparations are underway for the meeting in 2000, we meet the now-aging group: Carolyn, a semi-retired lawyer and activist; Ophelia, a physician; Faye, a sculptor; Agnes, a nun; Bettiann and Jessamine, both married to ambitious husbands. Sophy, the mysterious beauty whose disguise gave the group its name, disappeared some two years earlier, but still seems to haunt members of the group in various ways.

When Carolyn is asked to undertake the defense of an illiterate teenager accused of murdering her newborn baby, the various plot lines begin to align in epic fashion. Her opponent is Jake Jagger, a pathological woman-hater being groomed for high public office by a shadowy figure named Webster, head of the right-wing American Alliance, which has been secretly running all sorts of things for decades (part of the fun of such a near-future scenario is realizing how much of it has to be worked seamlessly into the fabric of recent history, and Tepper does a first-rate job of this). Meanwhile, Ophelia has noted a startling rise in suicide rates among men, coupled with a diminished sex drive and a radical drop in testosterone levels. Women, too, are losing sexual drives, and even some secondary sexual characteristics. And Agnes, an MBA who has built her convent into a profitable business, is ordered by her bishop to turn the business over to a group of less competent men and, well, get to a nunnery. What seems to be a pattern of organized and escalating hatred of women – including all-male marches during which women are routinely assaulted – is answered by an equally organized, if bizarre, series of attacks on tradition sex-role icons, as hordes of bag ladies riot to disrupt fashion shows.

The accused teenager, Lolly Ashaler, becomes the focal point for the debate about women and parenting that occupies much of the book, complete with a dynamite courtroom scene full of the kind of impassioned but informative argument you want to read aloud to someone. As the trial goes on, the surviving members of the club begin to suspect that Sophie may be not only alive, but somehow involved in the epidemic of sexual decline, just as Webster's organization may be involved in the attacks on women. What they discover about each of these figures escalates the narrative several notches into the fantastic, and as usual Tepper's manipulation of genres is bold and effective: her near-future world varies little from today (prisoners are "tanked" in cold storage to serve out their terms; armed guards ride in cabs through fortress neighborhoods), but what it gives way to is part Colin Wilson space vampires, part pulp SF, part even C.S. Lewis. By all rational standards, this ending ought not to hold up for a minute (and a brief coda nearly topples the whole thing); the real apocalypse Tepper shows us is the one we've nearly already made for ourselves through overpopulation, which seems far more scary than Tepper's cardboard villains. But Tepper's books always seem to be held together more by love and rage than by architecture, and never ought to work as well as they do. *Gibbon's Decline and Fall* is a work of considerable passion and substance, about real issues and a real crisis of real millennial dimensions.

One of the lessons I've been learning from some hard SF over the last couple of years is that I should be thrilled about the prospect of an SSTO, and upset that we don't already have one. For the benefit of clueless technophobes, an SSTO is a reusable single-stage-to-orbit vehicle – the kind of genuine space plane that might have resulted from the X-15 series had the cold war not sidetracked everyone into wasteful disposable rockets. The SSTO figures prominently in both Michael F. Flynn's **Firestar** and Charles Sheffield and Jerry Pournelle's *Higher Education*, and was the centerpiece of one of the stories in Sheffield's *How to Save the World* anthology reviewed last September (the story, James Kirkwood's "The Invasion of Space," bears a strong family likeness to the new Flynn novel).

It's hardly worth pointing out that the SSTO is far from a new idea; before about 1958, it's pretty much what everyone assumed real-life spaceships would be like, and it's never been anything less than a standard prop in SF. So why do we need to get excited about it now? The answer probably has less to do with SF than with the enervated space program itself, the various failures of NASA, and a powerful desire to see space exploration re-romanticized, and done right for once. This desire is what's really interesting; it's the space junkies' equivalent of going back and winning in Vietnam, and it's what turns the SSTO into an icon of the kind of techno-nostalgia that wants to recreate not only the rational optimism of Heinlein's heyday, but the social and economic structures of that era as well. In his *Locus* interview in April,

Stephen Baxter (who I would not count as one of this group) seems to feel it, too: he described his next novel as an alternate history that returns to the Apollo technology of the 1960s and follows it through the Martian mission that never happened. Flynn, Sheffield and Pournelle are reaching even further back, into the 1950s. The space program fizzled, they contend, because of social rather than technological shortcomings, and in order to bring it believably back into a near-future scenario, they have to deal with these social issues first, and the social issue of choice seems to be education; thus, we're beginning to get hard SF with a minimum of technical extrapolation and a lot of Dickensian prescription-writing about education, private enterprise, industrial management, and bureaucratic bungling.

Both novels are paeans to school privatization – a small irony in a year in which corporations doing exactly that are failing left and right – but Flynn's *Firestar* is by far the better novel, and the more thoughtful treatment of this unexciting topic. The first in a projected multivolume "epic" of space exploration, *Firestar* has all sorts of mainstream social novel aspirations, taking on not only a failed educational system, but everything else from childcare systems to the state of modern poetry (which, Flynn makes clear, can't hold a candle to Kipling). Flynn also makes it clear why education ought to be of interest to hard SF writers: it's the key toward re-motivating the citizenry to technological goals (and, one suspects, to salvaging the readership of hard SF itself). Flynn assertively makes this connection through his heroine, billionaire industrial heiress Mariesa van Huyten, whose twin obsessions are privatizing public schools and establishing a private space program, beginning with an SSTO. *Firestar* is the tale of her heroic, Ayn Rand-like triumph over fuddy-duddies and bureaucrats (who do not make very exciting villains).

This is not hard SF so much as its ideological cousin, free-enterprise SF. When van Huyten explains the importance of her space program to the heads of her various corporations, you halfway expect to see that Woody Woodpecker sales pitch from *Destination Moon*. When she visits one of her "Mentor Academies" incognito to find out what the teachers really think of their new management, she finds them not so much burned out as spoiled by tenure and too many vacations. (This doesn't stop her from falling in love and eventually marrying one of them.) To minimize government interference, she locates her spaceport and training facility in Brazil – and still has to outsmart the feds who try to subvert her at every turn. And the space jockeys chosen for training at this facility – especially Ned DuBois (does anyone outside hard SF name characters "Ned" anymore?) – are even more ruggedly individualistic than van Huyten; given to beginning every other sentence with "Hell, son . . .," they make Chuck Yeager sound like Pee Wee Herman.

Flynn generally has an awkward time trying to keep his characters up to speed with his provocative ideas, and the novel fails more in its mainstream ambitions than in these ideas. When van Huyten is being courted by teacher Barry Fast, she invites him to a fancy cocktail party; he takes her bowling. The kids we meet at the school wear unconvincing nicknames like Meat, Angel, Zipper, and Styx; the latter is a gloomy, sensitive girl who later becomes a famous poet, and whose unctuous doggerel is quoted throughout as representing a rebirth of poetry in the wake of obscurantist pedants. (If there's one thing Nabokov should have taught us all, it's that you don't quote a character's poetry unless you're prepared to satirize that character.) Still, the speech and behavior of these young people rings more true than the stilted dialogue of the rich or the gonzo posturing of the flyboys. As the novel ends, van Huyten's space program is about to launch a manned mission to an asteroid, and several former Mentor Academy students are involved – a dual triumph of private enterprise. No doubt we'll see more of these incipient space cadets in future volumes, but it's a good bet they won't be on government scholarships.

Space cadets, of course, are more readily associated with Heinlein juveniles than with free-enterprise epics, and for the last couple of years Charles Sheffield has been working, with varying success, on resurrecting the form in such novels as *Cold as Ice* and *The Ganymede Club*, as well as in such shorter works as "Higher Education" a collaboration with Jerry Pournelle which appeared in Sheffield's *Future Quartet* anthology (reviewed in September 1994) and was reprinted in Sheffield's *How to Save the World* (reviewed September 1995). Now Sheffield has begun a new series from Tor called "Jupiter novels," which states in its advance publicity that its aim is to provide contemporary readers with something of the same "thrilling, inspirational reading" that the Heinlein juveniles provided for earlier generations. Mind you, they aren't specifically calling these novels "juveniles" (something of a passé term in modern publishing circles anyway) probably because they know damn well that *real* juvenile readers are busy getting their hands on the last three weeks' worth of R.L. Stine books or Star Wars noveloids promising more of the early exploits of Lando Calrissian. So right off the bat there's a question of audience: are these books supposed to appeal to adults seeking to recreate the buzz which led them into SF in the first place, are they supposed to address the real concerns of today's teenagers, or – and here's my bet – are they likely to be purchased by the former group to be given to, or foisted upon, the latter?

For some possible answers, we can turn to the first of the Jupiter series, **Higher Education**, a novel-length version of that collaboration with Pournelle that Sheffield has already anthologized twice, as if to demonstrate that bad ideas need repeated flogging. Like the novella, *Higher Education* is a stiffly didactic tale which combines a facile savaging of educational bureaucracy with an uncritical celebration of the mechanistic universe (and grossly underplanned technologies) of Tom Godwin's "The Cold Equations"; at one point a character even says to another, "'The universe doesn't care how much people like each other'." Along the way, there are passing swipes at Job Corps, the welfare system, child abuse laws, politicians, lawyers, courts, various forms of political correctness, and stressed out teachers – hardly the sort of issues that young readers are likely to find gripping. Nor are the young protagonists as convincing as Flynn's; with names like Screw Savage and Vido Valdez and tough-guy dialogue straight out of *The Blackboard Jungle*, they come across as more nostalgic than cool. Even Anthony Burgess, thirty years ago, recognized that teen violence had already progressed far beyond the lamebrained practical jokes that pass for repressed rage and lost hope in this novel.

It's one such practical joke – a condom filled with water and propped over a door, believe it or not – that gets Rick Luban expelled from his useless high school and subsequently recruited by an asteroid mining corporation for its training program. The contempt that Rick and his fellow recruits feel toward reading, writing, and math comes out in wooden dialogue that might itself have come from an educational filmstrip: "'Why should I bother to know any of that math stuff? If I ever need it I'll pull it up on a calculator'." But even Rick and his uneducated pals could see what's coming next in this story: a succession of life-or-death training exercises which repeatedly place them in situations where such skills are crucial: "More than anything he had ever wanted in his life, he wanted to read that manual. And he couldn't." Rick learns his lesson but good: literacy and numeracy are the only way to prepare for a high-risk job in the mining industry. (Tell that to anyone under 20 and see how far it gets you.) And when Rick emerges near the top of his class, the bosses of the mining corporation want to send him back to earth to fight the educational bureaucracy as a teacher. Is this the tech equivalent of Christian young-adult fiction?

Or, perhaps more to the point, is it a Heinlein juvenile as it might have been written not by the inventor of modern SF, but by the loony, unedited Heinlein of later years? And for that matter, could anyone really bring off a Heinlein juvenile these days without it seeming oddly dated (Sheffield's own *The Ganymede Club* was far more successful in this regard)? The postwar period was a radically different environment educationally, economically, and science fictionally. The idea that a bad educational system was one that failed to prepare students for careers in industry might have made more sense then, and the idea that competitive private companies might soon be mining the asteroids with the unregulated abandon of U.S. Steel certainly would have – as would the idea that kids might actually be attracted into reading SF by such macho industrial parables. As far as today's kids are concerned, those of them likely to get past the first chapter of this novel probably don't need the homilies about math and reading – if they did, they wouldn't be reading SF in the first place. As a near-space adventure tale set in a conservative *Analog*-style future, the novel is competent enough – but it's competent in a way more likely to appeal to crabby oldsters than to today's nascent SF fans. R.L. Stine won't be glancing over his shoulder at this one, but Sheffield is a talented writer with many resources, and his next Jupiter novel – already scheduled for September, without Pournelle as collaborator – may yet get this promising series idea off to the start it deserves.

It's the kind of trick that has worked in the recording industry for years: fill an album with different versions of the same popular crowd-pleaser, say "Round Midnight" or the Pachelbel Canon, on the theory that true fans never o.d. So, on the apparent assumption that what's good for Pachelbel is good for H.G. Wells, here we have Kevin J. Anderson's **War of the Worlds: Global Dispatches**, a collection of nineteen pieces based on the conceit that since the Martian invasion in Wells's novel was supposedly worldwide, then it stands to reason that other accounts might also exist, either narrated by or featuring various celebrities and writers of the period. In his acknowledgments, Anderson reports that the idea came to him suddenly on a hike in California, and that's the sort of idea it is: stunning for the moment, until you stop to think that what you're proposing is a bunch of stories *all with exactly the same plot*, and with pretty much the same set-pieces. Either Anderson didn't stop to think, or he figured the gimmick of a celebrity-invitational Martian invasion would transcend the overwhelming sense of *déjà vu* inherent in the concept. It doesn't.

Individually, any one of these stories might have made an interesting little *tour de force*, which is what Howard Waldrop's "Night of the Cooters" (the only reprint) was when Waldrop first had this idea himself back in 1987. Waldrop's tale still stands up quite well, in part because he was playing with the conventions of the Texas tall tale as well as with Wells, and a similar edge of parody can be found in several other tales. George Alec Effinger not only deliciously captures the narrative voice of Edgar Rice Burroughs, but is practically the only contribute to concoct an original plot, set on a version of John Carter's Mars that somehow includes Wells's monsters. Daniel Keys Moran captures the cynical flavor of the later Mark Twain, and uses it to convey a sense of mordant tragedy as the Martians die. Barbara Hambly does a good job with Kiplingesque dialogue, and Gregory Benford and David Brin effectively reconstruct Verne's doggedly optimistic scientific rationalism in "his" account of the sacking of Paris. Robert Silverberg, on the other hand, craftily sidesteps the problem of trying to ape Henry James's literary prose by casting his story in the form of informal journal entries about James's adventures with his friend Wells; and Don Webb does pretty much the same with Lovecraft, who is the child protagonist of a tale that only fitfully tries to echo his style.

Is the whole purpose of this, then, to give us a catalog of literary pastiches? Not entirely – there are some historical pastiches as well. Mike Resnick takes on Teddy Roosevelt (who else?), Walter Jon Williams sets his piece in Imperial China, Dan Marcus concocts an almost cartoonish Picasso, and Allen Steele places Joseph Pulitzer at the center of a neat little fable about the futility of power. Only a handful of stories address the scientific issues implied by Wells's novel – the Benford/Brin takeoff on Verne, Doug Beason's contrived piece about Einstein, Anderson's own moving piece about Percival Lowell's dogged persistence in his canal theory. Rounding out the collection are pieces "by" or "about" Winston Churchill and Rider Haggard (Janet Berliner), Leo Tolstoy (Mark W. Tiedemann), Joseph Conrad (M. Shayne Bell), and Jack London (Dave Wolverton). Connie Willis's parody of a scholarly article about Emily Dickinson – whose death a decade before the invasion doesn't stop Willis's lamebrained academic from finding allusions to it in Dickinson's poems – is the funniest piece, but stretches its one joke far past the breaking point. By that late in the book, we're so overdosed on heat rays, tripods, and literary games that no amount of cleverness is likely to restore us. It's like the rising mania you must feel listening to that Pachelbel CD, as you work your way past the familiar versions and on down to zydeco Pachelbel, klezmer Pachelbel, Pachelbel yodels . . .

— June 1996, Locus #425 —

The Year's Best Science Fiction: Thirteenth Annual Collection ~
~ edited by Gardner Dozois

Year's Best Science Fiction ~~ edited by David G. Hartwell

The Year's Best Fantasy and Horror ~
~ edited by Ellen Datlow and Terri Windling

Best New Horror 6 ~~ edited by Stephen Jones

Walking the Labyrinth ~~ Lisa Goldstein

Science fiction is, of course, famous for resisting definition. For decades, each new attempt has been greeted with the sort of responses that in the real world are reserved for flaky proofs of Fermat's Last Theorem or claims of cold fusion using household cleaning agents — everything from undisguised guffaws to fatal nitpicking. When the dust dies down, we are pretty much left with the purely functional and largely circular definitions of the marketplace: SF is what I point to, SF is what SF readers buy, SF is what's in the SF magazines. For the most part, no one seems seriously disturbed about this conceptual fuzziness (at least, not until their own unarticulated definition is grossly violated by, say, something that looks an awful lot like an Ann Beatty story showing up in their monthly copy of *Asimov's*), but it gives rise to one of one of the field's most ingratiating paradoxes, which is this: even though none of us are very good at articulating what SF is, we don't hesitate for a moment when it comes to selecting its best examples. The fans have the Hugos, the writers the Nebulas, the readers of this magazine the *Locus* poll, and the editors — who already make those life-and-death decisions about what's good before the rest of us even see it — have their "best of the year" collections. And this year, for the first time in quite a while, Gardner Dozois's weighty annual is joined by a more modest but thoroughly enjoyable effort from David G. Hartwell, while Ellen Datlow and Terri Windling continue their creative mining of the even more ill-defined fantasy and horror fields, and Stephen Jones takes on solo editing of the horror annual that he and Ramsey Campbell had co-edited five times previously.

Looking at these annuals all together not only provides a rich jolt of good fiction, but makes one wonder exactly what that word "best" in the title is supposed to mean. It may well be that in the early years of such collections, going all the way back to the Bleiler and Dikty series in the late forties and early fifties, the purpose was simple: to rescue a handful of well-crafted and imaginatively stirring tales from the mountains of dross that made up a glutted SF short fiction market. "Best," in those years, may have simply meant "competent," or "pretty good," or "not as bad as most," and the problem of not having a clear definition of SF was irrelevant. But it didn't take long before a shrewd editor, Judith Merril, realized that this definitional problem presented a unique opportunity for a "year's best" editor. Constrained by no *a priori* understandings of what was or wasn't SF, Merril realized that the annual could *become* the definition. SF was by god what she put in her collections, and if she wanted to include stories by Steve Allen or John Steinbeck or Eugene Ionesco – well, who had the theoretical ammo to contradict her? By the later years of the Merril annuals, she deliberately blurred even the name of the field by using only the all-purpose rubric "SF" in her titles (science fiction? science fantasy? speculative fiction?). Merril had discovered something that no editor of an annual "year's best" has since forgotten.

And what she discovered is this: from the point of view of literary craft and general reader satisfaction, a year's best need only be a pretty good collection of pretty good stories. But from the point of view of the often-beleaguered SF community, it's far more: it's a position paper, a mission statement, a strategy of presentation, a prospectus. When it gains the kind of authority that the Dozois annual has earned over the last decade, it becomes something like SF's annual report. And yet despite all this baggage, the only thing an editor really has to sell is a particular view of the field that he or she wants to promote. If the Bleiler-Dikty collections seemed like innocent pearl-diving, Merril's were blatantly imperialist, reaching out to claim new territory for SF in precincts formerly controlled by the mainstream. Terry Carr's annuals (at least those done solo) were more like literary manifestos, arguing that SF could grow its mainstream values from within – a view more or less shared by Brian Aldiss and Harry Harrison in their series. By the seventies, the series edited (separately) by Donald Wollheim and Lester del Rey took on something of the aspect of barn-door closings, often trying to restore something like SF family values to a field rapidly dissolving at the margins.

Dozois, who has had the field more or less to himself for the better part of a decade, is clearly the heir of Merril, at least in terms of his virtually unchallenged market strength and his eclectic literary tastes, and he shares many of her strengths. Hartwell, who has had an enormous impact on the field in other arenas (as a book editor and general anthologist), identifies himself specifically with Carr and Wollheim, and frankly says his collection "announces itself in opposition to other extant anthologies" which have "so blurred the boundaries between science fiction and everything else that it is possible for an observer to conclude that SF is dead or dying out." His stories are ones that "a chronic reader would recognize as SF." All this may sound odd coming from an editor whose 1994 *Ascent of Wonder* anthology tried to convince us that Kipling and Hawthorne ought to be counted as hard SF writers, but it's consistent with the stories Hartwell has selected, and with the view of SF reflected in those stories – which is clearly different, if not totally at odds, with that of Dozois.

In one sense, Hartwell's challenge to Dozois could not have come at a better time, or in a better year for short-form SF. Dozois continues his remarkable streak of consistency and dependability, but a strong sense of *déjà vu* is beginning to creep into his pages. In fact, unsuspecting readers might easily be forgiven for thinking they've picked up last year's Twelfth Annual Volume by mistake, instead of this year's Thirteenth. Each collection begins with a Le Guin Hainish tale about a woman coming to terms with power, and closes with an ornate tale of far-future decadence by Brian Stableford. Each contains a *second* Le Guin story set in the Hainish universe, as well as a Robert Reed story about alienated outsiders, a hardboiled Pat Cadigan story about future urban violence, a William Sanders story about Native Americans, and a Joe Haldeman story about artists in love. Last year saw an Elvis story by Walter Jon Williams; this year has a Marilyn Monroe story by John Kessel. Last year had an alternate history by Lisa Goldstein; this year has one by Maureen McHugh. Last year's touching story of doomed relationships was by Michael Flynn; this year's is by Terry Bisson. Fine as these stories individually may be, we can't help but begin to suspect that we're looking at something like a template here – an anthology of assigned seats. Out of 21 authors in the 1996 collection, 14 were in last year's and 13 have made three or more Dozois annuals. Only Allen Steele and newcomer David Marusek appear to be making their first appearance this year.

The issue here isn't simply whether Dozois has put together another collection of readable and gratifying stories – he has long since established his skill at doing that – but whether, inadvertently or not, he's nailing down a kind of hegemonic aesthetic for SF. Dozois's topology of the field has little room for its pulpish past – the one selection which pays direct homage is Allen Steele's ironic "The Death of Captain Future" – and yet welcomes a kind of pseudo-folkloristic rusticana in such stories as Michael Flynn's very odd "The Promise of God" and William Sanders's "Elvis Bearpaw's Luck," set in the same world of post-collapse Native American resurgence as his story in last year's volume. Both stories involve psychic powers, which also provides the basis for Dan Simmons's "Looking for Kelly Dahl," with its shifting landscapes and echoes of Dick's *Eye in the Sky*. Michael Swanwick's "Radio Waves" is essentially a ghost story worked out with the mechanics of a hard SF story. Any of these stories are marginal enough that they might well have found a home in the Datlow-Windling anthology.

As is apparent from his editing of *Asimov's* (which is the source of a third of the stories here), Dozois is interested in stories about art and artifice, and he may exaggerate the degree to which these topics are represented in the field: Joe Haldeman's "For White Hill" – a stunning, formally structured far future romance that is one of his best stories to date – concerns artists trying to capture the essence of a dying earth while learning to understand one another. Robert Reed's

"A Place with Shade" – also one of this author's strongest performances – makes a neat connection between terraforming as art and the artifice of Shakespeare's *The Tempest*. In Mary Rosenblum's "Casting at Pegasus," the art involved is an interesting combination of electronic graffiti and astronomy, and the artists are risk-taking outsiders. A packaging designer (what a wonderful SF-nal occupation!) is the narrator of David Marusek's "We Were Out of Our Minds with Joy," set in a highly original and convincingly detailed future. Marusek gets my vote for Dozois's most impressive new discovery this year.

There are a few other trends apparent in the collection. Mathematics, long one of the most difficult themes to dramatize, is invested with a real sense of wonder in Greg Egan's "Luminous" (which also features a marvelous computer made of light), and a sense of tragedy in Nancy Kress's moving "Feigenbaum Number." Aliens, which generally do not seem to interest Dozois much, are admitted to the extent that they can be made to bear metaphoric weight, as they do in James Patrick Kelly's "Think Like a Dinosaur" and Greg Egan's "Wang's Carpets" (Egan surely now holds the record for deuces; this is the third time he's had two stories in the same annual). The near future, we learn from Geoff Ryman's brief but elegant "Home" (oddly, the only selection from *Interzone*), will be a tough, heartless place where (in Pat Cadigan's "Death in the Promised Land") murderers may track you even to your virtual reality haven. Cadigan's story is a better mystery than an SF story, strong enough to warrant consideration for an Edgar, if mystery readers catch wind of it. The far future, on the other hand, will be ornate and colorful, from the muted tones of Le Guin's Karhide to the formalized urban civilization of Paul McAuley's wonderful "Recording Angel" to the galaxy-spanning intelligences of Poul Anderson's "Genesis" – one of the few selections to represent SF's renewal of interest in Stapledonian perspectives. The past, on the other hand, is a barely averted nightmare of repression in Maureen F. McHugh's "The Lincoln Train," with its disturbing portrayal of a Civil War Holocaust following Lincoln's survival of the assassination attempt.

Dozois puts together a strong collection as always, and in the absence of any alternative it would be hard to second-guess his view of the shape and condition of the field. But this is where Hartwell comes in, with his inaugural **Year's Best Science Fiction**. More modest in scope (14 stories to Dozois's 24) and almost aggressively unpretentious (some of the story introductions are no more than magazine-style headnote hooks), Hartwell's volume actually draws on a wider variety of SF sources, including selections from *Tomorrow, Analog*, and *Science Fiction Age* (none of which are represented in Dozois). Only three stories overlap with Dozois: Kelly's "Think Like a Dinosaur," Haldeman's "For White Hill," and Le Guin's "Coming of Age in Karhide." It's interesting to note that each of these reads a little differently in the context Hartwell provides: the elegantly structured romance of the Haldeman story reveals a precisely worked-out hard SF underpinning; the Kelly takes on echoes of Budrys and Tom Godwin; the Le Guin seems more like a classic SF world revisited. Hartwell also includes a hardboiled VR crime story along the same lines as Cadigan's in the Dozois,

William Browning Spencer's "Downloading Midnight."

But it's about here that the resemblances end. Hartwell says he wants to show that SF — meaning SF with the barn door closed — is more vital and energetic than ever, but what he really shows is that SF's traditional machinery is still in good shape. He doesn't shy away from well-realized catastrophe stories like Robert Silverberg's lively "Hot Times in Magma City" (volcanos in California) or Nancy Kress's "Evolution" (an epidemic of drug-resistant bacteria). The Kress selection is an interesting benchmark of the differences between Hartwell and Dozois, who chose Kress's "Feigenbaum Number." Each story showcases Kress's keen eye for the telling details of strained relationships, but "Feigenbaum Number" is muted and restrained compared to the hospital bombings and social decay dramatized in "Evolution".

Hartwell's taste in general echoes a more innocent age of SF, when writers used tropes as though they were volleyballs and worried more about pace than character. His humorous selections — Roger Zelazny's "The Three Descents of Jeremy Baker" (black hole jokes) and Robert Sheckley's "The Day the Aliens Came" (alien jokes) — are more fun than the tall-tale rhetoric preferred by Dozois, and his selection of hard SF reveals a predilection for problem stories, sometimes almost in a classic Astounding mold. In Stephen Baxter's "Gossamer," explorers trapped on Pluto must figure out how to use a wormhole for escape. Wormholes in the sun are the hazard in Gregory Benford's "A Worm in the Well," with its freelance space jockey seeking quick bucks by offering to fly her uncertified ship into the sun. A puzzle involving unusual life forms on a planet slated for habitation leads to classic biochemistry speculation in Joan Slonczewski's "Microbe." There's even a space-program story: William Barton's alternate history "In Saturn Time" presents us with Walter Cronkite on the moon and may be the only story now or ever to celebrate the unrealized possibilities of a Morris Udall presidency.

Hartwell's major zingers not in the Dozois collection are Patricia McKillip's "Wonders of the Invisible World," a superbly convincing portrayal of Cotton Mather and Puritan New England reminiscent of Connie Willis's best historical time travel tales; and Gene Wolfe's "The Ziggurat," a profoundly disturbing and despairing meditation on men, women, parents, and aliens — all of whom seem hopelessly isolated from one another by story's end. There's no questioning the adroitness and technical mastery of such stories as these — item by item, Hartwell stands up pretty well to Dozois in the purely literary arena — but there is a distinct emphasis in Hartwell on concept over technique, and in Dozois on technique over concept. Since — as I said at the outset — none of us really know what SF is in the first place, it's useless to try to demonstrate who's right: each editor has arguably given us the best view of the side of the elephant he's looking at, and neither has captured the whole beast. The Dozois is literate, sophisticated, eclectic — and beginning to look a bit like a repertory company. The Hartwell is also literate, a little more fun, and a good deal more constructionist in its view of SF. While I don't quite agree with Hartwell's implication, in his introduction, that Dozois has to be stopped before he turns all of

SF into a copy of The New Yorker, I'm glad to see him offering a welcome balance, and returning a dimension of vital dialogue to the annual "best" sweepstakes. In other words, you have to buy both books.

Fantasy and horror, on the other hand, haven't really suffered the kind of ongoing mid-life crisis that has plagued SF for more than thirty years. There simply isn't enough generic cohesiveness to make invidious comparisons among stories, and the "pretty good collection of pretty good stories" rule applies here even more forcefully than it does in SF. Datlow and Windling's **Year's Best Fantasy and Horror** is up to its usual high literary standards, but as a genre-defining piece the book explains nothing, and draws broadly on everything from magic realism to mainstream suspense to psychological terror to surrealism. I've noted before that the Datlow and Windling elements of the collection have long since gone their separate ways, so that the final anthology, assembled in the lab, almost inevitably comes up looking a little like *The Fly* after that business with the matter transmitter: part one thing, part another.

Yet in some ways the collection seems more unified than in past years, toning down the jarring transitions from lyrical fantasy to brutal horror and strengthening the poetry selections both in quantity and quality. Some of the most aggressively violent stories, such as Stephen King's "Lunch at the Gotham Cafe" (about a lunatic maitre d') and David Schow's "Refrigerator Heaven" (about a bizarre kind of torture) are leavened with an edge of almost surrealistic humor, giving them a denser texture than the straight-ahead horror of Steve Rasnic Tem's "Blood Knot" or Michael Marshall Smith's "More Tomorrow" (which is one of the first, but surely not last, horror stories about Internet newsgroups). The Tem and Smith stories, along with Douglas E. Winter's "Loop" – all stories by male writers – share an unsettling tendency to draw their narrative effects from acts of extreme brutality against women.

Fantasy has never had a facile emotion tagline like SF's "sense of wonder," but one could easily come away from this collection with the impression that most modern fantasy, and much horror, is about a sense of loss. Looking through both year's best SF collections, you repeatedly find communities; here you find *isolatos* and collapsing or barely strung together family units. There you find connections; here you find failures to connect, or at best tentative gestures of trust. In Nina Kiriki Hoffman's poignant "Home for Christmas," a young woman isolated by her ability to communicate with inanimate objects joins a lonely divorcé at Christmas. A fragile friendship is derailed by the ghost of a dead husband in Terry Lamsley's "Screens," and a budding love affair is cut off by death in Christopher Kenworthy's "Because of Dust," a touching variation on the old film *An Affair to Remember*. A tragically burned child who tells a wonderful story turns out to be a haunting from a lost past in Gary A. Braunbeck's excellent "After the Elephant Ballet." A talking rhinoceros (animal stories are big this year) mediates a lifelong unconsummated love affair in Peter Beagle's wonderful "Professor Gottesman and the Indian Rhinoceros." Even vampires suffer lost loves: a poet in Peter Crowther's "Too Short a Death" refuses the immortalizing bite from his gay vampire lover, even as he faces death. The unicorn, a classic symbol of lost innocence and pure love, shows up in exactly this role, again involving a gay lover, in Ellen Kushner's "Hunt of the Unicorn." And the emblem of loss in Douglas E. Winter's "Loop" is a dead porn star.

This theme of loss also carries over into alternate reality tales, which seem to be gravitating from SF toward fantasy (where they probably belonged in the first place). Rick Moody's exceptionally well-written "The James Dean Garage Band" has the movie star junking it all to join a pickup rock band, but taking off just as success seems at hand. Pat Cadigan's "She's Not There" also deals with a rock star who never was, in a reality that may only be an illusion of the narrator – just as it may be in Lucy Taylor's "Switch," a twist on foster-child fantasies in which shifting realities lead to tragic alienation. In Ursula Le Guin's "Ether Or," a *tour de force* of multiple viewpoints, a whole Oregon town constantly shifts its location – not quite alternate history, but at least alternate geography – while its various denizens try to find solace in each other. S.N. Dyer's "Resolve and Resistance" is the most science fictional of the alternate-world tales, in attitude if not in substance; it concerns Jane Austen characters helping Lord Nelson save England from the yoke of French conquerors, and it has an optimistic ending uncharacteristic for this collection.

Fantasy and horror both have close family ties to folklore, which is one of the few remaining clear links between these two increasingly disparate genres. Both Datlow and Windling deserve credit for eclecticism here; the expected vampires and dragons are balanced by tales which capture the flavor of English balladry (Midori Snyder's "King of Crows"), draw on Chicano legends (Pat Mora's poem "Llantos de la Llorona: Warnings from the Wailer"), or derive from Gaelic folklore (poems by Mary O'Malley and Eiléan Ni Chuillenain). Delia Sherman's "The Printer's Daughter" is a first-rate original fairy tale set in Elizabethan England, and Patricia McKillip's "The Lion and the Lark" is even more impressive at capturing the traditional fairy tale magic of seamless transformations; these and Snyder's story are the only real examples of this challenging form in the book. Jane Yolen, our leading fairy tale writer, checks in with no fewer than three poems, covering everything from angels to swan princesses and women's stories. Other notable poems are by Nancy Willard, Neil Gaiman (two), Margaret Atwood, and Louise Glück. As the last two names might suggest, the collection also features its usual smattering of big literary names, including stories by Amy Tan, Joyce Carol Oates (with what may be the single creepiest story in the book), A.S. Byatt, and Stuart Dybek. All are excellent. Scott Bradfield's "Penguins for Lunch," while funny enough, mines the same lode as his *Animal Planet*, and it's getting pretty thin. Vivan Vande Velde's parody of "Little Red Riding Hood" – already the most parodied of fairy tales – seems somehow fresher and funnier than Bradfield's more original contrivance.

This leaves us with the usual mix of unclassifiable tales that almost always make up the seasoning of the Datlow/Windling volumes. Terry Dowling's oddly moving story of adolescent pranks "Scaring the Train" and Susan Moody's post-World War II tale of a refugee "The Guilty Party" both gain the power of nostalgia without losing a tough edge (and both barely seem to qualify as either fantasy or horror), while S.P. Somtow's "Dragon's Fin Soup" explores a painful generational conflict – involving real dragon's fins – in modern Bangkok. Martha Guthridge's "Henry V, Part 2" offers a delightfully goofy take on a woman's midlife crisis, while Charles de Lint's "Heartfires" is an odd fantasy set amid imagery that could derive from Samuel Beckett. The de Lint comes from a Canadian small-press chapbook, and thus is a good example of the enormous variety of sources Datlow and Windling have drawn on. Perhaps the clearest demonstration of the differences between the SF and fantasy/horror worlds can be found by looking at these sources: whereas both Dozois and Hartwell had only three or four anthologies to draw on and leaned heavily on the magazines, Datlow and Windling were able to take nearly two-thirds of their selections from anthologies, another dozen or so from literary magazines, and only a small handful (I count four) from the major genre magazines. If Hartwell thinks the boundaries of SF have gotten blurred by the year's best anthologies, wait'll he gets a load of this.

Much more coherent, at least in terms of our traditional view of the genre involved, is Stephen Jones's **Best New Horror 6**, a collection of 21 stories and a poem that comes to us a bit out of sync with the other annuals: originally published in England in 1995 and not reprinted here until late last year, it actually covers 1994 rather than 1995, and includes a couple of overlaps with last year's Datlow-Windling anthology. Like the first five volumes (which Jones co-edited with Ramsey Campbell) and like the long-running Karl Edward Wagner series (which ended only with his premature death), the collection shows little uncertainty as to what horror is all about, and with very few exceptions it doesn't stray too far from the traditions of the supernatural and the grotesque that have characterized genre horror since the heyday of *Weird Tales*. If Datlow and Windling (or more particularly, Datlow) seem to be bent on finding new kinds of expression for horror, Jones offers plenty of the familiar icons: vampires, werewolves, mad scientists, crazed doctors, nightmare monsters, shadow demons, body snatchers, even Jack the Ripper. No one who dislikes horror is likely to be converted by his collection, and no horror fan is likely to be disappointed.

There are a few trends over the past several years that show up in both the Datlow-Windling and Jones anthologies. One is what might be called an evolving aesthetic of mutilation. Michael Marshall Smith is a minor master at this, with amputations at the center of both his "More Tomorrow" in Datlow and Windling and "To Receive is Better" in Jones (the idea here is that the wealthy can afford to clone "spares" of themselves to later be farmed for body parts; it's hardly a new idea, but the notion of moving the act of mutilation to center stage is what I mean by a new aesthetic). Brian Hodge's "The Alchemy of the Throat" tells of a modern-day castrato (again a victim of the wealthy), while M. John Harrison's haunting "Isabel Avens Returns to Stepney in the Spring" (also in last year's Datlow/Windling) concerns a woman surgically rearranged in the direction of bird-dom. Elizabeth Massie's genuinely disturbing "What Happened when Mosby Paulson had her Painting Reproduced on the Cover of the Phone Book," probably the most mainstream selection in the book, details the unbearable life of a manipulated and psychically abused child, building toward an act of self-mutilation. The purest example of mutilation-fiction in the collection, however, is Richard Christian Matheson's short-short "Ménage a Trois," in which the third figure in the title arrangement is a knife (and you can pretty much write the rest yourself).

Another trend, as everywhere else, is toward multiculturalism. Robert Bloch's "The Scent of Vinegar" offers the most traditional vampire-in-a-spooky-house scenario in the book, but even this late master's vampire is no normal middle European parasite, but rather a weird Malayan variant that sends its disembodied head off, dangling entrails. The demons in Nicholas Royle's "The Homecoming" are shadows of the very real nightmare of Romania's Ceausescu regime, and in Garry Kilworth's "Wayang Kulit" they are Balinese shadow figures. The werewolf in Kim Newman's "Out of the Night when the Full Moon is Bright ..." is not only Mexican, but turns out to be Zorro himself. Kilworth's story partakes of another trend, also detectable in Datlow and Windling, toward mining earlier pop culture icons. Paul J. McAuley's take on Poe's M. Valdemar, set in an alternate renaissance Florence, is cast as a tribute to Ernest Thesiger, the actor who played Dr. Pretorius in *The Bride of Frankenstein*. Geoffrey A. Landis outdoes himself at this game in "The Singular Habits of Wasps," which manages to combine Sherlock Holmes, Jack the Ripper and H.G. Wells with SF's bodysnatching alien theme.

Of the remaining stories, Norman Partridge's "Harvest" is an unusual combination of horror and magic realism, while Ian MacLeod's "The Dead Orchards" is an equally odd combination of two of horror's most dominant but mutually exclusive traditions: Lovecraftian settings and sexual obsession. The shuttered cottage of Terry Lamsley's "Blade and Bone" also carries Lovecraftian overtones, but in a convincingly realized English village setting. Setting is crucial to the effects of much horror, of course; settings like Bali or Romania disorient by cultural alienation, while others disturb through their very ordinariness: Lamsley's mundane village, the rain-drenched London of Charles Grant's "Sometimes, in the Rain," or the decaying Birmingham of Joel Lane's "Like Shattered Stone." The phantom zombie village of Harlan Ellison's comeuppance-fable "Sensible City" is a direct metaphorical expression of the story's brutal theme. The shabby Tennessee resort hotel of Karl Edward Wagner's "In the Middle of a Snow Dream" descends from a thousand houses on the borderland, and serves exactly the same function all over again in the tale of a self-destructive stripper whose demons become real.

It's interesting to note that the two contributors who did not live to see their stories appear in *Best New Horror 6* are the two whose tales most clearly define what Jones's anthology represents. Neither Wagner's nor Bloch's are the best or worst in the book, but they're both benchmarks of technique and attitude as well as subject matter: cleanly imagined, crisply written, efficiently spooky – and neither too original nor too ambitious. It's the kind of work that built the tradition of horror that Jones's anthology straightforwardly represents, and that Datlow's touches upon on its way somewhere else.

Ever since her first novel *The Red Magician*, Lisa Goldstein has been quietly mapping out a territory for herself somewhere between genre fantasy and a kind of West-coast magic realism. Her stories, which often concern characters or worlds on the verge of some fundamental transformation, tend to be plotted along genre lines, with intelligent, alienated protagonists discovering unexpected new worlds mirrored by new revelations about themselves. But her imaginary worlds are apt to owe as much to Borges or André Breton as to the familiar stuff of genre fantasy, and this consistently gives a freshness to her work that is matched by only a handful of current writers. In **Walking the Labyrinth**, Goldstein shows what she can do with a familiar, almost clichéd plot: the idea that a troupe of stage magicians might secretly possess genuine occult powers, disguising their real magic as illusion (which, in turn, is disguised as "magic" in the performance). The notion that illusion might itself be illusory is irresistibly suggestive, and when Clive Barker got hold of it in "The Last Illusion" (which he turned into last year's film *Lord of Illusions*), the result was a familiar meat-and-fluid epic, but with resonance. Goldstein is interested in no such fireworks; all of her limited and tasteful special effects turn back on character: rather than using the gimmick to add depth to a shallow plot, she unfolds her plot in such a way as to add depth to the gimmick.

Molly Travers, whose lack of focus is evidenced by her infatuation with a vain celebrity biographer, is approached by a private detective named John Stow, seeking information about her family. Travers's great aunt, Fentrice Allalie, had belonged to a family troupe of vaudeville magicians which had disbanded sometime in the 1930s – and now a mysterious client is trying to track them down. Joining Stow in his investigation, Travers finds that her family's magical history dates back to Victorian England, to an untutored laundress named Emily Wethers and a secret London society called the Order of the Labyrinth. Traveling to the country home of the Order's patron, Stow and Travers uncover documents which reveal a web of class and family rivalries – as well as a basement labyrinth with apparently magical properties unknown to the house's present owners. A strange man who has been following them is murdered, and Travers begins to suspect that the Order of the Labyrinth may still be active – and that her own family (most of whom she had assumed dead) might be involved.

Goldstein paces her unfolding mystery with considerable skill, and introduces a variety of vivid and touching characters, both present and past – a retired reporter whose life was changed when he tried to interview the Allalies in 1935, the psychically gifted laudress Emily unable to gain full acceptance among the aristocrats who depend on her powers, Travers's guilt-ridden great-aunt Fentrice, the quirkily intellectual detective Stow, most of all Molly Travers herself as she tries to make sense of her own history. Goldstein has plotted out such a complex set of family relationships and rivalries, however, that a good chunk of the novel's second half has to work its way uphill just to get the lines unsnarled enough for us to understand them. This not only slows the pace, but leads to such a series of unexpected arrivals and startled surmises that we begin dizzily to feel in the midst of a Restoration comedy, only without the comedy. In the end, the novel is saved by the same techniques mystery writers often use to bail out overplotted narratives: the sheer likeability and substance of the characters, and the revelation of a single appalling crime committed by one of them against another. This not only gives Goldstein's conclusion a real punch, but sets up the possibility for Travers and her detective pal – now partners – to head off in search of sequels.

– July 1996, Locus #426 –

At the City Limits of Fate ~~ Michael Bishop

Synthesis & Other Virtual Realities ~~ Mary Rosenblum

Burning Your Boats: The Collected Short Stories ~~ Angela Carter

Ancient Shores ~~ Jack McDevitt

Behold the Man ~~ Michael Moorcock

Over the years, one of the most glaring omissions from both the Hugo and Nebula Awards (although not from the Bram Stoker, World Fantasy, or – I am pleased to note – Locus Awards) is a category for collections of stories by a single author. Not only must such books go unhonored by the two most prestigious awards from their literary community, but their sales seldom compare to those of novels by the same authors, and they tend to get reprinted far less frequently if at all. Yet the collection is the closest thing the literary world has to a gallery exhibit, and it often tells us far more about an author's visions and concerns than whole trilogies of novels. It also represents a purer form of that vision as well: short stories tend to get messed over by editors far less than novels, and story collections messed over even less. Thus the raw architecture of a writer's imagination is much more discernible in such collections, and authors take understandable pride in them, often even turning to less commercial houses to get them published.

For example, both Michael Bishop's new collection **At the City Limits of Fate** and Mary Rosenblum's *Synthesis and Other Virtual Realities* come from smaller presses – Bishop's from Edgewood Press, which has offered highly original collections from

Garry Kilworth, Gwyneth Jones, and Cherry Wilder; Rosenblum's from Arkham House, whose even more distinguished list of author collections includes Michael Bishop. Both Bishop and Rosenblum forgo the introductions, afterwords, and general persiflage that once characterized such story collections (and that Harlan Ellison raised to an art in itself), and in both cases it's a mixed blessing. For the benefit of readers less familiar with their earlier work, it would have helped to have notes explaining that Bishop's title story is a sequel to his "The Yukio Mishima Cultural Association of Kudzu Valley, Georgia" or that Rosenblum's is a prequel to her novel *Chimera* (and that three other stories are set in the same near future as her *The Drylands*). On the other hand, one can respect the authors' restraint in letting the stories speak entirely for themselves.

Bishop's collection is his first since 1986's *Close Encounters with the Deity* and could just about share that earlier collection's title; if anything, religion is an even more dominant theme here. God has his own TV show on CBS in "God's Hour," and "you die if you miss it." Judas is put on trial via software simulacra in "I, Iscariot," which carries sharply satirical overtones of the Simpson trial and other instances of media-driven jurisprudence. The crucifixion itself is at the center of "Beginnings," and one of the most bizarre offshoots of American Christianity, the Appalachian snake-handlers, is treated with sensitivity (and some rather dense dialect) in "Among the Handlers." In "For Thus Do I Remember Carthage," a St. Augustine living in a Hippo transformed by the early discovery of electricity listens with disbelief as his long-lost son describes the new scientific discoveries in China — including everything from digital wristwatches to relativity, black holes, quasars, and the Big Bang. Part of the fun here is recognizing these discoveries through the inventive terms Bishop has coined for them: light years become *annilumes*; galaxies are *lactastrons*; the Big Bang is the "Earliest Eruption Postulatum." Later, another visitor (this time from Africa) tells the weary philosopher of a new theory of the "Unfolding of Animal Types" based on ancient bones. While Bishop makes much irony out of what all this does to Augustine's ideas about the City of God vs. the City of Man, the story itself is an excellent example of a kind of narrative that has recently become quite popular in SF — what we might call the quasi-time travel alternate history story, which gains its effect by retroactively introducing modern ideas or technology into historical settings, but forgoes the clunky and overworked device of having a time traveler introduce them (the classic model for this may be Philip José Farmer's "Sail On, Sail On!").

Bishop has one of the most distinctive voices around, and one of the advantages of a Bishop collection is the opportunity it affords to see how he goes about achieving his characteristic effects. He is not afraid to cast a tale in dialect, even when it grates (as in "Among the Handlers"), or to narrate in the difficult-to-manage second person voice (as in "000-00-0000" or "Life Regarded as a Jigsaw Puzzle of Highly Lustrous Cats"). He's even willing to take a clichéd descriptive phrase ("buffeting gusts") and turn it into a mantra-like structuring device in "Epistrophy" (the title refers both to this rhetorical figure and to an old Thelonius Monk recording). He can be one of the funniest SF writers around, but he works his comic inventions out with such deadpan consistency – the stylistic equivalent of Buster Keaton's face – that you're not altogether sure he doesn't think a Yukio Mishima cult in rural Georgia is all that unlikely ("At the City Limits of Fate," or that butterflies might not be a real threat ("Snapshots from the Butterfly Plague"). He often seems to draw more from the traditions of magic realism than from SF, yet he can mount what appears to be straightforward *hommages* to Sturgeon ("Allegra's Hand") or even to *The Incredible Shrinking Man* ("The Ommatidium Miniatures").

Bishop approaches themes the way a jeweler approaches a rough stone: with a certain degree of obsessiveness and a fascination with uncovering all the possible facets. "000-00-0000" begins with a computer error that awards someone this null Social Security number, but turns into a meditation on the entire cultural history of the concept of zero. "Life Regarded as a Jigsaw Puzzle of Highly Lustrous Cats" explores a disintegrating personality through a flood of cat-images and cat-memories. "The Ommatidium Miniatures" not only revisits the familiar SF theme of microminiaturized exploration, but turns into an extended riff on the varieties and meanings of smallness. Sometimes, however, Bishop's imagination is at its best when it is most understated: one of the collection's best stories, "Icicle Music," traces its protagonist's unresolved relationship with his dead father through a series of brief hauntings, each ten years apart, each heralded by the sound of wind in icicles. This is the quieter Bishop that we met in *Brittle Innings*, and it suggests that the master of the thematic riff is also a poet of lonely morality, and one of the finest writers working in SF today.

Rosenblum is among the finest newer writers in the field (after three novels and several short stories she gets to graduate with honors from the category "promising"), and **Synthesis and Other Virtual Realities** tells us at least as much about her concerns and her talents as all three of her novels. She is concerned, perhaps more than anything else, with identity and environment, and in her worlds the two are more than casually linked. The title story "Synthesis," which is also the strongest piece in the book, concerns David Chen, a wealthy scion of a huge Chinese corporation who alienates his family through his preoccupation with creating VR environments, which have gained him considerable recognition as an artist. The tale risks playing with too many stereotypes – the rebellious artist-heir, the unyielding traditionalist father, the talented street-urchin hacker who repeatedly infiltrates David's VR worlds (such cyberpunk Oliver Twists seem to have become inescapable in stories like this) – but Rosenblum handles character with enough insight that you're willing to buy it, and she is careful to show how the VR environments reflect the preoccupations and anxieties of their creators.

In the Drylands tales, on the other hand, the environment seems to shape the characters. "Water Bringer," which made something of a splash when it appeared in *Asimov's* in 1991 by introducing the Drylands world, evokes a Dust-Bowl like setting in which – again – a son's talent for creating images out of nothing (without technical means; this is the older, psi version of VR) creates tensions with his crusty dad. In "Stairway," which takes its title from a famous M.C. Escher image, a crew member on an expedition to bring icebergs from Antarctica to water-starved Los Angeles is stricken with amnesia, adopts the name Escher after seeing a print of the engraving, and fears that his newly-constructed identity will be lost when his memory returns. But, he learns, constructing identity is an endless process, like climbing the endless stairway in the picture. The same character shows up much younger in "The Rain Stone," in which a young girl finds in herself the power to briefly control the weather.

Of the remaining stories, two focus on the dispossessed experience of Latin American immigrants ("Entrada" and "Bordertown"), two are us-against the elements adventures ("Second Chance," set in Antartica, and "Flood Tide," set on a sailboat), and one, "The Centaur Garden," treats another familiar Rosenblum theme, the isolated artist. In this case, a composer and flautist flees the city only to encounter, in the woods, a woman centaur who is herself an artistic creation; the tale evokes both *The Tempest* and "Rappacini's Daughter." Rosenblum's uncompromising and bleak environments – ice, water, dust, desert (I think she's yet to write about a single tree) – begin eventually to take on an almost talismanic quality for the characters who move through them, and the characters often develop strange new talents in response. In one sense, this is not at all new – wasteland mutants with special powers are pulp clichés even in the movies – but Rosenblum's gentle creators of illusory fireflies are very much her own, and her worlds take on convincing weight and texture even when we've seen the building blocks many times before.

During her career, Angela Carter published three story collections: *Fireworks* (1974), *The Bloody Chamber and Other Stories* (1979), and *Black Venus* (1985; published in the U.S. as *Saints and Strangers*). A fourth collection, *American Ghosts and Old World Wonders*, appeared shortly after her death in 1993. **Burning Your Boats: The Collected Short Stories** includes all of those earlier volumes plus six uncollected stories. Carter's reputation, already imposing at the time of her death, seems rapidly to be turning into legend, and rests heavily on the inventive and sexy re-imaginings of fairy tale materials in *The Bloody Chamber* (although there has always been a strong following for her novels as well, of which *Heroes and Villains* probably comes closest to identifiable SF). Carter was never really regarded as a genre writer, but her liberating influence can be seen in a wide variety of younger horror and fantasy writers, and she herself identified openly with the bourgeois post-Gothic tradition of Poe and Hoffmann. When she returned from Japan to England in 1972, she wrote in an afterword to *Fireworks,* she had a rude awakening: "We live in Gothic times," she wrote, and the tale – rather than the short story – may be better suited for reflecting and exploring those times.

Carter's fabulist bent is evident in her very earliest work, represented here by three stories from the early to mid-1960s. "The Man Who Loved a Double Bass" introduces a theme of fetishistic obsession which is echoed in several later stories; here the object of affection is the musical instrument of the title, but by the time we get to "The Loves of Lady Purple" from Fireworks, it's become a puppet with an erotic life of its own. The ironic echo of Pinocchio here represents an early example of what would become Carter's most famous trademark: her radical rethinking and resexualizing familiar materials, especially fairy tales, and especially in her most important book, *The Bloody Chamber*, in which she shows herself most fascinated by the beauty and the beast theme. "The Bloody Chamber" itself is a version of Bluebeard, while "The Courtship of Mr. Lyon" and "The Tiger's Bride" directly re-examine the role of Beauty; in the latter tale, she finds herself transformed into a tigress as the animal lover's rough tongue strips away her old skins. This, of course, becomes a central conceit in Carter's werewolf tales, "The Werewolf," "Wolf-Alice," and "The Company of Wolves," probably her most famous groups of tales if only because of the film Carter and Neil Jordan made from them (using the latter title). Later, these wild children from barren Gothic realms give way to actual historical figures such as Lizzie Borden, whose tale is retold in "The Fall River Axe Murders" (from *Black Venus*) and then combined with the beast theme in "Lizzie's Tiger" (from *American Ghosts*). Other historical figures who come in for Carter's brand of meditative mythologizing include Baudelaire's mistress Jeanne Duval, alchemist Dr. John Dee (in the *tour de force* multicultural fantasy "Alice in Prague"), and one of Carter's own mentors, Edgar Allan Poe. As Salman Rushdie notes in a brief but acute introduction, Carter seemed to be moving away from fantasy in her last two collections.

There is relatively little in *Burning Your Boats* that evokes Carter's most famous science fictional text, *Heroes and Villains*, although a near-future civil war in England provides the backdrop for "Elegy for a Freelance" and stories such as "Reflections" (a through-the-looking-glass fantasy) construct such dreamlike alien worlds that they might as well be SF. But what connects Carter to the best modern SF and fantasy traditions is not only her use of fantastic subject matter, but her oddly seductive combination of lyrical, sometimes florid prose with the reportorial inquisitiveness of the travel writer. The descriptions of Japan in several stories from *Fireworks* (most notably "A Souvenir of Japan" and "Flesh and the Mirror") suggest strong autobiographical content, yet present the country as virtually an alien world.

The same is true of her fictional lands. There is very little dialogue in her stories, but a great many digressive observations about the lands and people she writes of; the barren highlands of such tales as "The Executioner's Beautiful Daughter" and the fairytale revisions take on such a convincing texture that they begin to seem like a fully-realized alien planet – until Carter calls us back to earth by reminding us that the world of beauty and the beast is (at least in "The Courtship of Mr Lyon") also the world of cars breaking down and long-distance business phone calls. It's this juxtaposition of the mundane and the marvelous, together with that inimitable prose, that gives Carter her uniqueness; her plots, when they aren't openly borrowed, are often appallingly lame; once you get past the glittering surface of "Master" you realize that at bottom it's Defoe-inspired feminist pulp: a vicious great white hunter meets his match with a cat-woman. "Penetrating to the Heart of the Forest" is very nearly a classic shaggy god story – two thirteen-year-olds in a paradisical society descended from escaped slaves set out to find a mythic tree; it turns out just as Edenic as you think, but the tale is so hypnotically beautiful that you hardly worry about where it's going. There's a love of language at the heart of these tales that by itself is almost decadent; it's not for nothing that Carter's first collection was called *Fireworks*. Combine this kind of incandescence with a fierce intelligent that seems to transcend any labels you try to attach – feminist, postmodern, fabulist – and you have a body of work, represented nowhere as well as in this volume, that is undeniably one of the most important in all modern fantasy.

As I've mentioned before, there are certain kinds of SF narratives which we might call, for lack of a better term, Entry Level Texts. These are the novels and stories you can show to Mom: the science is easy and barely visible, the more challenging SF concepts are saved for late in the narrative, most of the characters might have walked in from a mainstream bestseller, and in general the reader is carefully and gingerly managed – brought into SF like a decompressing diver being protected from the bends. But to qualify as an Entry Level Text, the story can't cop out altogether; it has to have enough SF content and be challenging enough to at least entertain a veteran reader. It can't use its SF element as a mere maguffin on the way to an altogether different genre (as Stephen King often does), and it can't be so fainthearted and imaginatively lame that it looks as though it ought to be hosted by Truman Bradley (whose mid-50s TV series *Science Fiction Theatre* remains a quintessential example of the misappropriation of SF's name). In short, there's more to bringing these things off than it might at first seem.

Jack McDevitt's first novel *The Hercules Text*, published a decade ago, was a pretty good example of an Entry Level Text on the First Contact theme. It had some mainstream ambitions, but suffered from being overshadowed by Carl Sagan's similar and much-hyped *Contact* the year before, and by its own clunky attempts to reach for mainstream topicality via an ill-conceived Cold War subplot. Now McDevitt has returned to similar territory in **Ancient Shores**, which is much more successful both in drawing out its SF ideas and in managing the mainstream elements of the plot. Like The *Hercules Text*, *Ancient Shores* begins by introducing an SF concept into an immediate future made recognizable by allusions to current pop culture, and then expands the scope of the initial concept (in this case, an alien sailboat found in a remote part of North Dakota which was once the shore of an ancient lake) while tracking, in mainstream style, the political and economic fallout from the discovery. McDevitt balances these dual plot lines with skill and suspense, but when they finally converge in the end, the payoff is all for the SF readers, and involves a rescue of such jaw-dropping silliness that it threatens to unravel all the carefully built credibility that has gone before. Fortunately, the ending is never that important in an Entry Level Text (think of Clarke's original Rama novel), and for the moment let's just say that McDevitt gets away with it, but barely.

McDevitt begins with an SF motif so familiar to the mainstream audience that Stephen King was able to use it in *The Tommyknockers*: the buried alien spacecraft. Varying the formula slightly, he begins with a farmer discovering what appears to be an ultramodern sailboat on his land near the Canadian border. Only when a pilot named Max Collingwood and a scientist named April Cannon get involved does it become apparent that the boat — which must have sunk in the prehistoric Lake Agassiz thousands of years earlier — is the work of a radically advanced technology. A search for other remnants of this technology leads to the discovery of a buried building shaped like a roundhouse, which turns out to contain gateways to other parts of the universe. Needless to say, April pops off to the Horsehead Nebula in a flash (literally), and soon scientists are popping all over the galaxy, while anxiety over the impact of the new technologies — the promise of indestructible materials and instantaneous transportation — begins to wreak havoc with the stock market, employment rates, and the Department of Defense. There are various subplots — for example, the roundhouse is found on Native American land, and investors make increasingly outrageous offers in an attempt to buy it — but the bottom-line issue is whether the site might be destroyed, in order to prevent the massive social and economic dislocations that would result from the sudden introduction of so many new technologies. It's an interesting question, and one that McDevitt develops with care, although in order to keep his events sequenced, he has to portray the federal government as unbelievably passive in the early stages of the tale, unbelievably aggressive in the latter stages, and almost (but not quite) unbelievably dumb throughout. Nevertheless, with its likeable characters, its subtly developed romance, and its tantalizing glimpses of other worlds, *Ancient Shores* qualifies as the premier Entry Level Text of this season.

As noted above, Michael Bishop is one of the most interesting authors currently at work who regularly treats religious themes in an SF or fantasy context. But he is far from the first, of course, and this month brings us a 30th-anniversary reprint of Michael Moorcock's classic Nebula-winning novella **Behold the Man**, complete with an unspecified number of "author's corrections," and introduction by Jonathan Carroll, an autobiographical afterword by Moorcock, and several full-page illustrations by John Picacio. (You have to pile on the options if you're going to sell what is essentially a 50-page novella for $12.95.) In the years since its first publication, Moorcock's tight, ironic fable has been overshadowed by the more widely available novel which Moorcock developed from it in 1969, and that novel is what people usually refer to when they mention *Behold the Man*. In his afterword, Moorcock says he prefers this shorter version, and I'm inclined to agree with him. The novella length is ideally suited to certain kinds of SF narratives, and Moorcock's central conception – a time traveler searching for the origins of the Christ myth finds himself becoming the central figure of that myth – has the distinct flavor of classic inevitability. If Moorcock hadn't written the story in 1966, someone else would have written it by now.

Much of the appeal of the short novel derives from its elegant grafting of a formal tragic structure onto a popular SF motif – time travel into the past. Such tales always promise to reveal to us the unwritten aspects of history while permitting us to use our knowledge of the historical record in much the same way our knowledge of science enhances our reading of hard SF. Moorcock enhances the intrigue by choosing a highly mythified time and place – where there's a lot of wiggle room for the author – and by re-envisioning one of the central religious epics of western civilization. When Karl Glogauer discovers the historical Christ to be little more than a drooling idiot, he takes it upon himself to represent Christ's message (which is largely a message of political revolution), inevitably leading to his own capture and crucifixion. We are told just enough about Glogauer's childhood, his work as a psychiatrist, his debates with his lover Monica, and his own messianic tendencies that we can guess at what kinds of neuroses lead him to literally become Christ, but none of this slows down the forward tilt of the story, which still reads like classic SF, if a bit less blasphemous than it might have seemed in 1966 (Salman Rushdie should be envious that Moorcock could have gotten away with this as cleanly as he did, although his afterward reports a number of death threats after the book was made available to people in Texas.) When Moorcock expanded the story into a novel, he followed a pattern already common at the time (Daniel Keyes' *Flowers for Algernon* is another example, also coincidentally enjoying its 30th anniversary this year) of leaving the core SF story pretty much alone and wrapping a dense thicket of mainstream kipple about it. What this did was to greatly increase the significance of Glogauer's neurotic obsessiveness and his inability to sustain relationships, and to dilute the more ambiguous and austere central tale. The novella is a religious SF fable with psychoanalytic overtones; the novel is a psychoanalytic saga resolved through an SF gimmick. *Behold the Man* comes to us from an even smaller press than those publishing the Bishop and Rosenblum collections, and it's well worth seeking out.

Before ... 12:01 ... and After ~~ Richard Lupoff,
introduction by Robert Silverberg

Glory's People ~~ Alfred Coppel

The Fall of Sirius ~~ Wil McCarthy

Murder in the Solid State ~~ Wil McCarthy

In the middle of Richard Lupoff's career-retrospective collection **Before ... 12:01 ... and After** is a brief story ("Blinky Henderson Again") about a washed-up pulp western writer ignominiously applying for a typing job at a temp agency. In the headnote to the story, Lupoff tells us that he wrote it at a time when his SF career had collapsed, that it had appeared only in a convention program book, and that he couldn't even afford to attend the convention. This pretty much encapsulates the view of Lupoff's career that we get in this book — not only from Lupoff himself, but from Robert Silverberg in his appreciative but equally gloomy introduction. And yet, as Silverberg notes, Lupoff's career spans three decades in a variety of genres and an even greater variety of styles, highlighted by a handful of novels — *Space War Blues*, *Circumpolar!*, *Sun's End* — that almost but not quite edged Lupoff into the ionosphere of Name Recognition. So he comes to us now an experienced craftsman and almost legendary *pasticheur*, and a figure of some importance in the history of fandom (where he has always been highly regarded — his only Hugo was for his fanzine), and he's presenting himself as a kind of pulp Willy Loman, stopping just short of actually apologizing for asking us to read his stories, or to consider his career. The stories argue otherwise.

For all the first-rate writers who have emerged from communal SF over the years — I hesitate to say fandom, since fandom is only a part of it — there have been those whose authorial identities seem nearly to have been consumed by their good-old-boy fannish personae. One thinks of the careers of Wilson Tucker or Alexei Panshin, both with first-rate novels to their credit which are scarcely read today, both with deep roots in an SF community that never quite let them go (Panshin went on to collaborate with his wife on Hapsburgian histories of SF, while Tucker eventually retired to just being Bob). For such writers, what should have been the springboard turned out merely to be the pool. Lupoff almost — but not quite — could be counted the quintessential member of this group. Looking at the 23 stories in this collection, dating from 1952 to the present, two observations seem to support this: first, nearly half the stories are in some way *hommages* or pastiches clearly directed toward an audience familiar with the pulp cadences of SF history; and second, many of the stories originally appeared in specialized venues such as chapbooks, fanzines, original anthologies — even that con program book. Some of this can be attributed to

Lupoff's passion for the old pulp traditions – he even expresses disappointment that his clever aliens-among-us story "Venus – Ah, Venus!" had to be published in *Heavy Metal* rather than in an underfunded attempt to revive *Planet Stories* – but some is just bad luck.

What redeems Lupoff as a short story writer is not so much his skill at mimicry as his astute and highly professional sense of craft. It's interesting that although Lupoff's famed pastiches cover writers like Wells, Doyle, Lovecraft, Leiber, Dick, even E. Hoffmann Price, the short-story writers he says he admires are all consummate craftsmen: Thurber, Stanley Ellin, John Collier. And it's much harder to imitate craft than it is to imitate style; almost any undergraduate with a thesaurus can do a fair Lovecraft, and Lupoff's "The Doom that Came to Dunwich" is more than fair (although his often touching account of Lovecraft and E. Hoffmann Price in New Orleans, "The House of Rue Chartres," is a much better story). But it takes a well-developed sense of pacing and structure to bring off a tight little crime story like "Dogwalker" (built around the mundane observation that people who walk dogs often stop to chat) or a mordantly comic piece like "Mort in Bed" (based on the conceit that a jealous wife can suddenly see into her husband's dreams). Lupoff has the veteran's sense of how far an idea can be pushed, and when to back off. "The Woodstock West Killer" is that increasing rarity, a genuine mystery short story, and in the hands of many writers it would quickly have bloated into a novel.

Nowhere is this sense of restraint more evident than in the title story, "12:01," which is probably the most familiar piece in the book (it became an Oscar-nominated short film and later a TV-movie, and may or may not have been deliberately ripped off by the hit film *Groundhog Day*). It's a classic example of a neat idea which really has nowhere to go – in this case, only one man knows the world is recycling the same hour over and over – and Lupoff plays skillfully with it without asking it to bear too much weight. It's also one of a series of time-distortion tales which seem to be a Lupoff specialty. "Saltzmann's Madness" is about a computer engineer obsessed with the idea that time is somehow being stolen from us, and that he can find a way to reclaim it. This works well enough as a metaphor for something many of us feel, but Lupoff works it out as a horror story. "Snow Ghosts" and "A Funny Thing . . . " (the latter unpublished before this collection) each achieve a kind of tragic nostalgia by collapsing the lives of their protagonists into a few key events, seemingly only moments apart. These stories are among the most rewarding in the book, and are far more satisfying than the one pure time-travel story, "Nebogipfel at the End of Time," a rather unconvincing tribute to Wells.

For the most part, Lupoff is a blessedly unpretentious writer of well-shaped tales, and this collection is a thoroughly entertaining sampling of his range. When he's in his pulp vein, his affection for the material never becomes cloying, and is often hilarious: an inspired Yiddish take on Leiber's sword-and-sorcery heroes (here transformed into "Flayshig and the Goyish Meshugge"), a Sherlock Holmes (or more precisely, Dr. Watson) story which segues into a Farmerian pantheon of interrelation superheroes. But on occasion, he can attain unexpected power as well; "After the Dreamtime," with its interstellar sailing ships and allusions to Australia and Old Earth, at first looks like another pastiche, this time of Cordwainer Smith, but suddenly turns into a brutal and disturbing parable of racism. "With the Evening News" begins as another bit of throwaway paranoia — what if news organizations actually made news happen? — and ends up making us think about the extent to which this already happens. There may not be a great story in the book, but there's hardly a bad one (although the first three early tales are a bit trying), and Lupoff may not be a great writer, but he has enough passion, intelligence and humor to keep us engaged, and for that alone he's grown into one of more admirable figures in recent SF and mystery fiction. It's a collection worth having.

Last month, I mentioned that Jack McDevitt's *Ancient Shores* might serve as a good example of an SF entry level text — the kind of novel that might help attract non-SF readers into the genre. But what about readers of such science-fictionoid texts as, say, *Star Trek* novels? Are they really likely to become general SF readers, and if so, what kinds of novels might help them make the transition? This idea isn't new, of course; in the early days of the Trek industry, writers like James Blish and Joe Haldeman turn out Trek tales, presumably not only for the big bucks but with the hope, however faint, that at least a portion of that inflated readership might later turn to their other books, and thus almost inadvertently discover what real SF was. It probably didn't work, for pretty much the same reason you don't see LaVyrle Spencer readers moving on to Anne Tyler: people aren't inclined to give up stability for challenge. And it probably won't work today, either, although if I thought it might I would be urging you all to go out and buy Alfred Coppel's *Glory* series as a first-rate tonic for rampant Trekkidom. **Glory's People** is the third in this series, which is an odd but compelling mixture, in almost equal parts, of *Star Trek*, Cordwainer Smith, and what colleges have taken to calling "culture studies".

The basic conceit is similar to that of the TV series: a vast starship with a likeable multicultural crew travels from planet to planet, getting involved in the problems of locals and occasionally squabbling among themselves. But the specific nature of the ship and its crew are borrowed shamelessly from Cordwainer Smith: the *Glory* is an immense goldenwinged solar sailing ship, the crew members are "Wired" into the ship when on duty, and they are assisted by telepathic cats — who perceive a shadowy monstrosity in distant space as either a rat or a dragon. (This not only borrows from several Smith stories, but conflates several eras of his future timeline for the Instrumentality of Man.) So right off the bat, Coppel has found a way to integrate one of SF's most familiar and reassuring pop conventions with one of its most baroque and idiosyncratic visions. The third element in this mix is always (at least in the first three novels) a planetary society which strongly reflects and exaggerates the cultural traits of its parent society on earth: South Africa in the case of *Glory*, the Middle East in *Glory's War*, Japan in *Glory's People*. But the real focus of *Glory's People*, as the title suggests, is the team that runs the ship: the Scots captain Duncan Kr, the German "cybersurgeon" Dietr Krieg, Sailing Master Anya Amaya from the feminist society of New Earth (presented in unsubtle asides as a joyless dystopia), Damon Ng from the tree cities of a planet called Nixon, and two crew members added from the racist society of Voerster in the series' first novel. Plus the cats. And the cyborg "monkeys" who do the dangerous work in the ship's superstructure. It's an attractive enough family to reassure even the most codependent media fans.

In none of these novel has Coppel made much effort to thematically integrate his starship plotlines with those of the planetary society, and I suppose he doesn't need to in what seems designed as an ongoing series. In this case, the planet Yamato was settled by the Japanese many centuries earlier, and still retains such ancient traditions as the samurai and the ninja. (Coppel is far from alone in portraying far future societies as displaying astonishingly cultural continuity over millenia, but Japanese culture, given its history, seems far more credible than Coppel's earlier colonies, and Coppel knows enough to be able to show us just how Japanese traditions have functioned to preserve old traditions; in that sense, this is his best job so far in giving us a fully-textured planetary society.) But the factional problems of Yamato pale in comparison to the real threat, introduced toward the end of *Glory's War*: the nameless, formless Terror that threatens the galaxy, sucks power from planetary atmospheres, and seems drawn toward turmoil and hatred. The crew of Glory wants to enlist the aid of the Yamatans, who have developed a faster-than-light technology involving mass reduction, to fight the Terror, but soon a ninja assassin is loose on board the ship, the monkeys and cats seem paralyzed by terror, and the Terror is just down the block. While the pace suffers momentarily from the almost endemic problem of all waiting-for-the-terror plots (see Wil McCarthy's *The Fall of Sirius*, below) – namely, what do you do between the initial horrifying reports and the final confrontation? – Coppel keeps our interest, and delivers another satisfying, swashbuckling finale. Is someone like to come to this novel from *Star Trek* and leave it looking for Cordwainer Smith? Not likely, but wouldn't it be pretty to think so?

Wil McCarthy's debut novel in 1994 was *Aggressor Six*, a modest but thoroughly competent space war adventure whose plot turned, a little surprisingly, on the sheer alienness of the enemy Waisters, rather than on their awesome power or ugly mugs. **The Fall of Sirius** is a sequel set more than two thousand years later, although the event of the title actually takes place sometime before the events of *Aggressor Six*. A military investigator named Malyene Andreivne has herself, her children, and a few others placed in cryonic suspension during the Waister attack on the Sirius system in the 32nd century, expecting to be revived in a few days. But the Waisters don't merely attack – they annihilate whole populations – and it turns out that Malye and her companions stay in the deepfreeze until the 53rd century, when they are (rather grudgingly) revived by a bunch of green-haired, blue-skinned half-aliens who are facing another possible Waister attack. In Aggressor Six, a team was assigned to try to replicate Waister thought for military purposes; now, in the far future, a whole societal unit called the "Finders Ring" has devoted itself to physically becoming more like the Waisters — although the information on which they base their transformation is far from complete. They hope to learn more by reviving and interviewing the only survivors and eyewitnesses of a Waister attack.

Malye and her companions are initially more puzzled by the strange ways human society has evolved into hundreds of specialized work teams, complete with queens and drones, in those areas that survived the initial Waister attacks. McCarthy works hard to make this interesting — introducing various intrigues among the Finders and the other rings as well as tensions among the revivees themselves — and he knows he'd better, because he's stuck himself with another waiting-for-the-terror plot, like Coppel. When you start a novel by waking someone up and telling them, basically, that the worst thing in the universe is coming by the end of the book, it's pretty difficult to convincingly get them to focus on anything else. So all of McCarthy's carefully worked out Human Suzerainty comes across as little more than marking time until the Waisters arrive, flavored with another favorite SF subplot: namely, that for all their fancy technology, humans of the far future just aren't as spunky and competent as we are. By the time the Waisters arrive, wanting basically just to chat, it's Malye who takes over negotiations and more or less saves the universe. By the end, she's nattering away with her new buddy, the Waister queen (who talks in an unfortunate amalgam of Tweety Bird and Buckwheat), when she learns of the "Blue Star Plague," which is far worse than the Waisters ever were. Only this time we have to wait for the next novel.

McCarthy's chief attractiveness as a new writer is his lack of pretension; like its predecessor, *The Fall of Sirius* is craftsmanlike and efficient, its large-scale backdrop only hinted at, its philosophical questions confined to a few introspective asides. But for the most part, it's a pretty undistinguished novel, flawed by occasional clichés and facile character riffs, and almost (but not quite) redeemed by its detailed examination of how really difficult it would be to communicate effectively with a genuine alien society. If McCarthy shows a particular gift, it may be with his portrayal of aliens.

Which is why it comes as something of a surprise that his first hardback novel, **Murder in the Solid State**, should retreat so radically from McCarthy's more space-opera-oriented scenarios. *Murder in the Solid State* is a better novel, with better characters, better structure, and a much more fluid style than *The Fall of Sirius* — but it is also less ambitious (which, as is often the case in SF, may paradoxically mean more ambitious in a marketing sense; McCarthy is careful in this novel not to do anything that might scare off mystery or mainstream readers). Despite its almost quaint title ("solid state" is a pun on a political slogan and pre-nano electronics), the novel is less a murder mystery than a chase melodrama set in a repressive 21st-century America dominated by the conservative "Gray Party." The SF content — which is little more than a maguffin to drive the chase — revolves around the emerging science of molecular fabrication, which is just beginning to promise all the amazing benefits (and economic chaos) we've already seen in a dozen other nanotech novels. McCarthy handles the discussions of microtech and nanotech with sophistication and inventiveness, but it's largely window dressing: at bottom, *Murder in the Solid State* belongs to the tradition of what we might call promethean paranoid thrillers – someone discovers or invents or finds something that will be an inestimable boon to mankind, but powerful forces conspire to suppress the discovery and kill the hero. Here it's molecular-sized machines, but it might as well be the Ark of the Covenant. McCarthy actually invokes Prometheus at the end of the novel.

A graduate student named David Sanger has invented a remarkable substance called MOCLU – "molecular caulk and lubricant" – which threatens to render obsolete a security device called the "molecular sniffer" developed by an influential molecular scientist name Otto Vandegroot. After a violent altercation with Sanger at a scientific conference, Vandegroot turns up dead, with Sanger the likely suspect. Next, Sanger's lab is trashed and all his data has disappeared, even off-site backup copies. Thugs dressed as cops break into Sanger's apartment and beat him up. Sanger's faculty adviser turns up dead – again with Sanger as chief suspect. By now Sanger, aided by his VR-addicted lover Marian and his unlikely-monikered lawyer Bowser, is able to reach the conclusion that no one – police, FBI, colleagues – can be trusted, and that he'd better hide out among poor people (who, it is understood in such thrillers, always look out for each other and uniformly detest authority). With the panache of ET building an interstellar transmitter from old toys, Sanger steals a machine and sets out to recreate five years' worth of research in a few days, *and improve on it to boot*. Then he's ready to stage a trap for the bad guys.

This may be more of the plot than is really needed, and may actually give away too much to anyone who hasn't seen this plot before. But in formula fiction like this, originality of plot is less important than competence of performance. Does the mystery hold up? Is enough really at stake? Does the pacing work? On all counts, McCarthy shows considerable skill and energy, and while *Murder in the Solid State* is far less original than his *Aggressor Six* novels, it's also far more fun. His political background, with its sinister but believable Gray Party, lends a comfortable texture to the work and complements the intelligent speculations on nanotech with some good old-fashioned dirty pool. While McCarthy's view of the relationship of technology to politics is at times confusing – MOCLU is at once a hazardous material that needs to be regulated and a libertarian's delight that can protect citizens from government regulation – the issues he raises are real, as is the excitement he offers.

Holy Fire ~~ Bruce Sterling

Quicker than the Eye ~~ Ray Bradbury

Over the River & Through the Woods ~~ Clifford D. Simak

Starlight 1 ~~ edited by Patrick Nielsen Hayden

If you go back far enough, you can trace a sizeable chunk of SF (and a bigger chunk of utopian fiction) to a mutual parent genre of travel writing. When, for various reasons, distinctions between fiction and nonfiction became important, travel writing spun off the imaginary voyage subgenre, which in turn begat tales of imaginary societies and imaginary adventures. So it's not really surprising that many of the more thoughtful modern SF writers should bear genetic markers of these older ancestors. The Grand Tour — whether of the galaxy or a future earth — has long been one of SF's easiest and most entertaining expository devices, and with intelligent writers like Kim Stanley Robinson and Bruce Sterling taking a hard look at the workability of various social structures and schemes, that old utopian sensibility seems to be enjoying a kind of minor renaissance. But today, we rightly expect utopian ideas to be explored in more densely realistic contexts, free of the kind of ideological sucker-punches and textureless landscapes and characters that nearly caused utopian fiction to die out early in this century. I'm not saying that Bruce Sterling's **Holy Fire** should be described as a utopian work — that would be the kiss of death for a first-rate novel these days — but he does explore the merits and hazards of a future gerontocracy with the discipline of a social scientist and a sensibility toward character that goes far beyond anything he's shown before. Good social thought and good characters are rare for utopian fiction, and they're not all that common in SF, either. Sterling has visited this utopian-futurist territory before, most notably with *Islands in the Net*, but while there his occasional tendency to pontificate gave the novel overtones of a corporate long-range planning report, here the people are almost as interesting as the ideas.

Holy Fire is set exactly one hundred years in the future, in 2096. Someone once pointed out that such round-numbered displacements from the present — 50, 100, 1000 years — can be taken as a signal that the author wants to underline the immediacy of the text by reminding us of the year of its publication. I'm not sure that works in all cases, but it does with *Holy Fire*, which examines the social and economic impact of biomedical advances through the story of Mia Ziemann, a wealthy 94-year-old who chooses to undergo a rejuvenation process so radical and disorienting that those who survive it call themselves "posthuman." (The term has appeared before, mostly in the work of prefix-happy theorists, but here for the first time it seems self-evidently right.) Ziemann is easily the most convincing and interesting character Sterling has so far created, and the core of the novel is her sometimes confused but always resilient attempt to forge an identity for herself in her "new" 20-year-old body in a gerontocracy that both honors and exiles her. She is at once nearly a century old and barely two weeks old, and Sterling makes the most of the inherent dramatic irony. Along the way, he offers us rich glimpses of a colorful 21st century in which dogs host TV talk shows, computers are made of smart fabrics, whole city blocks are made of edible fungi, and virtual reality has advanced several generations to create a mystical, posthuman alternative consciousness called "holy fire".

After undergoing her experimental rejuvenation treatment, Ziemann rebels against the lab-animal circumstances of her recovery and escapes to Europe, where she takes to calling herself Maya and meets a succession of thieves, artists, and intellectuals who offer her what amounts to Sterling's version of the familiar utopian lecture-tour, mostly through Prague and Stuttgart, which become emblems of different aspects of Sterling's future world. For the most part, the story is so richly textured and the characters complex enough that the pace never really flags even when they begin speaking in bumper stickers: "The human condition is over," says Paul, a university lecturer who is explaining to Maya the high-tech Dadaism that passes for late-21st century art. "Nature is over. Art is over. Consciousness is ductile. Science is an infinite powder keg". Paul and his compatriots are seeking Maya's assistance to prepare for the "singularity," a crucial moment when human history passes into the posthuman, when life extension treatments have advanced far enough to guarantee virtual immortality. Needless to say, there is considerable tension between the younger generation of incipient immortals and the gerontocrats already long in power, and Maya finds herself caught in the middle.

There are aspects of *Holy Fire* that call to mind novels by authors as diverse as Norman Spinrad, Joe Haldeman, and Neal Stephenson, but what is noticeably missing is the swaggering hipness of much cyberpunk writing, of which Sterling was the original theorist. But Sterling's ideas always seemed too complex to be entirely comfortable in such a surface-worshiping mode, and he may temperamentally have never been cyberpunk in the first place (although, of course, one of the most useful definitions of a cyberpunk writer is any writer who has occasion to deny being a cyberpunk writer). He does, however, write well about *characters* who are cyberpunk, and they show up in *Holy Fire* as well, but with a depth and substance we haven't seen before. It may be Sterling's best novel, and it's certainly one of the best of the year.

After decades of collecting, Ray Bradbury finally owns all the exclamation points. He is the most irrepressibly enthusiastic of all major living American writers (Walt Whitman would have given him a good tumble), and for more than half a century this attitude has helped shape what is probably the most unmistakeable prose style ever to escape from the SF pulps (even though that style has long since demonstrated more influence outside the SF field than within it). In his new collection **Quicker than the Eye**, you only need to read the first story – no, the first paragraph, the first sentence, the first *clause* – to know you're in Bradburyland: "They drove into green Sunday-morning country ... " This is the sort of warmly reassuring baritone that has fed a generation of breakfast cereal commercials, Ronald Reagan campaign ads, theme park "villages" with fake front porches, and movies from *Big* to *E.T.* (not to mention the oddly unsuccessful attempts to translate Bradbury directly to film or TV). If the voice has largely faded from the SF world (which Bradbury himself all but abandoned decades ago), the reason isn't lack of affection for the man or his work – it's simply that he never belonged there in the first place. His aesthetic owed less to Heinlein or Stapledon than to Thornton Wilder or Aaron Copland (whose music, incidentally, has been appropriated for some of those same breakfast food ads). He's an American author who got out in time, escaping the small-town midwest before it could turn him into Sherwood Anderson (or David Lynch) and the decaying boardwalks of Venice, California before growing into the cynicism of Nathanael West. He's the only author to destroy the world in a nuclear holocaust and turn it literally into a picnic.

Yet among non-SF readers, Bradbury is still the name that most often comes to mind when SF is mentioned, and one of a handful of writers anywhere who can command a first printing of 50,000 copies (according to the promotional material for *Quicker than the Eye*) for a volume of short stories. So even if, by a fairly generous stretch, there are only three or four stories here that could remotely be called SF, the book commands attention as Bradbury's first collection of recent stories in many years. And for those who had long since concluded that Bradbury had forsaken the short story form in favor of ill-conceived detective stories and appalling poetry, it may come as something of a pleasant surprise. There is, to be sure, a fair measure of cloying sentimentality (such as "Remember Sascha?," about a poor couple in Venice, California – he bears the trademark autobiographical-signature name of Douglas Spaulding – who get cheery messages from their unborn child), and there is precious little of the hard-edged young Bradbury of *Dark Carnival* (although "Free Dirt" strives for the horror-story tone), but there are a good number of lightly entertaining tales that often recall earlier stages in Bradbury's career. The book isn't a retrospective collection of stories, but it is of themes.

For all that's been written and said about Bradbury, I don't recall ever seeing him discussed as a ghost story writer, even though ghosts of one sort or another figure in several of his most memorable tales, as they do here. "Night Meeting," one of the most popular stories from *The Martian Chronicles*, gets recast in *Dandelion Wine* country in "That Woman on the Lawn," about a cross-time encounter between a grown man and a young girl who turns out to be his mother. Earlier tales like "The Exiles" and "Usher II" grew out of Bradbury's fear that some of his favorite imaginative writers might be banned or forgotten; in "Last Rites," he sends a time traveler back to assure Melville, Poe, and Wilde that this hasn't been the case. The ghosts of Laurel and Hardy get similar assurances in "Another Fine Mess." In "The Witch Door," one of the few tales to echo *Fahrenheit 451*, a fugitive in a dystopian future hides in an ancient cubby once used to hide witches – and trades places with a witch hidden there centuries earlier. There are distinct echoes of "The Million Year Picnic" in "The Other Highway" in which an overgrown road almost lures a family to spurn their fast-paced urban life. And Bradbury's favorite haunted places are here as well: small-time carnivals ("The Electrocution," "Quicker than the Eye") and libraries ("Exchange").

While there has always been a mordant humor to some of Bradbury's more grotesque tales (one thinks of "The Handler"), his later attempts at comedy (dating perhaps from his stint in Ireland with John Huston) have seemed far less edgy and often just too damned jolly. His attempt to blend a Sherlock Holmes *hommage* with an Irish tall tale in "The Finnegan" succeeds as neither, while "The Ghost in the Machine," his latest tribute to the bicycle (also celebrated in several of his Irish tales), lays out its one idea and then pounds it into pavement grease. The conceit in "At the End of the Ninth Year" is so lame it doesn't even need the pounding. Humor requires a certain amount of bile, and Bradbury only occasionally manages to subdue his cheerfulness long enough to bring it off. "The Very Gentle Murders" is a genuinely funny story about an aging married couple trying to do each other in but getting innocent bystanders instead, and "Zaharoff/Richter Mark V" features the grandly loony paranoid fantasy that earthquakes are caused by architects to drum up more business. "Unterderseaboat Doktor," with its magic periscope and U-boat captain turned psychiatrist, is so off the wall I'm not sure what it's meant to be.

It's both reassuring and dismaying to think that on the basis of the evidence in *Quicker than the Eye*, Bradbury has hardly changed as a writer in decades. As always, it's virtually impossible to speak his dialogue aloud with any hint of conviction – people simply don't talk with all that boisterous punctuation. As always, he views plots as optional accessories, like adjustable lumbar seats, while the main business – the chassis – of all his fiction is that famous cadenced language. There's no denying that the language works: it's marketed an evanescent dream of a Waukegan that probably never was to generations of readers and a handful of genres; it's finessed its way past the second dumbest Mars on record (Burroughs gets the honors) and probably *the* dumbest Venus; it's colonized high-school creative writing classes the way kudzu colonized Georgia. But it must also be said that no one can do it like Bradbury, that Bradbury can make it work a surprisingly good part of the time, and that the best device for imposing some restraint and discipline on this ebullient voice is the short story. There are no masterpieces in *Quicker than the Eye*, but there's some good innocent fun, and a master's voice.

Clifford D. Simak is another classic SF writer who staked out a distinctive territory based on his rural midwestern roots – only a couple hundred miles north of Bradbury's – but he never strayed very far from a few classic SF themes, which he treated with considerably more rigor than Bradbury, if sometimes with as much sentimentality. Simak's *City* is at least as important to the history of SF as Bradbury's *The Martian Chronicles* – some would say more so, given its more challenging conceptual framework – and his other short stories are among the most enduring in the genre, as **Over the River & Through the Woods** (a new limited edition from Tachyon Publications) attests. Yet Simak, like Sturgeon, seems in danger of fading into the limbo of historical anthologies; while his work was once as widely available as that of any of the giants, today these stories seem almost like new discoveries – and are just as fresh. Part of the reason may be not that Simak's folksy language seems to belie the underlying sense of alienation and tragedy that characterizes much of his work; part may be due to the rediscovery of American regional idioms among younger SF writers from Terry Bisson to Nancy Kress (with some further examples to be found in Patrick Nielsen Hayden's new anthology *Starlight 1* [see below]). Simak's territory isn't entirely Simak's any longer, and it's not a bad thing.

Over the River & Through the Woods contains eight Simak stories from 1951 through 1980 – which means it includes none of the classic stories, like "Desertion" or "Huddling Place," which later went to make up *City*, but does include his late Hugo and Nebula-winning masterpiece "The Grotto of the Dancing Deer" and the Hugo-winning "The Big Front Yard." One of the first things that comes to mind when rereading the latter story after several years – it concerns a characteristically laconic farmer with a dog named Towser (the only name Simak seems to have permitted for dogs) who finds on his property a gateway to distant worlds – is that few contemporary writers would have let such a simple and elegant premise be confined to a novella. One thinks, for example, of Jack McDevitt's *Ancient Shores* (reviewed here in July); like McDevitt, Simak eventually brings in the U.N. and hints at the political and social implications of such a discovery, but it's clear that Simak's focus is on the unimpressed rustic whose very lack of response to the wonder at his doorstep intensifies our own. When a rustic is impressed by an alien presence, such as in "A Death in the House," it is less likely to be from a sense of wonder than from a sense of companionship. Simak's roots may be firmly in SF, but he writes of alien encounters in a way bizarrely suggestive of the way Willa Cather might have written of them. Aliens are strange but unthreatening, and in some cases (as in "Neighbor") they can turn the entire neighborhood into a pastoral Shangri-la, isolated from the outside in a way that encapsulates what must be Simak's own dreams of lost innocence.

But Simak could write about more than wonderful things happening to remote farmers. "Good Night, Mr. James" is a very early treatment (1951) of what we would today call a cloning story, done with the kind of cynical humor that is needed for what is essentially a double- and triple-cross tale. It reveals Simak's healthy streak of humor, as does "Dusty Zebra," in which trivial objects are zapped into another dimension in return for high-tech wonders. "Construction Shack" ironically explores an almost Stapledonian notion of whole solar systems being engineered by ancient aliens (Pluto is the construction shack of the title), cast in terms of the matter-of-fact space jockeys so familiar from pulp SF. Simak may be at his best, however, when his theme is isolation and abandonment. The title story (widely familiar from its inclusion in LeGuin and Attebery's *Norton Book of Science Fiction*) concerns children from the future sent back to the refuge of the 1890s. The best tale in the collection and one of the high points of Simak's late career, "The Grotto of the Dancing Deer," concerns an anthropologist who comes to realize that his assistant seems to know far too much about certain ancient cave paintings, and may in fact have been their creator. Simak's evocation, in a few pages, of the sheer loneliness of immortality and the daunting perspectives of time involved, again could be a lesson to a generation of younger writers, and reminds us brilliantly of what Simak was capable of.

Patrick Nielsen Hayden's **Starlight** 1 is a worthwhile and entirely admirable attempt to recreate the SF original anthology series in the mold of Damon Knight's *Orbit* or Terry Carr's *Universe* – series in which each volume was less ambitious than say, Bantam's more recent *Spectrum* series, but more fussed over than the average issue of the average magazine. Such series have been an important source of short SF since the decline of the pulps, and part of their purpose has always seemed to be to present a kind of "state of the art" report on current SF for readers who may only occasionally explore the field in its short forms. But such anthologies also inevitably argue for a certain approach to SF favored by the editor, leaving readers with uncertainty as to whether SF really looks like this or if the editor *wants* it to look like this. Hayden, for example, shows a predilection for SF playing with history and – overlapping with this – SF which gains its effects by deliberately colliding two disparate frames of reference.

The latter technique is more often associated with humor, and there is a good deal of gentle humor in Jane Yolen's "Sister Emily's Lightship," which describes Emily Dickinson's encounter with aliens in a way that seems entirely consistent with her poetry, and that never becomes the kind of joke that Connie Willis made of it in her contribution to Kevin Anderson's recent *War of the Worlds: Global Dispatches*. Carter Scholz's "Mengele's Jew," on the other hand, uses the collision of themes – in this case, Mengele's experiments and Schrodinger's – to achieve nothing much more than a nihilistic grimness. There are also traces of Holocaust themes in John M. Ford's unusual and experimental "Erase/Record/Play," which gradually reveals a nightmare future by describing a production of *A Midsummer Night's Dream*; in Mark Kreighbaum's "I Remember Angels," about a riot-torn future; and in Maureen F. McHugh's "The Cost to be Wise." The McHugh story, which describes the brutal effects of intolerance on a colony planet, is not only one of the cleanest SF stories in the book (it calls to mind Le Guin's best Hainish stories, with its carefully controlled point of view), but is clearly one of the best.

SF's repeated recent attempts to colonize historical fiction are represented here by Gregory Feeley's convincingly textured tale of 17th century optics, "Weighing the

Ayre," Susanna Clarke's excellent Victorian magic tale "The Ladies of Grace Adieu," the Yolen piece, and perhaps Andy Duncan's "Liza and the Crazy Water Man," set in a world of 1930s country radio that is as meticulously detailed as any of the more exotic historical settings. The Duncan story is a surprise and a delight, not only because of the freshness of its setting, but because Duncan is a genuinely new writer, who graduated from Clarion only in 1994. A similar vernacular voice lends power to Susan Palwick's "GI Jesus" (the title refers to an image of Jesus that seems to appear on an upper gastrointestinal x-ray, not to anything military), although it takes a fairly generous frame of mind to accept this fine story as either SF or fantasy. Martha Soukup's "Waking Beauty," on the other hand, is a clear Collieresque fantasy of office romance realized through spellcasting.

Of the remaining stories, perhaps the most unusual and moving is Robert Reed's dreamlike "Killing the Morrow," which ingeniously conflates the theme of time travel (or at least crosstime communication) with that of the strange pregnancy, to examine the ways we create and destroy futures. The almost obligatory nod to punk-decadent futures is Michael Swanwick's "The Dead," a chilling but fairly predictable tale of a world in which corpses become sex toys. Both of these tales lean rather heavily on the polished style of the authors, and in general Hayden has an excellent ear for style and craft – there's actually not a badly written or structured piece in the book. And in a sense, that's all we need to expect from such an anthology series as this one promises to be. If, along with that satisfied expectation, we get a vague feeling of self-absorption with technique, of younger writers straining a little uncomfortably against the genre's historical preoccupation with neat new ideas, it's hardly worth complaining about. *Starlight 1*, it's a fair guess, is what we can expect much SF to look like in the coming year or two, and it's not at all a bad prospect.

– October 1996, Locus #429 –

Idoru ~~ William Gibson

Humpty Dumpty: An Oval ~~ Damon Knight

Blade Runner: Replicant Night ~~ K.W. Jeter

Little Sister ~~ Kara Dalkey

William Gibson's most famous sentence remains his first: "The sky above the port was the color of television, tuned to a dead channel." Knowing when he's on to a good thing, Gibson doesn't let us out of his new novel **Idoru** until we've seen a sky like a "paint-chip submitted by the contractor of the universe," a sky "like mother-of-pearl," a sky crawling with "oil-slick colors," a "serious sky," a "gasoline sky," endless gray skies that are pressing down, and at least one rare sky that's "beautiful but empty . . . like pale turquoise." Mostly, the skies are rainy, and the rain generally ends up in greasy puddles on streets, casting distorted reflections of neon lights in seedy retrofuture cities. In short, Gibson knows his territory, and it's a territory as distinctive — and by now as familiar — as that of Hammett or Chandler. But for all its sardonic edginess, Gibson's world is seldom quite as tough or ruthless as those of his hardboiled ancestors, and never as heroic. When he shifts fully into hardboiled mode — as he does toward the conclusion of *Idoru* — the result is deliberately comical, as much parody as *hommage*. It may be that all the grimness and the glitz have caused readers to overlook the considerable wit underlying Gibson's deadpan hipness, but in *Idoru* it's impossible to ignore.

Like *Virtual Light*, *Idoru* is more user-friendly, and thus more likely to appeal to a broader mainstream audience, than the earlier novels. Instead of a complex multilevel plot involving worldwide conspiracies, we get a simple two-track narrative focusing on a problem of daunting tabloid triviality: why has the lead singer of the rock band Lo/Rez announced his intention to marry an *idoru*, or computer-generated "idol singer"? (These artificial-personality media stars are compared to similarly constructed "synthespians" in the movies.) Instead of burned-out cyberjockeys, we get a spunky teenage fan from Seattle and a grown-up orphan whose youthful exposure to an experimental drug has given him a kind of psychic ability to perceive "nodal points" in vast fields of information, making him a useful data detective. And instead of brutal shadowy villains, we get B-movie molls and gunsels.

The young rock fan Chia has been sent to Tokyo by her chapter of the Lo/Rez fan club to make contact with the local chapter and get to the bottom of the rumor that Rez intends to marry a data construct, or "software agent," named Rei Toei. The detective, Colin Laney, who had established a reputation with Slitscan (a kind of reality-TV program turned international megacorporation), is hired for a similar mission — to examine Rez's data fields in order to get clues to his intentions. Exactly why all this is important to anyone is unclear, but skewed perspectives are an important part of the Gibson universe. As Laney moves through theme bars devoted to Kafka or chewing gum, landscapes of Giger-like nanotech buildings, or a decadent club called the Western World in a ruined building caked with solidified urine, we get the impression that no one in this future delves much beneath the surface: what is important is what is in front of you. Part of the reason Gibson hinges his plot on a rumor barely worthy of a minor gossip-column item is to show us a society in which it really seems important.

Chia represents a kind of innocent idealism unusual to the Gibson universe. She spends time in a virtual Venice given to her by her father, and meets her fellow club members in richly textured virtual environments; her world retains both color and promise. En route to Tokyo, however, she naively agrees to carry a suitcase for a stranger, and inevitably gets mixed up with spies trying to smuggle nanotech generators, which are as illegal as nuclear weapons. For a while — for a long while, actually — it seems as though we're in the middle of a bizarre conflation of young-adult suspense and *fin de siècle* techno-decadence: Harriet the Spy turned bladerunner.

The novel's tough-guy villains — an ex-con bodyguard named Blackwell (nicknamed "Toecutter") and a blowsy blonde named Maryalice who totes a cigarette lighter in the shape of a gun — add a note of comic-book excess to a narrative that seems increasingly slapstick. By the final confrontation — Chia trapped in a love-hotel by Maryalice and her partner, with Laney racing to find her — the dialogue has turned into full-fledged parody and the action into something resembling screwball comedy. Although lightweight by comparison with almost anything else he has written, *Idoru* is entertaining, funny, and slyly subversive of the whole cyberpunk aesthetic.

Damon Knight is also a fairly subversive writer, but one whose reputation as a novelist has long been overshadowed by his considerable achievements as a critic and editor. If it weren't for that work, it might be said of Knight that his impact on the field has been the least memorable of all major current figures in SF; ask an average reader to name two or three Knight titles, and you might get vague memories of recent novels like the CV series or the mordant tale "To Serve Man" (mostly famous from *The Twilight Zone*), but you won't get the instant recitation of classics like you would for Blish or Bester or Pohl — Knight's closest compatriots in the picaresque/satirical dimension of SF that emerged during the 1950s. With *Humpty Dumpty*, however, Knight pulls out most of the generic stops that have constrained his earlier work, and storms happily into territory we more often associate with Kurt Vonnegut or James Morrow. It's as though he always belonged there.

Humpty Dumpty: An Oval is the hallucinatory picaresque tale of Wellington Stout, an aging lingerie executive who is shot in the head while delivering a mysterious package for his brother in Milan. Waking in the hospital, Stout first notices something is wrong when he keeps hearing distorted women's voices, whose punning gossip recalls that of Joyce's washerwomen in *Finnegans Wake*. Spirited away from the hospital by a shadowy figure named Roger Wort, Stout learns that the package has disappeared, but that the information it was supposed to contain may have been hidden in a business card he had given to a woman he met on the plane, Rosemary Sanchez. Stout's attempts to track down Sanchez through a wildly distorted Europe and America provide the skeletal plot frame on which Knight hangs an astonishingly inventive series of dreamlike transformations and slapstick interludes.

A new planet has appeared, christened Mongo by the media, and aliens seem to have taken over the shoestores, using their new ultra-comfortable shoes to implant tracking devices in people's feet. An ancient conspiracy of dentists threatens to rule the world. Meteors open huge craters throughout North America — including one that wipes out the entire northeast — and alien soldiers begin to march out of the craters, plotting to freeze the world with a secret machine. Stout himself, as he retraces the path of his own life in pursuit of Sanchez, finds figures from his past appearing everywhere, as he himself undergoes strange transformations. At one point he is led about by an implanted umbilical cord; at another he slowly turns into a bus. Sometimes he is told that his entire experience is the result of the bullet in his brain, or that he is a secret agent of the aliens, or that he has been suddenly given the power to see things as they really are, or that he is leading the world into a new reality.

Easily the most impressive display of Knight's imagination to date, *Humpty Dumpty* is an antic fable distinguished by it's author's unwillingness to yield to easy SF solutions; while there are enough clues to enable us to resolve the narrative into a kind of Dickian mind-bending game, it's far from a giveaway. Most important, Knight has the courage of his own surrealism: he knows it's the endlessly transforming and looping text that is at the core of the novel, and not some hidden infodump. Along the way, he offers a catalog of anarchic, satiric jibes at everything from religion and medicine to automobile security systems and motels. Although it's pretty much unlike anything else he's written, this may turn out to be the novel Knight is remembered for.

K.W. Jeter, who did a yeoman's job of reconstituting a film experience in last year's *Blade Runner 2*, seems determined to let us know that his second sequel, **Blade Runner: Replicant Night**, is very much his own construct; even the subtitle echoes Jeter's earlier *Morlock Night*, a similar original riff on inherited material. But the novel will hardly be a disappointment to devotees of the film: not only are the settings and characters familiar, but even exact sequences are reproduced. The film began with the android-hunting blade runner Holden being blown away during an interrogation of the replicant Kowalski; *Replicant Night* almost begins with exactly the same scene, only cleverly displaced.

The film, it turns out – apparently the film that we know as *Blade Runner* – is a docudrama being shot in an orbiting soundstage and based on Rick Deckard's famous hunt for four renegade replicants; Deckard himself has been hired as consultant. But in traditional Hollywood murder mystery fashion, someone is putting real bullets in the prop guns. Holden, on a mission to deliver a talking briefcase to Deckard (the briefcase turns out to be all that's left of super-replicant Roy Batty), gets caught up in the mayhem. Deckard flees back to the Martian hovel he shares with the generally pissed-off Sarah Tyrell, who is waiting to shoot him, only she shoots the dancing clock instead after being invited back to earth by a mysterious pair of agents claiming to represent the shadow corporation behind the destroyed Tyrell replicant empire – but wait. Either I'm getting ahead of myself here, or Jeter is having some off-the-wall fun with us, and with the welter of texts and subtexts inherent in a project like this. After all, we are dealing with a sequel to a sequel to a movie alteration of a novel which, way back when Philip K. Dick had something to say about it, was already a game of codes and discourses.

So Jeter knows he's working with a complex palimpsest, and that's what makes this novel far more interesting than the average movie tie-in. *Blade Runner* has become such an iconic film that the only way for Jeter to escape it – to claim the narrative as his own – is to subsume it, reducing the source text to a plot element and weaving an original narrative around it. Jeter laid the groundwork for this in *Bladerunner 2* by introducing the evil Sarah and developing a substantial backstory about an ill-fated interstellar mission in the early days of the Tyrell corporate empire. At its best, *Replicant Night* is a sequel to that novel, and not to the film or the Dick novel. By the time we get done, we know we're in a Jeter novel, not a Dick *manqué* or a Ridley Scott film, and this is underlined by such marvelous set-pieces as a nightmarish confrontation with the past aboard a submerged spacecraft in the North Sea. At the same time, Jeter's fatal attraction for overheated hardboiled melodrama often undercuts his own narrative ingenuity. For example, Sarah's such a sucker for Bogart dialogue that whenever she gets a gun on Deckard (at least four times by my count – she's determined), he talks his way right into a romantic clinch. "Could you kiss me?" she whimpers. "The way you kissed her?" There may still be room for retro-*noir* in this material, but not for lines that would have made Bacall gag.

Enamored as librarians and booksellers may be of the term, I've never quite been comfortable with "young adult" as any way of describing a book. Even when describing a readership, it's a polite euphemism if not an outright oxymoron, unless you're willing to accept as "adult" anyone within shouting distance of puberty. The problem is further exacerbated when the kind of literature involved is fantasy, a genre whose history and canon confounds even the more traditional distinctions between children's and adult literature. (One could even argue that the basic trope of fantasy, toward discovery and maturation, would place most of it in the realm of childlike or adolescent concerns – but that's another debate.) Look at a bibliography of young adult fantasy and you'll find listed major works by Richard Adams, Ursula Le Guin, Lewis Carroll, Diana Wynne Jones, Patricia McKillip, Jane Yolen, and any number of other writers who may or may not have had some mythical "young adult reader" in mind when they set about creating their worlds; at times it seems that all it takes is a youthful protagonist to send a novel into the admittedly lucrative ghetto of YA-dom.

This is not a fate to be sneered at from a marketing point of view, of course, but how many fine novels escape the notice of us Not Very Young Adults because of it? Jane Yolen, who has demonstrated her acumen at editing adult fantasy through her *Xanadu* anthology series, has for some time now had her own imprint at Harcourt Brace, and some of the titles in that series deserve note simply as fantasies, "young adult" or not. In this case, it's Kara Dalkey's **Little Sister**, a superbly realized short fantasy set during the Heian period in twelfth-century Japan. The "little sister" of the title is Fujiwara no Mitsuko, 13-year-old daughter of an Imperial court administrator, who sees her entire identity in terms of relationships with her elders. When the family is forced to flee from a violent rebellion of renegade monks, Fujiwara's new brother-in-law is killed, her older sister Amaiko reduced to near-catatonia at the shock, and her mother and other siblings captured by a neighboring warlord. Fujiwara escapes with Amaiko, and soon finds herself involved with a shapeshifting *tengu*, who assists her in a quest through several dimensions of Japanese mythology, including a powerfully realized underworld journey and confrontations with intimidating gods. Fujiwara's initial goal is only to find the spirit that has apparently left her sister's body, but by the end of the novel she has arranged to free her family from the warlord and even arrange a convenient political alliance.

The supernatural quest plot is standard issue, of course, but it's also standard issue in much of what passes for adult fantasy. In fact, it's hard to figure how you would improve on this tale by converting it into an adult fantasy (although it's not hard to imagine the same tale done with an older male protagonist and padded out with a few treacherous seductresses and several hundred pages of overwrought action). What gives Dalkey's tale its unique value is the masterful way in which she balances a convincing portrait of an historical epoch – one so remote from us, she notes in an afterward, that it predates most of our conceptions of Japan – with a carefully derived mythological realm that seems consistent both with the historical setting and with the more familiar conventions of fantasy. Dalkey has apparently written at least one other fantasy set in Heian Japan, and she's clearly a writer who knows what to do with her research – how to use it as a source of imagination, rather than as a replacement for it. I hope *Little Sister* does big business among the teenage girls for whom it is apparently aimed, and who already seem to control most of the American economy. But like most of the economy, giving this only to them would be a waste.

– November 1996, Locus #430 –

Voyage ~~ Stephen Baxter

Visions of Wonder: The Science Fiction Research Association Reading Anthology ~~ ed. David G. Hartwell & Milton T. Wolf

Spares ~~ Michael Marshall Smith

The Wall of the Sky, the Wall of the Eye ~~ Jonathan Lethem

It's rare that we get the opportunity to watch science fiction transformed into historical fiction in a single generation, and even rarer when that historical fiction gets reconverted into SF. But that seems to be exactly what has happened with NASA's manned spaceflight programs of the l960s. Of course, near-future, near-space adventures had been the stuff of SF since its infancy, but by the late 50s and early 60s writers could extrapolate from actual policies and plans; I recall reading a Sunday-supplement voyage-to-Mars tale allegedly by Wernher von Braun himself, and a number of pedestrian aeronautics writers like Kenneth Gantz and Jeff Sutton (whose 1963 *Apollo at Go* is the mediocre classic of this period) could briefly break into SF with thinly fictionalized accounts of actual long-range planning reports.

(Their prose may have been as lame as their imaginations, but give them thirty years of improved book-marketing and several hundred extra pages per novel and they might have become Tom Clancy.) During and after the Apollo program, we could watch the transformation of our understanding of spaceflight simply by noting its movement from genre to genre: from SF to tech fiction (Sutton et al.) to journalism to "new journalism" (Norman Mailer, Tom Wolfe) to backdrops in mainstream fiction (like John Updike's Rabbit Redux) to memoirs, histories, and finally historical dramas like James Michener's *Space* or Ron Howard's film *Apollo 13* (at a showing of which I overheard a teenager telling his wide-eyed date, "You know – it's a true story!").

But apparently SF never wanted to give up what was once its sole property, especially since almost every SF writer who has written about it is convinced that NASA never made a logical policy decision when a loopy one would do. What should have been the decade of triumph for the kind of pristine technological rationality that had been promoted by SF at least as far back as Wells was instead being undermined by the very people who were supposed to implement it. So in the last couple of years we've begun to see an odd but fascinating effort to snatch Apollo and all it supposedly stood for from the jaws of an uncaring history. A number of hard-SF writers – Sheffield, Pournelle, James Kirkwood, William Barton – have begun to reimagine near-space exploration in a series of retro-corrective stories and novels, the best example of which is probably Michael Flynn's *Firestar* (reviewed here last May). (At the same time, we're getting new nonfiction books like G. Harry Stine's *Halfway to Anywhere: Achieving America's Destiny in Space*, which echo such awestruck manifestoes of the fifties as Clarke's *The Exploration of Space* – only this time in the context of making an argument for the development of a single-stage-to-orbit vehicle, which seems to be a large part of these hard SF writers' agenda.)

Whatever all this means, it's hard to imagine that this historical reclamation project can carry things much further than Stephen Baxter's **Voyage**, which reimagines the entire Apollo program in such a way as to lead to a manned landing on Mars by 1986. *Voyage* isn't really an alternate history tale, even though Baxter described it as one in his interview here last April. He posits essentially two pivotal changes in history – Kennedy surviving the 1963 assassination attempt to become a champion of a Mars program, and Nixon deciding in 1970 to back the Mars project over the Space Shuttle – but then pointedly avoids allowing a full-fledged alternate history to develop from them. Nixon, Carter, and Reagan still get elected, Vietnam is still a national trauma, Apollo 13 is still a near-disaster. In other words, Baxter isn't playing by alternate-history rules: he wants to change only just enough to make his point about how a Mars mission might have come about. Some of the changes are a bit jarring, as when he replaces Buzz Aldrin on Apollo 11 with his own character, Joe Muldoon. Some are unconvincing, as when he has the crippled Kennedy turning into a champion of manned spaceflight, or Reagan buying enthusiastically into a Mars landing. But, by and large, Baxter gets away with it amazingly well.

The danger in writing what amounts to an institutional history novel (the institution here being NASA) is that most of what happens in an institution, most of the time, simply isn't very interesting – and *Voyage* has its own rather trying share of RFP's, contractor presentations, and hardware specs, which Baxter tries to keep interesting through occasion irrelevant jaunts into melodrama, as when a chief contractor's neglected wife takes an overdose of sleeping pills. But Baxter skilfully keeps his dramatic thrust going by weaving a number of personal narratives into his larger picture. The actual 1986 Mars mission is described in alternating chapters with the historical material, and as the novel unfolds, we learn how each of the three politically correct crew members (a jock, a black, a woman) came to be on the mission. Natalie York, a geologist who earlier had an affair with a doomed astronaut, is the strongest of Baxter's characters, and it is her story that finally frames the entire novel. But for sheer dramatic impact, Baxter's *tour-de-force* is the story of that doomed astronaut, an extended episode (almost a novel within a novel) about a mission to test the nuclear-powered rockets that have been chosen for the Mars flight. The catastrophe that ensues is Baxter's tribute to both the Challenger and Apollo 13, although it's more horrifying than either – and makes you wonder how we could ever have thought seriously of using such a propulsion system.

It's probably premature to say that Baxter is the next Arthur C. Clarke (since we aren't quite done with the first one yet), but he's certainly the most important writer in the Clarkean tradition to emerge in recent years, and his favorite themes echo those of Clarke, right down to the odd juxtaposition of cosmic epics of eternity (*Ring* or *The Time Ships*) with conservatively-imagined technical scenarios and vanilla main-stream characterization. In the early 1950s – at the same time he was producing those cosmic epics – Clarke did much to stoke our imaginations with the romance of real-life spaceflight, both in his nonfiction and in novels like *Prelude to Space*. It's ironically appropriate that his heir apparent, writing decades after the events that Clarke made us dream of, and at the same time that he's producing his cosmic epics, should set out to ignite those dreams all over again. It's even stranger that he should succeed.

David Hartwell and Milton Wolf's gingerly subtitled **Visions of Wonder: The Science Fiction Research Association Reading Anthology** (note that it doesn't actually say "teaching anthology" or "scholarly anthology") once again raises the question of how SF should be approached in the college classroom, assuming of course it should be approached at all (the now-hackneyed "get it back in the gutter" approach seems moribund except as applause-bait at cons). I would have thought that the 1970s boom in college-level SF courses, spurred largely by a desire to lure *Star Wars*-dazed kids into lit classes, had tapered off, but a census in November 1996 issue of the academic journal *Science-Fiction Studies* tracks down no fewer than 402 courses in North America alone (including some fantasy and utopian fiction courses). In the most literal sense, the matter is purely academic, since SF has never been dependent on the educational system for its next generation of readers. In fact, the claim can be made — with the kind of conviction made possible only by the absence of hard data — that few SF readers have ever been created by a good SF class, and even fewer have been derailed by a bad one.

Nevertheless, the classroom is perceived as a rarefied hearts-and-minds battlefield over the nature of SF, and text anthologies have appeared with some regularity for decades. To look at them now in light of the new Hartwell/Wolf anthology is to see a gradual disintegration of consensus, both as to what SF is and what represents it. Any SF reader would have recognized almost all the stories in Robert Silverberg's 1970 "critic's anthology" *The Mirror of Infinity*, Robin Scott Wilson's 1973 *Those Who Can*, or Silverberg's high-canonical *Science Fiction Hall of Fame: Volume I*, which were among the most commonly used classroom books in the 1970s (in the current Science-Fiction Studies survey, the *Hall of Fame* still tops the list of anthologies). When the Science Fiction Research Association first got into the act in 1978 (Hartwell and Wolf's is actually the third SFRA anthology), the results were only slightly different; *Science Fiction: Contemporary Mythology* added to the recognizable classics a few more contemporary "literary" tales by Le Guin, Dick, Carr, and a handful of others.

One could almost see lines beginning to be drawn, though, and James Gunn's monumental four-volume *Road to Science Fiction* (1979-1982) persuasively reasserted the claims of historicism over eclecticism. The most popular of Gunn's series was volume 3, "From Heinlein to Here," which was again filled with recognizable stories by Heinlein, Asimov, Bradbury, Clarke, Sturgeon, Ellison, Delany, Ballard, Aldiss, Le Guin, Russ, Haldeman, etc., and covered the early 1940s to the mid 1970s. It provides a remarkably complete and balanced picture of the development of SF from in this period, and it quickly became one of the most popular teaching texts. Fortunately for those instructors who felt at sea when the Mentor edition went out of print, this third volume has been reissued in an attractive trade format (albeit with a lot of new typos) from White Wolf. It remains the best historical anthology of its kind, and is enormously enjoyable on its own terms: it's exactly the kind of thing that might intrigue new readers enough to send them off exploring, but it's hardly risk-taking from the point of view of challenging consensus. When the Science Fiction Research Association produced its second anthology in 1988, it had relatively little to add to what Gunn (a former SFRA president) had already achieved. If frequency-of-anthologization is any measure, a clearly defined classroom canon of short fiction emerged from the Silverberg, Gunn, and SFRA anthologies, and it was a canon based largely on a postwar historicist model of the genre. Understanding SF meant beginning with *Astounding* and ending somewhere just this side of the New Wave (later, just this side of cyberpunk).

Things changed radically with the appearance of Le Guin, Attebery, and Fowler's *Norton Book of Science Fiction* in 1993. By eliminating all authors but North Americans and all stories before 1960, the editors chose to sacrifice breadth for depth, historical perspective for contemporaneity and style. Any teacher or reader seeking the kind of comfort level provided by the Silverberg/Gunn canon wouldn't find it here; only a handful of selections were familiar to most SF readers (and for teachers who worry about "preparations," the Norton book meant a lot more work than the earlier, more familiar anthologies). The new Hartwell/Wolf SFRA anthology (which appears to have had a lot less input from the general SFRA membership than the first two) may not be intended exactly as a response to the Norton book, but it certainly stakes out much of the same ground − post-1960 North American SF in the case of Norton, post-1980 and mostly American in the case of SFRA − and it offers just as little in the way of historical context (except through a selection of nine critical essays interspersed with the 31 stories). Its stated goal, to represent "SF in the 1990s," is modest for a text anthology but ambitious for a trade book, and *Visions of Wonder* clearly aspires to be both.

I should mention at this point that I had a number of discussions with the editors of *Visions of Wonder*, offered suggestions (some of which have made it into the final book), and contributed an annotated bibliography of scholarship. One point I tried to make was that not all classic stories teach well in the classroom, and that not all stories which teach well are classics. But even an obvious point like that leads into the question of what you are teaching when you teach SF, and that in turn leads into the usual morass of conflicting definitions. For example, Hartwell and Wolf have decided to include fantasy stories like Charles de Lint's "Paperjack" or Suzy McKee Charnas's "Boobs" (there's even a slice of a Robert Jordan novel), but it's not clear what an instructor is supposed to do with these, other than raise the question of why they're not SF (although the Charnas story arguably carries some additional weight as an important feminist rethinking of familiar fantastic tropes). Several stories − Le Guin's "Sur," Aldiss's "A Tupolev Too Far," Judith Tarr's "Them Old Hyannis Blues," Lisa Goldstein's "Split Light," Walter Jon Williams's "Wall, Stone, Craft" − give the collective impression that modern SF is obsessed with alternate or variant history. Maybe it is, and maybe their historical content renders them especially appropriate for academic discussion (although Williams's sophisticated variation on Mary Shelley's inspiration for Frankenstein stands a good chance of being taken as gospel by more than one naive reader). But are such stories representative of a major dimension of SF, or merely of a current trend?

Another group of stories, almost certain to be successful in the classroom, present satiric extrapolations on hot-button social issues: welfare in the case of Philip Jose Farmer's "One Down, One to Go," health care in Nancy Kress's "The Mountain to Mohammed," cult religion in Frederik Pohl's "Redemption in the Quantum Realm," urban crime in Susan Shwartz's "Getting Real." (One of the real strengths of the anthology is the inclusion of excellent recent stories by such older masters as Aldiss, Pohl, Farmer, and Jack Williamson.) These at least provide a taste of *Galaxy*-style social consciousness, and suggest that the genre still has a great deal to offer beyond self-reflexivity. Still another few stories − McCaffrey's "The Ship Who Sang," Bear's "Blood Music," Card's "Ender's War" − serve partly as stand-ins for the novels they became, and seem cleverly chosen to send the readers toward those novels (there is virtually no other reason I can think of for including the Jordan piece, as if he needs the extra readers).

Although the late cutoff dates for inclusion apparently precluded anything by Philip K. Dick, he is everywhere in evidence in the collection, either through tales of shifting identities and realities or cyberpunk settings: James Patrick Kelly's "Mr. Boy," Benford's "Doing Lennon," John Varley's "Overdrawn at the Memory Bank," Tiptree's "The Girl Who Was Plugged In," Gibson's "Burning Chrome." This is probably what many younger students will find most familiar in terms of both setting and attitude. Those looking for more traditional hard SF, though, have fewer choices: Saberhagen's early Berserker story "Masque of the Red Shift" is virtually the only hint of the long tradition of the series tale (although Andre Norton's "Spider Silk" is set in her more fantasy-like Witch World), and Charles Sheffield's "A Braver Thing" – one of his very best stories – is the only realistic exploration of scientists at work. While none of the stories are less than first-rate, the Sheffield shares with Kate Wilhelm's "Forever Yours, Anna," Gene Wolfe's "The Death of Doctor Island," Bisson's "Bears Discover Fire," Joanna Russ's "Souls," and the Le Guin and Aldiss pieces the distinction of being teachable for sheer elegance of writing.

This leaves us with the nine critical essays included, all of which are provocative and almost all of which predate even the earliest stories in the collection. Damon Knight's "Critics" dates from 1952, Judith Merril's introduction to *England Swings SF* from 1968, and the most substantial historical piece, Algis Budrys's "Paradise Charted," from 1980. (There's even an old John W. Campbell, Jr. editorial.) While the more theoretical of these essays (especially those by Delany, Russ, and Stableford) offer insights that are fairly applicable to any of the stories that surround them, there's at least a small irony in the fact that the entire body of SF literature alluded to in the essays is excluded from the fiction selections. This may not confuse readers (and remember, many of the prospective readers are students, a species distinguished by its low threshold of confusability), but I suspect it will. Imagine a mainstream equivalent: a collection of post-Raymond Carver/Donald Barthelme short stories, accompanied by essays discussing Maupassant, Chekov, and Mansfield. I think the idea of including some criticism in a volume like this is an excellent idea – especially since the criticism is by people who really know what they're talking about (an earlier Dick Allen text had essays by Arthur Koestler, Susan Sontag, and Gerald Heard). But uncoupling the criticism so completely from the fiction seems questionable.

As an overview of the last decade or so in SF and a trade anthology whose goals include being "fun to read," *Visions of Wonder* is as fine a book as you'll see this year. As a text – unless of course supplemented by other books – it's far more problematical. It offers neither a systematic exploration of characteristic themes, tropes, and techniques nor a sense of the field's development. But it's shrewd in other ways: a handful of its selections (Bear, Wolfe, Bisson, Le Guin, Russ, Gibson) have already begun to take on a ripe canonical bouquet, suggesting that the book might not date as rapidly as its narrow chronological focus would suggest. And the other stories are enjoyable and provocative enough to make for good classroom or coffeehouse arguments; overall, the book passes the teachability test with flying colors. It may not explain much about SF, and it may not win many new readers, and the prospect of an ill-informed teacher (there are some, I've heard) let loose with this in a class of ill-informed students is fairly unsettling. But could it hurt? Is a first-rate anthology ever a bad thing?

With due respect to Coleridge, some disbelief can be willingly suspended, and some has to be beaten down with a stick. This may be one of the things SF has done to us as readers; a brilliantly executed metaphorical horror story such as, say, Kafka's "In the Penal Colony" can lose a lot of its steam if we are expected to buy into it as rational extrapolation of real behaviors and trends. In other words – as Kafka teaches us – it's better not to explain a fantastic trope at all than to explain it badly. This is the main problem with Michael Marshall Smith's otherwise harrowing second novel, **Spares**, which has already begun to garner substantial attention with a sizable U.S. advance, an equally impressive movie option, and enough violence and pathos for easy bestseller marketability. It probably won't bother too many readers that two of the novel's three main SF premises don't really hold water. The central premise, which will be familiar to readers of Smith's story "To Receive is Better" (reprinted in Stephen Jones's *Best New Horror 6* last year), is that the day will come when the wealthy will be able to clone exact duplicates of themselves as insurance against mutilation, dismemberment, and the attendant problems of tissue rejection during transplants. These clones, or "spares," are raised like vegetables on "farms" where, stripped of all human rights and not even taught to speak, their only function is to provide the requisite arms, legs, lungs, or whatever when their real-life doubles get into serious trouble. They are, of course, gradually whittled to pieces until they die.

This is a truly horrifying proposition, with all sorts of metaphoric weight, and one can't fault Smith for doing all he can to make it work. But unlike Robin Cook's *Coma*, with its much tamer scenario of brain-dead patients harvested for an international black market in transplants, Smith's novel asks us not only to believe in immense corporate and social evil, but in an astonishing degree of amputation-worthy klutziness among the wealthy (just about every one of Smith's spares has suffered multiple "harvestings" by the time they reach their twenties). The wealthy may be different from you and me, but it's hard to believe that getting replacement parts is something they spend much time worrying about, let alone being mean enough to want one under such circumstances. In Smith's world, however, the wealthy fall apart faster than a cheap suit – mostly through accidents or recklessness – and you suspect the only reason for this is to rationalize the horrific premise.

In other words, *Spares* is a good example of what might be called back-formation SF: an SF world contrived specifically to support a particular conceit, but not really thought through on its own terms. In addition to the spares, the other major SF element of Smith's setting presents similar problems: five-mile square, 200-storey-high "Megamalls" which, for completely incomprehensible reasons, also serve as scheduled airliners. The idea of such urban monads is an old one in SF, but why would they ever need to be airborne (apart from the daunting aerodynamic questions involved)? Smith's third major SF element – and one which fortunately almost comes to dominate the novel in the second half – involves a much more convincing future Vietnam-style war fought largely in a kind of alternate cyberworld called The Gap. Smith's explanation of how the Gap works is sheer handwaving, but these sequences achieve a kind of dramatic integrity that much of the rest of the novel lacks.

Despite these conceptual problems, Smith follows through with maniacal conviction, and produces a suspenseful chase narrative with several unexpected turns. Jack Randall, an ex-cop and veteran of the war in The Gap, has worked for five years as caretaker of a spares farm, where he has begun to educate and humanize his charges. When one of them faces certain death to provide organs and skin grafts for her double, he helps a group of them escape to the Megamall of New Richmond, where he finds himself the target of pursuit by several shady characters. The outcome, which leads back into The Gap and to secrets in Randall's own past, is satisfyingly complex. Smith's style is also smooth and often elegant, although he's not above the occasional ancient cliché ("It's because I'm a whore, isn't it?") and the aforementioned handwaving. As a horror/mainstream novel with powerful metaphoric overtones of real social injustices, *Spares* can be moving and even powerful; as SF, it gets off the ground about as smoothly as a Megamall would.

On the strength of two novels and a handful of stories, Jonathan Lethem has established a reputation as one of the most quirky and original fantasists to emerge in the last couple of decades. Both *Gun, with Occasional Music* and *Amnesia Moon* celebrated sheer artifice through the creation of self-consciously literary worlds, and Lethem's enthusiasm for his own narrative inventions was contagious. **The Wall of the Sky, The Wall of the Eye** collects seven of Lethem's stories, and provides further evidence that Lethem is a writer not much given to repeating himself, and highly eclectic in his tastes and influences. The tone of these stories ranges from the comic/nightmarish "The Hardened Criminals" (who are literally hardened, and made part of the wall of the prison) to the drawing-room comedy of "Forever, Said the Duck" (which consists almost entirely of dialogue, set in a cyberspace "party" where a husband and wife have brought together recorded versions of the personalities of their former lovers – the sort of scenario William Gibson might dream up if he were possessed by Noel Coward). Lethem's characteristic wry humor informs even his darkest scenarios (such as his vision of hell in "The Happy Man"), but it is the distorted, reflective humor of the true surrealist, rather than the easy whimsy of much comic fantasy. Like a true surrealist, Lethem is also a bit of an obsessive, and his tendency to worry an idea to death leads to some stories being far longer than they really need to be.

For example, there's "Vanilla Dunk," a novella-length tale about a degraded future NBA in which basketball players compete by enhancing their own skills with exosuits that mimic the moves or "subroutines" of great players of the past. When an arrogant white kid wins the right to use the Michael Jordan subroutines, the result not only reduces the game to lopsided exhibitionism, but brings to the surface many of the racial tensions that already inform professional sports. (Racial themes crop up in a couple of other Lethem stories, as well.) But Lethem seems so fascinated with his fannish knowledge of basketball that he lets the details of individual games almost overwhelm the larger narrative. (As always, the difficulty in writing sports fiction is avoiding the temptation to be a sports reporter, and Lethem doesn't quite avoid it.) Lethem's satire works better when blended with his peculiar brand of surrealism, as in "The Happy Man," in which a typically troubled family is not quite held together by the father, brought back from the dead by the courts in order to keep earning a living. The rest of the father's time is spent in an inventive existential Hell, which in turn is mimicked by a computer game played by his son back in the real world. The story achieves considerable resonance among its various themes, just as – along with all Lethem's best fiction – it retains its mystery.

Lethem is in no sense a science fiction writer, and when he borrows an SF trope, he's only borrowing the metaphor. Virtual reality merely stands in for a kind of Beckettian limbo in "Forever, Said the Duck," where ex-lovers can be brought together to compare notes on a husband and wife. The transdimensional alien "sufferers" that dog the footsteps of criminals and druggies in "Light and the Sufferer" might as well be demons, except that Lethem takes pains to emphasize that these panther-like creatures imply no moral judgments. The tale of the narrator's edgy and tragic relationship with his downward-spiraling brother is far more important than the question of what aliens are doing among us (which is never even really addressed). Like "Light and the Sufferer," "The Hardened Criminals" takes place in a grimy tough-guy world reminiscent not so much of Chandler or Hammett (whose fingerprints were all over *Gun, with Occasional Music*) as of the juvenile delinquent fiction of the fifties. There is a similarly nostalgic tinge to "Sleepy People," in which chronically somnolent people, connected somehow with a strangely diffident local militia, haunt the lives of small town residents.

What Lethem does best is evident in this story, as it is in "The Happy Man," "Light and the Sufferer," and "The Hardened Criminals": namely, to introduce a single bizarre and ambiguous central metaphor in a story otherwise played straight, and see what happens. In the most ambitious story in the collection (at least in terms of scale), "Five Fucks," the metaphor is simply the one-night stand that seems to last forever. When a woman returns from what she thought was a single night with a lover, she finds she's been gone for two weeks; each of the successive title fucks carries the situation further into myth and legend, until the whole thing becomes a vaulting metaphor of sexual alienation. Even when Lethem is working at being realistic, he writes with the mystery-drenched tone of a Paul Auster; when he tries to get cosmic, as he does here, he can't resist a touch of Tex Avery – or perhaps more to the point (and more like Lethem's worlds than anyone else) of George Herriman. In other words, Lethem is a relentlessly unexpected writer, and that's the best reason I know to keep reading him.

– December 1996, Locus #431 –

The Invisible Country ~~ Paul J. McAuley

Catch the Lightning ~~ Catherine Asaro

Blood Brothers ~~ Steven Barnes

Ferman's Devils ~~ Joe Clifford Faust

It's been argued from time to time that the imaginary settings of SF and fantasy novels are at least as important as character, plot development, or style; they are, the argument goes, formidable aesthetic constructs in their own right, and an experienced SF reader can vet a Cordwainer Smith universe or a Philip K. Dick psychoscape in a page or less. I think to some extent this valorization of setting has come about because it's thought to be something that fantastic literature does *better* than mainstream fiction, a way of leveling the playing field in SF's ongoing struggle for the hearts and minds of people who still pay attention to the *New York Times Book Review*. The SF or fantasy writer faces unique challenges in placing the reader in a world with substantially fewer signposts than our own, whereas the mainstream writer merely reports. The argument doesn't hold water, of course. For one thing, mainstream literature can use settings as distinctively as SF, and experienced readers can recognize Hardy's Wessex or Chandler's Los Angeles as readily as the SF reader can recognize a trademark world. For another, not all – not even the majority – of SF and fantasy settings are worth thinking about as much more than backdrops. It's still a rare writer who can create a world as rich and brilliant as, say, the future Europe Paul McAuley gave us in *Fairyland* (reviewed here in August 1995). No fewer than four of the nine stories in McAuley's new collection **The Invisible Country** return us to that phantasmagorical Europe, and offer further evidence of just how compelling a place it is.

If we're going to view imaginary worlds as artistic structures on their own terms, then surely one of the tests of such a world is how many different narratives it can support. Fantasy worlds which may seem richly detailed as long as there's a quest going on can dry up like dead leaves as soon as we try to imagine anything other than a quest ever happening there; it's the only plot such worlds can support. (No one wants to read *Pride and Prejudice* set among Hobbits.) Nor do most of SF's various galactic empires offer much of interest beyond adventures of oppression and rebellion: the Death Star is there to get blown up, more special effect than setting.

But McAuley is one of those writers who sees a world as a story-generator, not merely a backdrop, and this is as true of his Renaissance Florence in *Pasquale's Angel* (another setting revisited here, in "The Temptation of Dr. Stein") as of his transformed Europe. What is especially impressive is that he does this without an excess of bells and whistles; only one of the stories in *The Invisible Country*, the elegant "Recording Angel," is set in a baroque, alien far future, and part of the strength of that story comes from the ways McAuley familiarizes and domesticates the unfamiliar setting.

In his brief notes that accompany these stories McAuley mentions that future Europe is still rarely made a subject for SF, despite the turbulent changes going on there already (one could quibble: Brian Aldiss has consistently looked at changing Europe in his later fiction, and Bruce Sterling's *Holy Fire* is another recent example). Using EuroDisney as a focal image, *Fairyland* showed how the Europe of today might be transformed through genetic engineering and nanotech into a radically different, potentially posthuman environment of the not-too-distant future. Looking at the other European stories in *The Invisible Country*, we can get a glimpse of how this idea evolved in McAuley's own work. The "dolls" – blue-skinned subhumans designed for manual labor and sexual games – first show up in "Prison Dreams," in which a medical technician convicted of murdering her abusive husband serves her sentence doing triage on brutalized dolls in the Hague. "Dr. Luther's Assistant" varies this plot only slightly: a doctor arrested for drug trafficking (the drug is called Hux, and is actually an infection of nanomachines called "fembots") serves part of *his* sentence as assistant to a Moreau-like doctor conducting gruesome surgical experiments on the dolls. But then he encounters and falls in love with a "fairy," a kind of evolved, intelligent, and more human-like doll.

Both "Children of the Revolution" and "Slaves" explore different aspects of how society changes as the fairies organize a liberation movement which threatens the hegemony of humans; "Children of the Revolution" is an odd sort of Peter Pan story which – perhaps more than any of the other tales in this cycle – illustrates my point that McAuley's future Europe can support a wide variety of narratives. "Slaves," the longest story in the book, recasts the fairy revolution from the perspective of Katz, a young woman living in a community of ecological activists. McAuley's tales are peppered with allusions to Wells (he sometimes refers to the dolls as Morlock-like, and "Slaves" even features a rampaging tripod straight out of *War of the Worlds*), but – perhaps because of the European setting, perhaps because of the slave-rebellion theme – there are also clear echoes of Karel Capek (*War with the Newts* more than *R.U.R.*) There is more than a hint of contemporary satire in these tales, and in "Gene Wars," which is not part of the *Fairyland* cycle but covers similar territory, McAuley gives a brief whirlwind tour of a world in which corporate greed and designer genes lead rapidly to a posthuman environment.

SF history also shows up plainly in a diptych of stories about Dr. Pretorius, the classic mad scientist portrayed by Ernst Thesiger in The Bride of Frankenstein. "The Temptation of Dr. Stein," set in the alternate Florence of *Pasquale's Angel*, offers a Hoffmann-like take on the Frankenstein story as a physician visiting Venice encounter Pretorius's claims to be able to raise the dead. In "The True History of Doctor Pretorius," an opportunistic journalist uncovers evidence that a Mengele-like doctor offering AIDS treatments in Mexico might actually be the same Dr. Pretorius who shows up in documents dating back to the 15th century – and who therefore might possess the secret of immortality.

What is perhaps most interesting about McAuley's short stories (this is his second collection) is their relative narrowness of focus, at least in SF terms. He returns not only to the same or similar settings, but to the same themes of betrayal, revolution, and transfiguration – all cast in rigorously hard-SF terms. By no means does this suggest that he is a writer of limited range, however – merely that he knows what settings are really good for in SF, and knows when they are good for more than a single story. In fact, one could make an argument that McAuley may actually be better suited to the short story form; the richly varied Martian colonies of *Red Dust* could have generated a whole gaggle of stories, and pretty nearly did just that in the middle of the novel (there are no Martian stories here, however). Once McAuley works a setting out, he turns his attention to characters, to incidents, and to the passions which strongly motivate his fiction. And eventually, the settings themselves do begin to seem like separate works of art – they do what SF settings are supposed to do, both in terms of conveying surpassing strangeness and supporting solid, intelligent, and always provocative stories.

Now I have here a copy of an actual issue of the tabloid *Weekly World News* from last September, and in it is an article called "How to Tell if You're an Ex-Alien" (among the warning signs are "creativity," "restlessness," and "sensitivity to humidity"). What's interesting about it – apart from the deliciously psychotic tone that accompanies such accomplished tabloid writing – is that its basic conceit is a degraded version of an SF trope familiar since the days of the pulps: the notion that an unprepossessing misfit in our own society may turn out to harbor secret powers crucial to the outcome of vast galactic conflicts. Even therapists who never got above a B- average in grad school could quickly deduce why such a theme might appeal to socially wounded adolescent SF fans, or why it eventually began to show up even in SF movies and finally the tabloids. It's SF's own illustration of the old anthropological concept of *gesunkenkulturgut*, an idea so broadly appealing that it can go on endlessly being made more stupid. Despite this, SF writers seem to have no intention of abandoning the idea, and it remains at the core of novels such as Catherine Asaro's **Catch the Lightning**, her second novel and the second in her series about the vast interstellar Skolian Empire. Of course, we expect more of SF writers treating this theme than we do of tabloid writers, and Asaro delivers a rousing enough tale – but there's still that edge of vengeful wish-fulfillment, that pulpish longing that reduces her characters nearly to cartoons just as she's spent half the novel making them into believable, complex figures.

And that of course is the main problem with the undiscovered hero motif: it tends to break novels in half. Asaro's narrative begins with a compelling opening line: "I last saw earth in 1987, when I was seventeen." The narrator, Tina Pulivok, is an immigrant of Mayan descent living in the Hispanic community of Los Angeles in a curiously altered 1987 (instead of the U.S.A., for example, her country is called the "Federated States of America"; we later realize this is a tale of alternate universes rather than time travel). She meets a golden-skinned stranger named Althor who claims to be a space pilot, and with whom she immediately feels a mysterious kinship – especially after he rescues her from a neighborhood thug. Asaro gets credit for launching unapologetically into the development of this unlikely relationship, and the growing romance between Tina and Althor – who turn out to share both ancestry and empathic psychic powers – is what gives the first half of the book its considerable charm (Althor's idea of romantic swooning consists of lines like "Your influence has migrated to all my processors"). As a Mayan, Tina is a perfect candidate for the kind of alienation that her role requires – displaced from Mexico to LA, a kind of outsider even in the Hispanic community. When Althor's starship is discovered by the government, Tina is able to marshal her small group of friends to help him retrieve it. Then, of course, he takes her to the stars, where she is to play a crucial role in an intergalactic war.

And Asaro takes us along for the ride. There's nothing particularly wrong with the space-opera second half of *Catch the Lightning*, but the shift in tone is jarring. In place of the interesting characters we met on earth, we get a Ming-the-Merciless villain named Kryx Iquar, who buys Althor and Tina then tortures him and rapes her, and a group of minions who talk more like street thugs than the more believable street thugs Asaro described back in LA. There are plenty of chases, fights, and escapes, a lot of big numbers tossed about (5,000 year old rivalries, a hundred billion people owned by Iquar) to give some sense of cosmic sweep, and a sentient spaceship armed to the teeth but with the personality of an angry puppy. It's space adventure assembled pretty much with off-the-shelf parts (although Asaro's physics of "inversion" is an interesting hard-SF add-on), and with plenty yet to come. But for the most part, Althor and Tina were much more intriguing back in LA.

Oddly enough, Steven Barnes's **Blood Brothers** shares some of the same structures, and structural problems, as the Asaro novel: hidden identities, an unlikely pair of heroes (one a minority), and a narrative that splits between contemporary LA and a remote time and place. Only in Barnes's case, the remote setting comes to seem more real and compelling than the contemporary one, as he takes us not to a galactic empire, but to a 19th-century slave plantation. This may seem to invite comparisons with Octavia Butler's *Kindred*, but Barnes is after something entirely different. Barnes has an impressive track record as a slick writer in that hybrid genre of bestseller SF, where he has often collaborated with Larry Niven and Jerry Pournelle. On his own, in novels like *Streetlethal*, he's shown a more punkish sensibility, but he's not at heart a cynic, and he really seems to want to see things work out the way they do in his bestsellers. When Derek Waites, a black computer game designer and Barnes's main protagonist, agonizes over his conflicting feelings about the 1992 Rodney King riots, you feel the agony is Barnes's own. When Waites finds himself thrust into an unlikely collaboration with a white supremacist named Austin Tucker – and even protected by Tucker's associates at a survivalist compound – you get the sense that Barnes may be treating these wormy characters with far more understanding and good will than they deserve. The real enemy, after all, is not racism, poverty, or riots. It's sorcery.

Waites and Tucker, it turns out, are descended from a common ancestor, and this makes them targets of a particularly terrifying threat: Tucker's daughter, some years earlier, burned to death in what appeared to be spontaneous combustion, and now Waites's daughter seems in danger of the same fate. But the heat turns out to be a by-product of a kind of psychic possession, and Waites's daughter is able to transmit messages from Dahlia Childe, a favored slave on the plantation of Augustus DuPris. And it's Childe's narrative, cast in the form of her diary, which gives *Blood Brothers* its real source of emotional power. Not only is Childe a complex and intelligent woman who learns to manipulate her master to guarantee her survival (and continued youth), but her story takes on a near epic quality, involving ancient African sorcery, inhuman tortures, and a Cronus-like character whose survival depends on consuming the generations of his own children. (It may be possible to assign too much metaphoric weight to this last, but it works as a powerful imagery of the legacy of slavery.) Barnes's contemporary narrative – except for a few moments of family bonding and that passage about the Rodney King riots – never seems to attain quite this level of authentic feeling. Tucker does not for a moment seem to be a believable white supremacist, and Waites learns to trust him far too easily. The various chases and gunfights that pepper this part of the narrative make for good suspense reading, but never slow down enough to examine the real issues of racism and cruelty that are the novel's main concerns. Instead, it's the almost Lovecraftian pair of villains – DuPris and the sorceror known as The African – and the quiet dignity of Dahlia Childe, haunted by her own Faustian bargain, that makes *Blood Brothers* worth the trip. We've seen the horrors of slavery in novels from Octavia Butler to Toni Morrison; Barnes is one of the first writers to directly make use of horror story traditions in approaching the topic – while being careful to avoid trivializing the already appalling history. It's a technique not without some risks, and it works better than you would suspect.

The world of advertising has always been easy satirical fodder for mystery novelists (such as Dorothy Sayers) and mainstream writers (such as Joseph Heller), but mention it in connection with SF and the only thing anyone thinks of is Pohl and Kornbluth's *The Space Merchants* (and perhaps Pohl's much later sequels). Actually, Pohl wrote a great many more stories in a similar vein, and the mind-bending possibilities of futuristic advertising attracted writers from Sheckley to Dick.

But many of these stories dated from the fifties and sixties, and the ad world they portrayed derived from the hard-sell tactics and gullible consumers of that era. Joe Clifford Faust is an ad copywriter of much more recent vintage, and he brings to his new SF-advertising novel **Ferman's Devils** a keen understanding of how modern ads are generated and how they work. Interestingly, he doesn't project much in the way of future technology for the industry; most of the many sample ads he scatters throughout the text are simple video or audio presentations, although software has become one of the major media for commercials. These ads, presented in the form of scripts written by the ace copywriter Boddekker, also provide an entertaining way for Faust to introduce his comically *noir* future: the products include a heroin-like drug called "Daily Jones," a nuclear toilet-bowl cleaner, a doll called "Baby Barely Alive" which mimics the symptoms of several horrible diseases, and an agency offering "self-termination services" ("Service not available in Utah"). Advertising, in Faust's view, is not so much the corrupting consumer brainwashing of *The Space Merchants* as an amoral industry signing on cheerfully to whatever a disintegrating society wants to sell itself.

Faust's voice is less that of the cool social satirist than of the angry urban absurdist; less Pohl than Paddy Chayefsky. His initial situation, at least, is very Chayefskian: Boddekker wanders into a dangerous part of Manhattan controlled by franchised street gangs and talks his way out of an ugly situation with one such gang, Ferman's Devils, by offering them a spot in a commercial. The product being advertised, "NanoKleen," is a kind of nanotech laundry detergent which enables garments to continually clean and even repair themselves (it's one of the most convincing if unglamorous potential applications of nanotechnology I've seen described), and Boddekker's ad strategy is to recreate his own confrontation with the gang – using the real gang in the commercial. The discussions in the ad agency about whether to use urban terror to sell a laundry product ring disturbingly true, and when the ad succeeds, its catchphrase ("I handled it!") becomes a national craze. For all the dark comedy that makes *Ferman's Devils* a superior entertainment, it seems to be one of the most believable and deadly accurate portrayals of the ad world in all of SF. For all the scenes of near-slapstick brutality – such as when Ferman and his followers (who sport names like Jimmy Jazz and Rover) take their re-enactment too seriously and nearly beat to death an obnoxious commercial actor – there's an underlying sense of conviction that this world is not much displaced from our own, and the advertising strategies not displaced at all. And at the center of it all is the engaging character of Boddekker himself, a rising star of only twenty-eight whose only dream is to buy a fancy house in Princeton and escape the city.

Faust has been writing SF for something like a decade, and has demonstrated a wicked sense of humor before. But with this novel (the first of a pair of novels about Boddekker), he's staking out a territory that seems fresh and inventive despite a near-future scenario that seems already familiar from the work of Neal Stephenson and other post-cyberpunks. The phrase that comes most readily to mind to describe

Boddekker's world is one coined by Kingsley Amis to describe dystopias in the mold of Pohl and Kornbluth: "comic inferno." Faust shares something else important with those earlier comic infernos: a welcome lack of pretension and substantial skill in both plotting and character observation. Boddekker's tale, when completed, may well turn out to be one of the funniest SF satires of recent years, as well as one of the more intelligently plotted and convincingly detailed.

INDEX OF TITLES